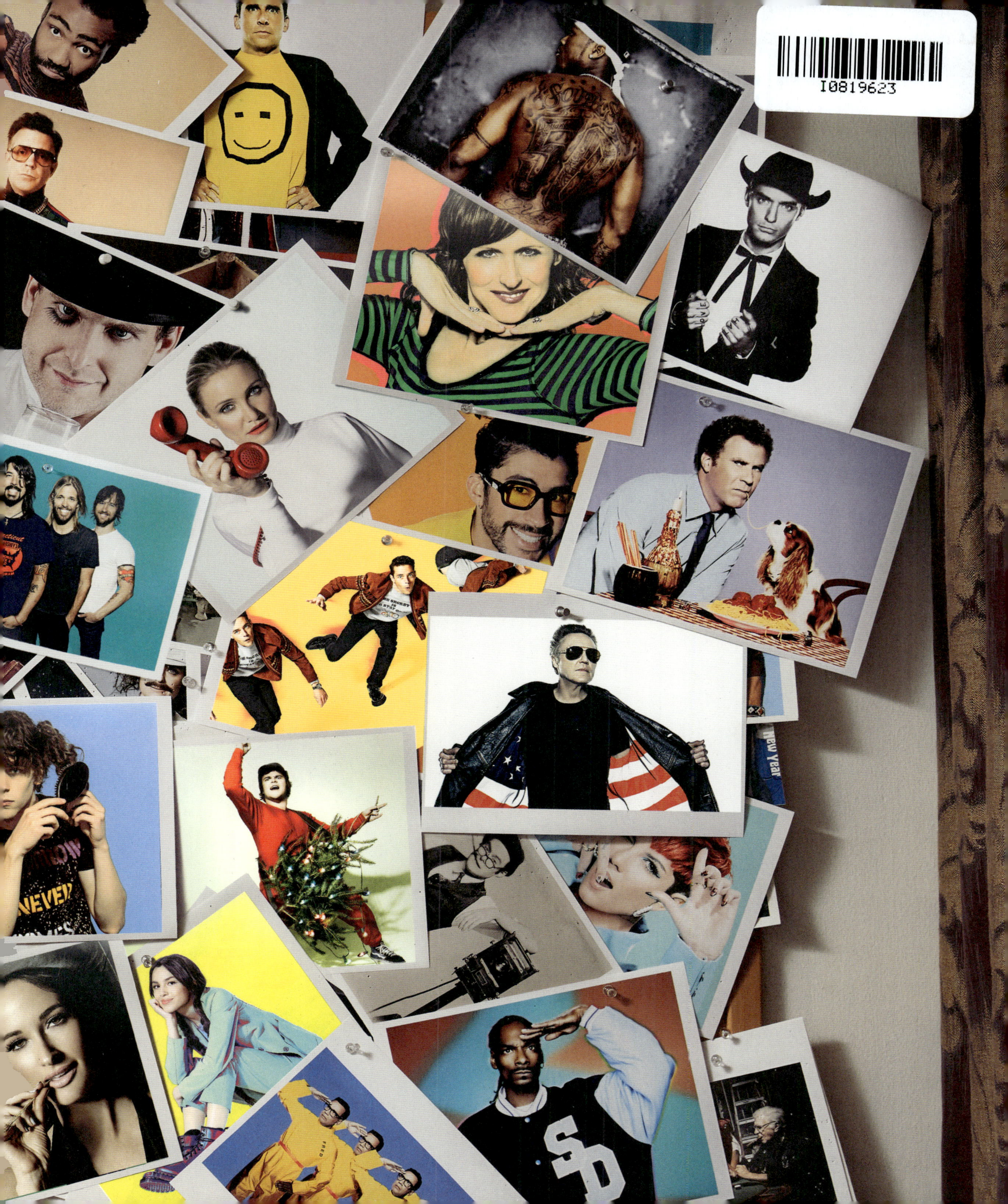
I0819623
NEVER
New Year
SD

THE ART OF THE SNL PORTRAIT

MARY ELLEN MATTHEWS

THE ART OF THE SNL PORTRAIT

Concept and Image Selection by
Alison Castle, Mary Ellen Matthews,
and Emily Oberman

Writing and Editing by Alison Castle

Foreword by Lorne Michaels

Design by Pentagram

Abrams, New York

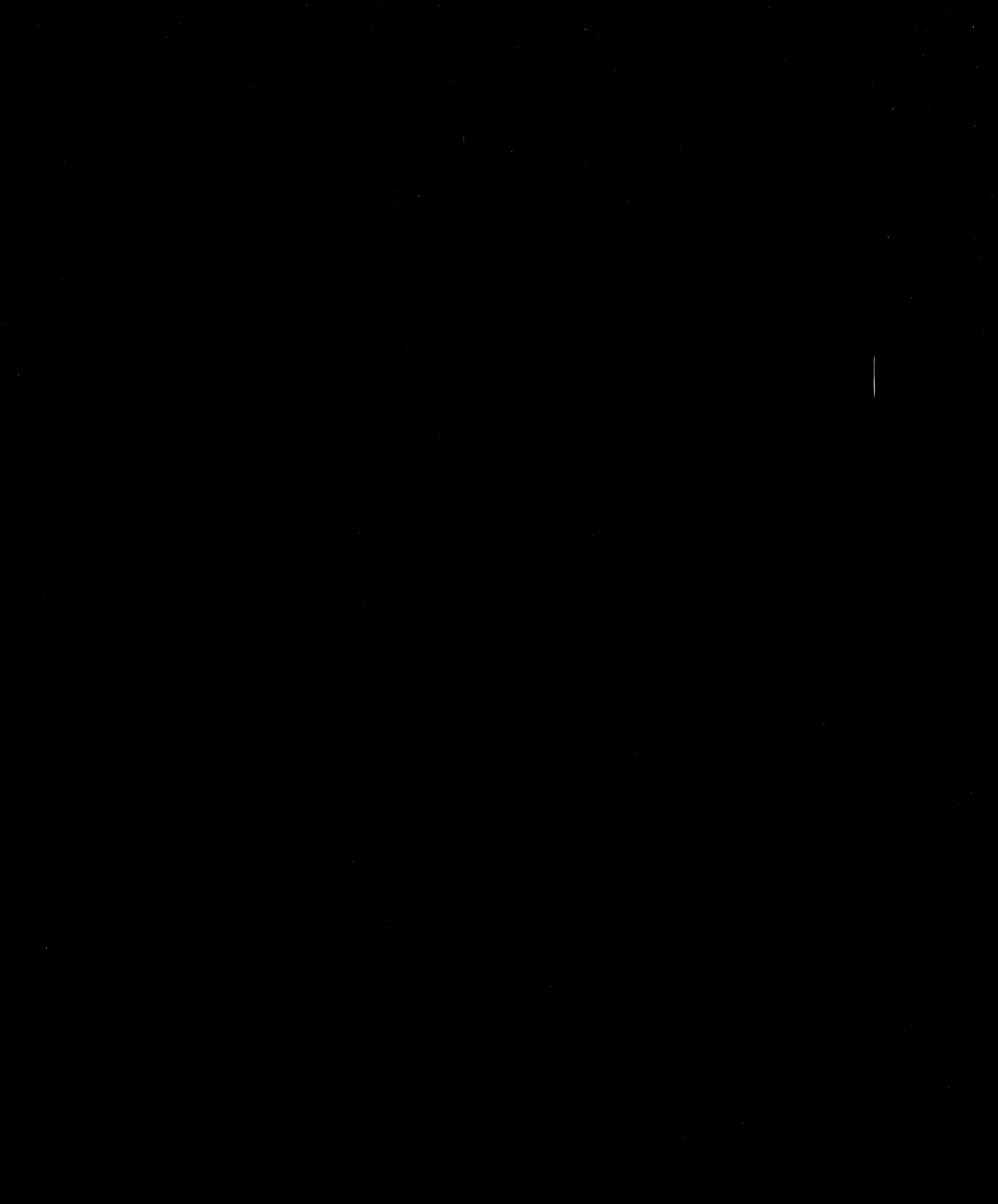

CONTENTS

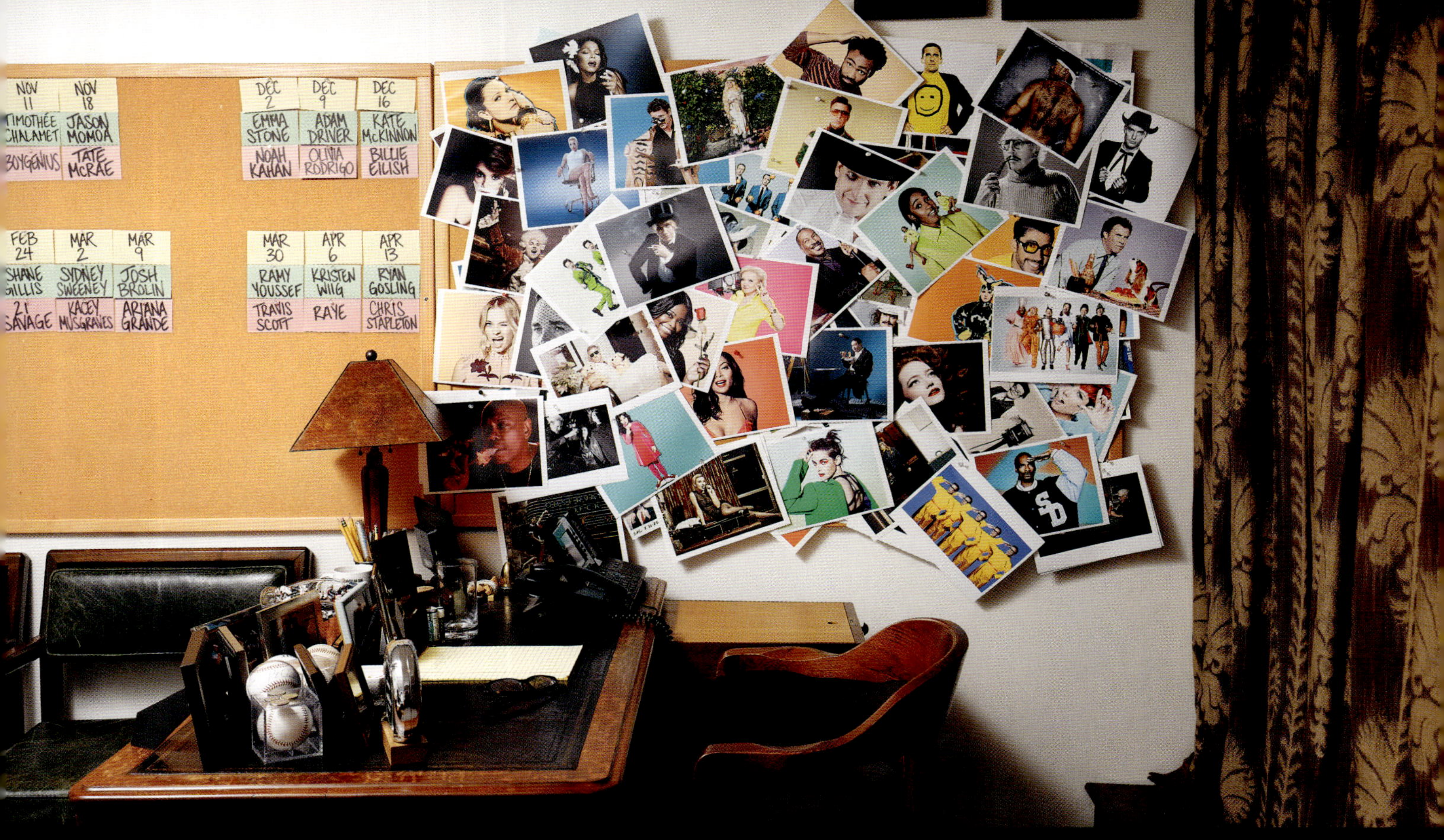

orne Michaels's desk in his ninth-floor office

FOREWORD

by Lorne Michaels

When Studio 8H was turned over to SNL in 1975, we inherited the *Tonight Show* format, which had been ninety minutes with Johnny Carson. Before each commercial break, as a signal to the affiliates that they were to cut away and do local commercials, they would put up a bumper that would say something like, "More to come," and it would have a picture of Johnny Carson. At that time comedy sets were cartoonish, but our comedy was going to be different. We wanted the show to be reflective of the way New York looked and felt—which was essentially urban decay, as the city was bankrupt at the time—as opposed to the West Coast Hollywood romantic version of New York. So I wanted hard wall sets, realistic architectural environments to play against. And as the city came back, things changed in our graphics and design, too. But it always starts with New York.

When it came down to the bumpers, we adapted them from the *Tonight Show* format to something that fit the show. Since the host and musical guest changed every week, we decided their portraits would be the identifying things on the bumpers, with the SNL logo in there somewhere. So Edie Baskin established the portrait tradition, and her signature thing was hand tinting. Sometimes you'd see the bumper for the full five seconds; sometimes you'd just see it as a flash, because the affiliates were hungry to have more commercials in that space. It became a thing that was different every week—the approach to it was the same in the sense that it was the same artist doing it, but the work varied and it changed over the years, with both Edie and of course, Mary Ellen. And when Mary Ellen started to innovate with things like graphics that moved, we realized that worked, too. She's always reinventing what she's doing; she keeps it fresh. But the core thing is her on a Thursday, photographing the host and musical guest, making them feel comfortable, taking their input and working with them—but also giving her ideas, which involve a lot of thought on her part, and finding her way visually—and then turning out these remarkable things. The bumpers are probably the least appreciated part of the show, but anybody who knows the show knows how much they mean.

Occasionally, Mary Ellen will pick one of the bumpers and put it on the bulletin board in my ninth-floor office, which is now crowded with ones that I love from over the years. They just make the week that it was, for me, vivid. And the same for the guests, who usually sign one of the prints just before air that then gets hung in the hallway. People ask me, "So you just see the bumpers when they're done?" And I say yes, because I have a full-time job in another part of the show. I'm famously good with people I trust. We talk, of course, and sometimes I speak up, but it's really their work. When people feel that they're admired and trusted, it leads to a different kind of work. When Mary Ellen is meeting, say, Kim Kardashian, or whoever is hosting, they know who she is and they're comfortable with her. They know she's going to make them look good. And the look on the host's face could be a smile or it could be a scowl, but it's something that feels right, for that moment. It's the style of the show, but it's them.

To put it simply, Mary Ellen is both an artist and a star.

PREFACE

by Mary Ellen Matthews

I've often thought about this gig I have that allows me to create with the best and most interesting talent—both from within the show and all the performers who come through the doors of Studio 8H. And how lucky I am that Edie Baskin brought me in and taught me so much. And that Lorne Michaels inspires me and trusts me with this work. And all that, of course, makes this what I believe is the best job in the world and, quite certainly, the only one like it.

About 3,872 of my images made it to your television from 2000 to 2024. And all of those images were on-screen for about three seconds. So we decided to give them more of a chance to be seen, and make a book.

It was a near impossible task to choose from all these images to fill the mere 272 pages here. It was an interesting process in that the design and flow—the selection—really dictated how the layout came to be. So many were left behind, and I would like to apologize to those photos still waiting their turn: I love you all and hang tight; maybe we can do another book soon.

THE ART OF PORTRA

THE SNL
T

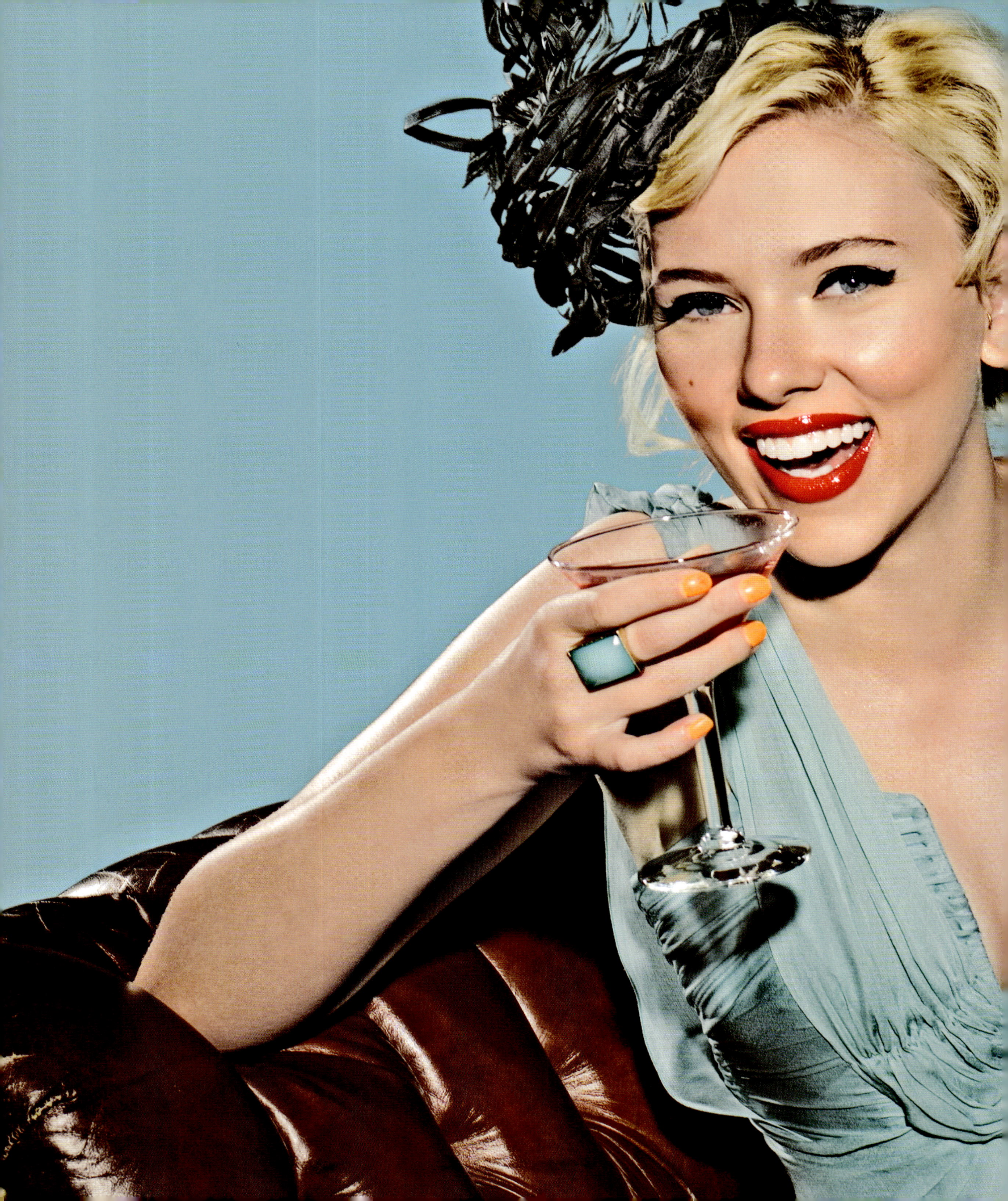

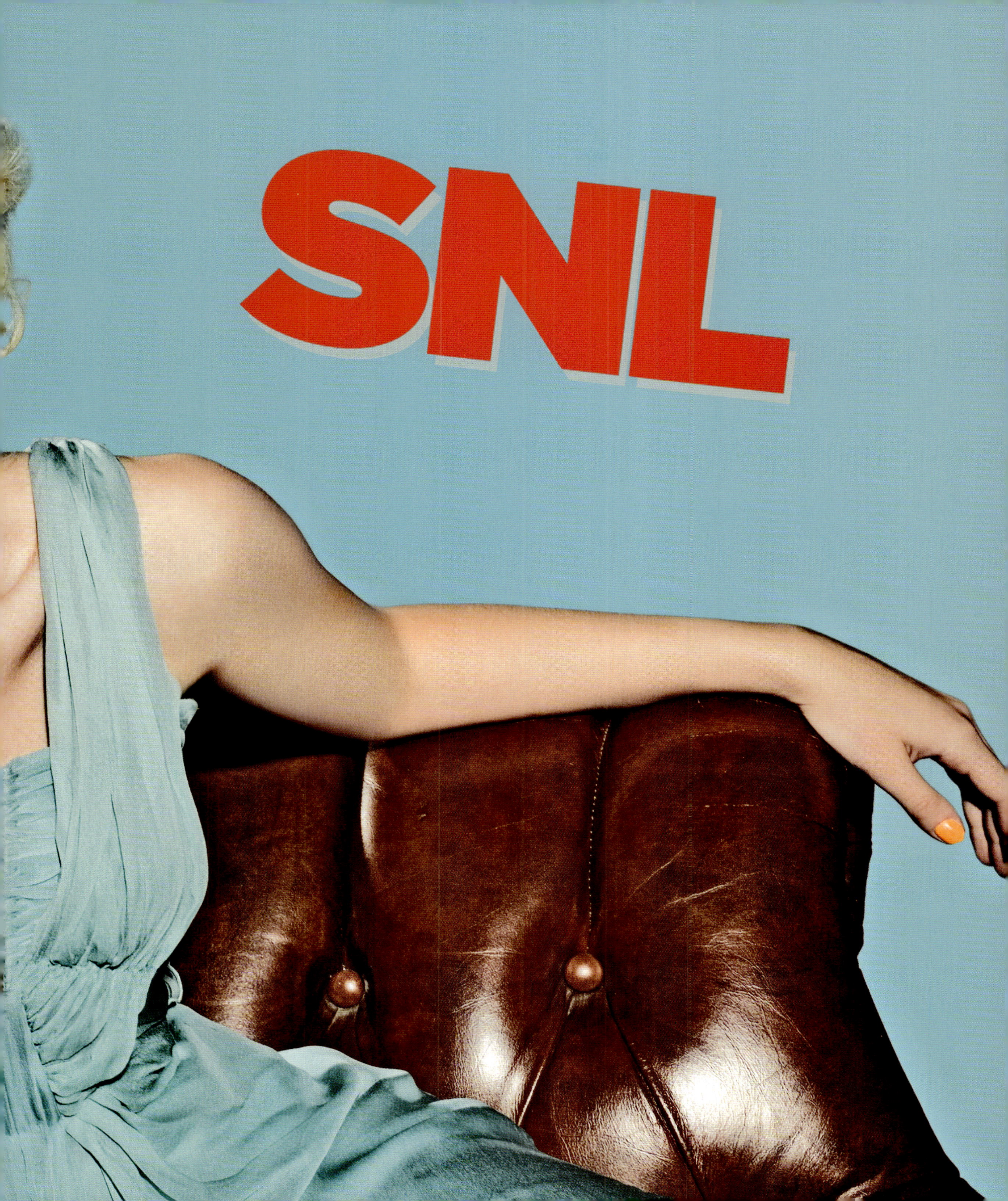
SNL

INTRODUCTION

When *Saturday Night Live* debuted in 1975, the TV bumper was already on its way into obsolescence. "Bumper" is broadcasting lingo for the graphics displayed on-screen as a show cuts to and returns from commercial breaks. Sometimes bumpers were accompanied by a voiceover saying, "And now, a word from our sponsor" or "We'll be right back after these messages." Part of the reason for bumpers was technical: they signaled to affiliates to roll the commercials. By the late 1970s and early 1980s, most TV shows had stopped using bumpers, with the exception of some live and children's programming. Most of these, too, eventually dropped the bumper, with one very notable exception: the SNL bumper, which was and still is an integral part of the show's identity.

From the first episode (the fantastic Edie Baskin was the photographer then), artistic portraits of the host and musical guest, and sometimes of New York City itself, provided the transitions to and from breaks.

Held for three seconds on-screen, SNL bumpers did much more than remind viewers who the host and musical guests were. Funny, clever, glamorous, edgy . . . they gave the show an aesthetic and conceptual personality that can be aptly described as "very New York." Mary Ellen Matthews has carried the torch handed to her by Baskin, her predecessor and mentor, for over two decades, during which time she has developed and expanded the bumper into an expansive art form—variously abstract, sublime, slick, cheeky, or goofy. Matthews has a special talent for mining art history and pop culture to create hilarious and often surprising spoofs: Aziz Ansari in a recreation of a Salvador Dalí photograph, Alec Baldwin as the Godfather, John Mulaney as Patti Smith from the *Horses* album cover, Emma Stone as Gilda Radner's Roseanne Roseanadanna, Aubrey Plaza as Sharon Stone in *Basic Instinct*, Edward Norton as all four subjects in Edward Hopper's *Nighthawks* . . . It's hard to believe that each of these bumpers, like every SNL bumper, was completed in just a few days.

The creation of each show, as many may not realize, spans six days, beginning on Monday afternoon and capping off with the live broadcast on Saturday night. Broadly speaking, the week looks like this: Monday is the writers' meeting, when the entire cast and writing staff cram into producer Lorne Michaels's office to pitch ideas to the host; Monday night through Wednesday afternoon (often through the night), the writers labor over the sketches they will present during Wednesday's read-through, when everyone gathers around a massive table and each sketch is read aloud; Wednesday evening, as soon as the sketches selected for dress rehearsal are announced, writers meet with producers, costume and set designers, hair and makeup artists, and music supervisors to discuss their vision for each sketch; on Thursday, rehearsals begin in 30 Rockefeller Center's Studio 8H and promos are shot; Friday and Saturday morning are when the sets, props, costumes, hair, makeup, etc. start to come together and "pretape" shorts are filmed, all while rewrites happen continuously; on Saturday night from 8 to 10 p.m., a dress rehearsal is performed in front of a live audience; between 10 and 11:30 p.m., cuts and final changes are made and cue cards are updated; and at 11:30 p.m., the show goes live on TV.

Amidst all of this flurry of activity, Matthews must conceive, plan, shoot, and post-produce her photographs. Most weeks it isn't until Thursday that she can pull the host and musical guest away for the shoots, most of which take place right in Studio 8H. That leaves about forty-eight hours for her to do image selections and retouching—often making changes up to and even during the live show. To say it's intense doesn't quite do the experience justice, and one must not forget that this happens week after week, with twenty-two episodes per season and sometimes three or even four episodes in a row without a break. To be consistently creative and inspired week after week, year after year, takes some serious grit. And because Matthews has grit in spades, she never stops pushing the envelope as far as it can go and consistently gracing each show with portraits that perfectly embody the visual DNA and fighting spirit of *Saturday Night Live*. With this book, these photographs that once existed only on-screen are forever committed to print so that we may, finally, properly enjoy them.

Alison Castle
New York, 2025

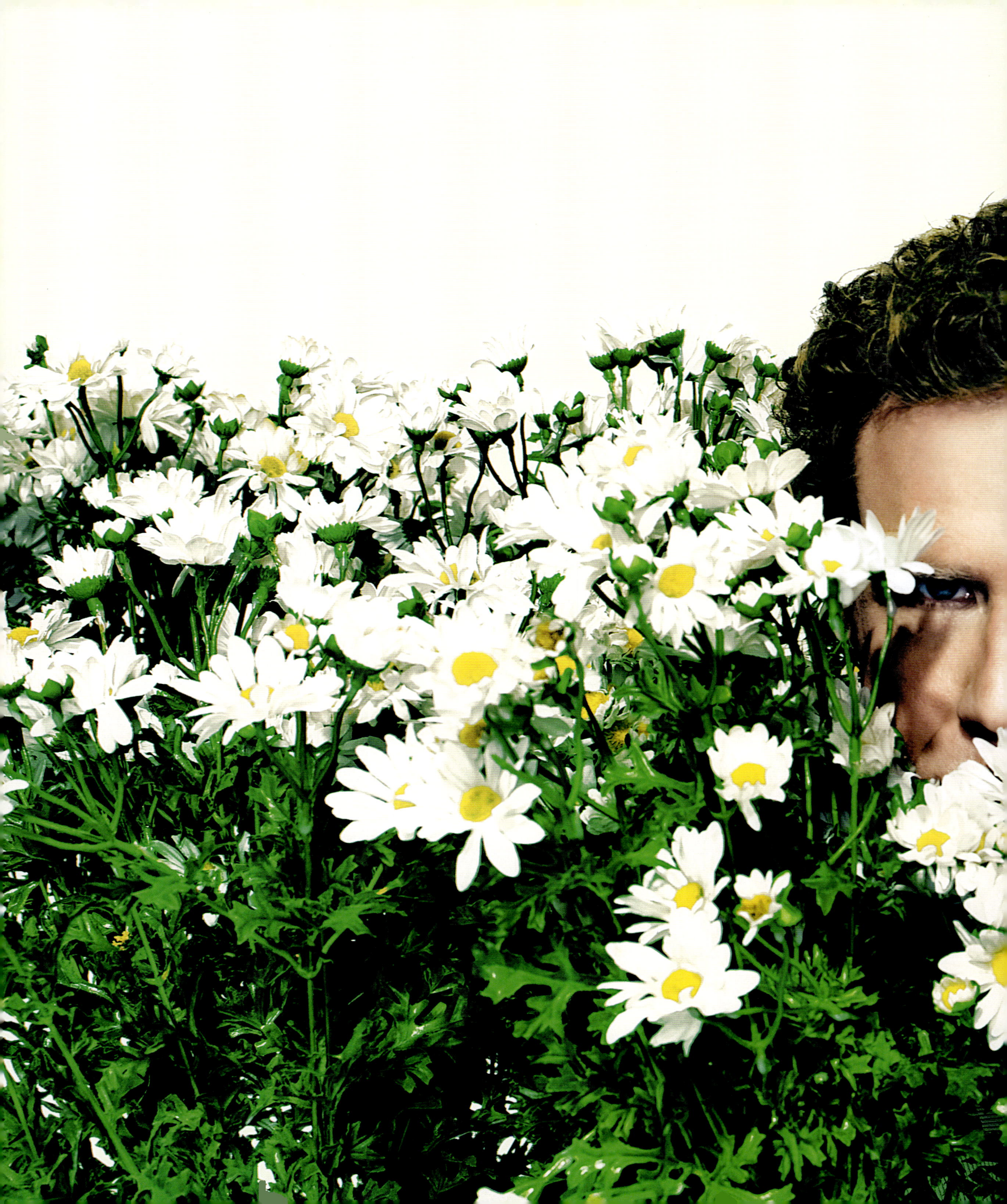

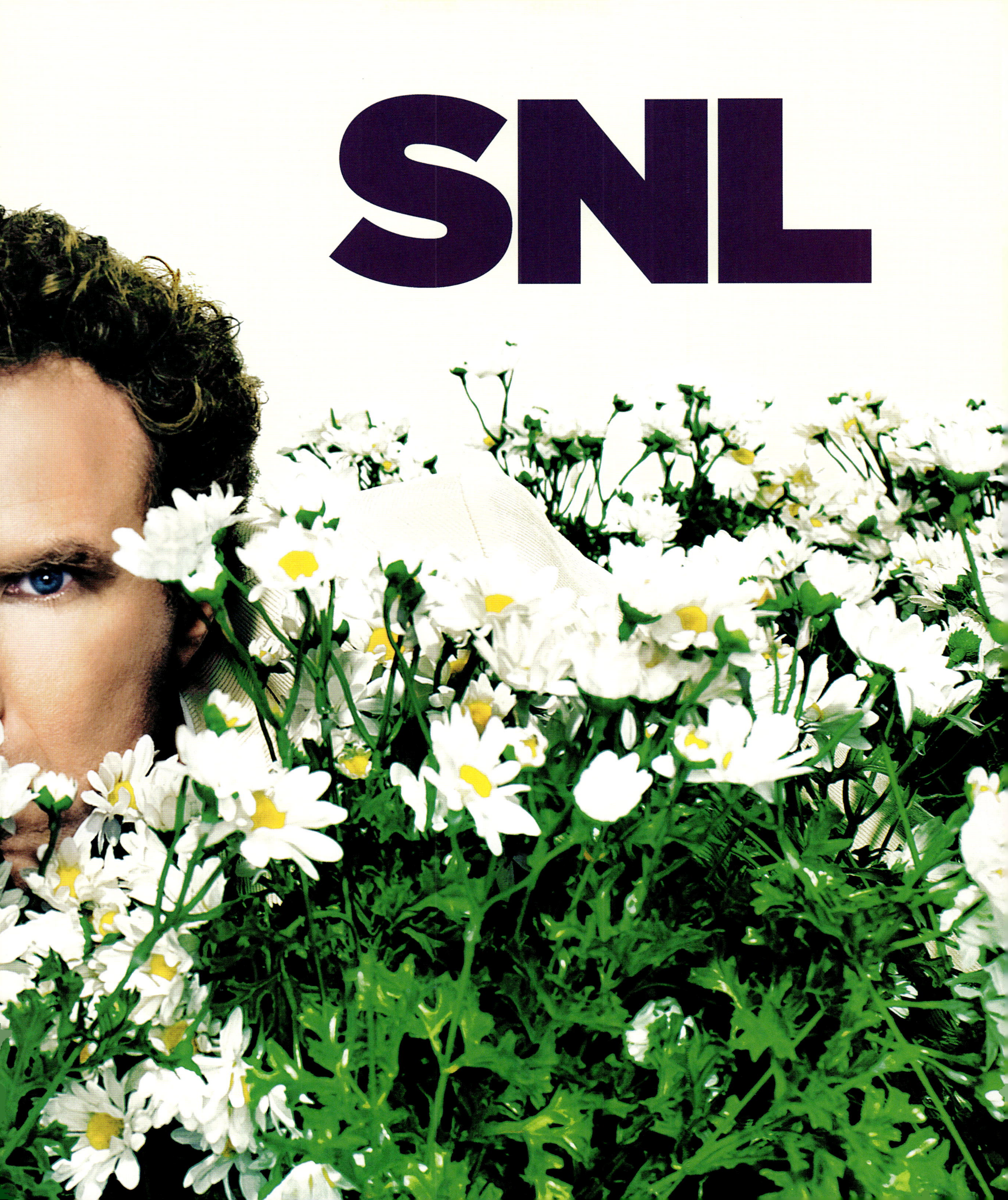
SNL

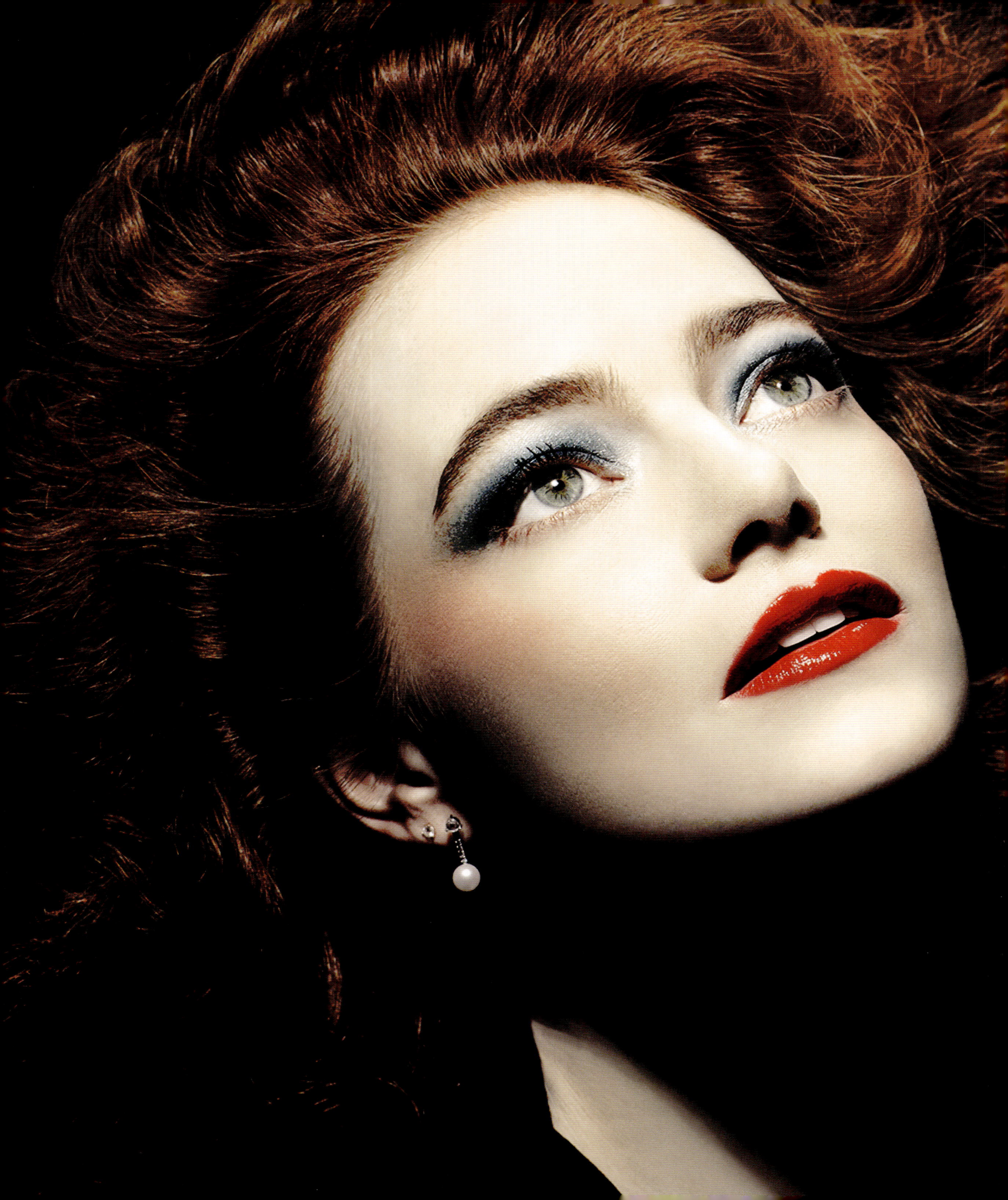

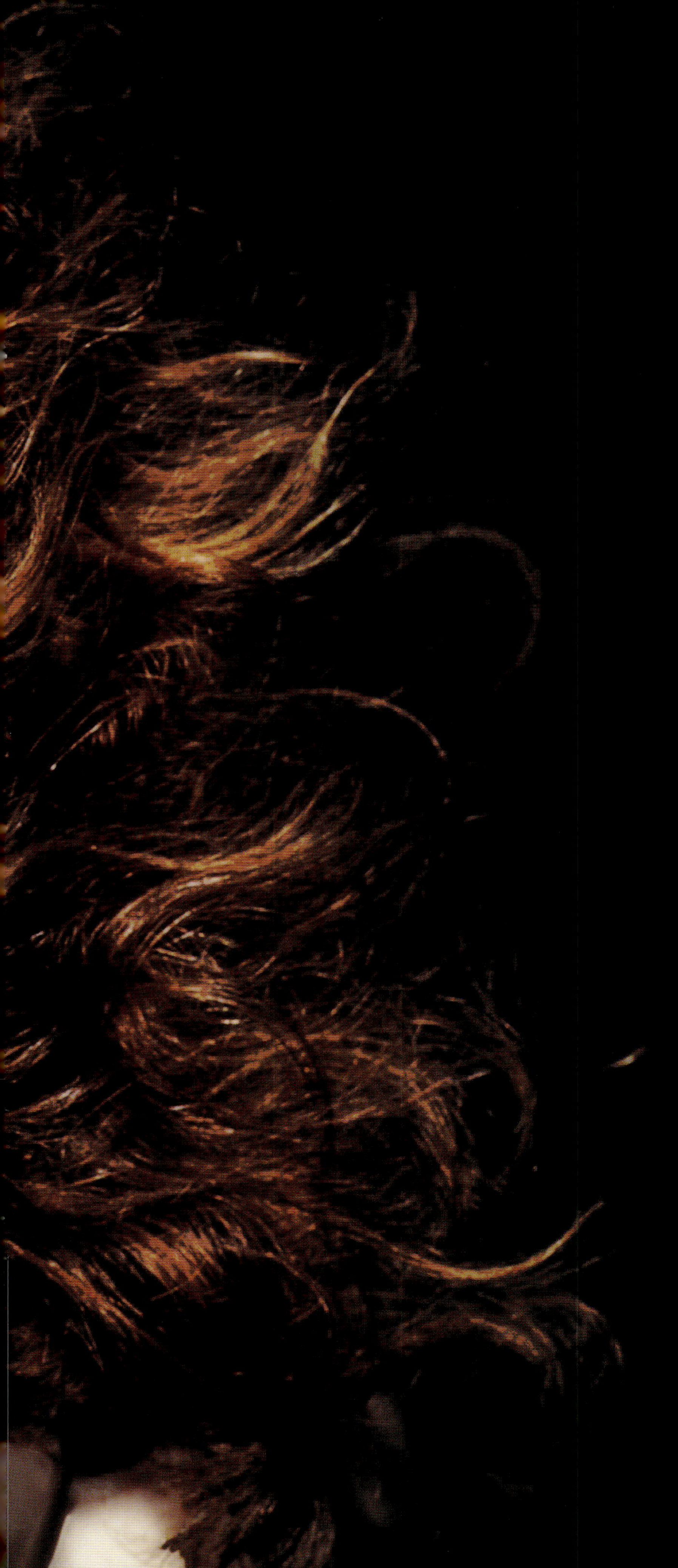

S L

N

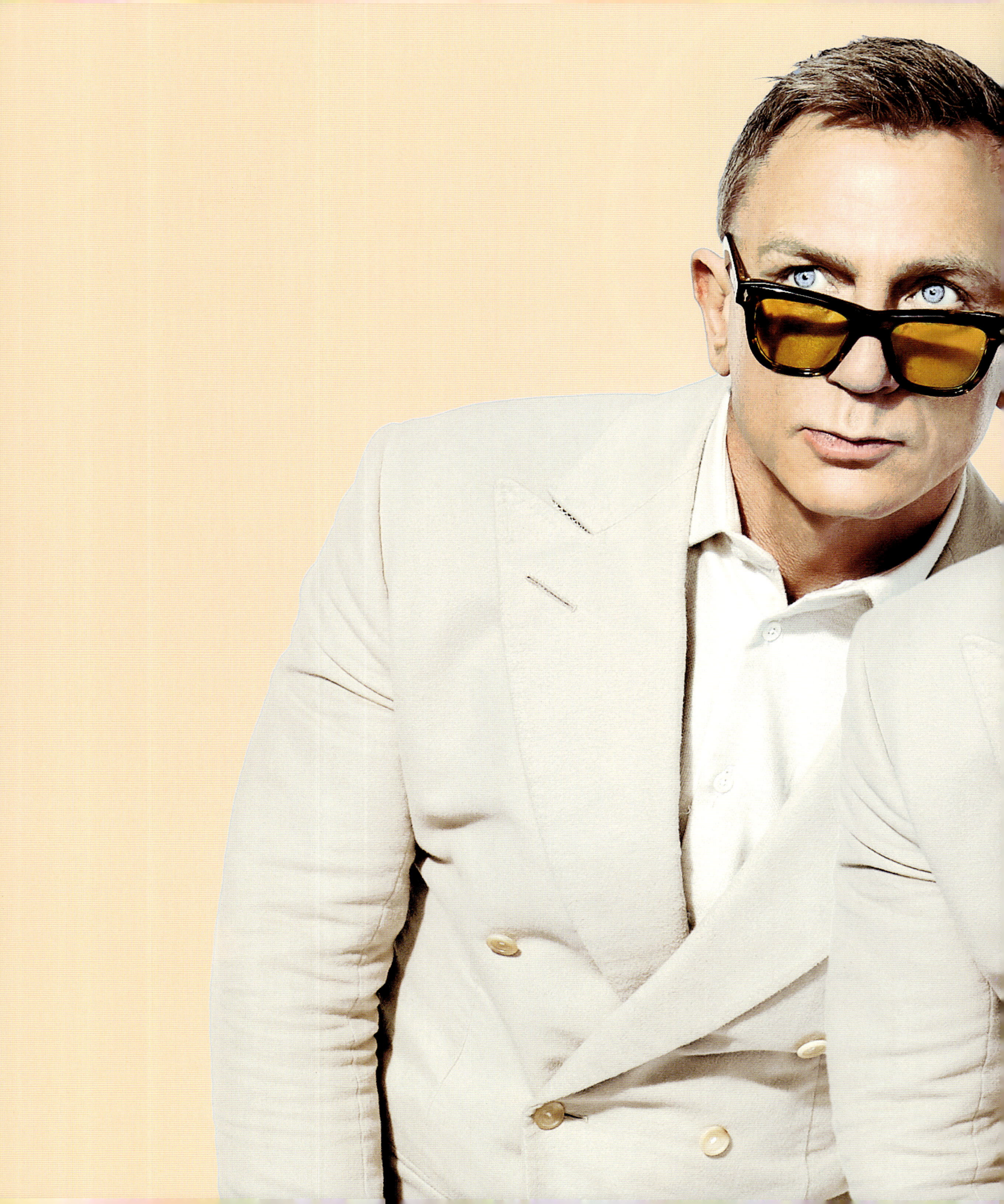

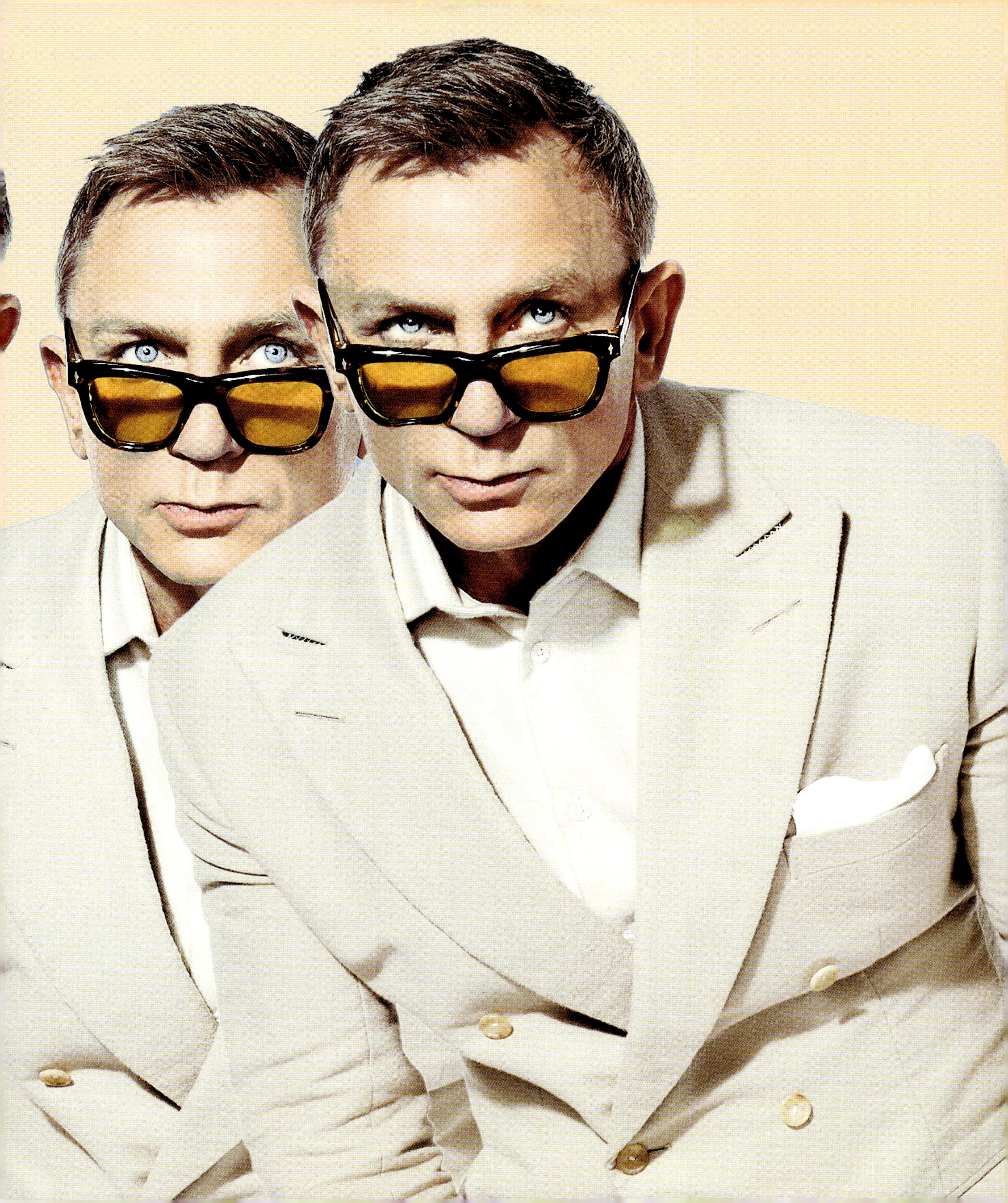

SNL

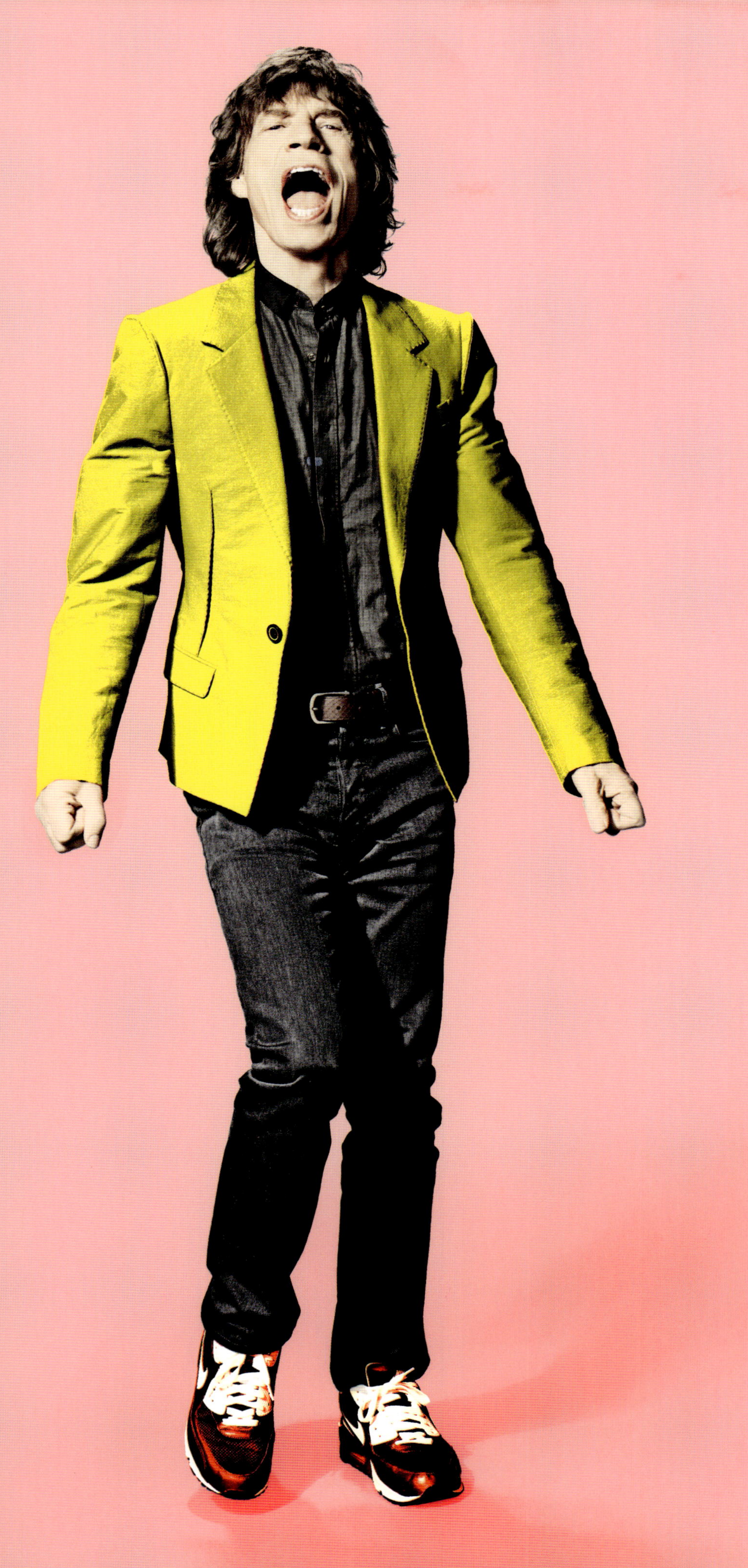

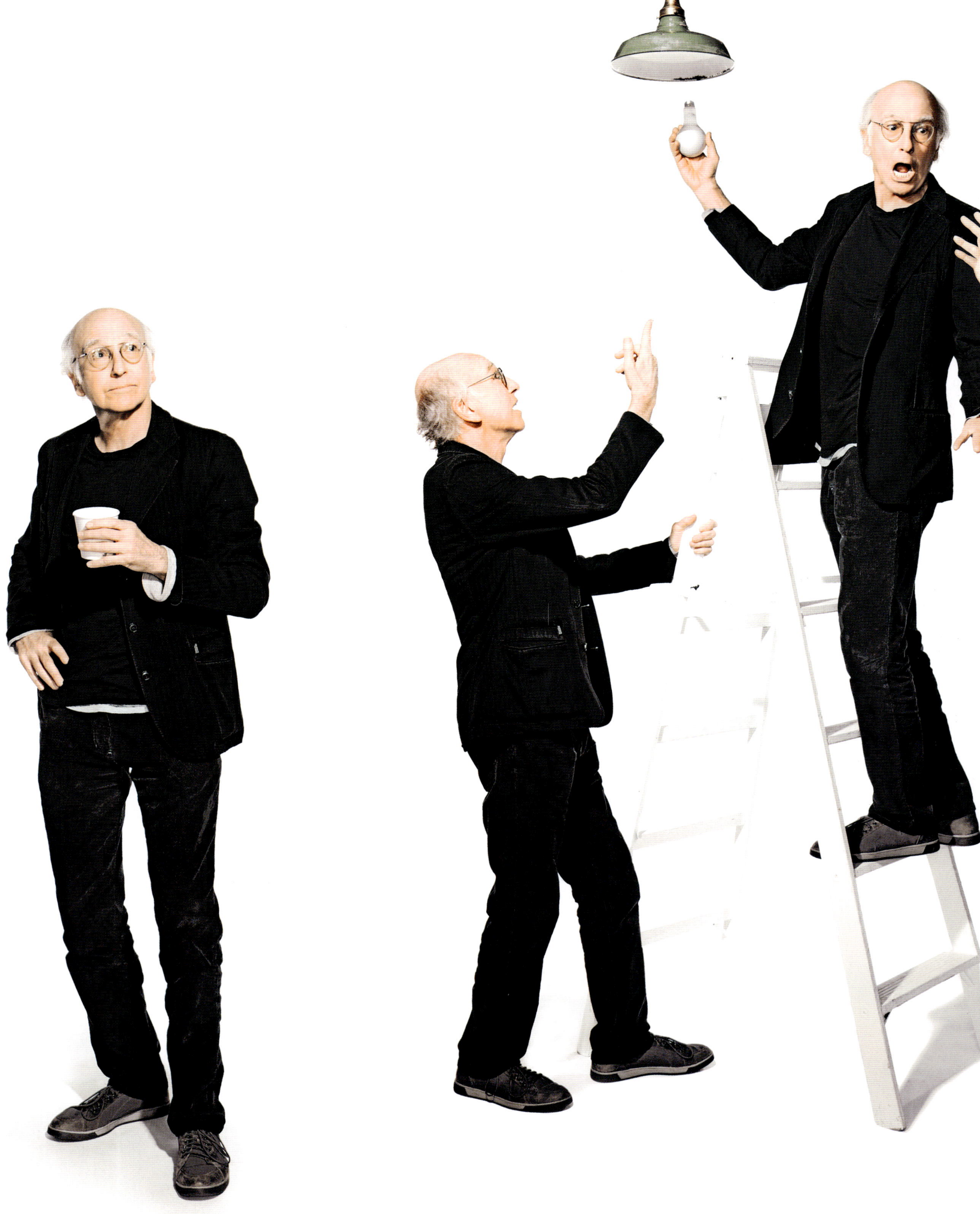

SNL

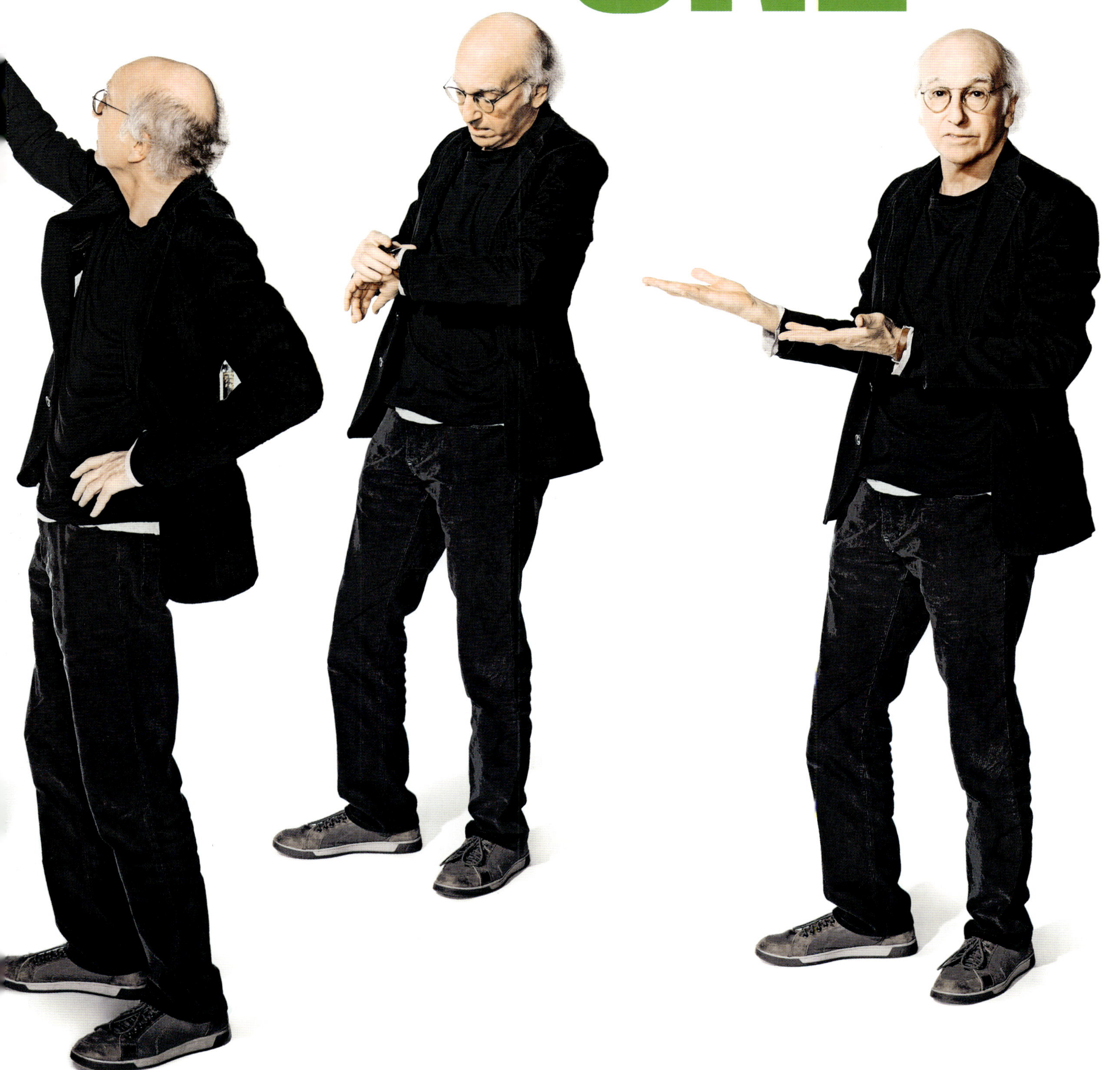

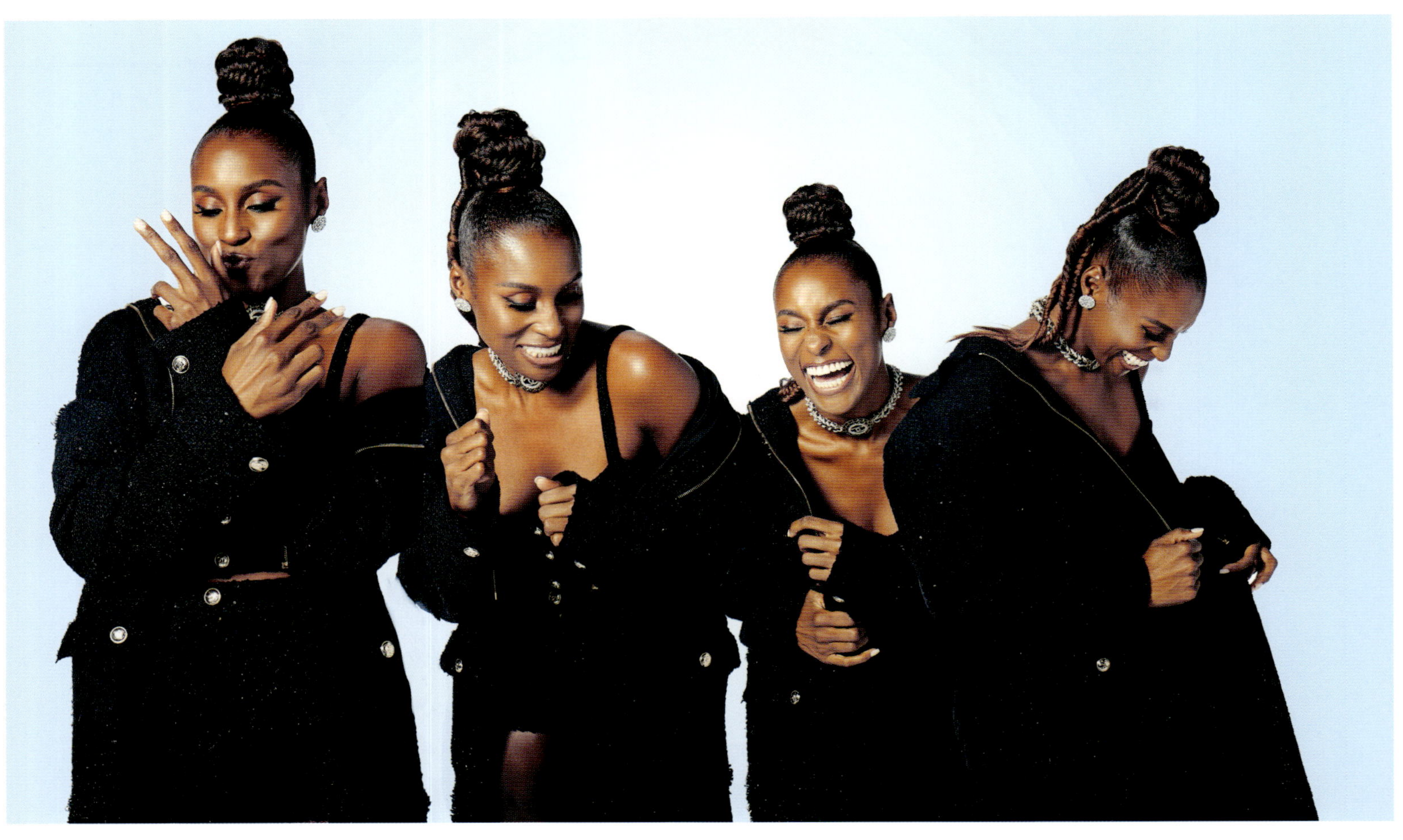

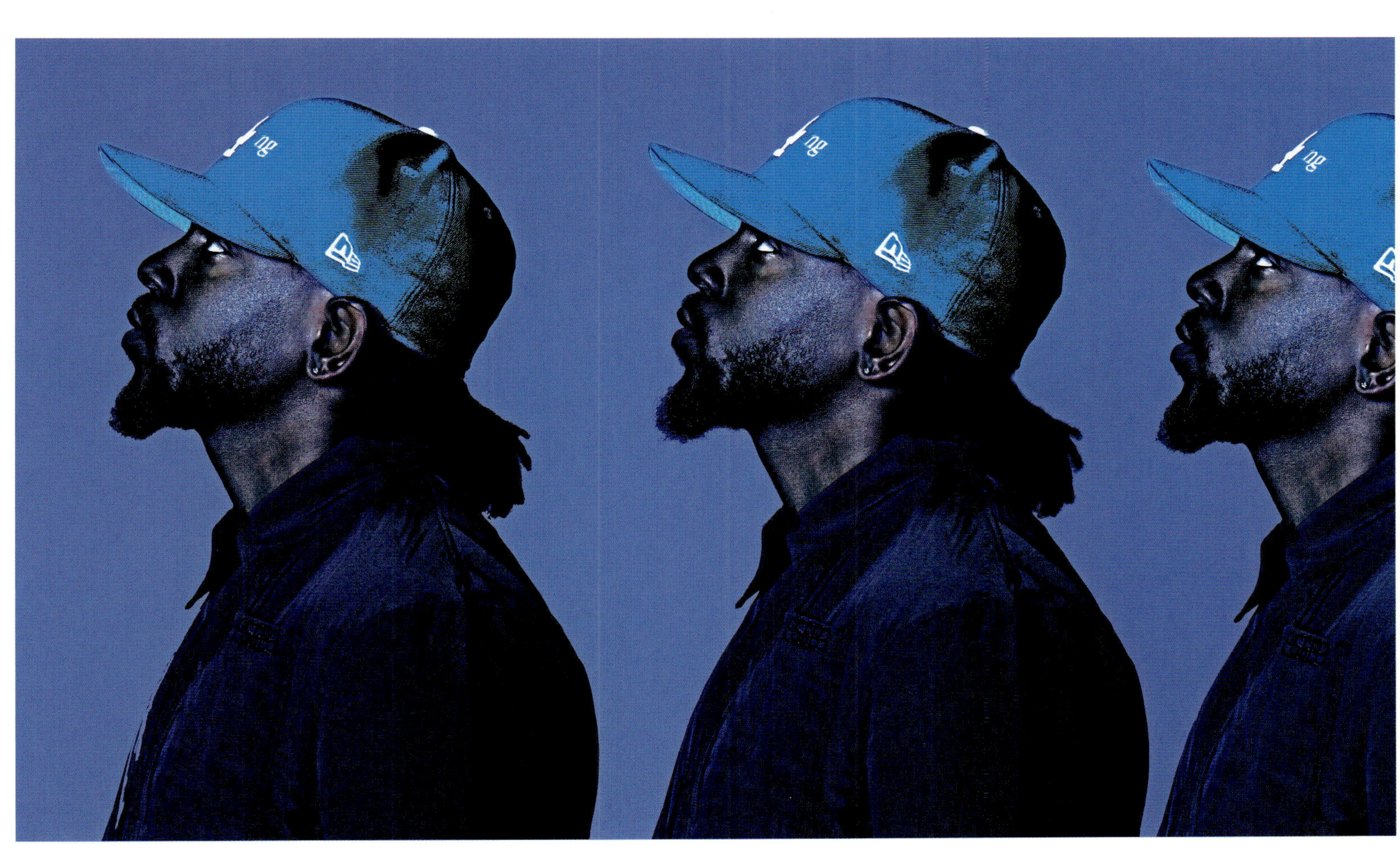

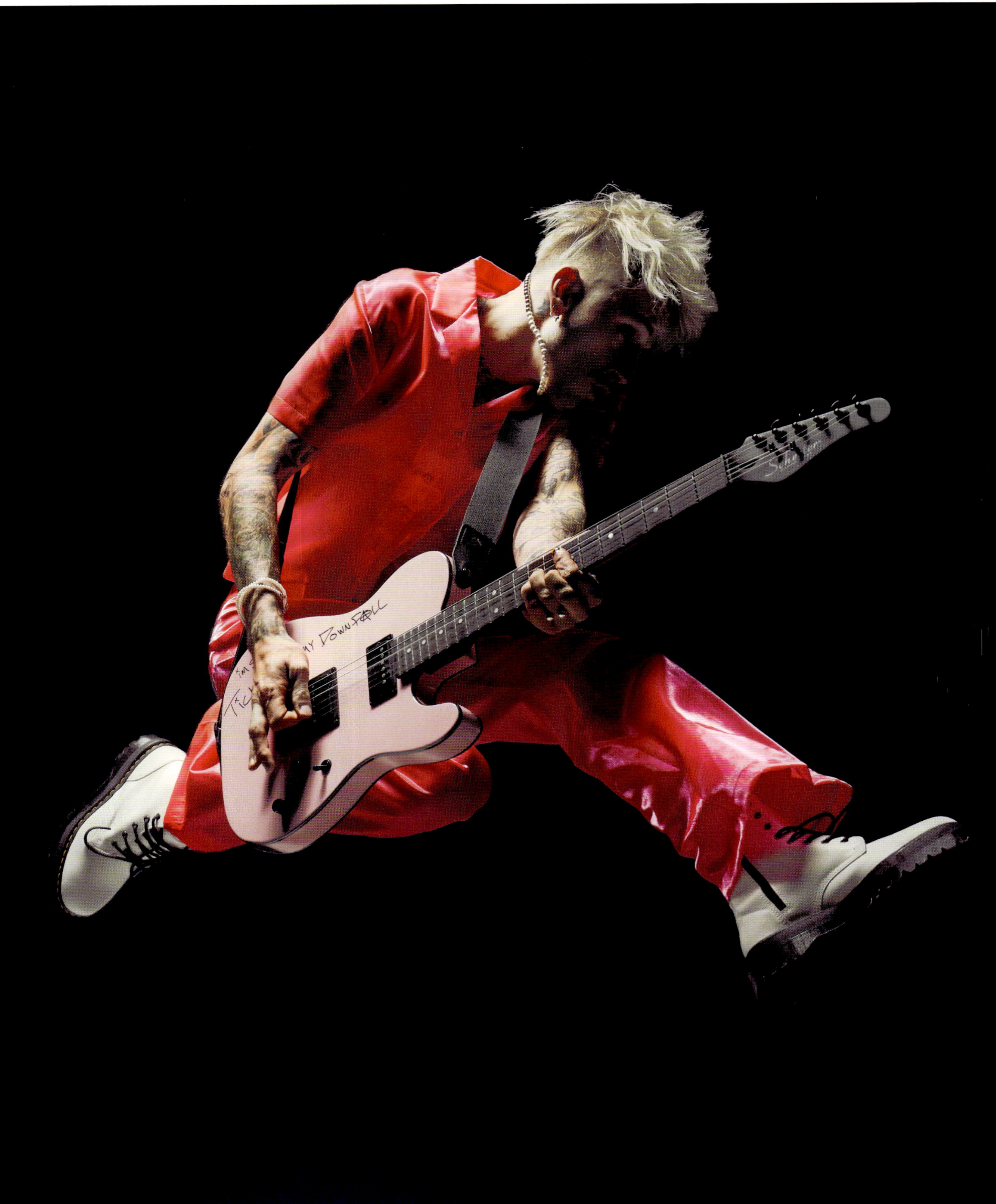
MY DOWNFALL

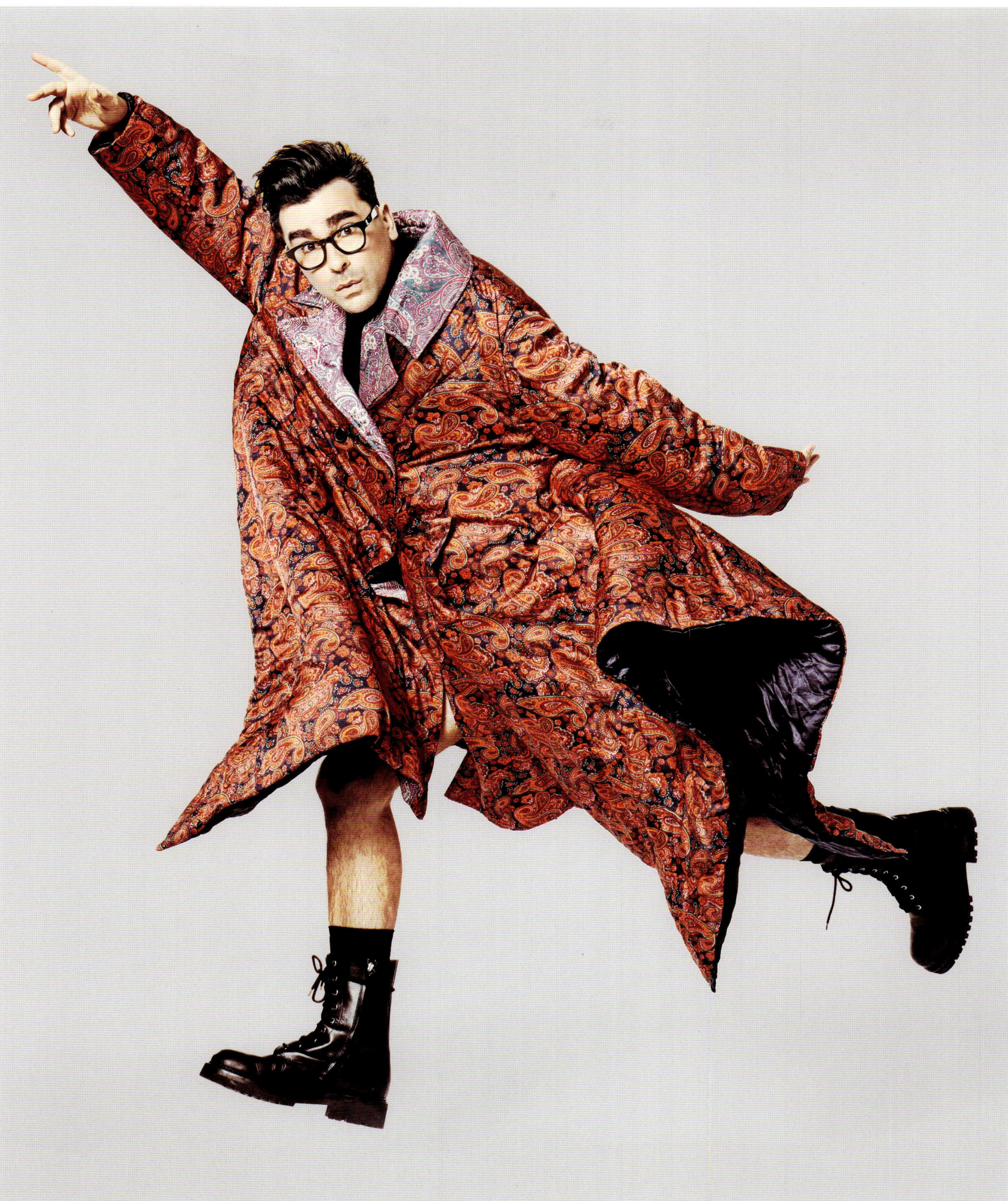

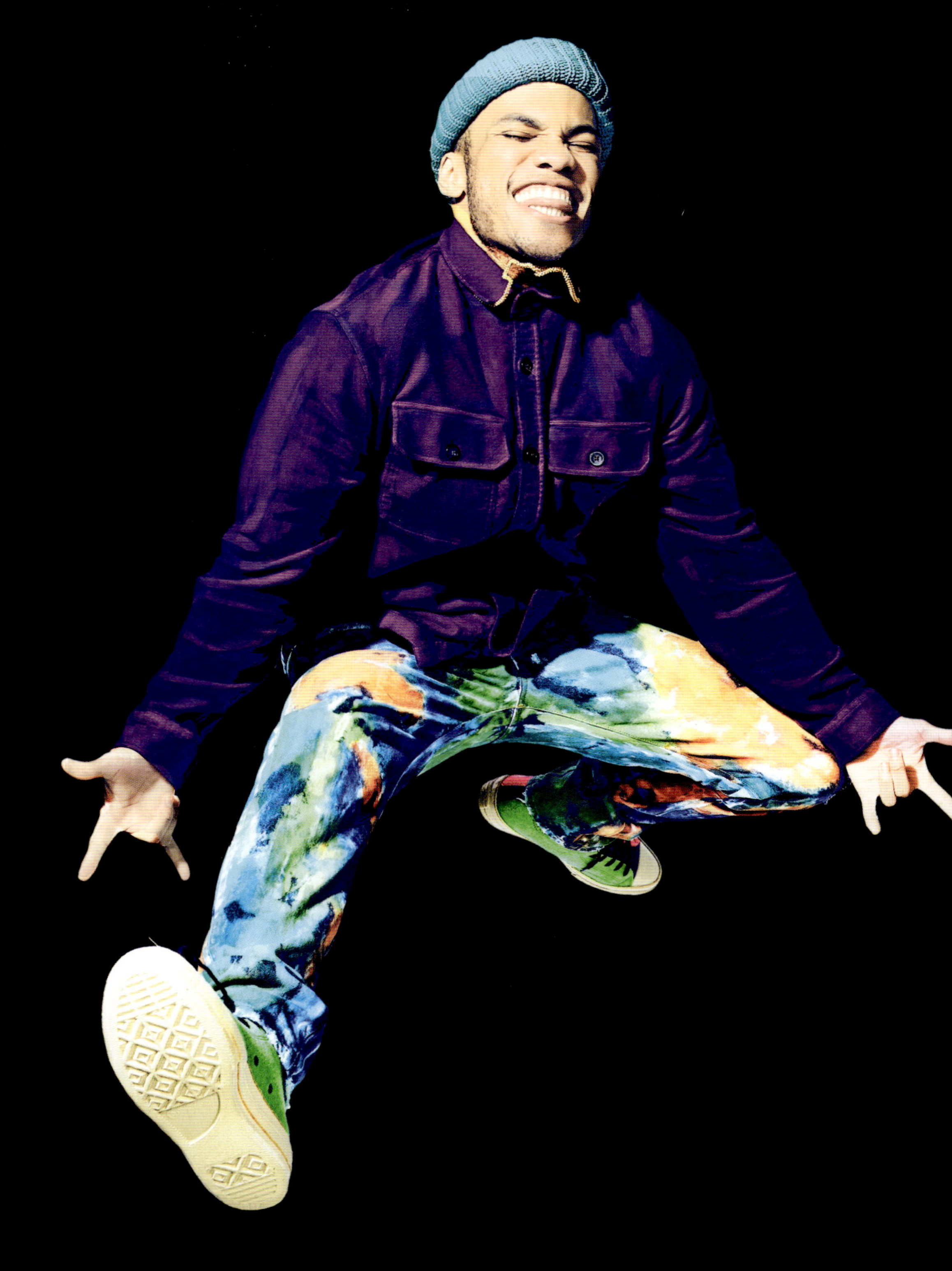

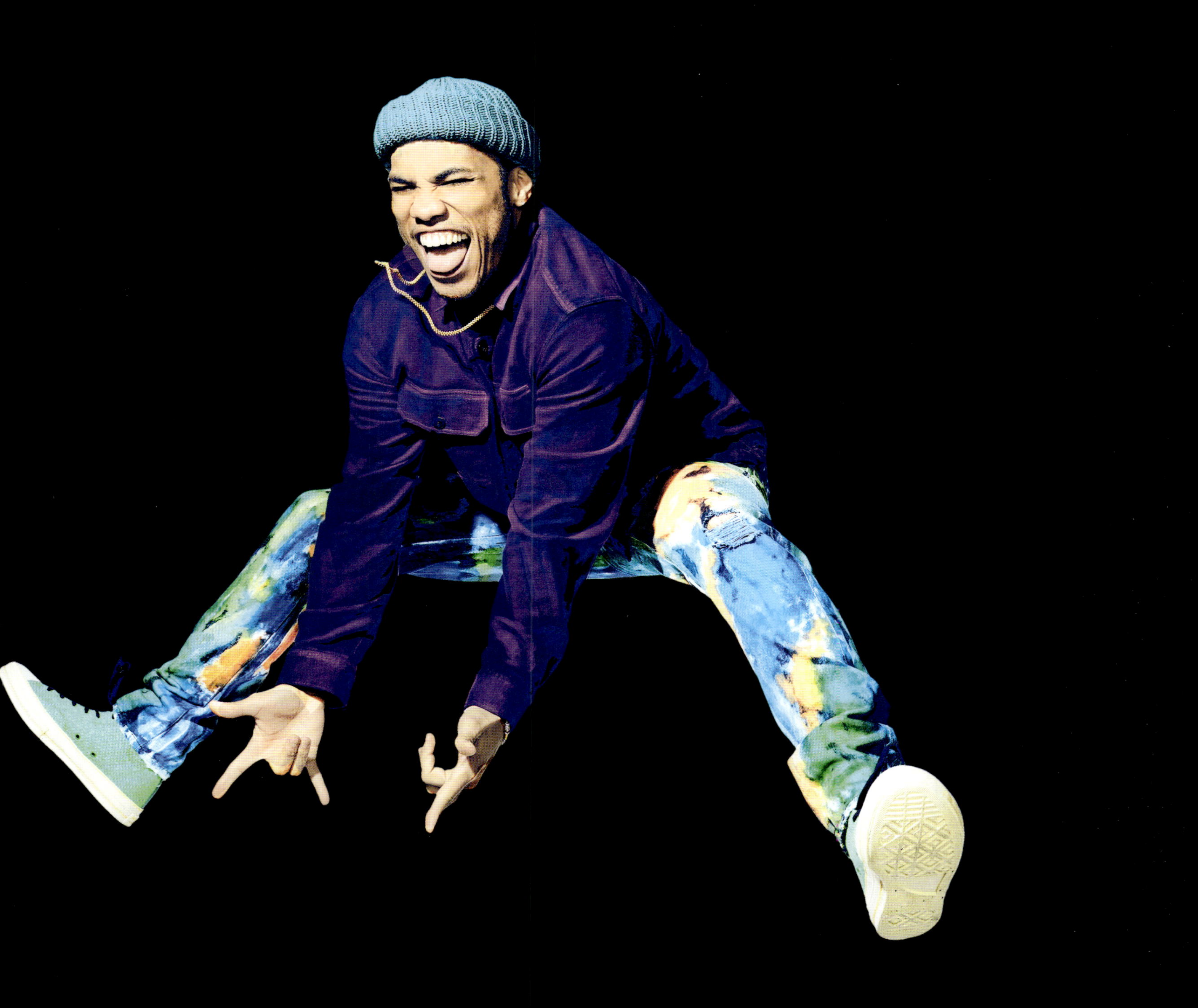

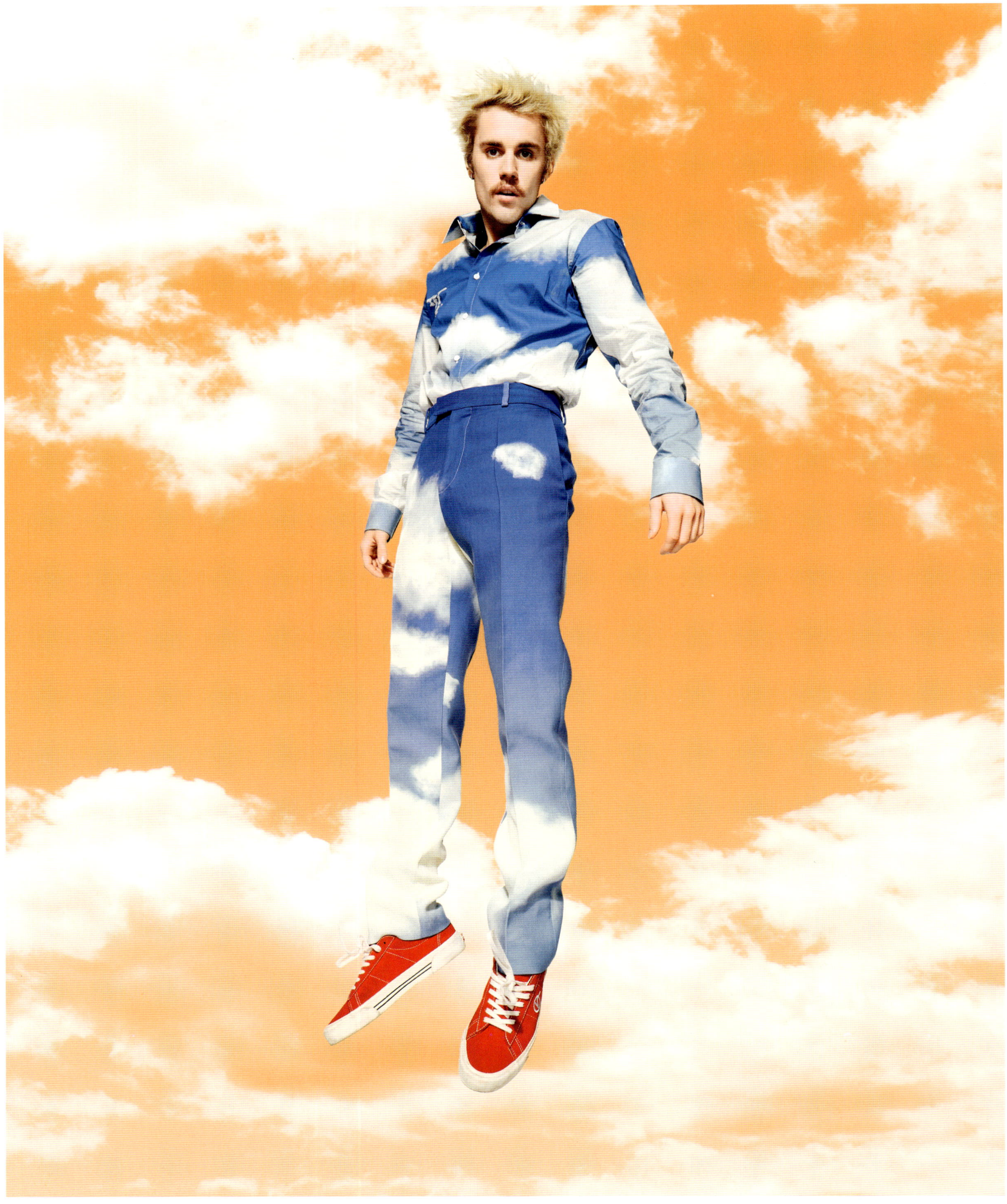

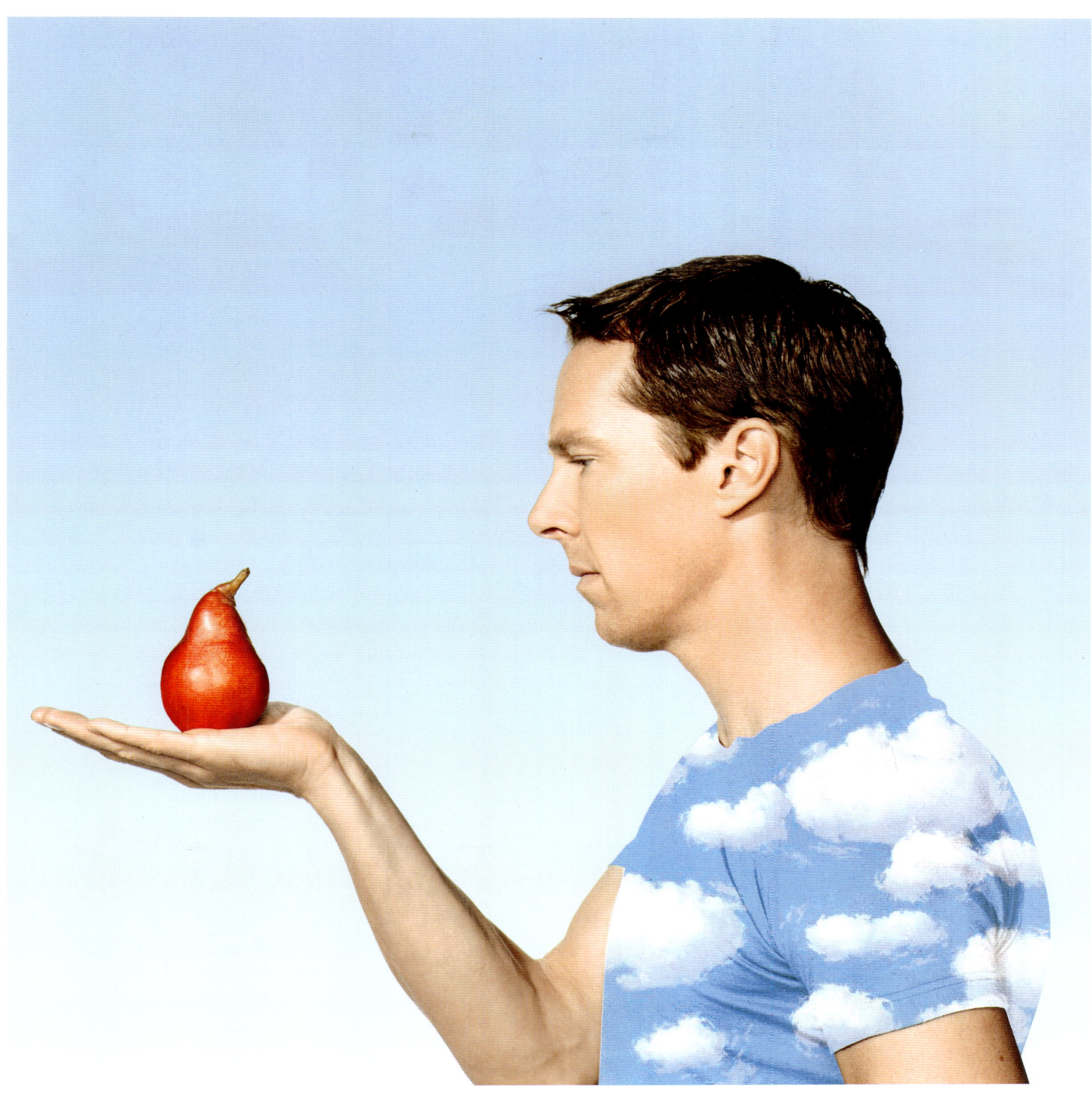

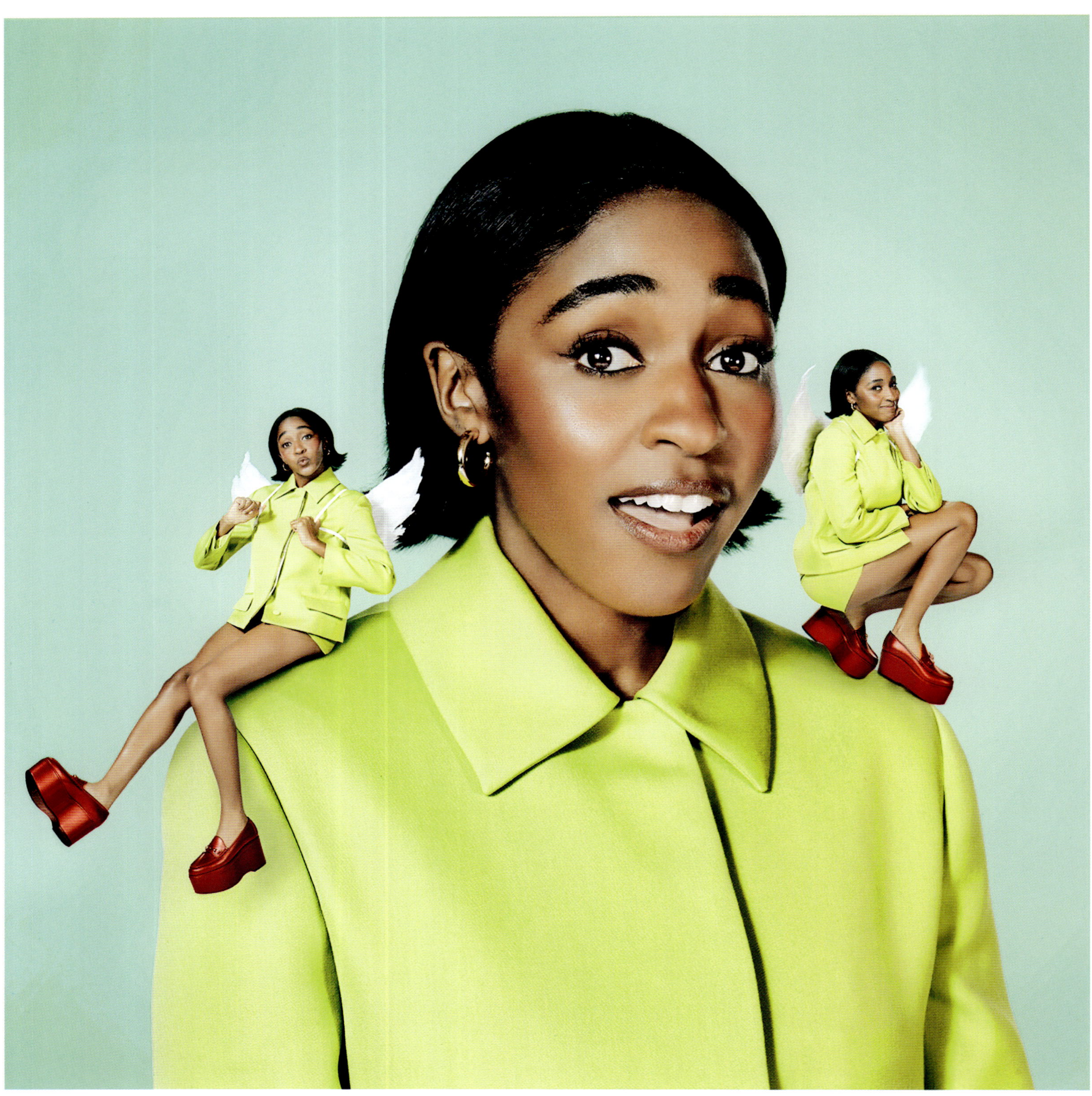

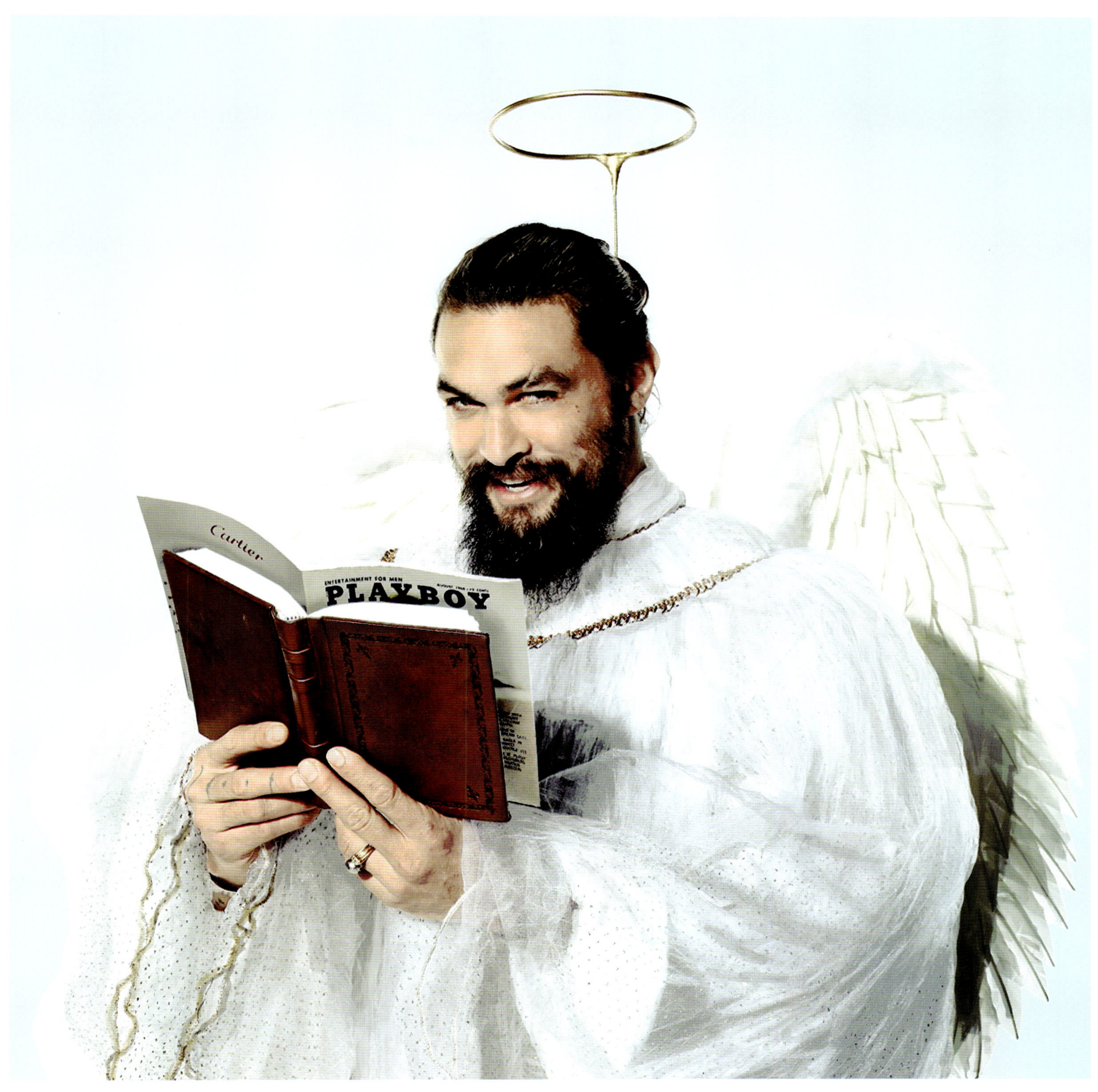
Cartier
ENTERTAINMENT FOR MEN
PLAYBOY

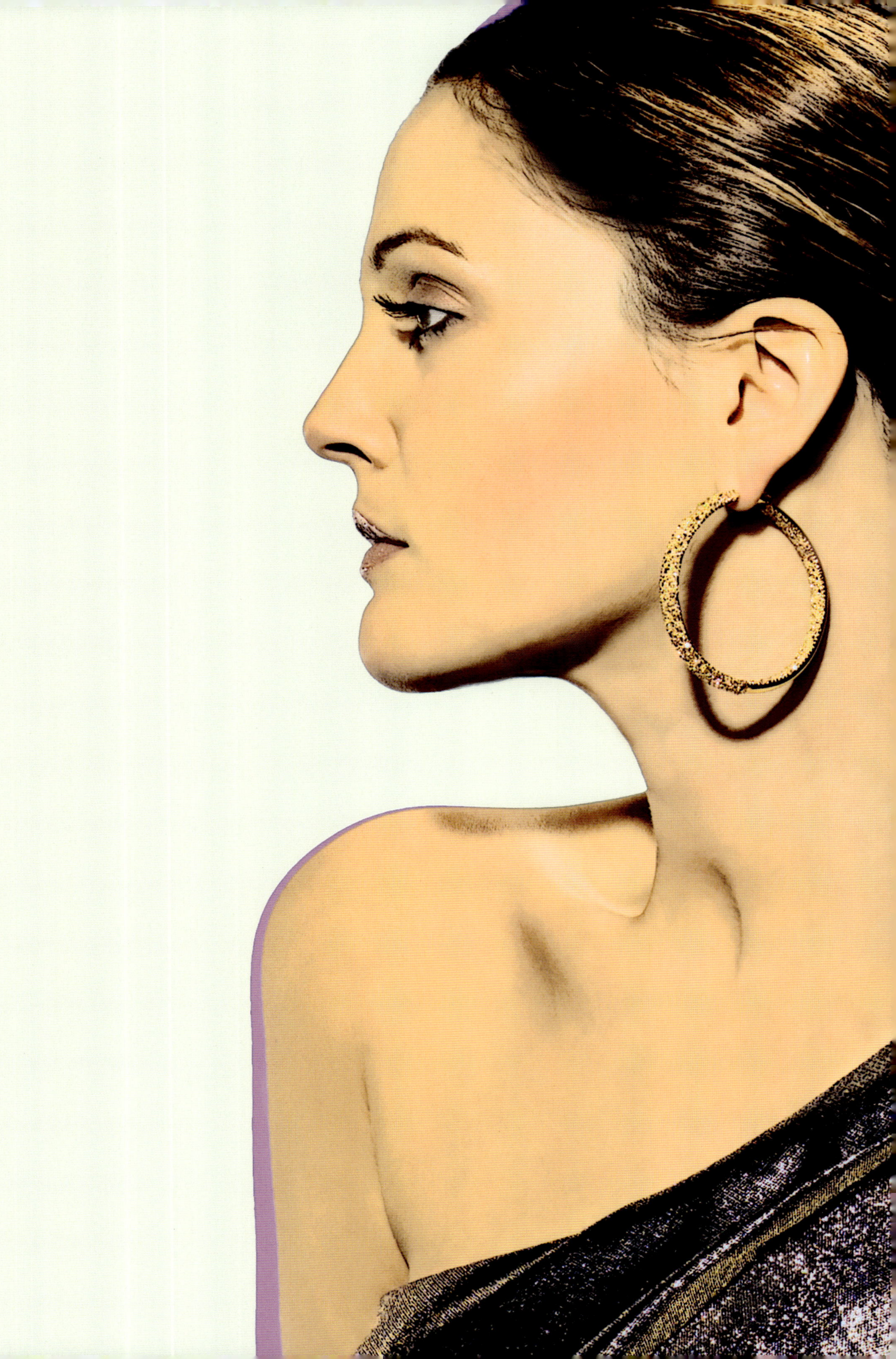

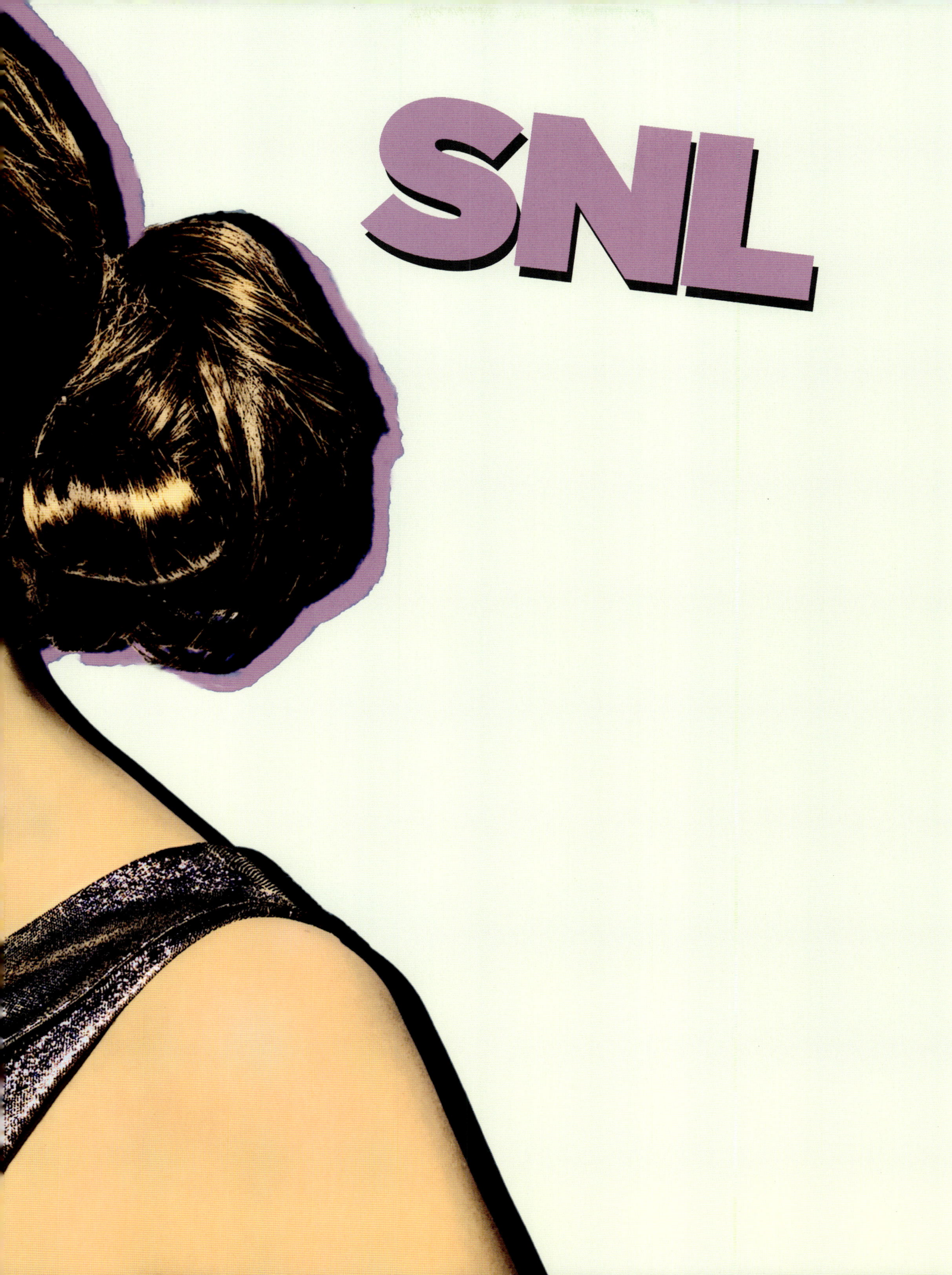
SNL

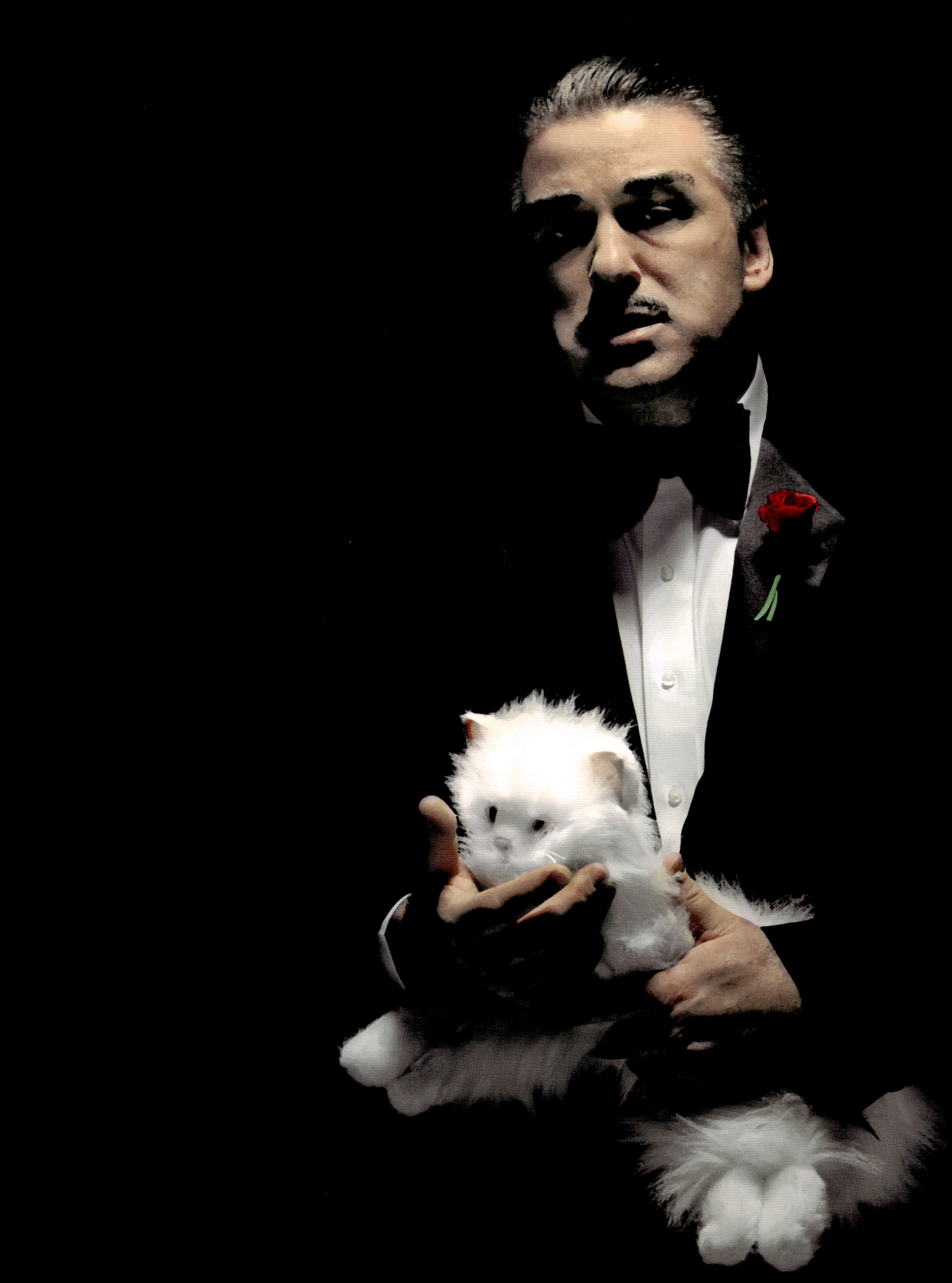

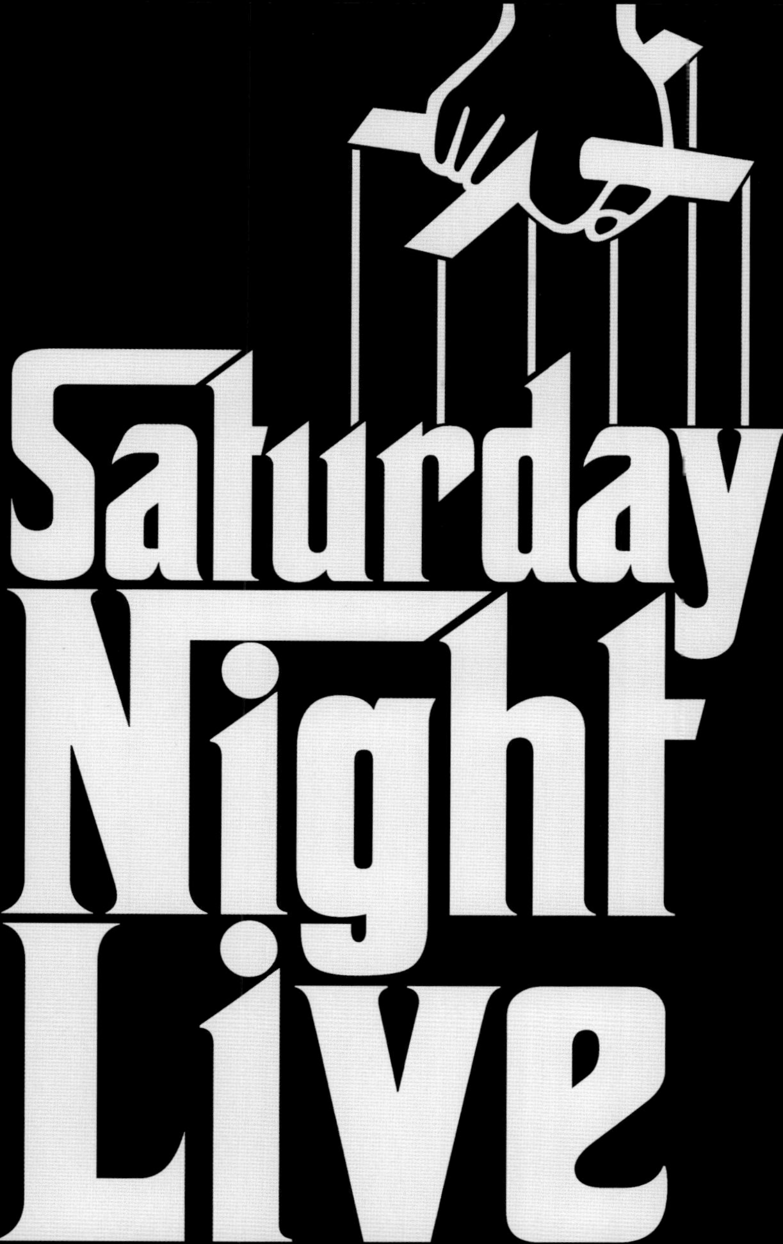
Saturday
Night
Live

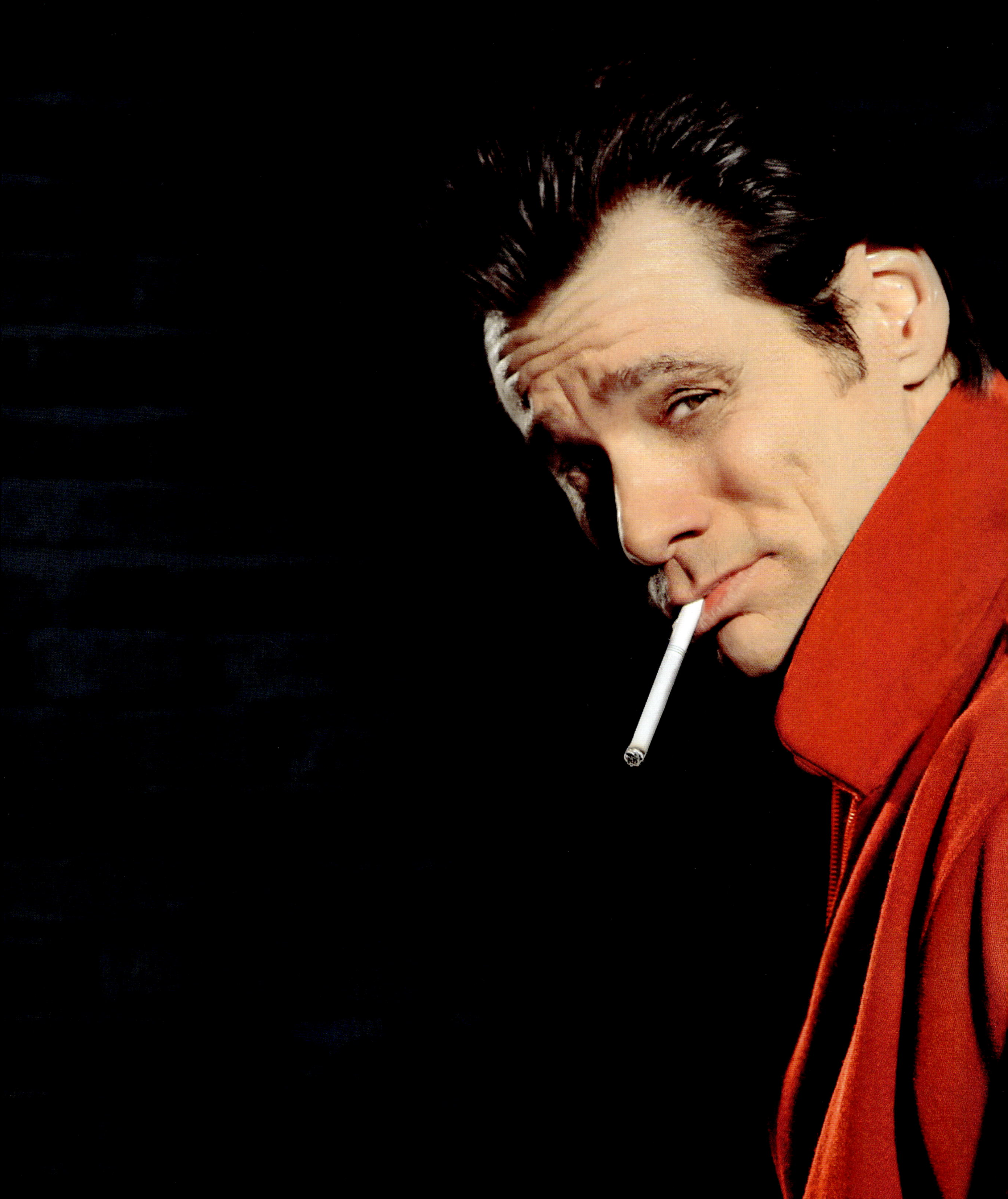

JIM CARREY

IN

"SATURDAY NIGHT LIVE"

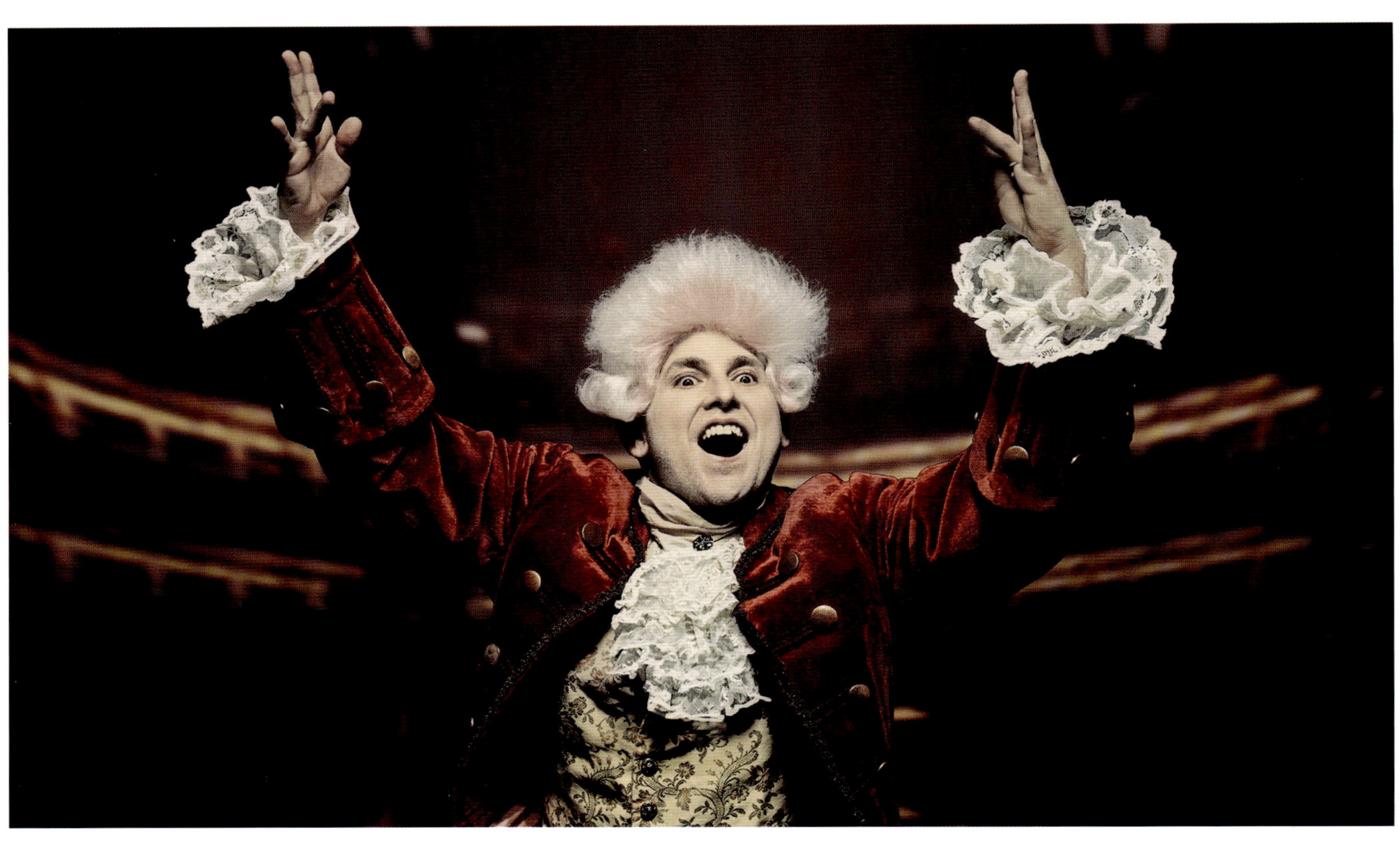

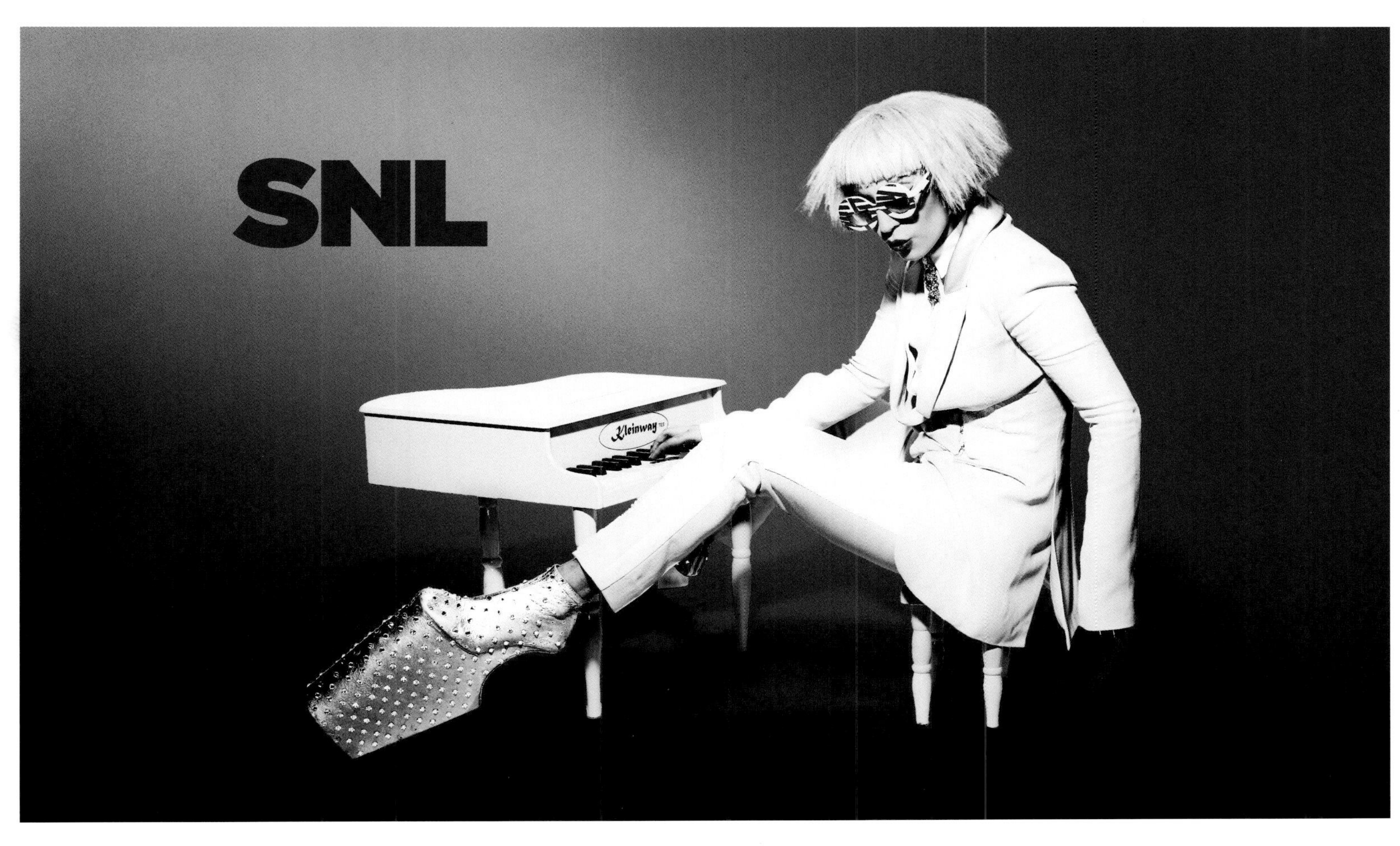
SNL
Kleinway

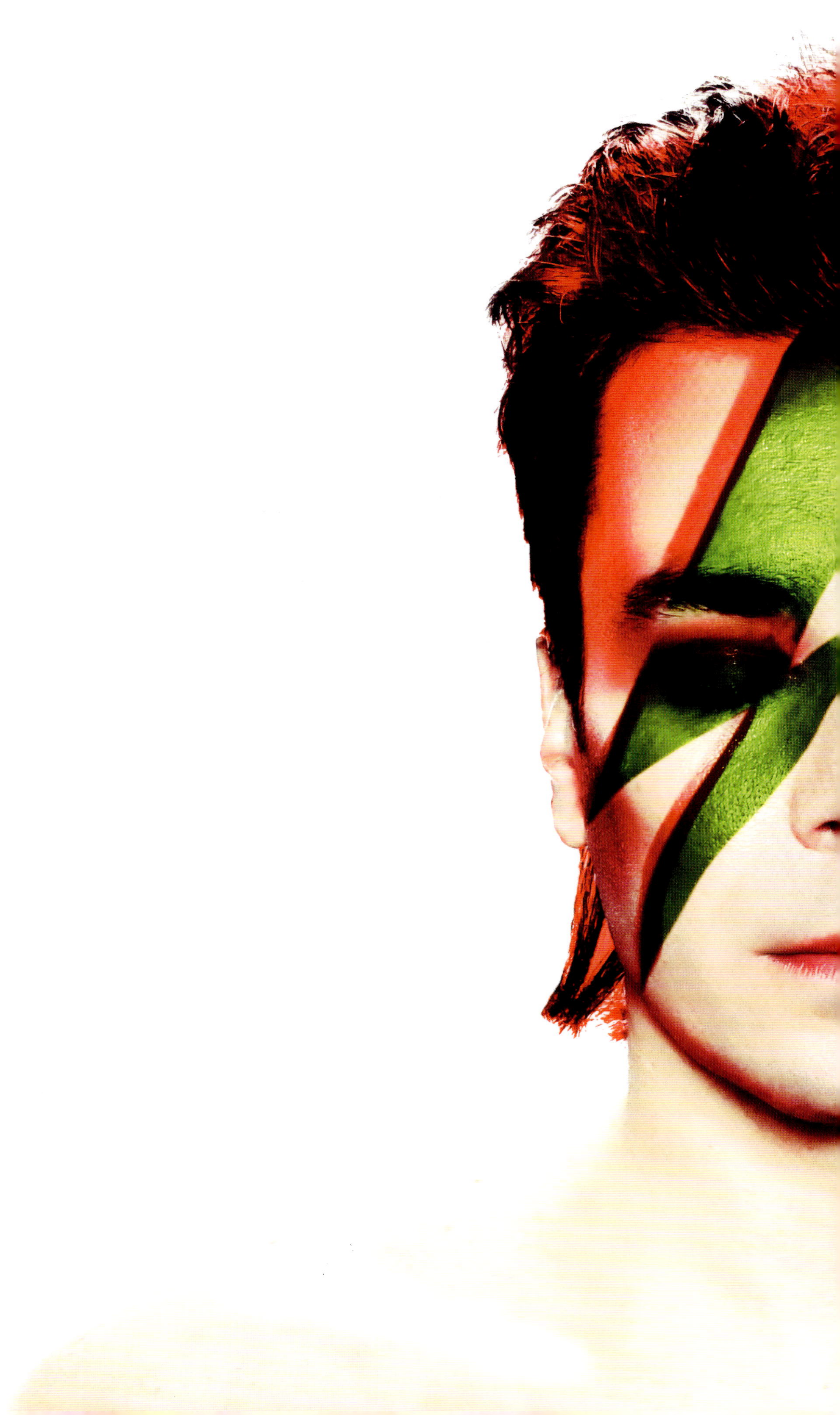

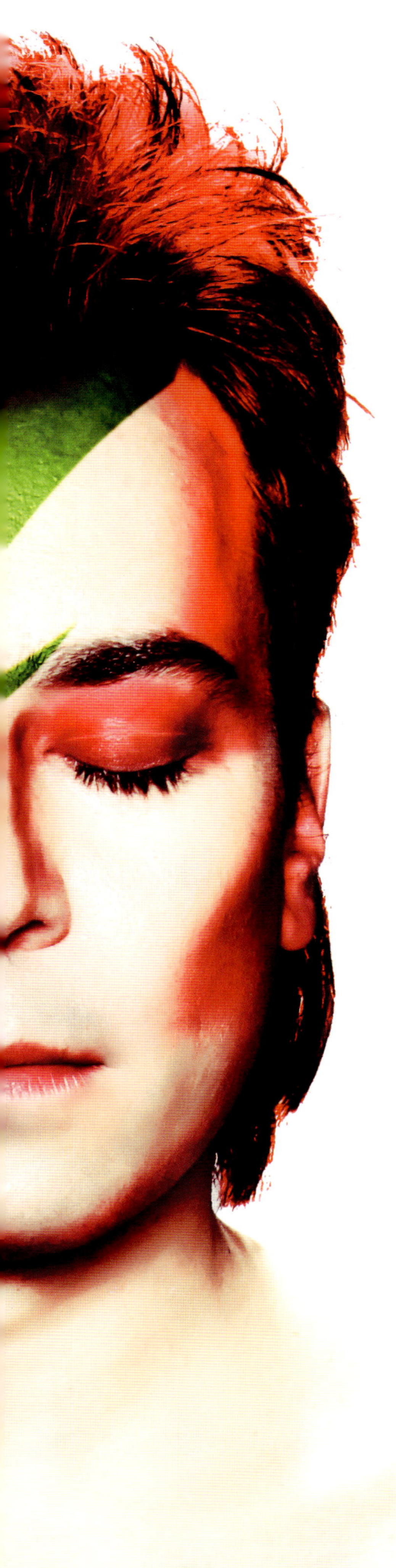

SNL

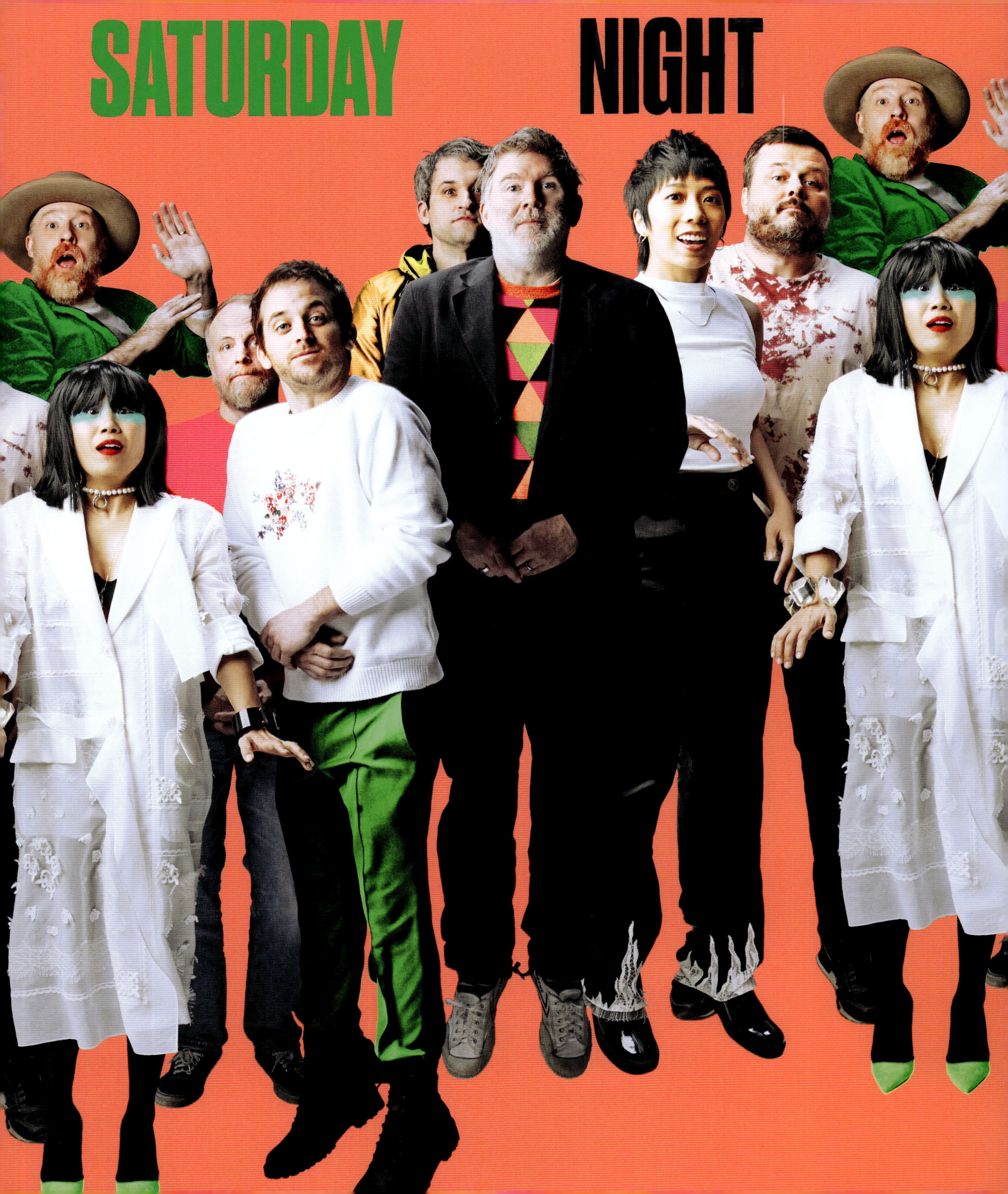
SATURDAY
NIGHT

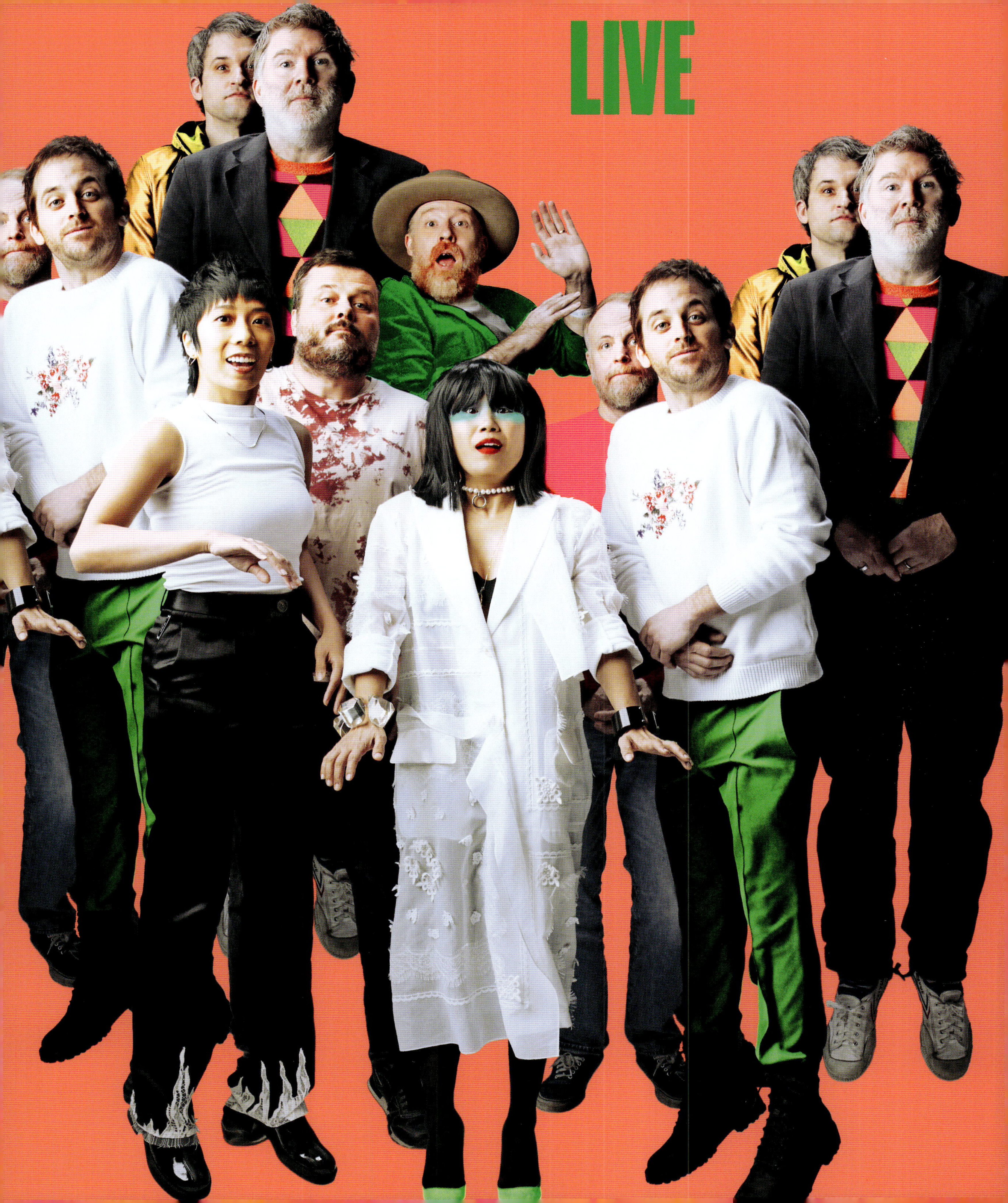
LIVE

SATURDAY NIGHT LIVE

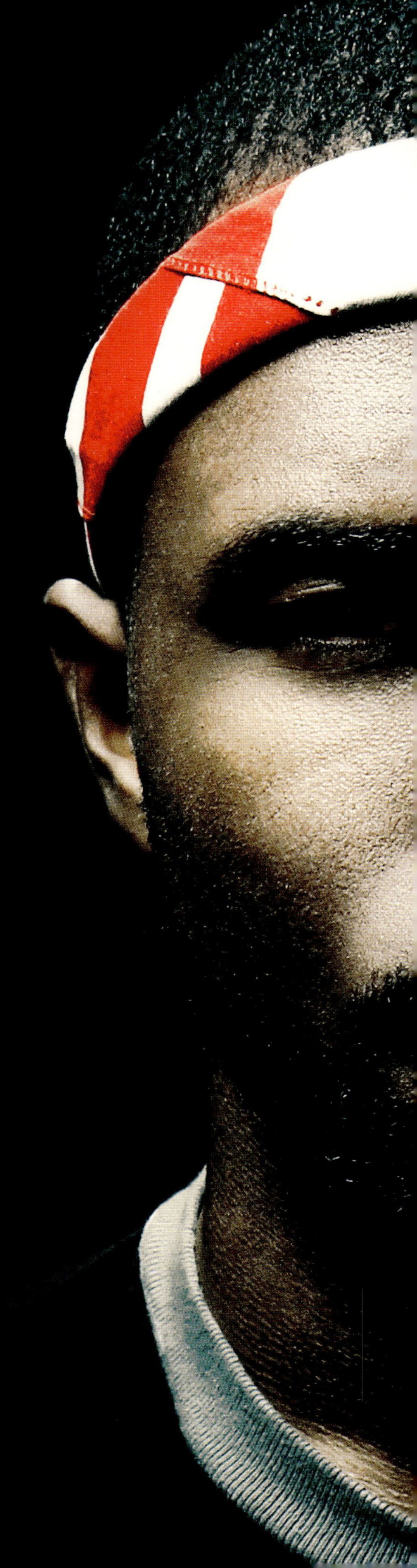

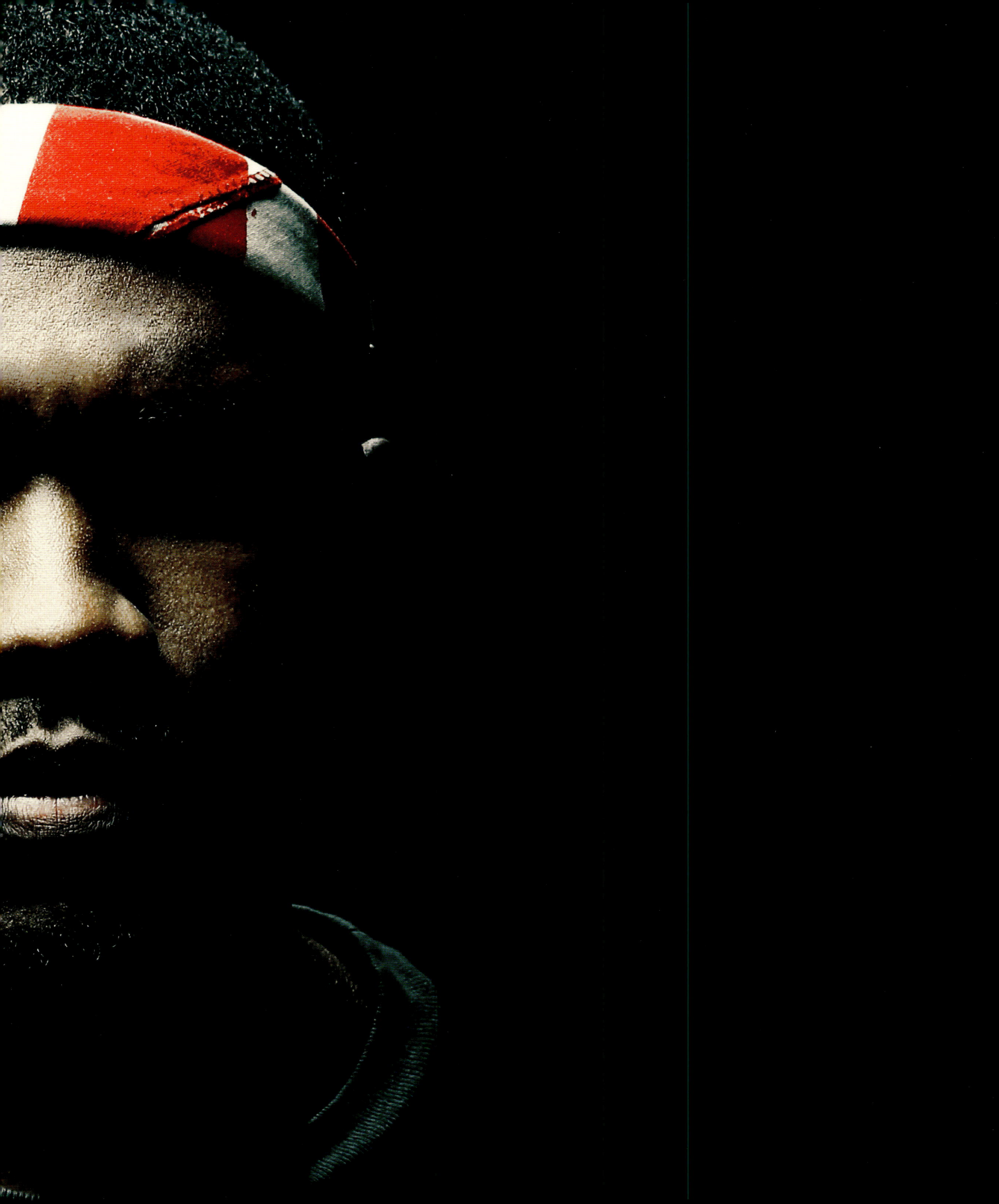

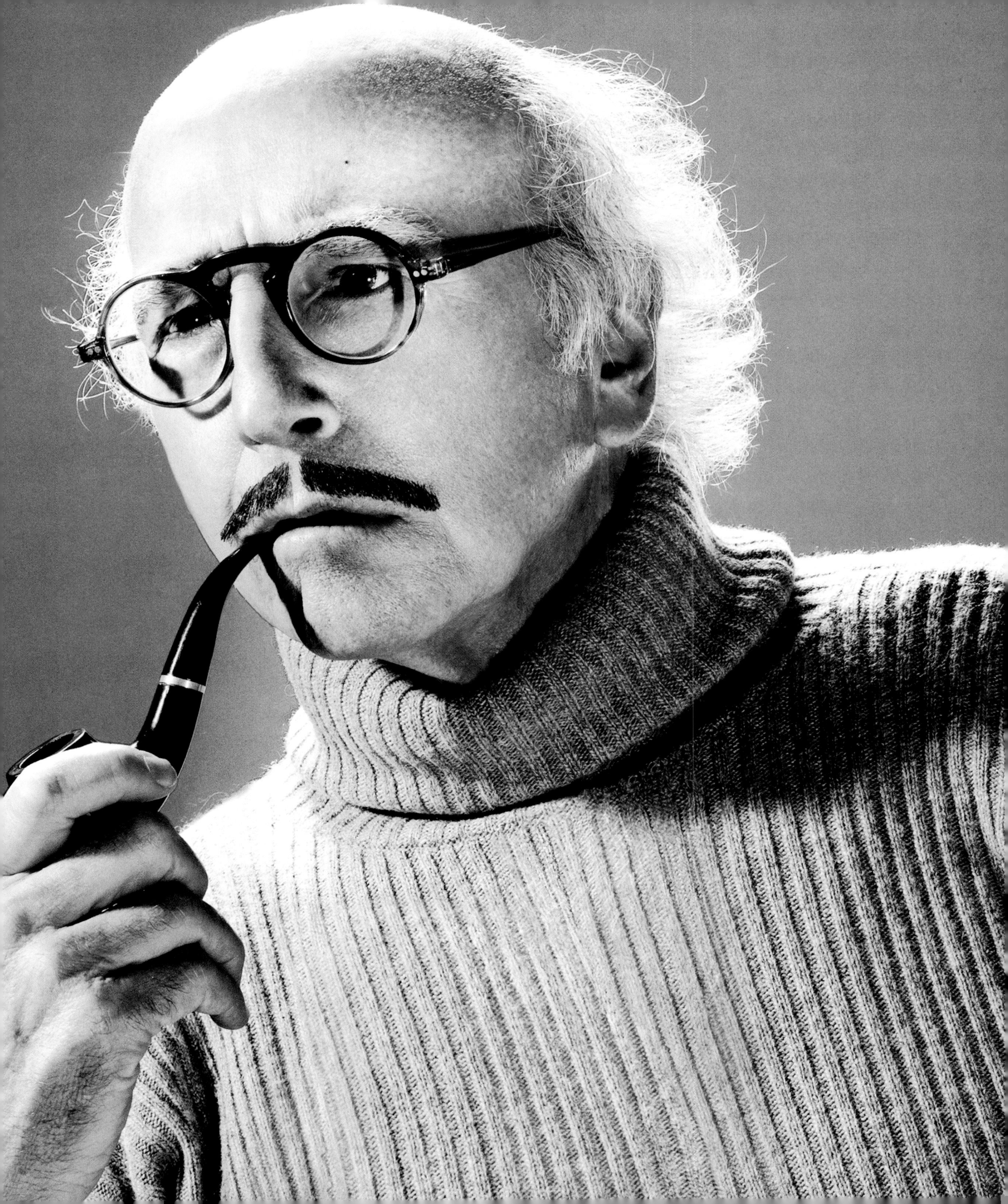

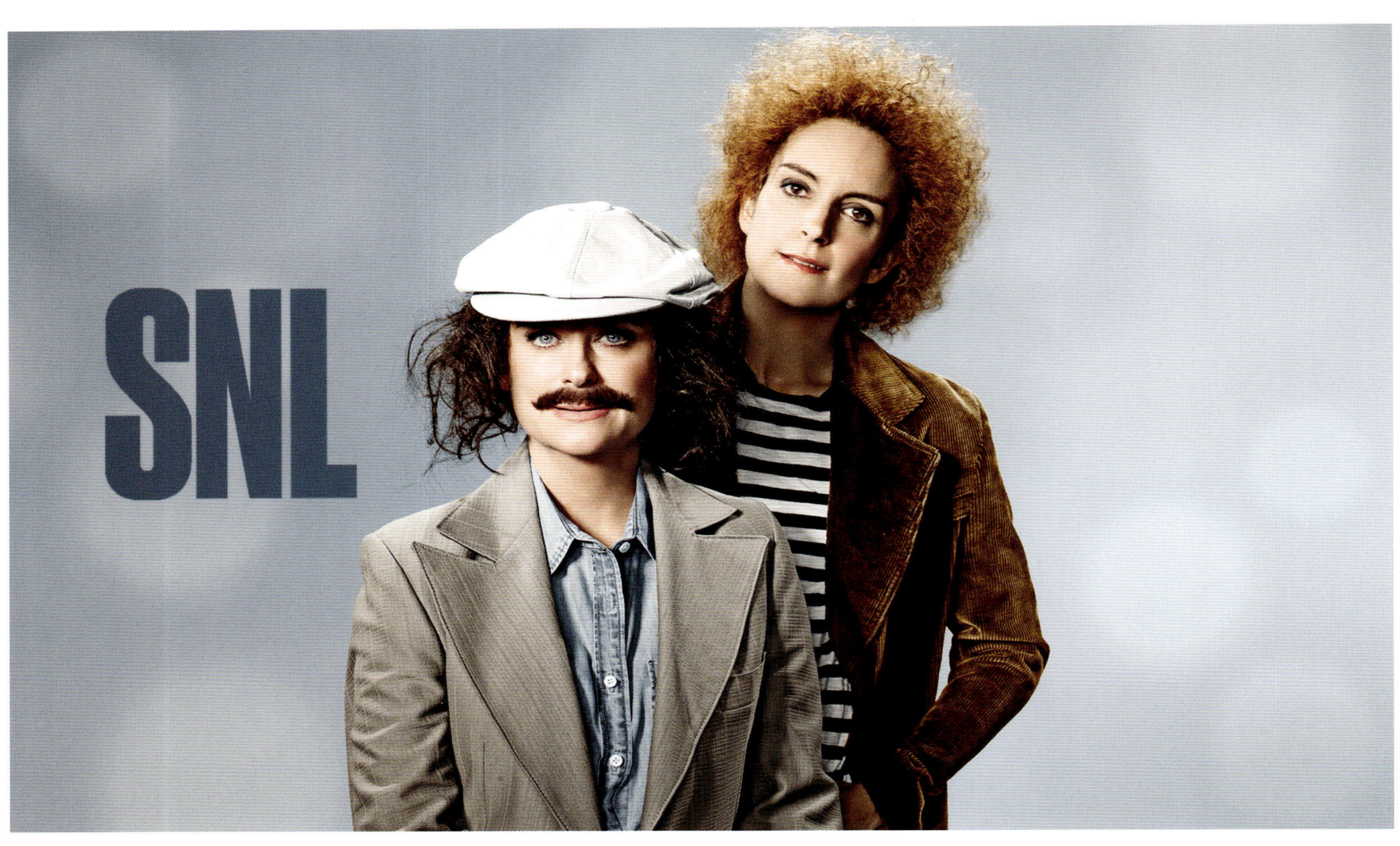
SNL

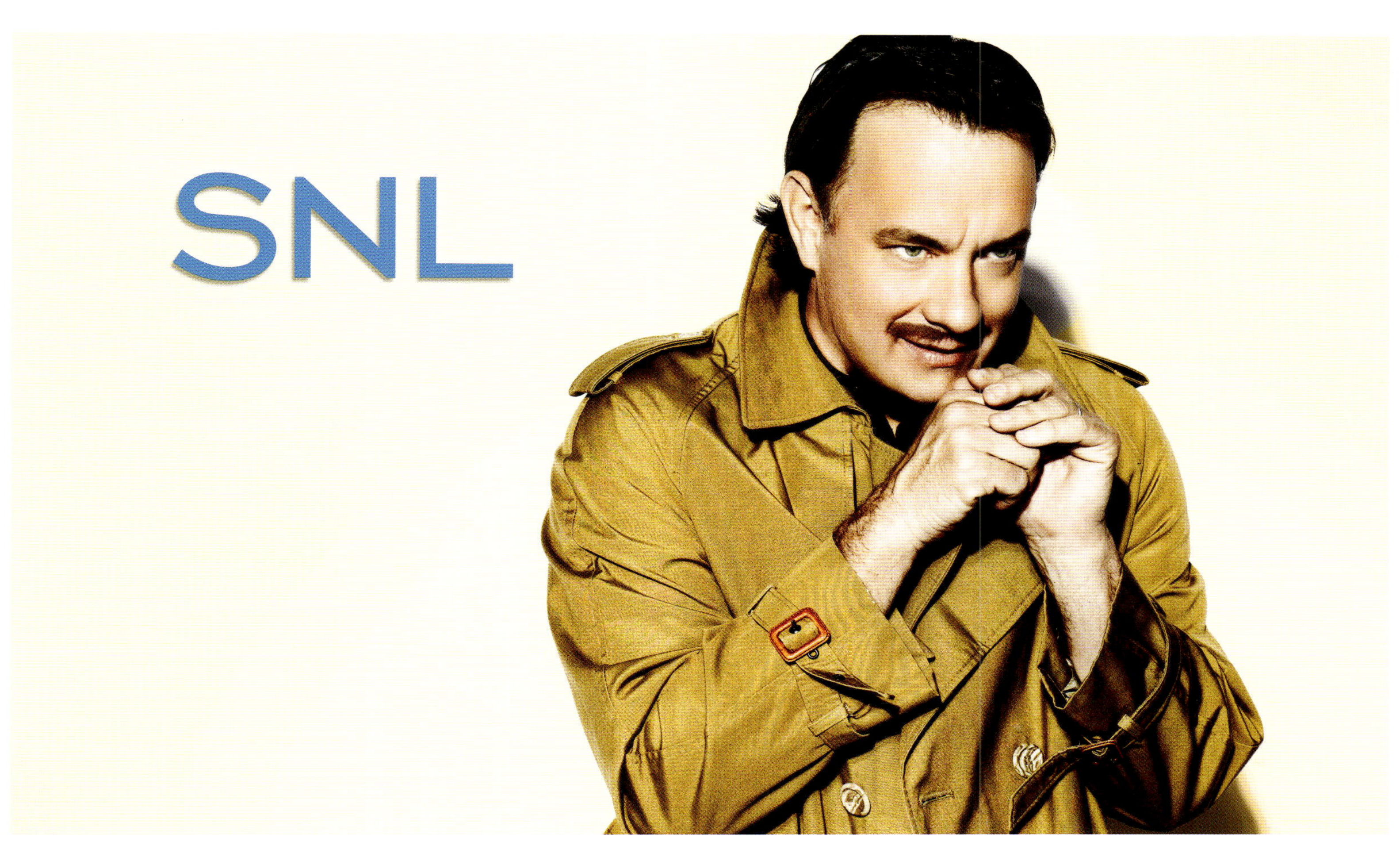
SNL

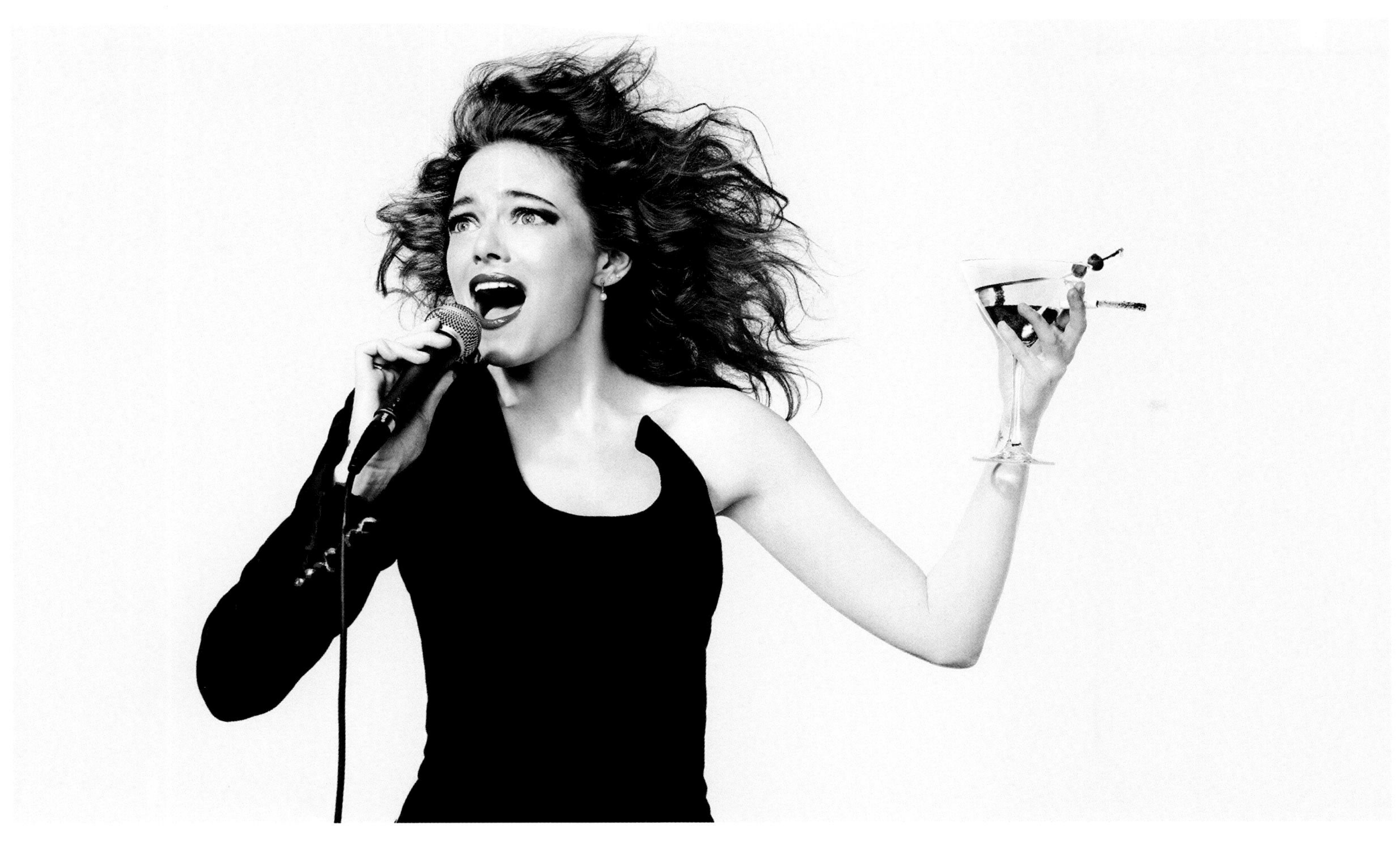

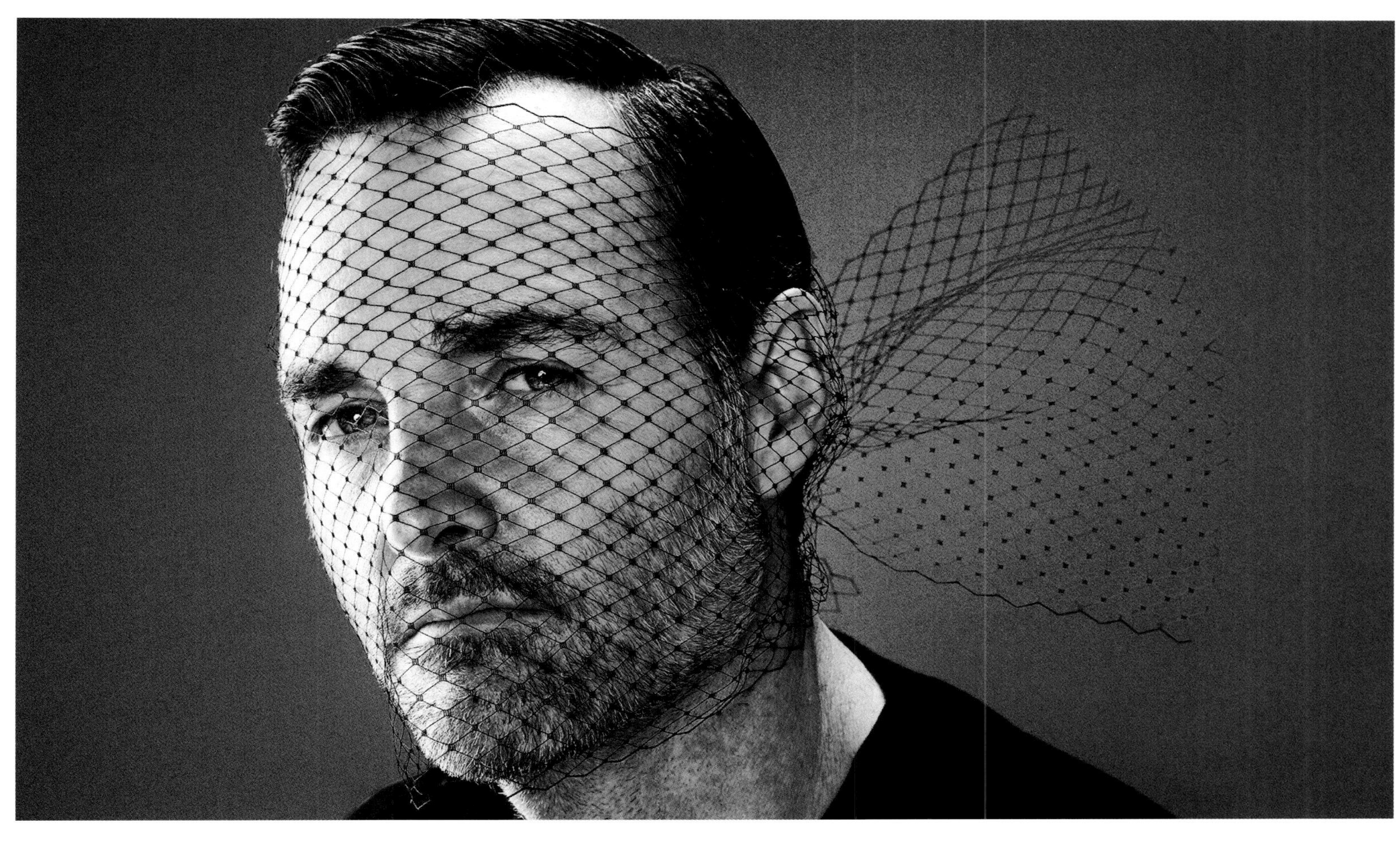

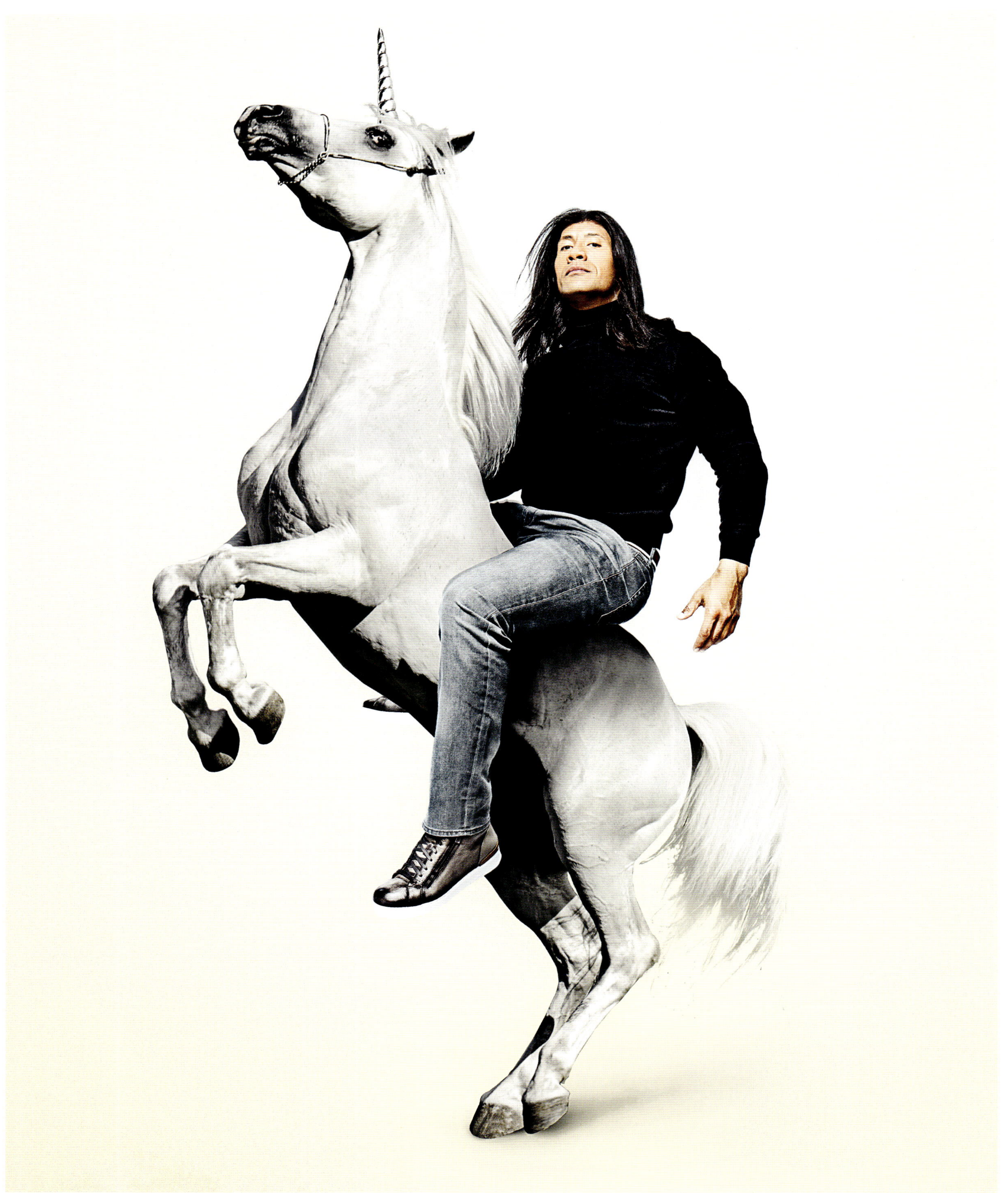

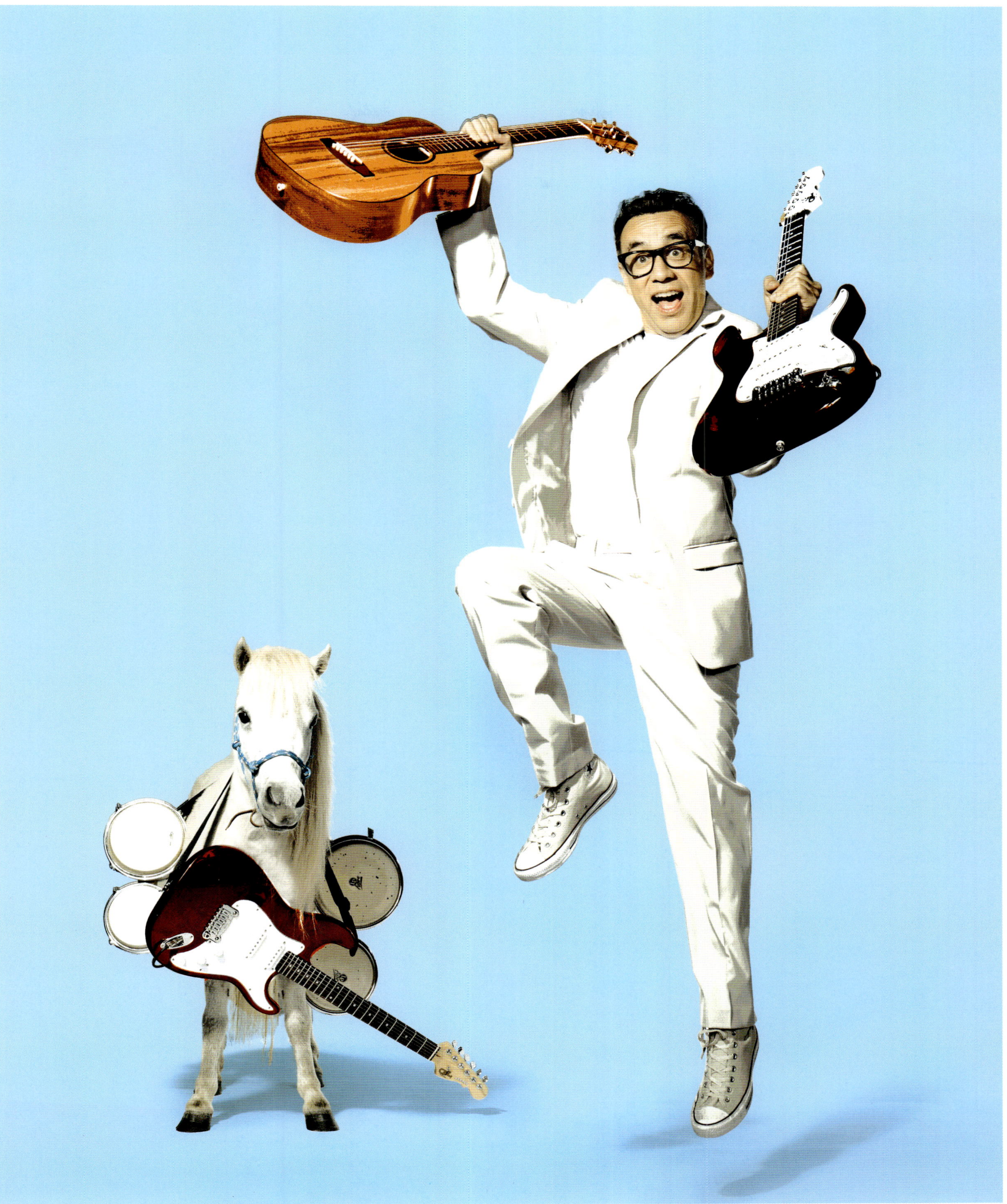

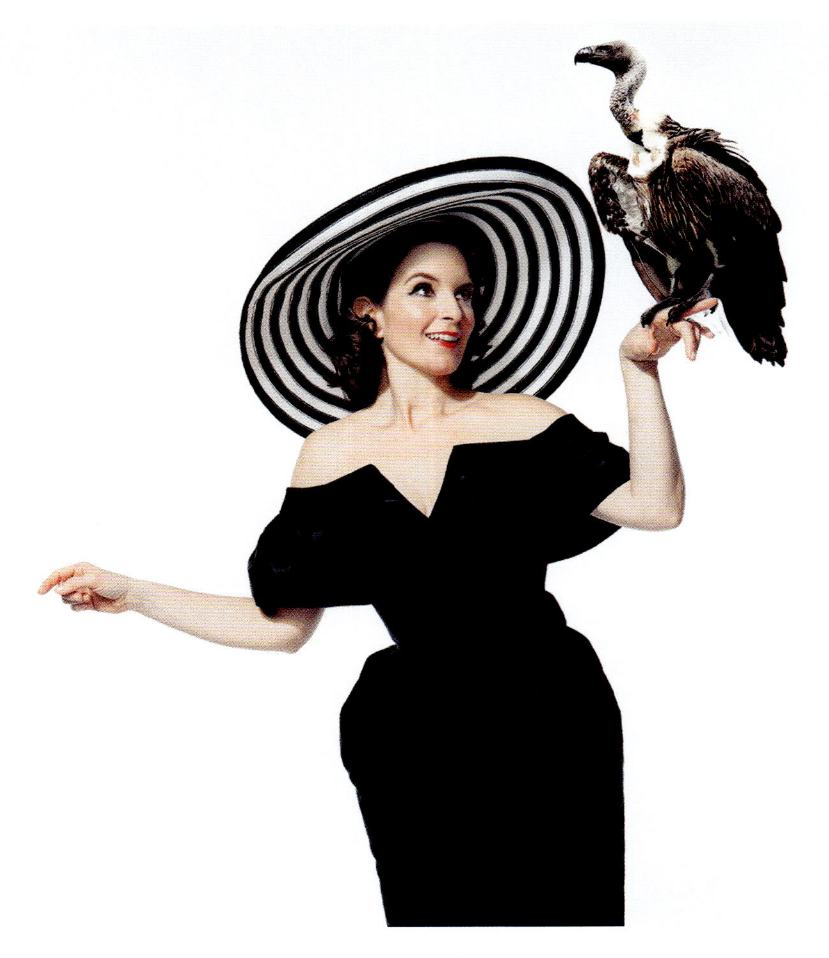

SNL

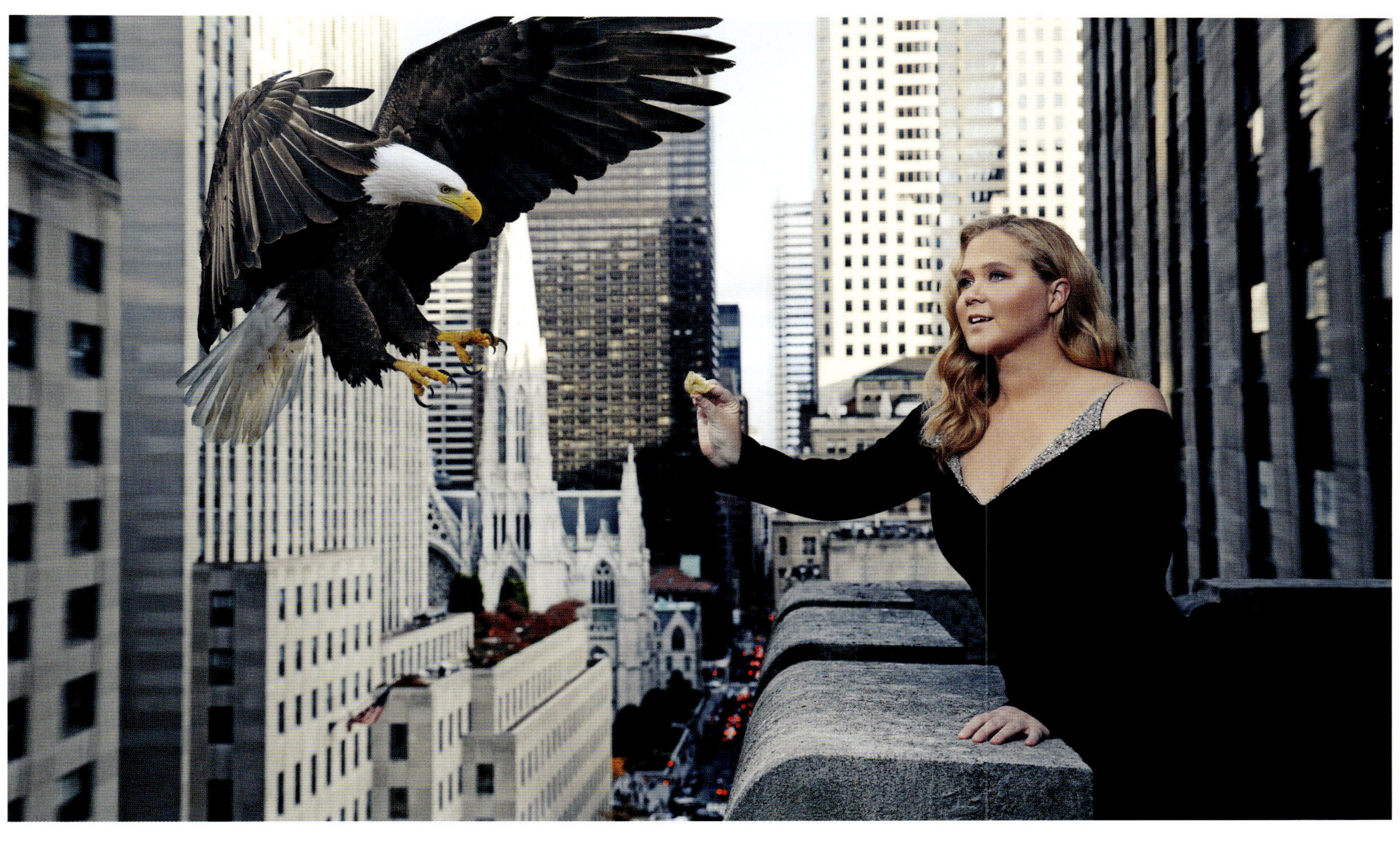

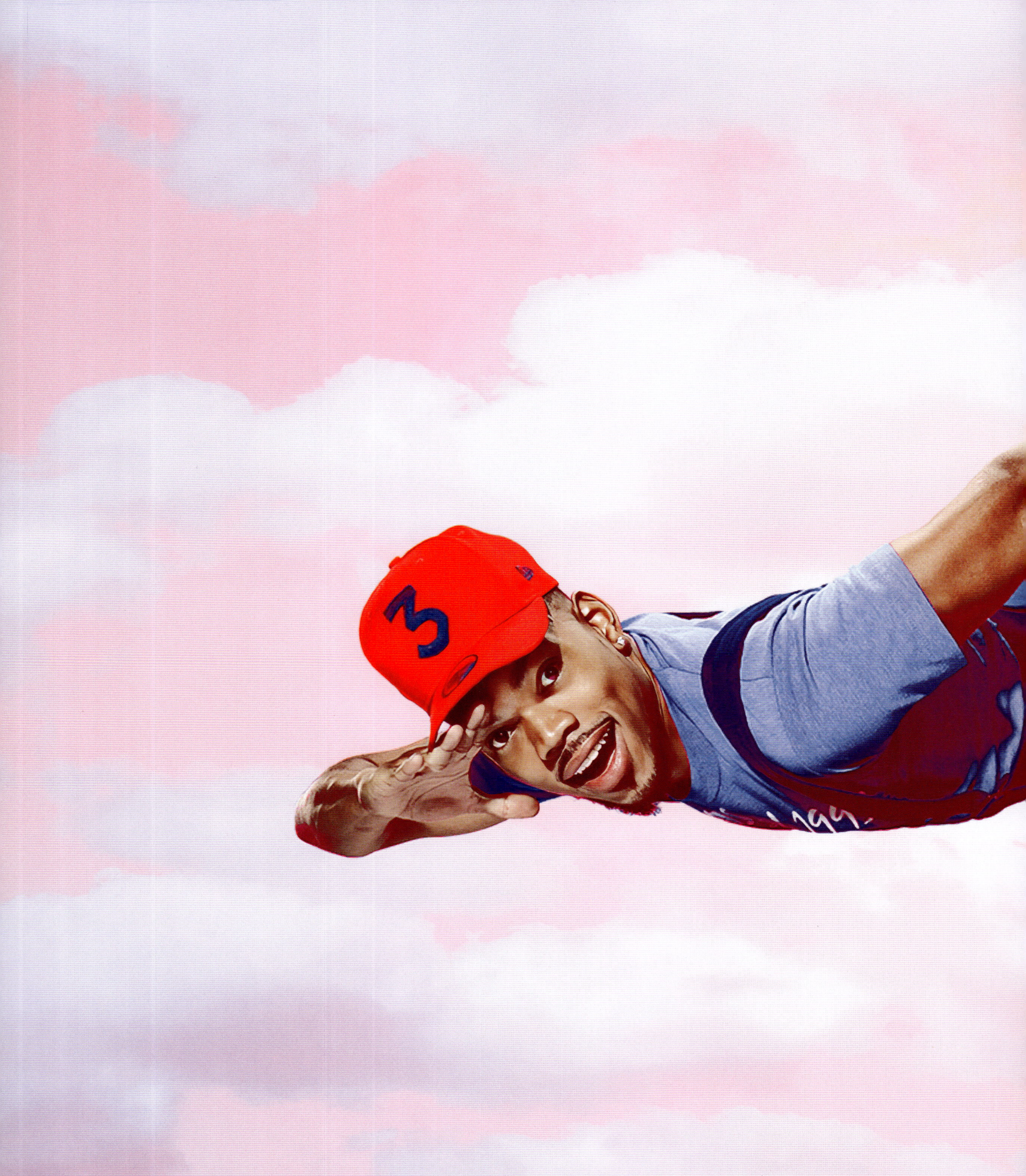
3

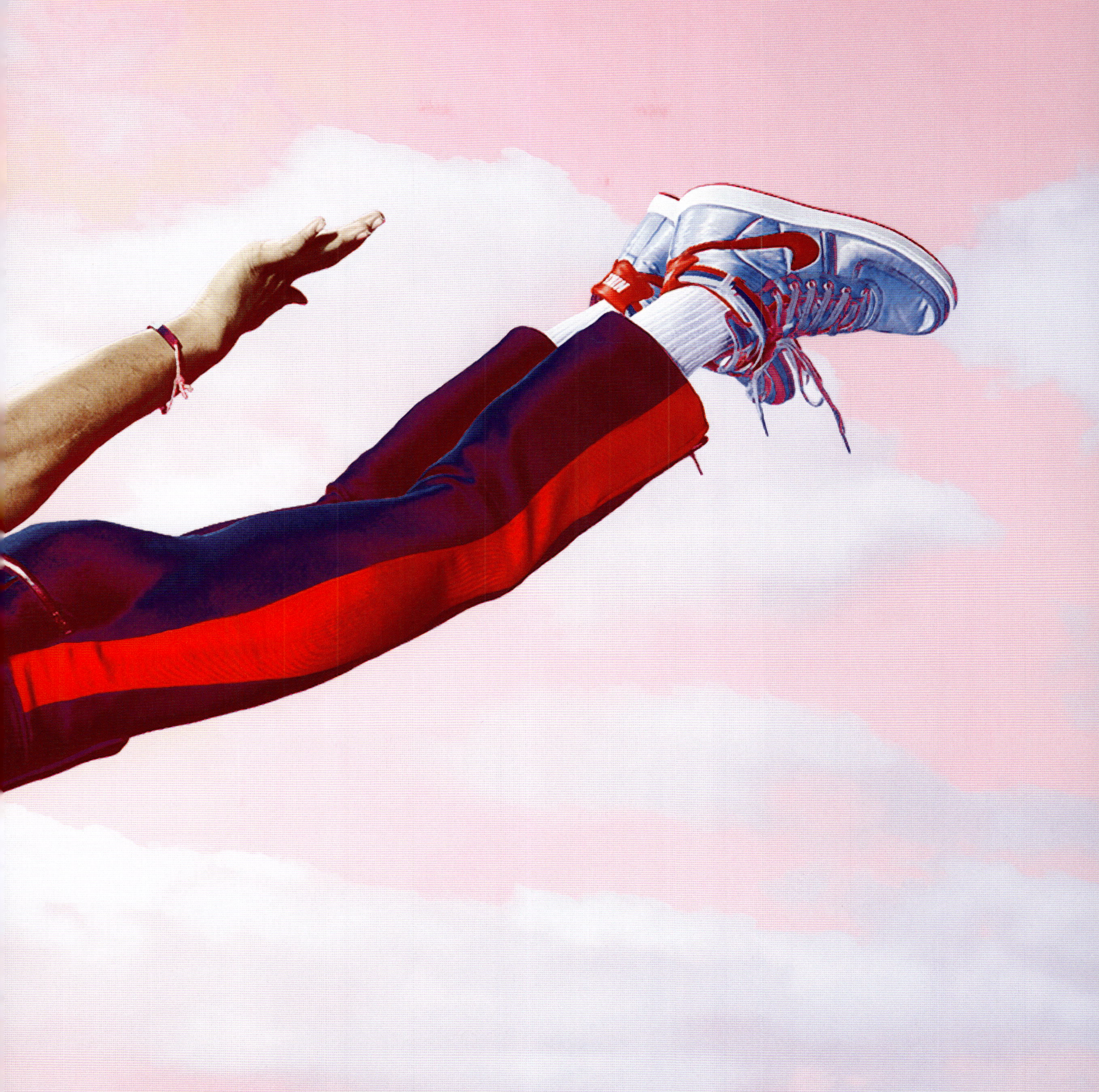

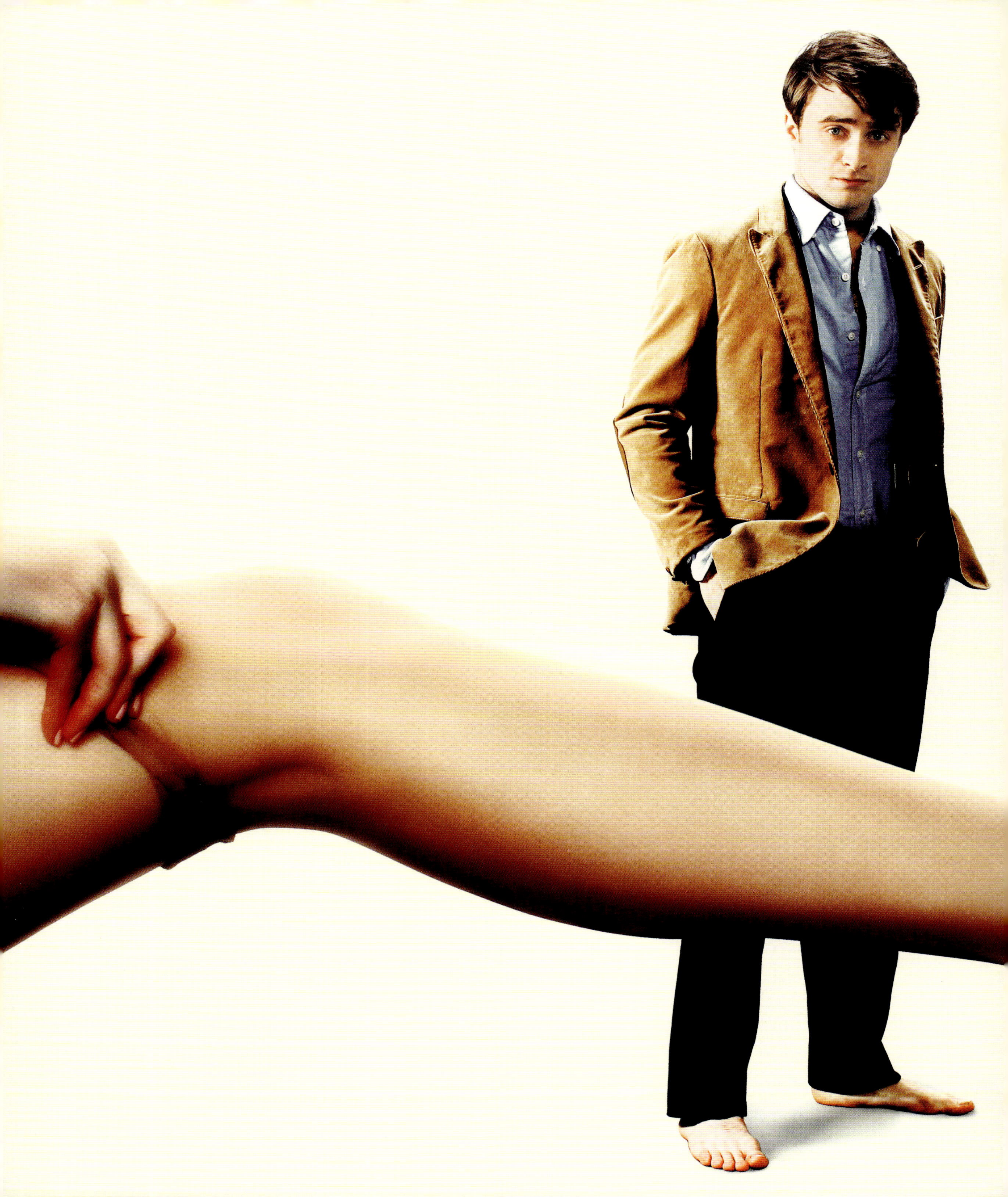

SNL

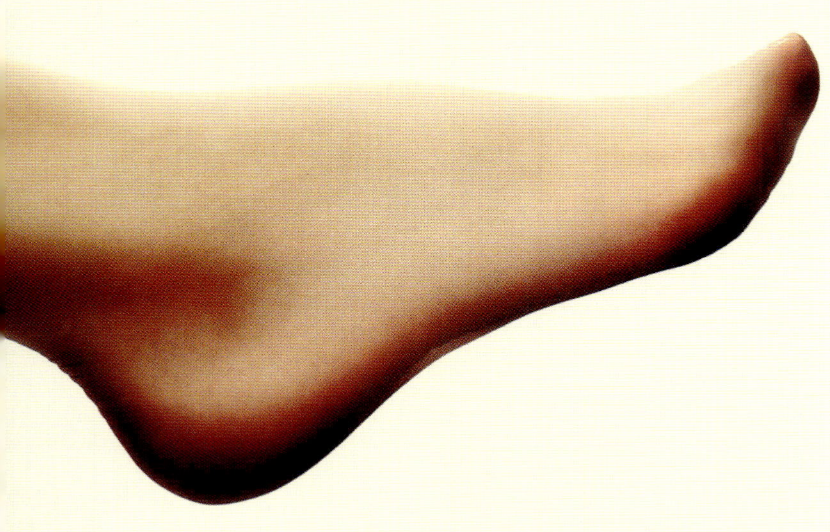

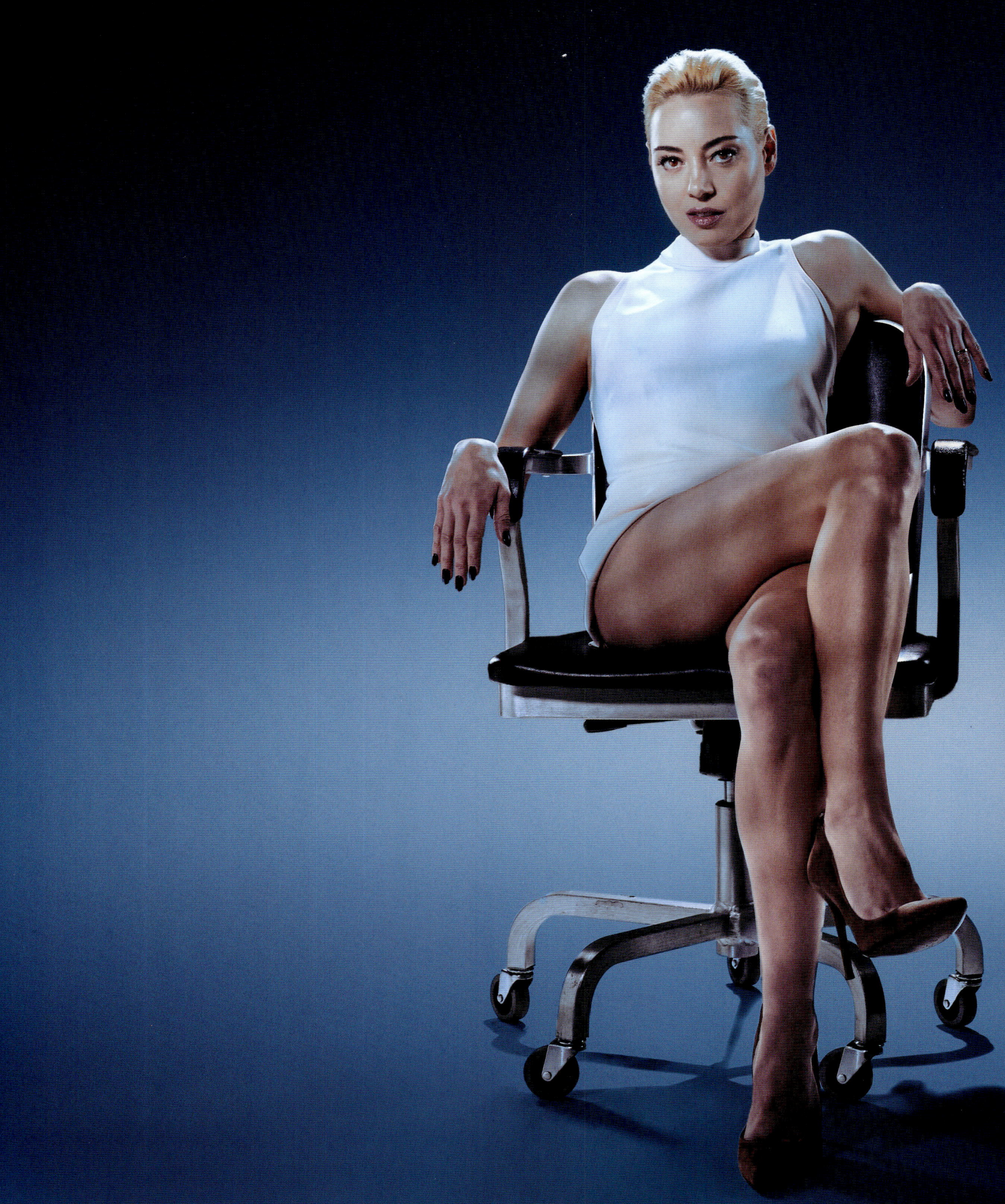

SATURDAY NIGHT LIVE

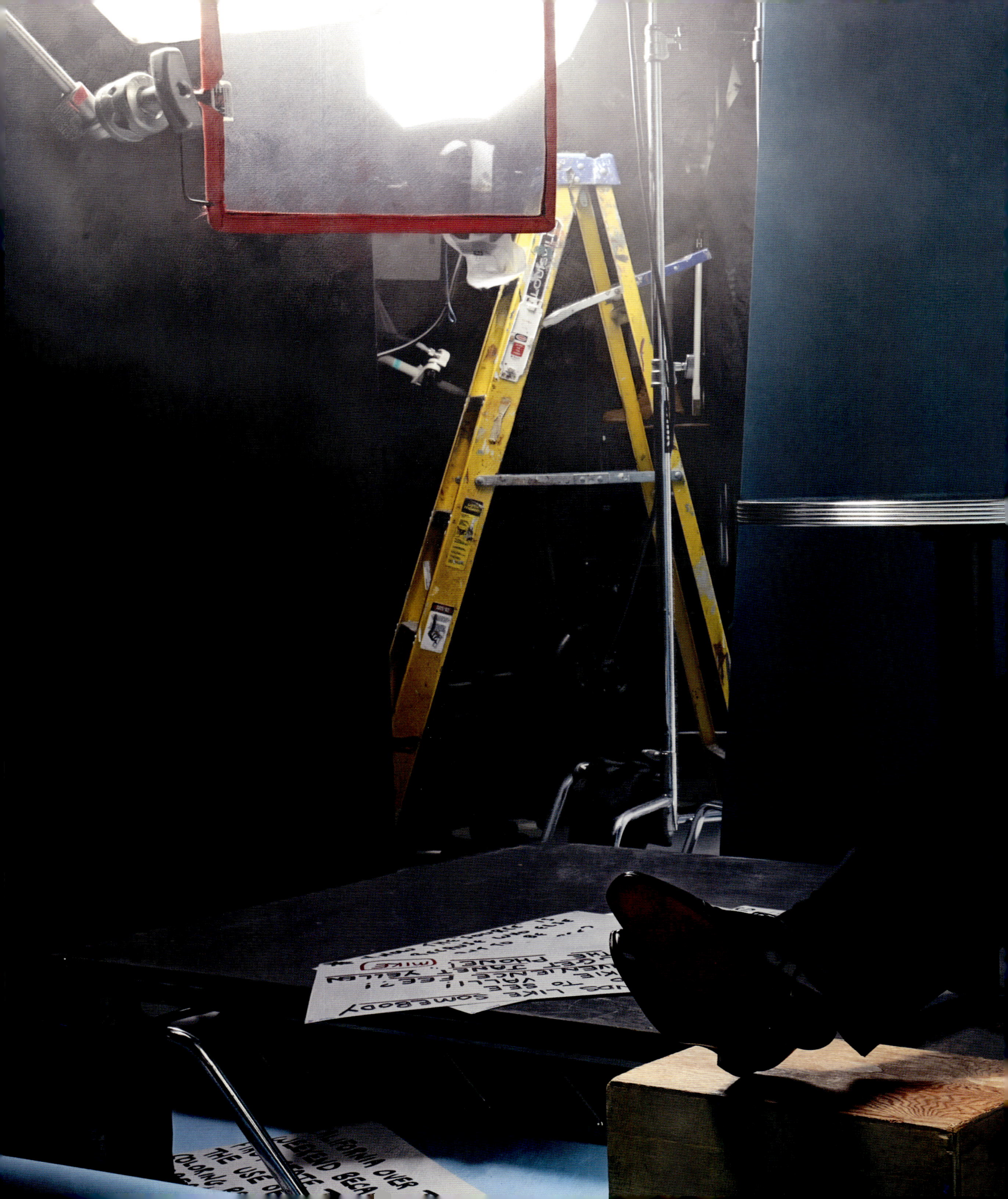

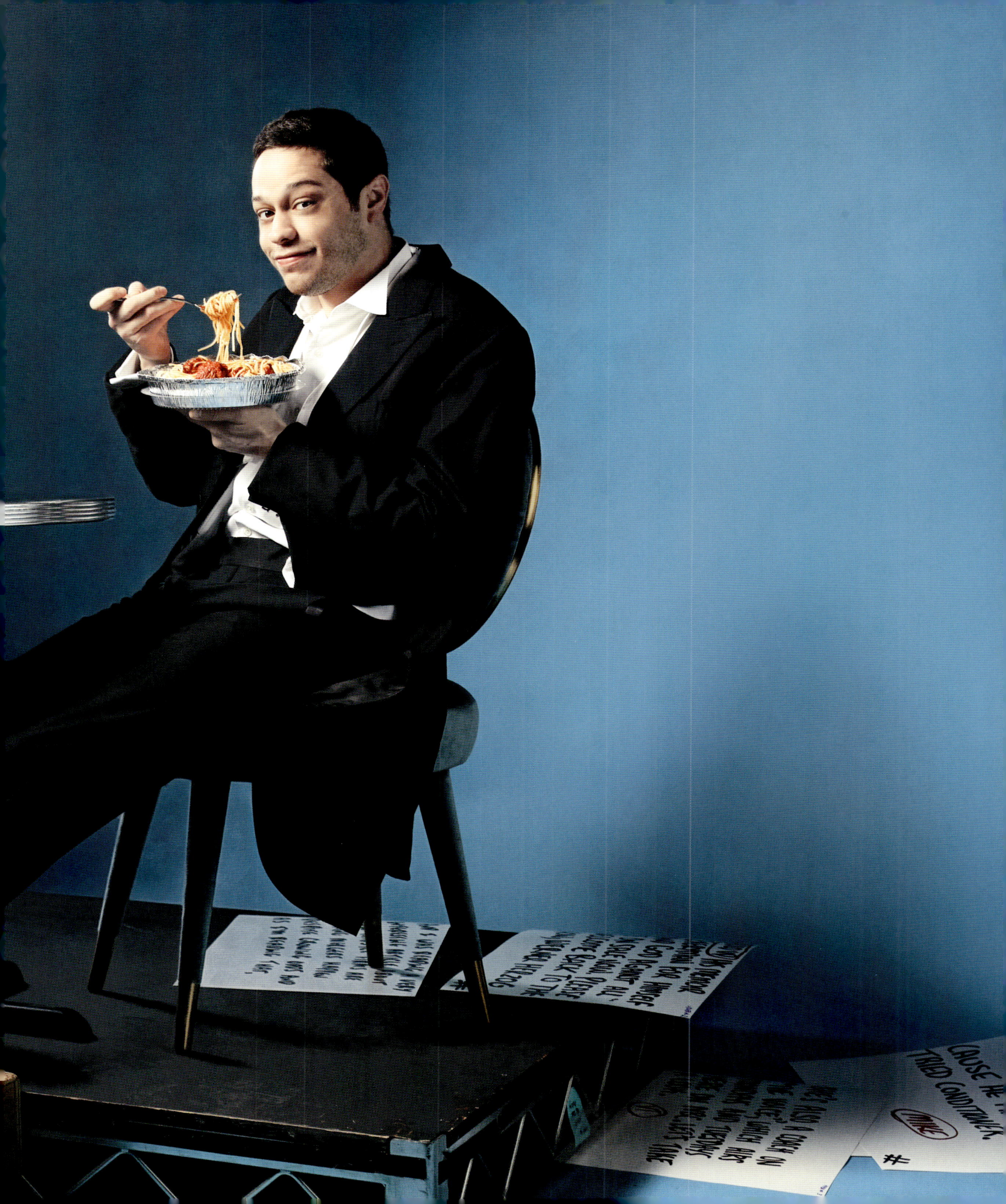

SATURDAY NIGHT LIVE

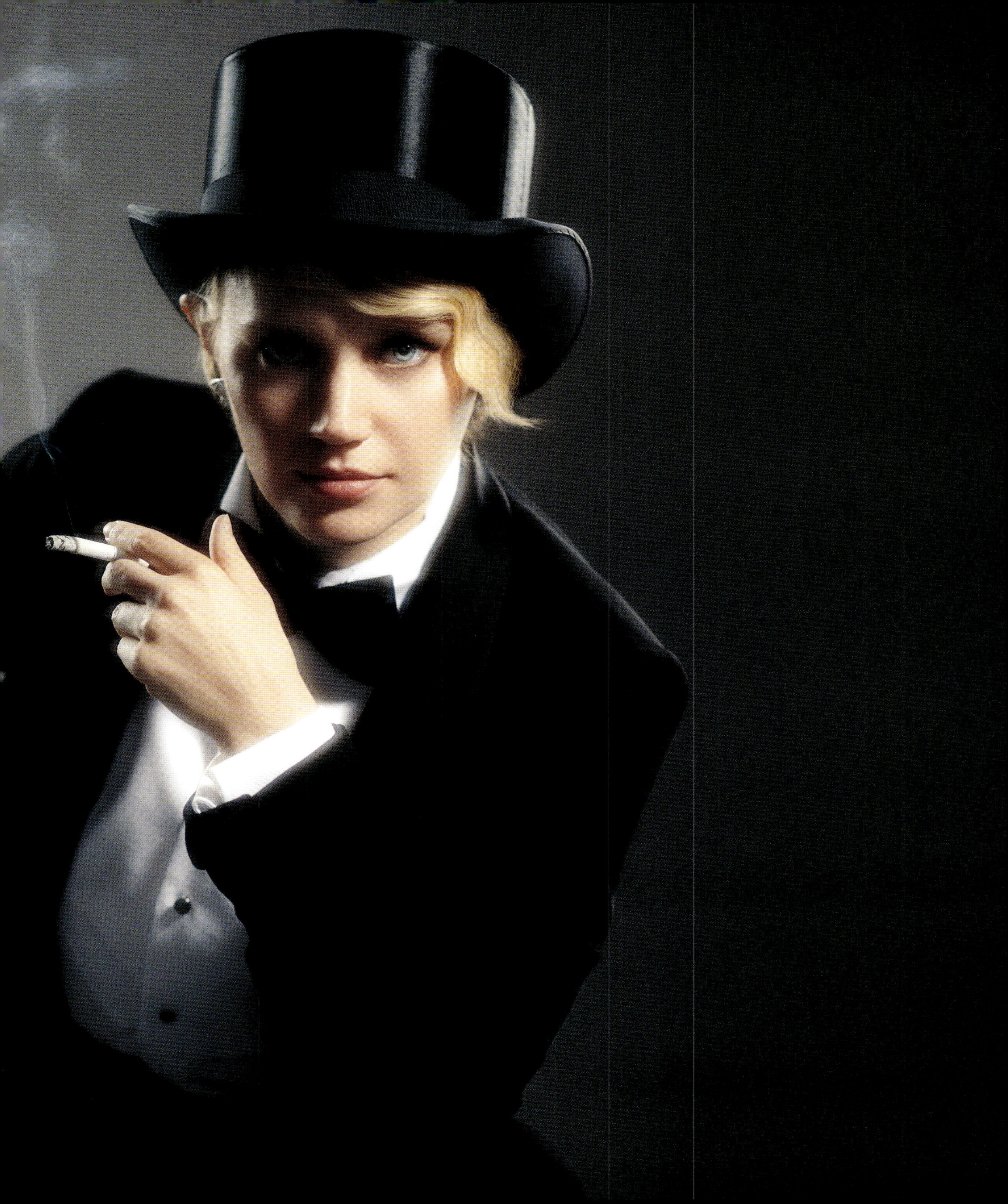

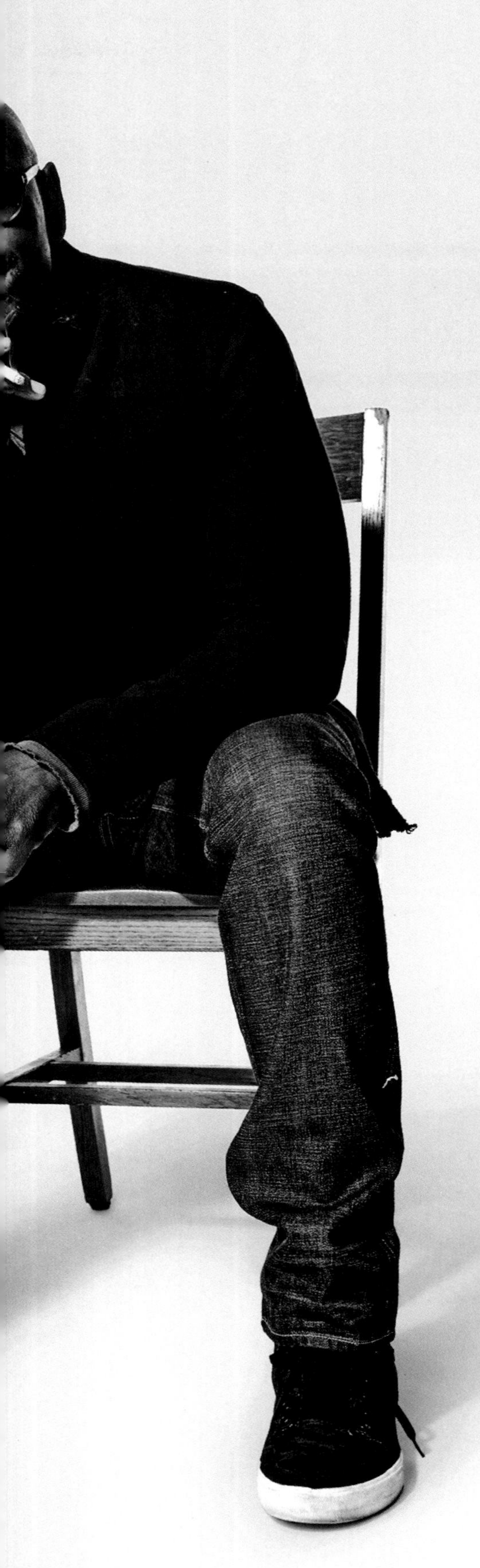
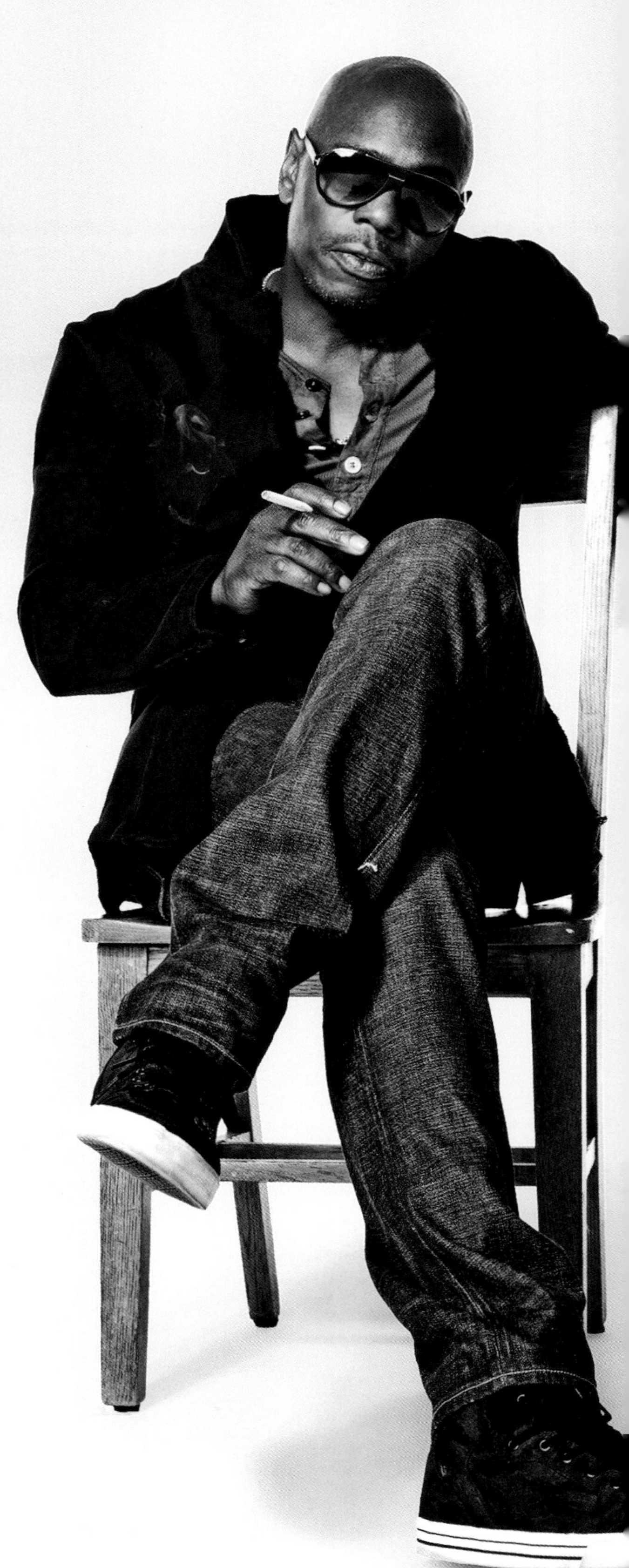

SNL

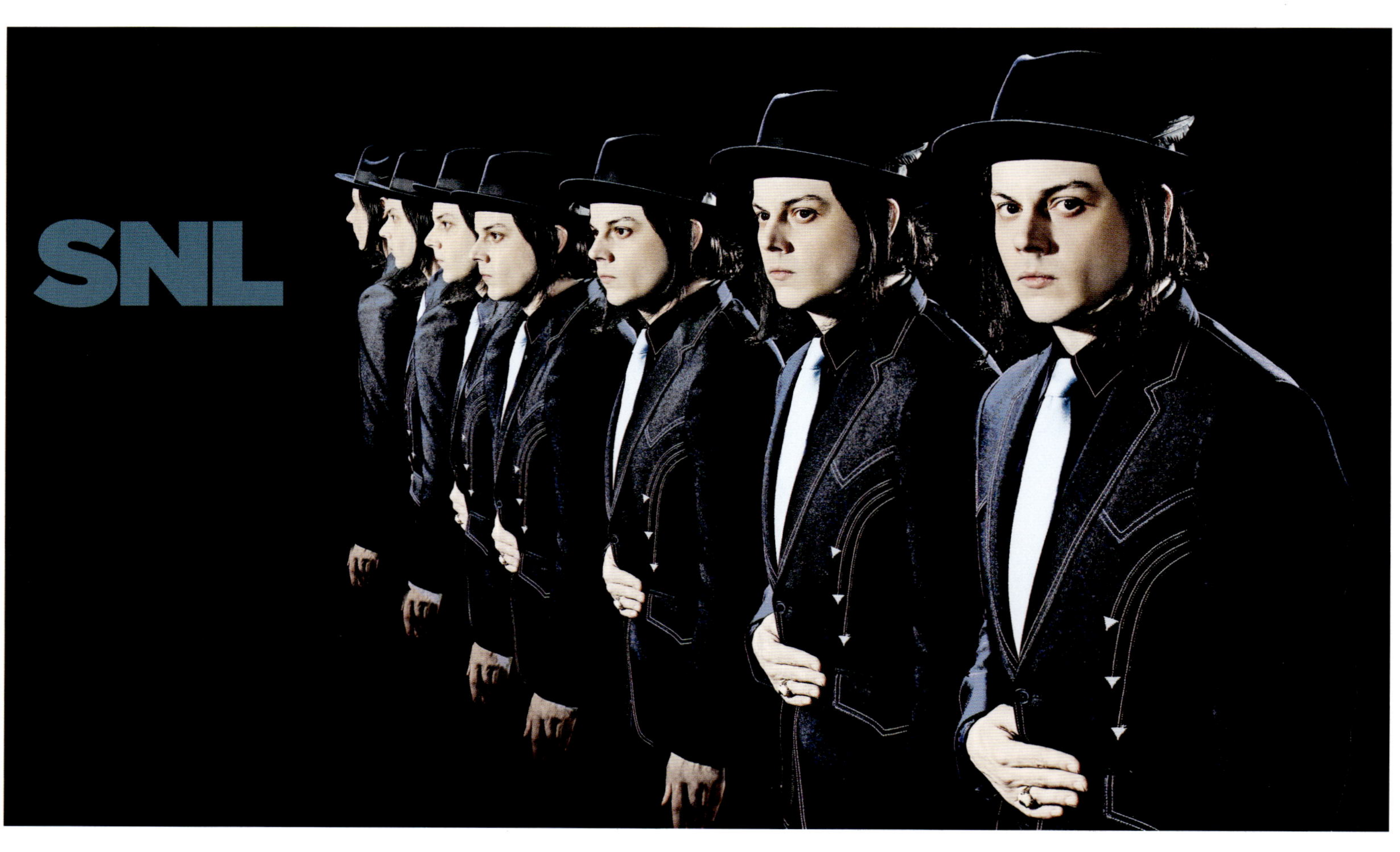
SNL

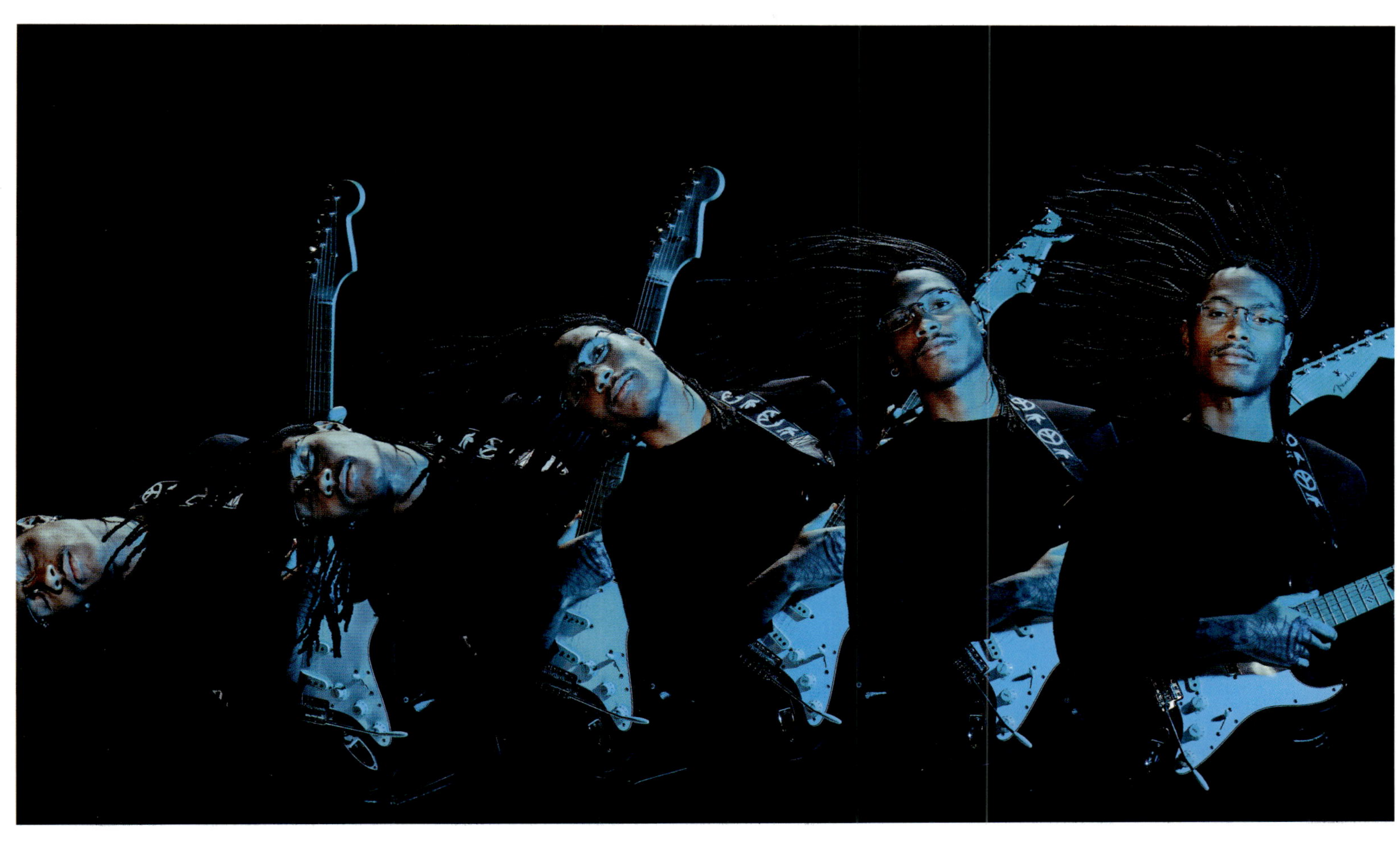

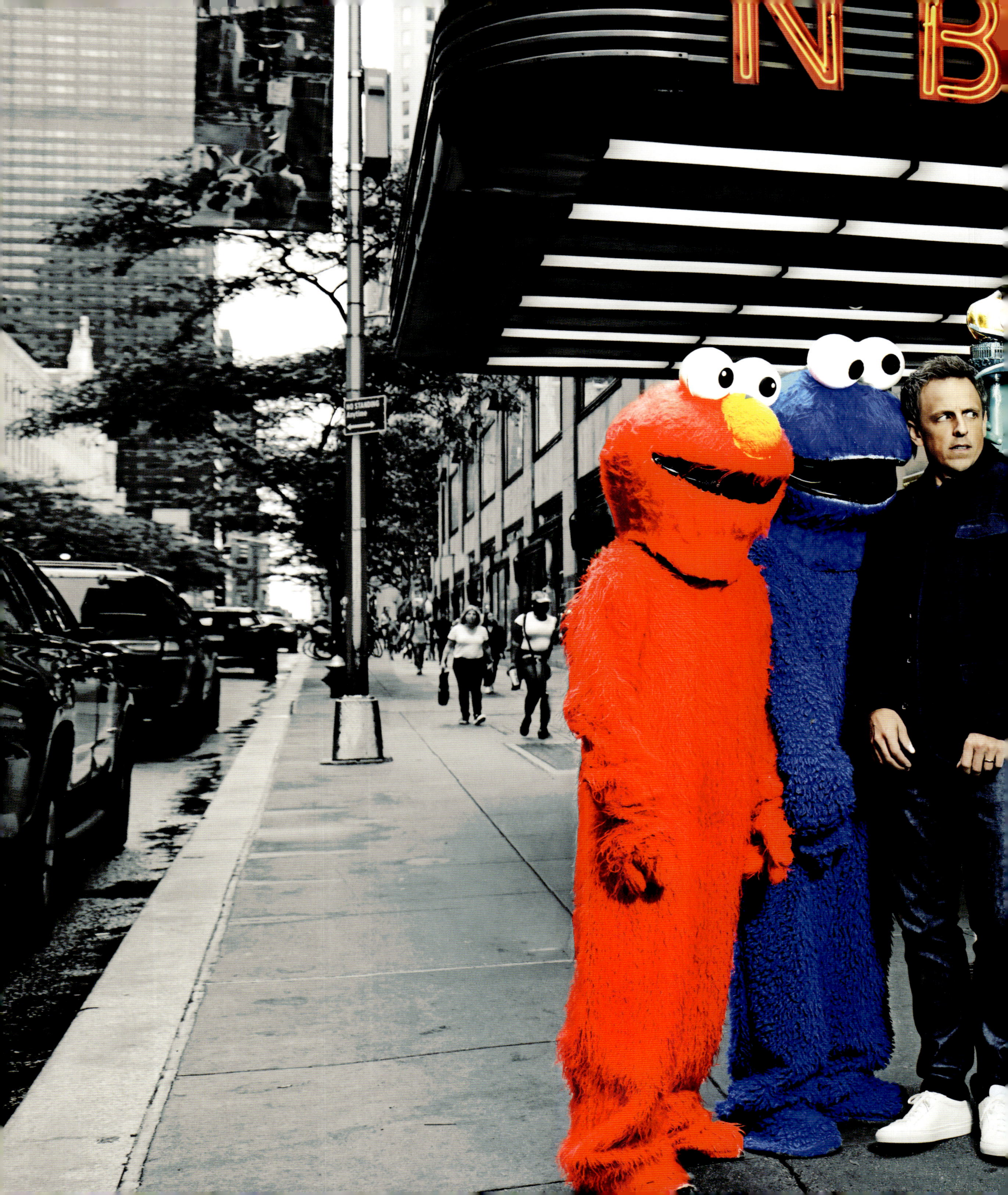
NB

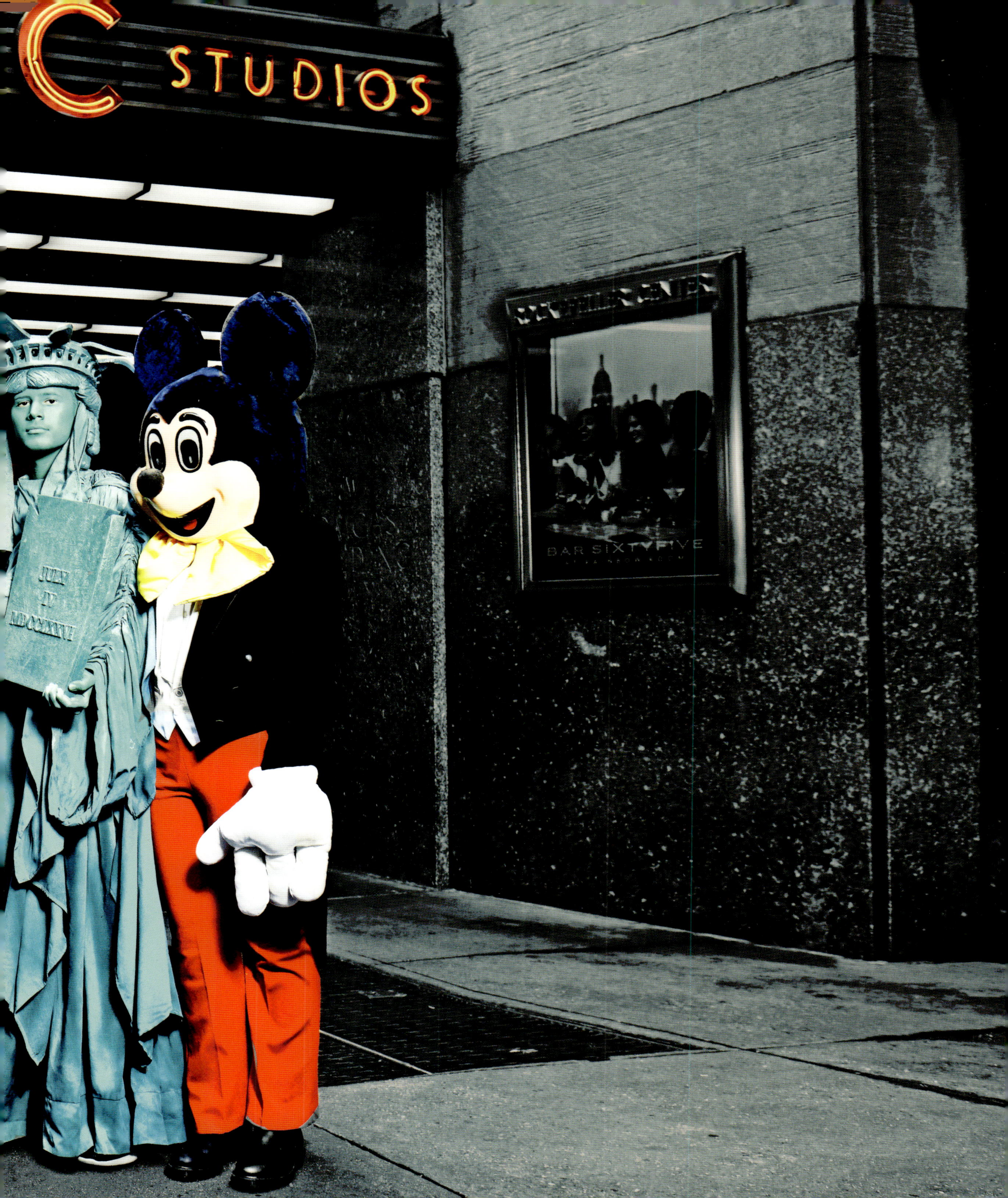
STUDIOS
BAR SIXTYFIVE

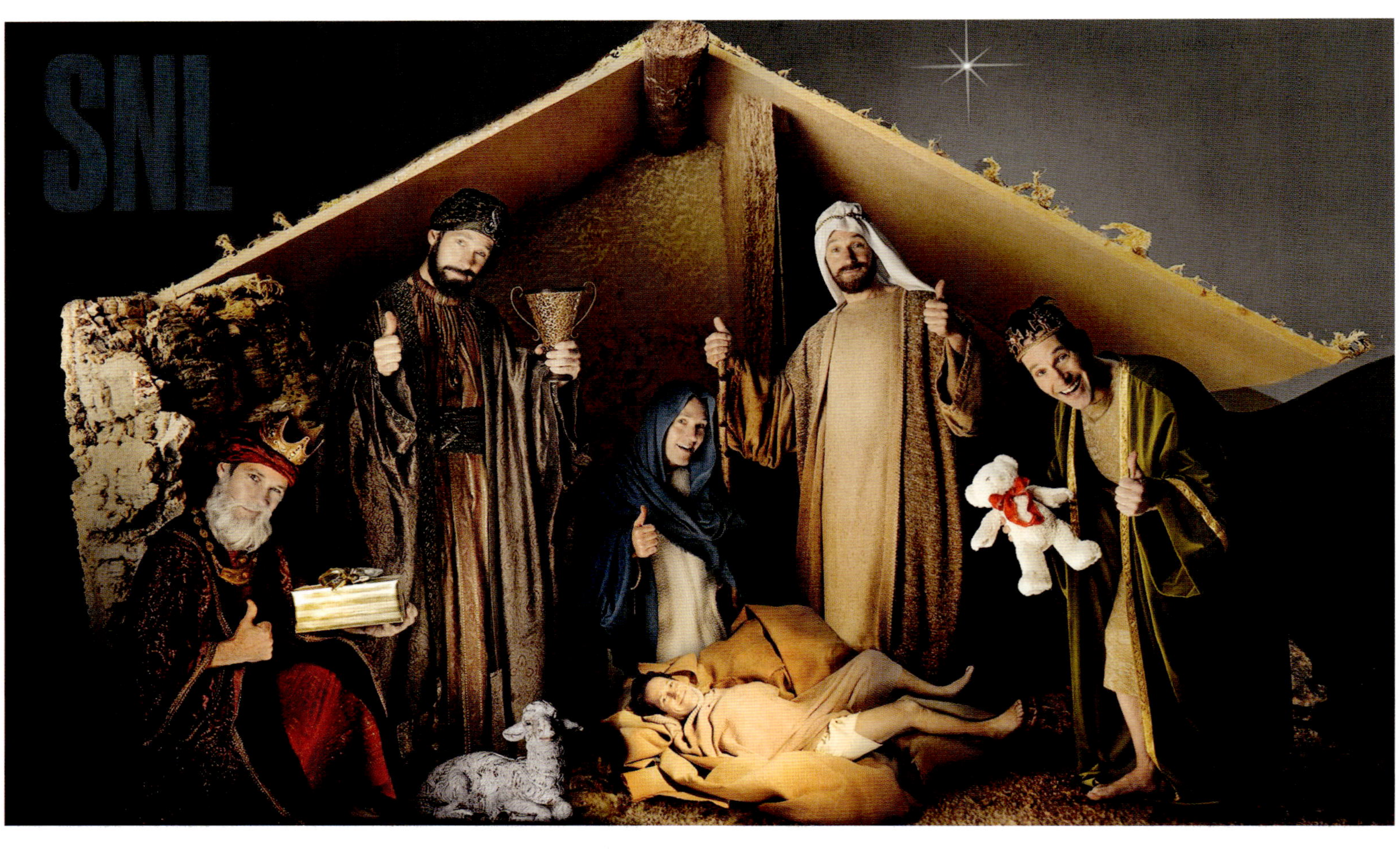
SNL

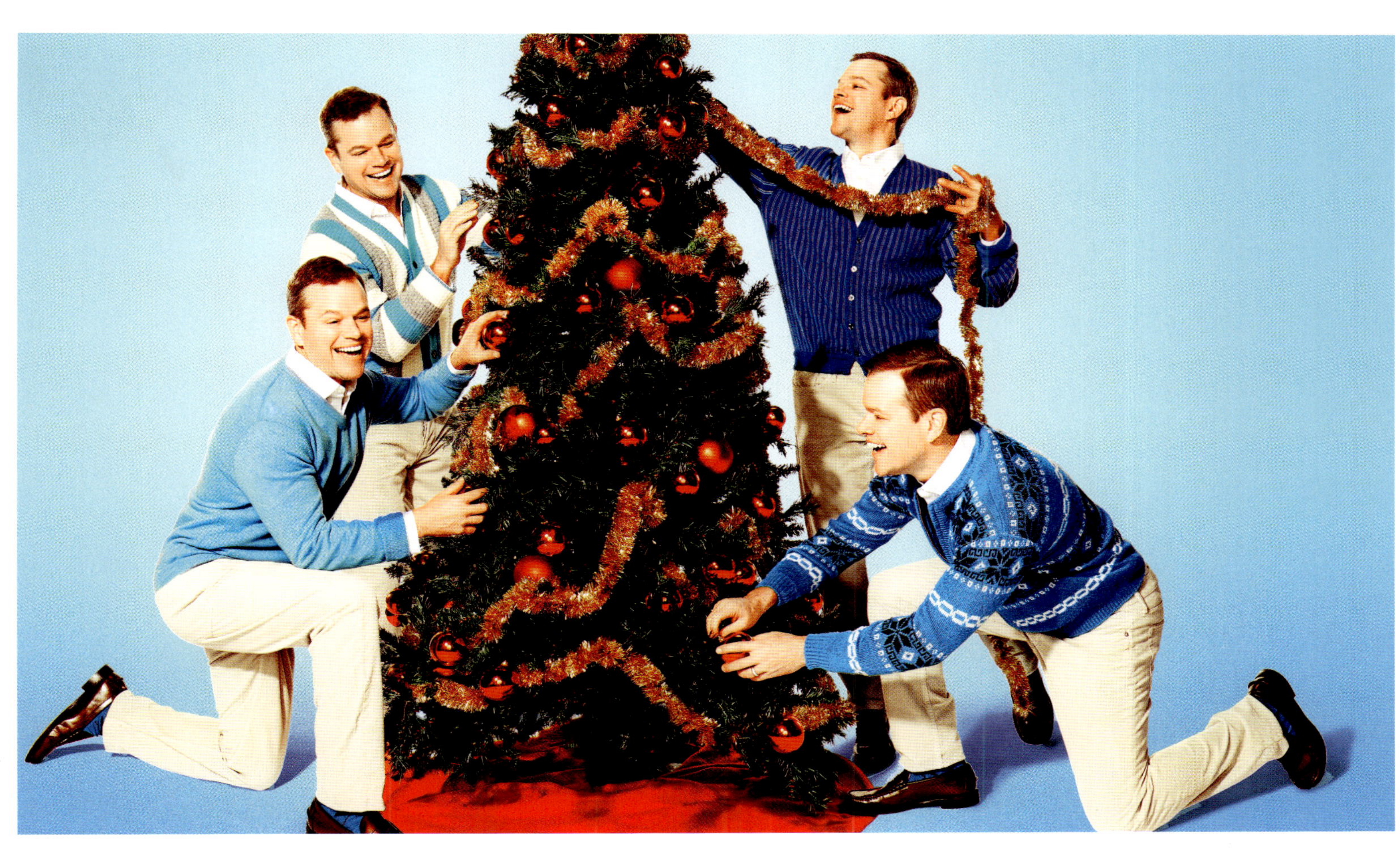

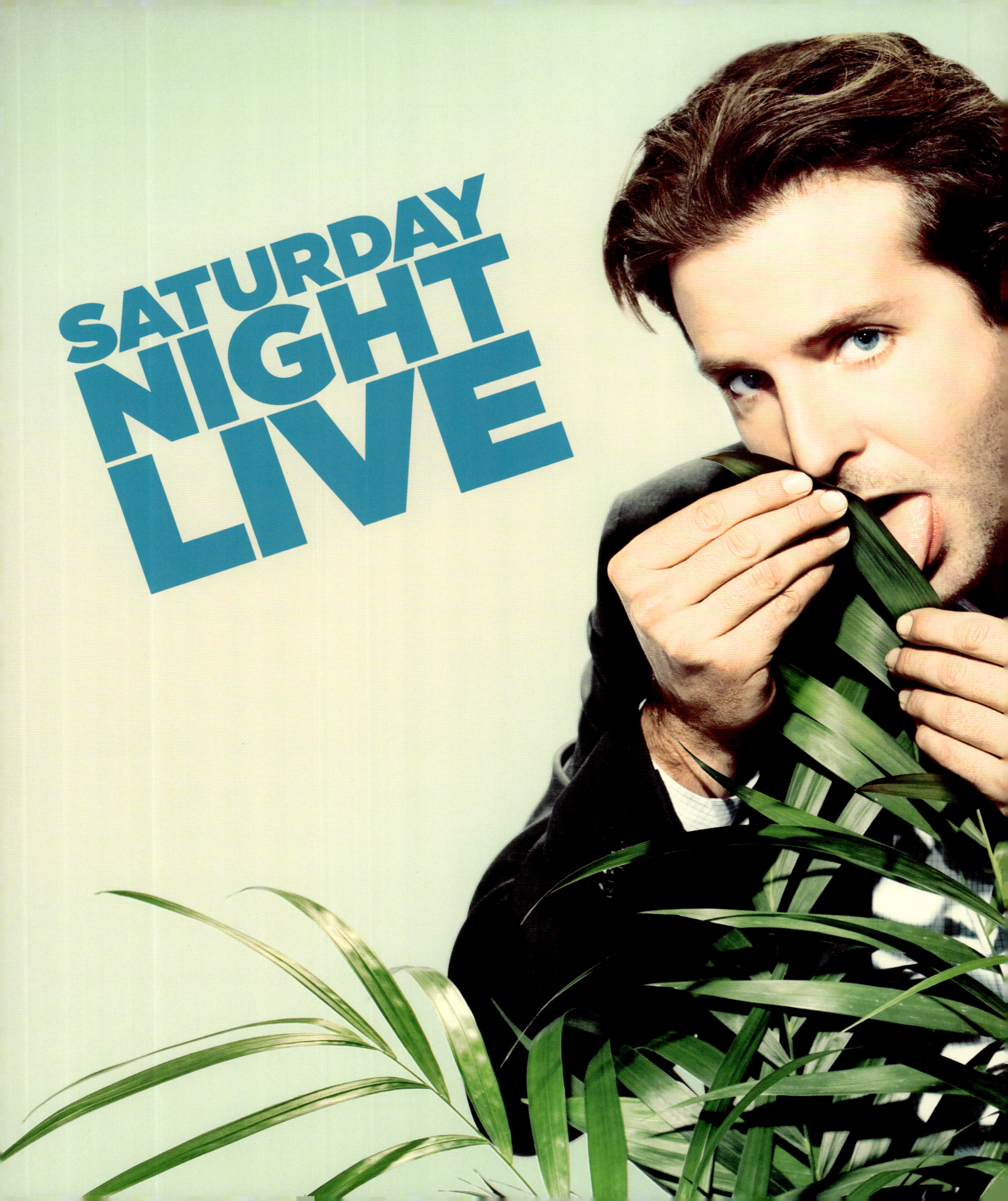
SATURDAY
NIGHT
LIVE

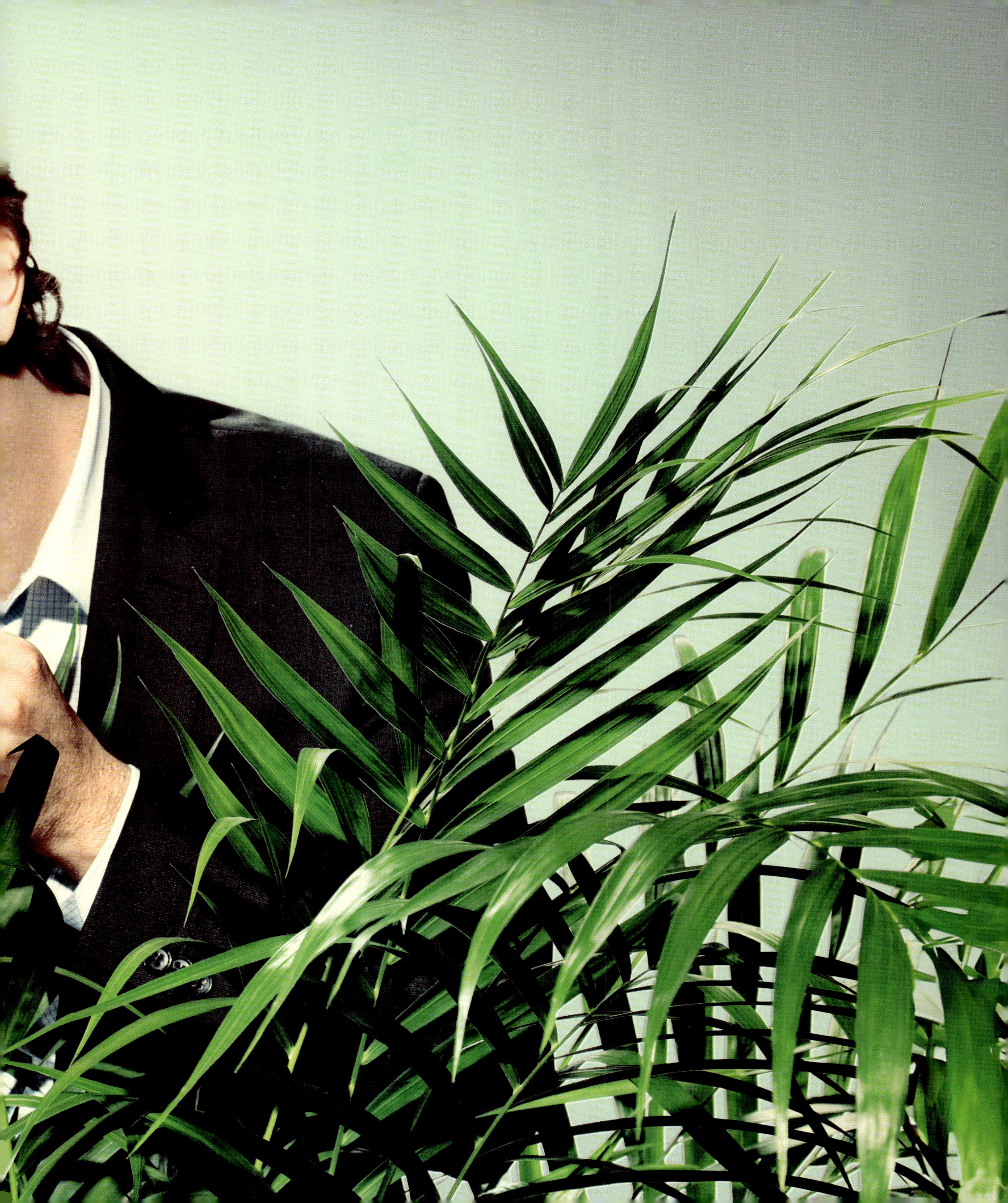

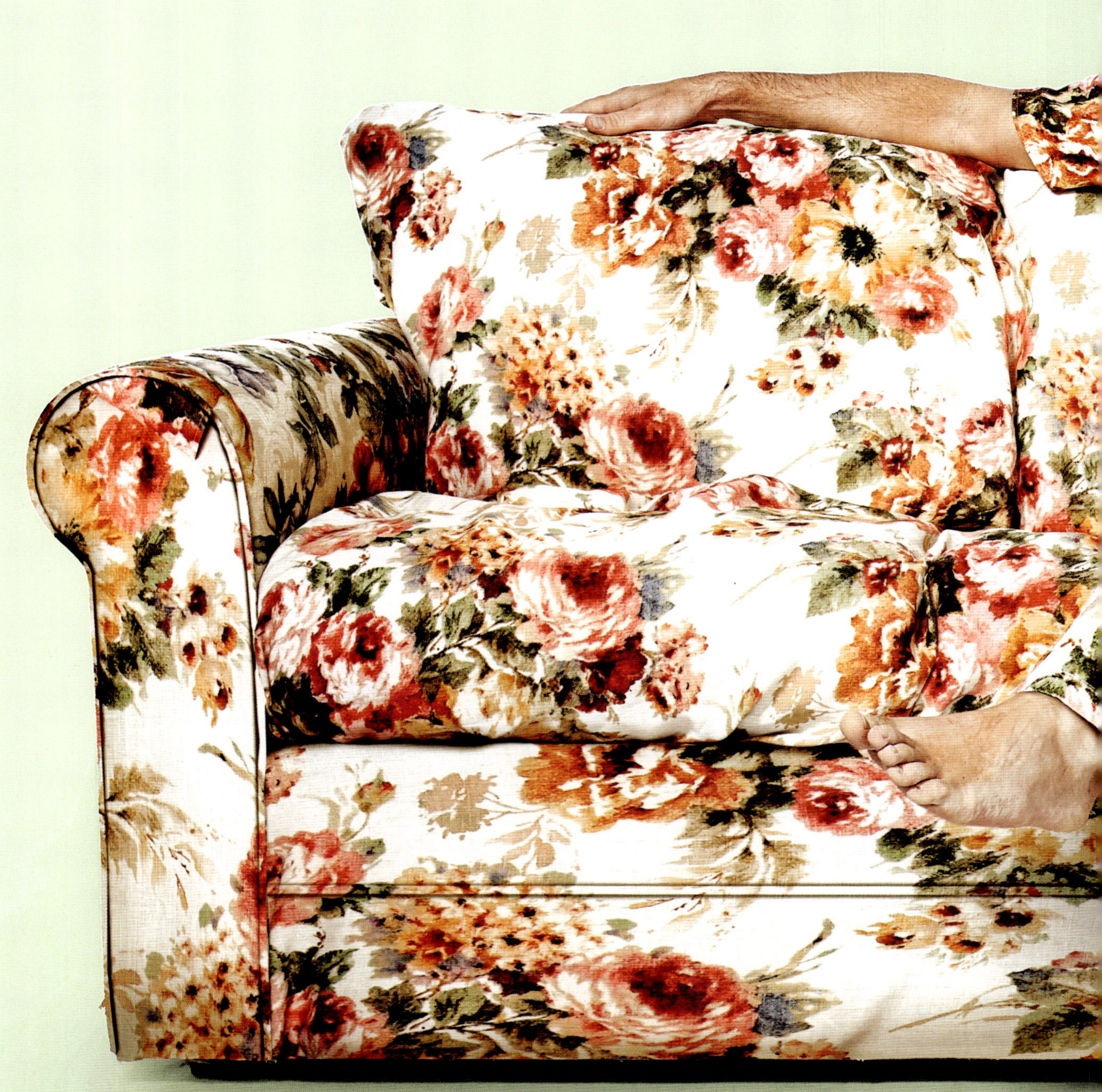

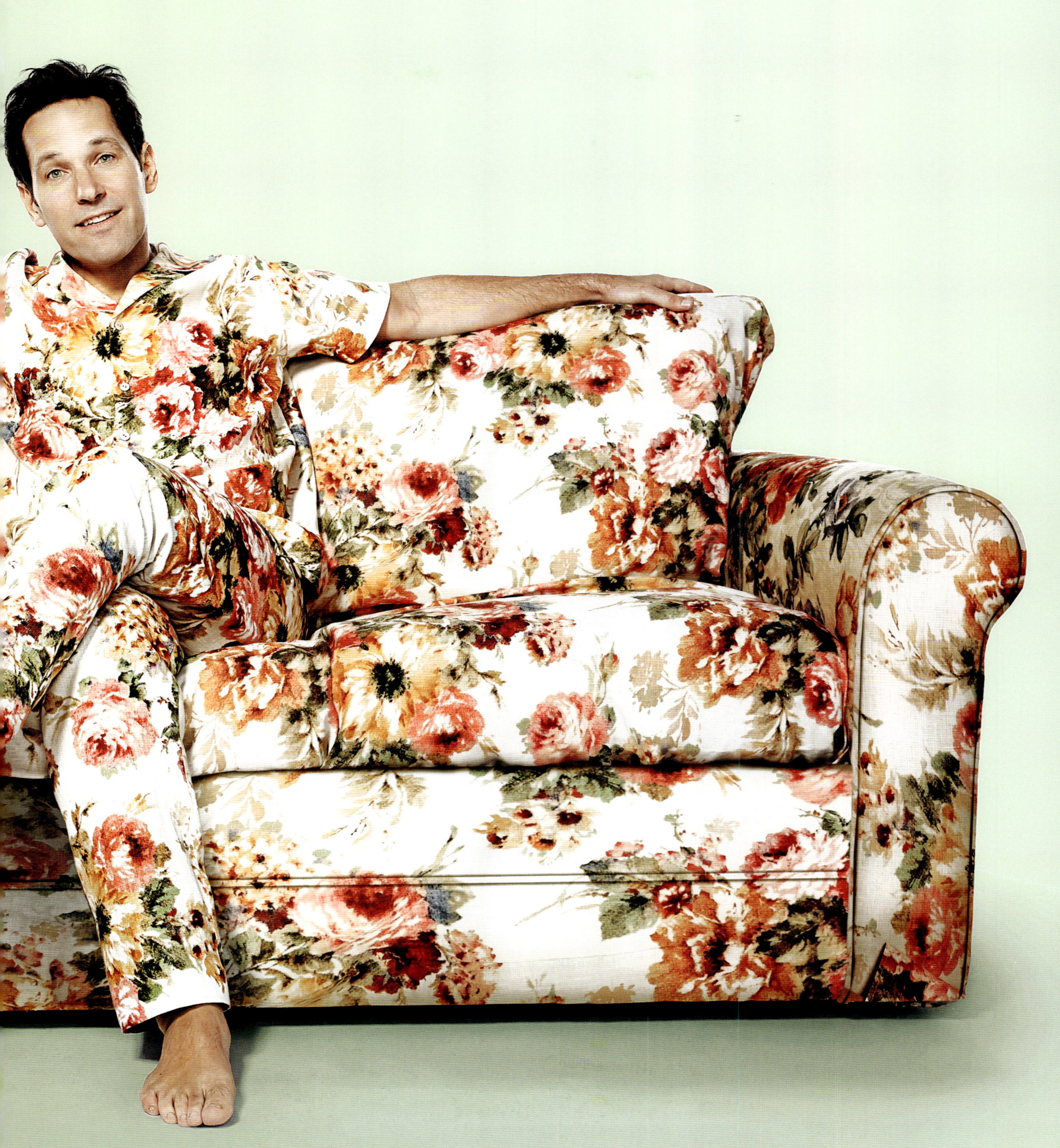

SATURDAY NIGHT

LIVE

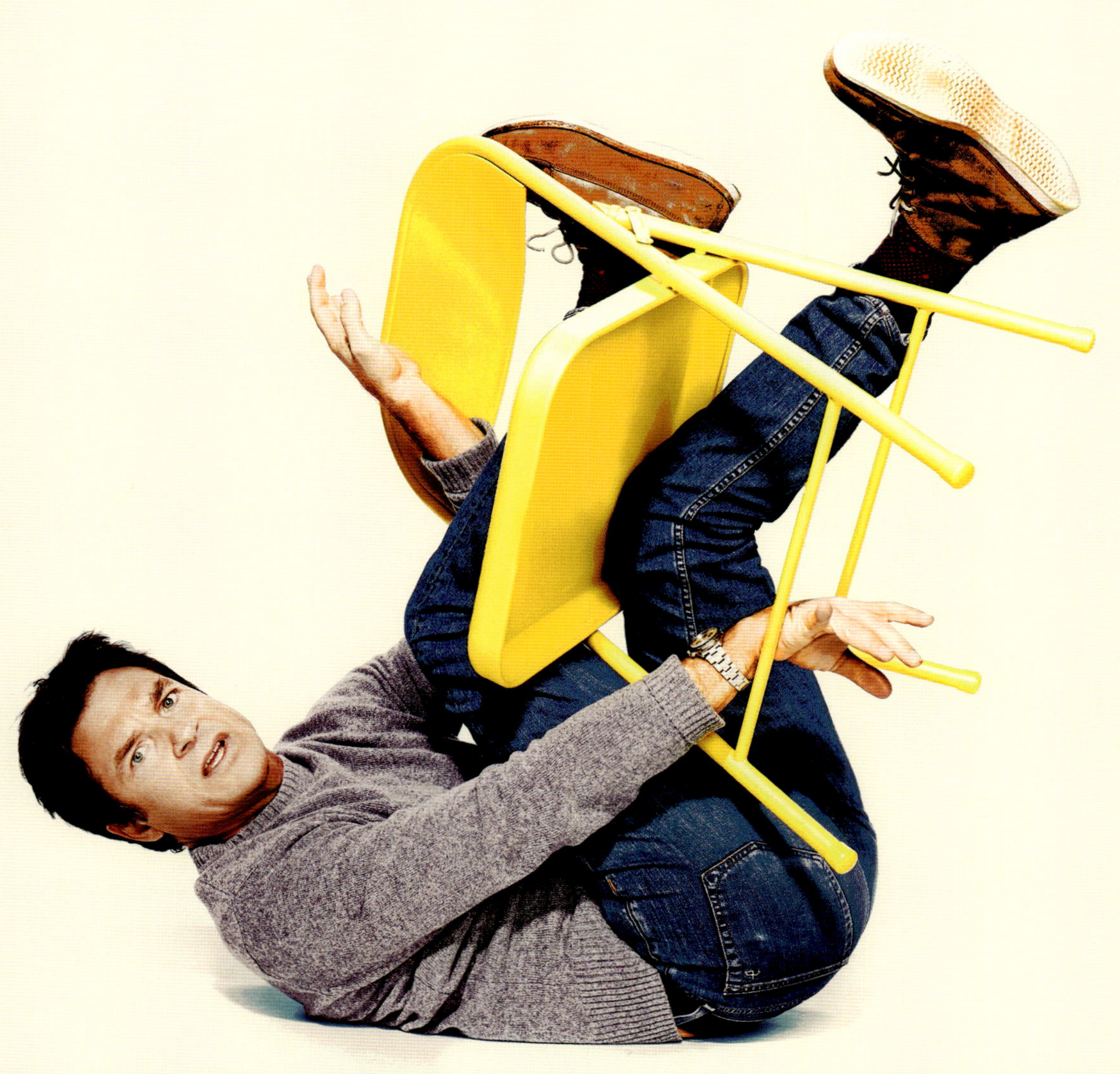

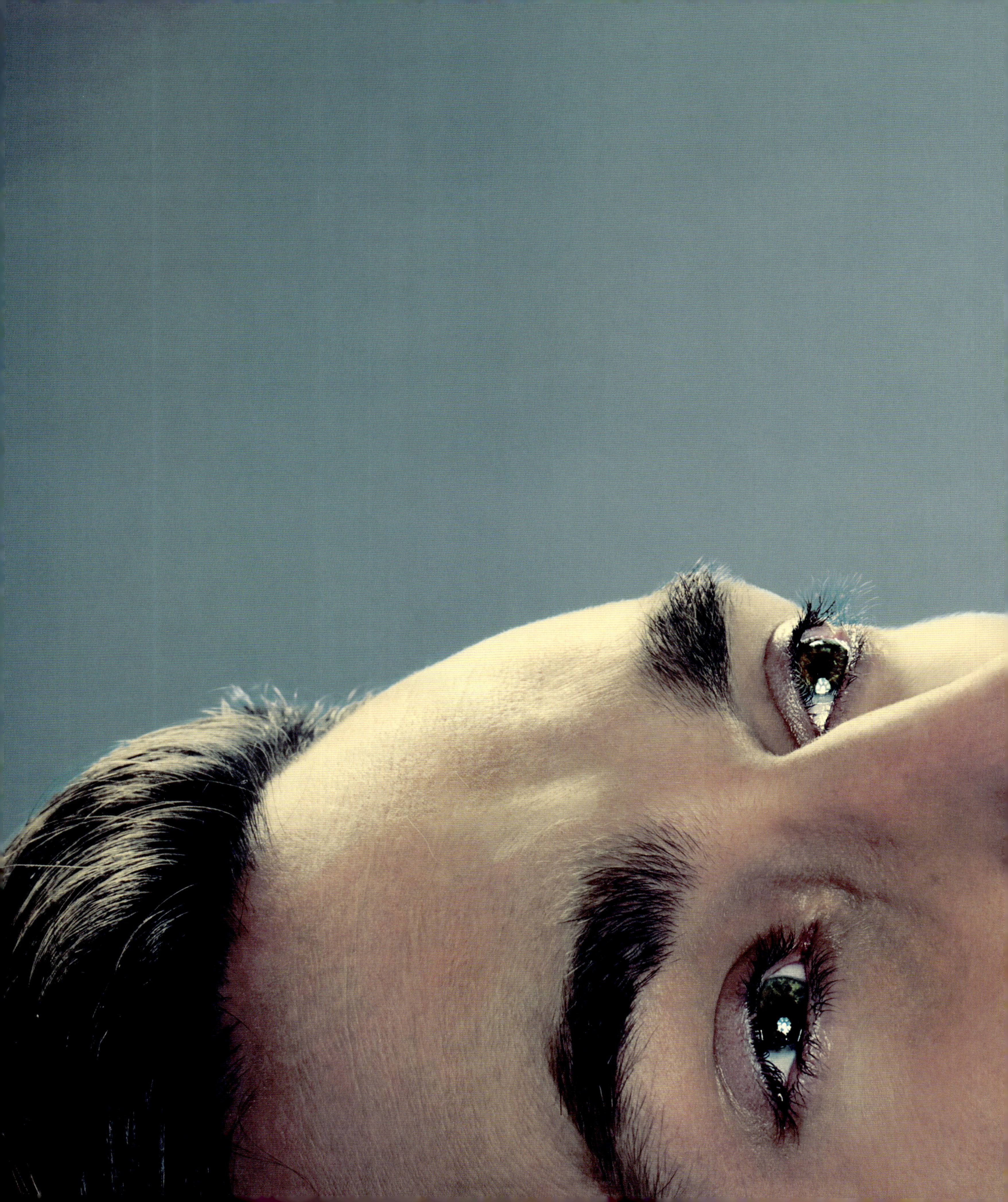

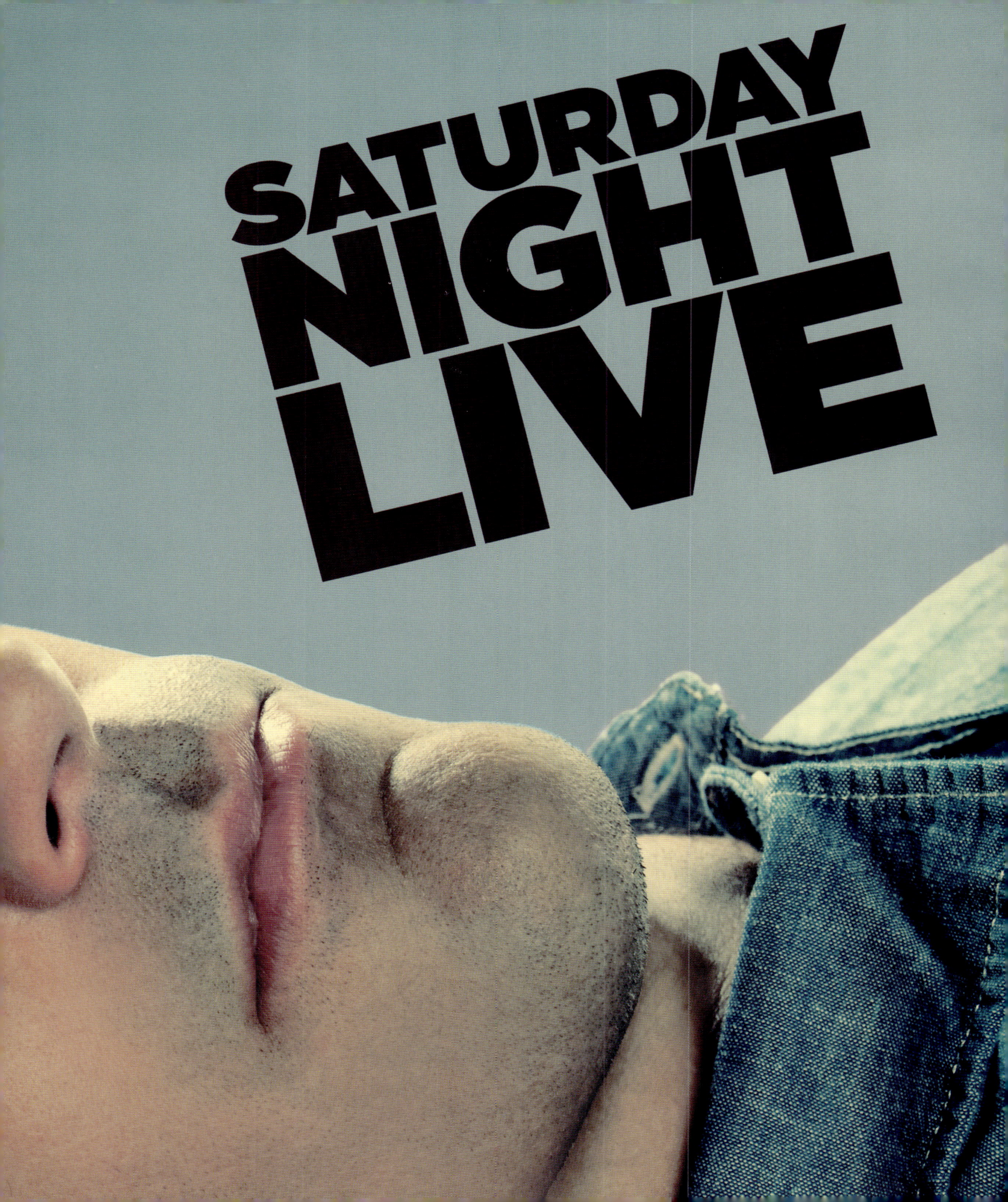
SATURDAY
NIGHT
LIVE

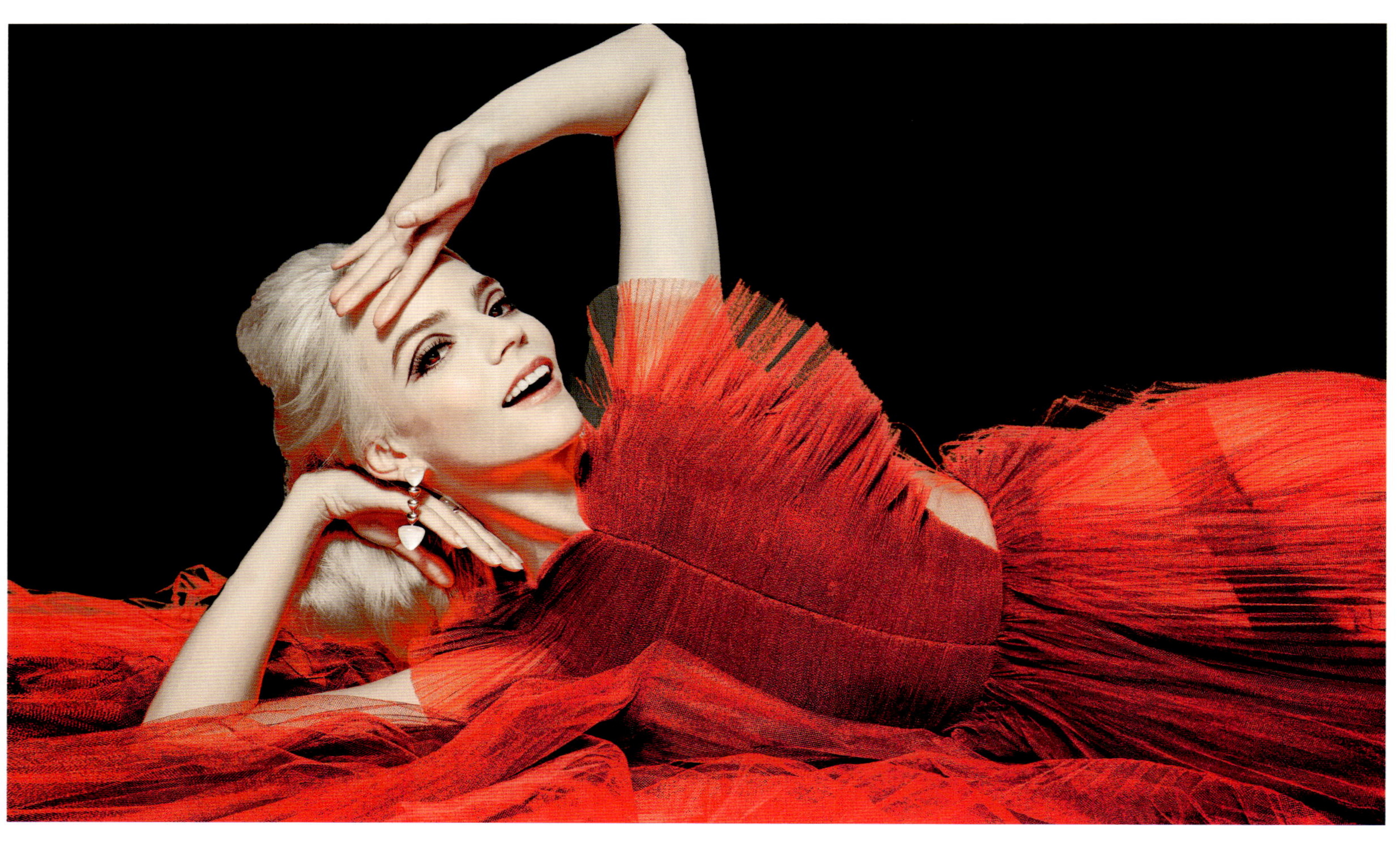

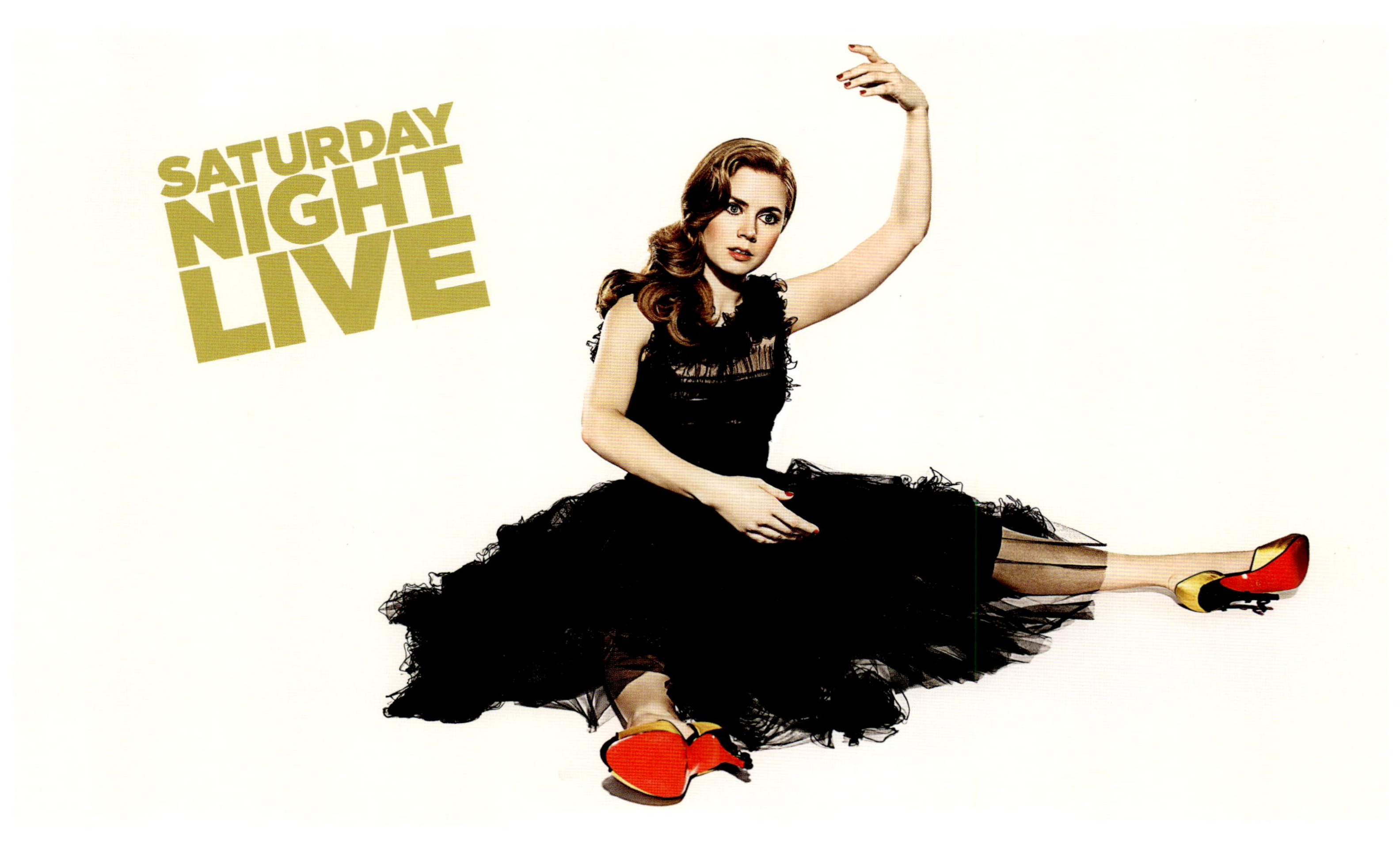
SATURDAY
NIGHT
LIVE

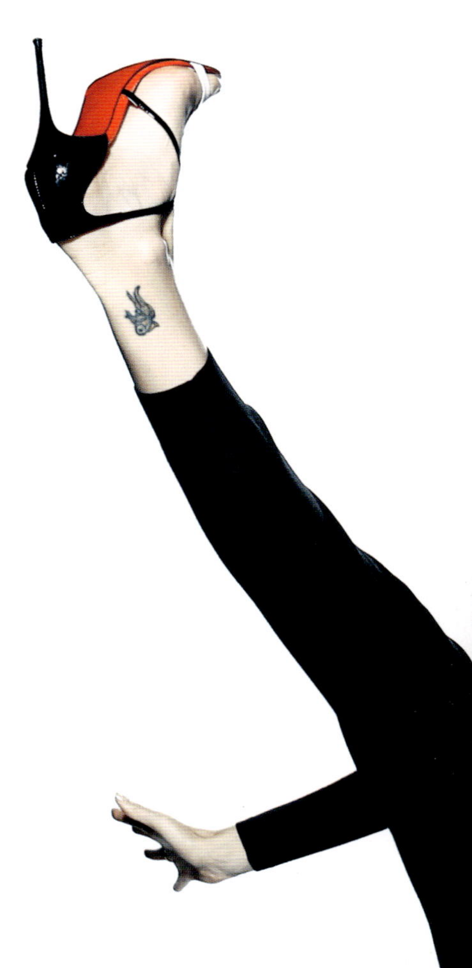

SNL

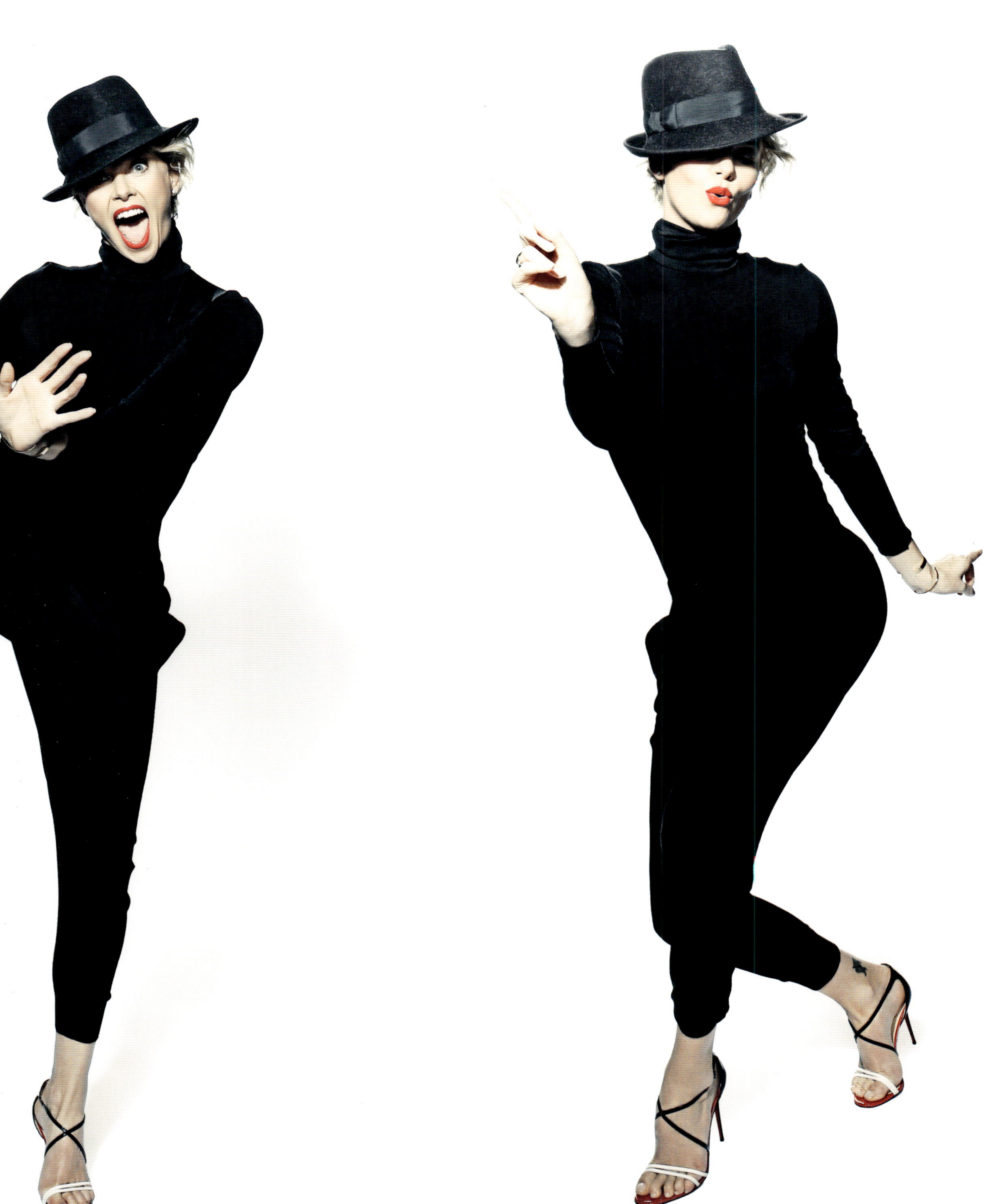

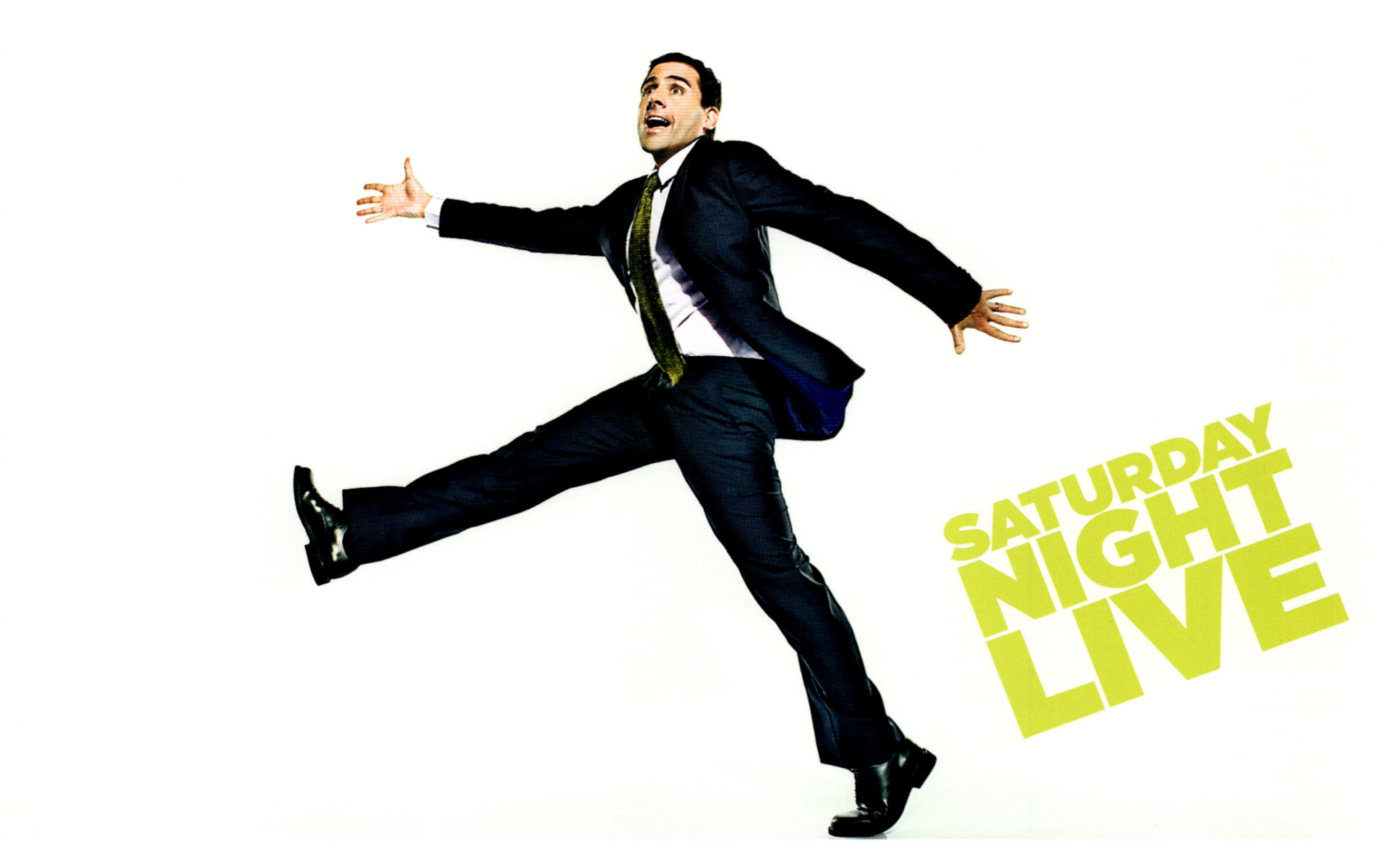
SATURDAY
NIGHT
LIVE

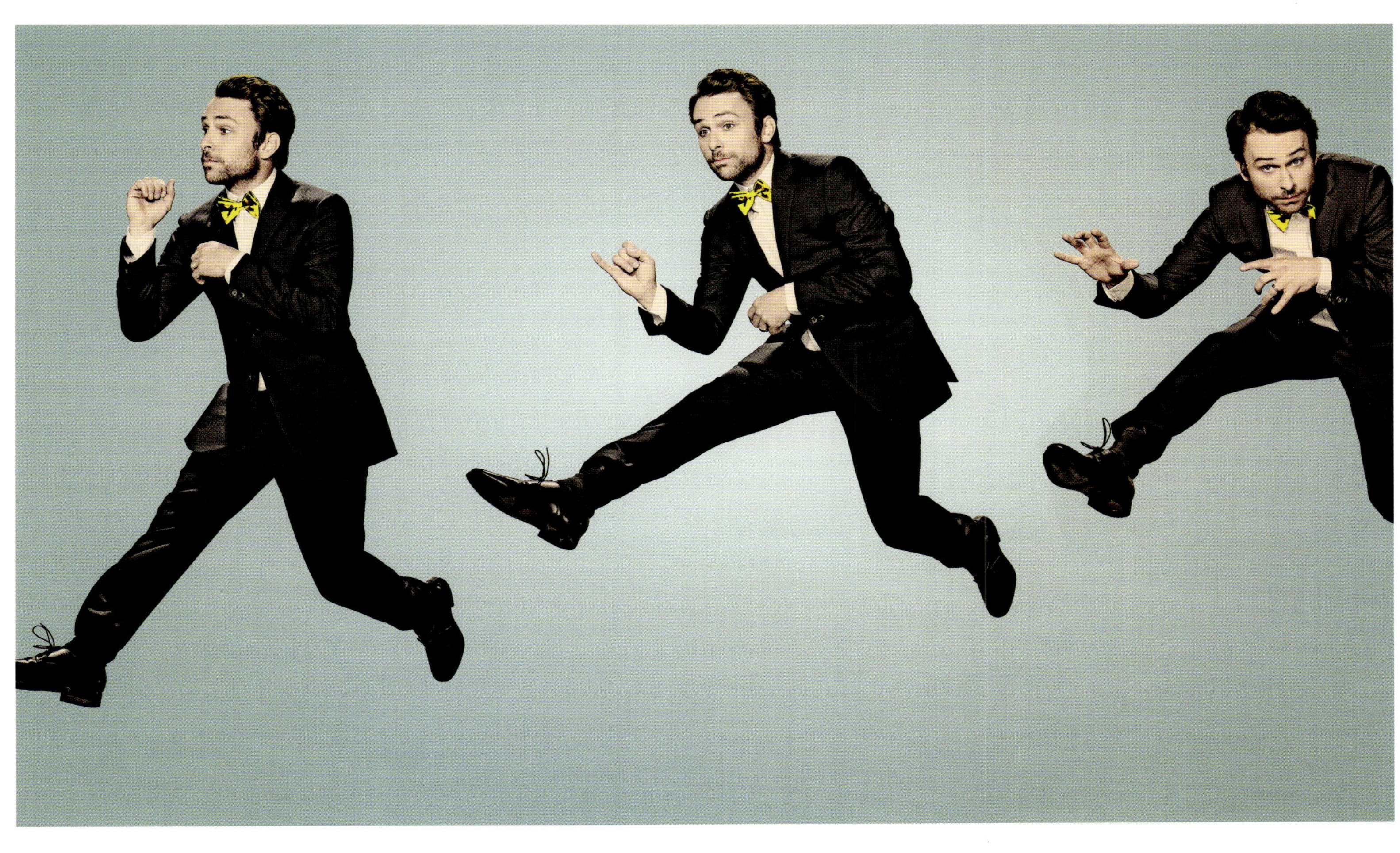

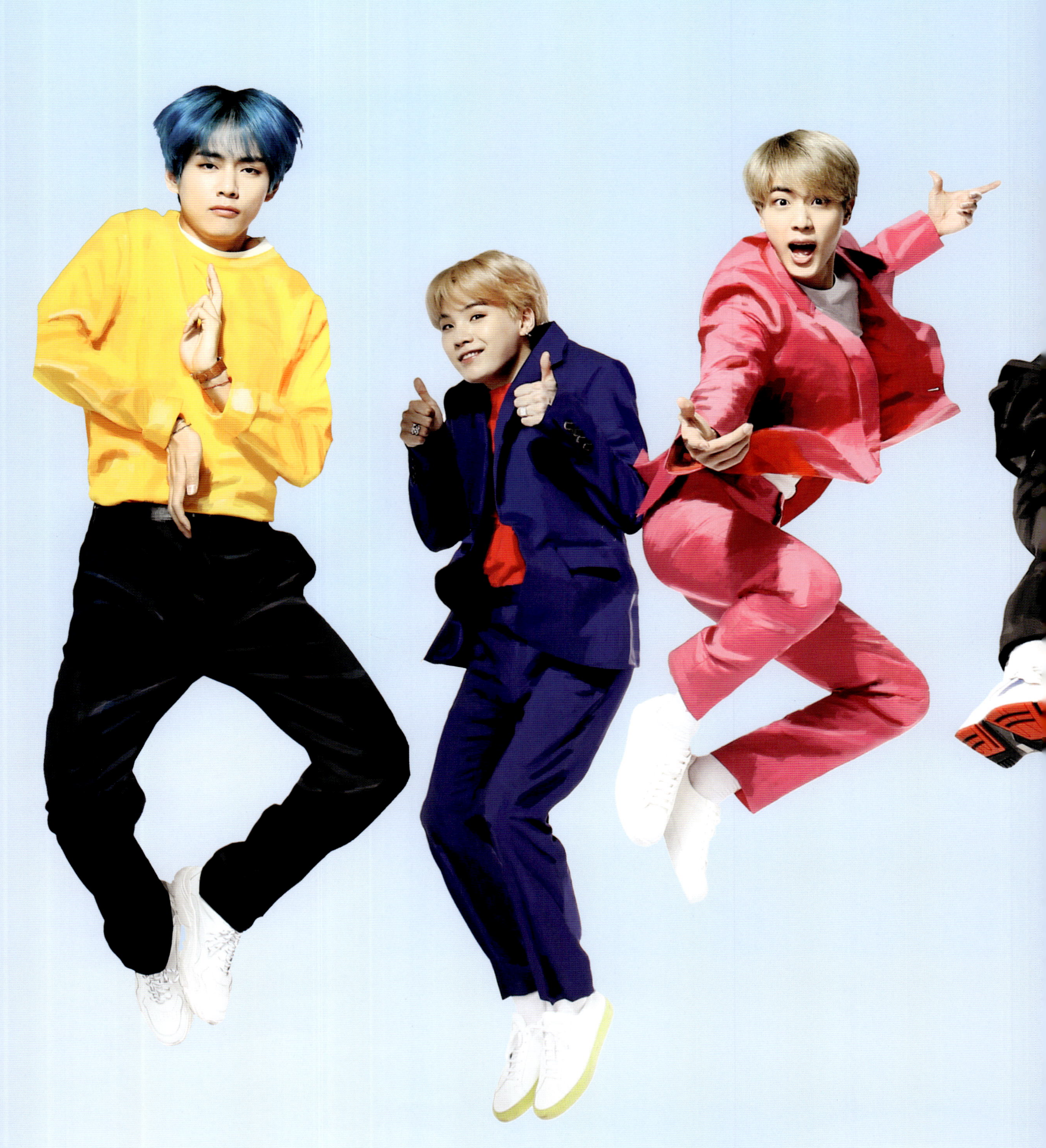

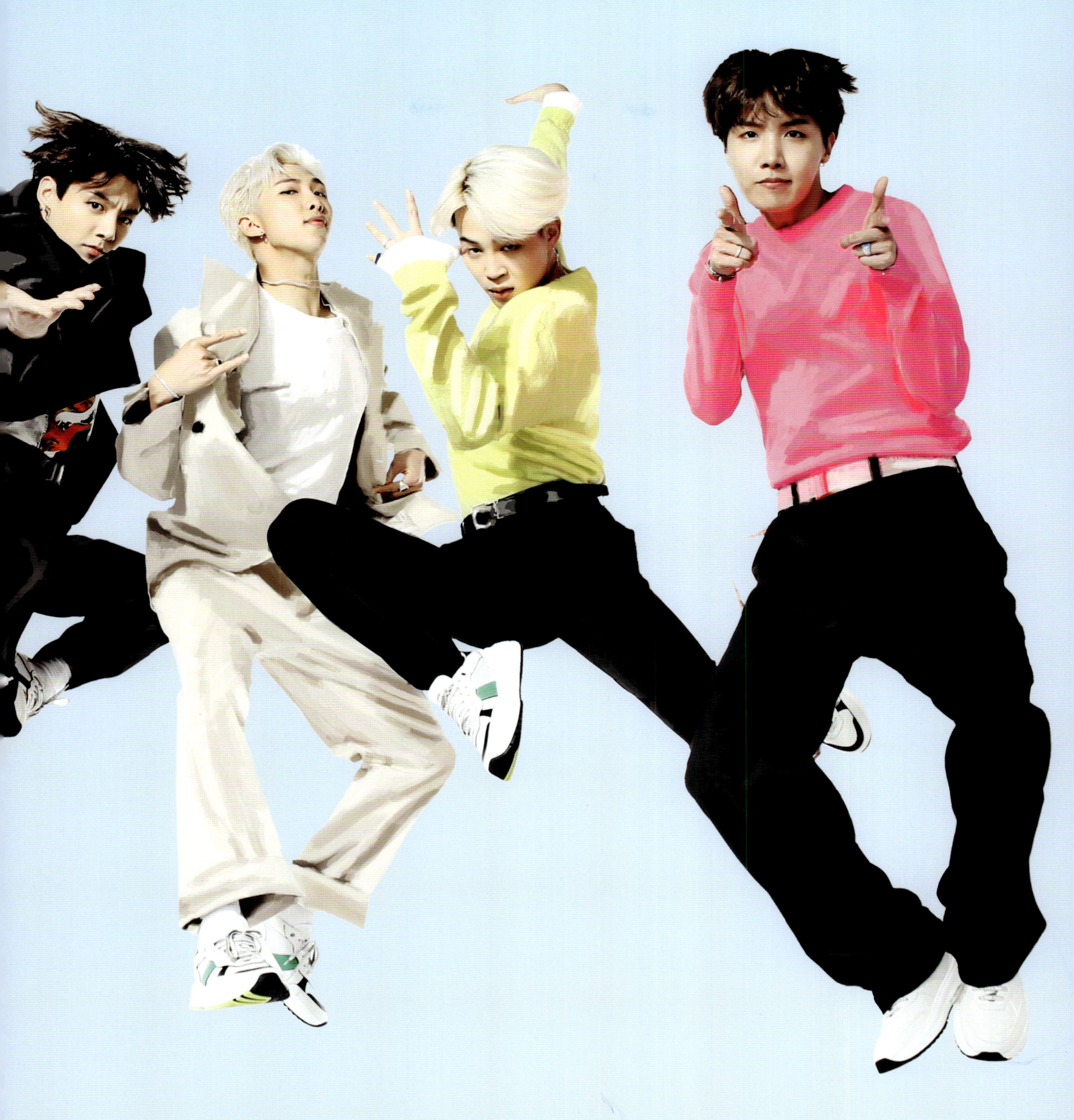

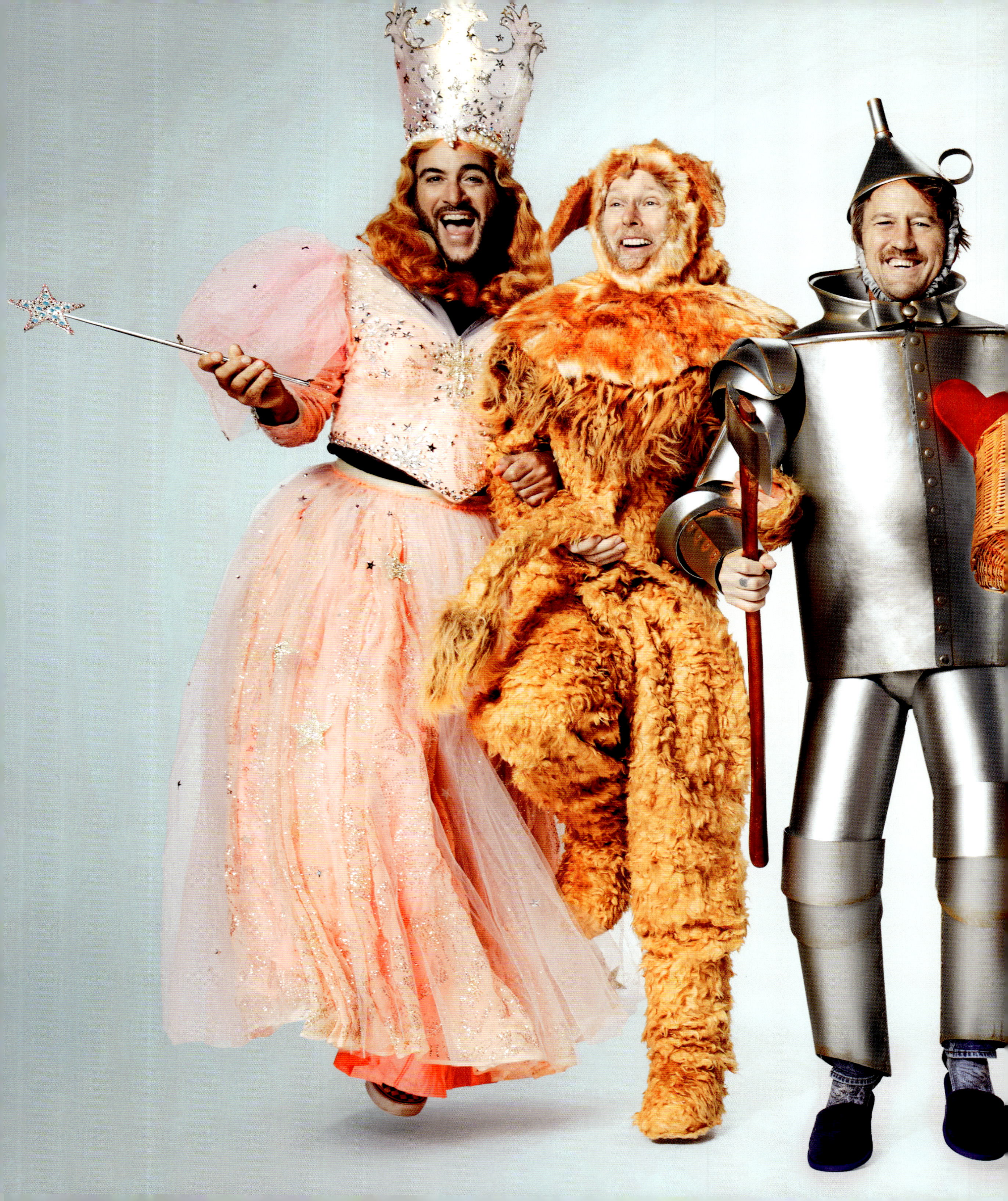

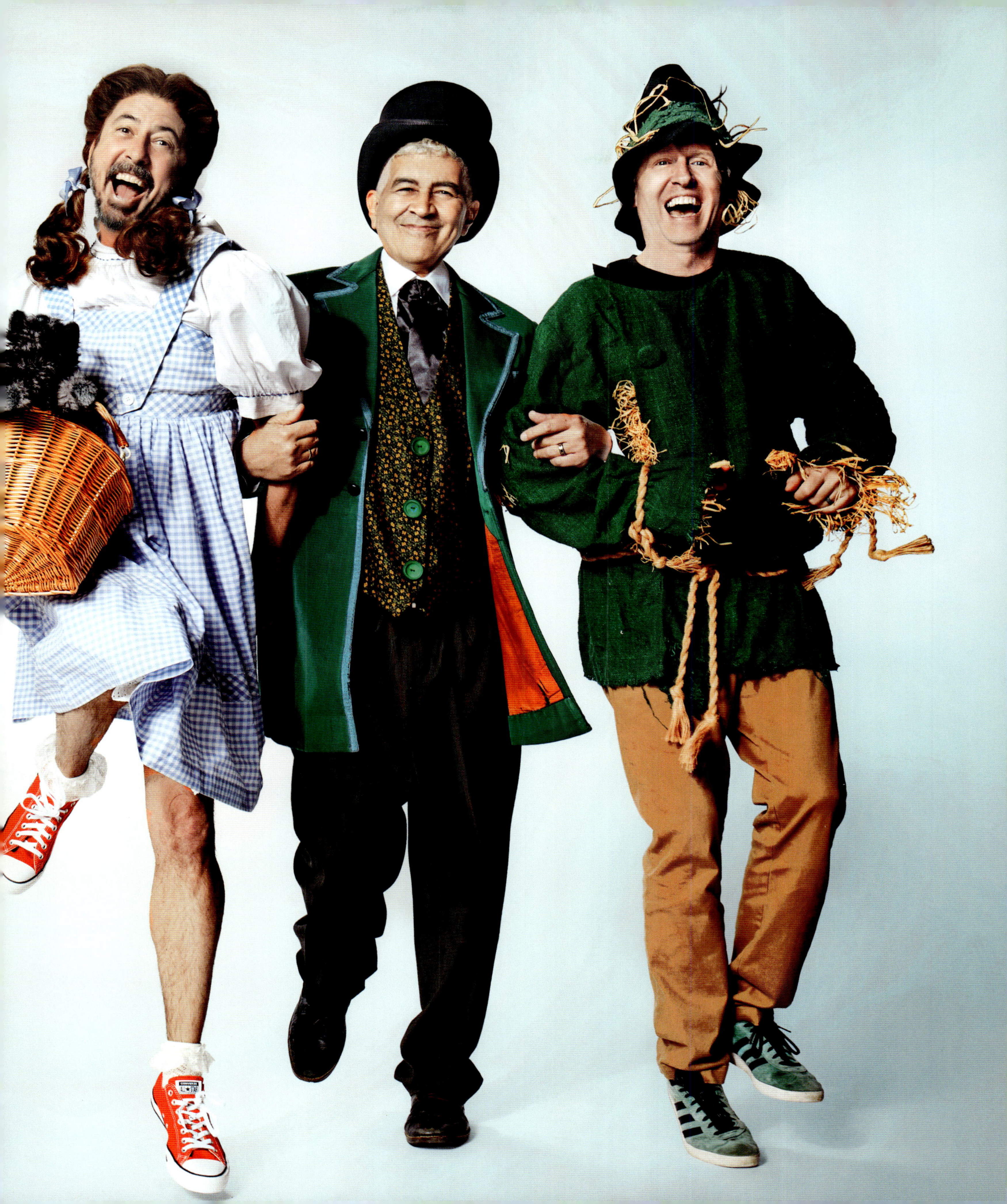

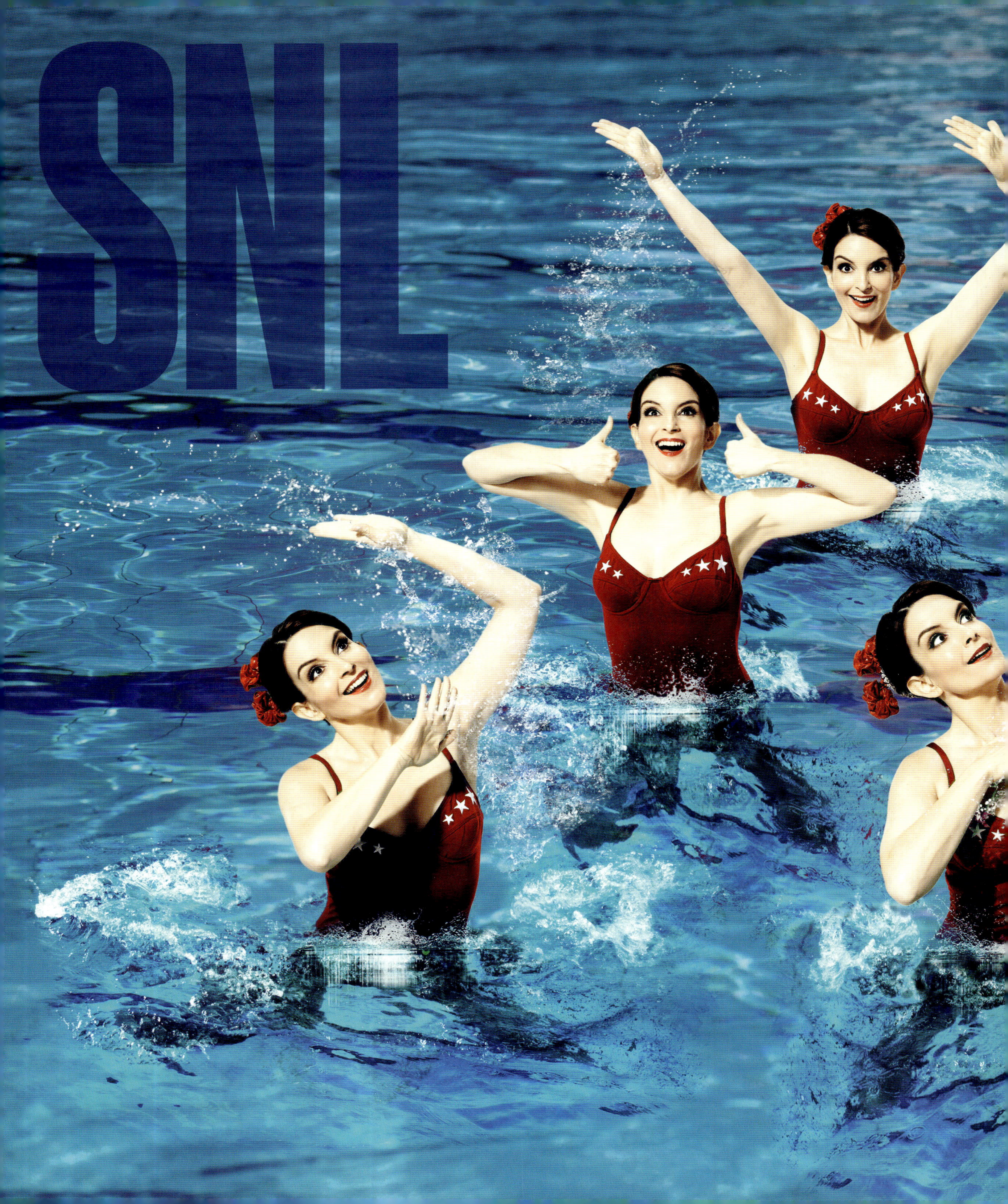
SNL

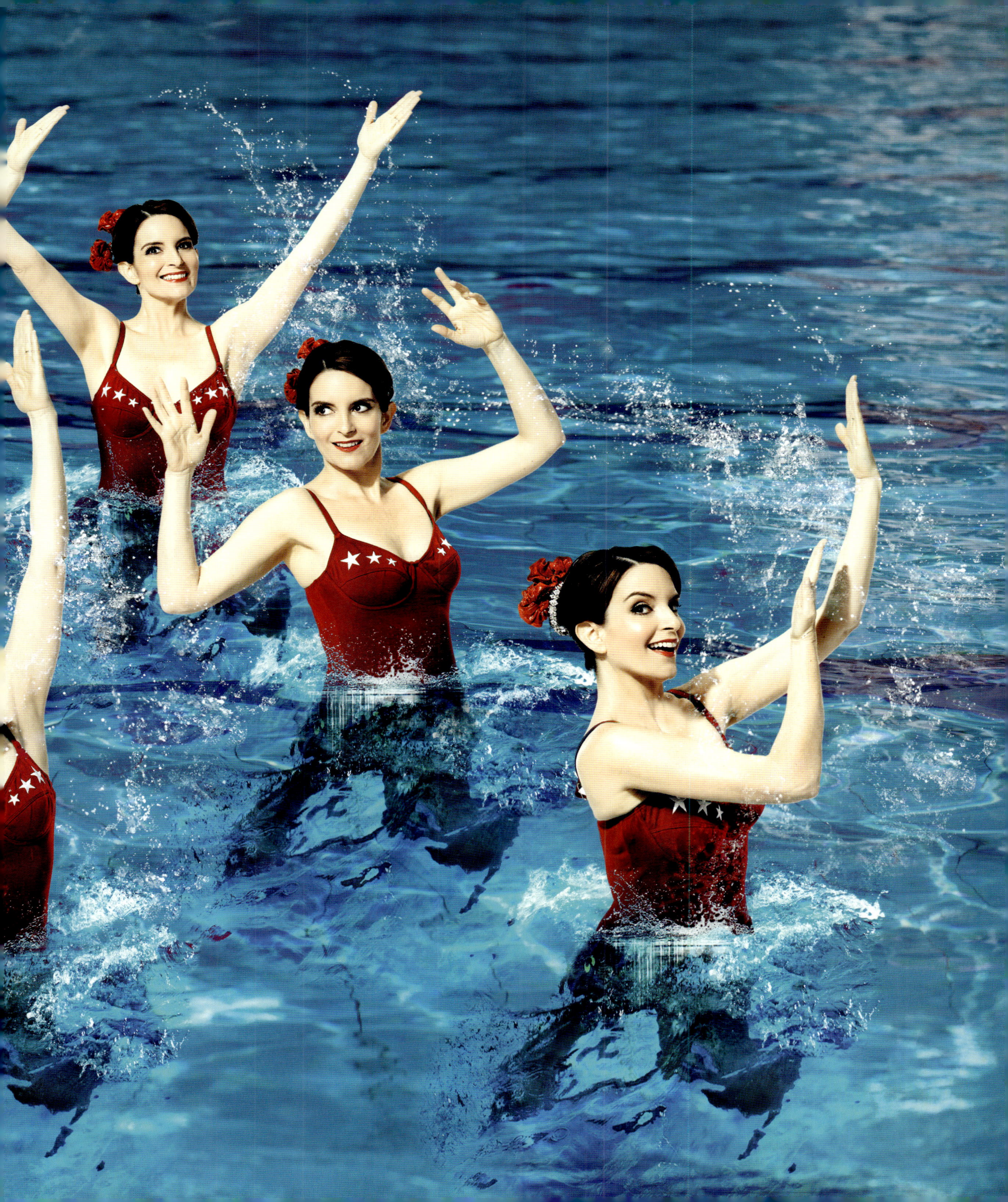

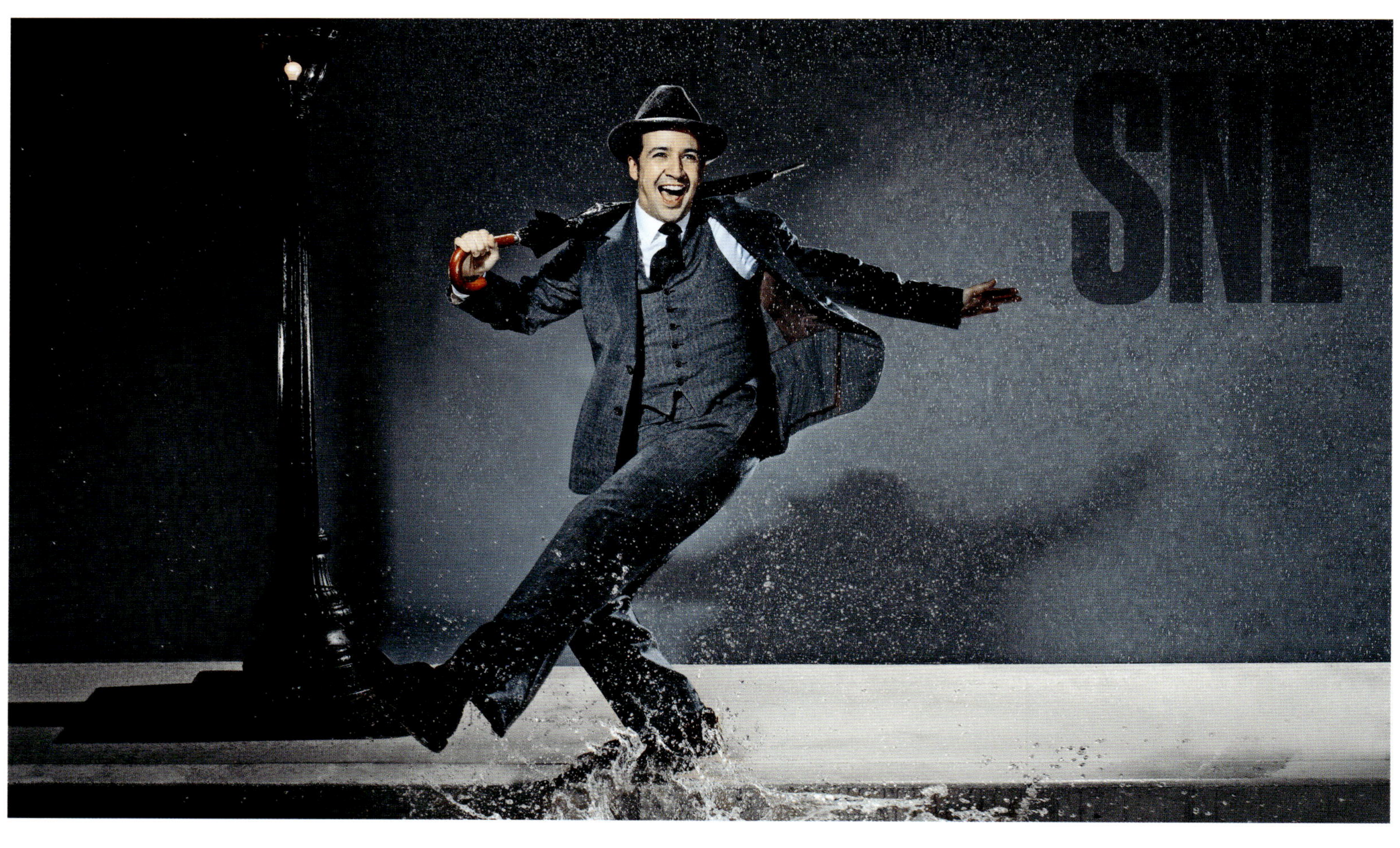
SNL

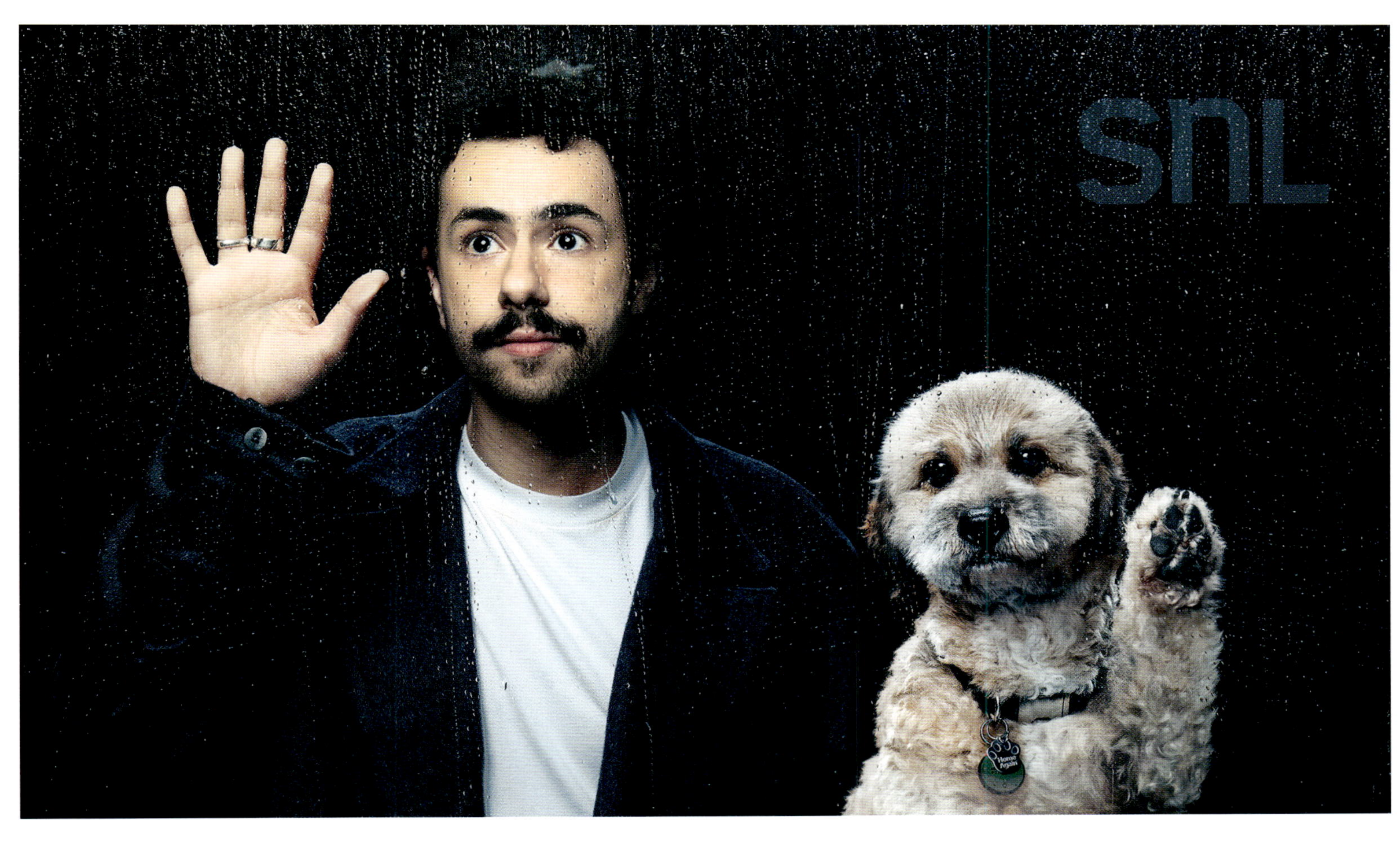
snL

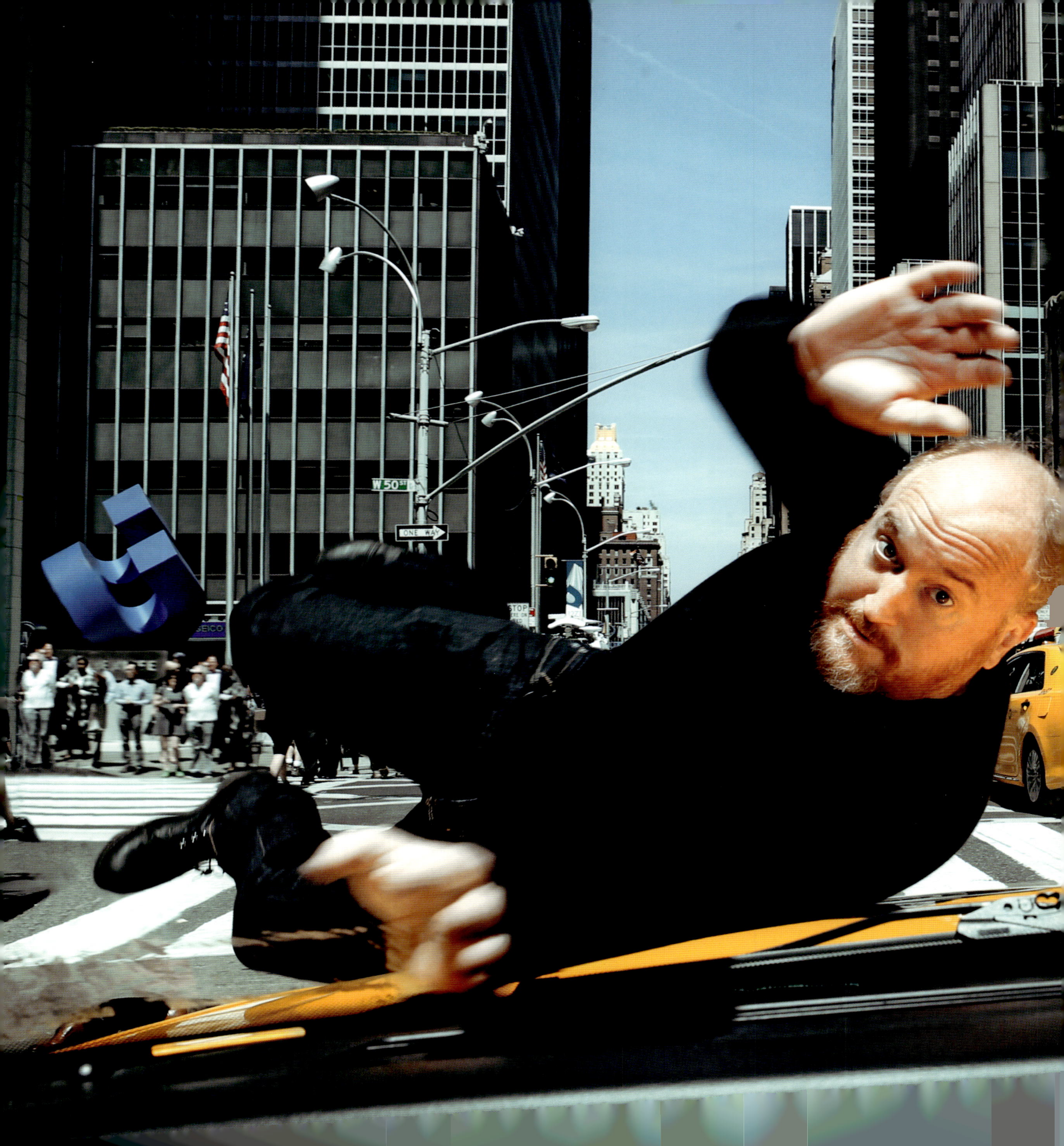
W 50 ST
ONE WAY
GEICO
STOP

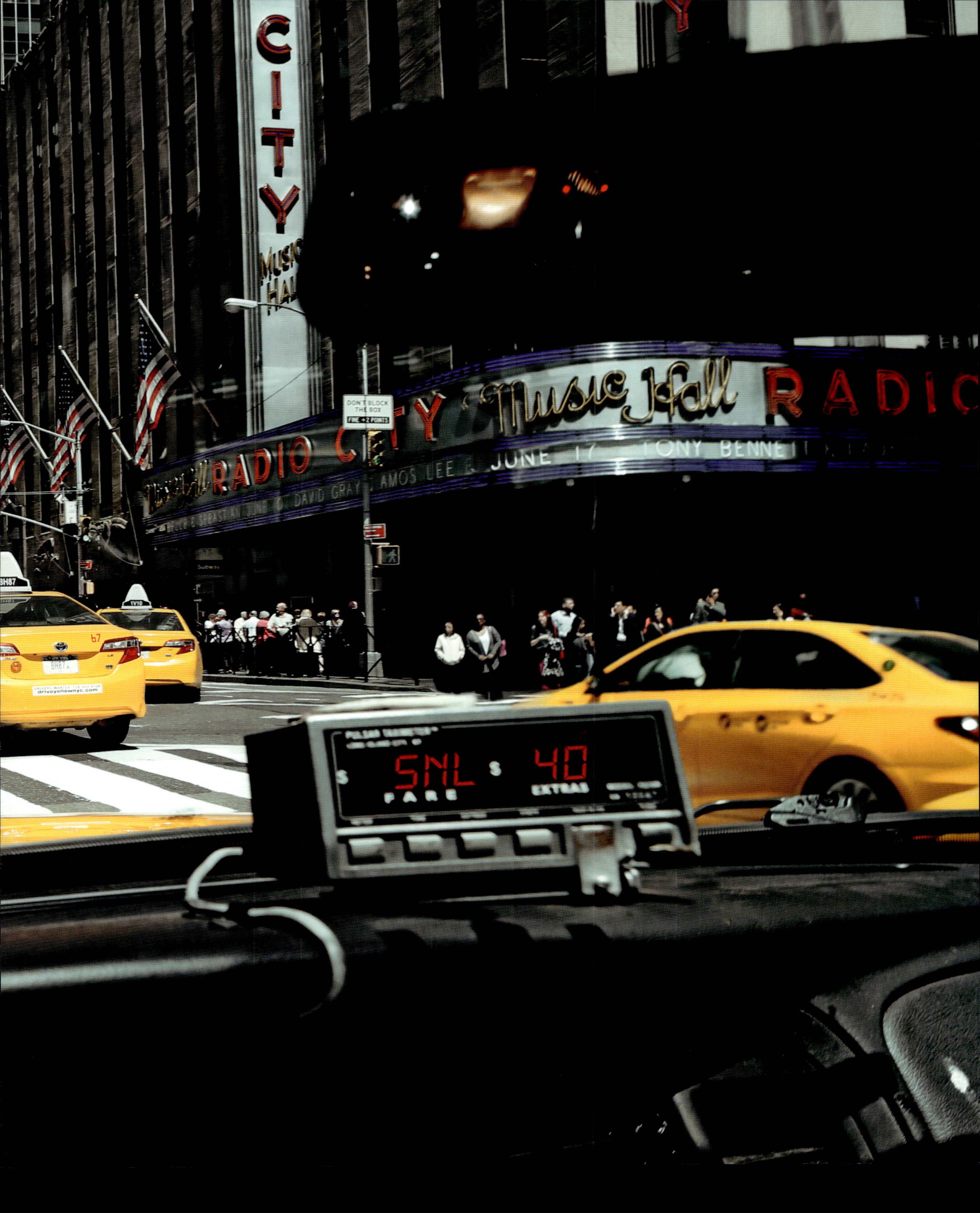

RADIO CITY
Music Hall
DON'T BLOCK THE BOX
FINE + 2 POINTS
JUNE 17
AMOS LEE
DAVID GRAY
SNL
40
FARE
EXTRAS

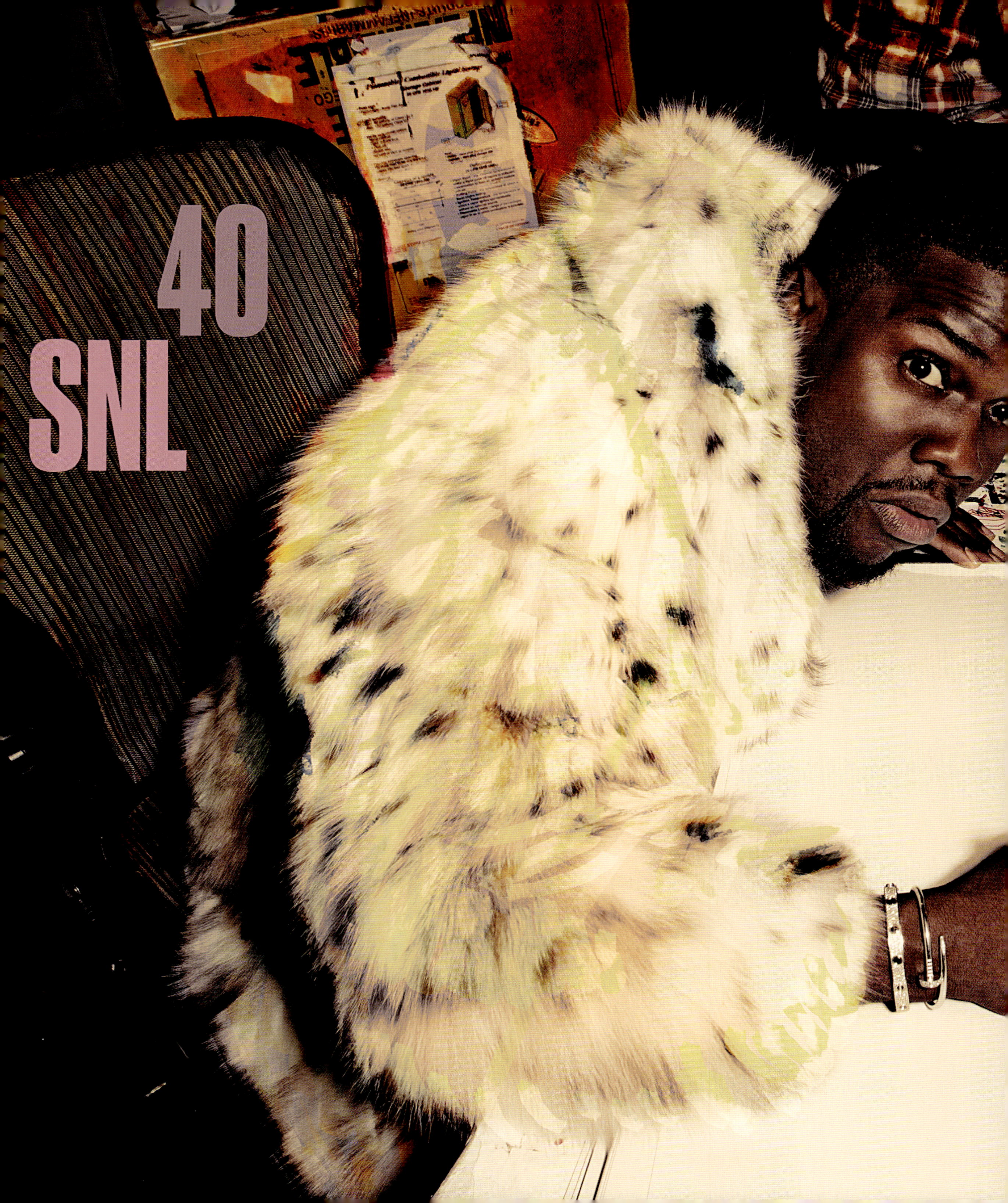

40
SNL

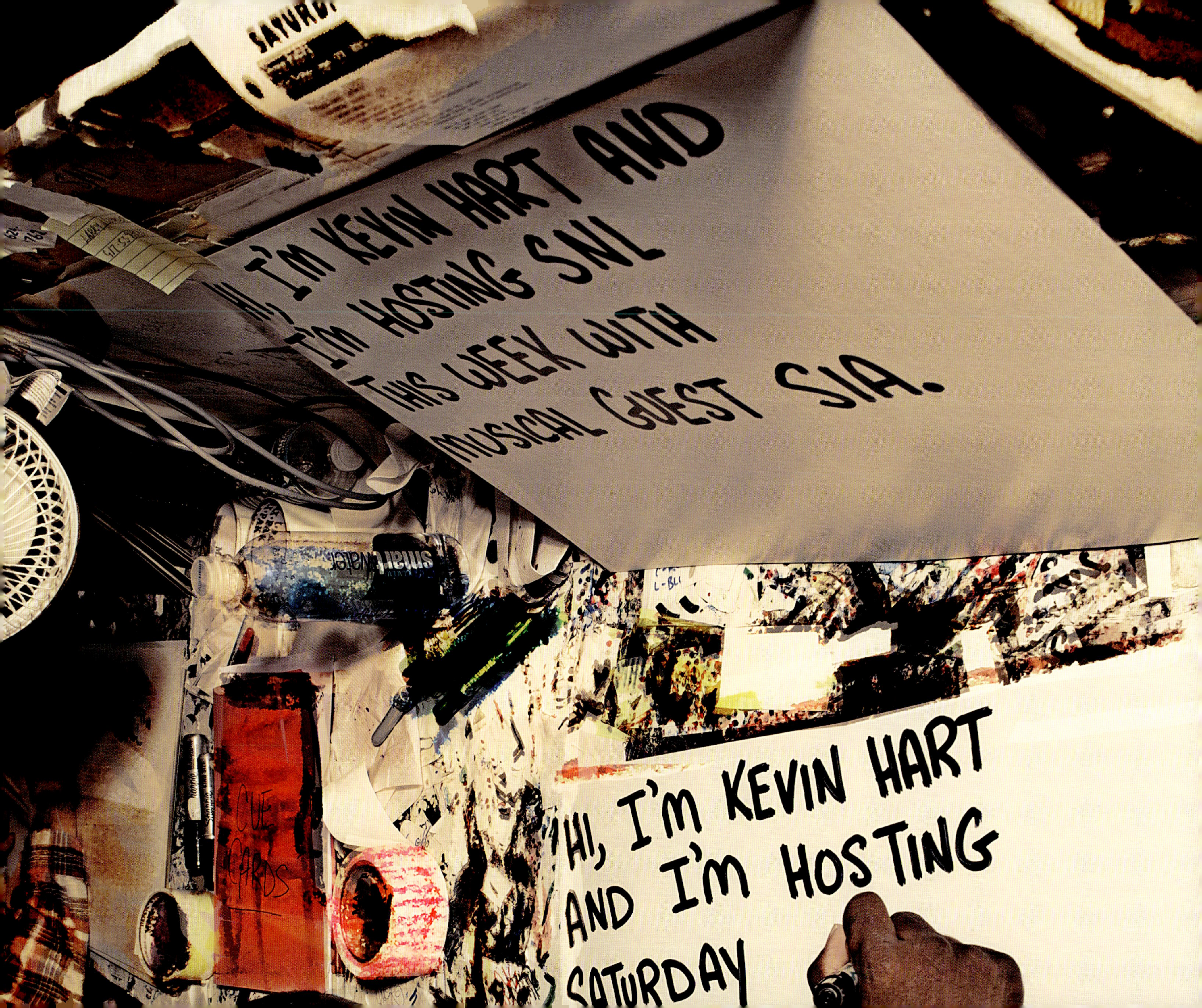
HI, I'M KEVIN HART AND
I'M HOSTING SNL
THIS WEEK WITH
MUSICAL GUEST SIA.
CUE CARDS
smartwater
HI, I'M KEVIN HART
AND I'M HOSTING
SATURDAY

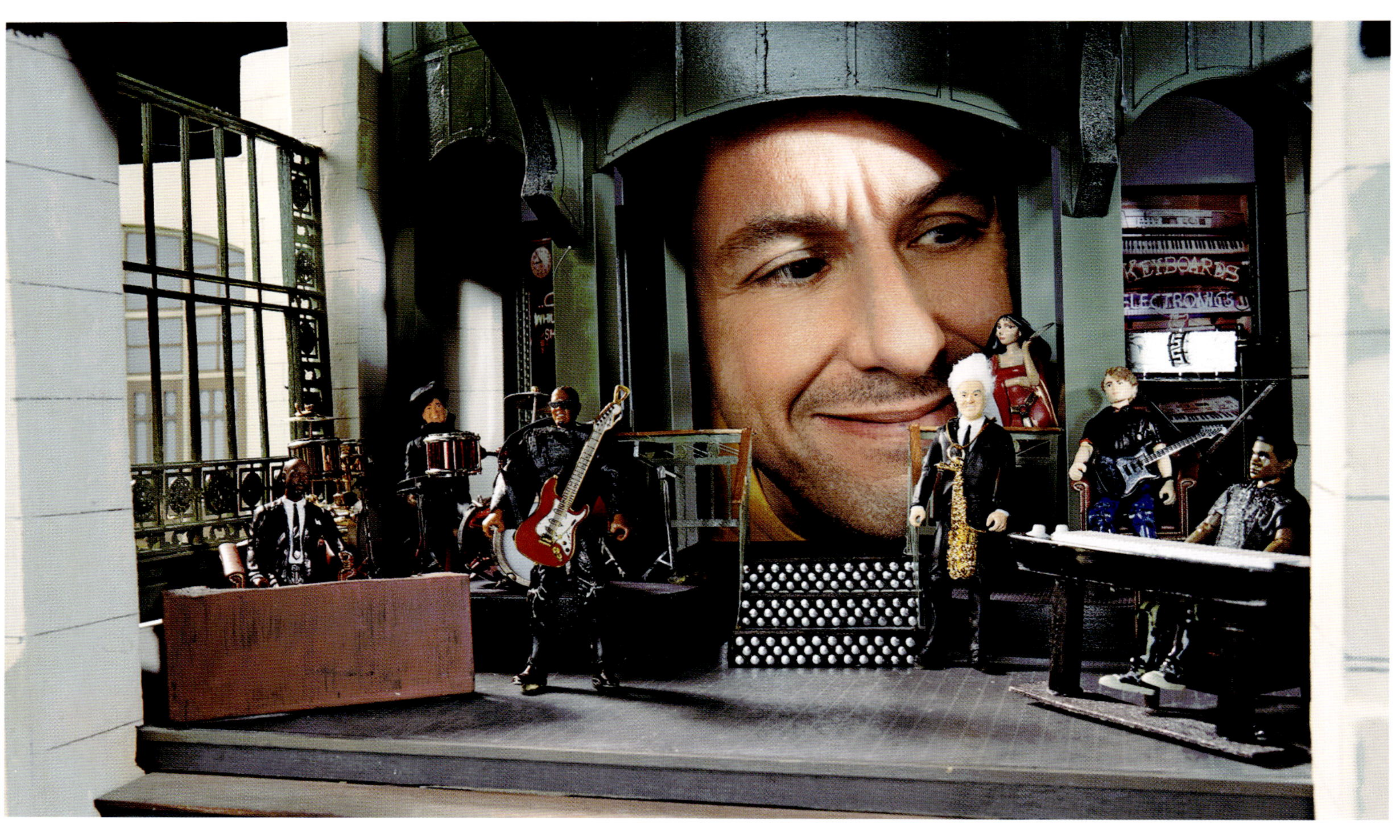
KEYBOARDS
ELECTRONICS

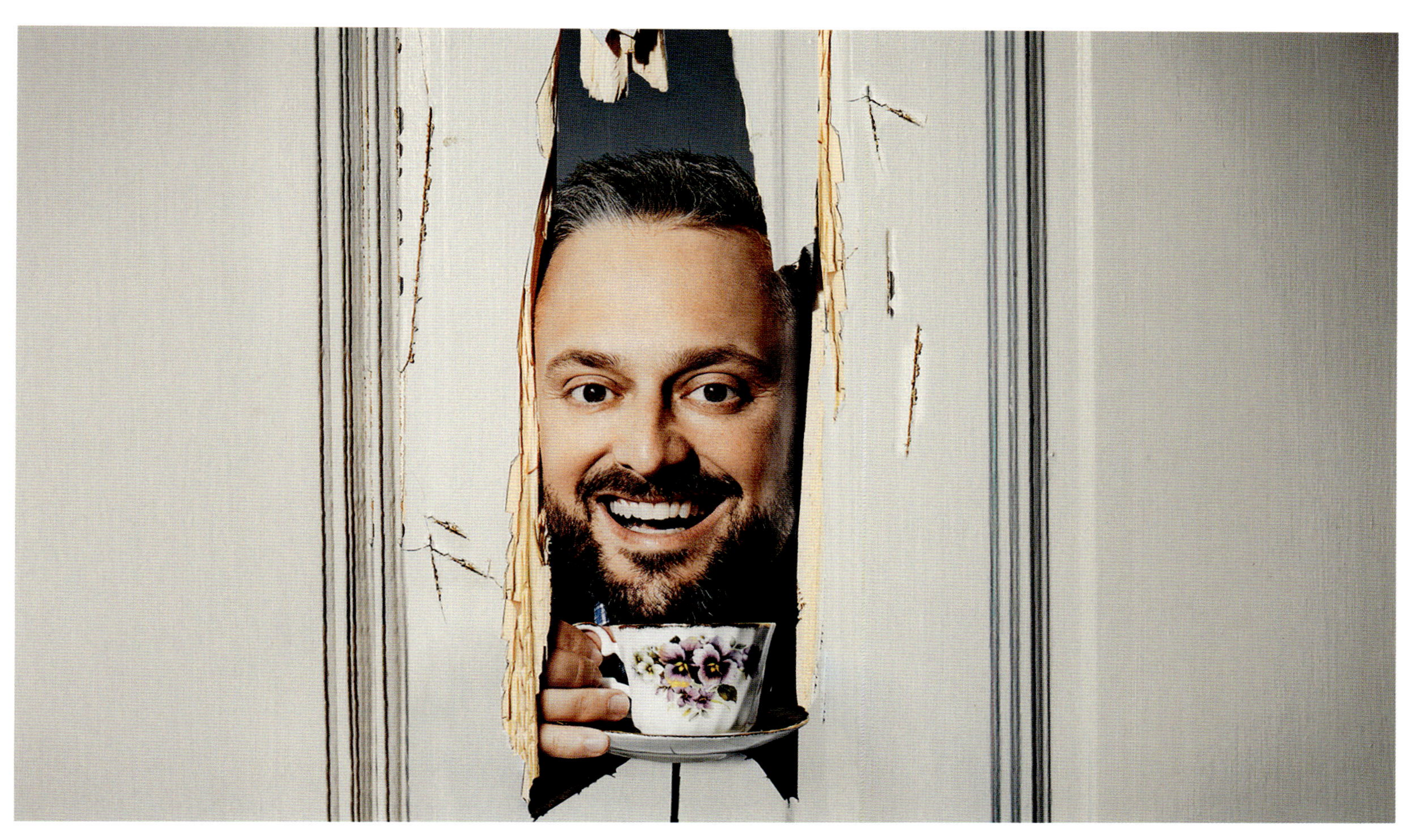

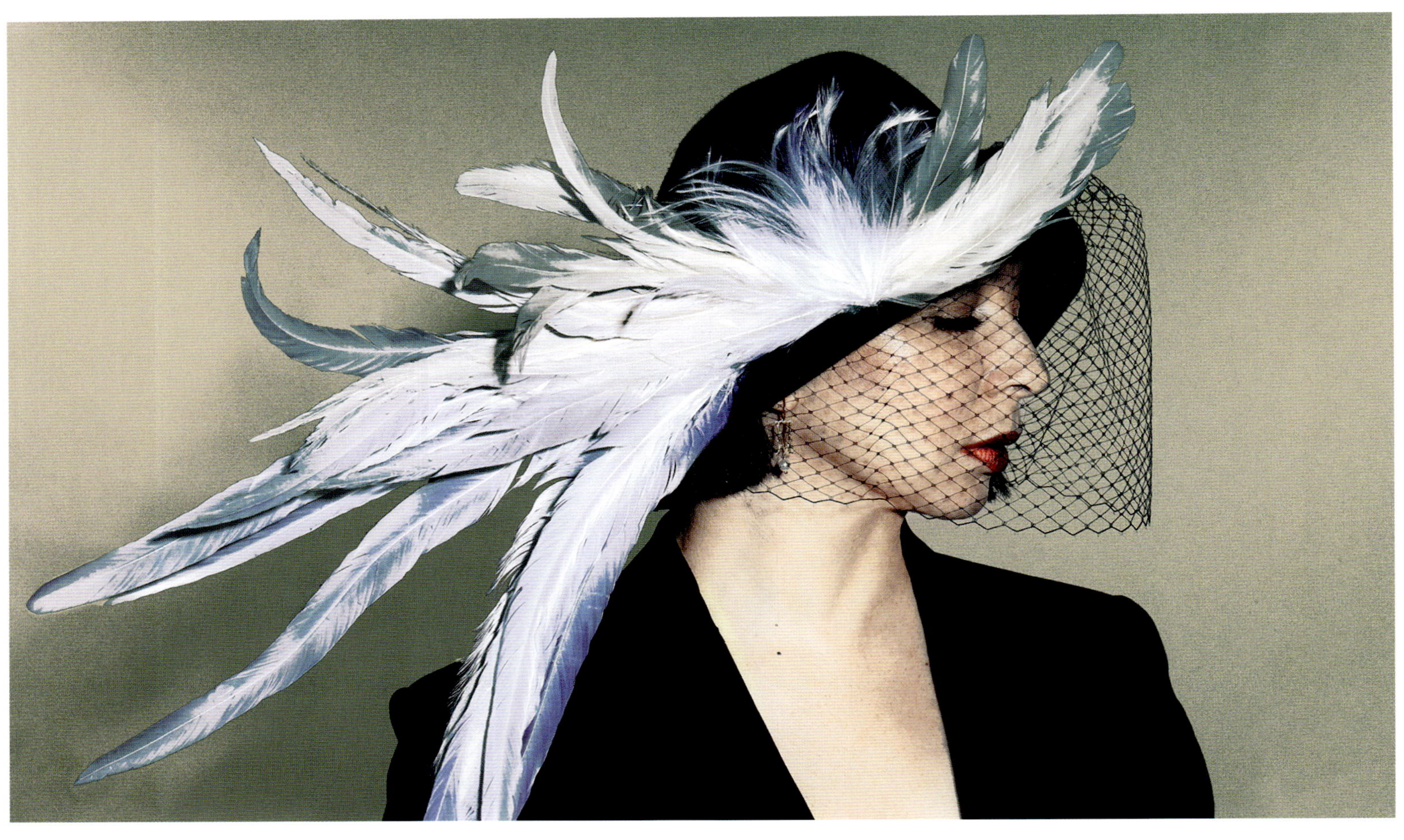

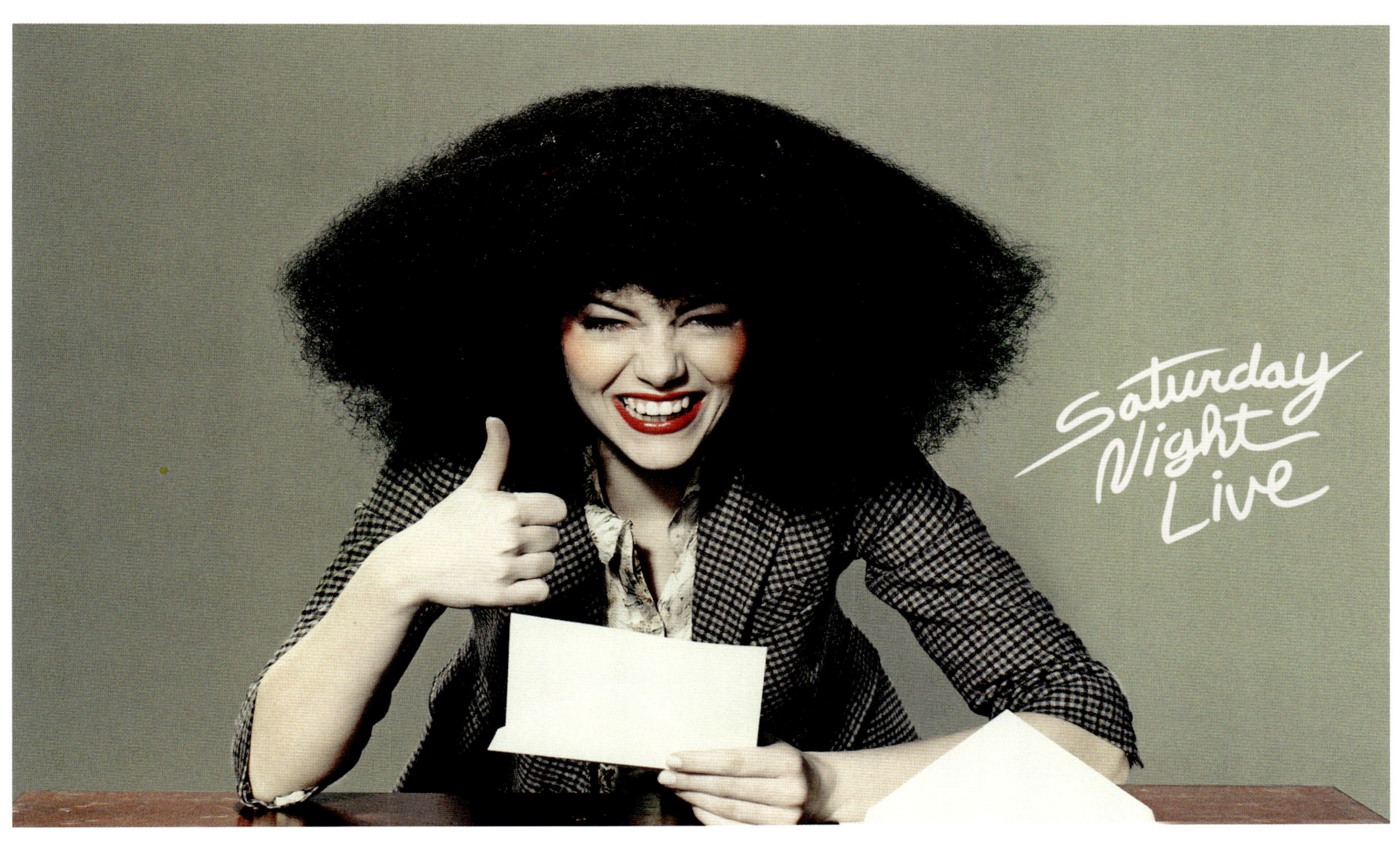
Saturday
Night
Live

THE ONE-CIRCUS

WOMAN

HOW DOES SHE DO IT?

MARY ELLEN MATTHEWS IN CONVERSATION WITH ALISON CASTLE

Alison Castle: Let's start with a bit of background: you grew up in suburban New Jersey, you were the youngest of five, and you got interested in photography at a young age.

Mary Ellen Matthews: Yes, I grew up in Madison, New Jersey, and my dad was a hobbyist photographer. We had a big darkroom in the basement, a lot of photography books, and that's how it all was revealed to me. It has always been an interest of mine. I used to develop pictures with my dad, mixing the chemicals, using the enlarger.

But then in high school and in college, you were really into athletics.

Yes, I was a gymnast my whole life. I went to college for gymnastics. I rode horses my whole life. I was a competitive diver and a swimmer. I actually won the state diving championship.

How did you end up coming to work at SNL?

I was working for an independent record label called TVT Records. And I was shooting the bands a lot. I did a lot of things there, but the last part of my time there I was a publicist and we used to go out and see bands all the time. And I would always have my camera. I spent a lot of time doing that, but also I was going down that path, I was just pulling people aside in the East Village and asking to take their picture or just getting the word out there to any bands that might want band pictures, and just kind of putting my skill set together. Honestly, I can't remember if I was fired from TVT or I quit, which is probably a sign that I was fired. Our office was on Fourth and Lafayette, and the day that job ended, I walked out and was like, "Let me check my answering machine," and there was a message from Leslie Weiner, who was working for [SNL photographer] Edie Baskin, saying, "I'm leaving and Edie wants to talk to you about taking this job," which was working for Edie as an assistant. I was really just her support system at first, helping to archive her photography and assist her on the shoot days, which then was on Tuesday. I saw how good she was, and wanted to gain that knowledge.

Did you have a feeling from the start that there was a potential for you to be her successor?

No, I did not know that. But I was so enamored by the job, by the energy on set, by the creativity, by being part of this show. You know, it's like stepping into an institution. But actually I wasn't working out of the show at first. She had an office downtown on Lafayette and Spring Street. So I wasn't really that involved [with SNL] at the beginning, but I would meet her on Thursdays for the band shoots. So I got to go to 30 Rock, I got to go to [Studio] 8H, and I think she must have seen my enthusiasm for it, and she became a mentor of mine.

So you got to watch how she worked, to watch her process?

Yes, and to work with the talent and also learn what it is to be a voice for *Saturday Night Live*. You are the look, a piece of the mechanism, you learn the sense of "cool" and what it represents and how to work within the show, to represent it in the right way.

How many years were you in that position?

That was '93. And then I took over in 2000. I must have proven to her that I was the right choice. And I think in the back of my mind, I was trying to do that. Not for the job specifically, I just wanted her approval, for her to see I was learning something. And I was developing as a photographer, because I would do a lot of stuff outside the show, for next to nothing, like headshots and bands and just taking on work, which I would show her and, you know, she would encourage me. I wanted her critique. I wasn't somebody who was going out and assisting other people. I wish I had done that, you know, to learn from other photographers in different ways.

You essentially went to the School of Edie Baskin.

Yes, but I also learned by doing. I learned how to do a very specific job very well. It's not just photography, it's learning how to deal with talent, with the schedule, how to maneuver within that show. There's not another job in the world like this.

And there's no way to prepare for it unless you've already been there. You do every show in a week. There's nothing that can replace experience and being around and understanding how it works.

And the built-in timeline that will never change. There's a set schedule, the day in, day out, which is not to make it sound monotonous, but it is something to be reckoned with every week.

Do you remember what it was like at the point where you took over as the photographer? Do you remember any feelings of worry or great anxiety?

Yes, great anxiety. I didn't want to copy what Edie was doing, because it was so iconic. I wanted to shift enough, but to also stay in that same playing field. It was a very shaky feeling.

It's tough to fill someone's shoes without trying to emulate them.

Right. The way that the show works is, you do what you do. It's hard. There's not an approval process there. You're trusted to do what you do and you do it, and that is such a beautiful way to work in a way because you feel so backed up, it's just built in.

Over the years, you've had certain moments when Lorne has really shown his appreciation for your work and his gratitude to you, and I know that means a lot, because he's not effusive with his praise. Obviously, over time, you realize that if he's hands off, there's a reason.

Right. And you feel like you really are owning the job. And at the end of the day, he's the person that you have to keep up with.

And he knows that you're not going to put something on air that's going to offend anybody.

We know that. I'm not going to do a rogue nude shoot with somebody. We know what works and what's not going to work, and like all art, you want to keep edging towards what's new and what's fresh. And what's going to be inspiring.

Because you'd been around for many years, you already had a feel for the rhythm and the way it works to pitch an idea to the talent, what their various reactions might be to certain ideas, whether some people pull back on something that they think is too silly, etc.

I started to think of the bumpers in a new way. Introducing concepts instead of just portraits. So that came out of the urge to do something new.

Do you remember the first time you did a "concept" bumper?

I think it might be Anne Hathaway. I gave her a steering wheel and made this kind of noir light. She's driving and she's looking in the rearview mirror. And it's just in this limbo. You know, it's like, "Let's give them something to do." It was a way to make it something different than what Edie did. So, props are something that we started.

Luckily, you also cover the spectrum, doing beautiful glamour photography, doing amazing lighting and beautiful postproduction. It's nice to have that range, so you don't have the pressure for every single picture to be some clever reference to something.

You want a range in the show, you want a quiet moment. I love to have a quiet

"THE WAY THAT THE SHOW WORKS IS, YOU DO WHAT YOU DO. IT'S HARD. THERE'S NOT AN APPROVAL PROCESS THERE. YOU'RE TRUSTED TO DO WHAT YOU DO AND YOU DO IT."

portrait, maybe it's a profile, maybe it's a silhouette, but something a little more introspective, and a range of ideas. There's concepts, there's letting them be themselves, and then a quiet moment, like a mixture of all of that. Letting them be themselves, that's the gold, when you can get that portrait and somebody's shining from within, and they're laughing, they have a standalone look that's only themselves.

Generally, it's from Thursday to Saturday night that's your start to finish. Do you have a notebook where you keep running ideas, and then you think about which host or musical guest will work for an idea?

Yeah, it's actually on my phone now. As soon as I know who [the host] is, then I'll start a folder and just start putting ideas in, because it's not about having ideas and then giving them to people. It's about bringing ideas into their folder, if that makes sense. Usually we know the host a couple of weeks in advance, but sometimes the show doesn't get booked until the week before, if somebody has to shift to something.

Do you meet with them to pitch ideas?

It depends. If it's a complicated ask or a complicated concept, before we spend the money to get, say, a pony or something, you want to make sure that they're on board with it. Or if someone's making a specific wig, or we're asking Tom [Broeker, costume designer] to make a costume, I'll ask talent to meet with them on a Tuesday or Wednesday and run it by. Otherwise, I'll have more than enough ideas, so we can throw out some. Say there's five ideas and maybe we just need three. And sometimes the performer is going to bring something else to the table. You know, it is the only job like it and it just constantly gives. From everybody on my crew to the talent . . . to be able to collaborate with these amazing, amazing people, to be part of the show, to be part of the visual language of the show . . . it's just amazing that I'm that person. It's super nuts.

Let's drink to that! And with the 50th anniversary coming up, it's nice to reflect on how many people have been working for the show for so many years. That's one of the legendary things about the show, how long so many people stayed with it. My suspicion is that once you've worked in that atmosphere, and you've sort of drank the Kool-Aid, and you're into that energy, it might be hard to imagine what else would compare.

Yes, I mean, the opportunity to be so creative on a weekly basis, with these incredibly talented, creative people, to put it in the context of this institution, this legendary show, to put it on television and then get to do it again the next week and do better and do something different . . . You learn from the last show and then bring it to the next show.

You had a title idea for this book, "All This for Three Seconds", which I think is quite funny, although probably wouldn't translate, as people wouldn't understand what that means.

But it's true, it's an incredible amount of work for three seconds on-air. From the concept to the discussions with the talent, follow-through with costumes, if wigs are involved, perhaps set pieces need to be sourced . . . And then the post-production, to the delight of seeing it all come together. But because we are on such a tight schedule, the bumpers air when they aren't quite finished, and just as Lorne has always said about the show itself going on not because it's ready but because it's 11:30 p.m.—the same is true for the bumpers. I always say that these images are meant to be on television, with luminosity on them. I produce them on a computer and they aren't meant for print, really. Of course we print them and hang them on the walls of the studio or give them as gifts, but this is the first time they are being presented as a collection. And also, some aren't fully perfected

"IT'S A MIRACLE. IT'S EVERY WEEK! AS SOON AS YOU START TO KIND OF TAKE IT FOR GRANTED, ALL OF A SUDDEN, YOU REALIZE, WAIT A MINUTE, THIS IS UNBELIEVABLE."

because of the rush of it all. I wish I had time to do more finishing work on the photos, and I went into this book project with a little anxiety knowing that. But that is the nature of how this show works, and I still wanted to present them that way, in all of their authenticity.

Yes, I really think that it's important for us to highlight the fact that this book is one of the very few times that these things actually get printed. They've always existed, but the only time they ever really were shared was for three seconds on television. It's obviously very unusual for a photographer to have work where the principal output is on television. I can't even think of another show that still does bumpers.

And this is not cheap to do. I mean, they're paying me, they're paying my staff. You know, it's a lot. And it's a lot of time to ask of the host.

And the fact that on streaming, which is the way most people watch SNL now, they don't show more than a couple bumpers per show. SNL could say, "Well, we really don't need to spend this money on them." But they don't, and that's why we love the show so much. This is part of its identity. And the talent, I've seen so many people come up to you after the show and say how much they loved the photos, it really is special for them, too. So there's a lot of reasons why it makes sense to keep doing them.

It's part of the weekly experience, and that is another thing that I just lean into and smile deeply about, that I am part of that experience. That's why it's just about having fun, it's just about joy.

Everybody's really excited to host SNL. And in the same way that it's exciting to get your yearbook pictures, I would think that for the hosts, the pictures are like a special souvenir.

Well, I don't know if you know this, but we give each host a book. It's a leather-bound little photo book that we have embossed. We put in a photo from each sketch and all the bumpers. You know, the hosts work really hard at this. It's not nothing to change five times in an hour, and become, like, a lion tamer, or pretend that you're walking on a tightrope or whatever it is. It's a lot of hoops to jump through.

But still, especially the ones that are on the goofy side or more on the cheeky side, you can really sense them enjoying it.

Yes, and there's a lot of trust there too. It's a trust fall to even start the process.

And of course all this is supported by every single department, who are all busy preparing the show at the same time.

My god, for me to say to Jodi [Mancuso, hair designer], can I get a wig? That's like her saying to me, can I get a photoshoot?

Yeah, because they make those wigs from scratch. It's unbelievable. Let's talk a little bit about costumes.

Tom is a huge collaborator on every show. Really, you know, I can't talk about any of what I do without him. For example, the [Paul Rudd] nativity scene, I'm like, "Tom, I have an idea," and he never says no. Never. So he'll support my idea in a way that is from the highest level. Sometimes these ideas don't come until an hour before or while we're doing it. And of course he's also working on the show at the same time. The Paul Rudd as Paul McCartney, I was thinking about in the moment. Jodi did the wig and Tom pulled together the suit, he got the Beatles skinny tie, the whole thing, and Jodi got the Beatles cut . . . and—this is the best story—it's a left-handed bass, a very specific one. And Paul McCartney had it on set, but of course we couldn't use it, because it's priceless. So [music technician] Speedy [Rosenthal] found a replica somewhere in New York City at some guitar shop, and got it in there in time before it all fell apart.

Wow. That's amazing. I suppose you could have Photoshopped that, but it's so much better that you didn't. It's all hands on deck, right? And there's a lot of overlapping things going on at the same time.

What we want to do is we want to create, and we're given a stage to create and all these tools to work with, and all these talented technical people, and everybody comes together . . . it's just astonishing.

You still feel that way.

I still feel that way. You come to the show and you can't believe it. It's a miracle. It's every week! As soon as you start to kind of take it for granted, all of a sudden, you realize, wait a minute, this is unbelievable. It really is true. The lighting and the sound. And of course, the designers and the writers—we don't have a show without them.

Not to mention the number-one honcho.

Of course, and he is incredible to work for. Listen, the fact that I've gotten to work with Lorne Michaels for more than twenty years has been such an honor.

I know you as somebody who's endlessly curious about different kinds of art, photography, cinema, cultural references, art history, and you've managed to weave that into a lot of what you've done. Let's talk a little bit more about that.

All true. First, let me say that living in NYC is constantly inspirational. You get to experience so much culture, obviously the world's best museums, but also I make it a habit of trying to go to galleries as much as I can, to constantly be inspired. I have stacks and stacks of magazines I collect, photo and art books everywhere. And I really love keeping those and paging through them. We all know that the internet offers us a lot, but I'm a fan of sitting on the floor with a stack of books. It's a very big splurge in life, to keep buying artists' books, but a really important one.

Speaking of books, it has been really interesting but difficult to make the photo edit for this book. There are so many great images, so many great subjects, and yet the book needs to have the right tone, the right flow, needs to feel current and avoid things that feel really dated . . . That's been a crazy process, hasn't it?

Yes, it has been excruciating!

We, yourself included, decided that we wanted to base this book on a flow, a "greatest hits" type of thing. Not chronologically. And once you get into a flow, image to image, they all start to relate and it sort of sets itself up from start to finish. Literally, magic happens when you find these connections between two photos that you think would never have anything to do with each other, like Dwayne Johnson holding a big rock with Dana Carvey holding a lobster—Rock Lobster! That's what I try to shoot for, is the joy that these images give you, the unexpected pairings that introduce us to a whole other realm of visual cadence.

One thing that has been really challenging is to balance the subjects and the art itself, the artistry of the photographs, in terms of the image selection.

A hundred percent. It has been so, so difficult! We have a page limit and that means there are so many we have to leave behind. There are so many people I love and loved working with that didn't make it into the book because it just didn't work from an art and design perspective. And there are some people who made it in more than once because the pictures were really strong and worked so well together. The good news is, we can always make another book.

SNL at Home

The show was on a two-week hiatus in March 2020 when the pandemic was declared. The following three episodes were canceled while the cast and crew scrambled to adjust to this unsettling new reality. The final three episodes of season 45 were filmed remotely, with cast members writing and performing sketches from their homes. The first episode of "SNL at Home" featured a tribute to Hal Willner, the show's beloved music supervisor who died of COVID in early April.

For the bumpers, Matthews leaned into the stuck-at-home concept by creating still lifes in and around her apartment and setting up scenarios featuring her dog, Daphne. These low-fi, homemade shots were relatable to an audience similarly cooped up at home; they were also a comforting sight because they helped reassure us that "the show must go on."

"I actually felt lucky to have something to do, and I loved doing these," says Matthews. "I was grateful for the creative challenge of making content for the show at home. Even stepping outside for the one with the birdseed was odd, as the streets were empty and you really felt the desolation. I tried leaning into Warhol and Jackson Pollock for inspiration, some of my art heroes. The broom leaning from the roof was a reference to a Marilyn Monroe photograph, another was a reference to a photo by Bob Gruen. It was especially fun to feature the cast in the fridge one, as they are never in the bumpers. The only true challenge was getting my dog, Daphne, to sit in the bathtub."

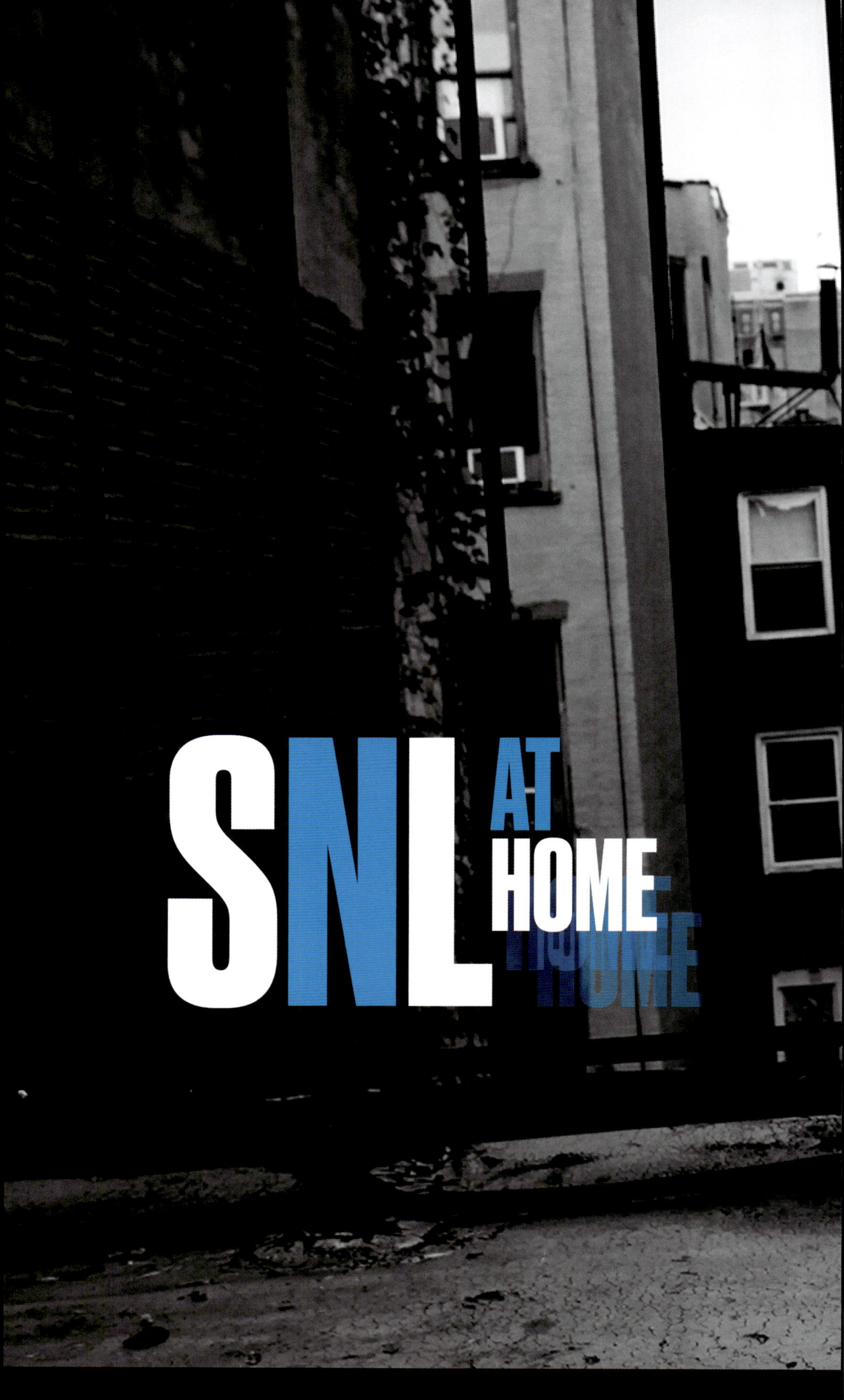

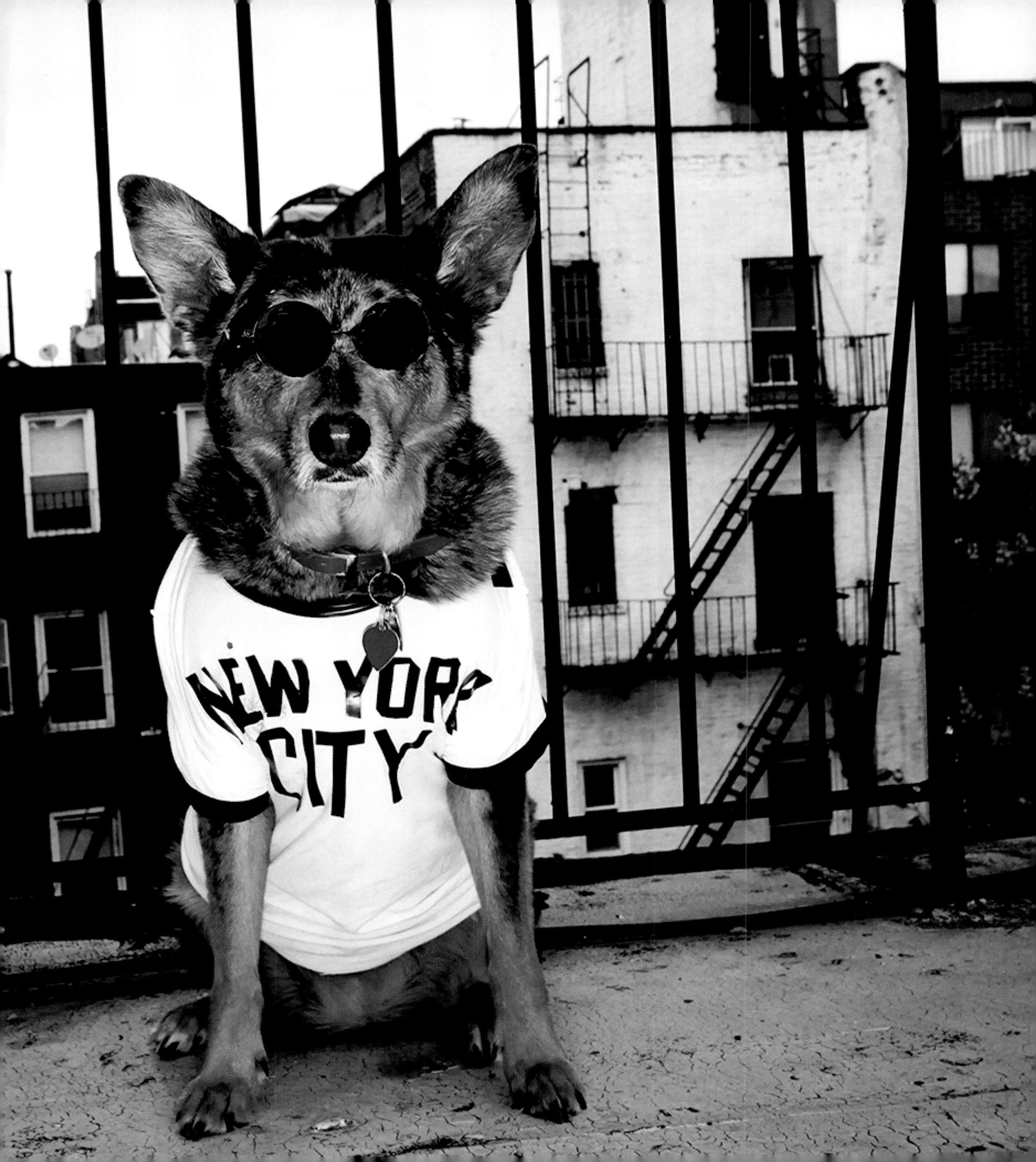
NEW YORK
CITY

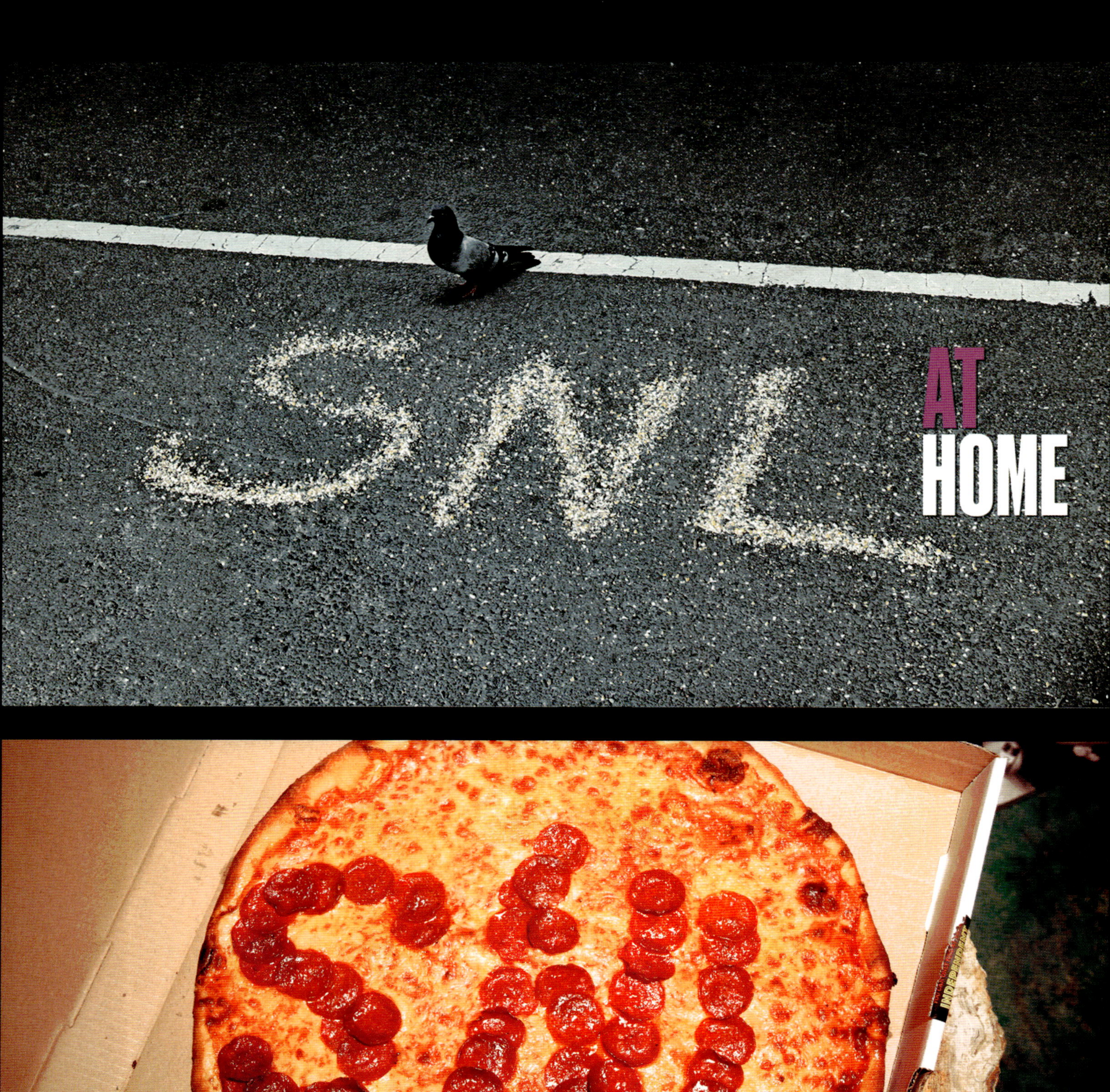
SNL
AT
HOME
SNL
AT
HOME

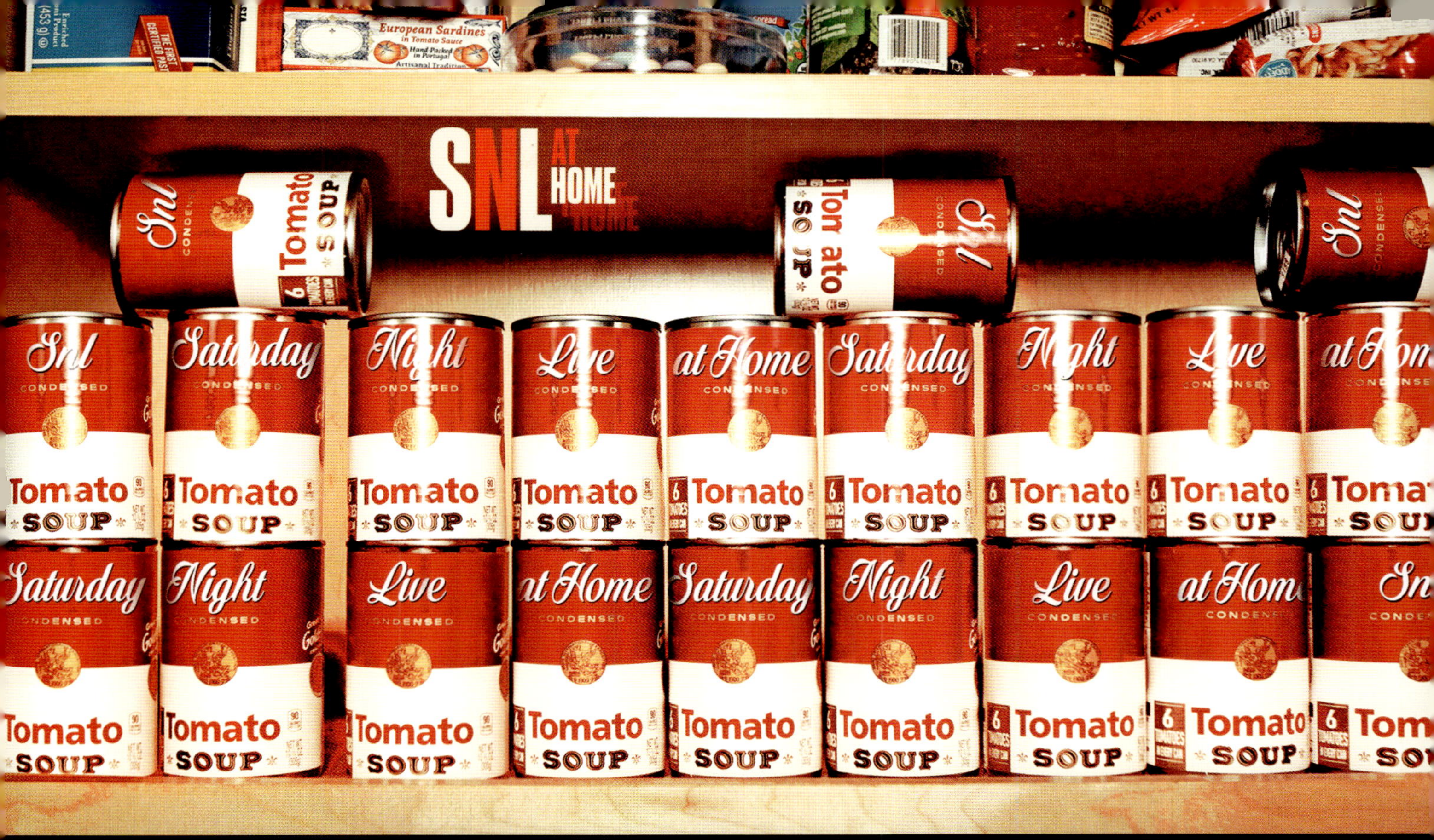

SNL AT HOME

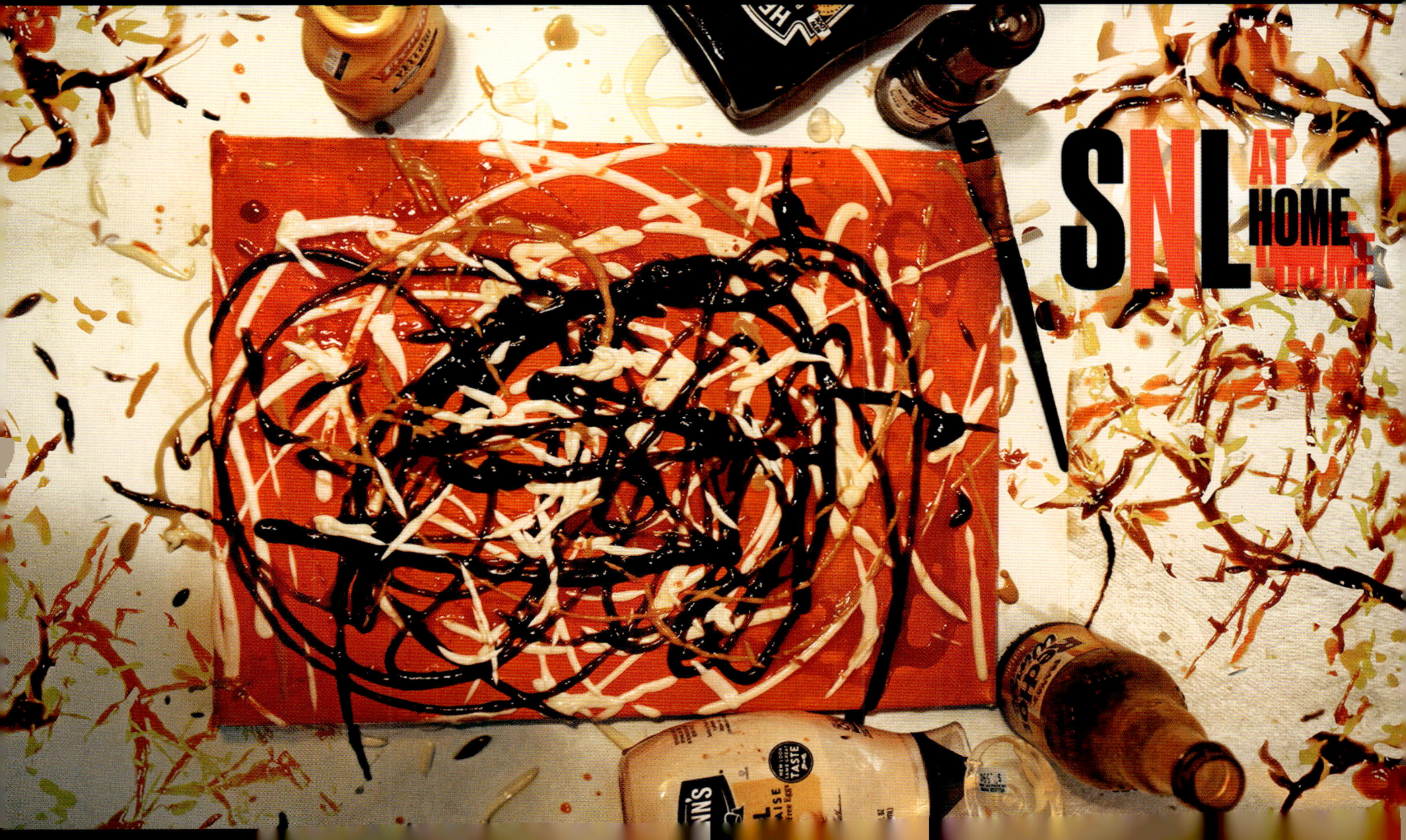

SNL AT HOME

"The only true challenge was getting my dog, Daphne, to sit in the bathtub."

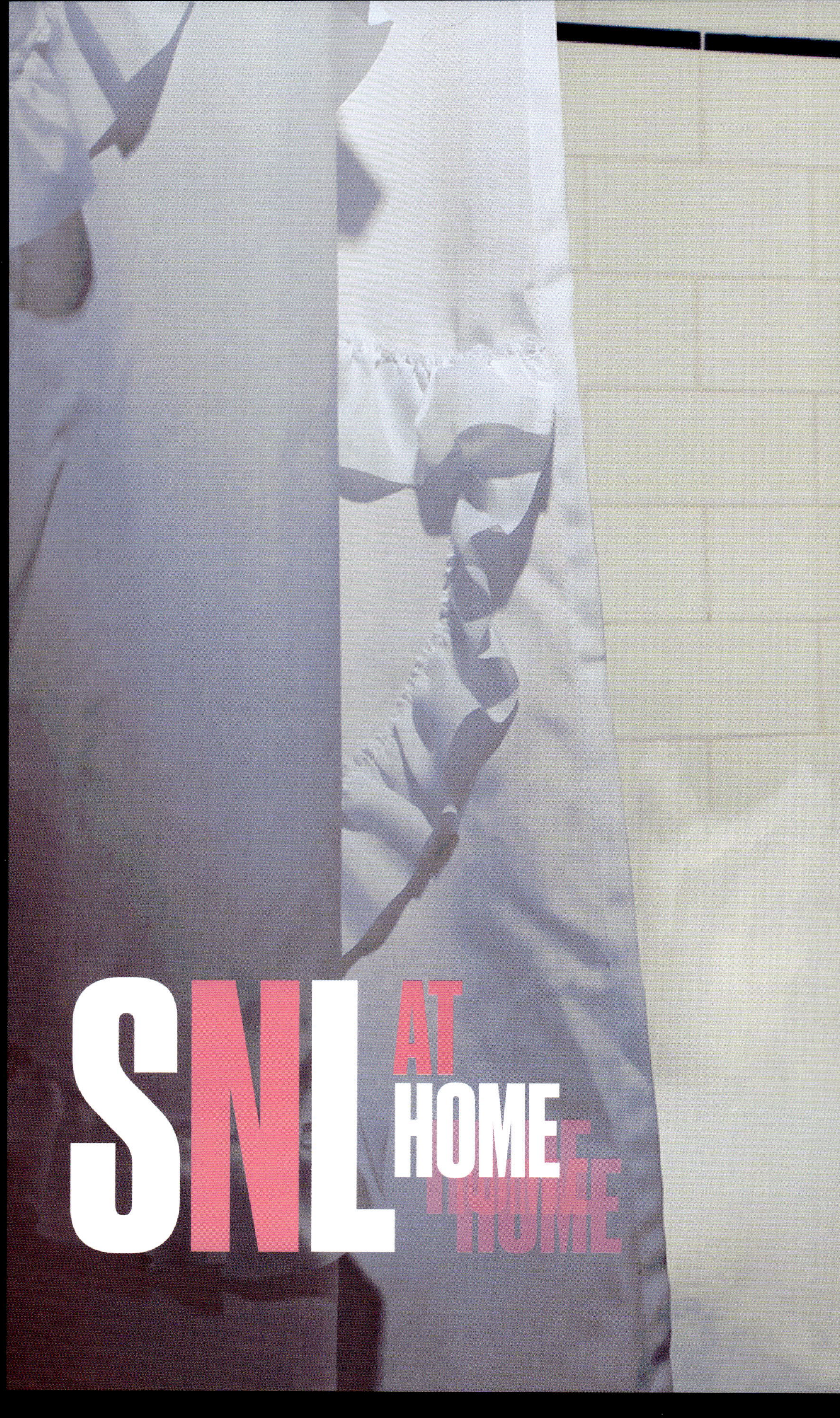

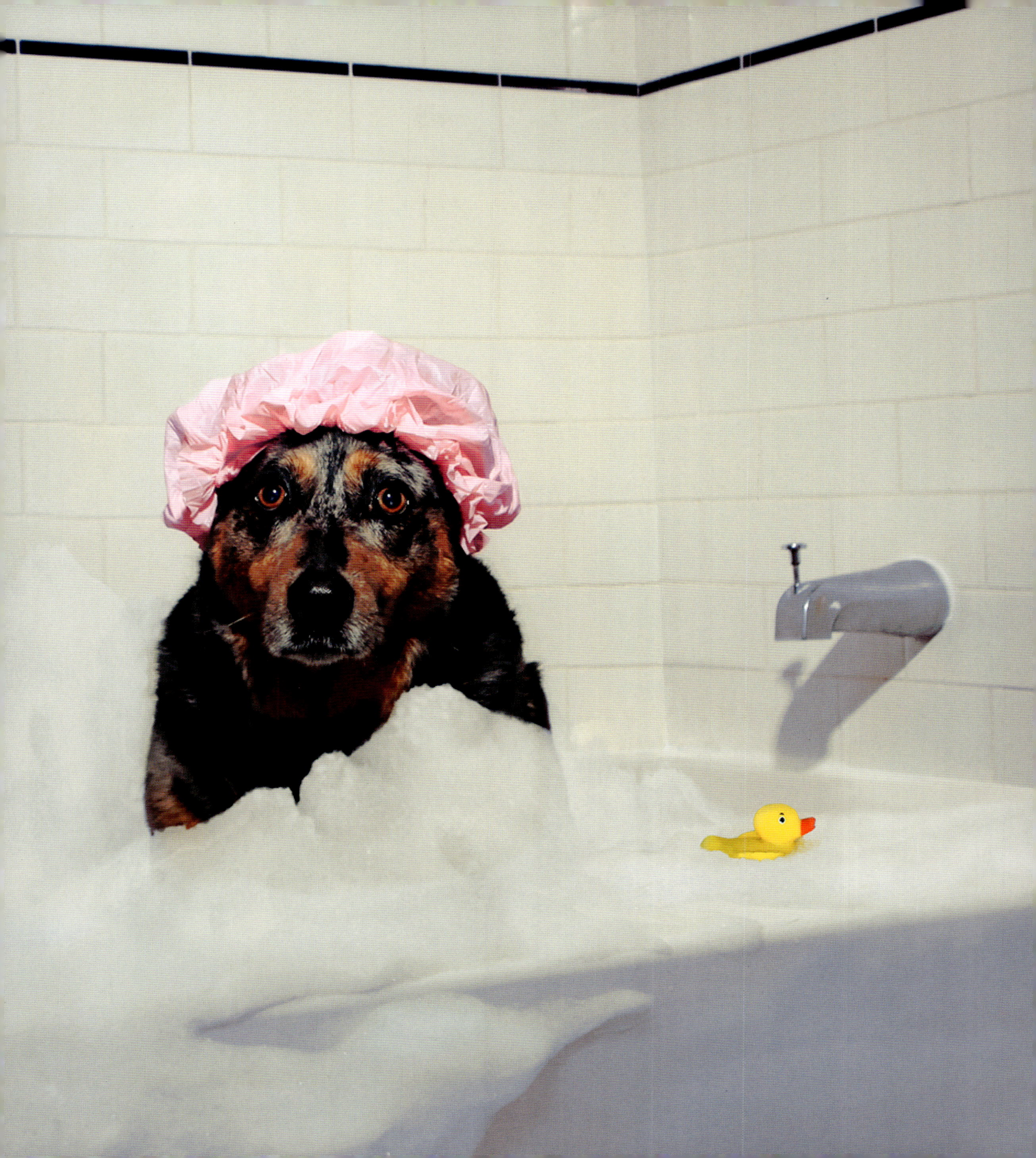

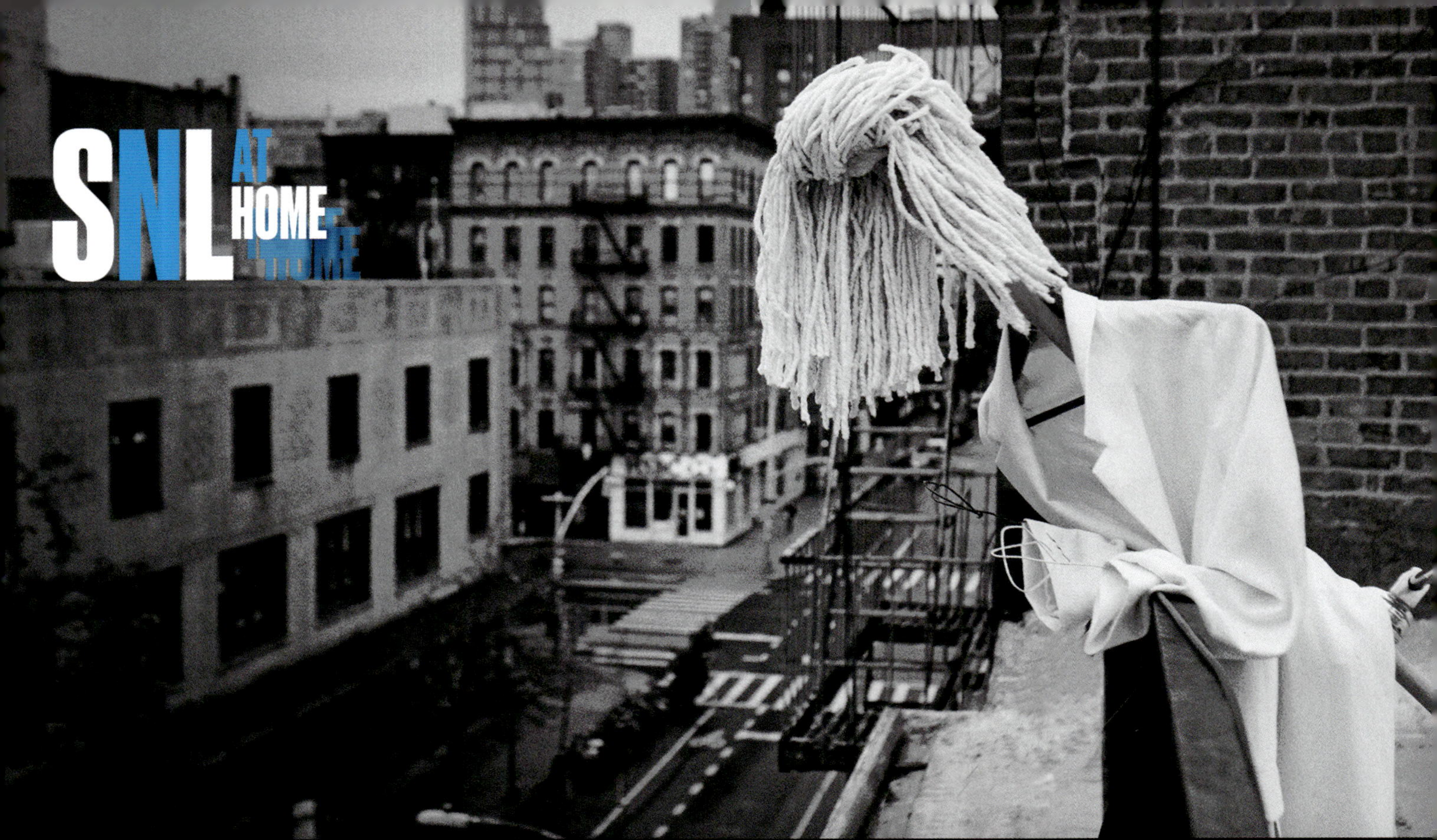

SNL AT HOME

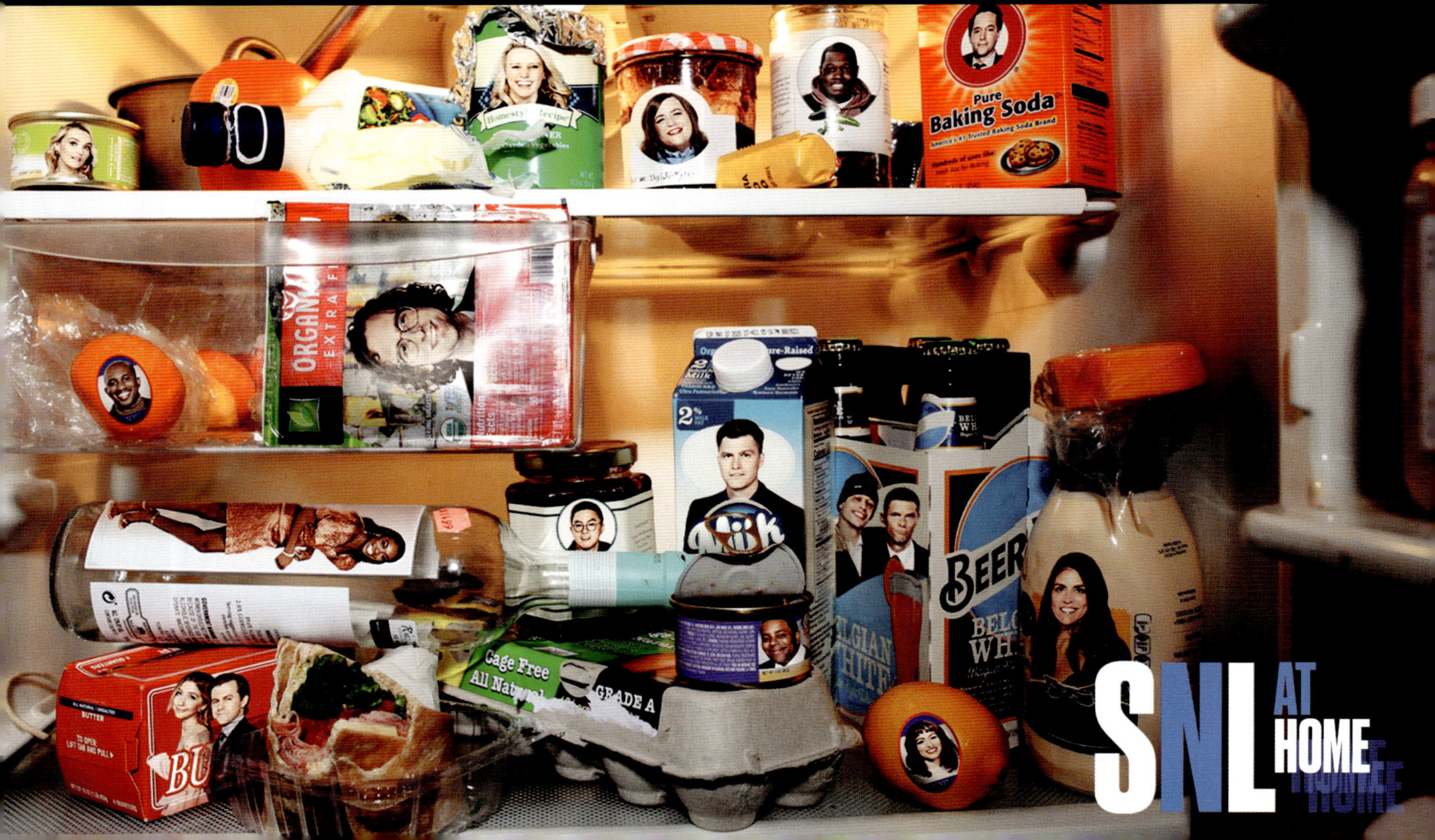

SNL AT HOME

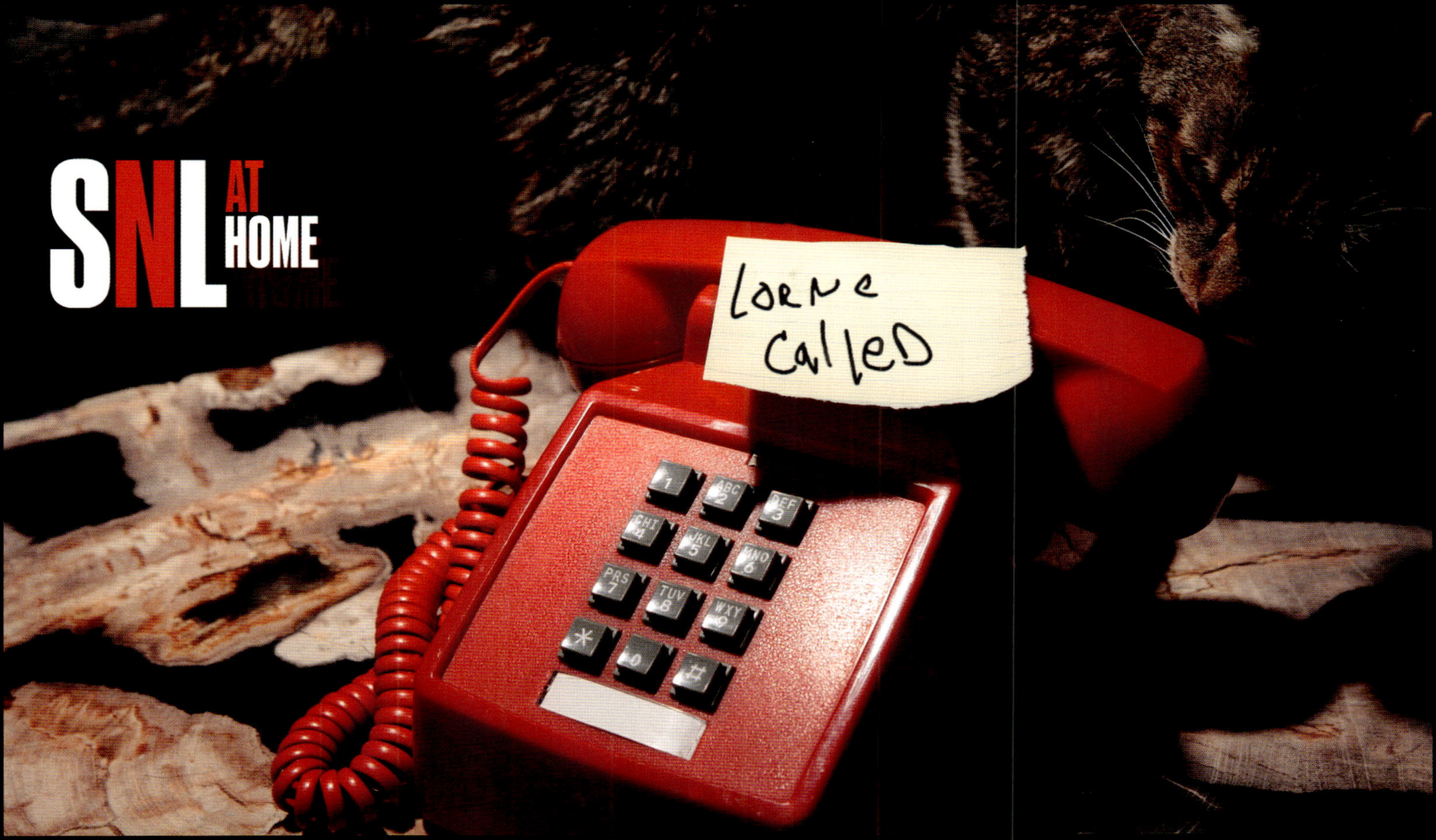

SNL AT HOME
Lorne
Called

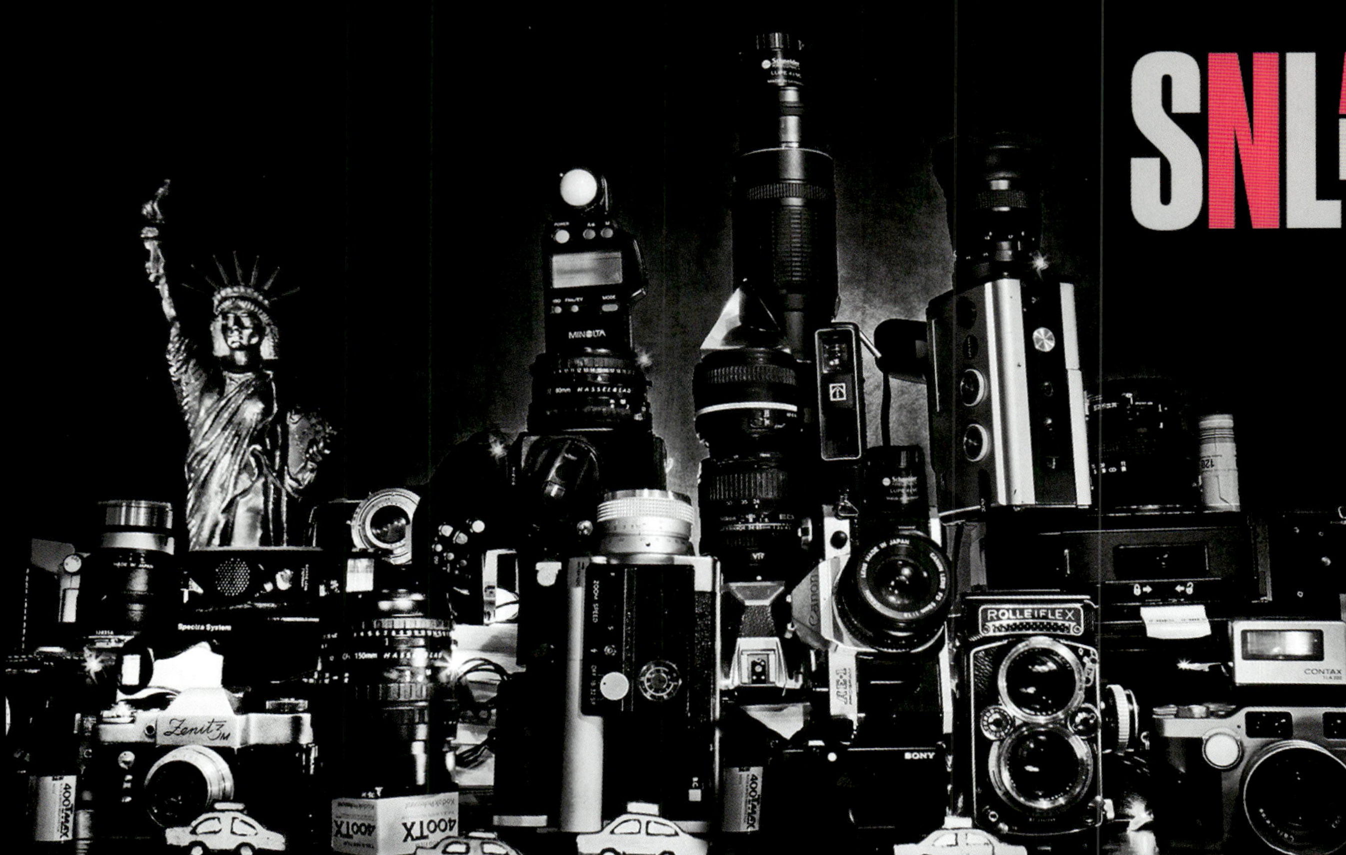
SNL AT HOME
MINOLTA
ROLLEIFLEX
SONY
CONTAX
400TX

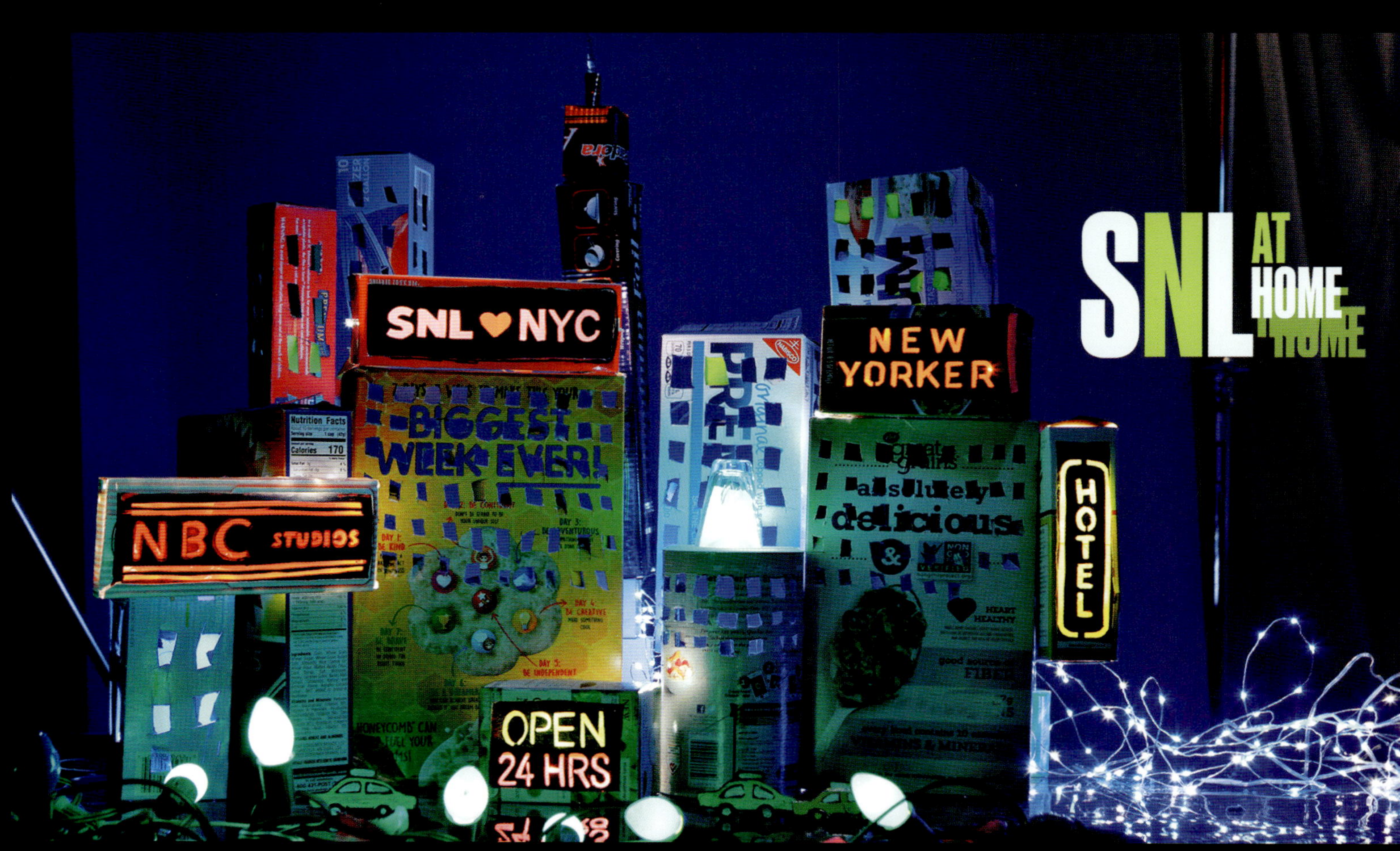
SNL AT HOME
SNL ♥ NYC
NEW YORKER
NBC STUDIOS
HOTEL
OPEN 24 HRS
BIGGEST WEEK EVER!
Nutrition Facts
Calories 170
great grains
absolutely delicious
HEART HEALTHY

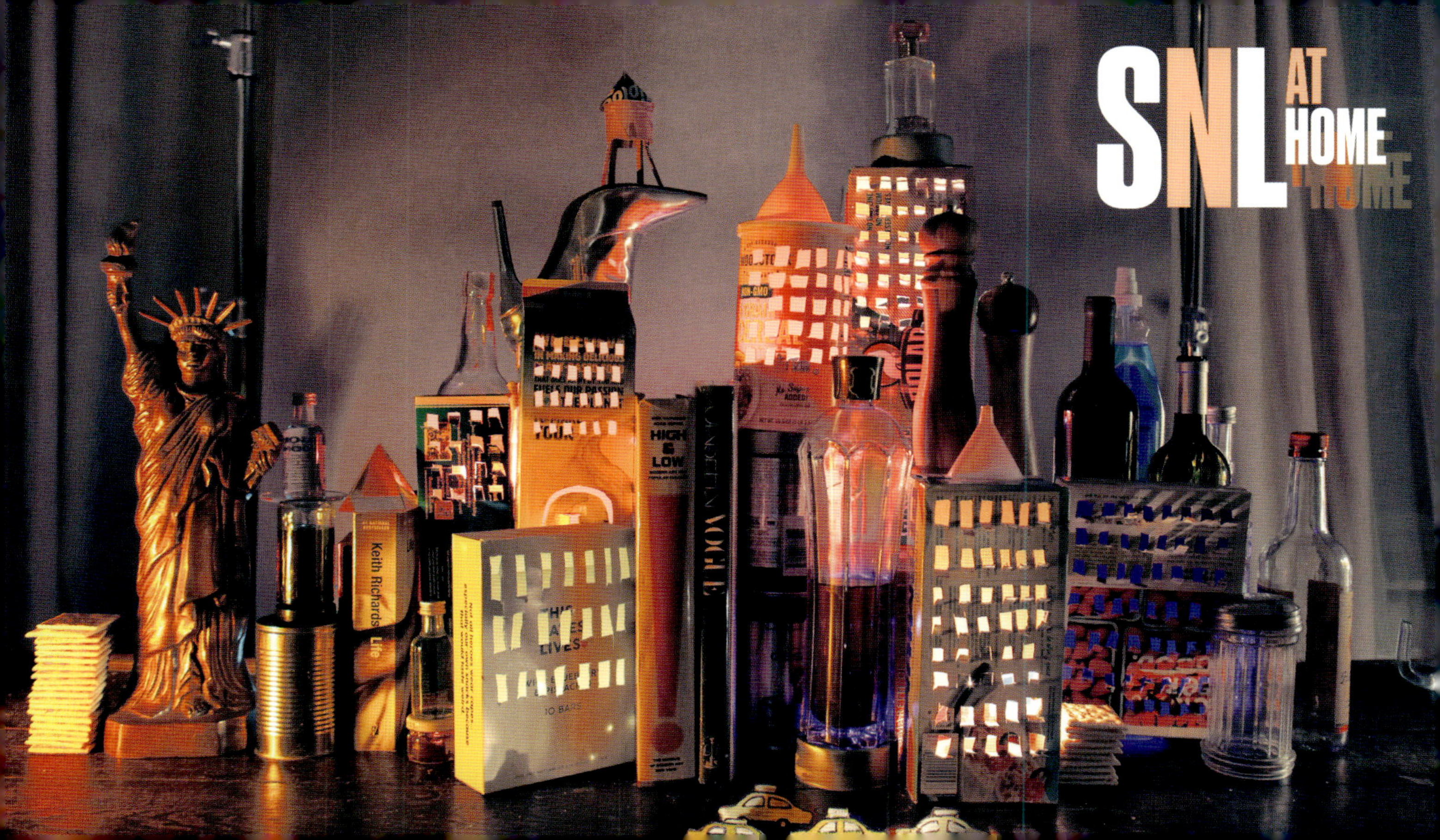
SNL
AT
HOME
HIGH
&
LOW
VOGUE
Keith Richards
Life
10 BARS

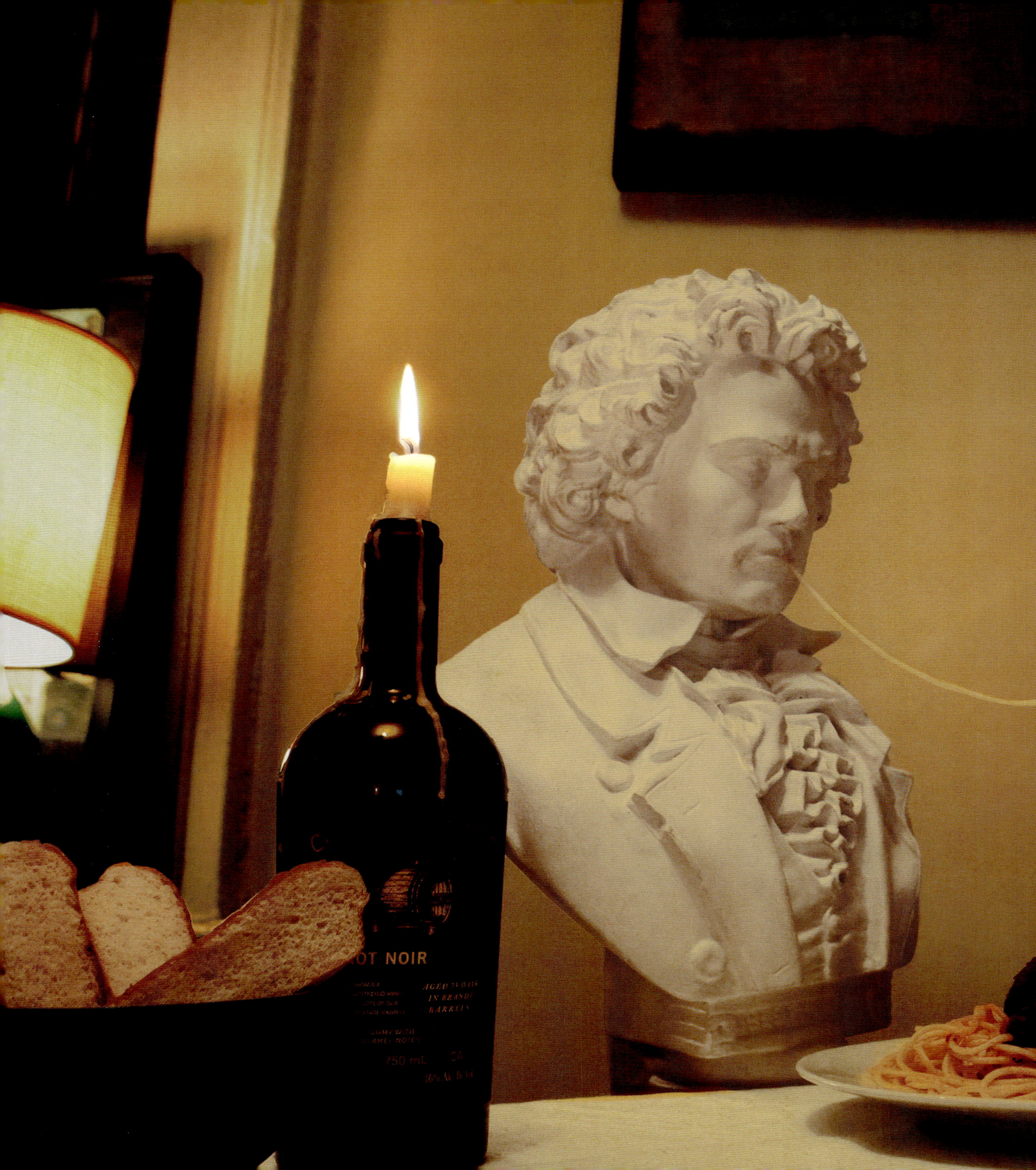
OT NOIR
750 mL

SNL AT HOME

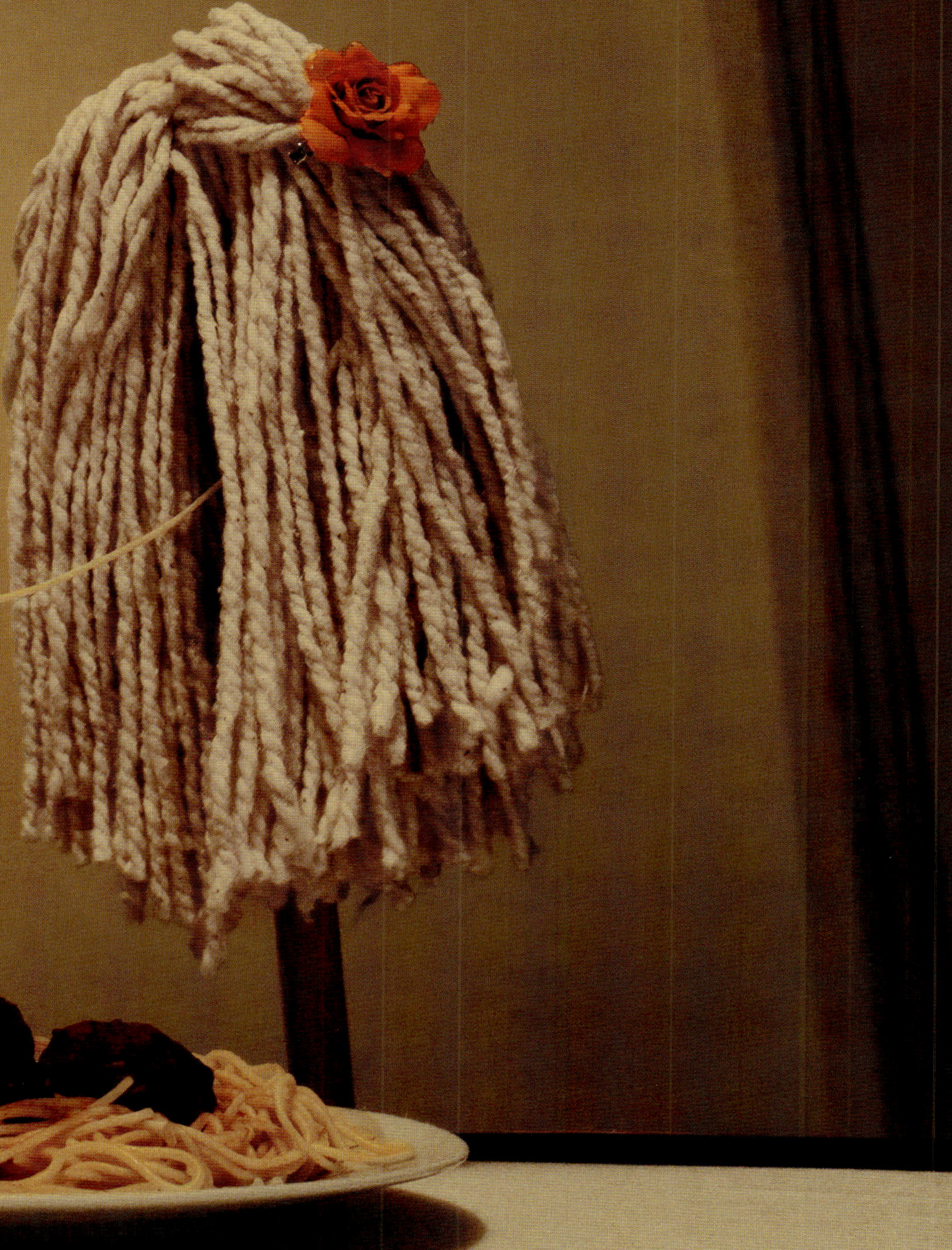

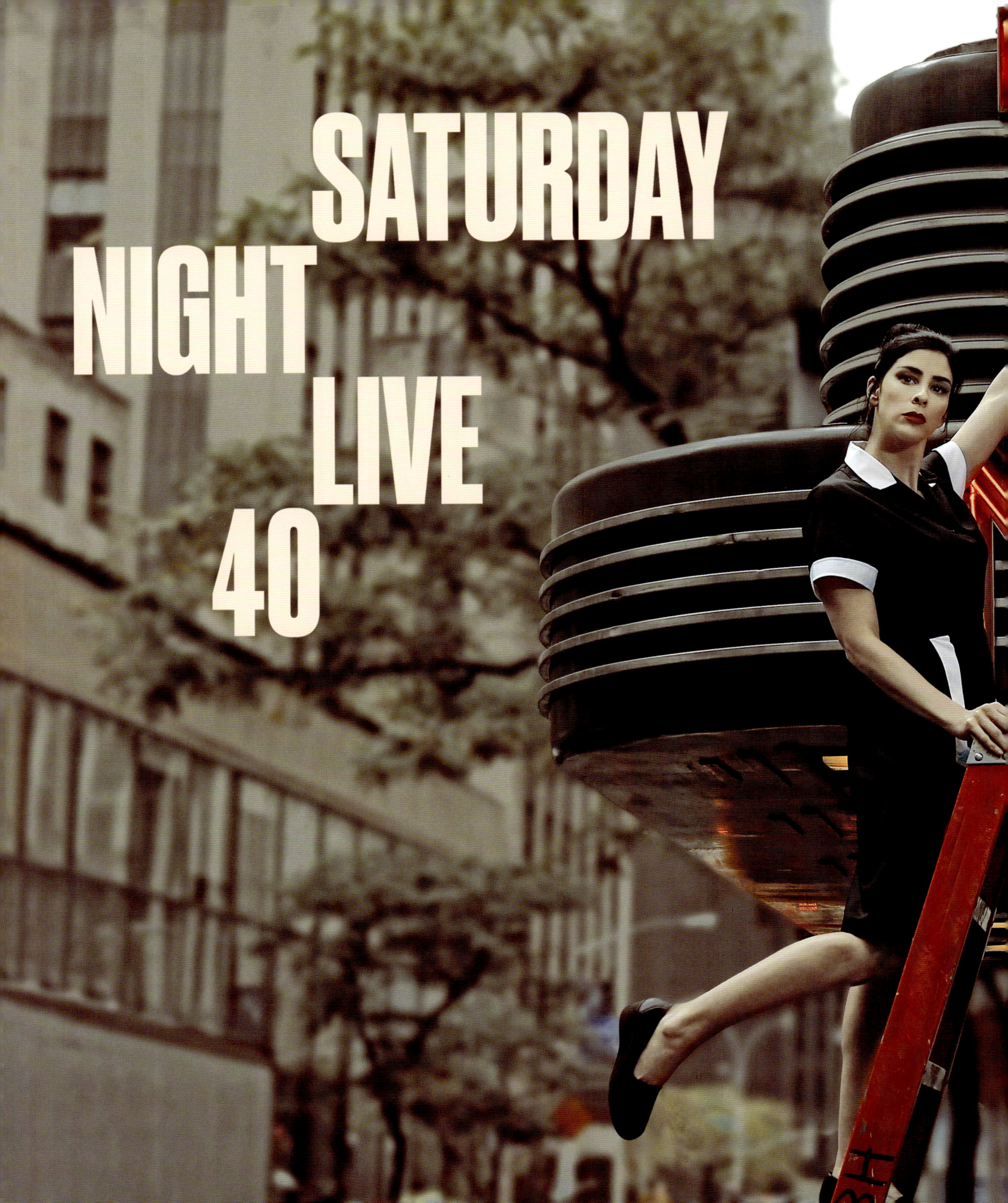
SATURDAY
NIGHT
LIVE
40

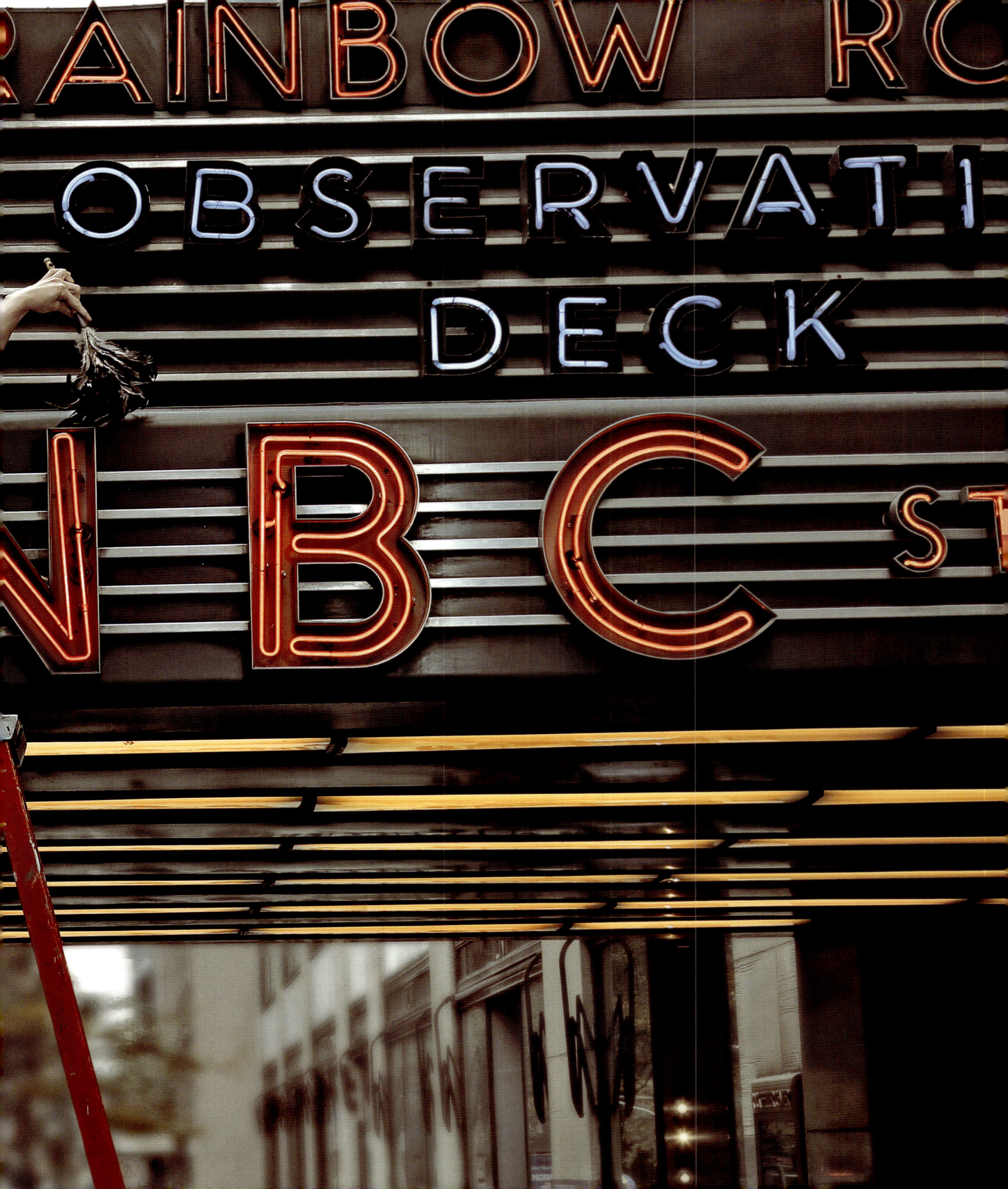

AINBOW RO
OBSERVATI
DECK
NBC
ST

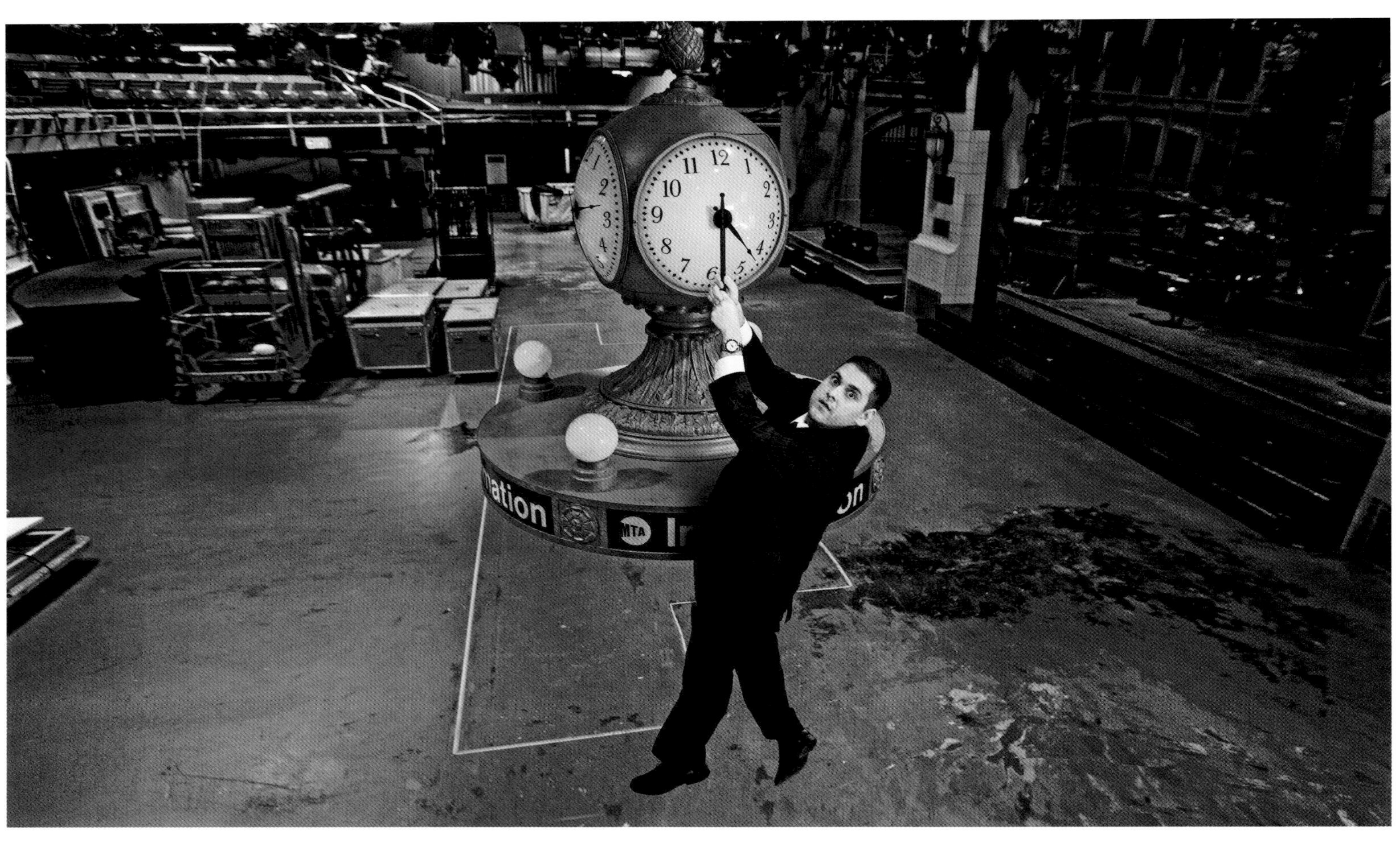

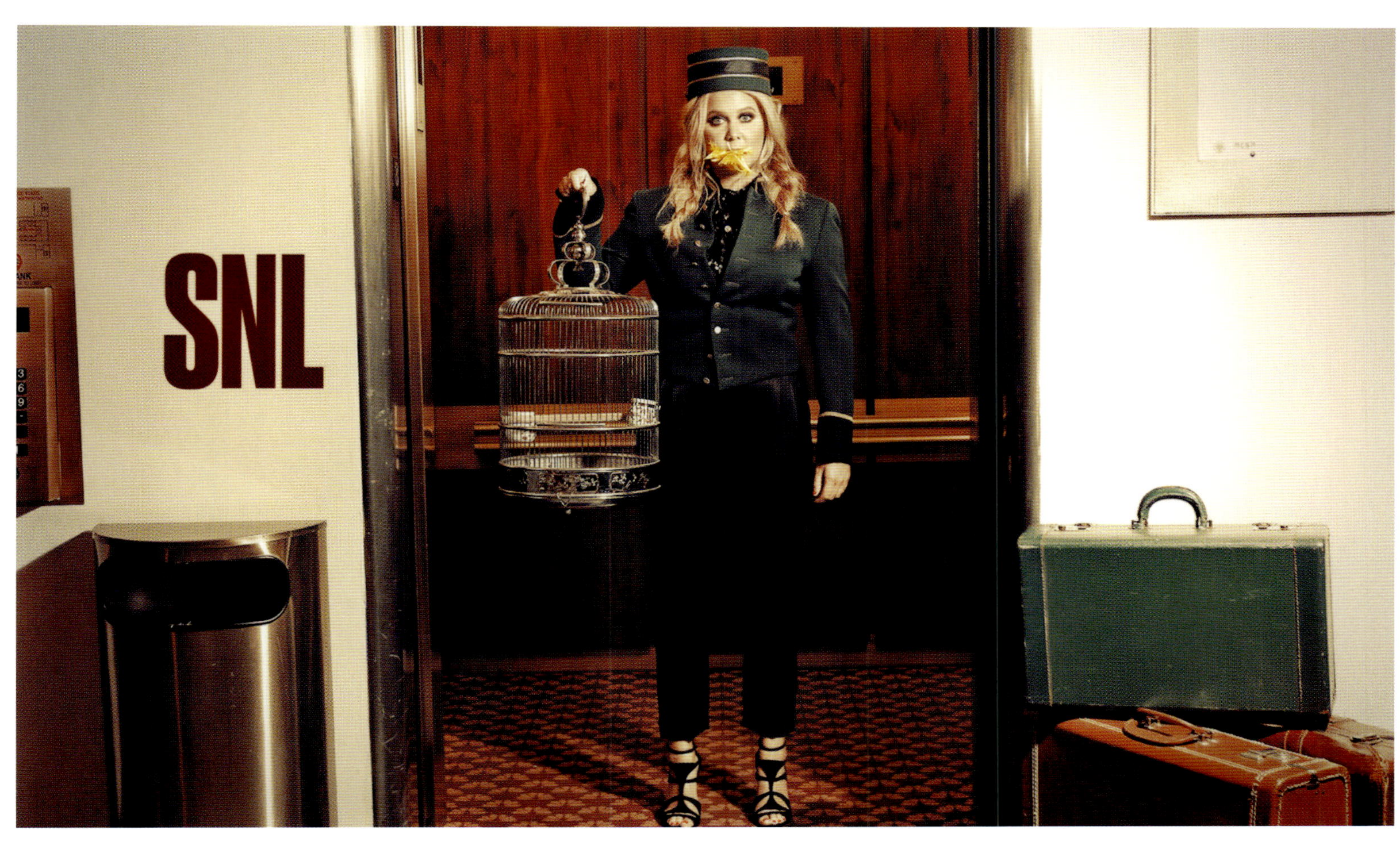
SNL

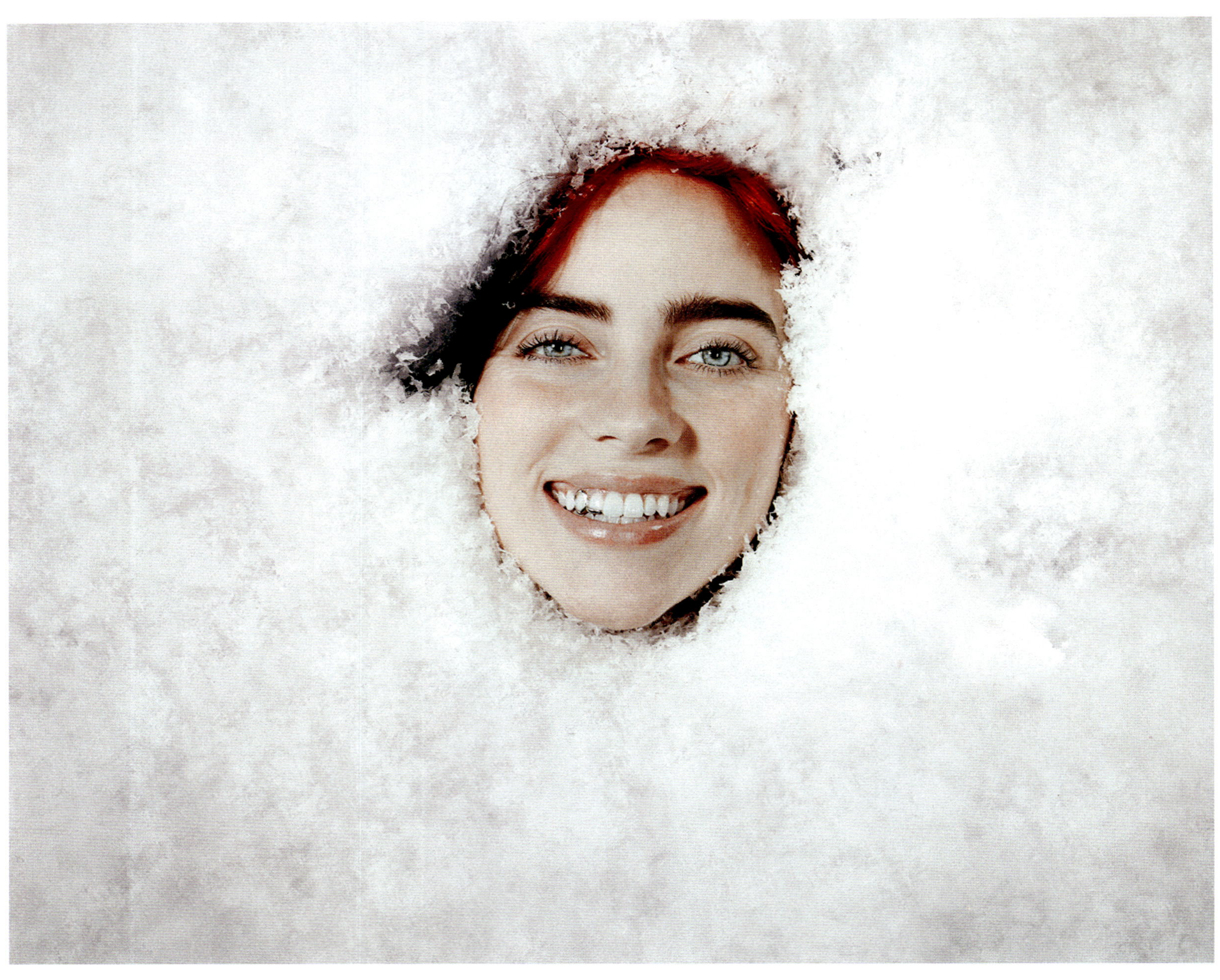

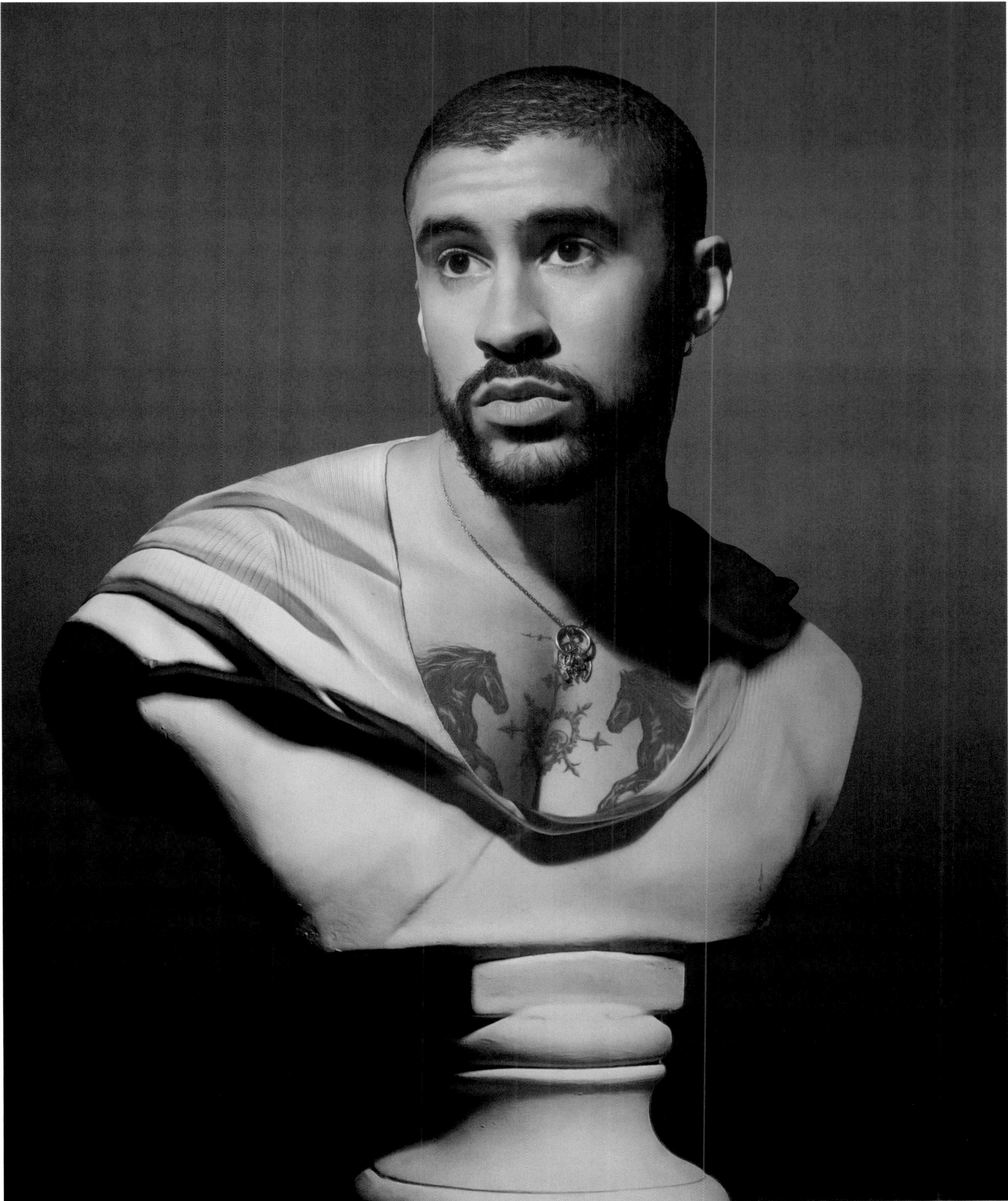

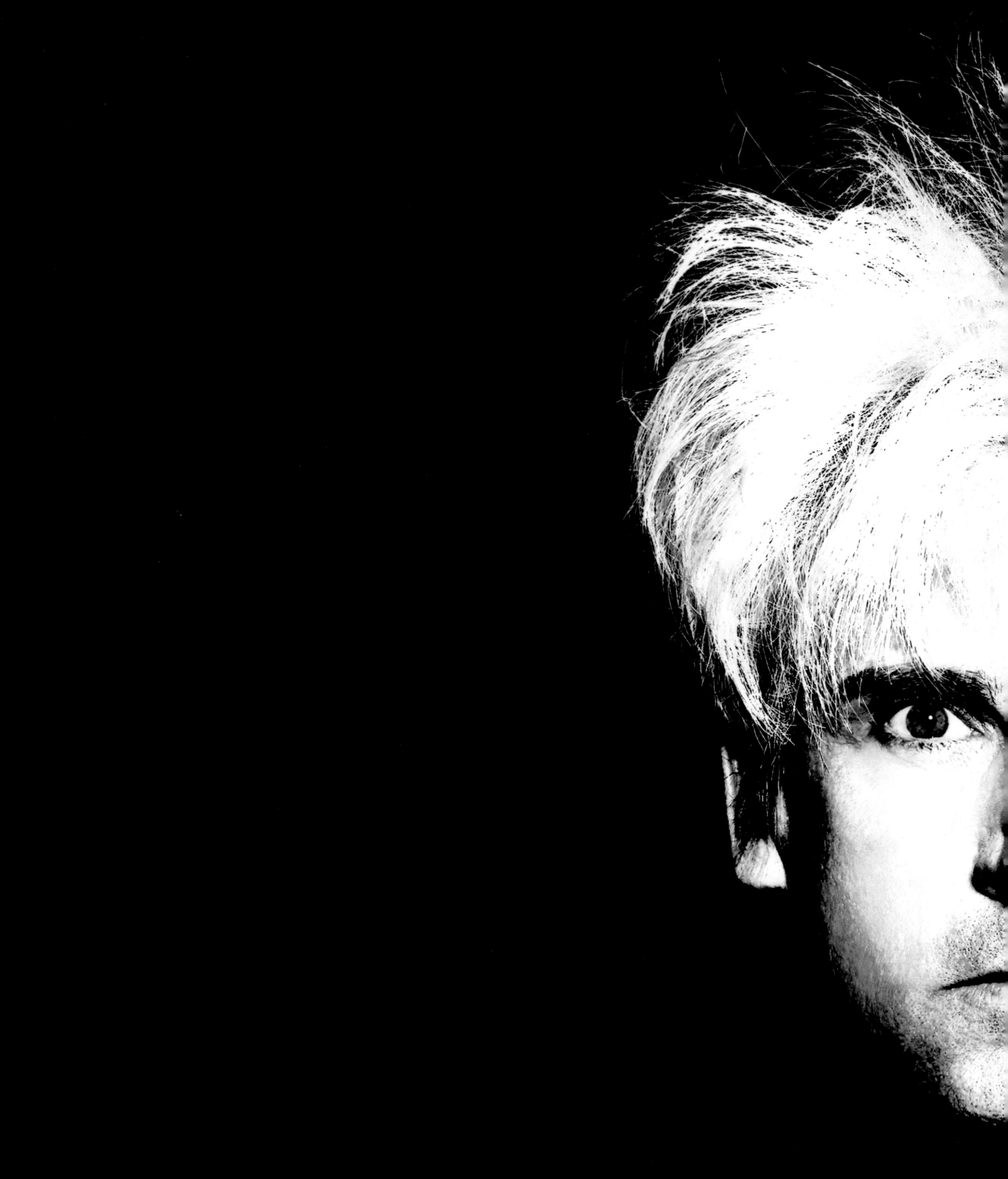

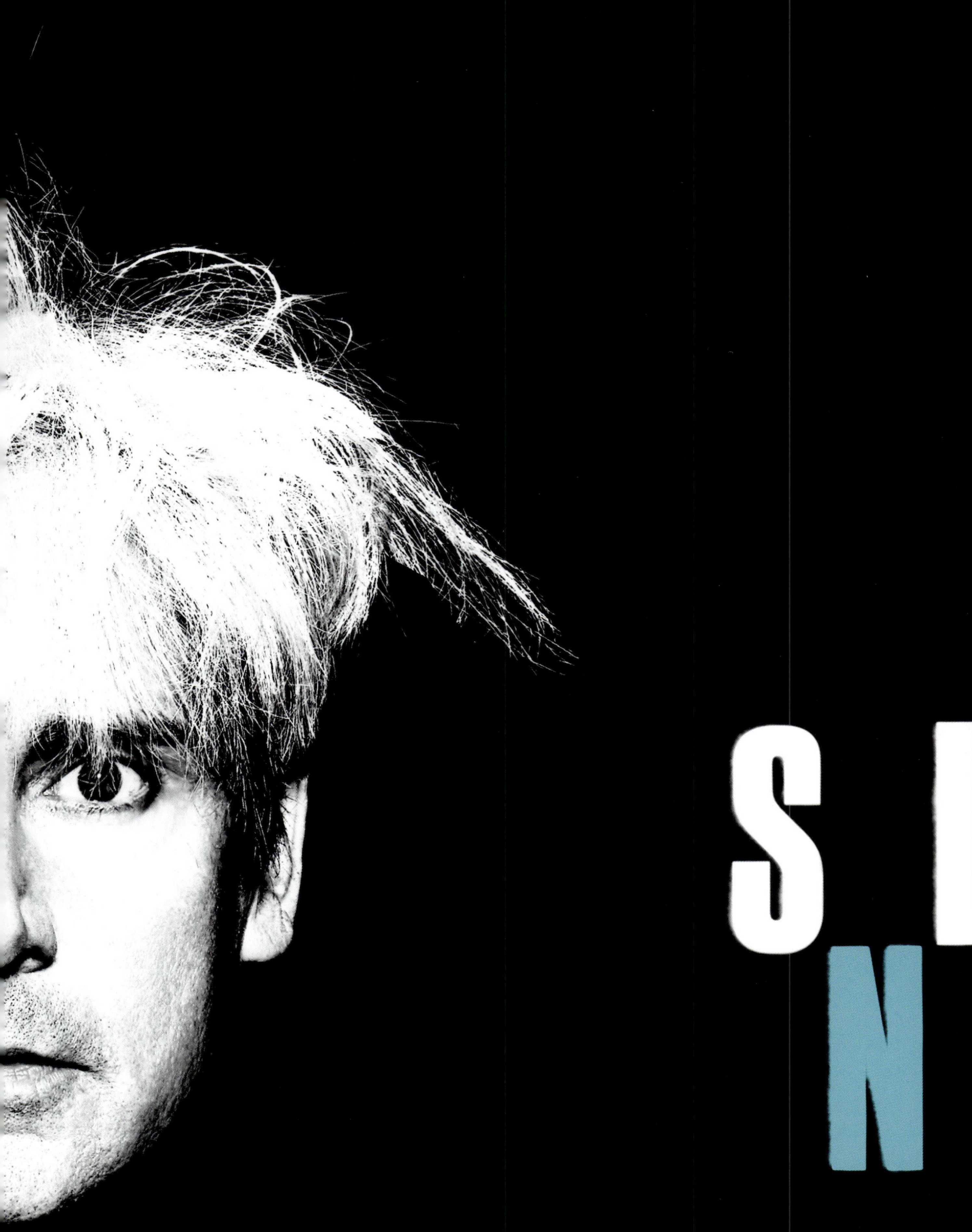

SNL

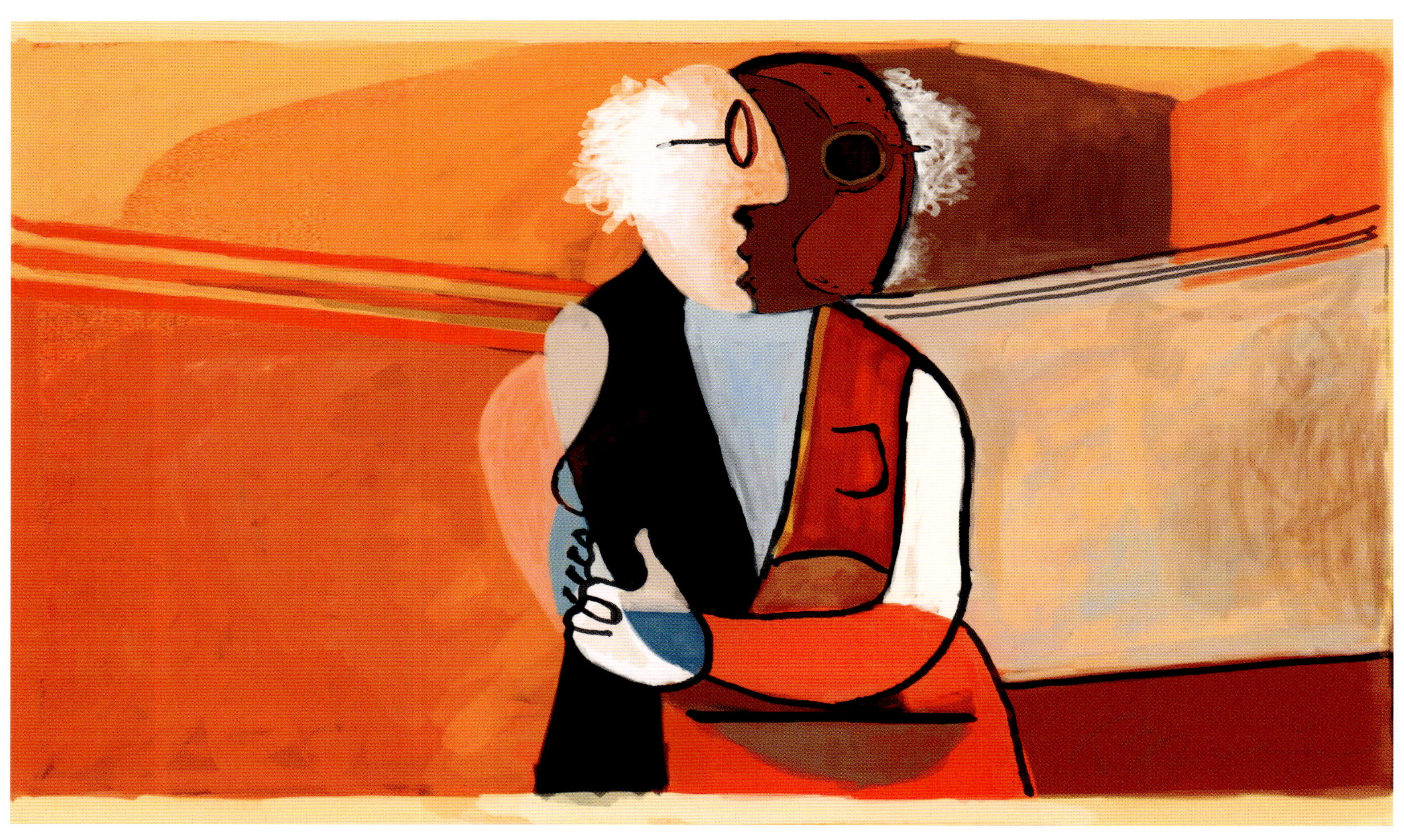

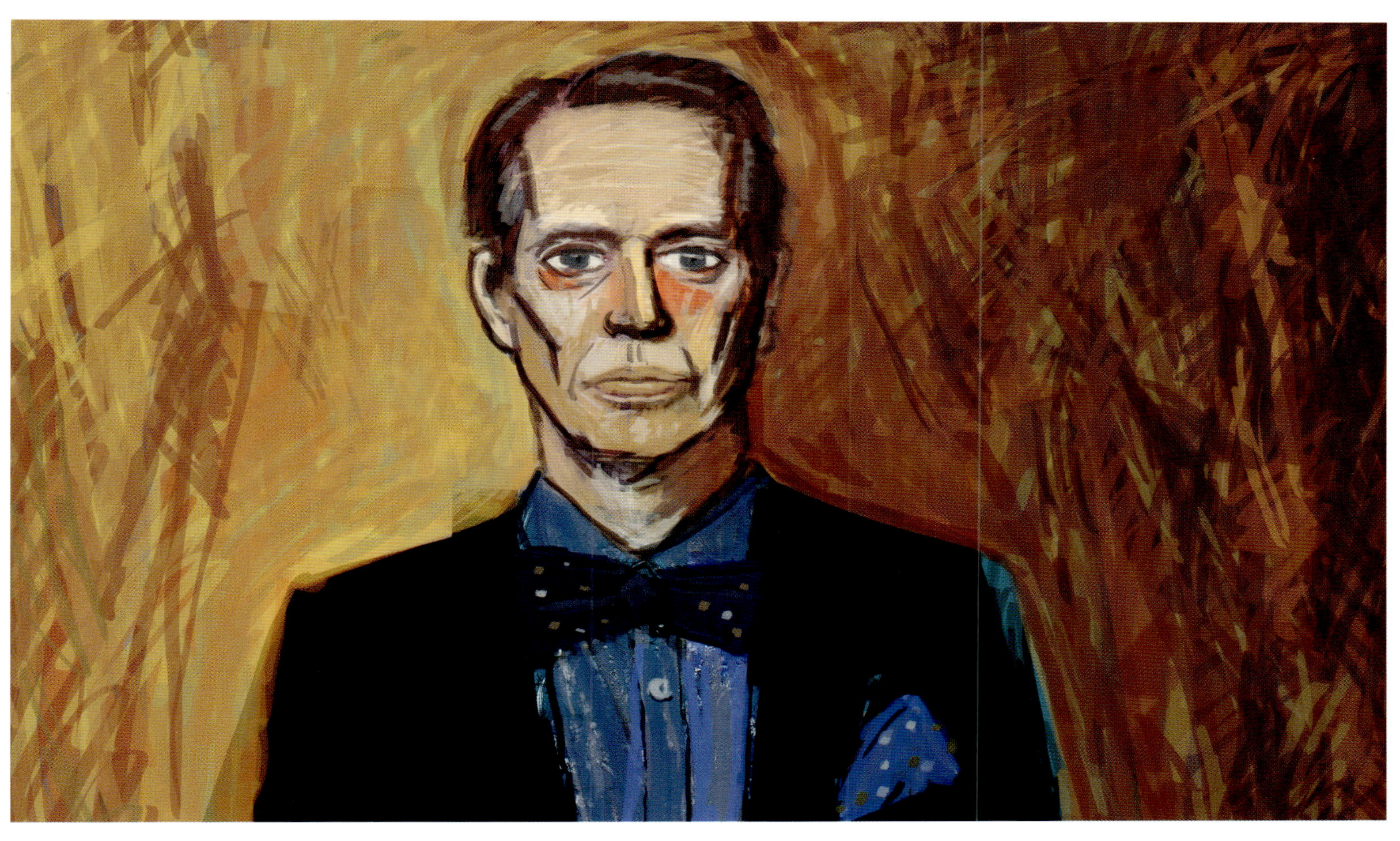

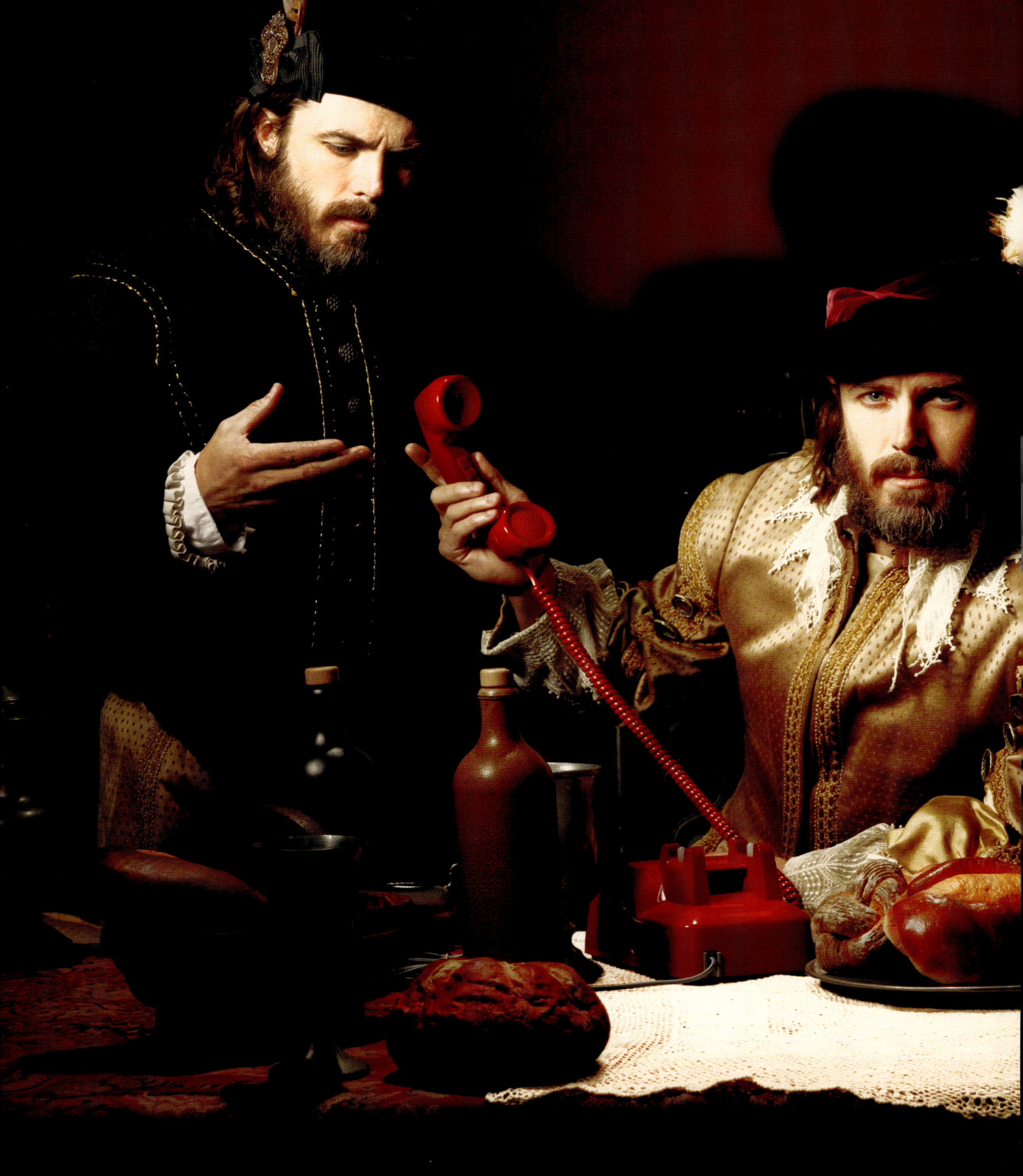

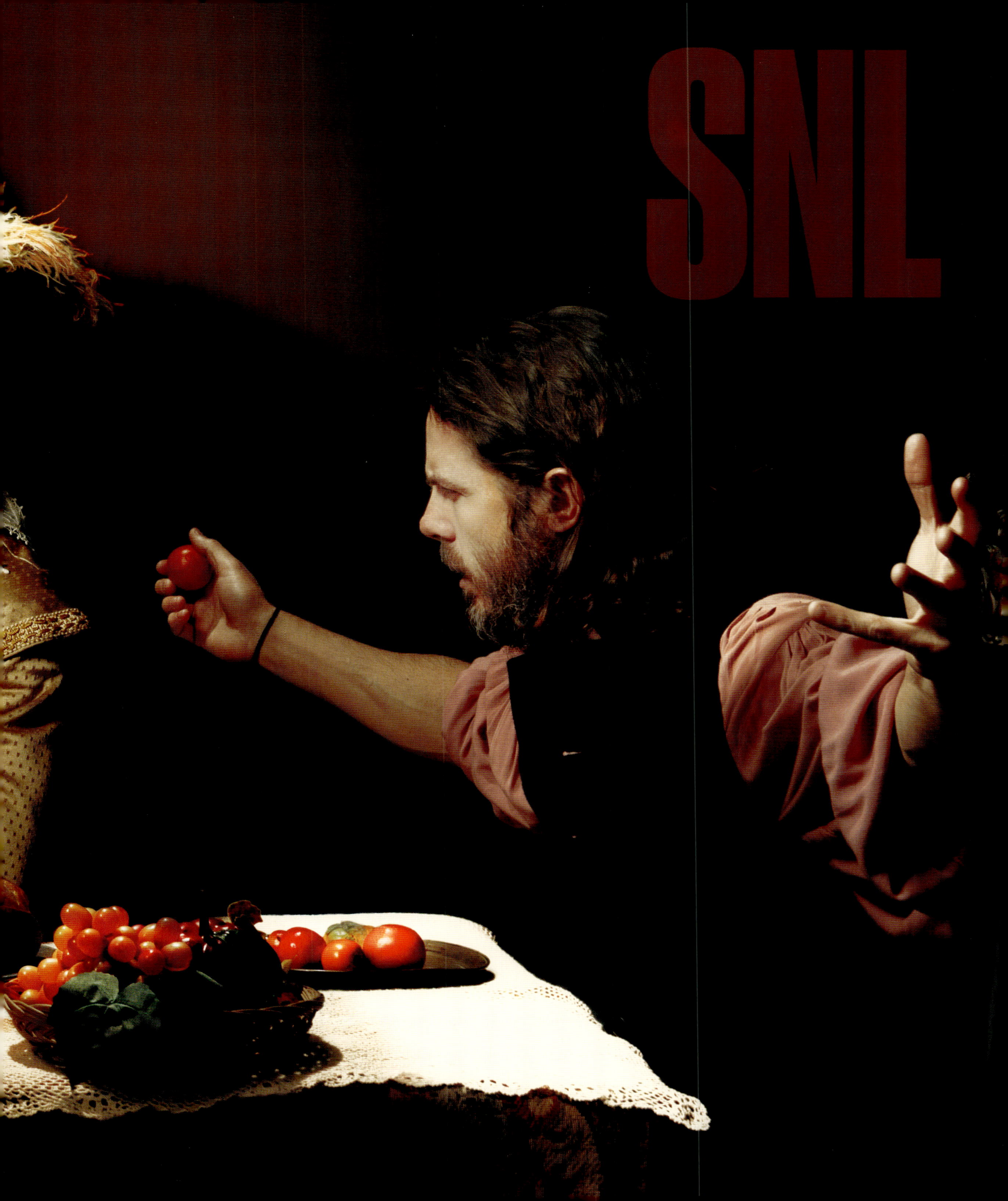
SNL

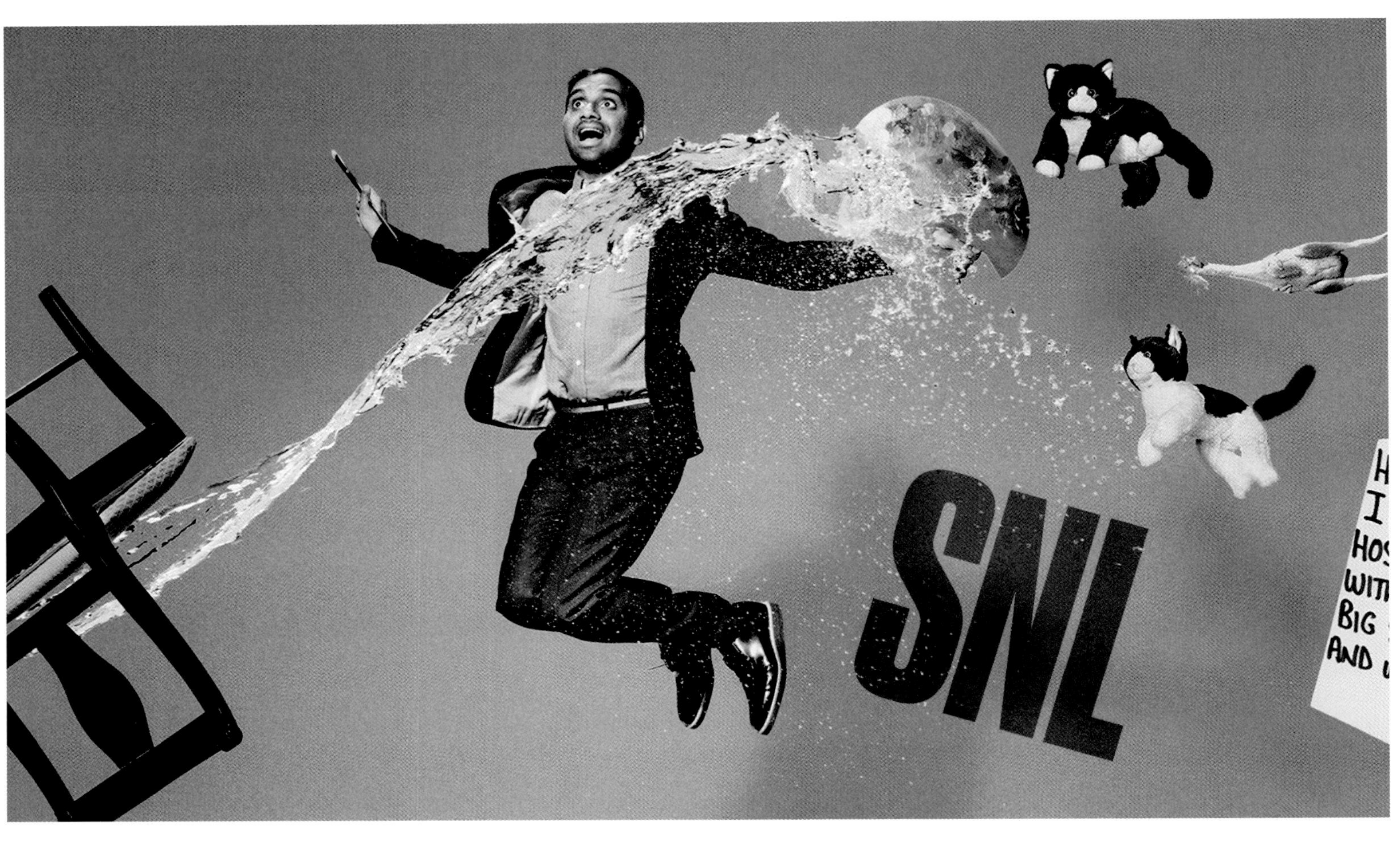
SNL

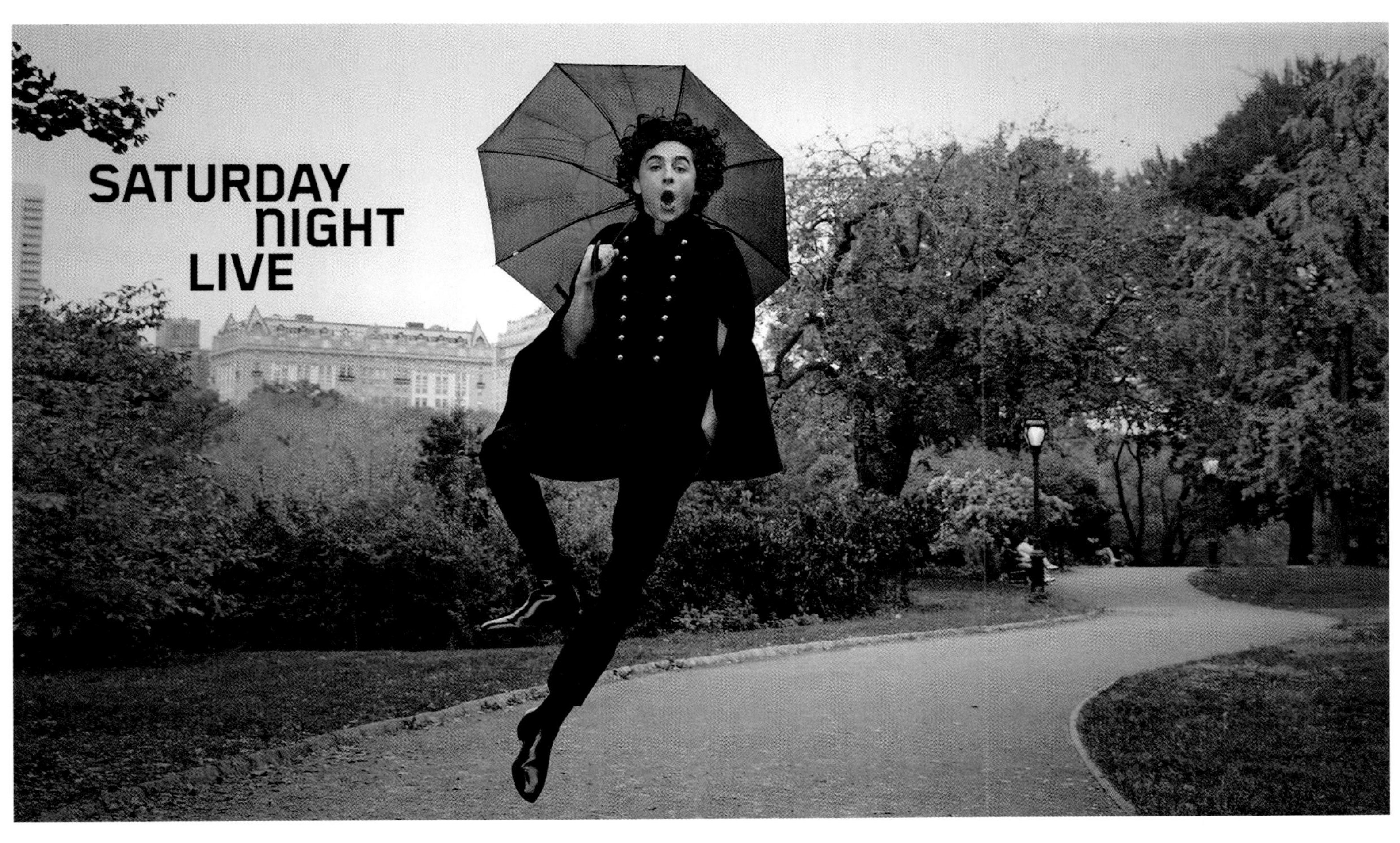
SATURDAY
NIGHT
LIVE

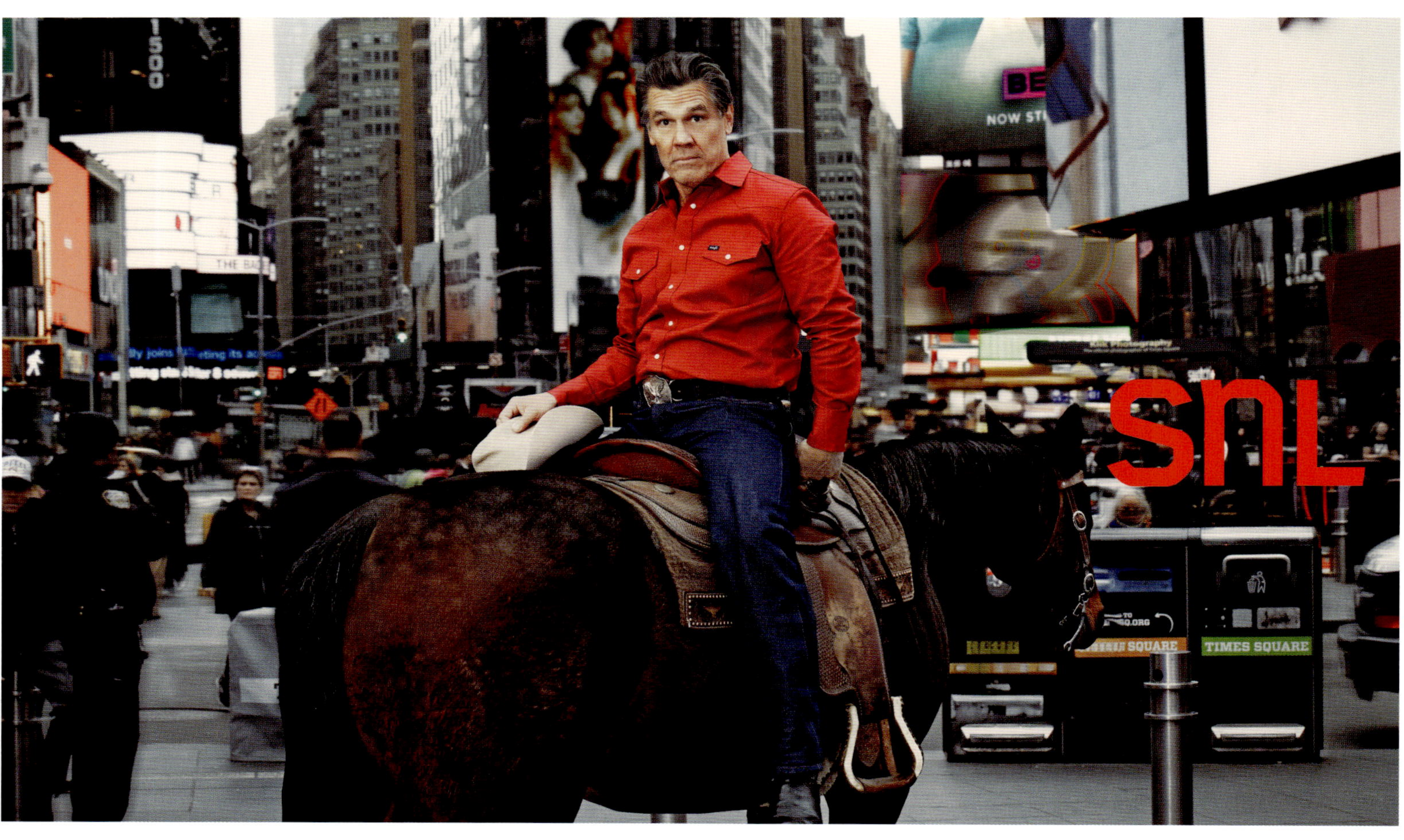
1500
SNL
TIMES SQUARE

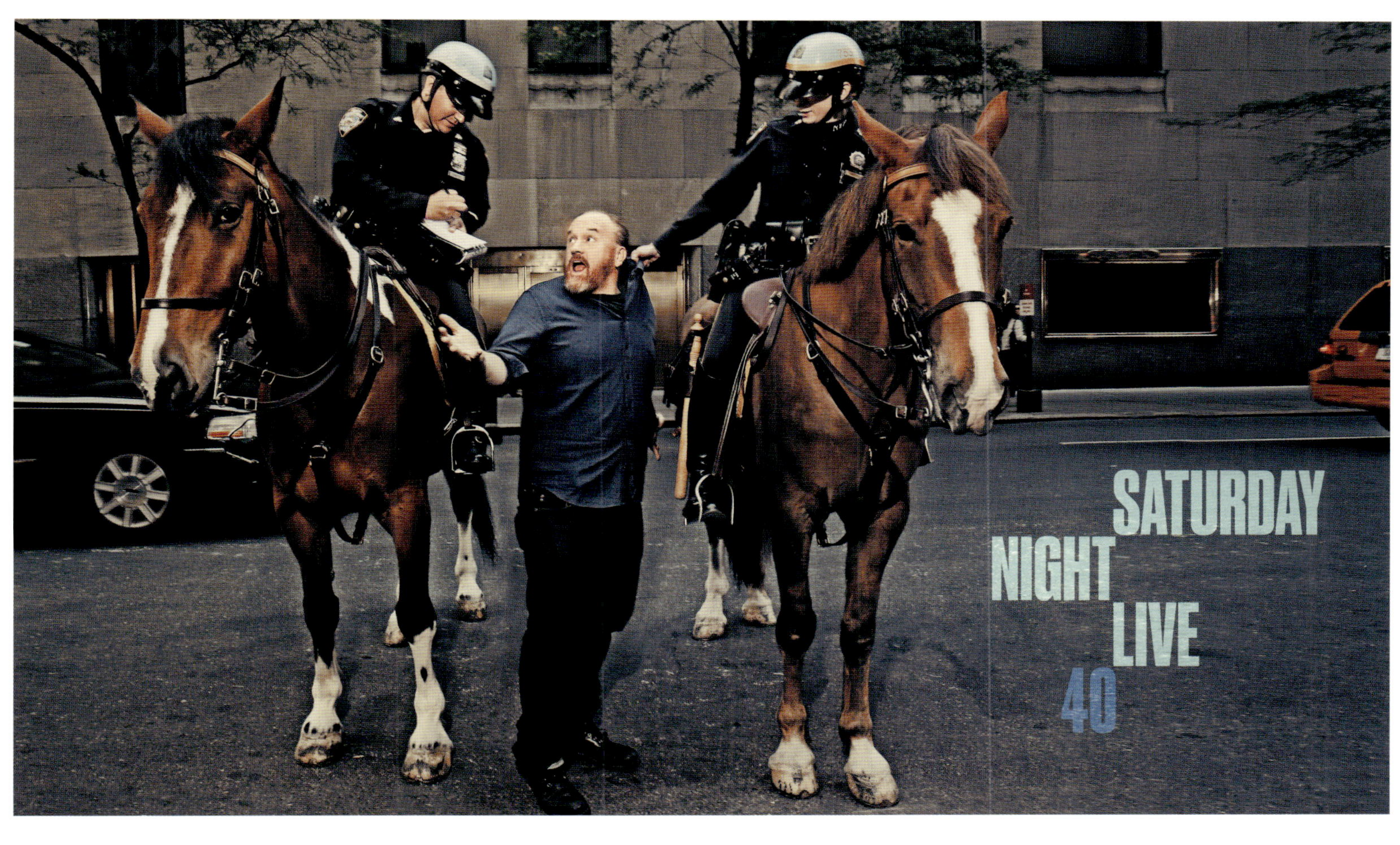
SATURDAY
NIGHT
LIVE
40

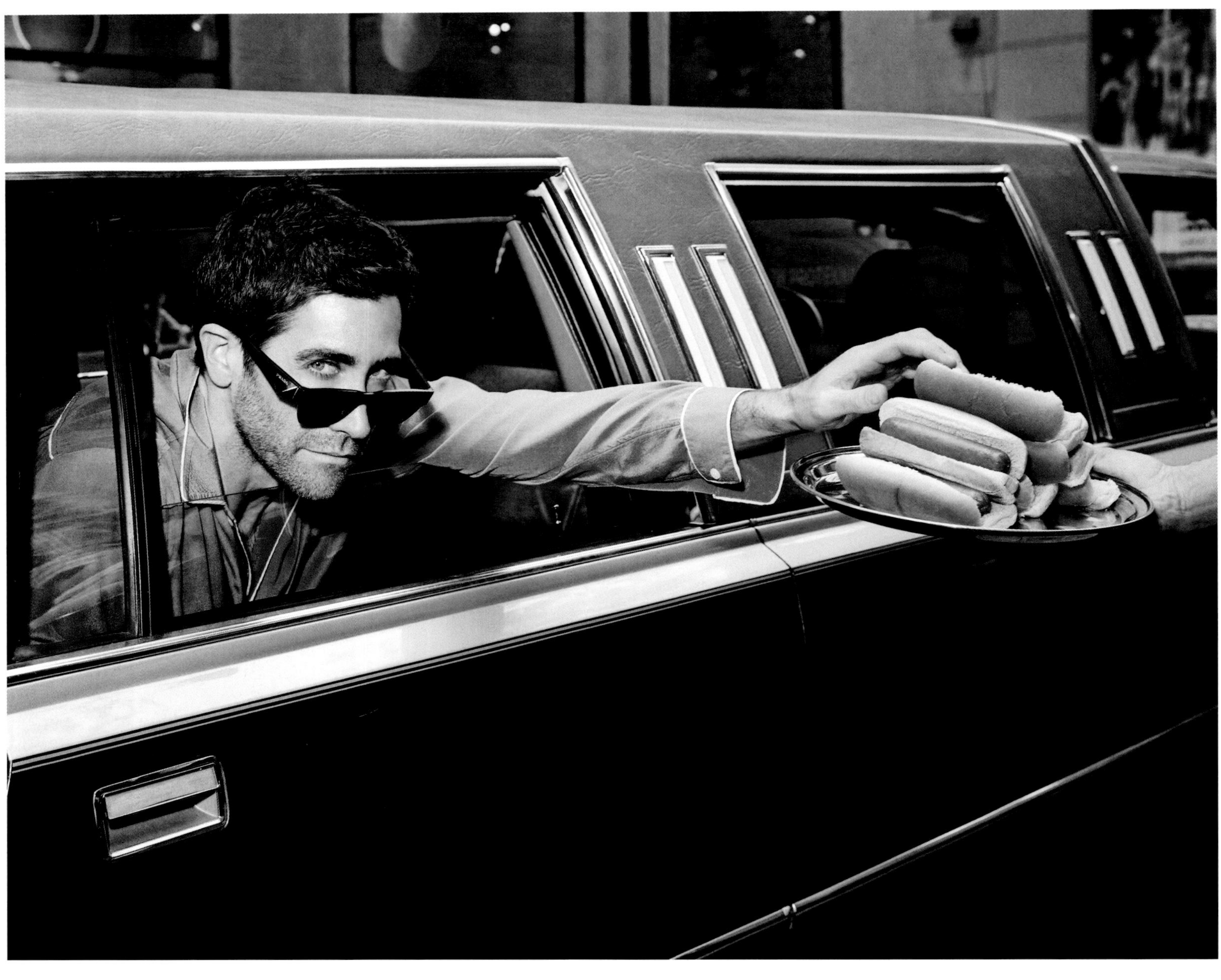

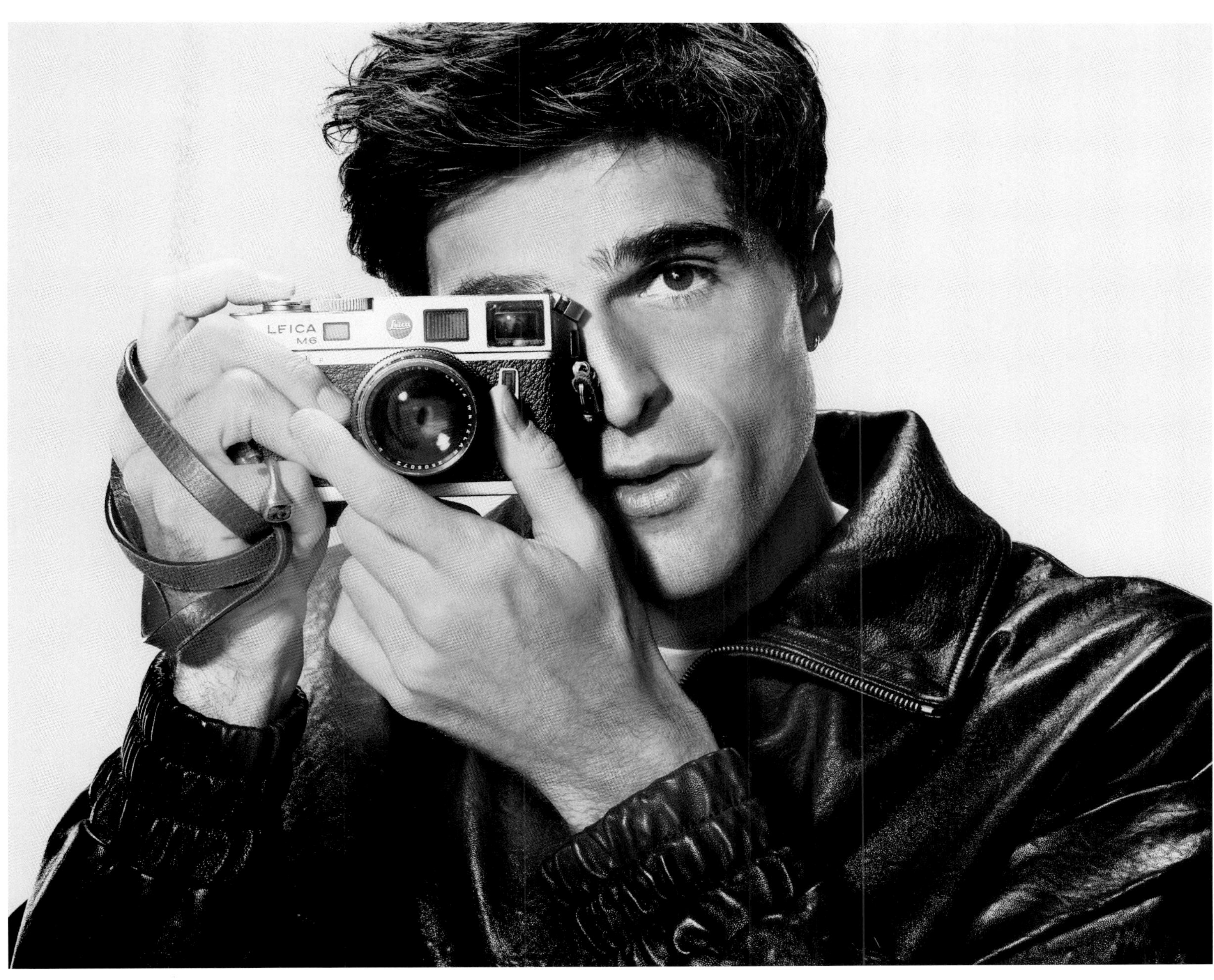
LEICA
M6

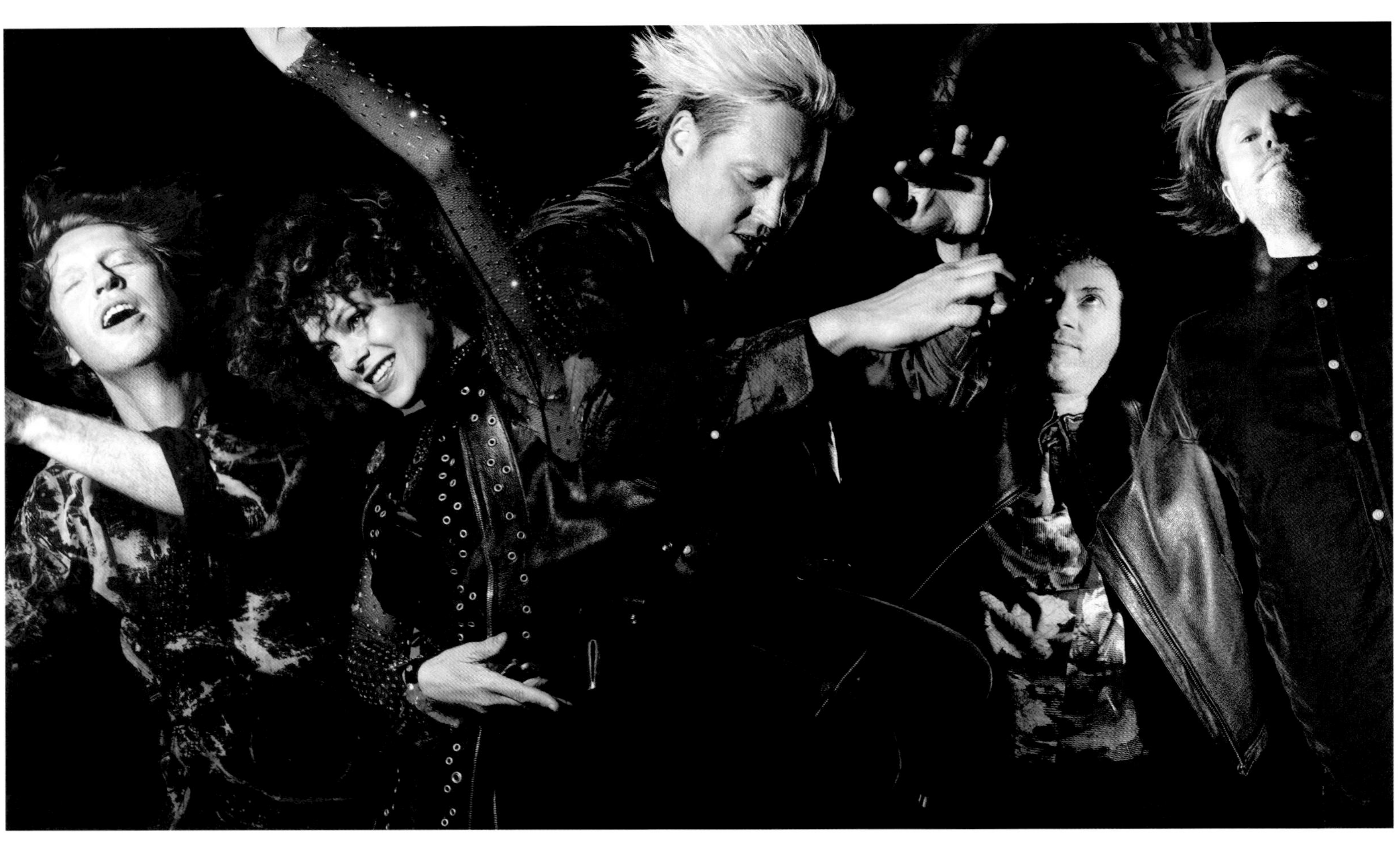

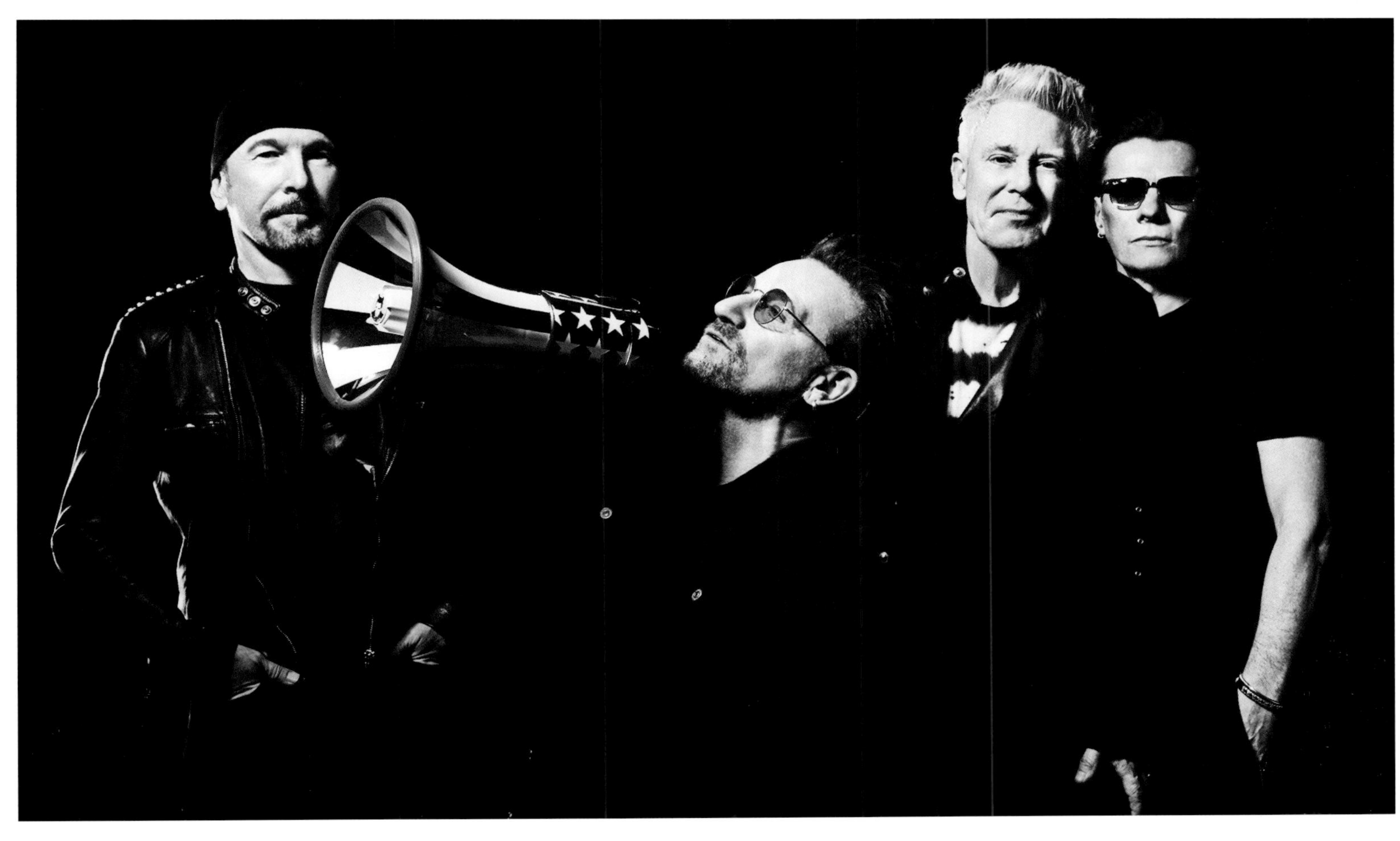

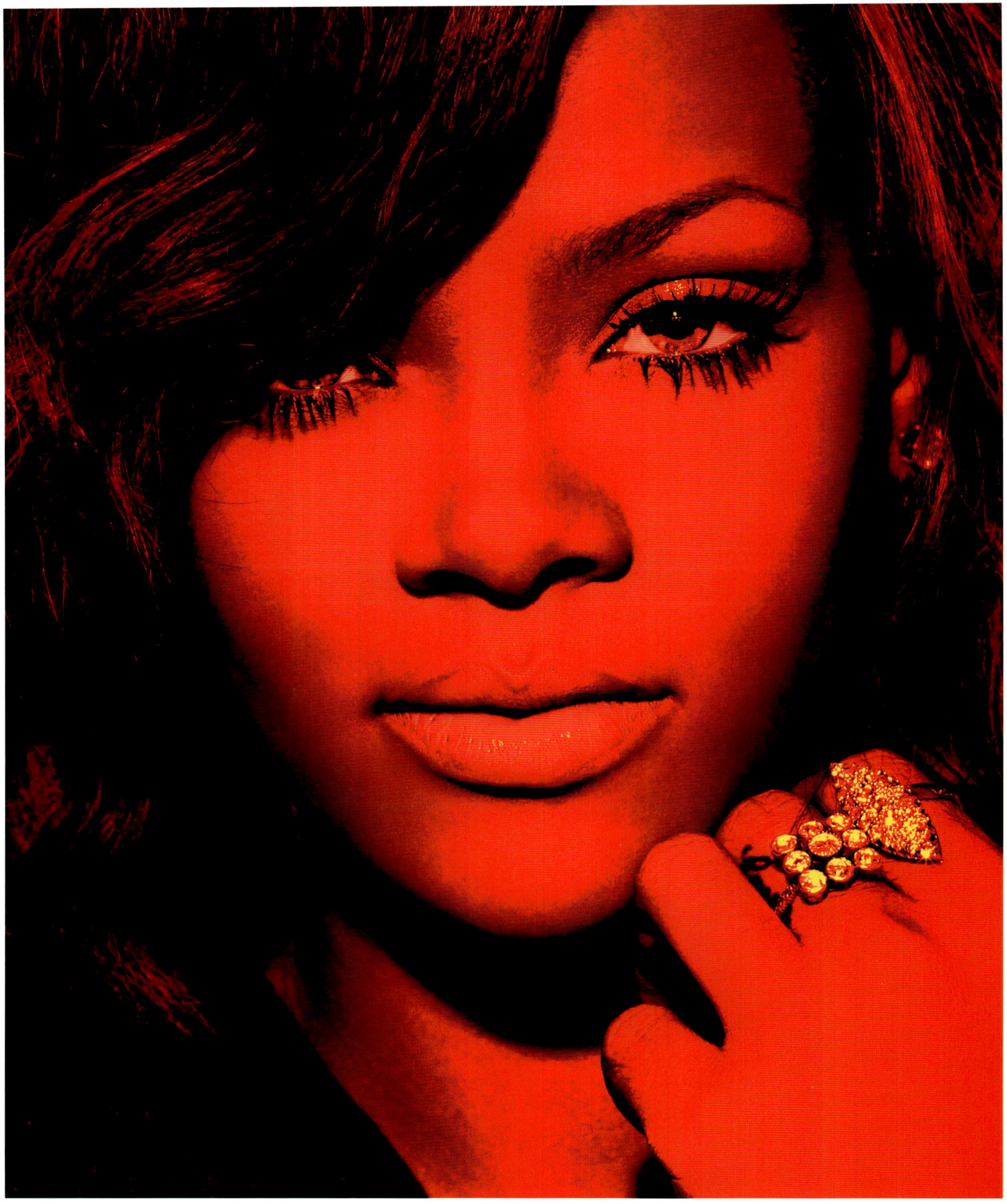

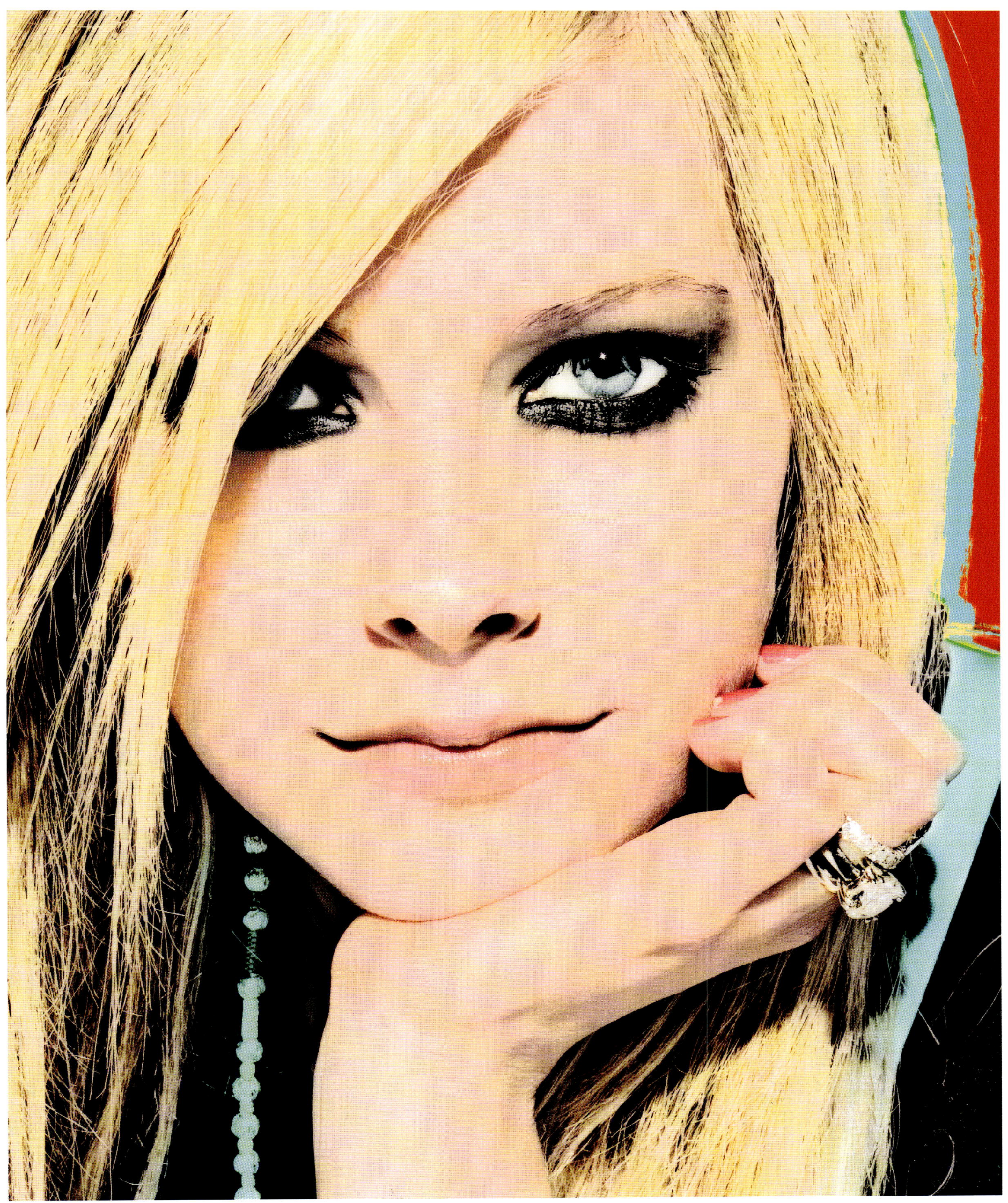

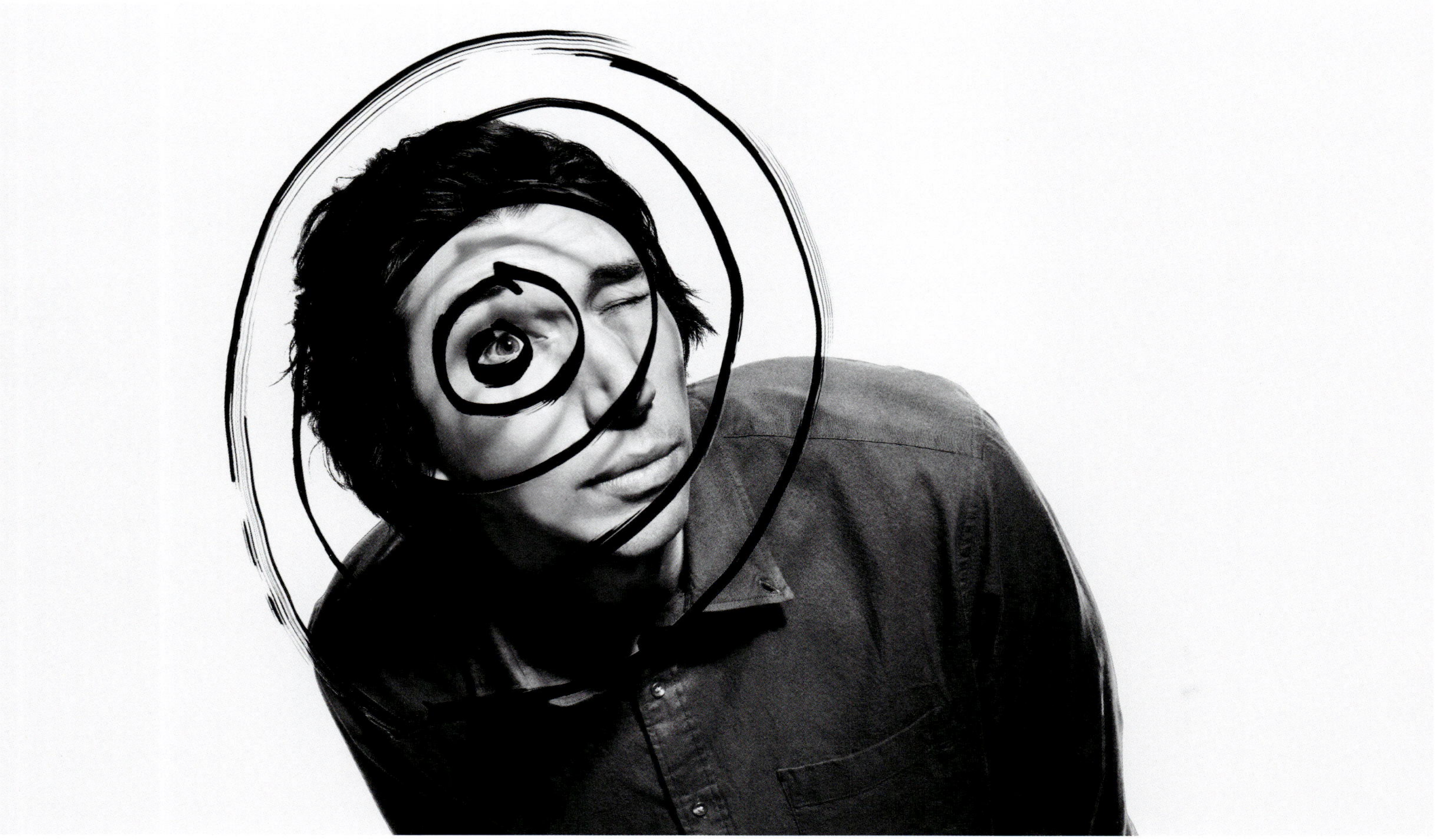

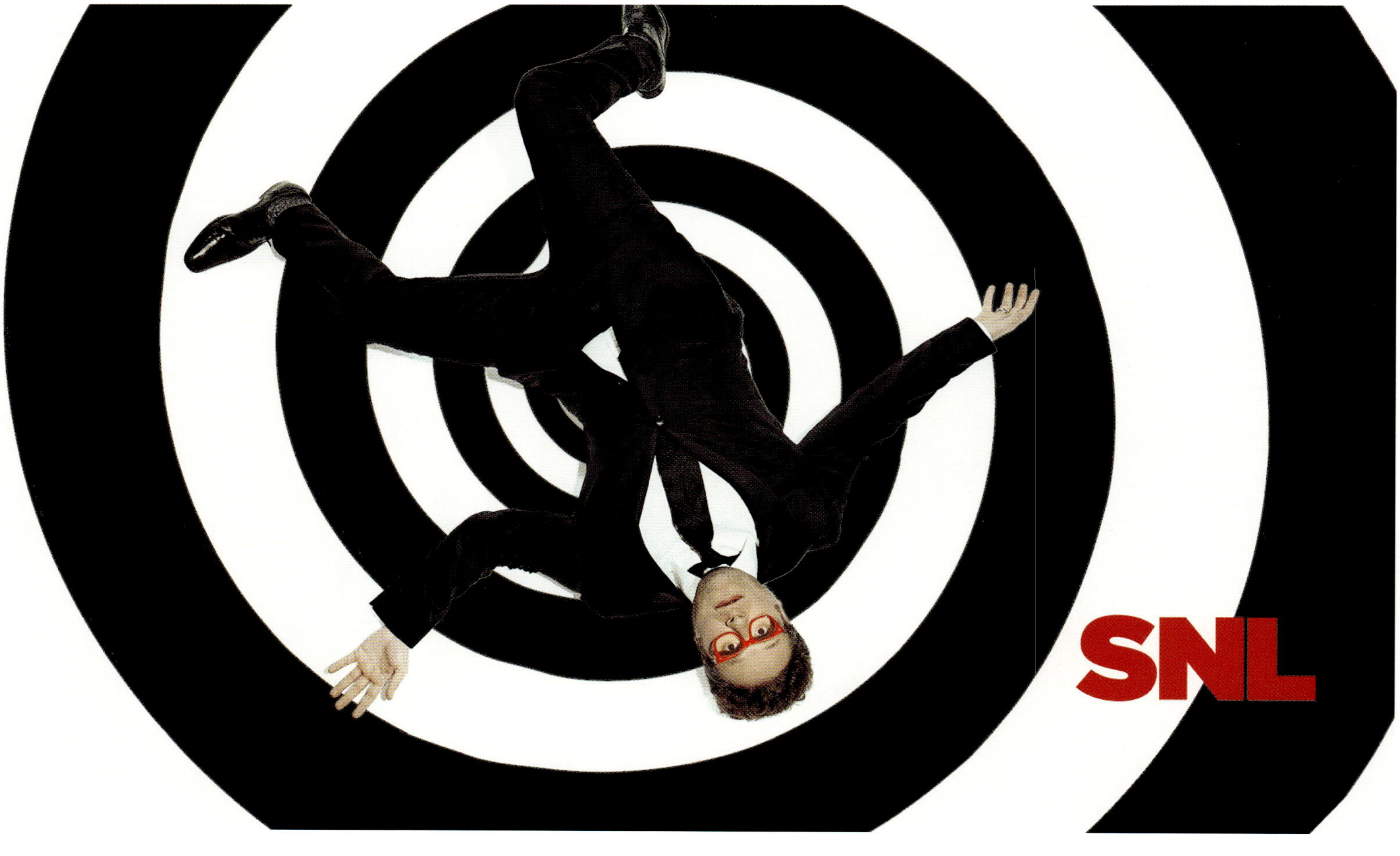

SNL

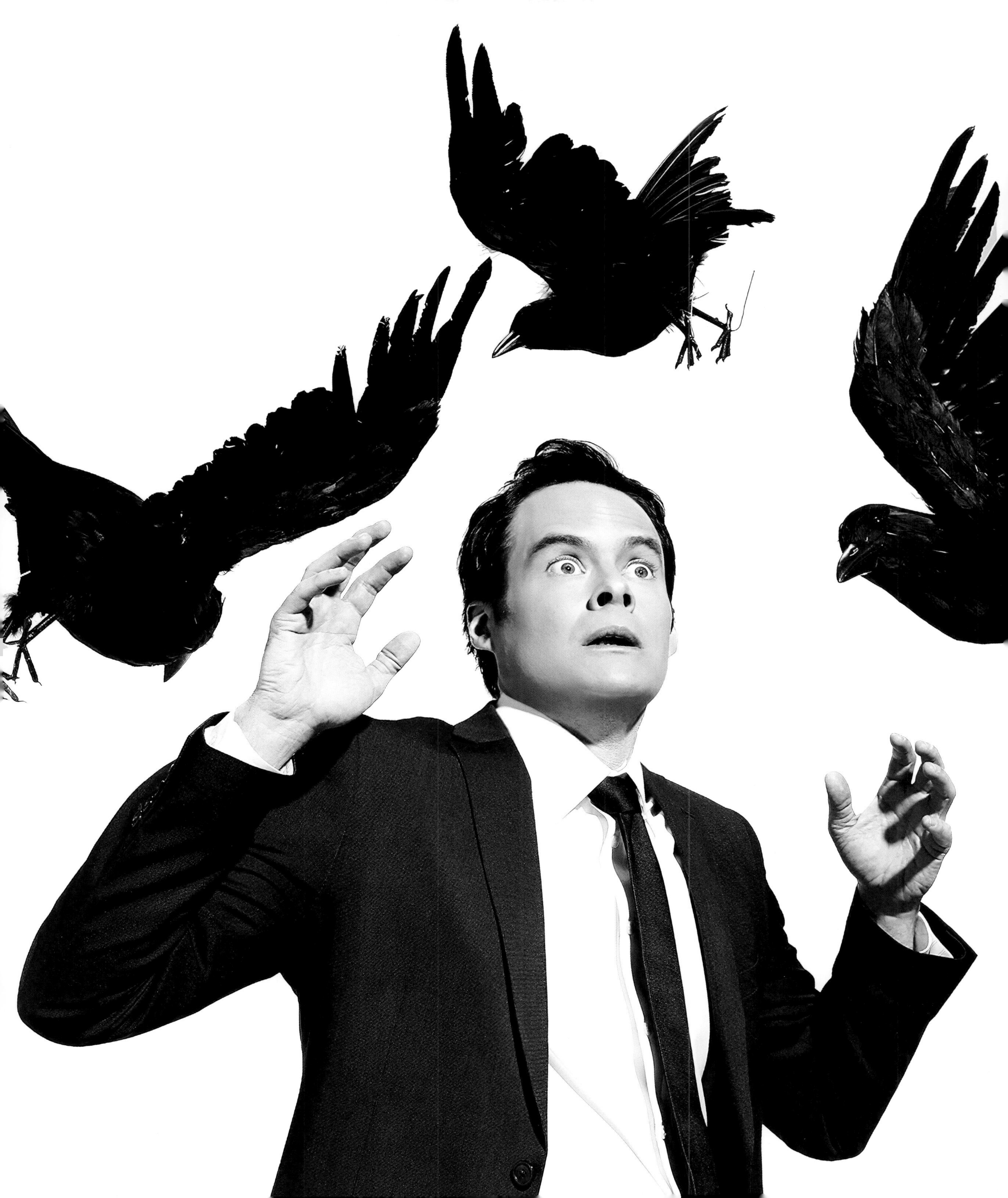

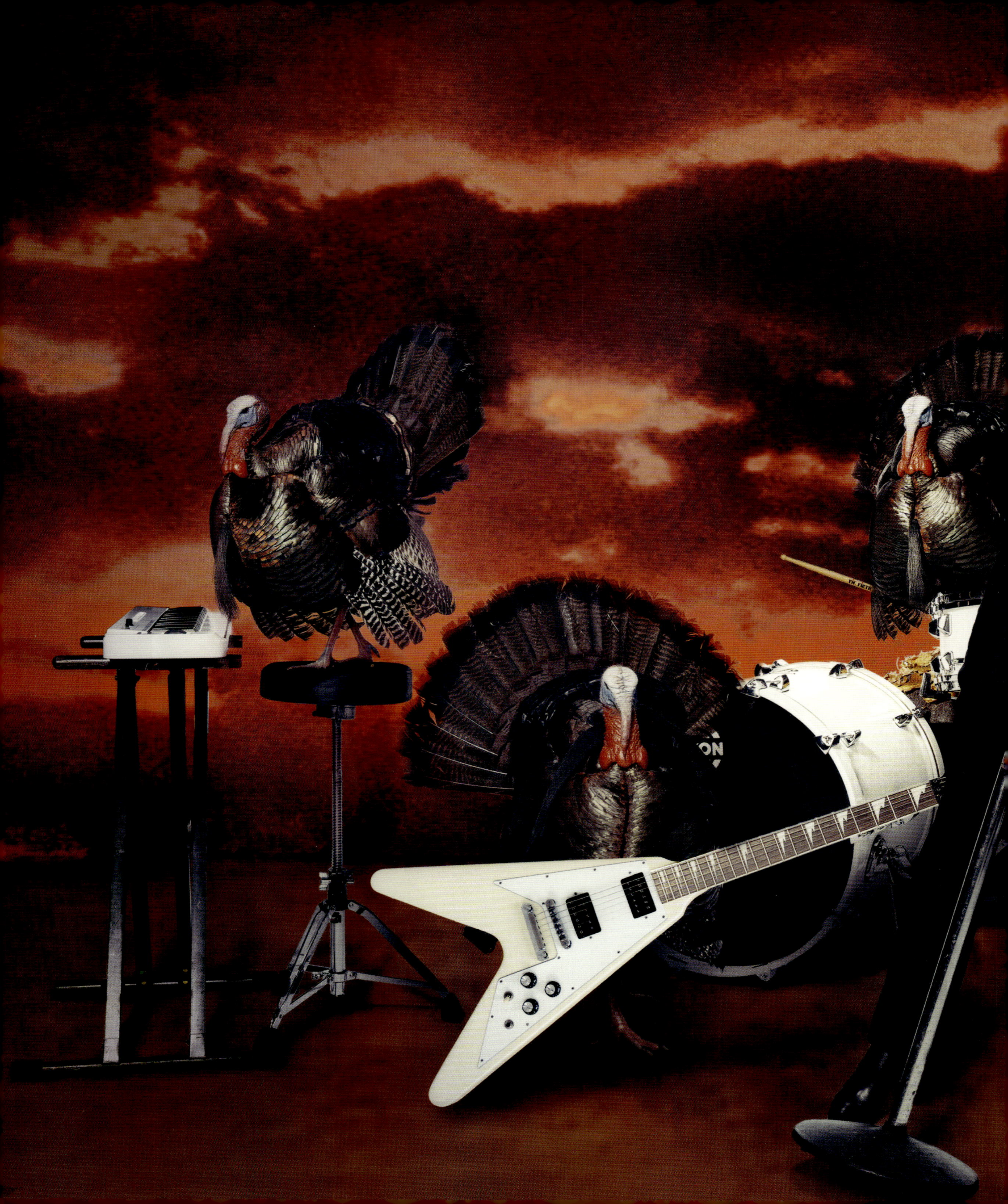

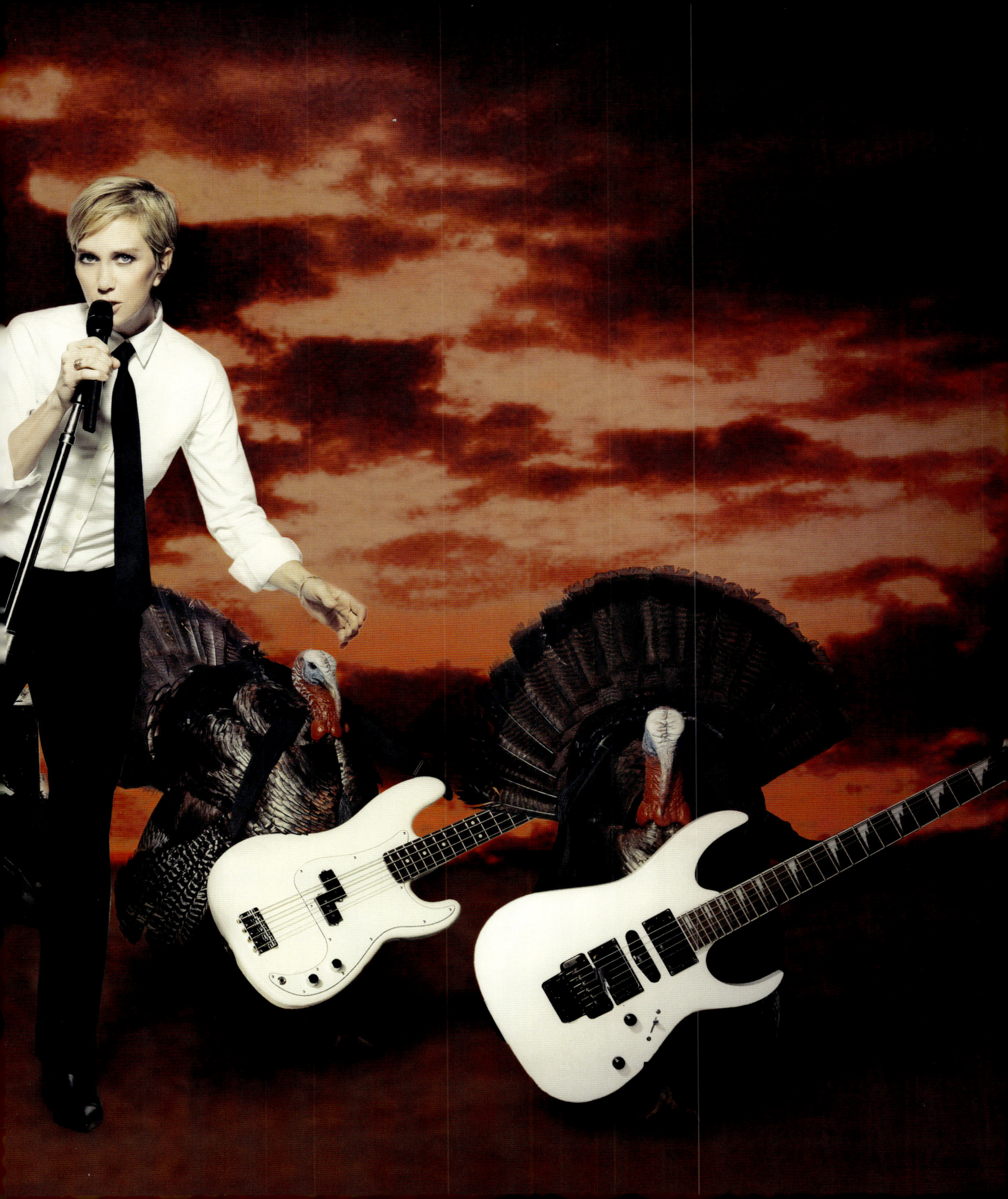

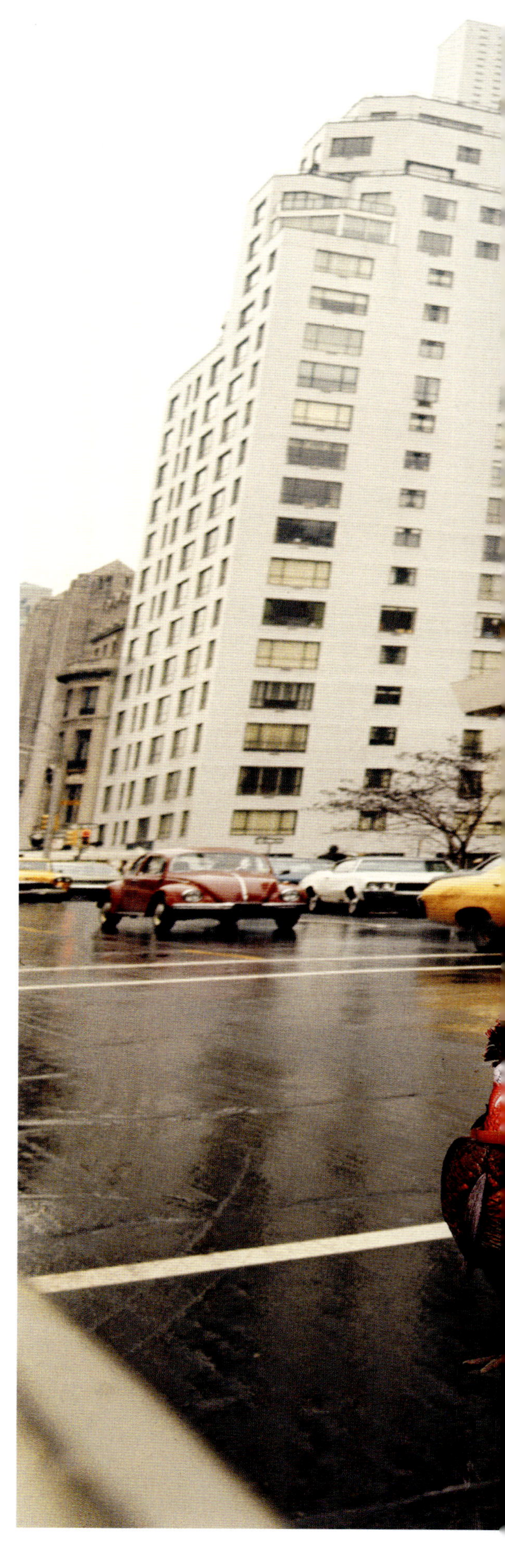

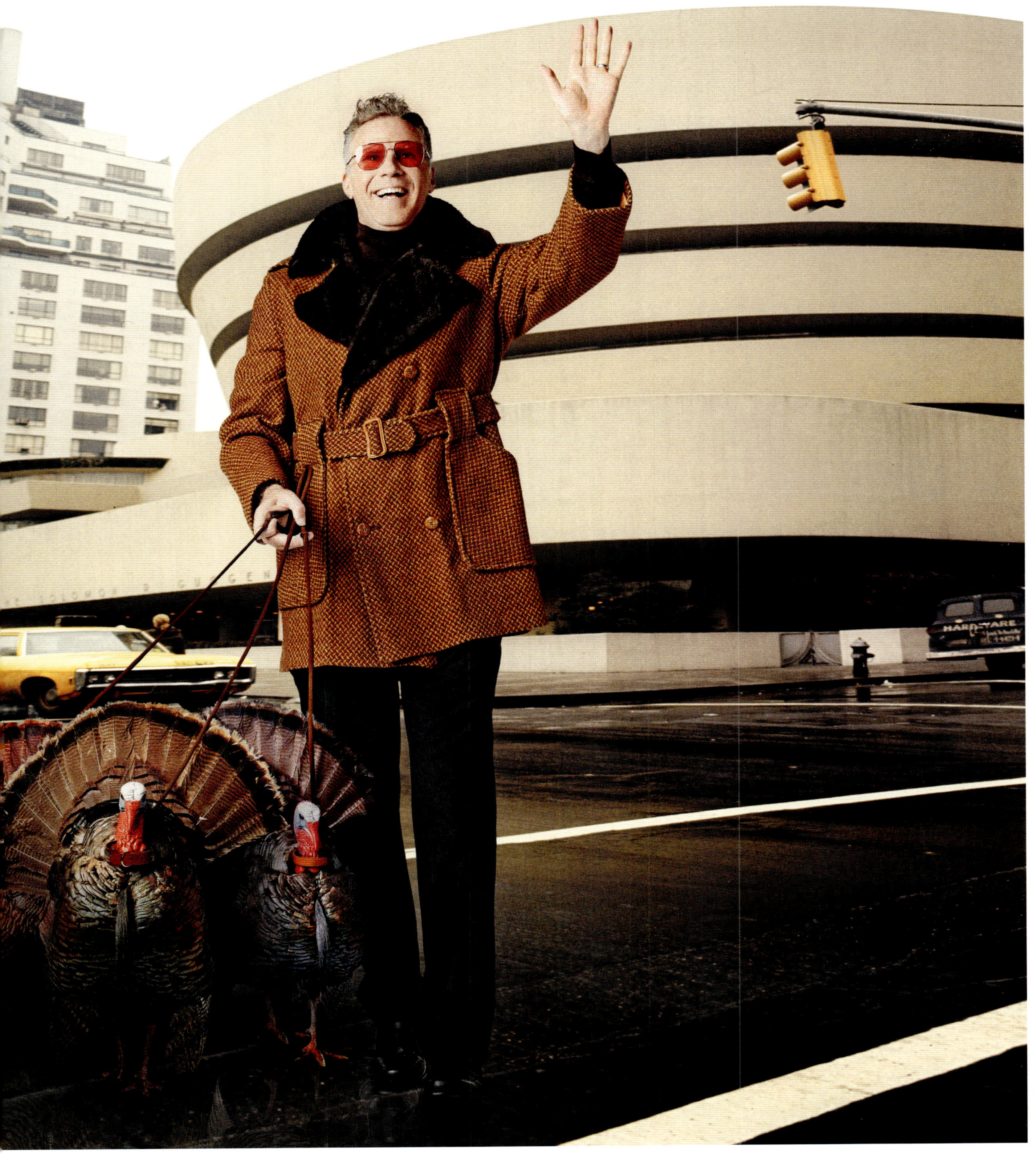

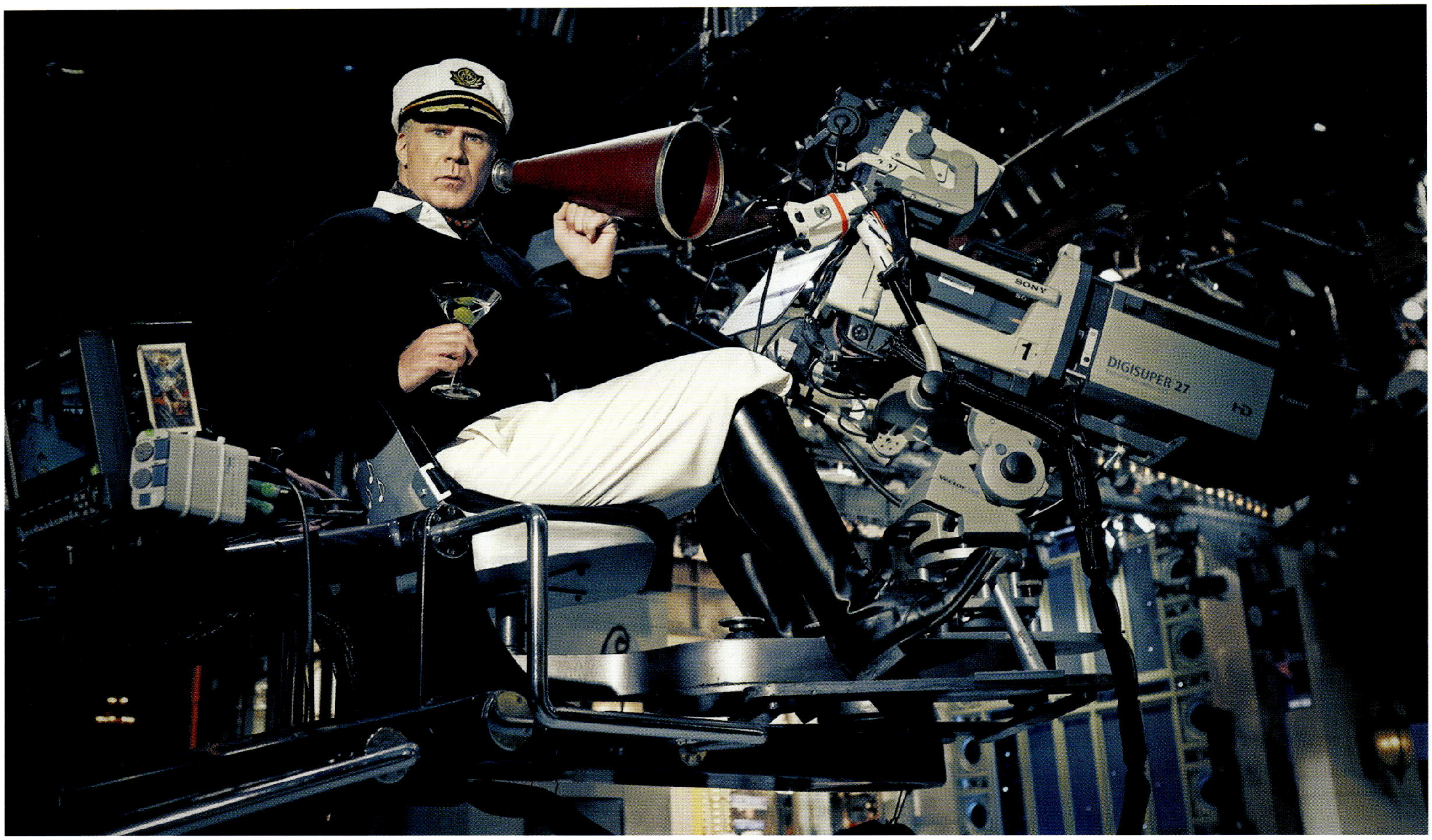

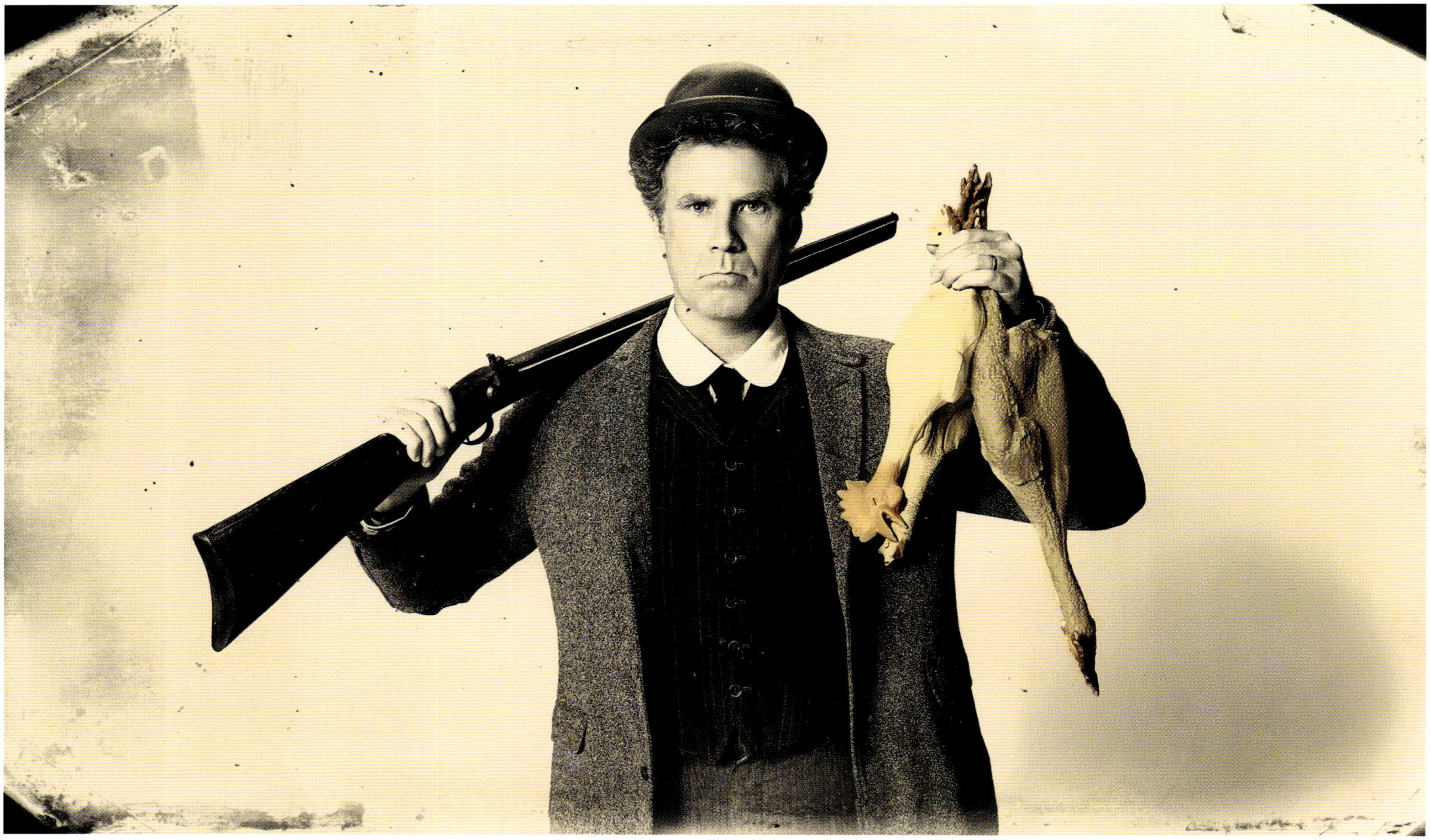

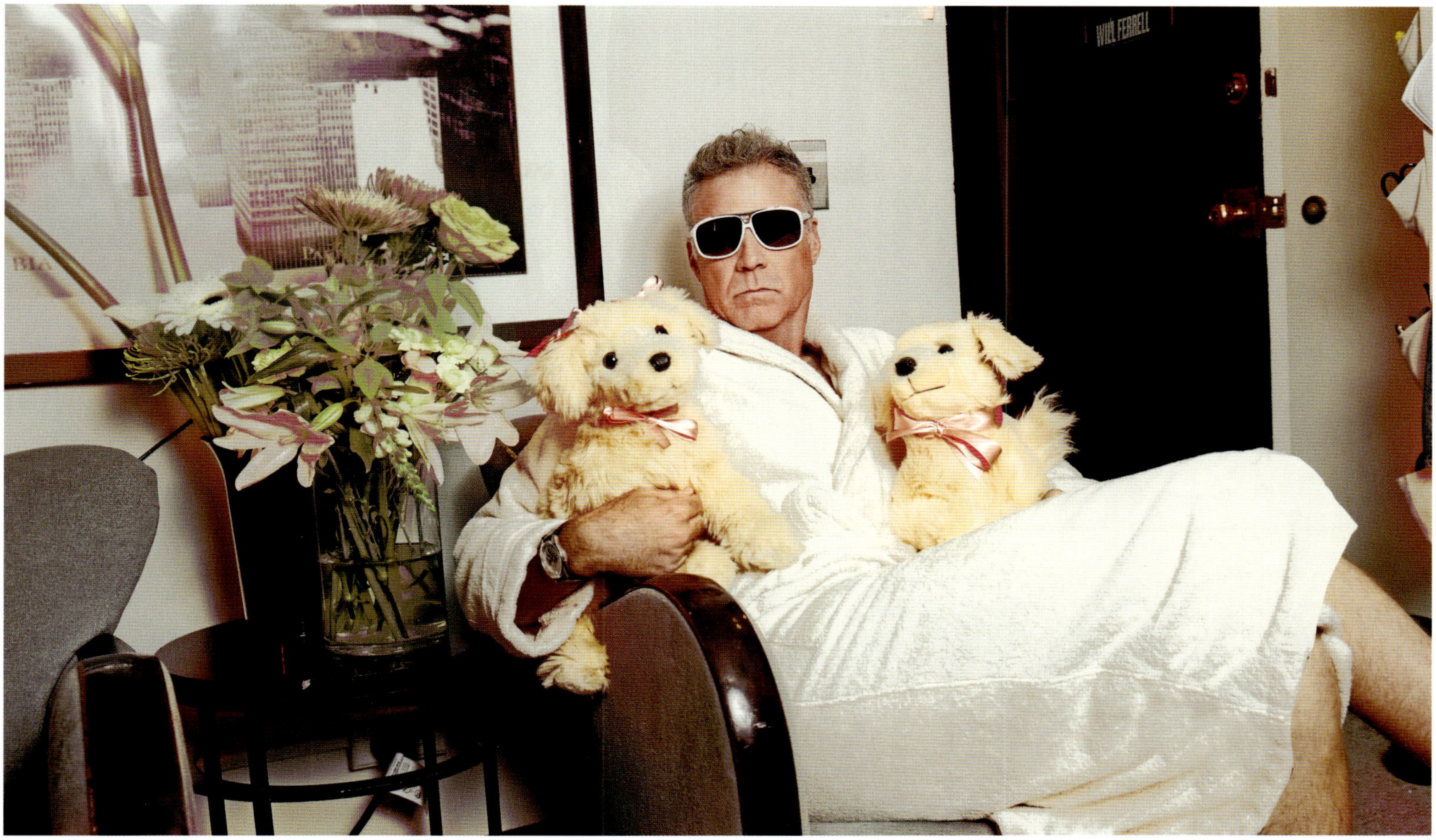

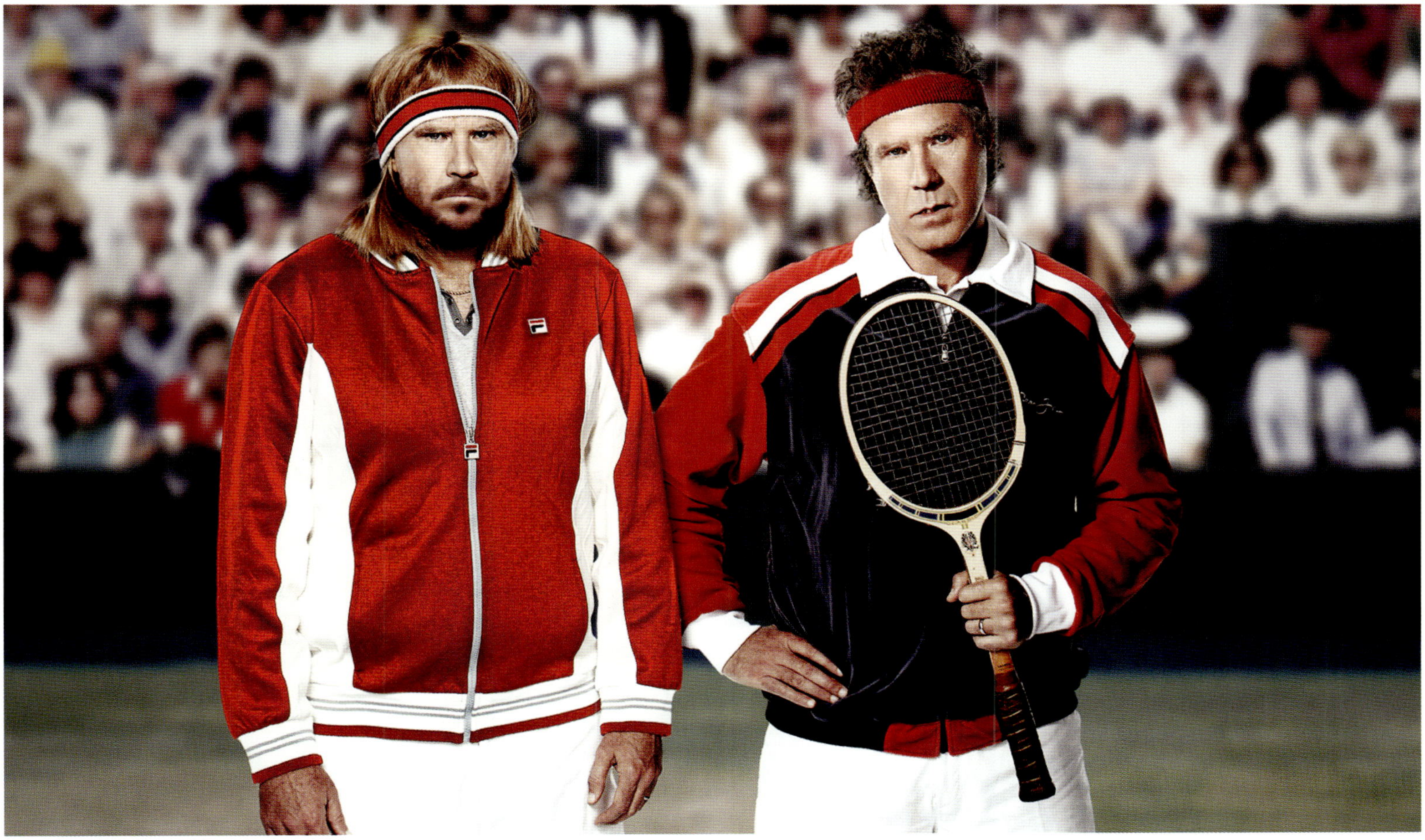

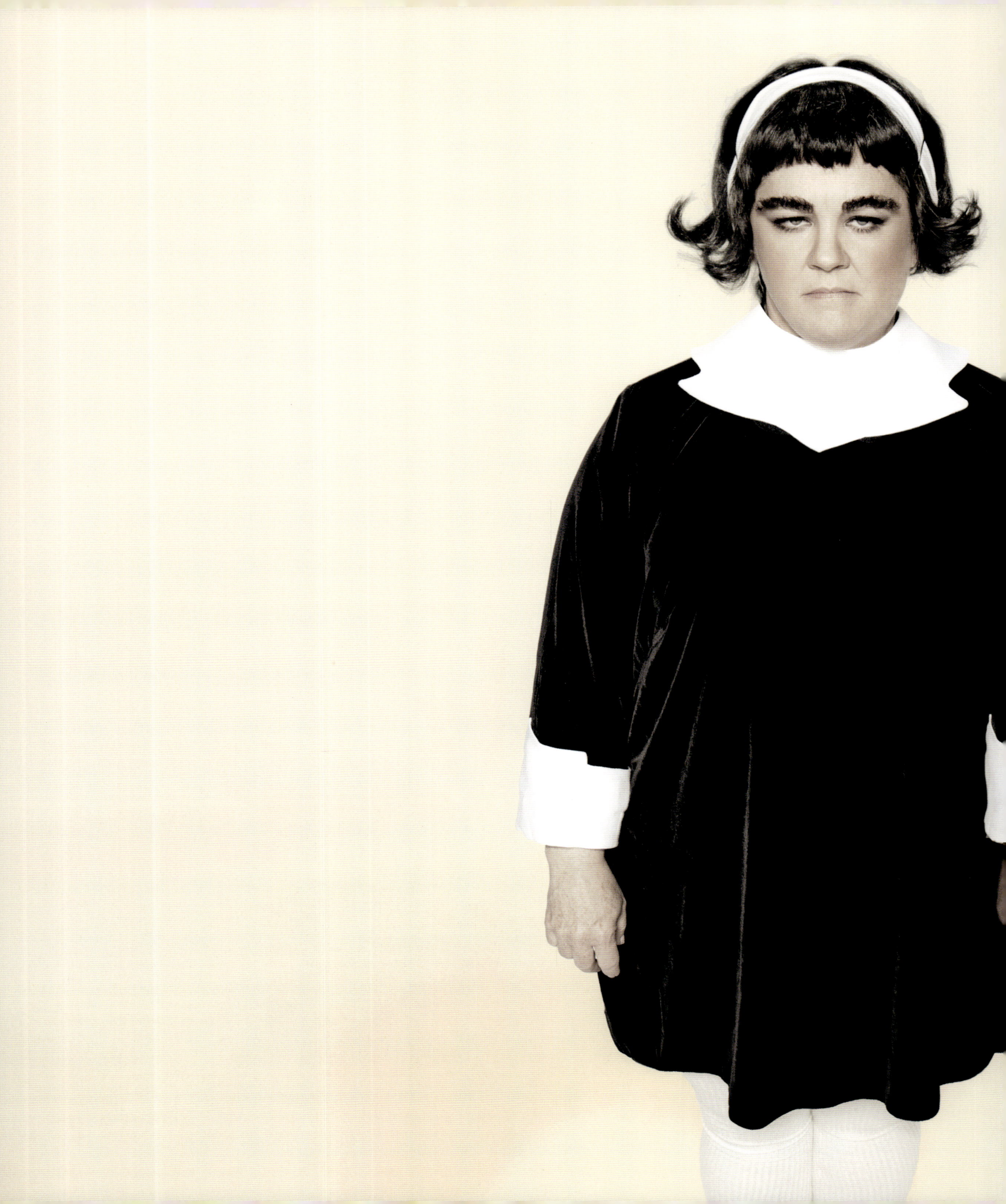

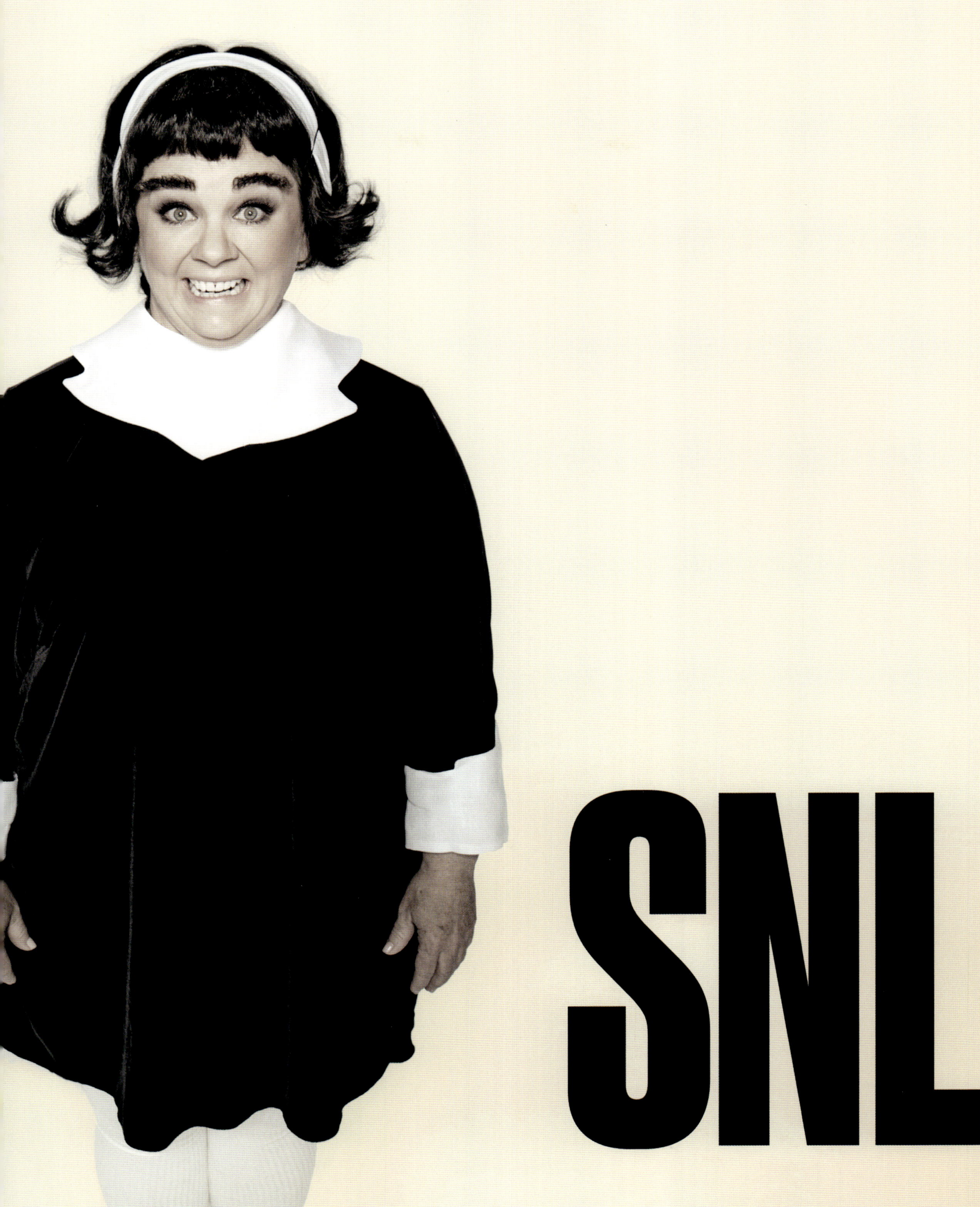
SNL

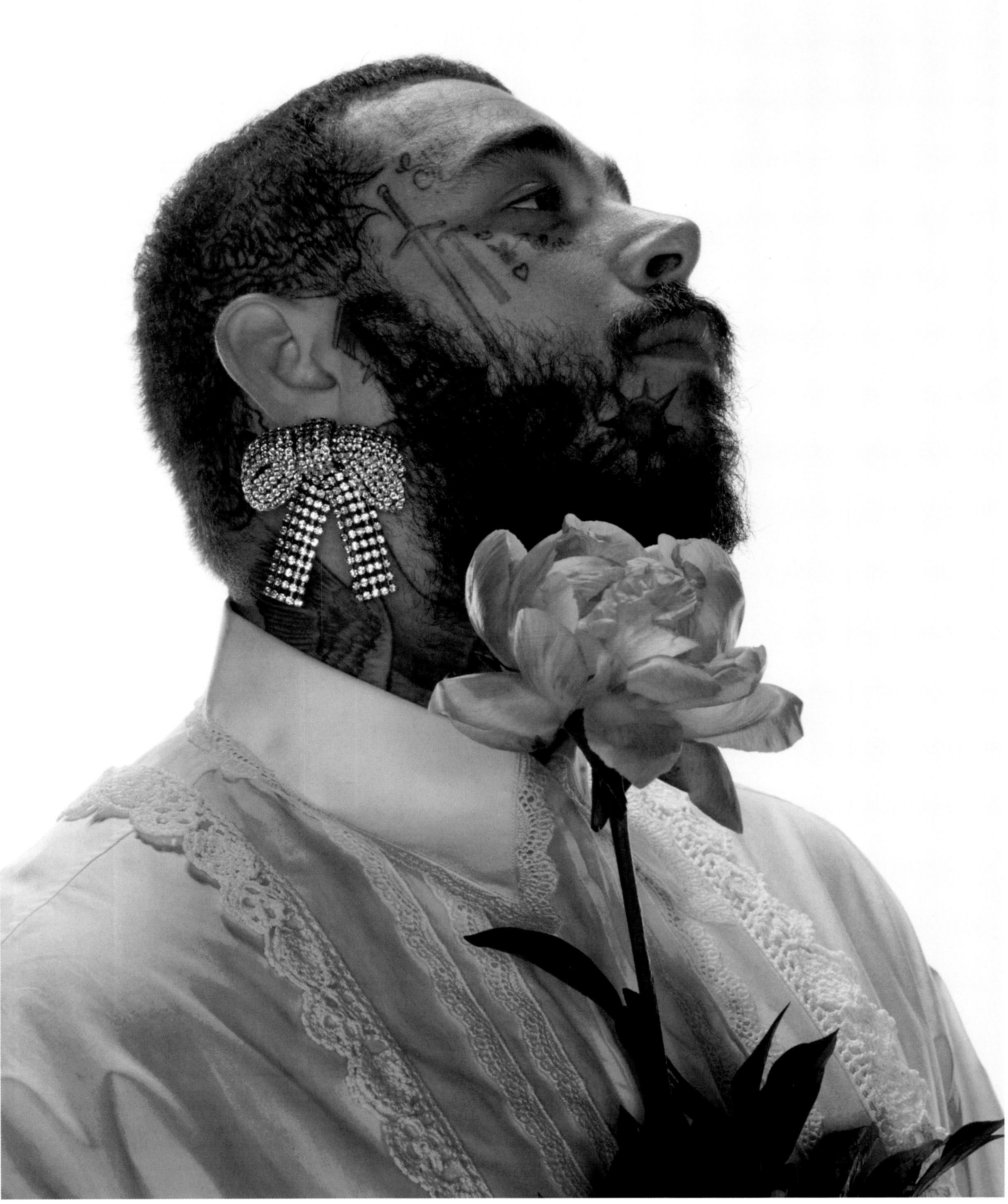

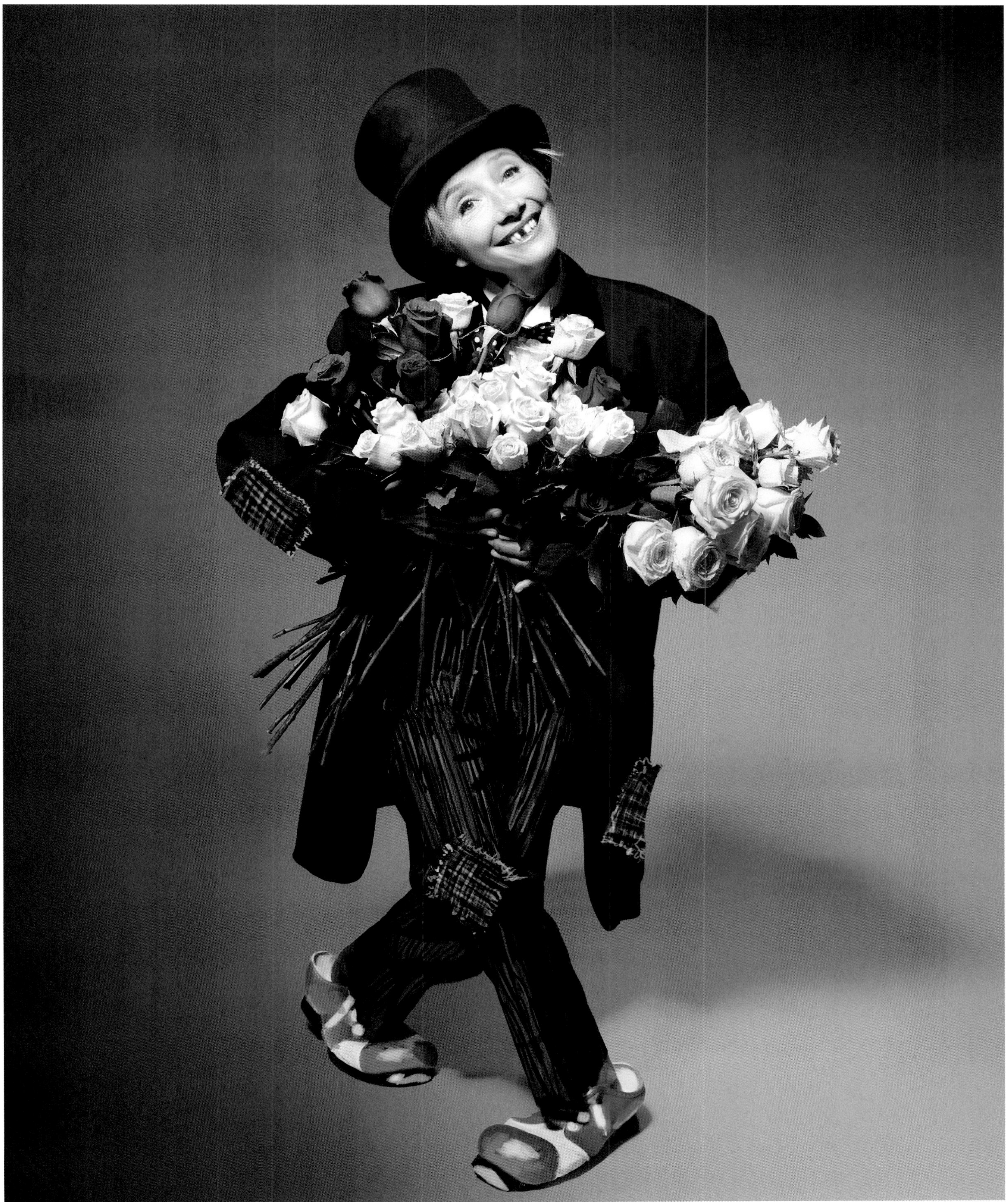

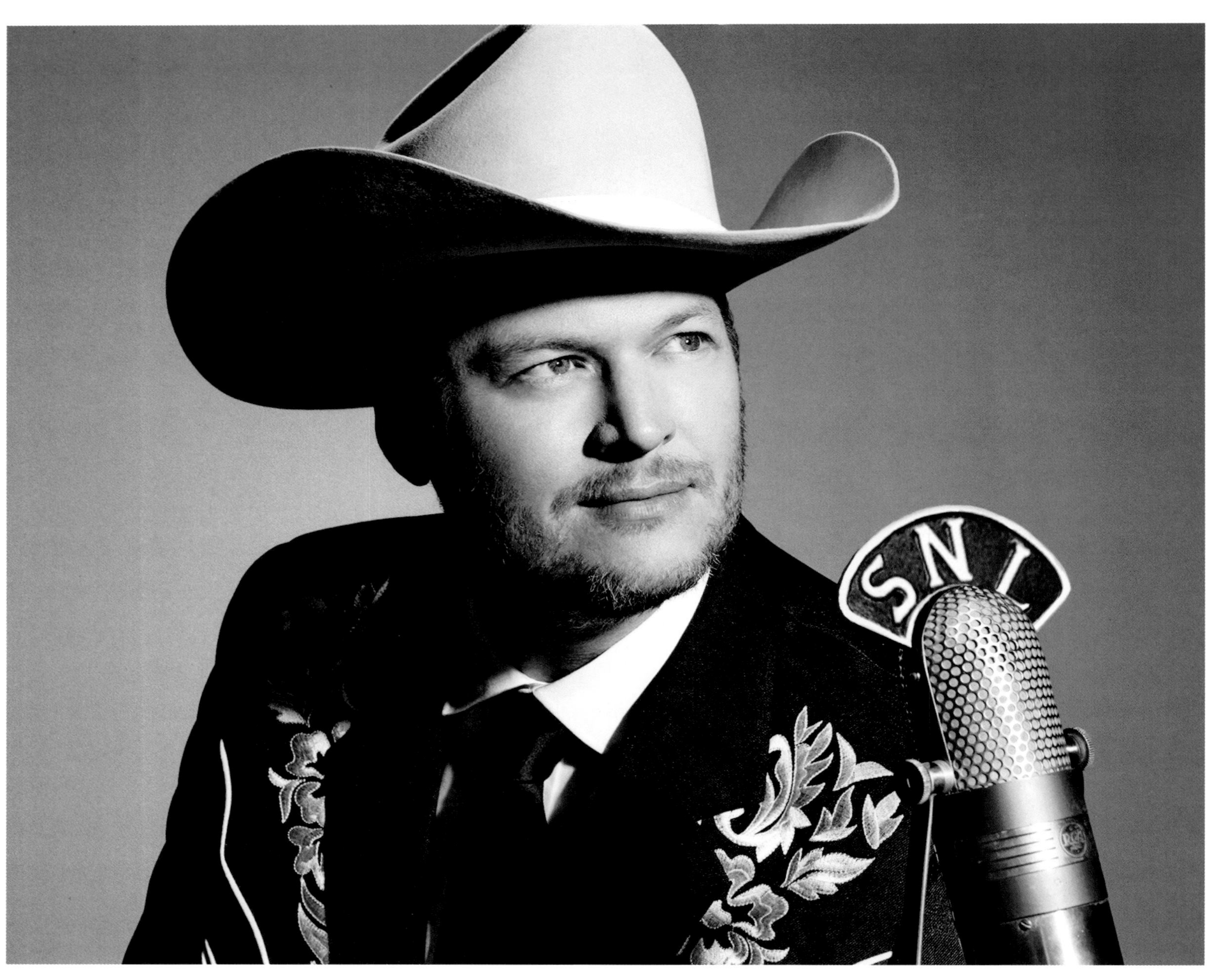
SNL

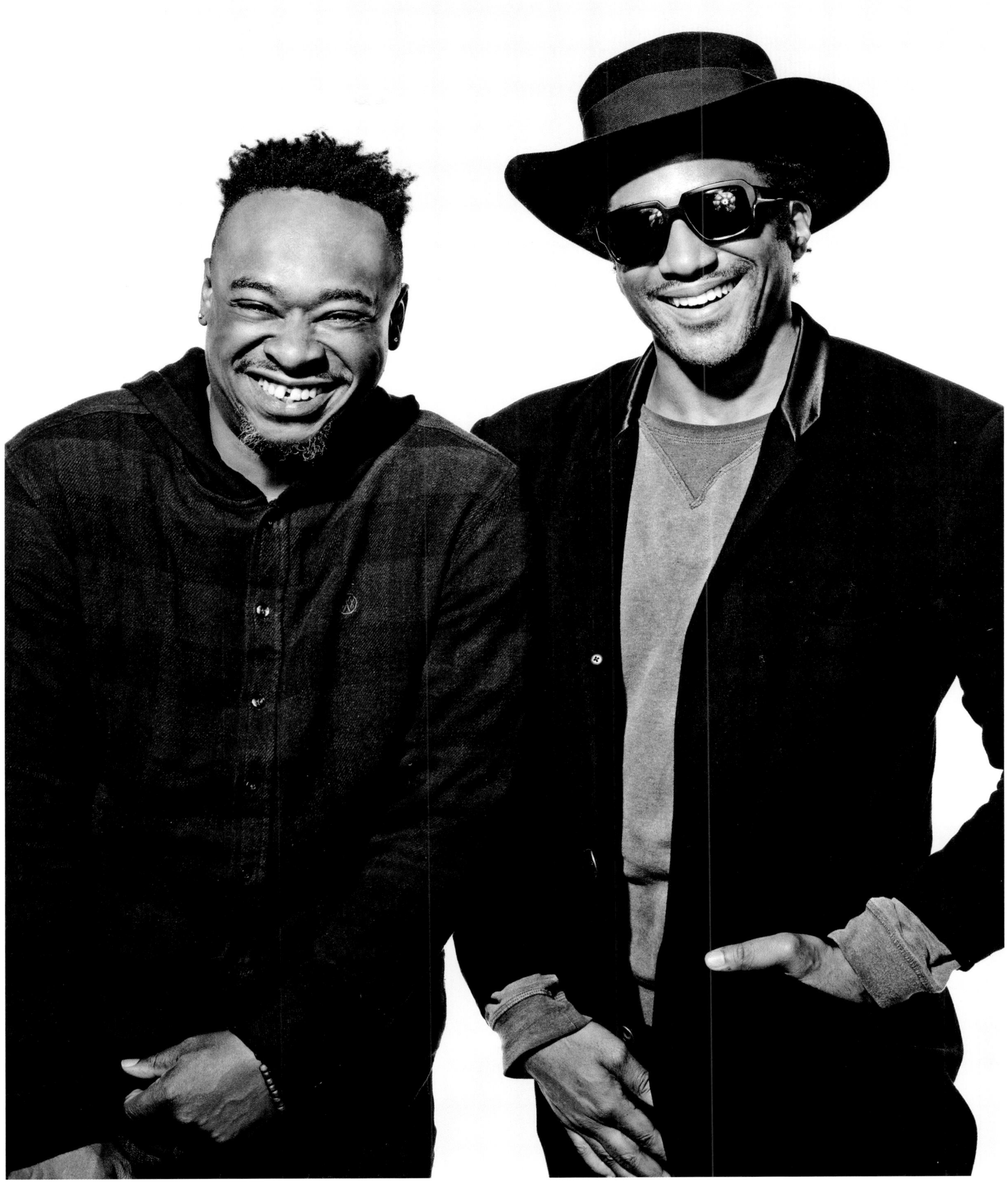

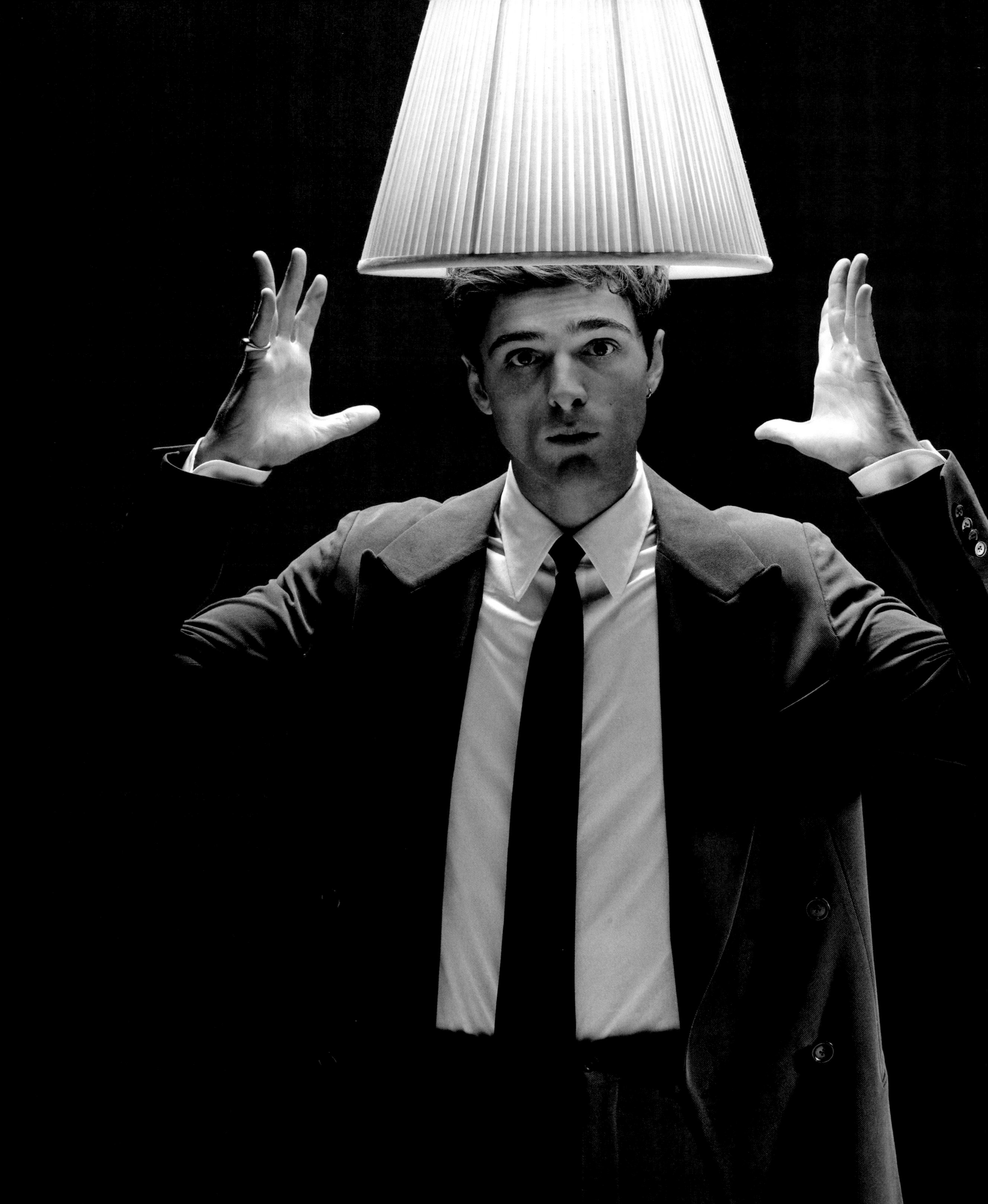

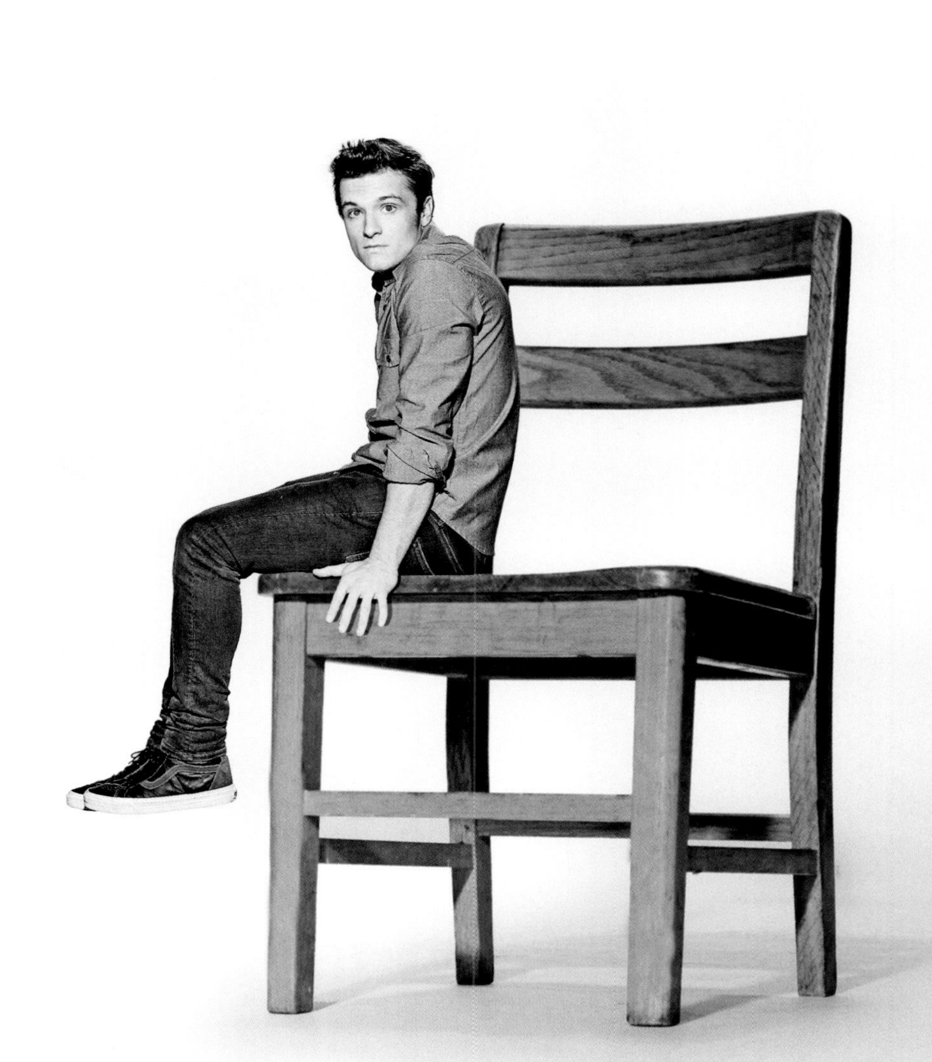

SNL

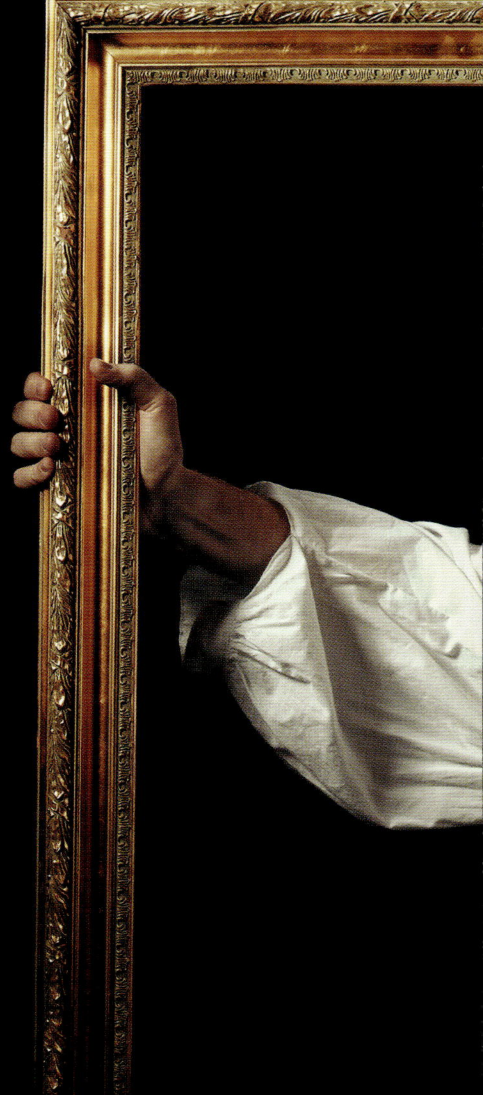

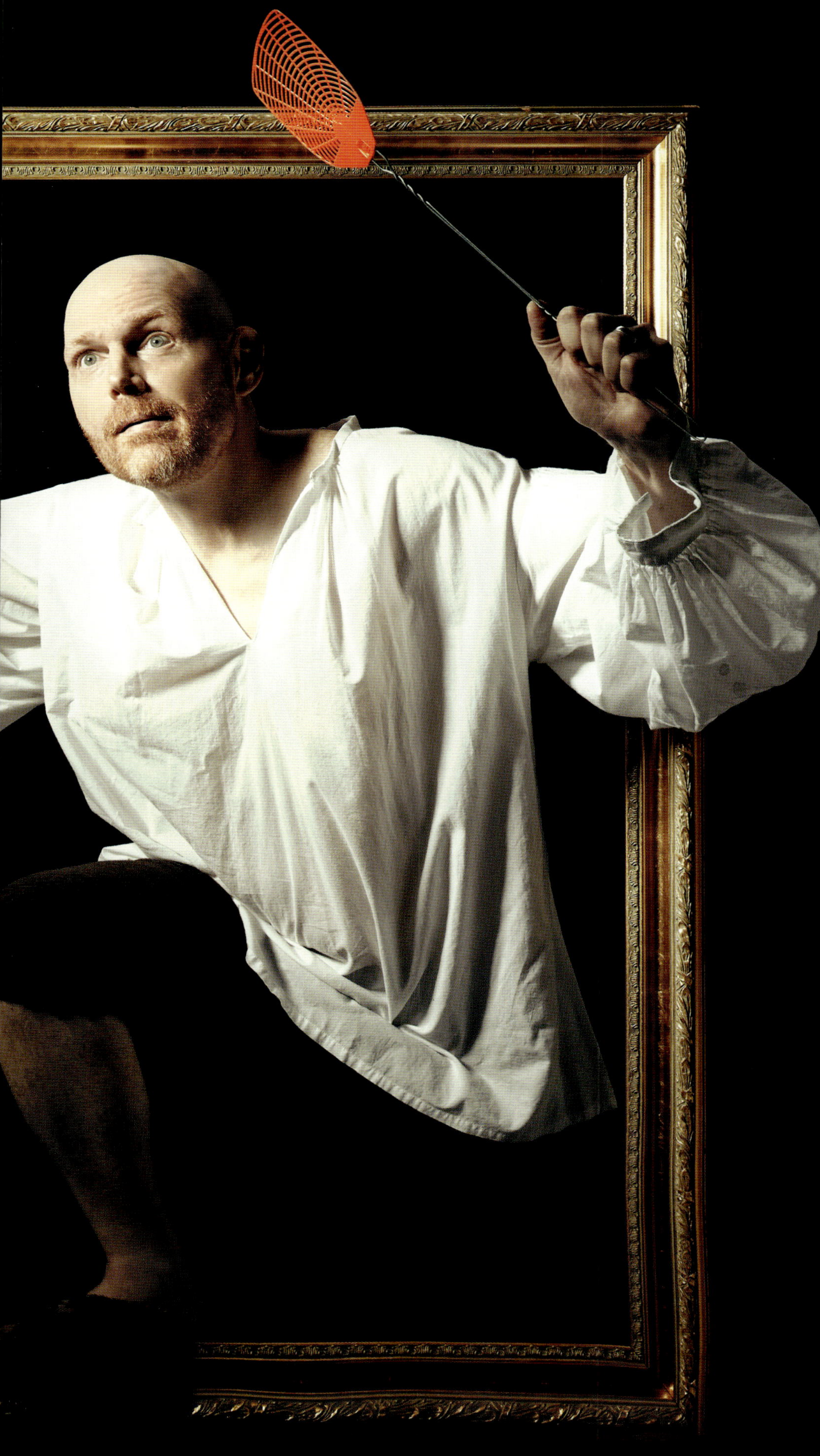

NIGHT

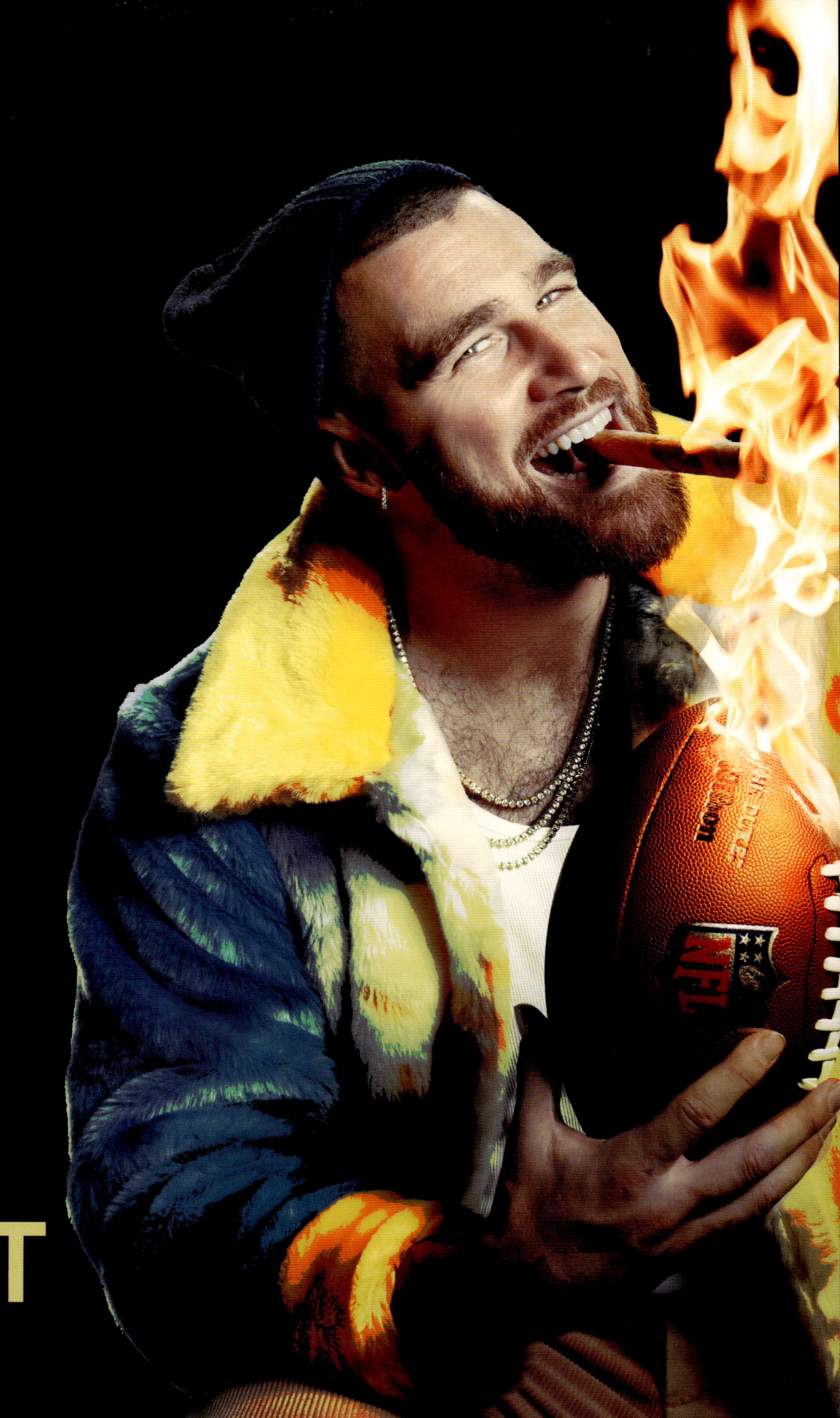

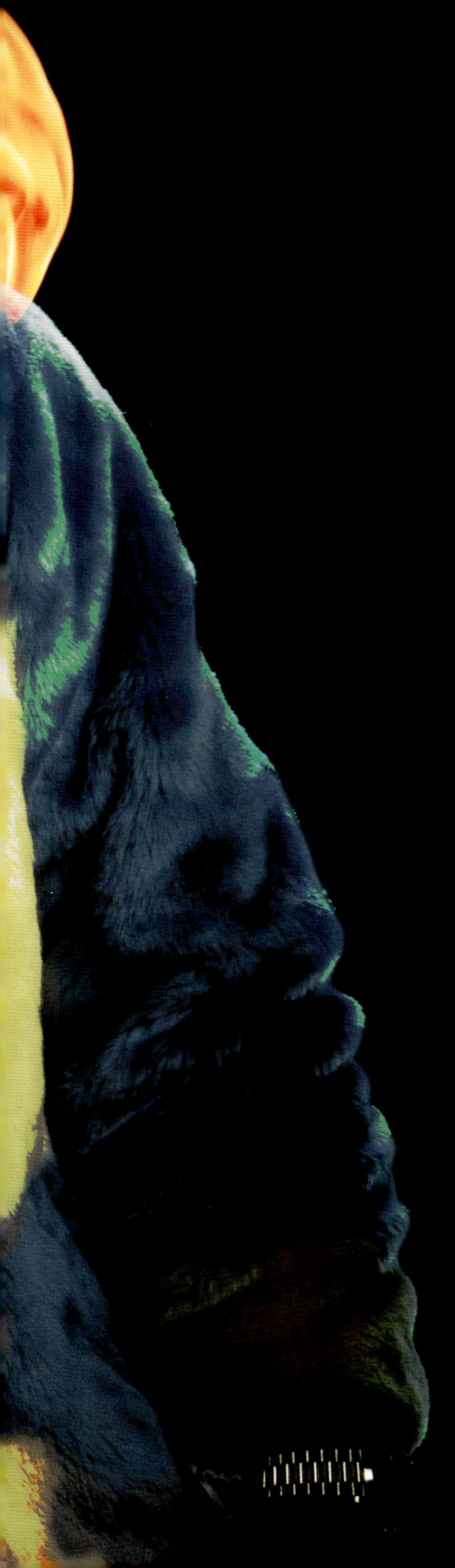

SATURDAY

LIVE

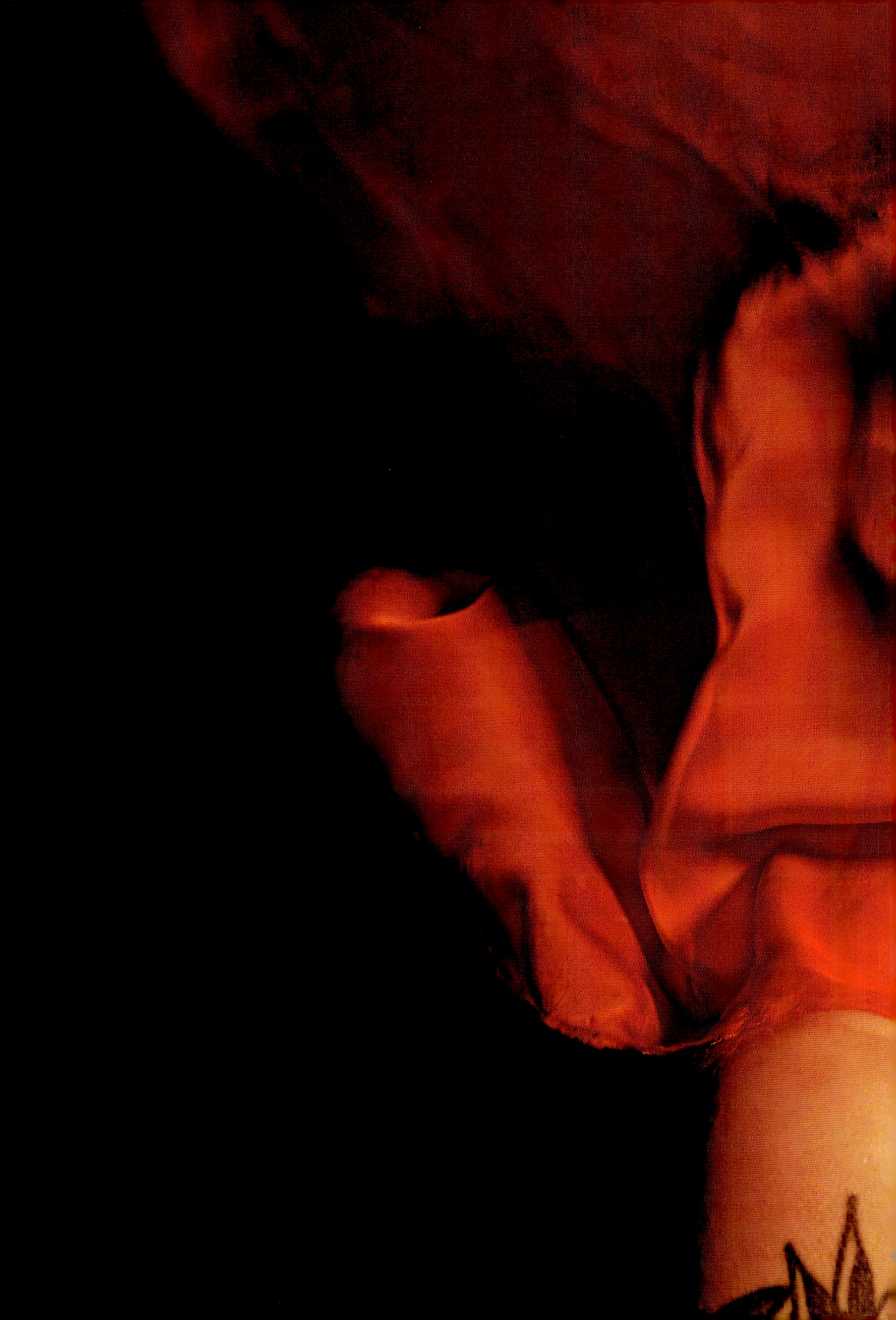

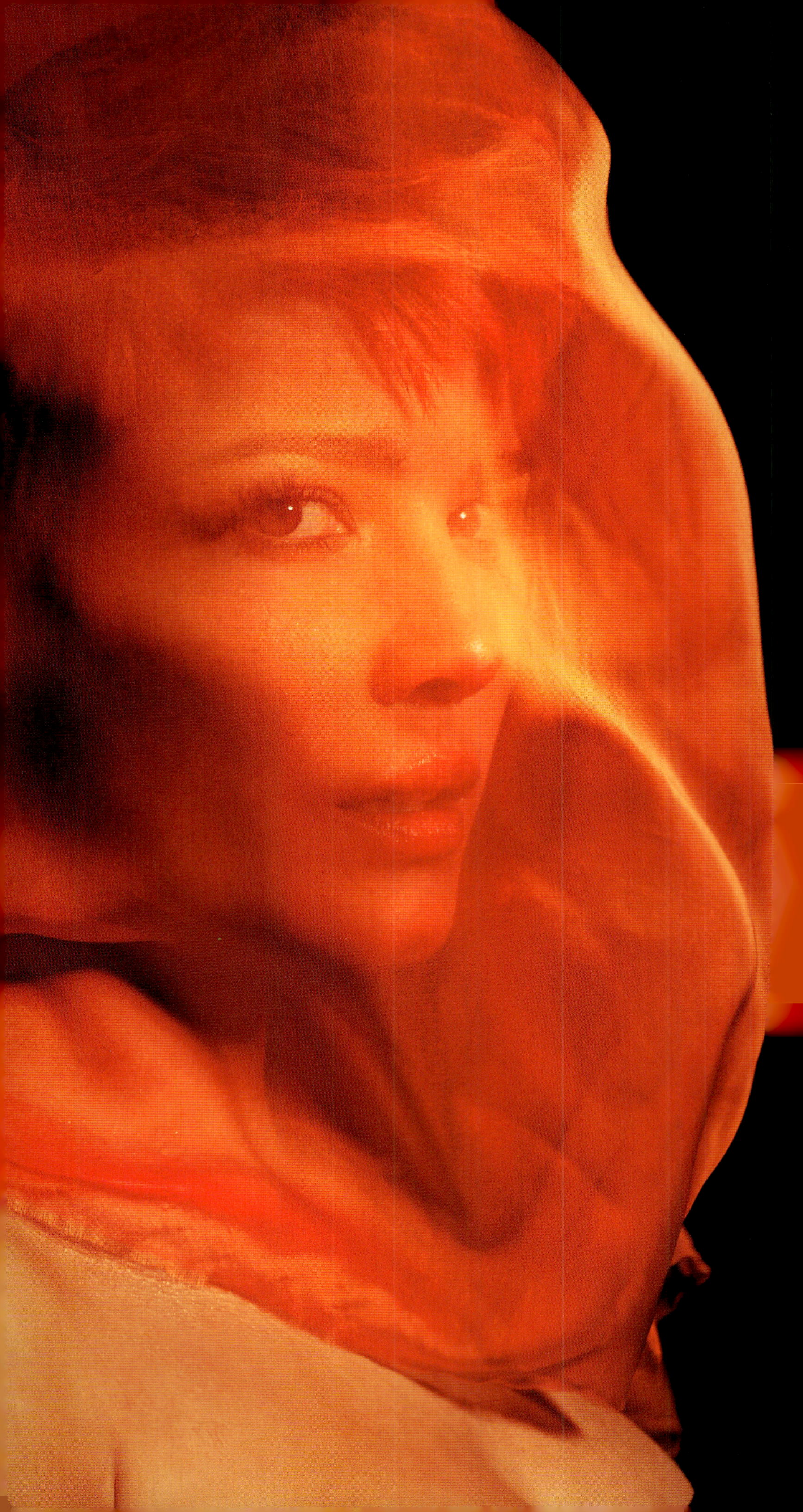

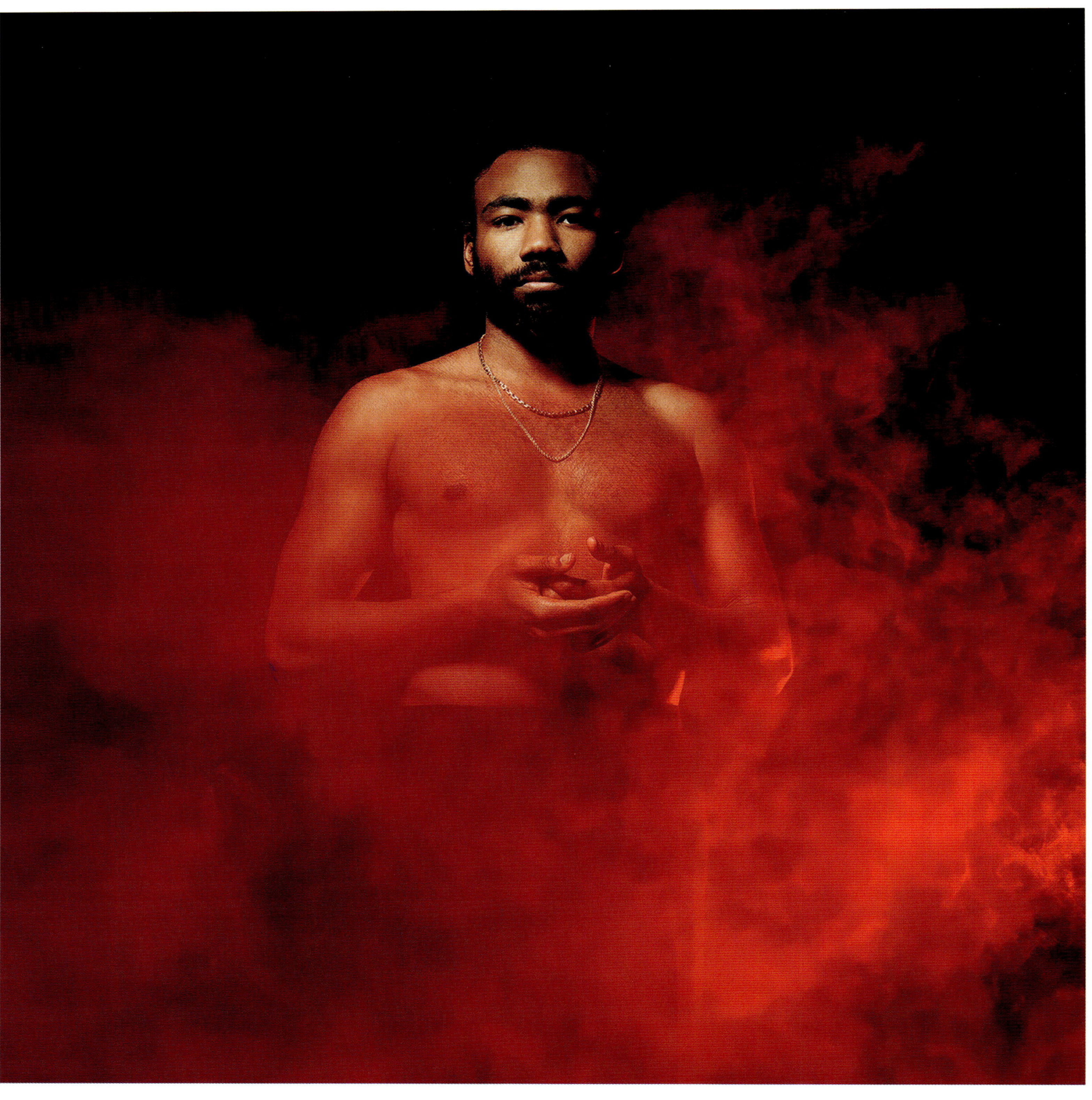

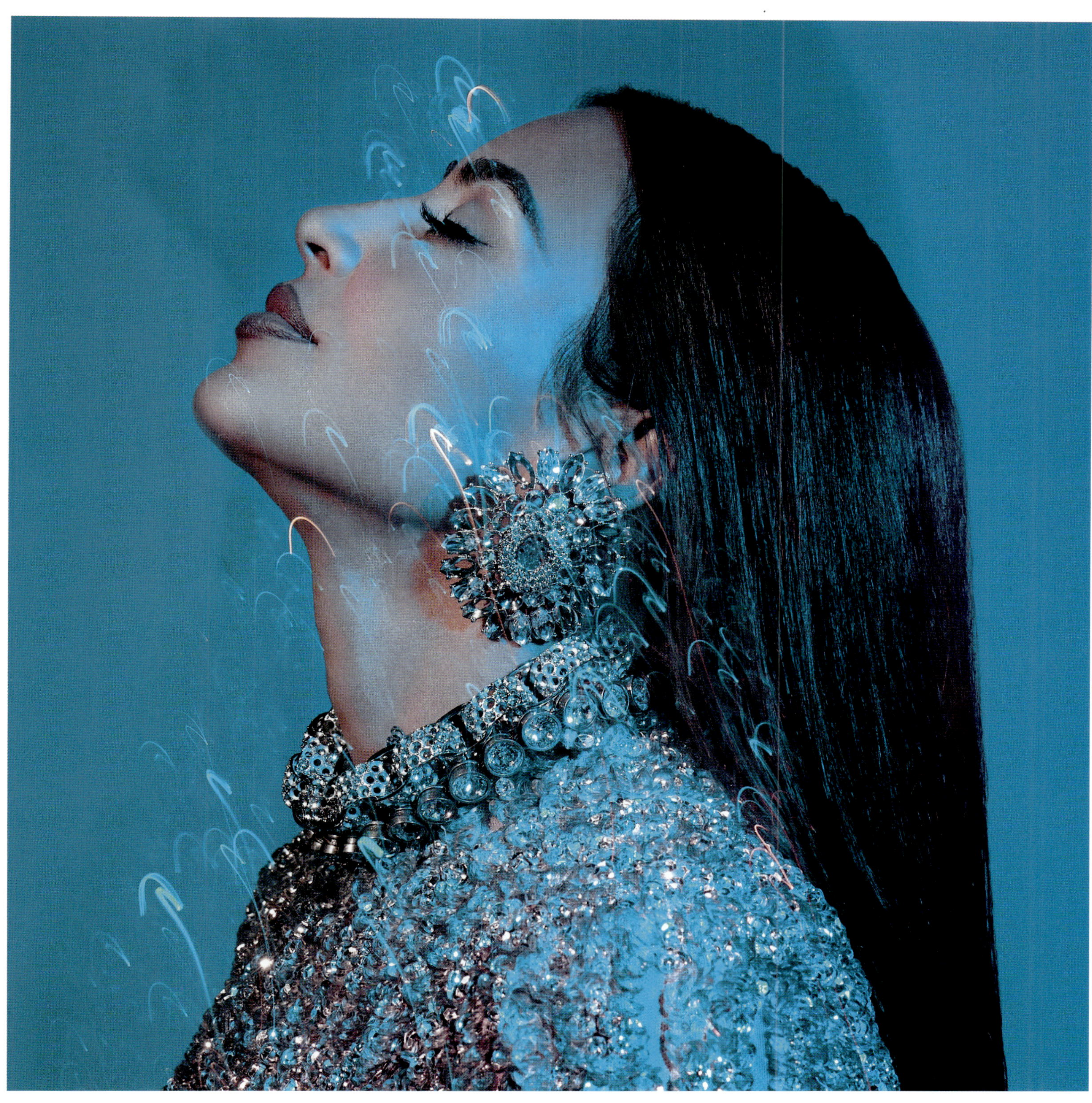

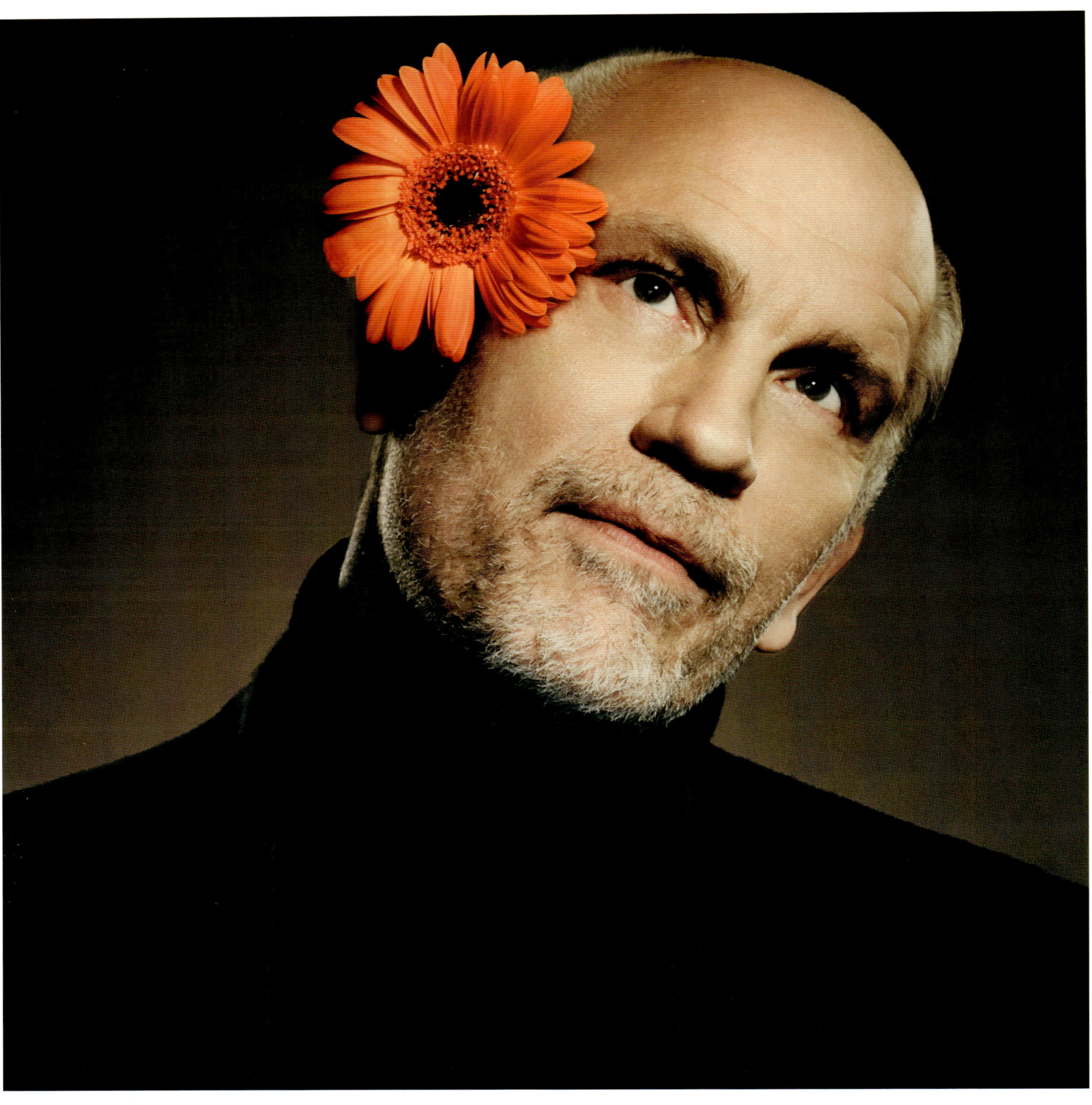

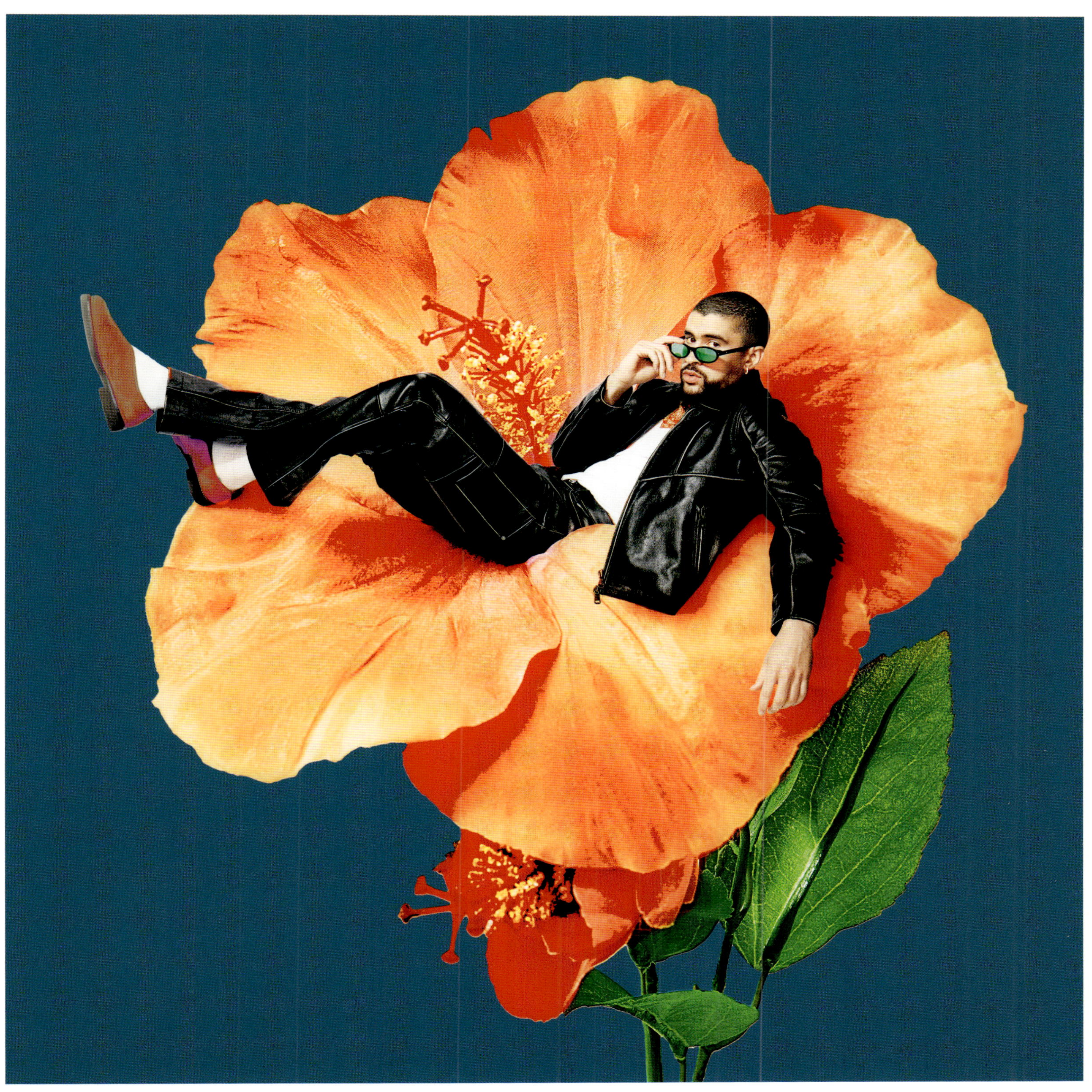

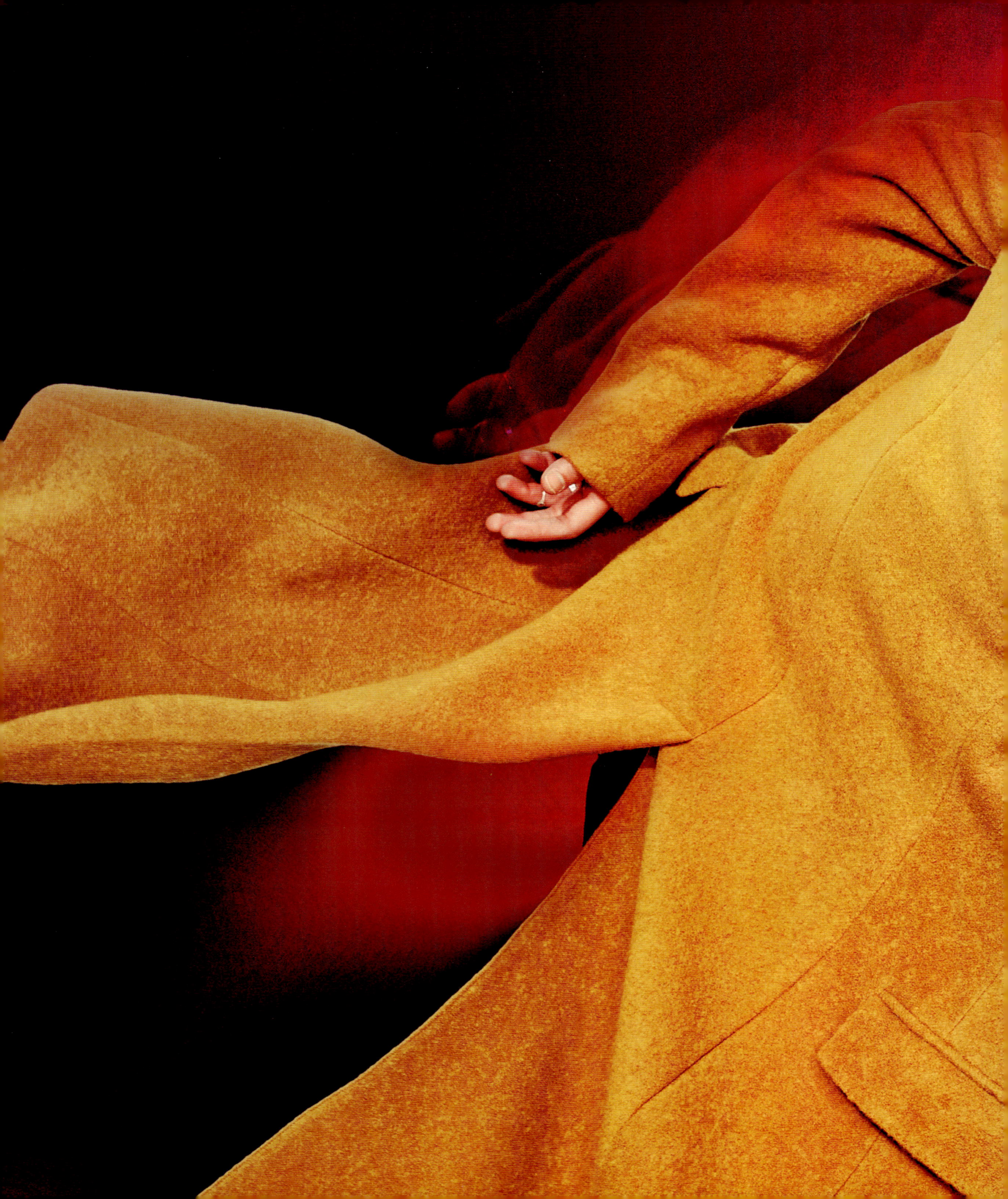

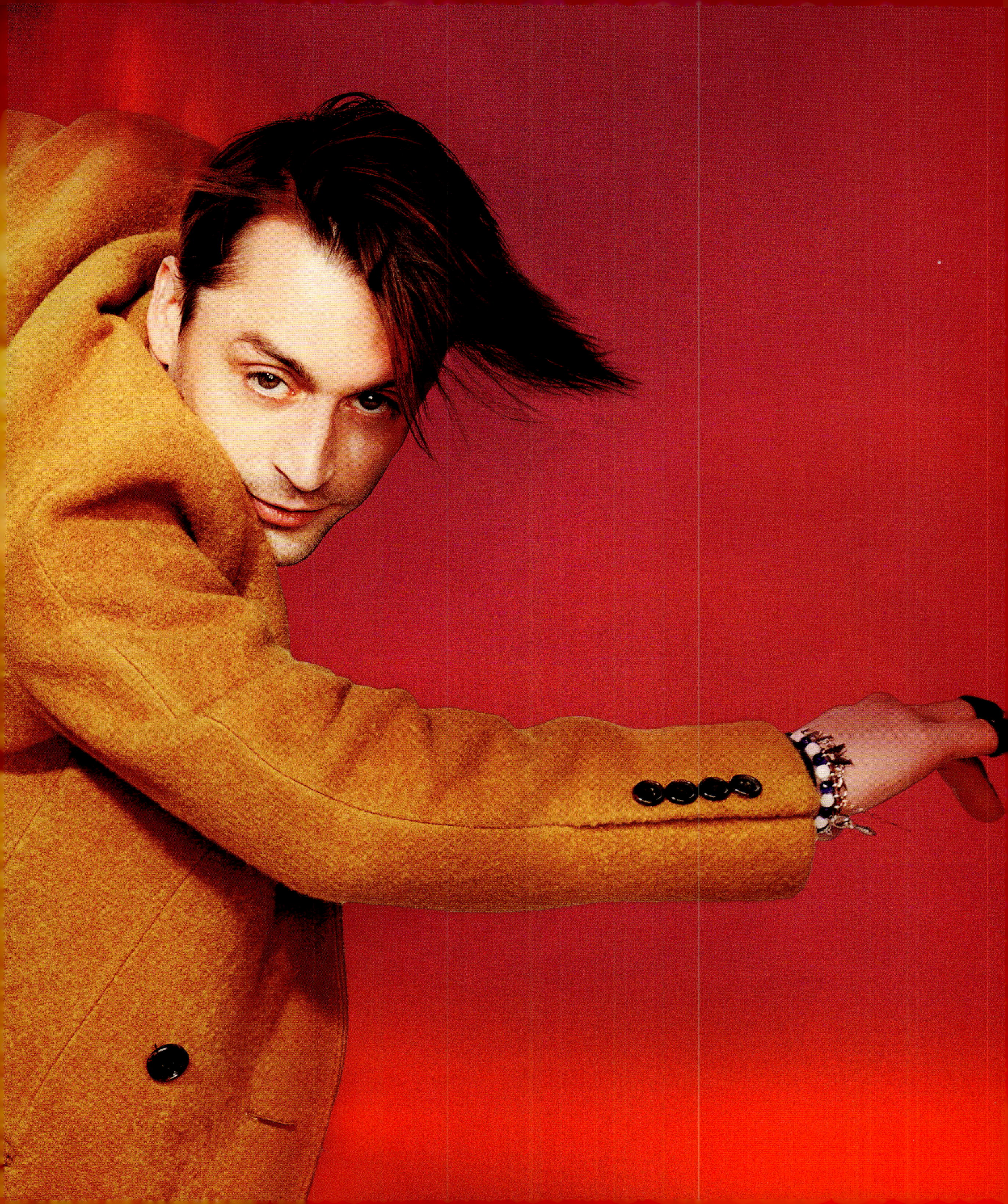

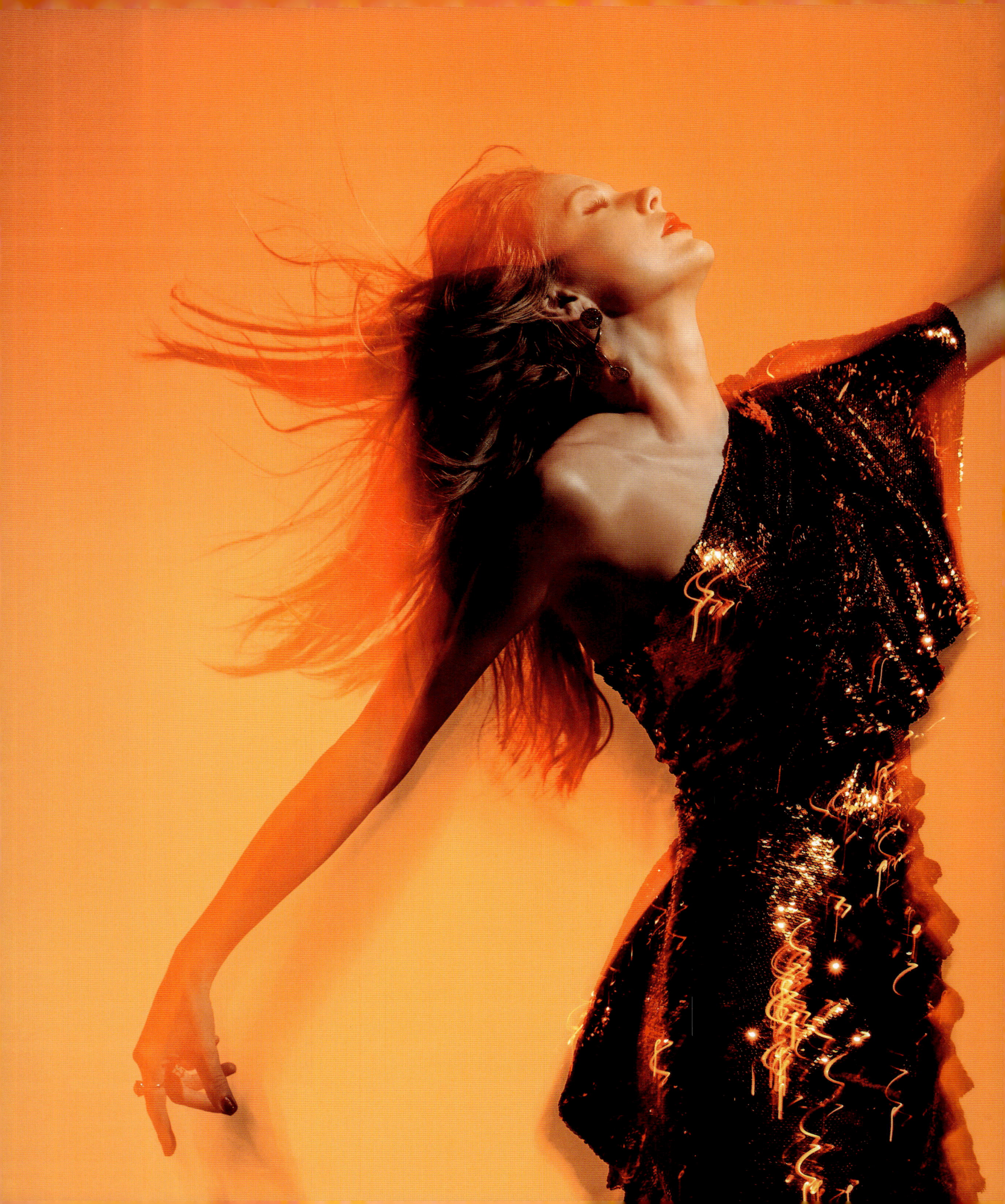

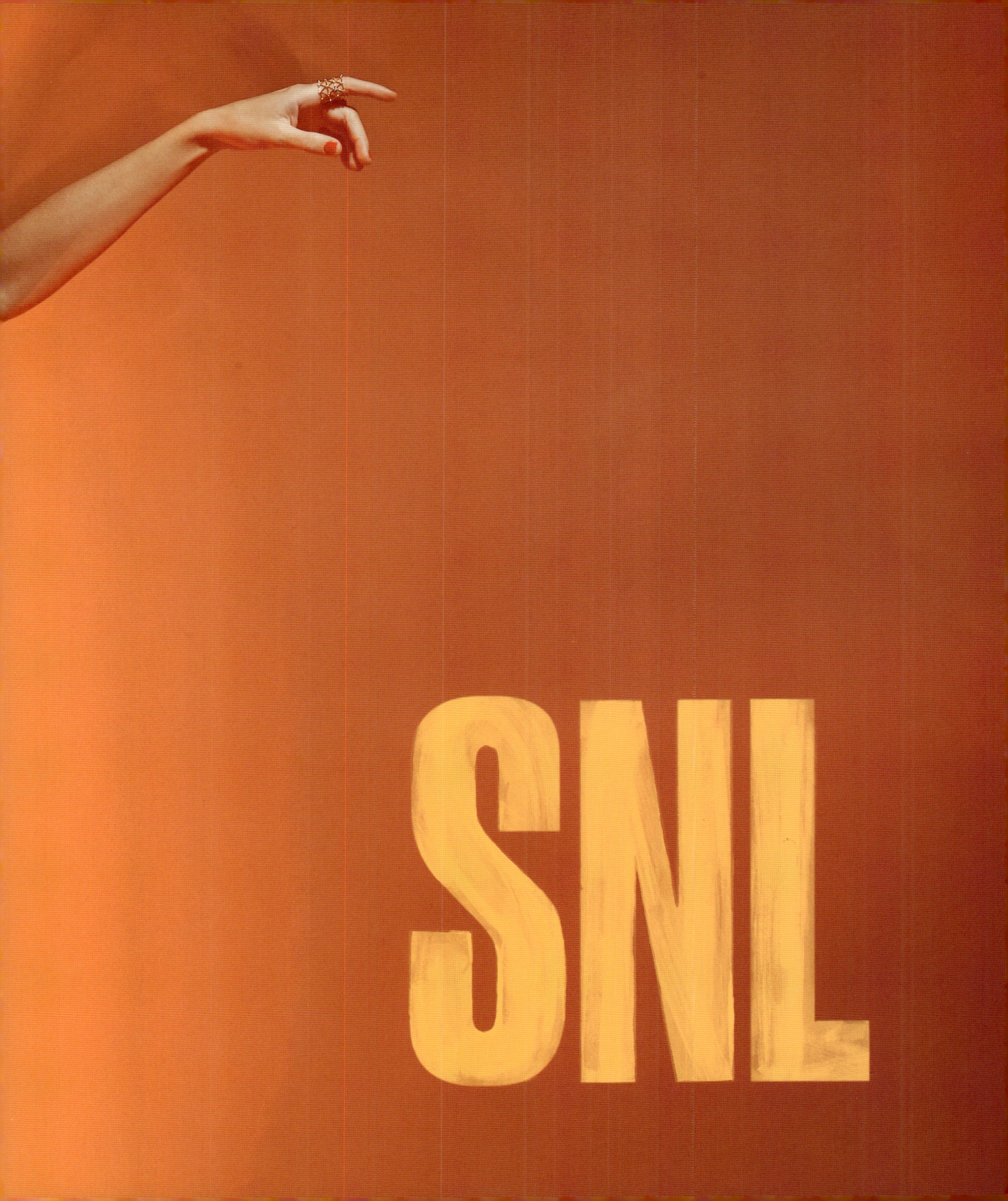

SNL

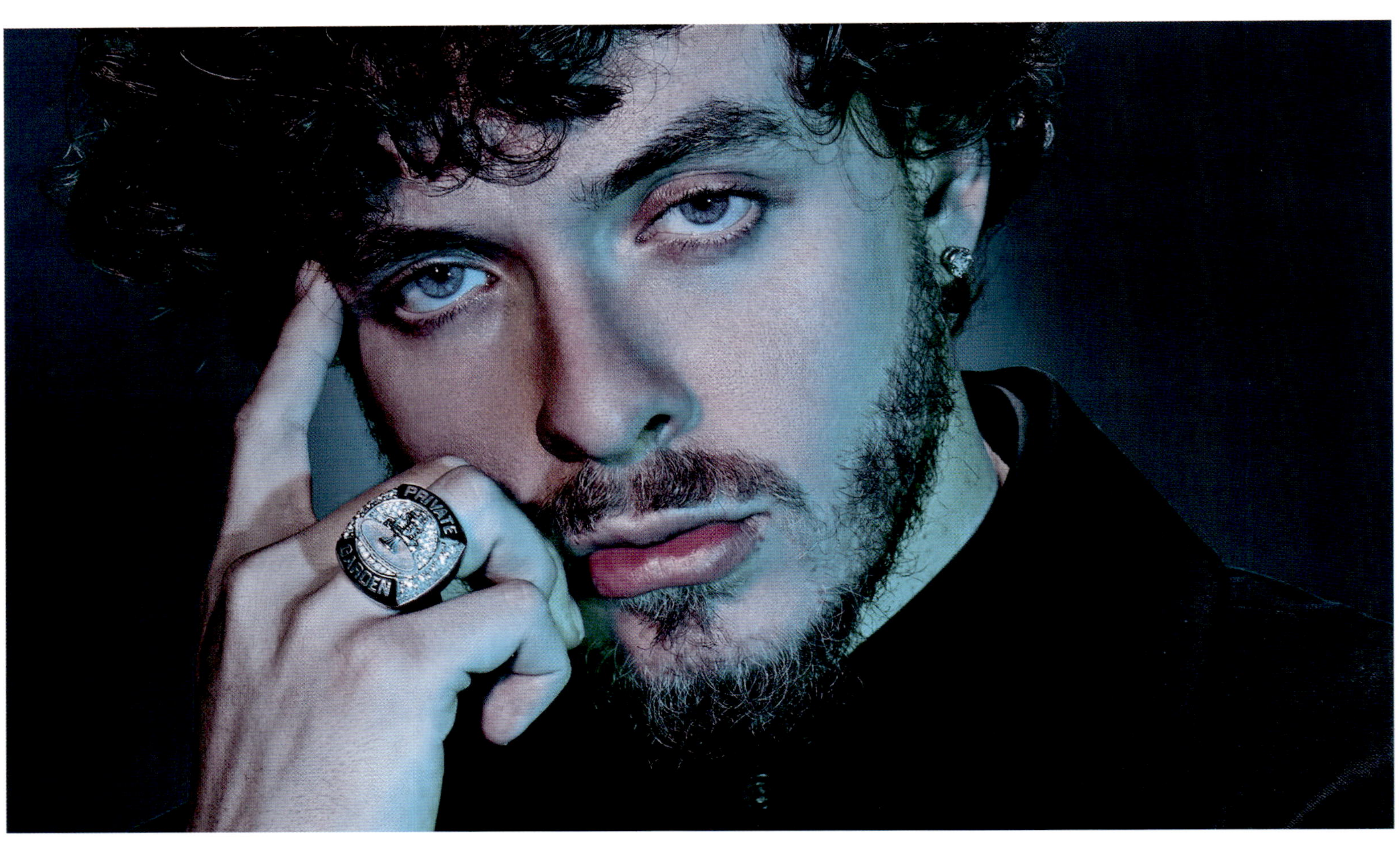
PRIVATE
GARDEN

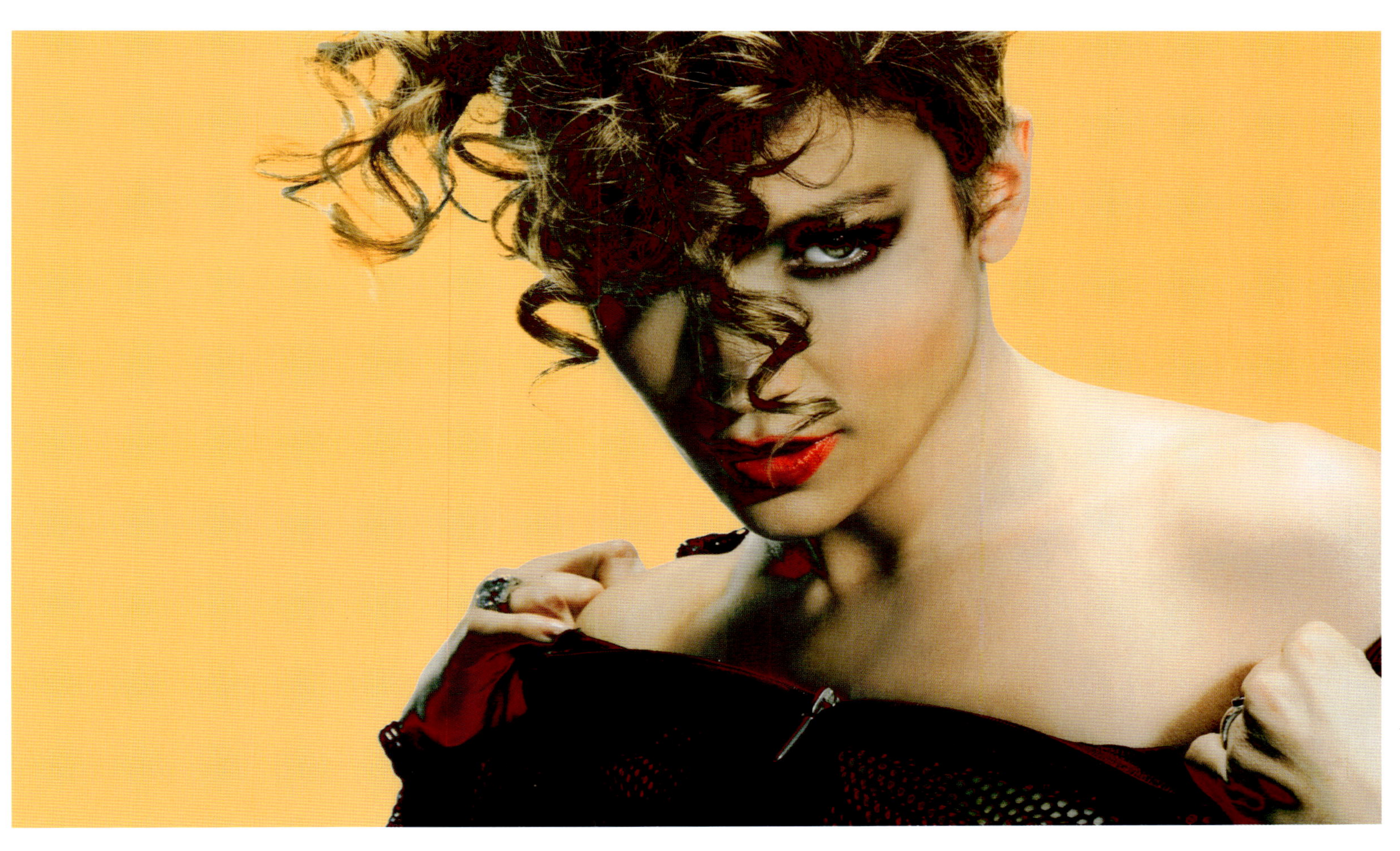

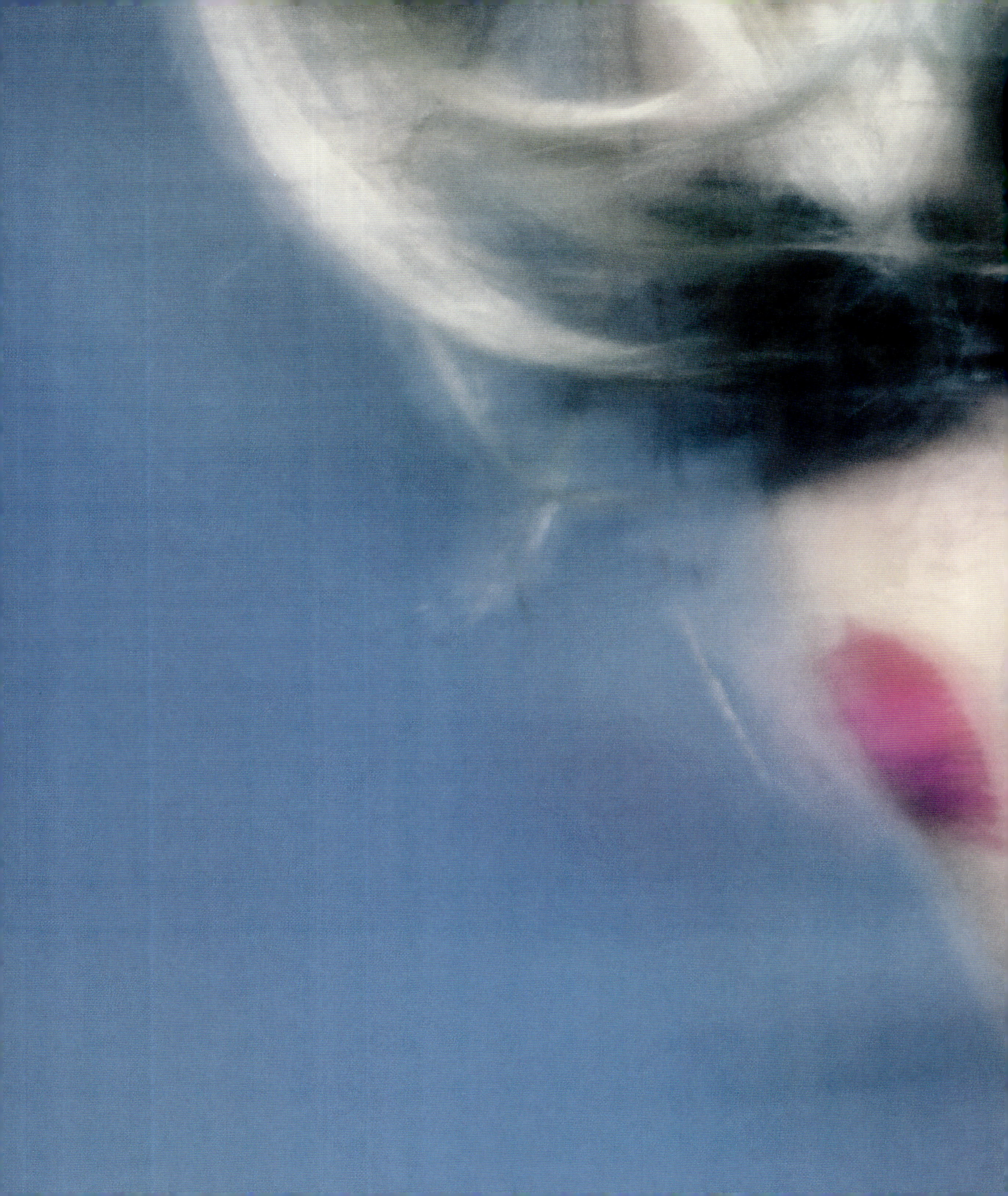

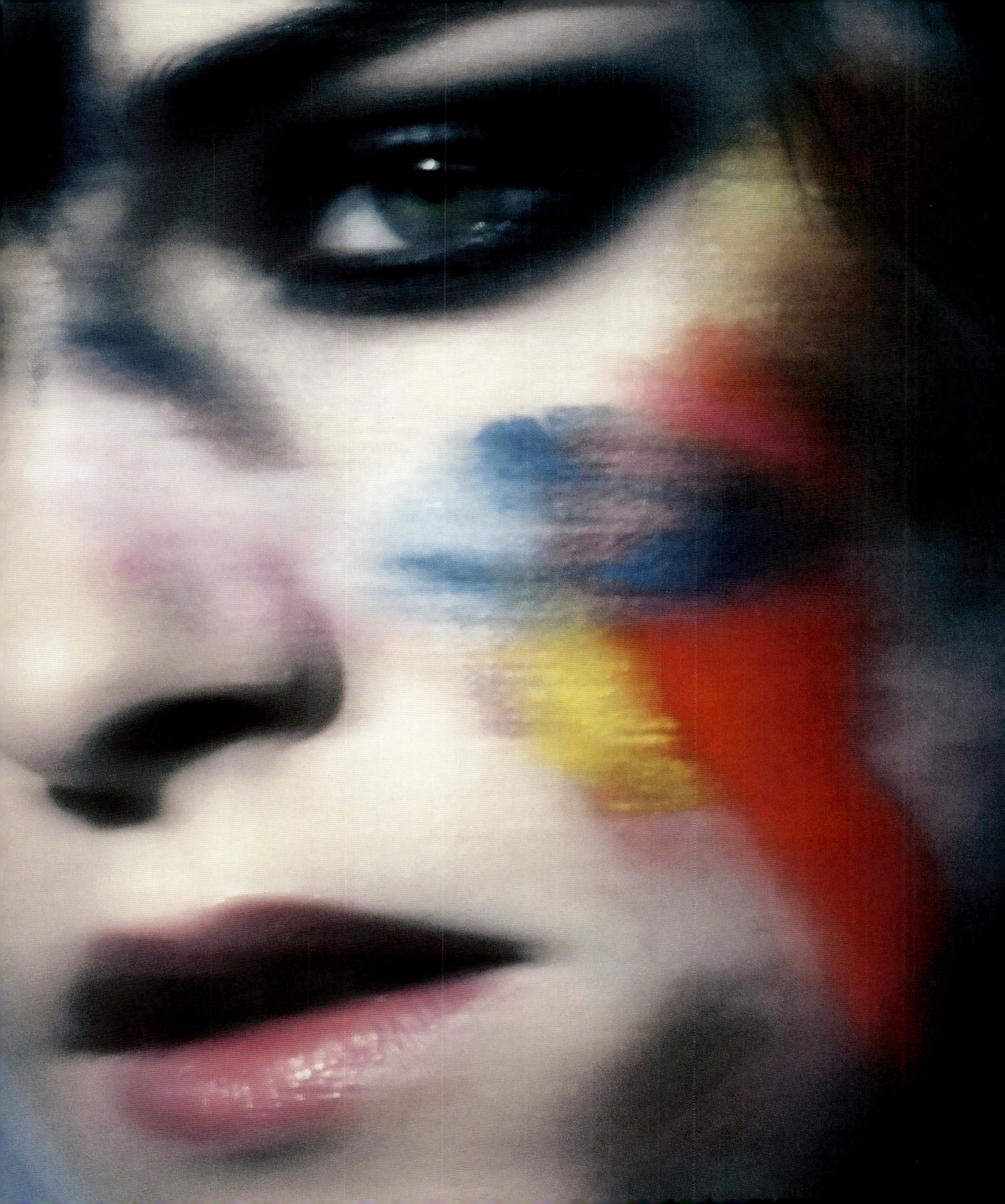

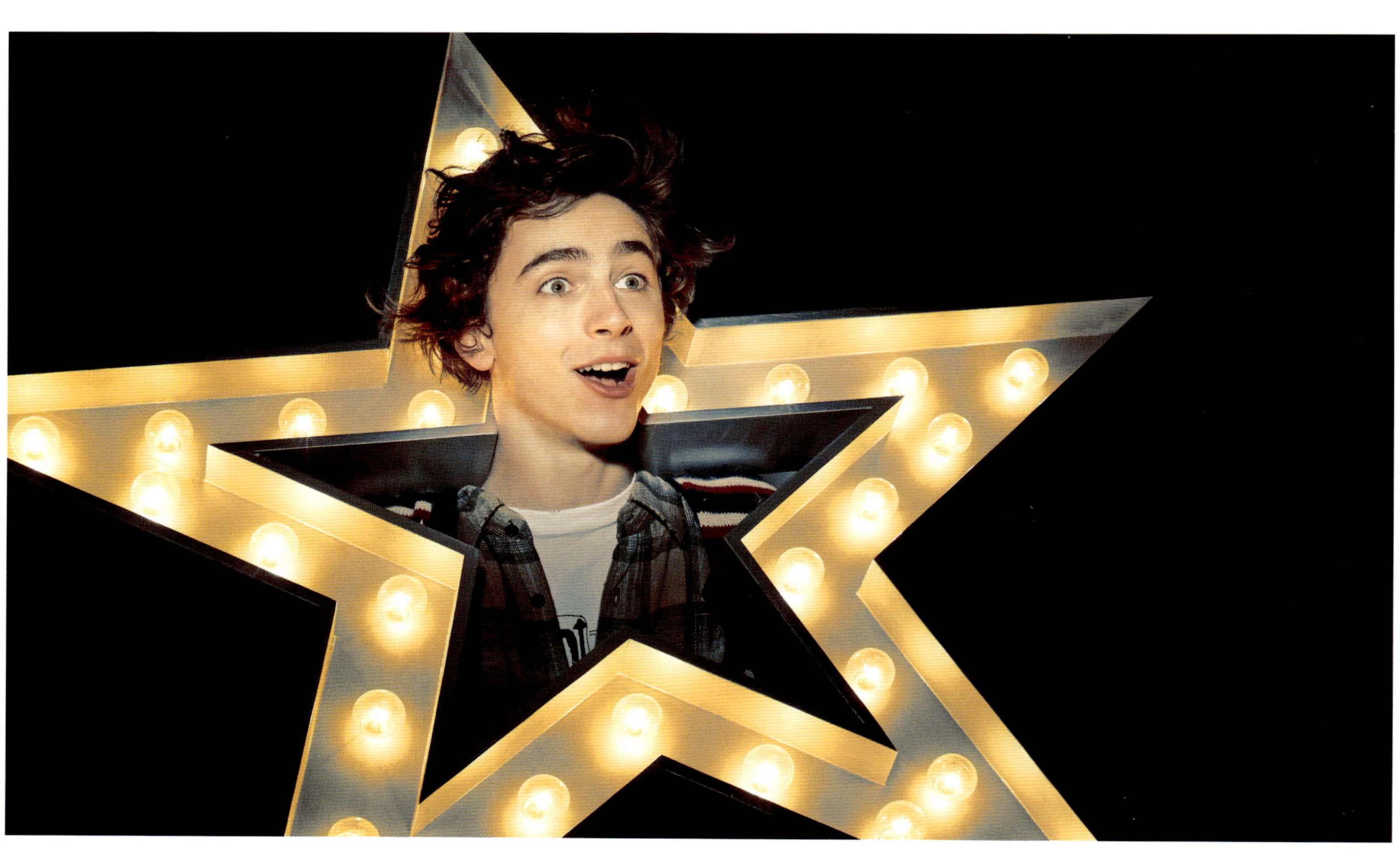

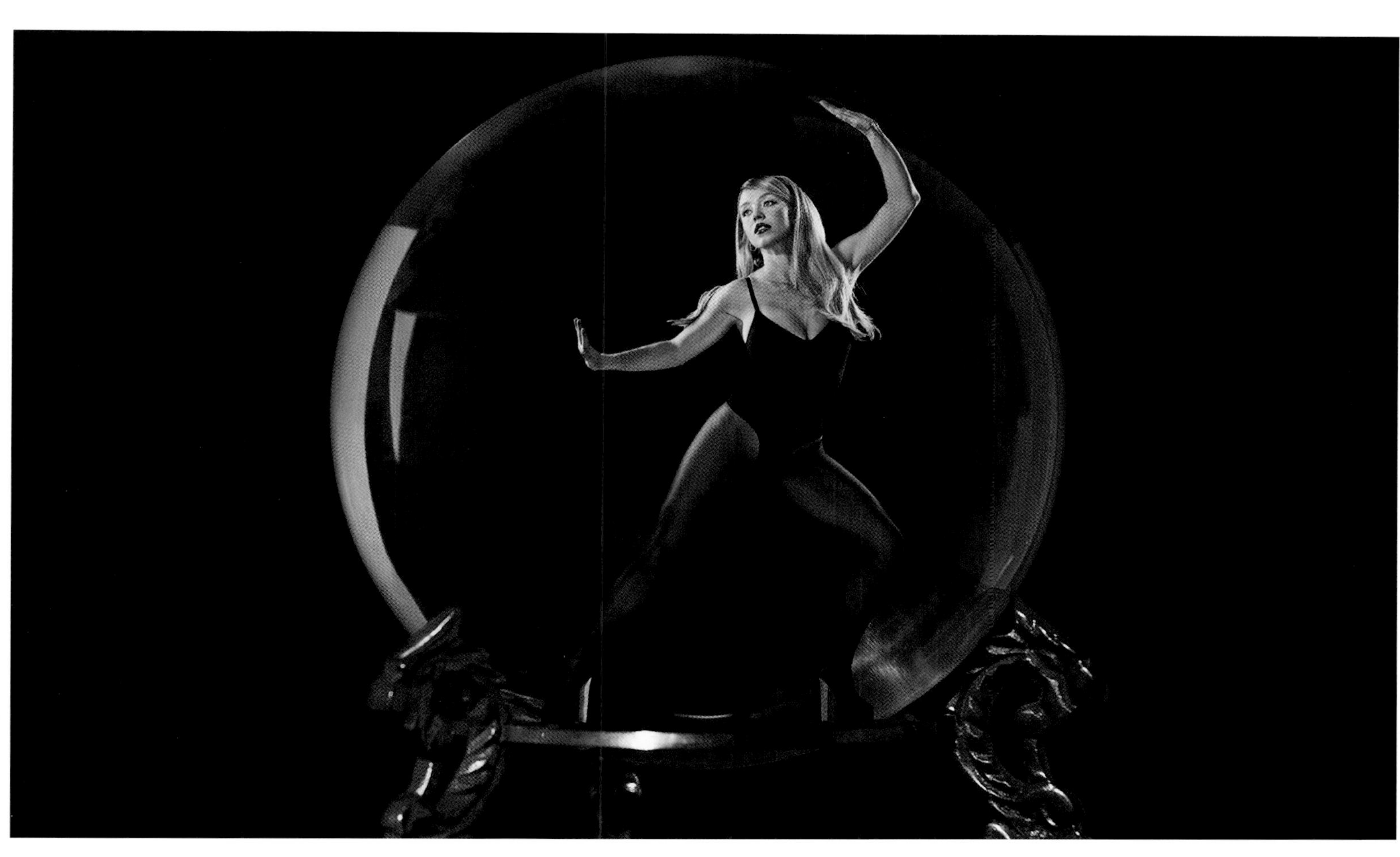

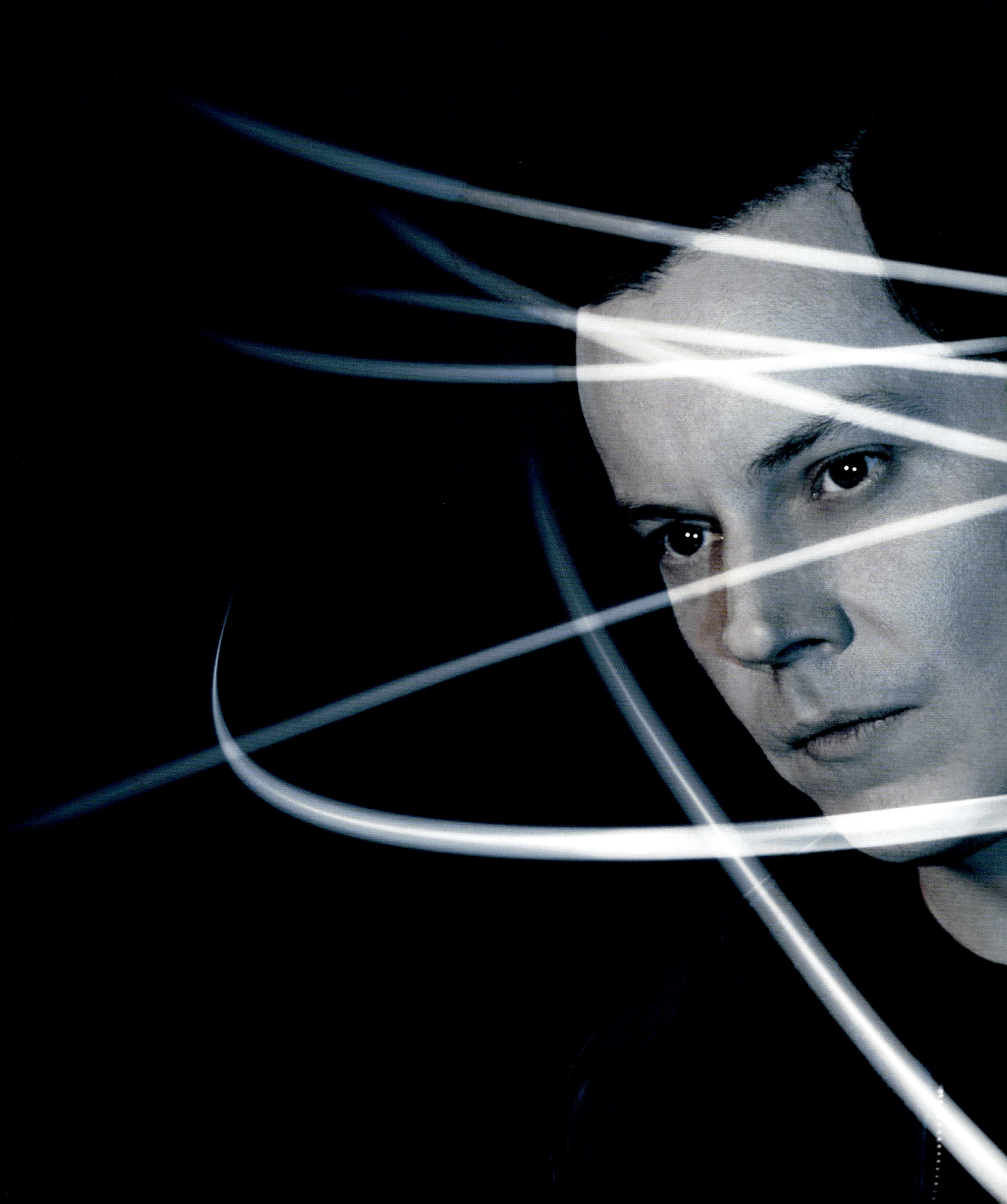

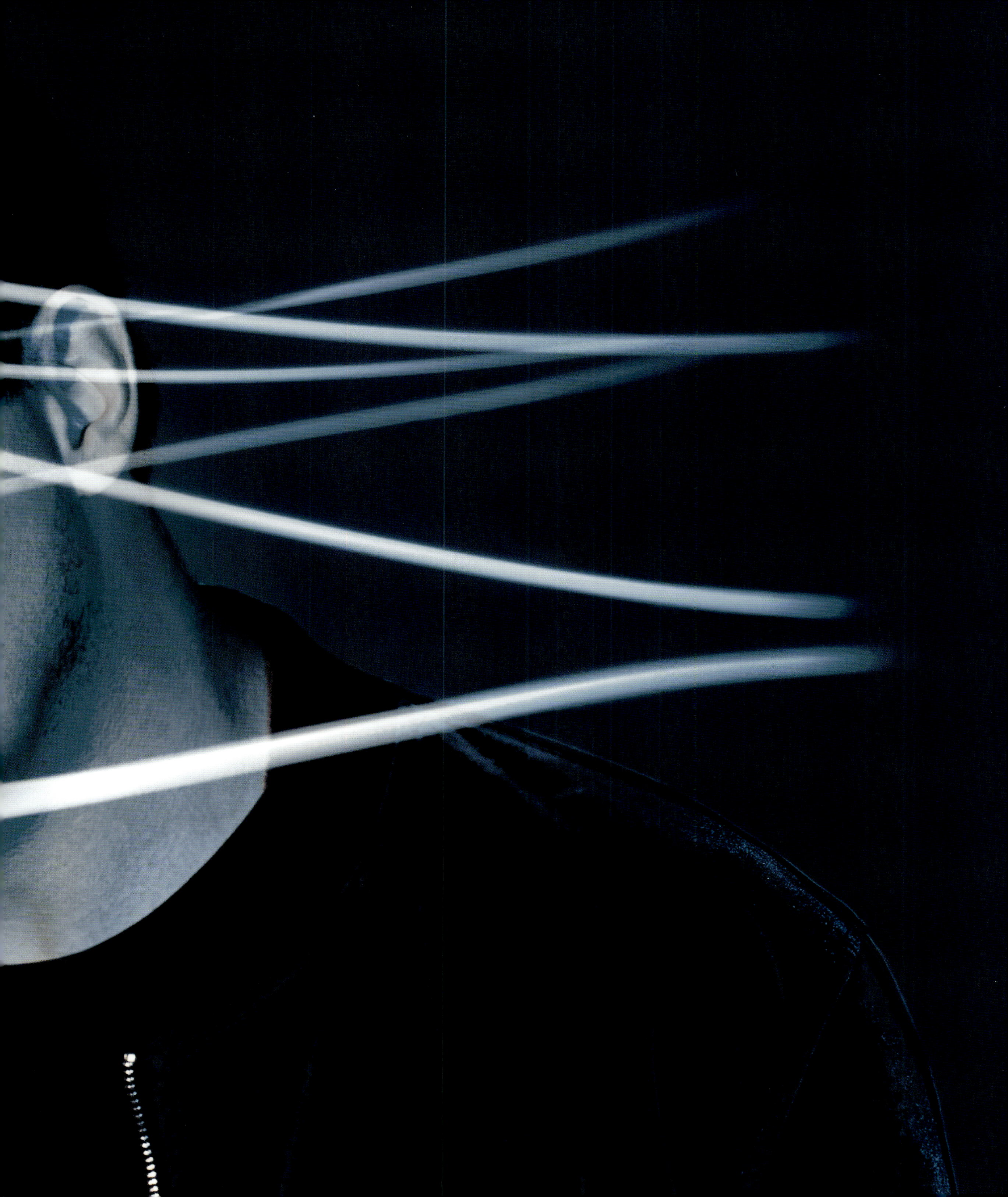

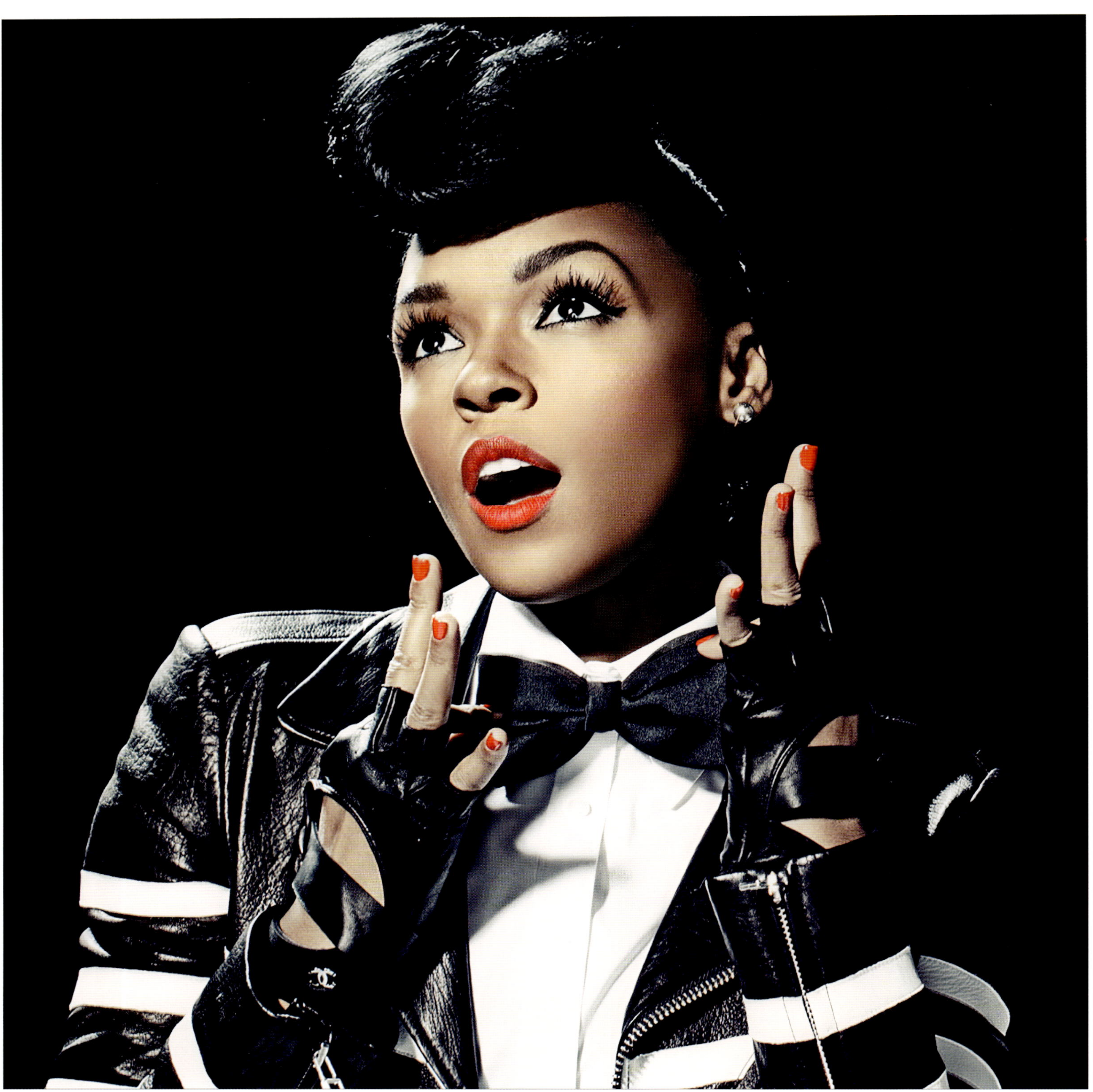

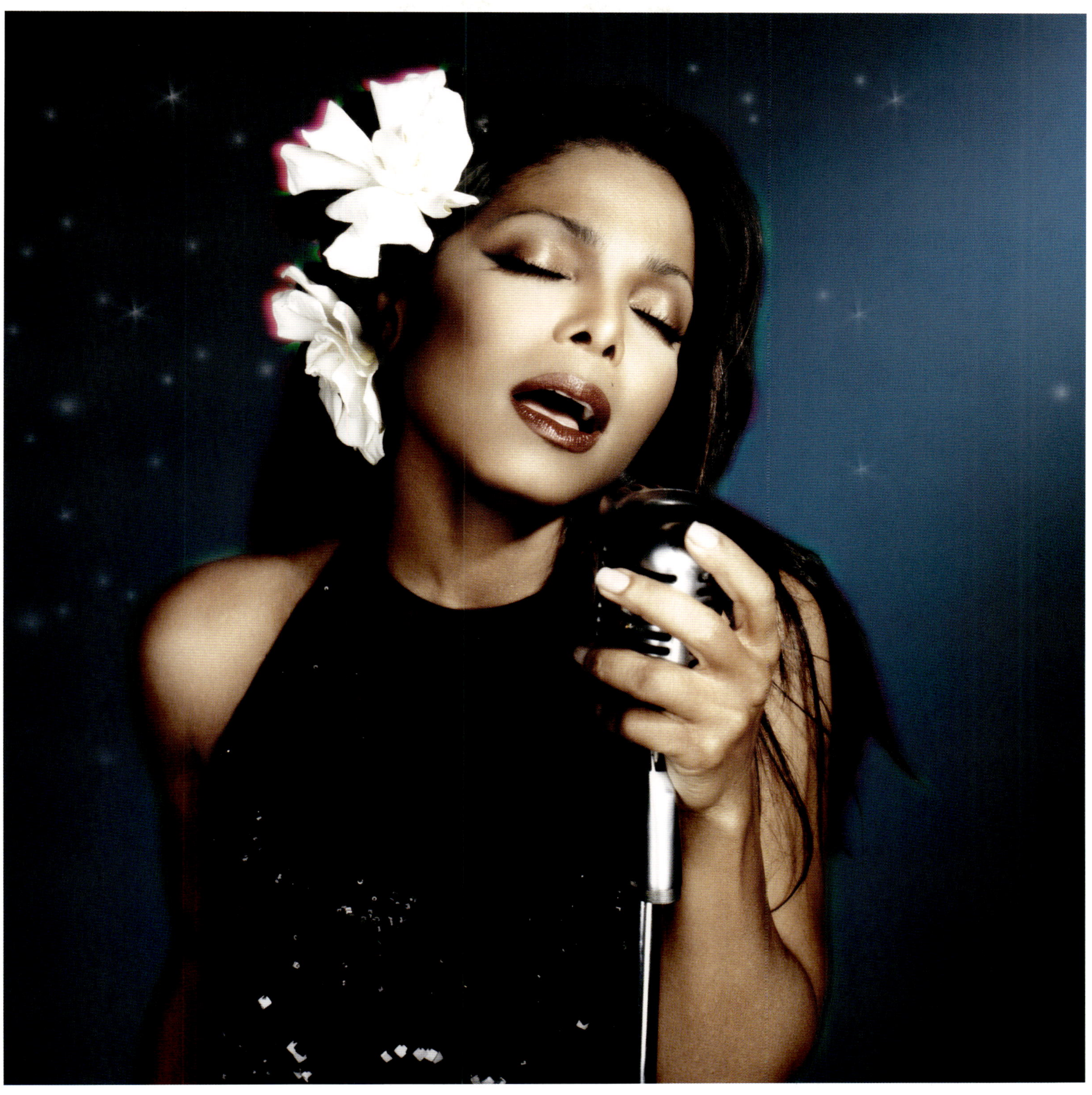

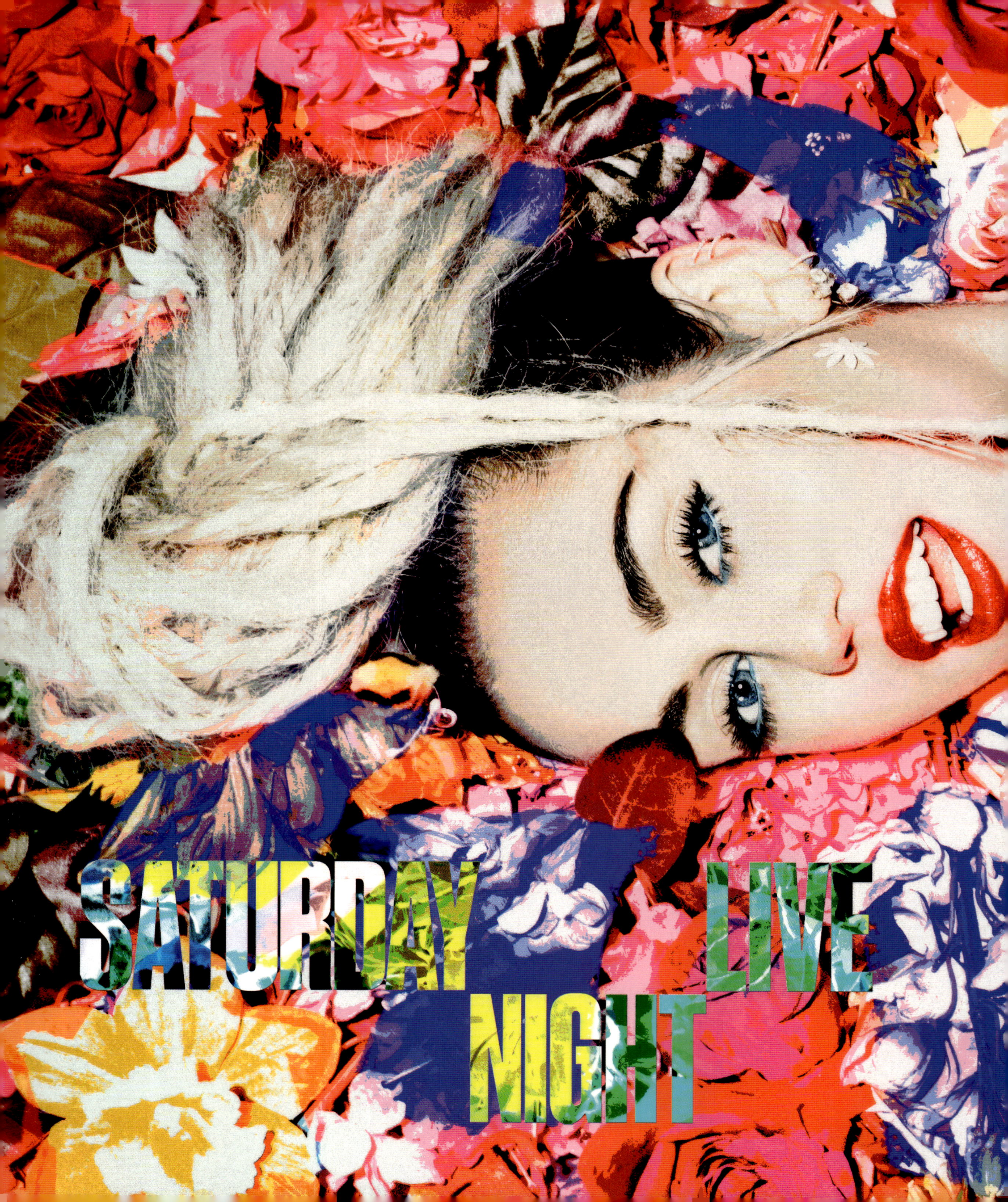
SATURDAY NIGHT LIVE

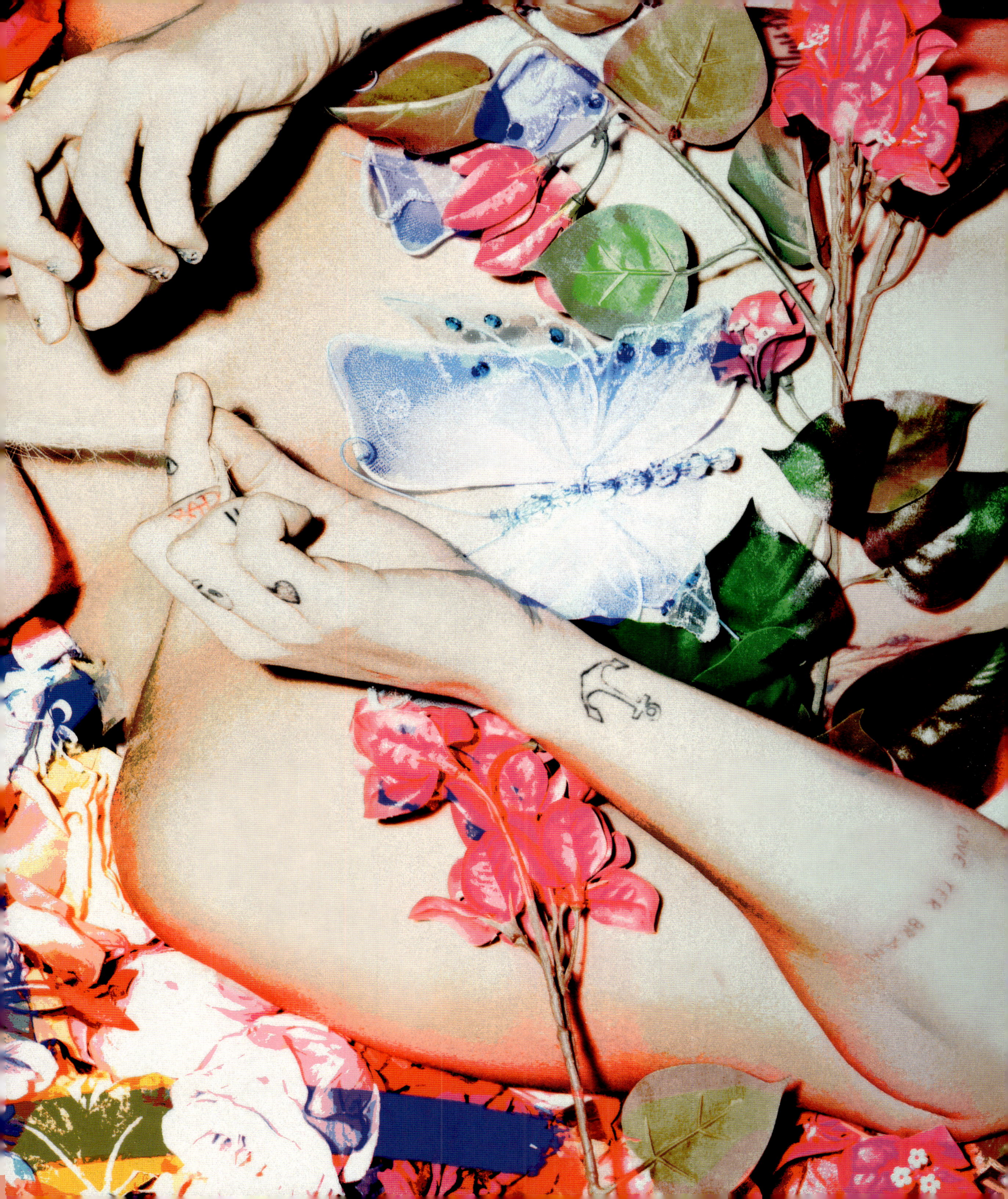

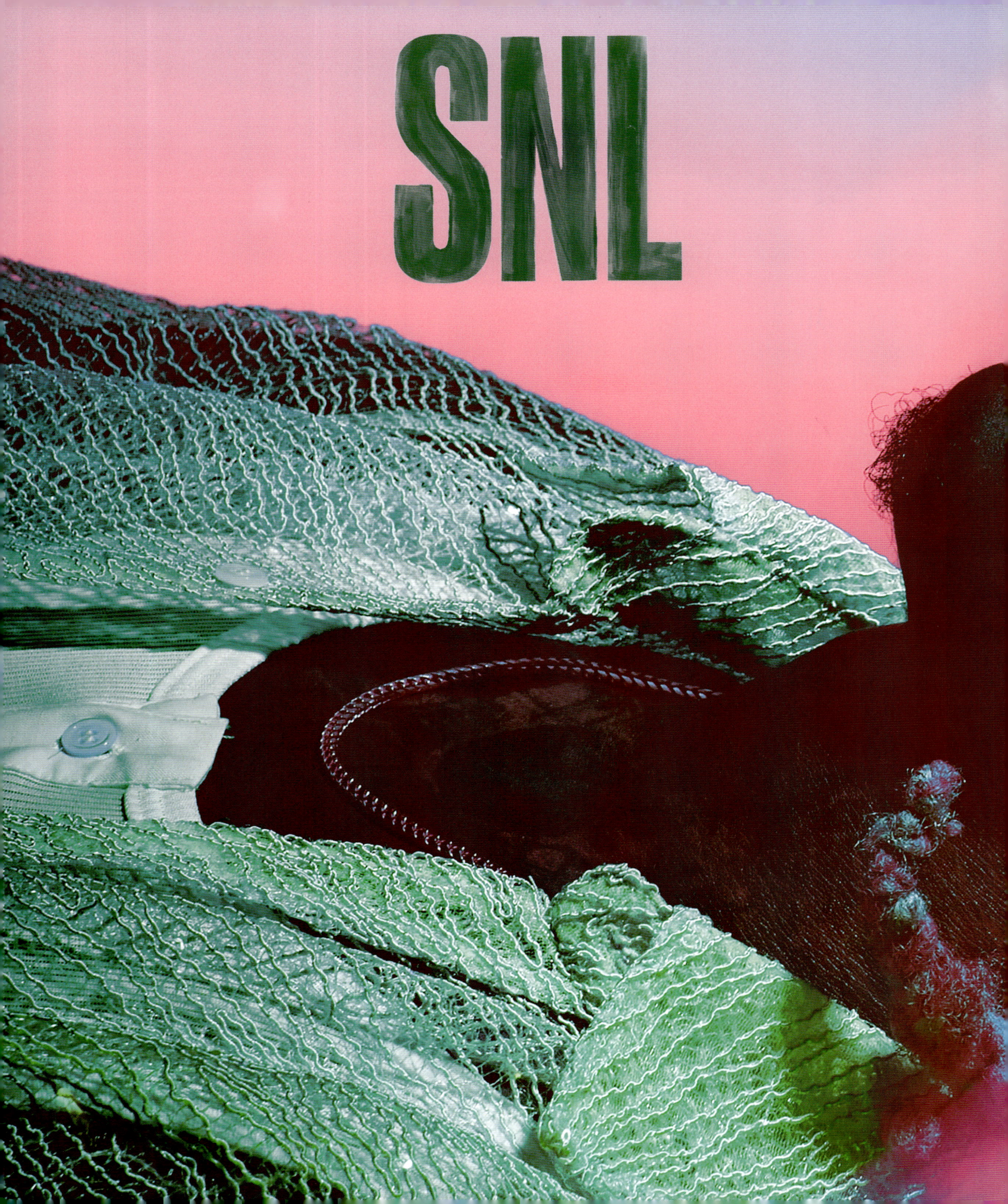
SNL

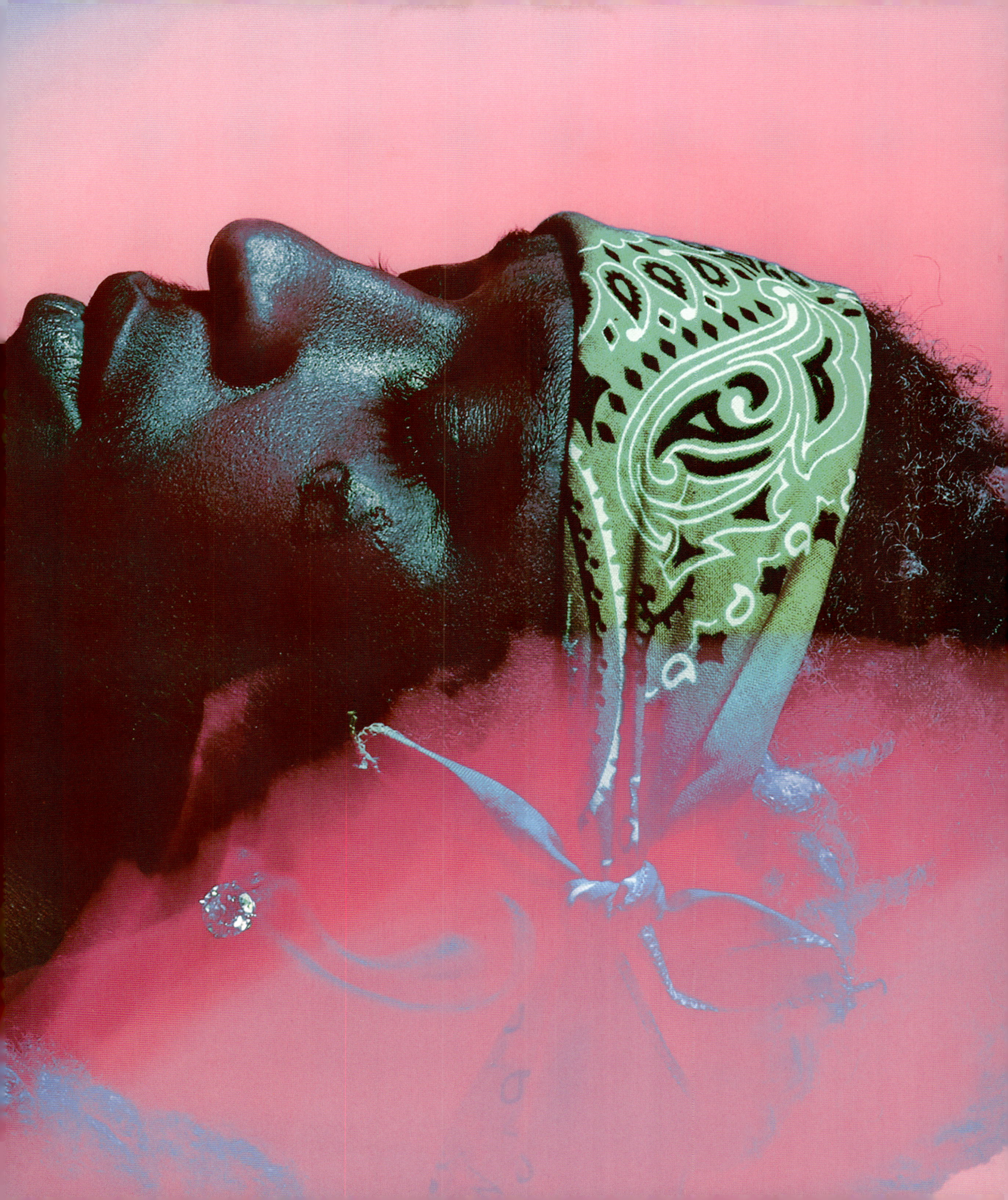

SATURDAY

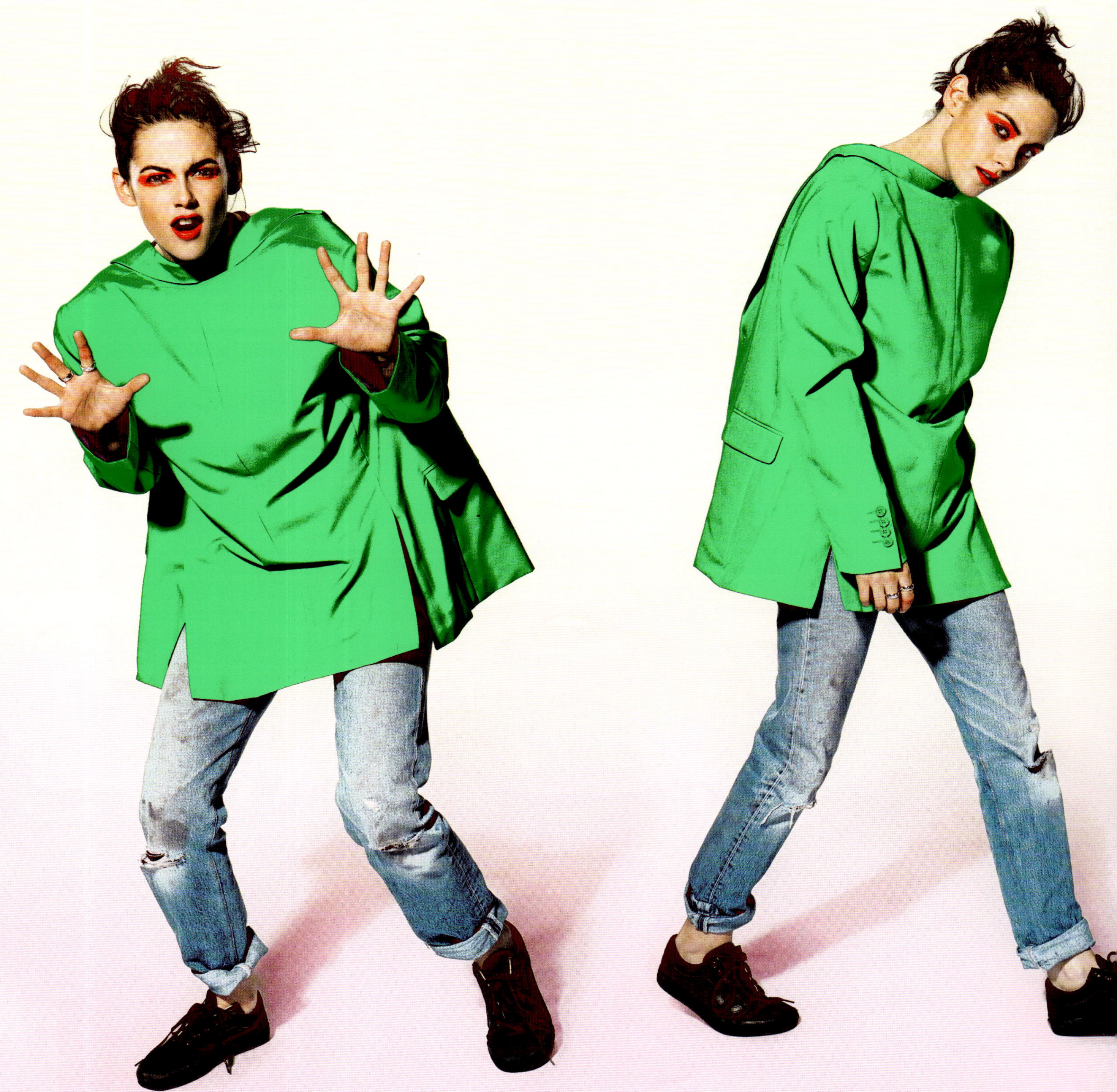

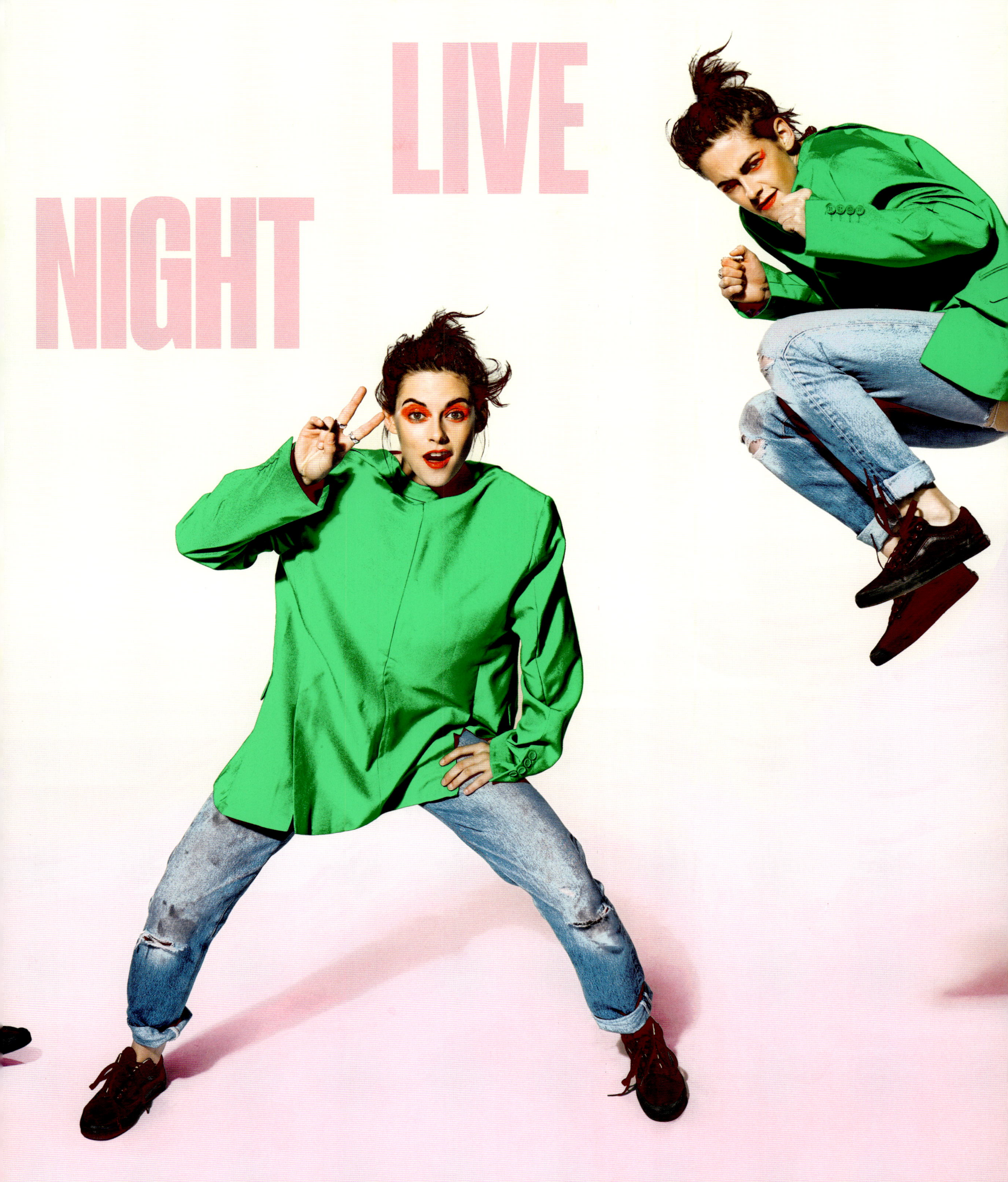
LIVE
NIGHT

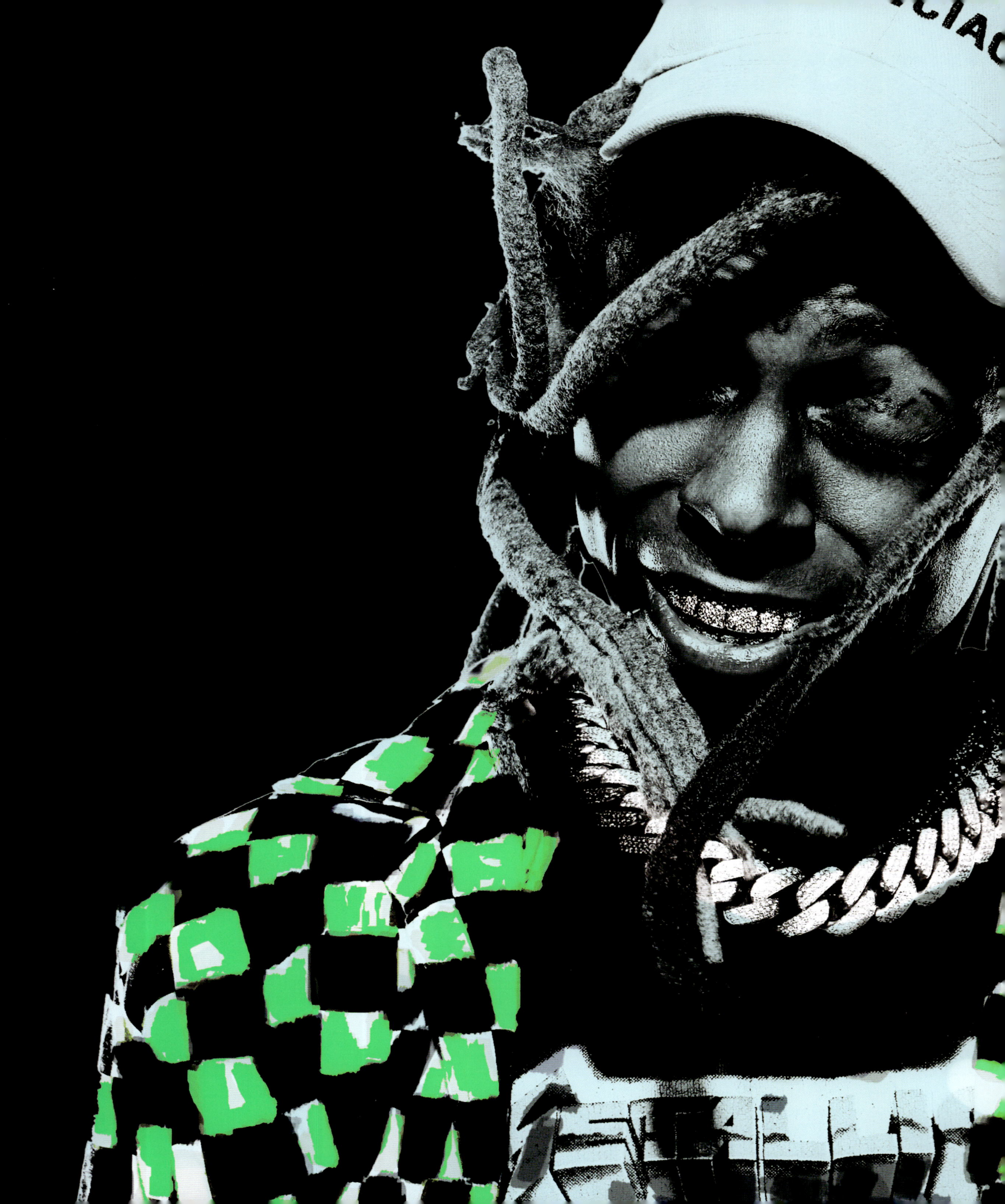

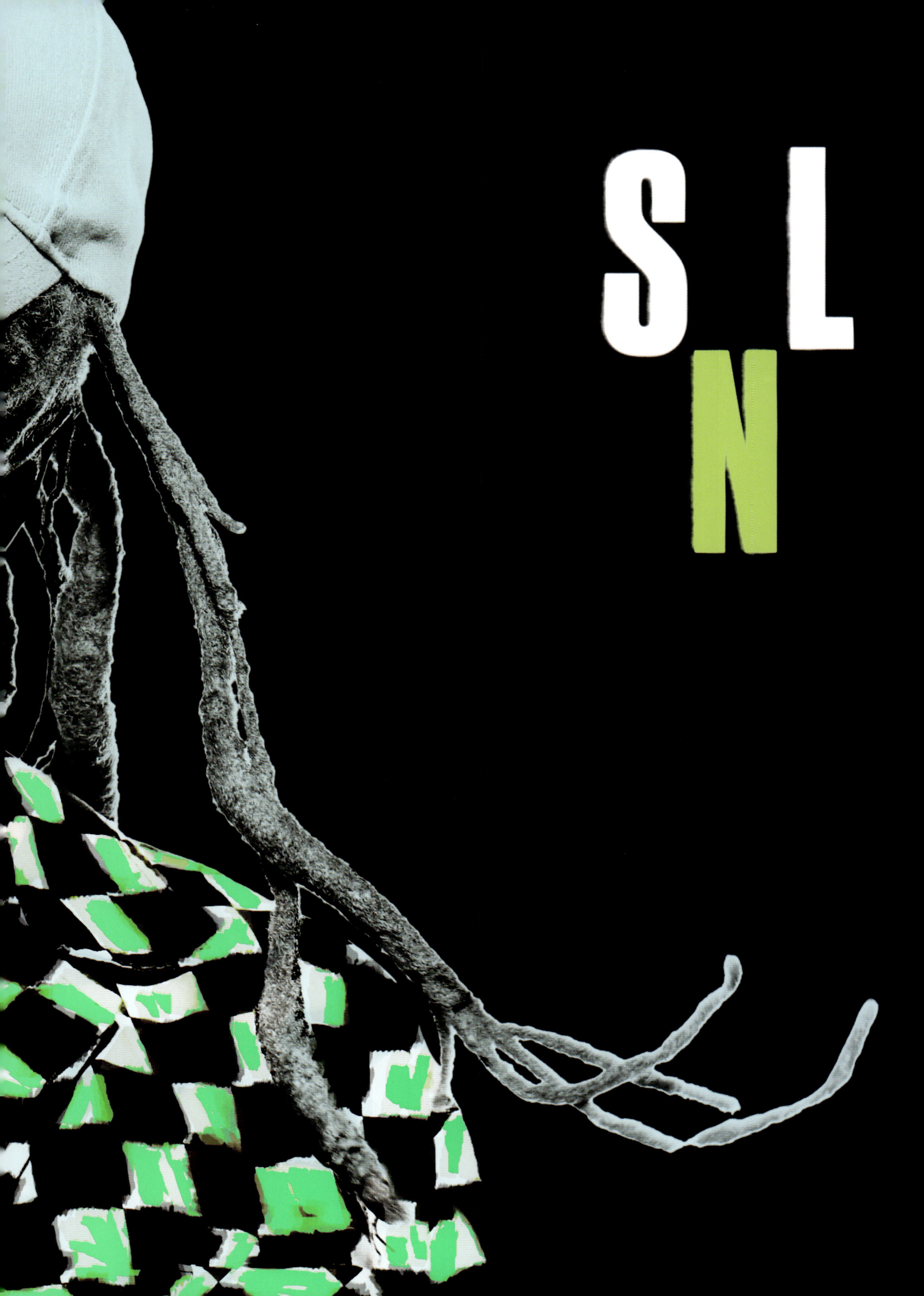
S L
N

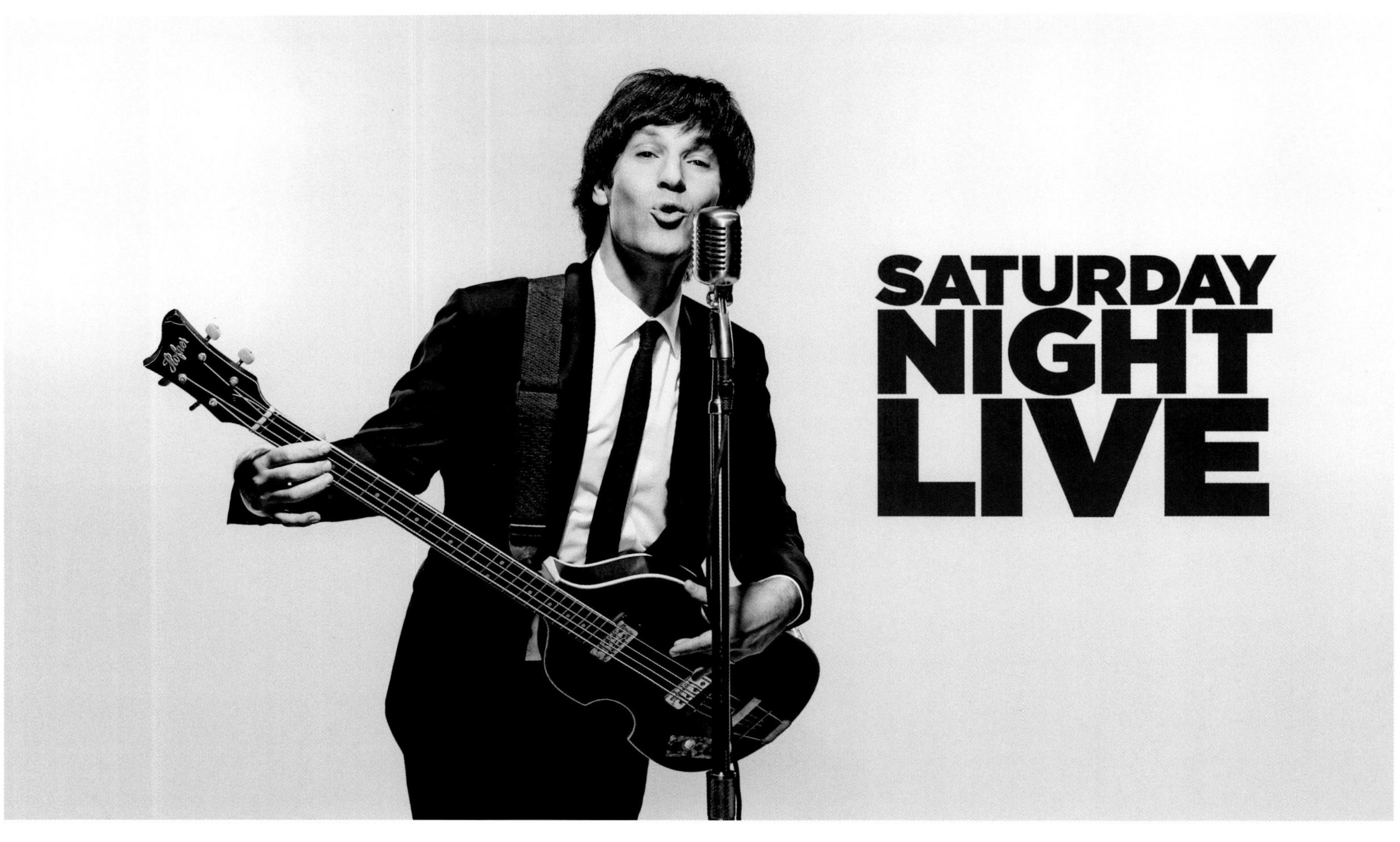
SATURDAY
NIGHT
LIVE

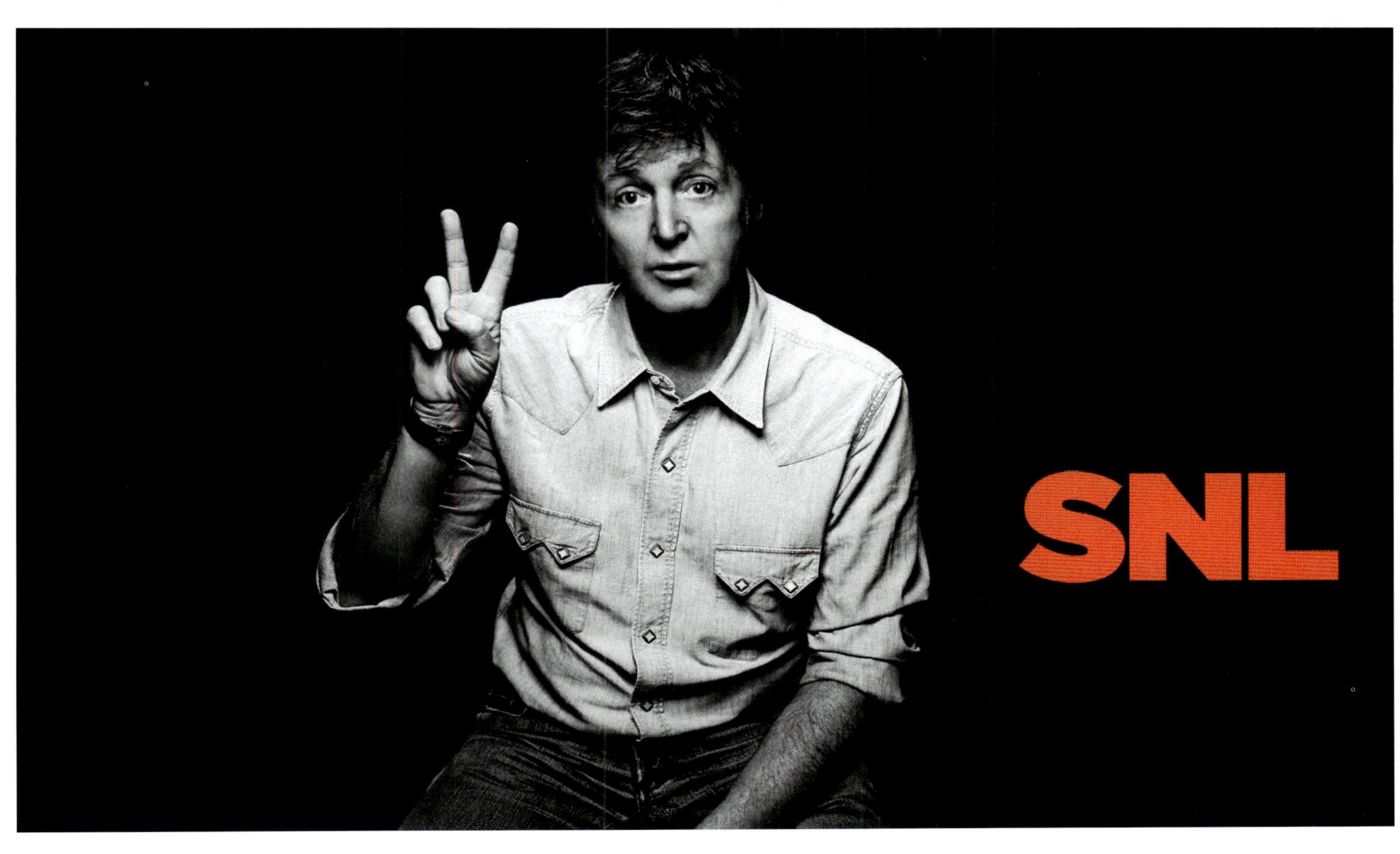
SNL

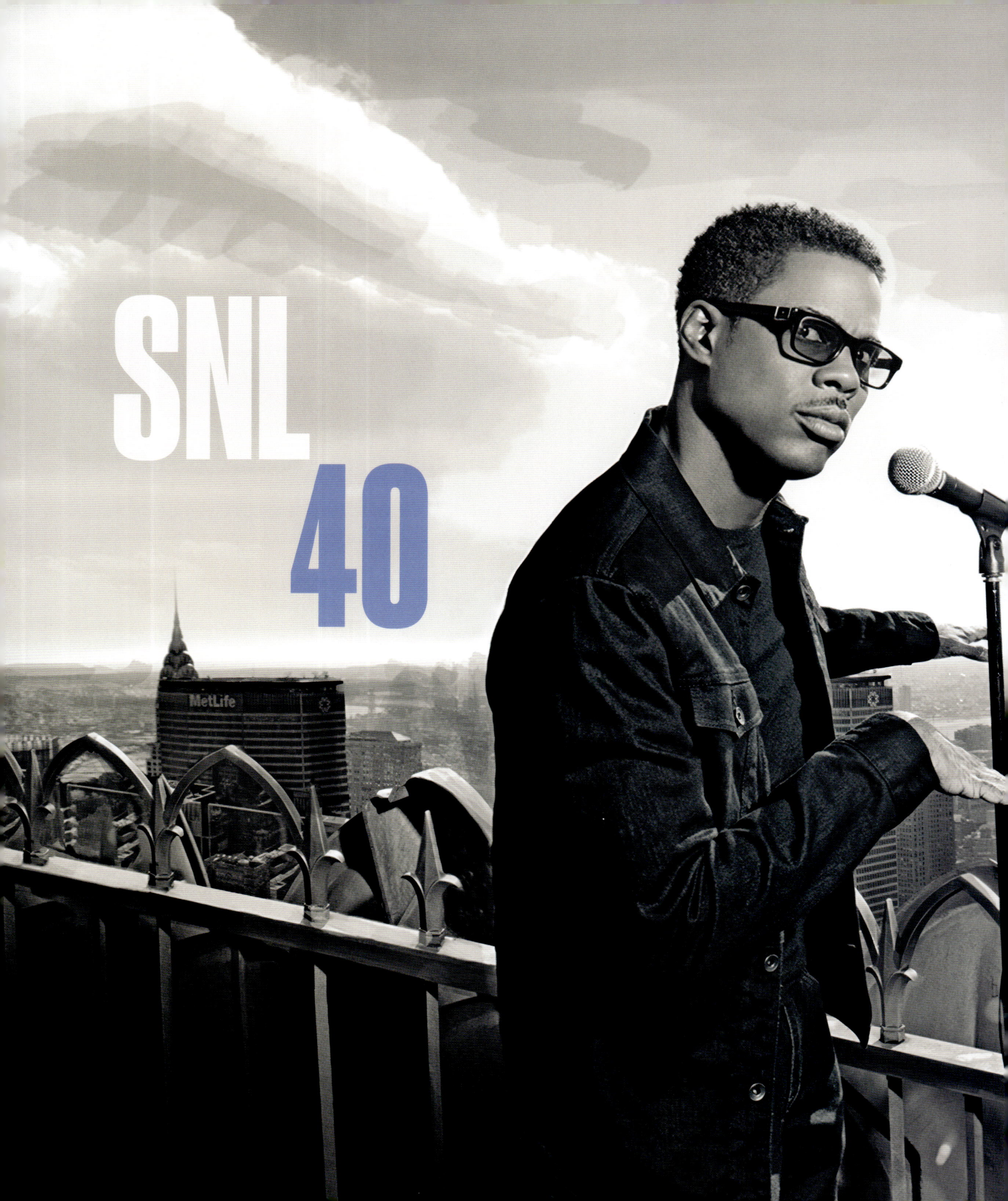
SNL
40
MetLife

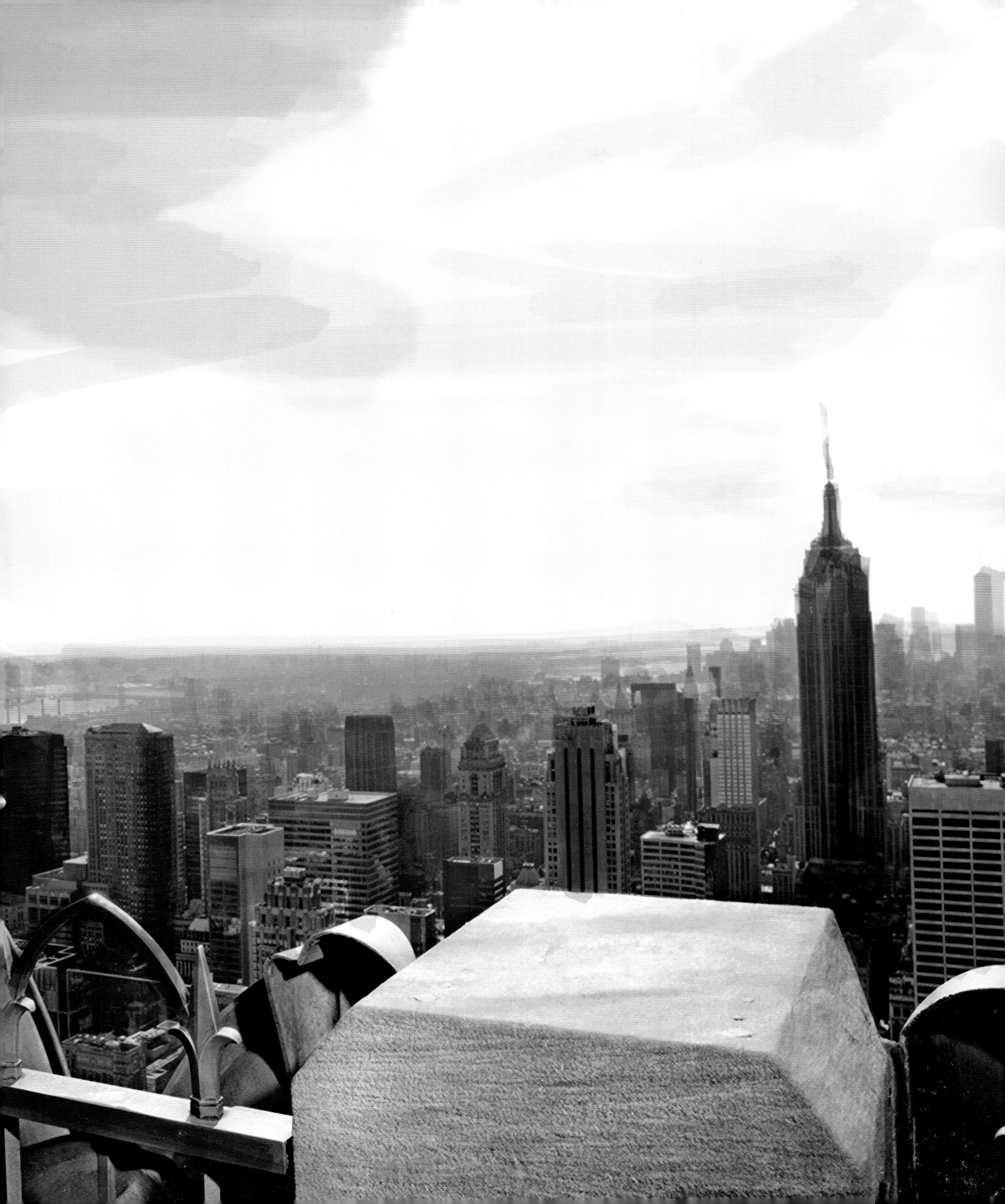

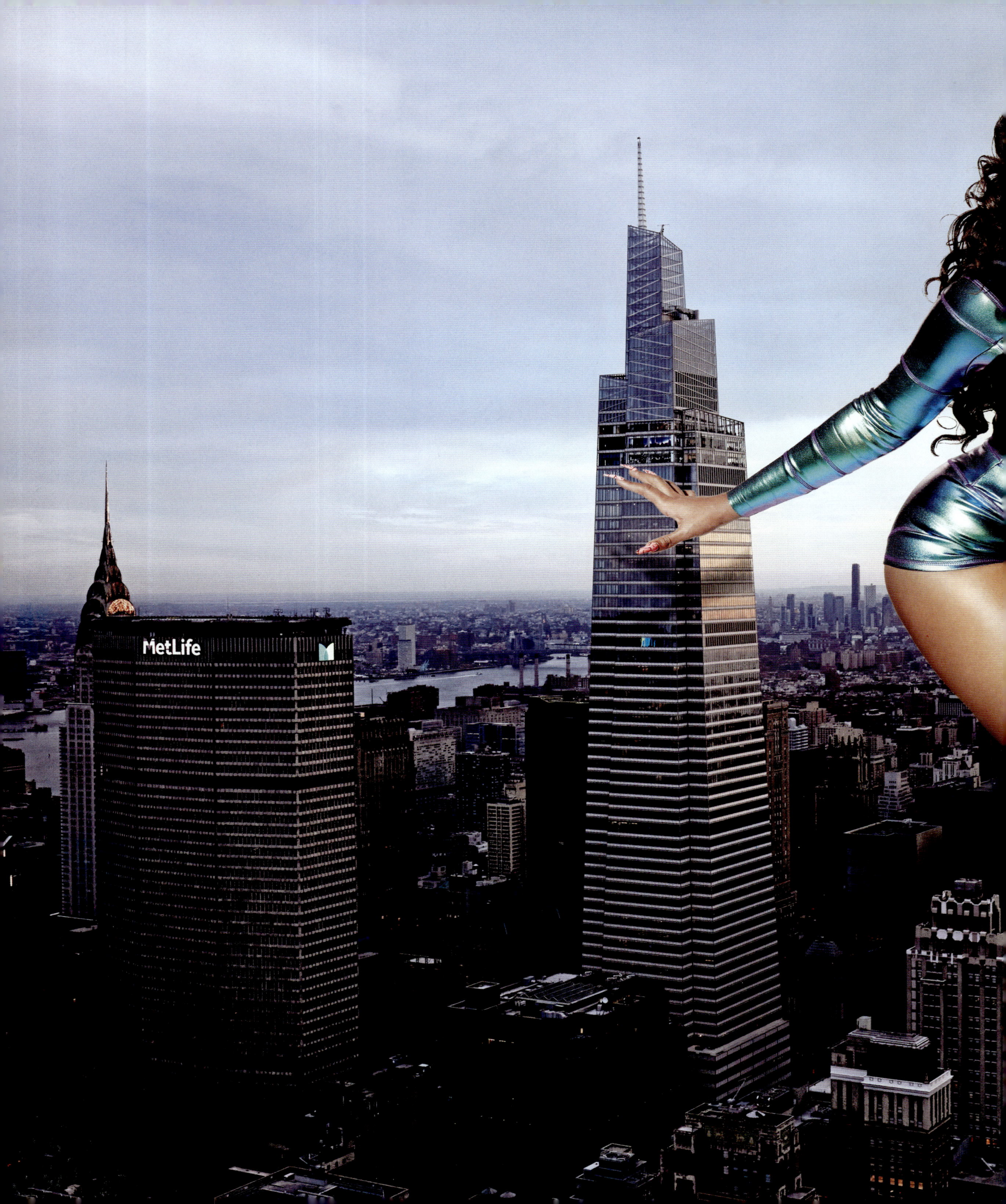
MetLife

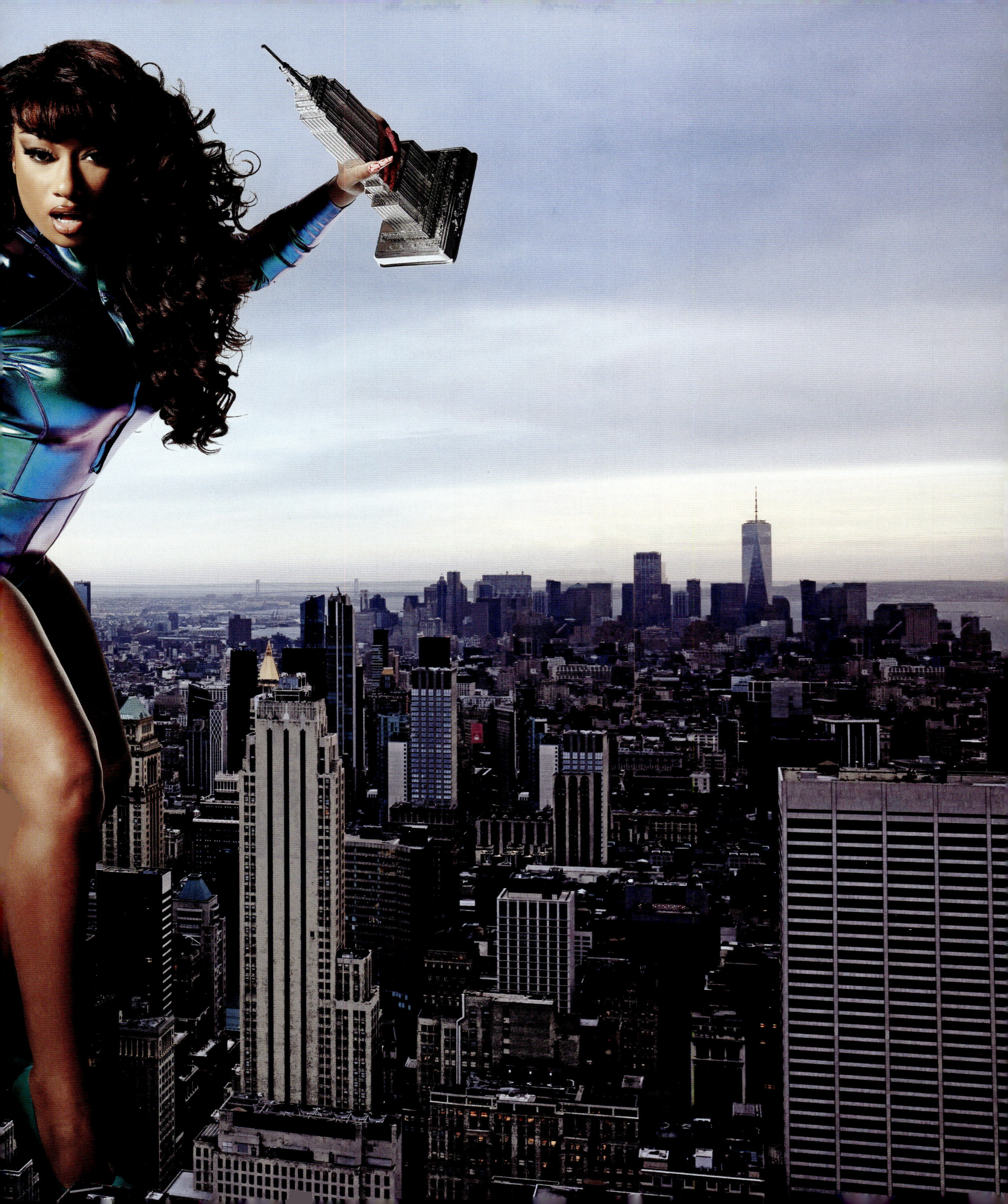

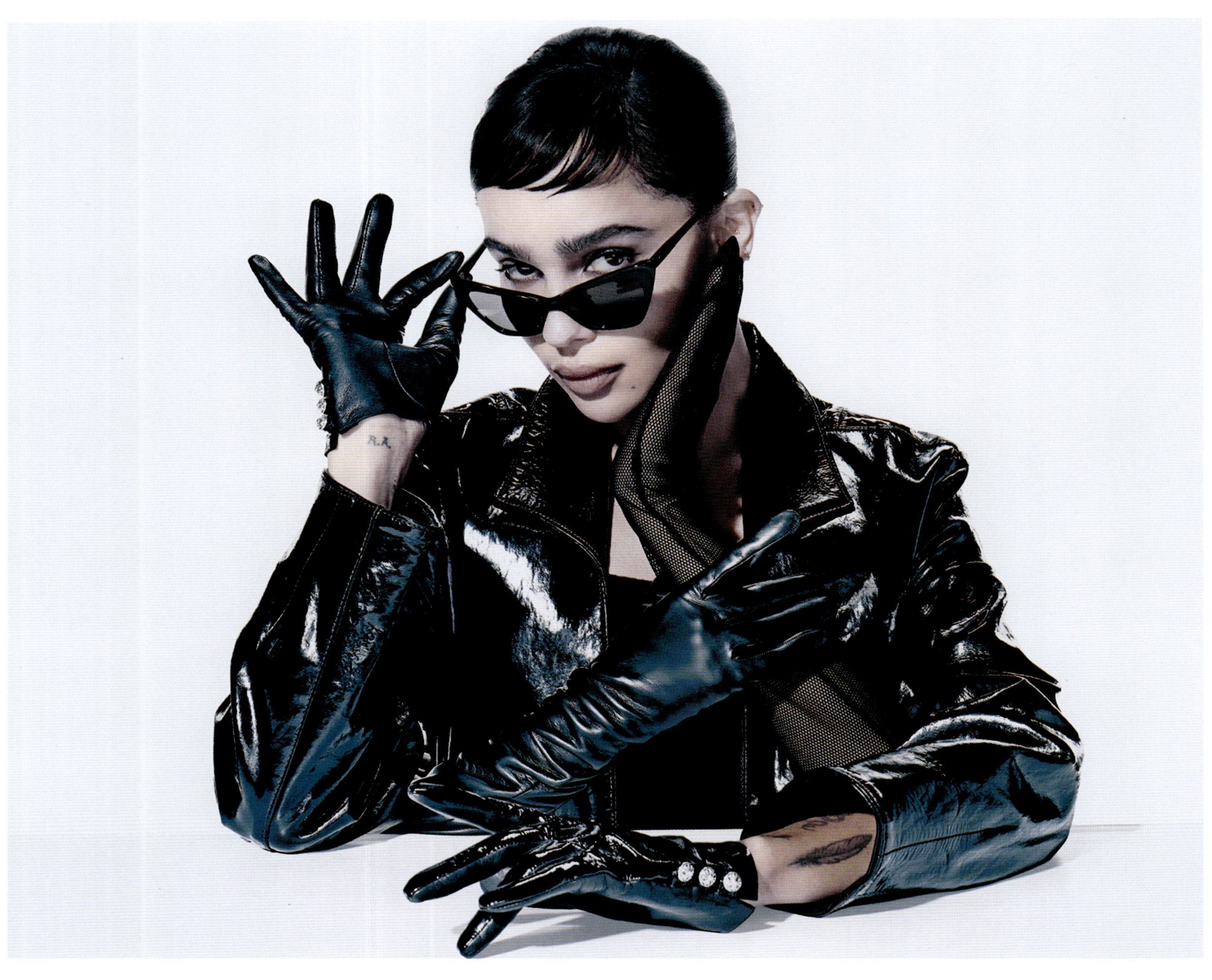

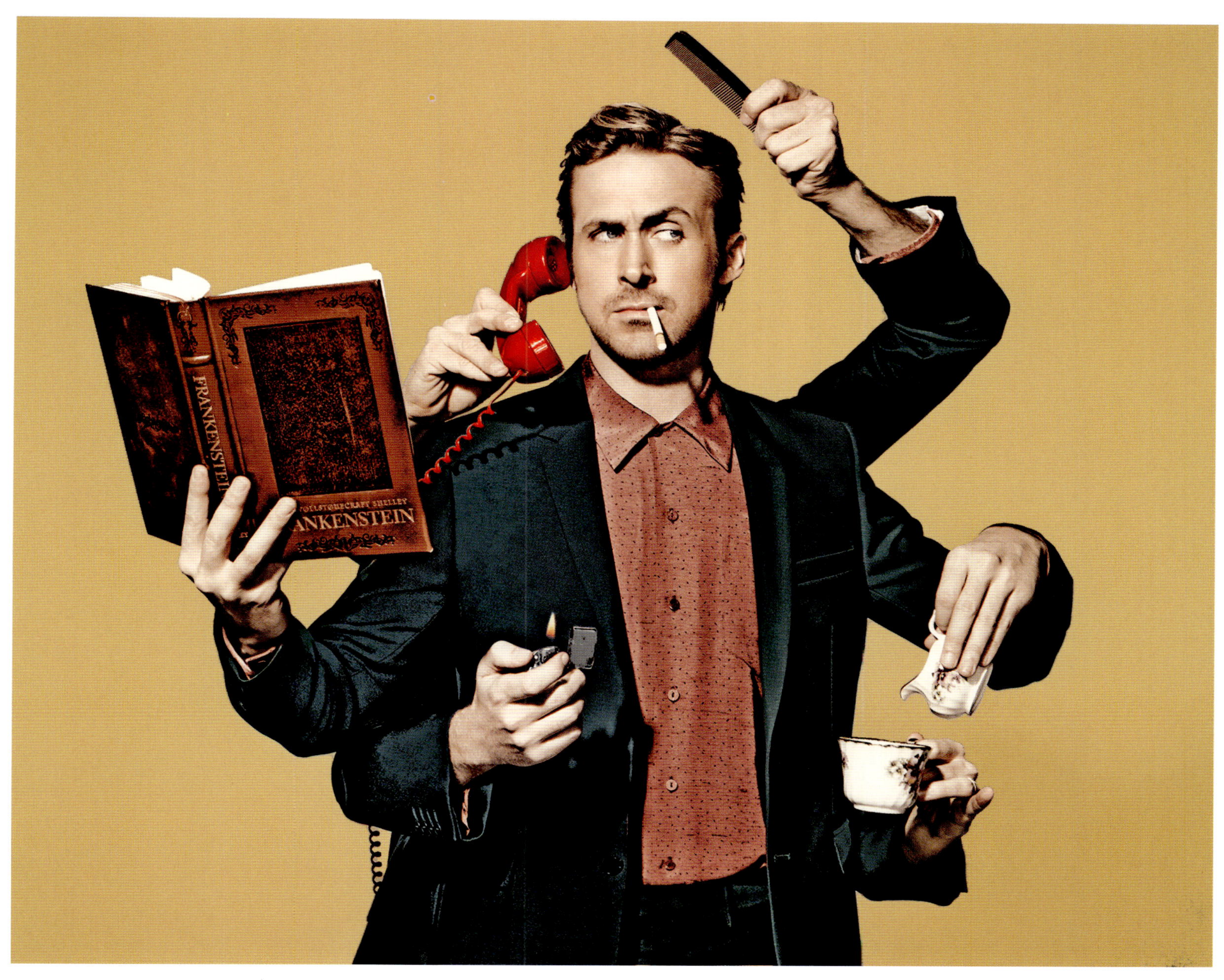
FRANKENSTEIN

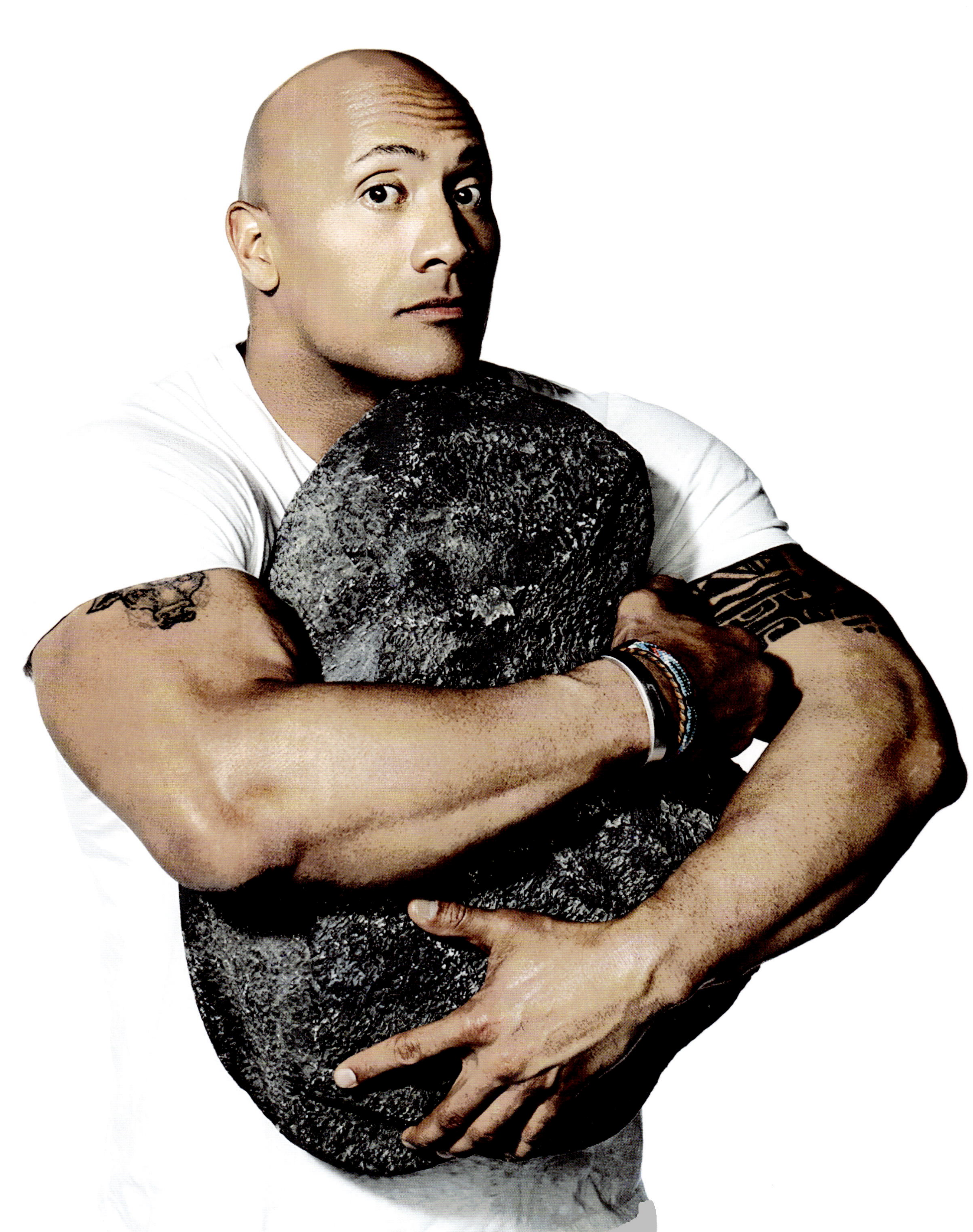

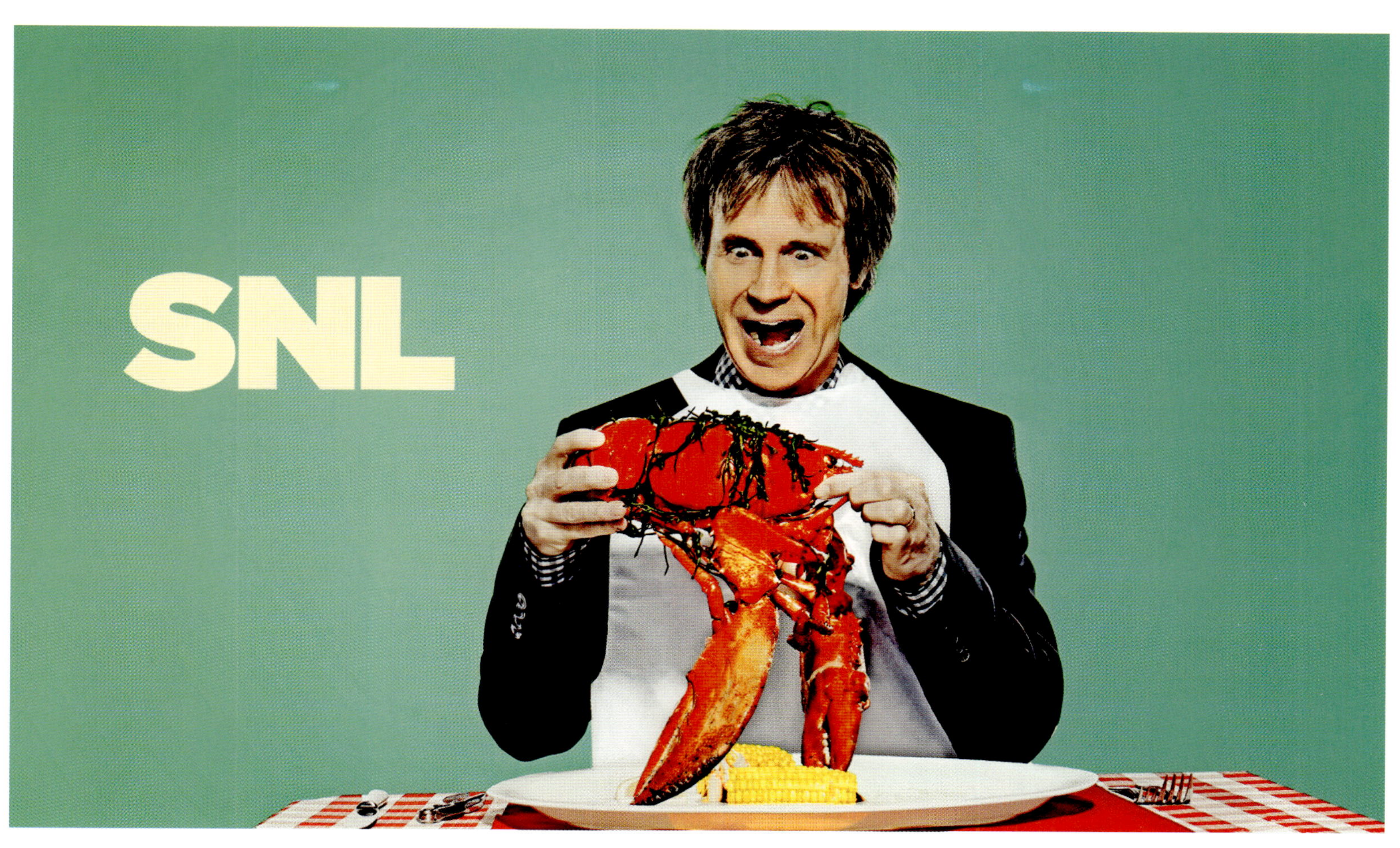
SNL

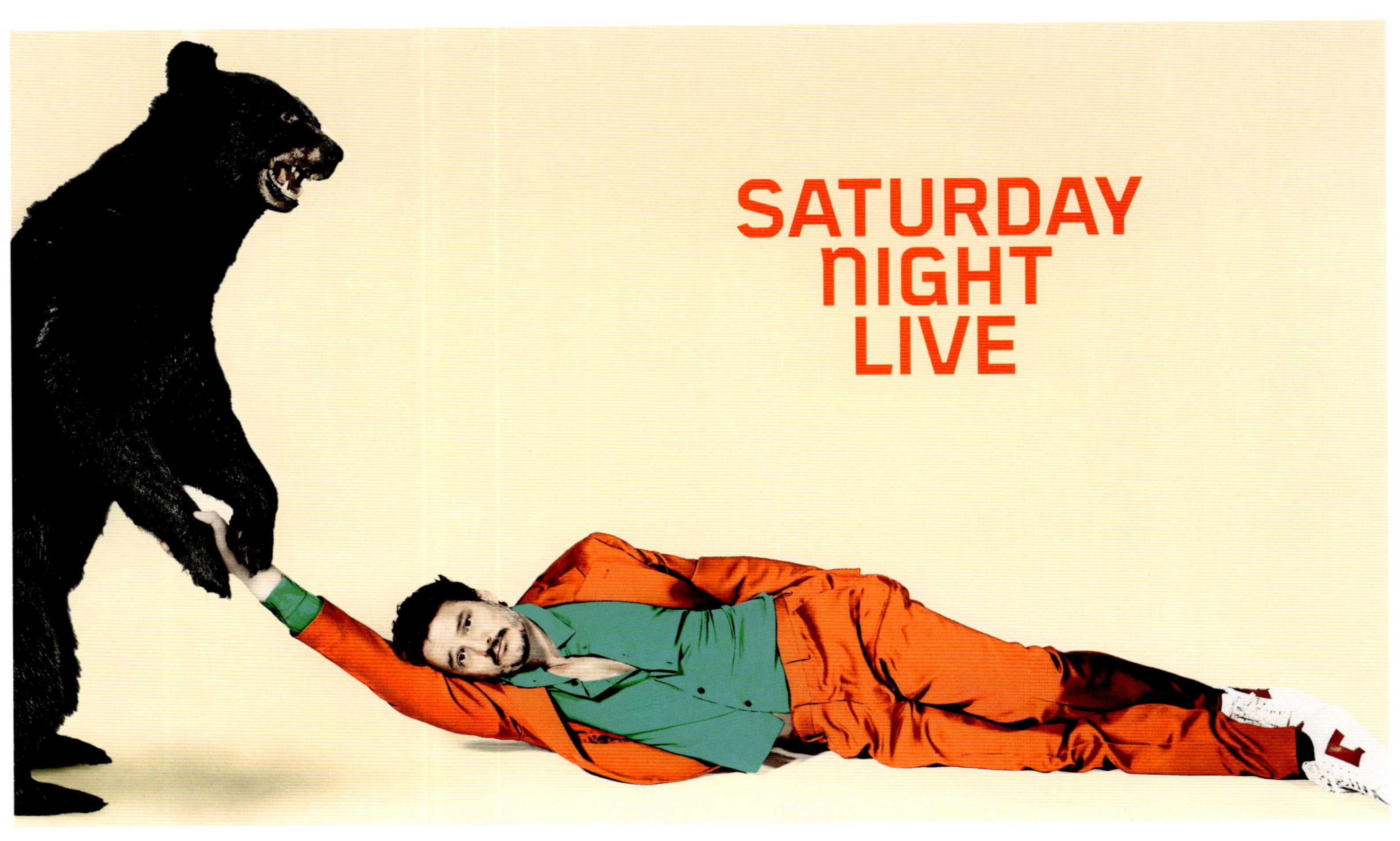
SATURDAY
NIGHT
LIVE

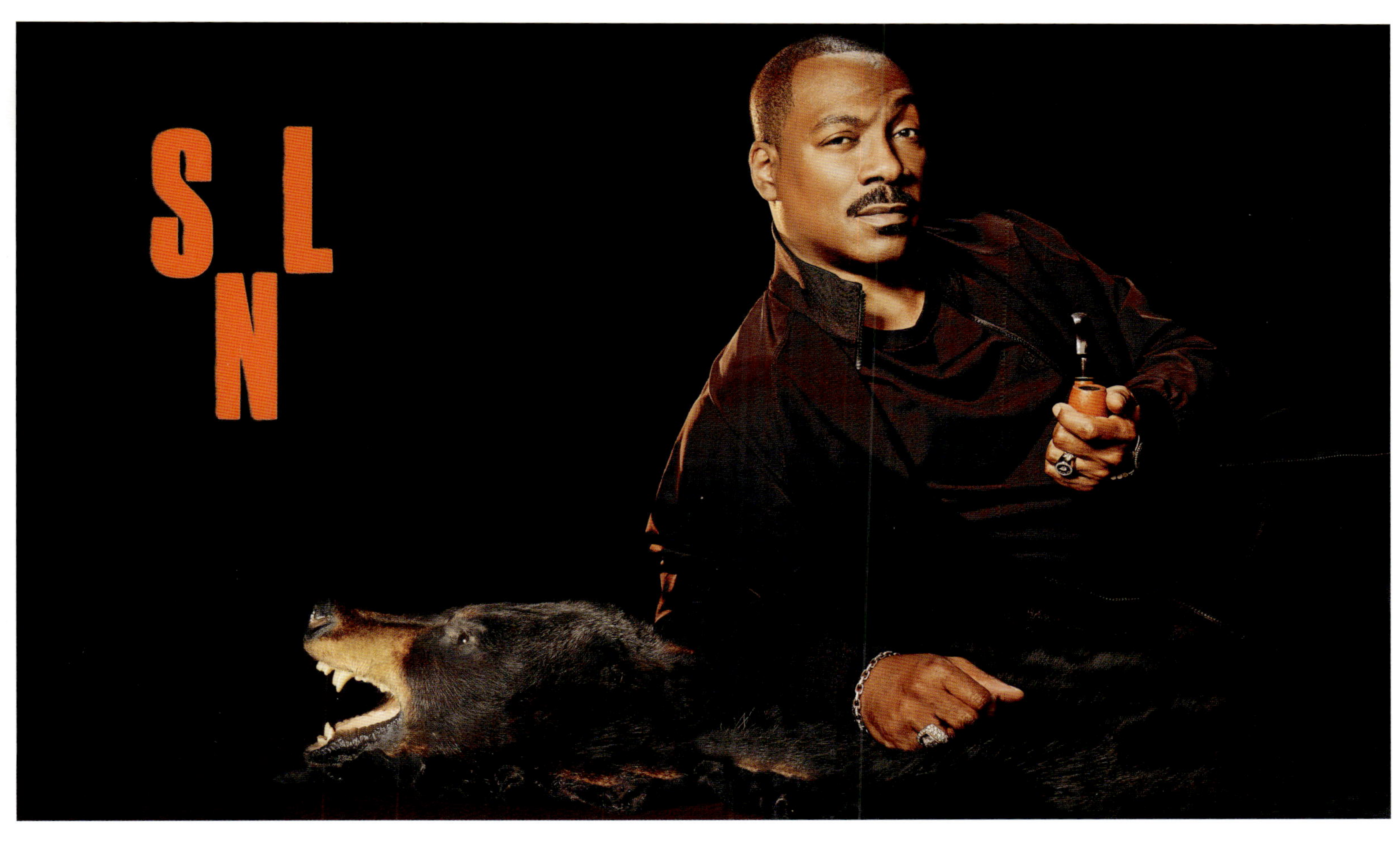
SNL

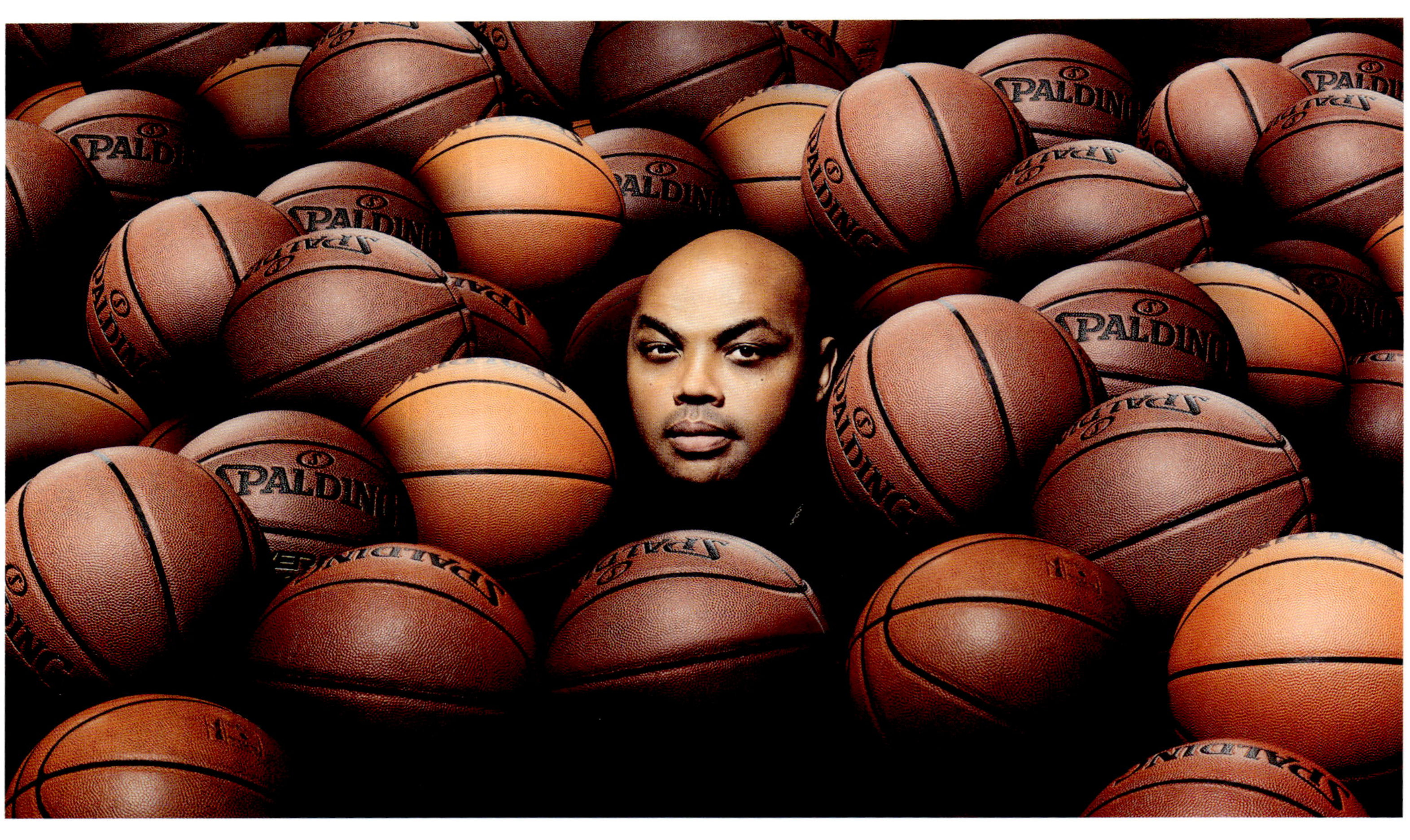

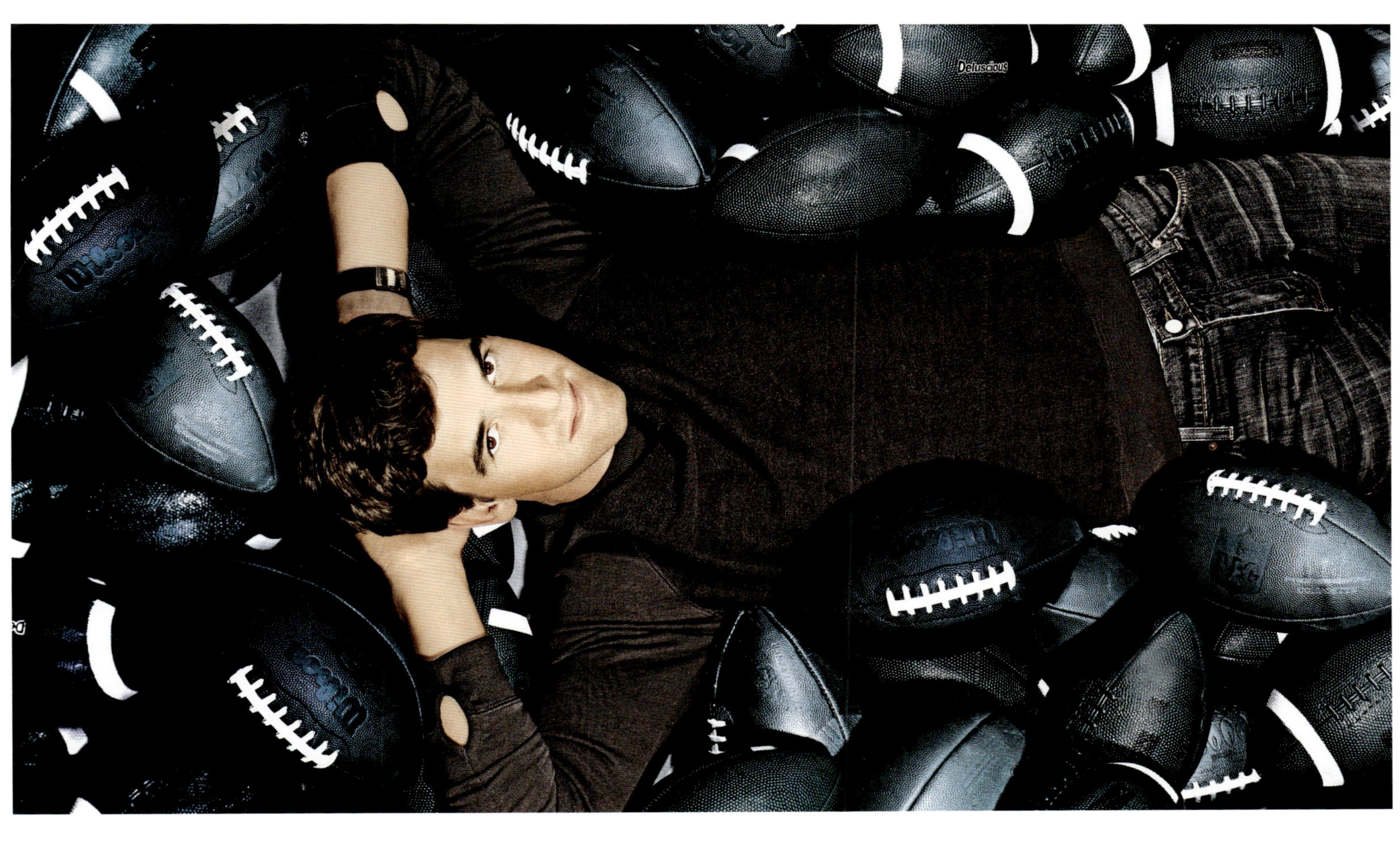
Deluscious

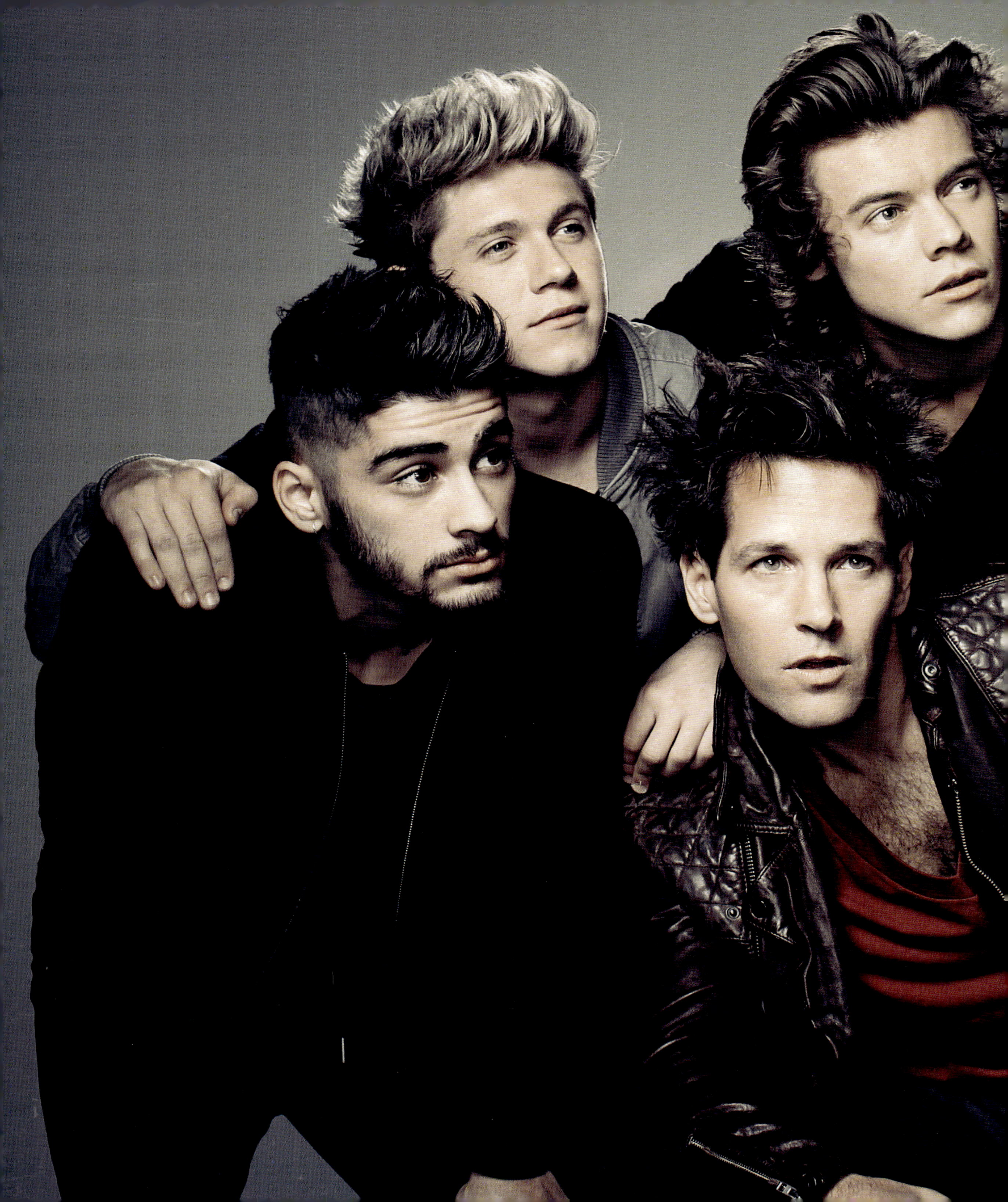

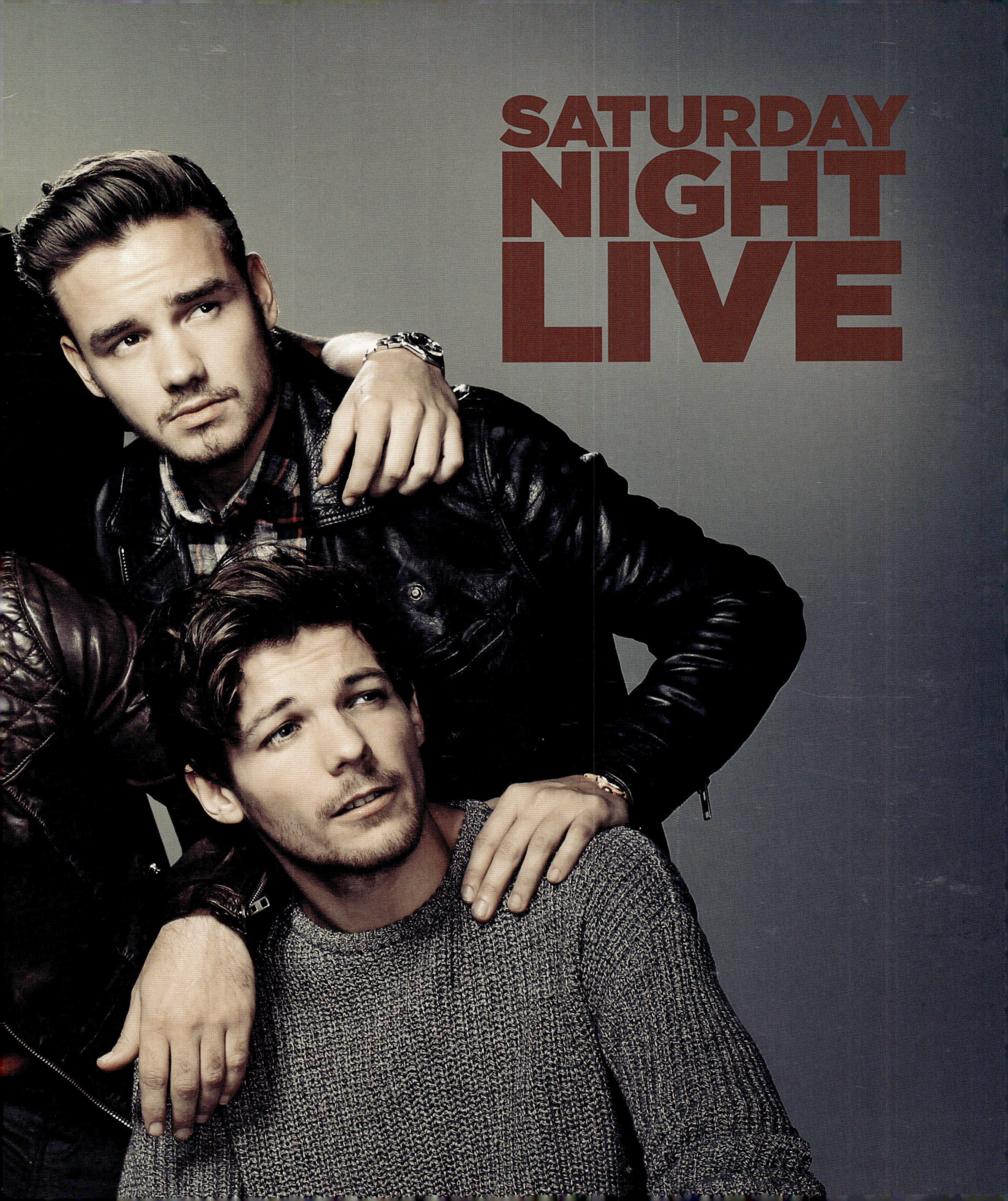
SATURDAY
NIGHT
LIVE

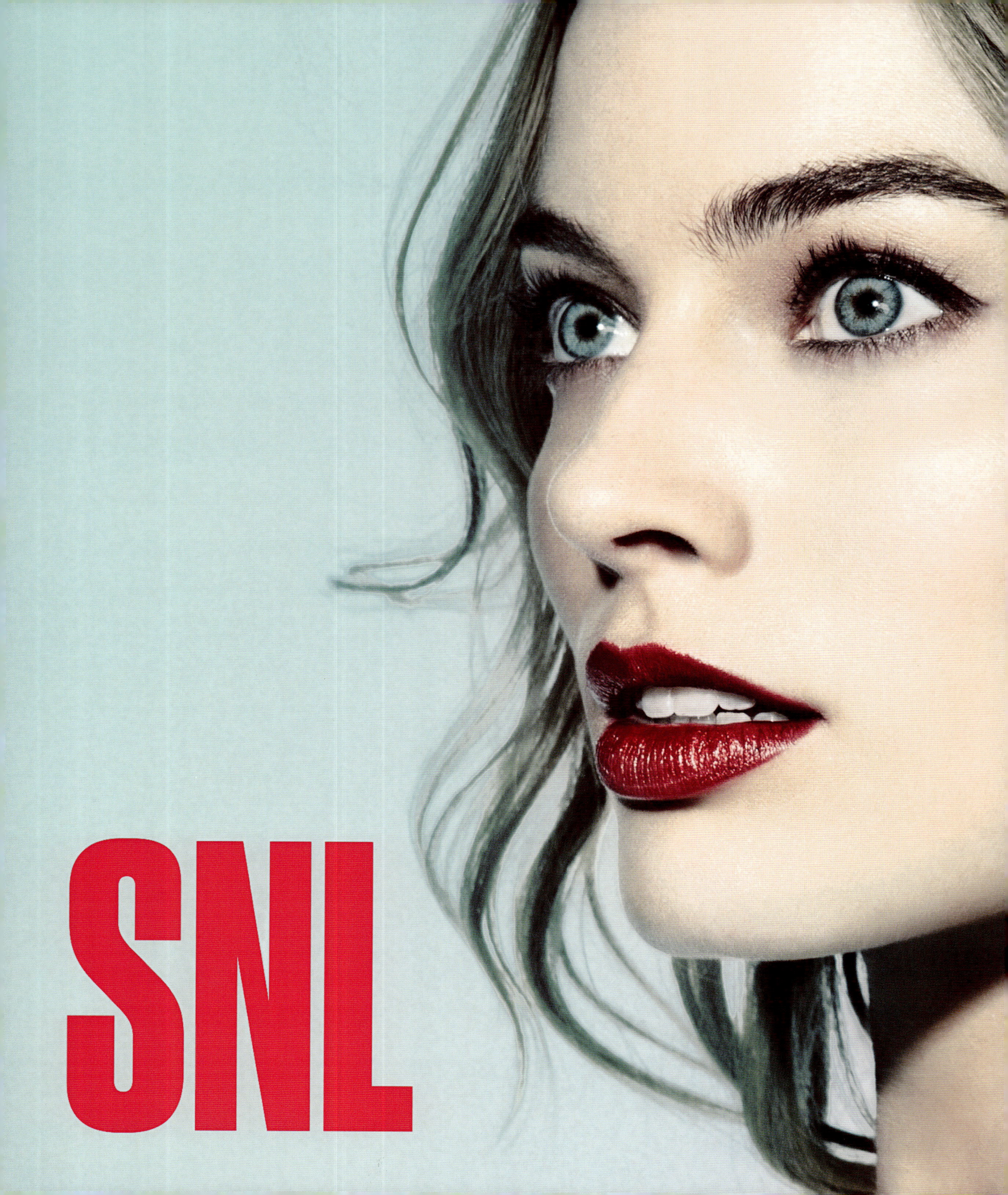
SNL

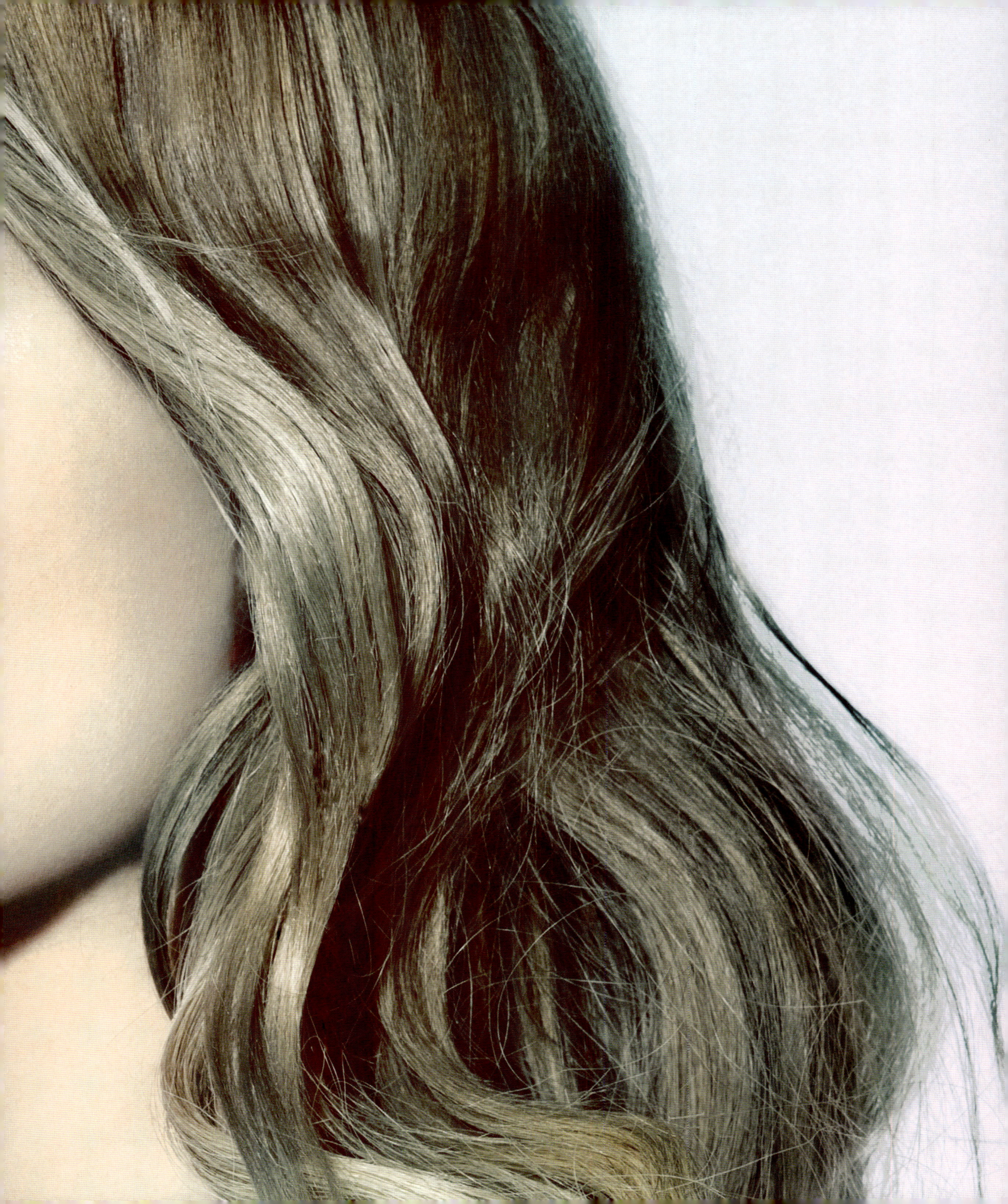

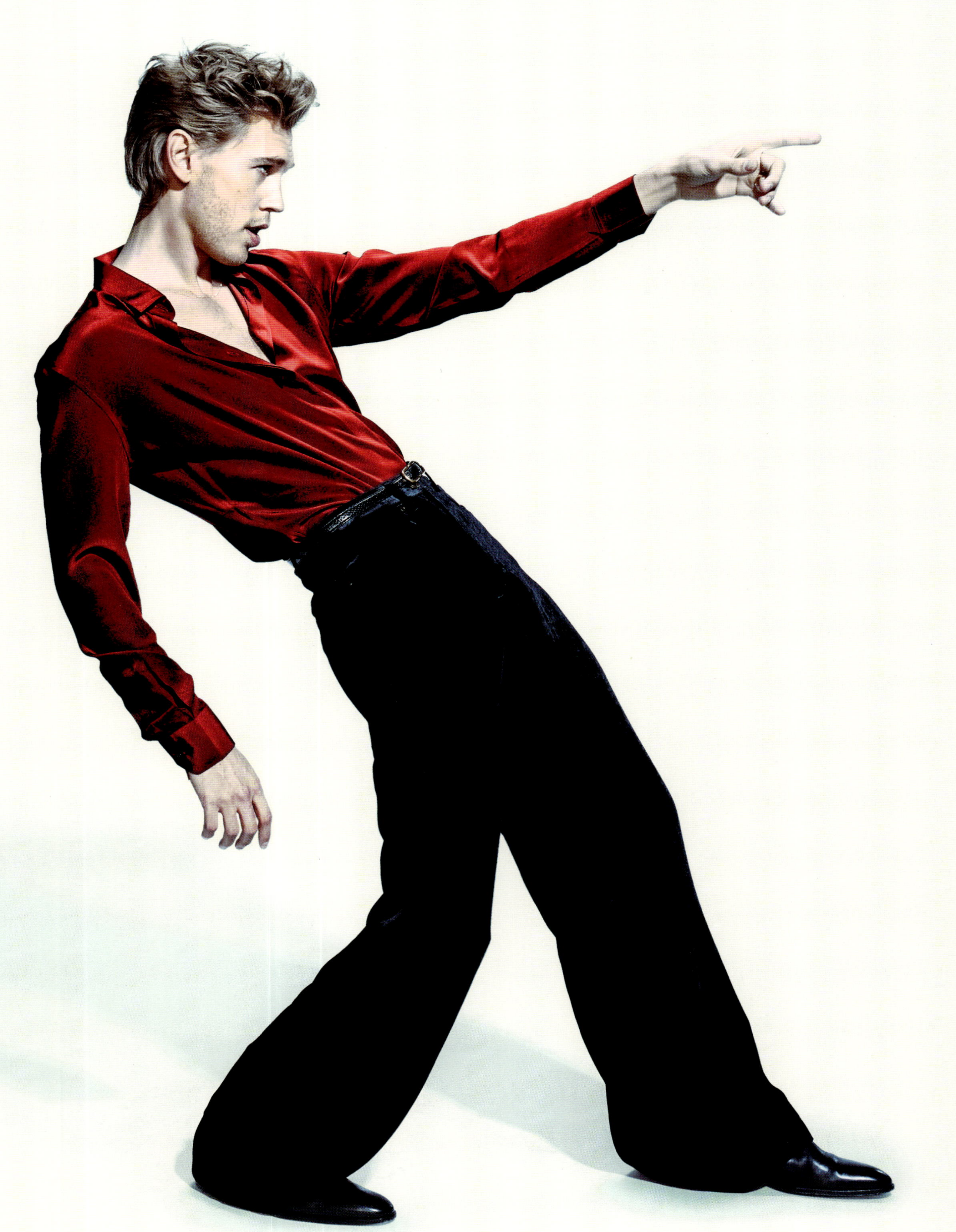

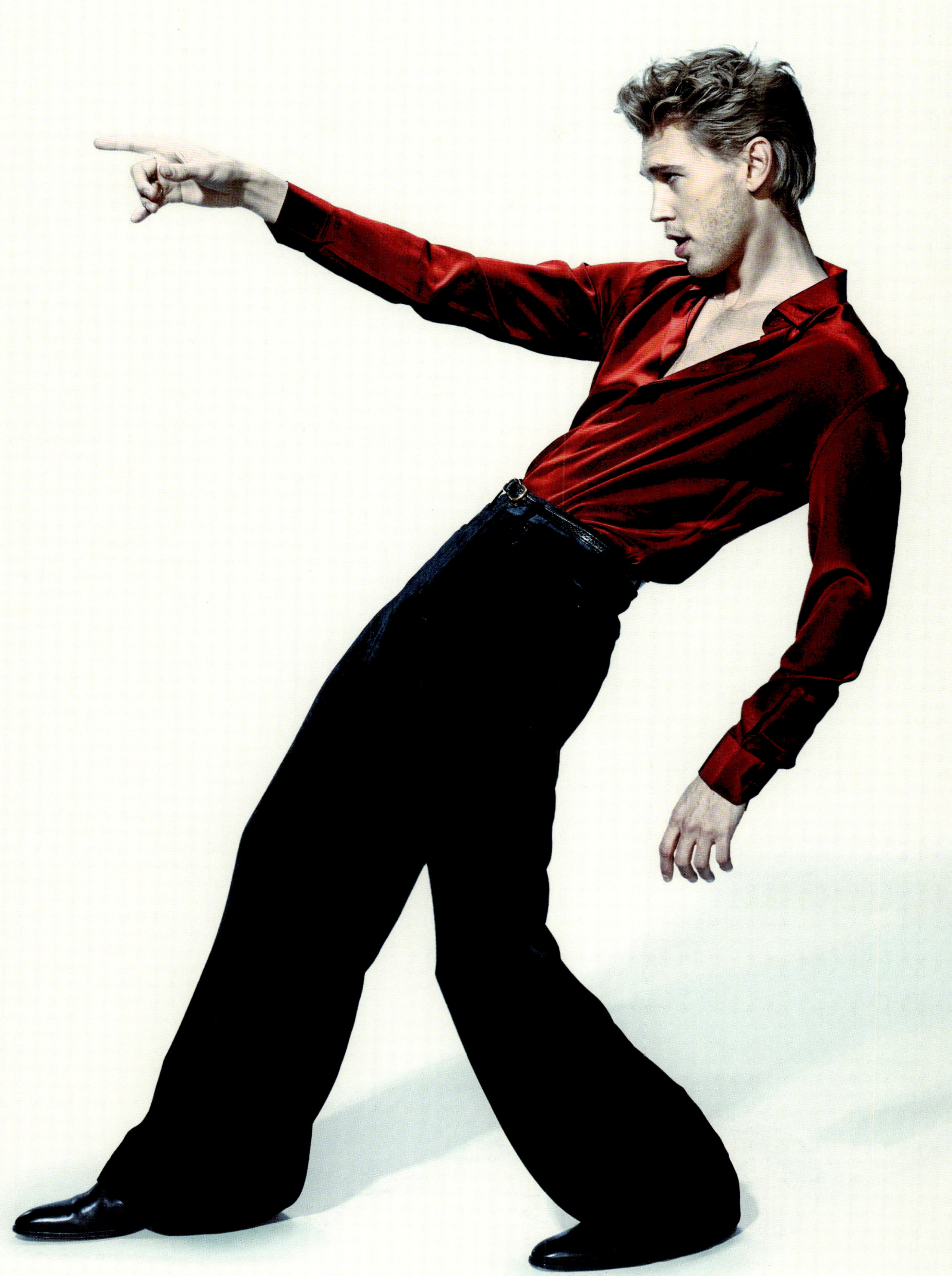

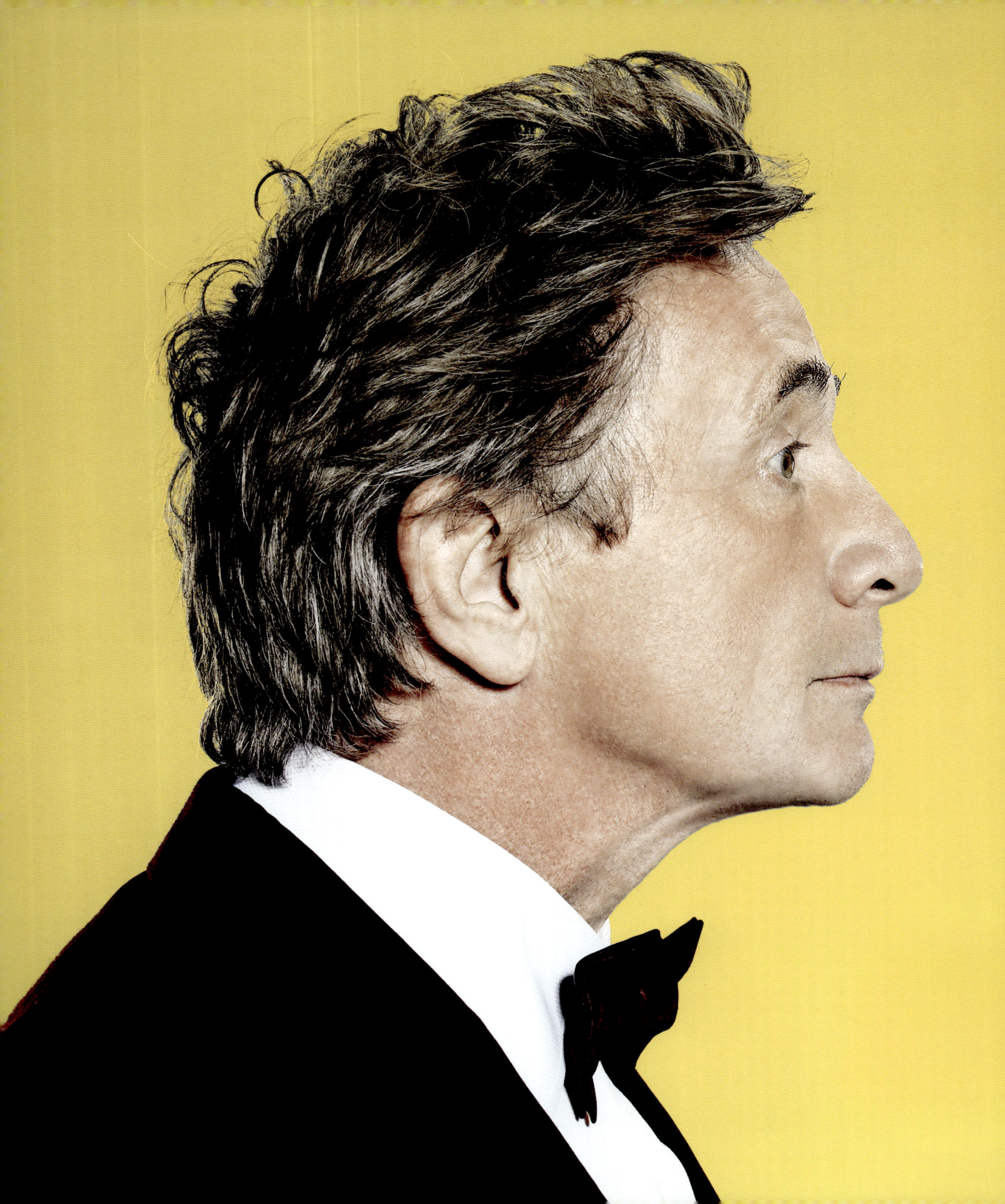

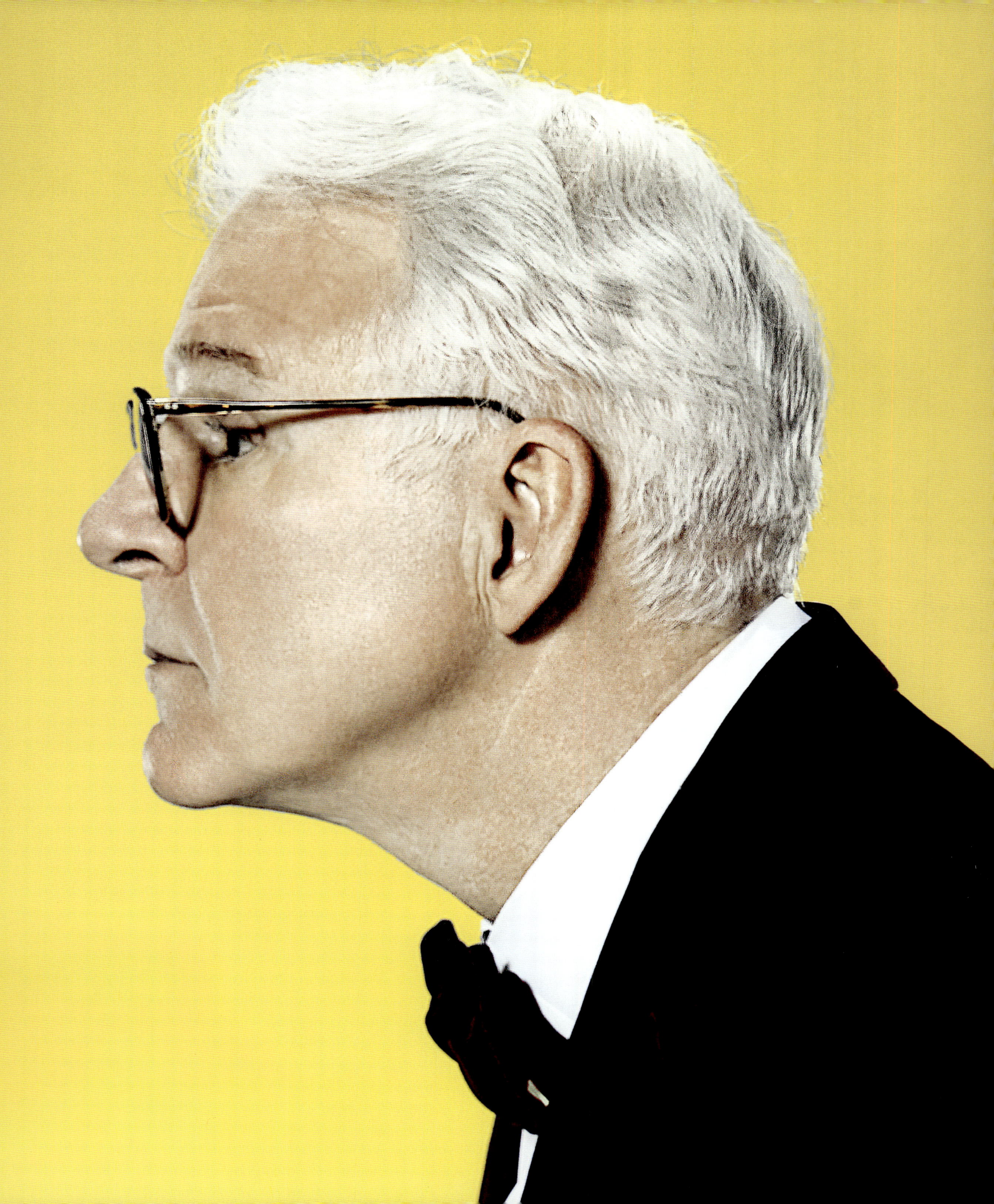

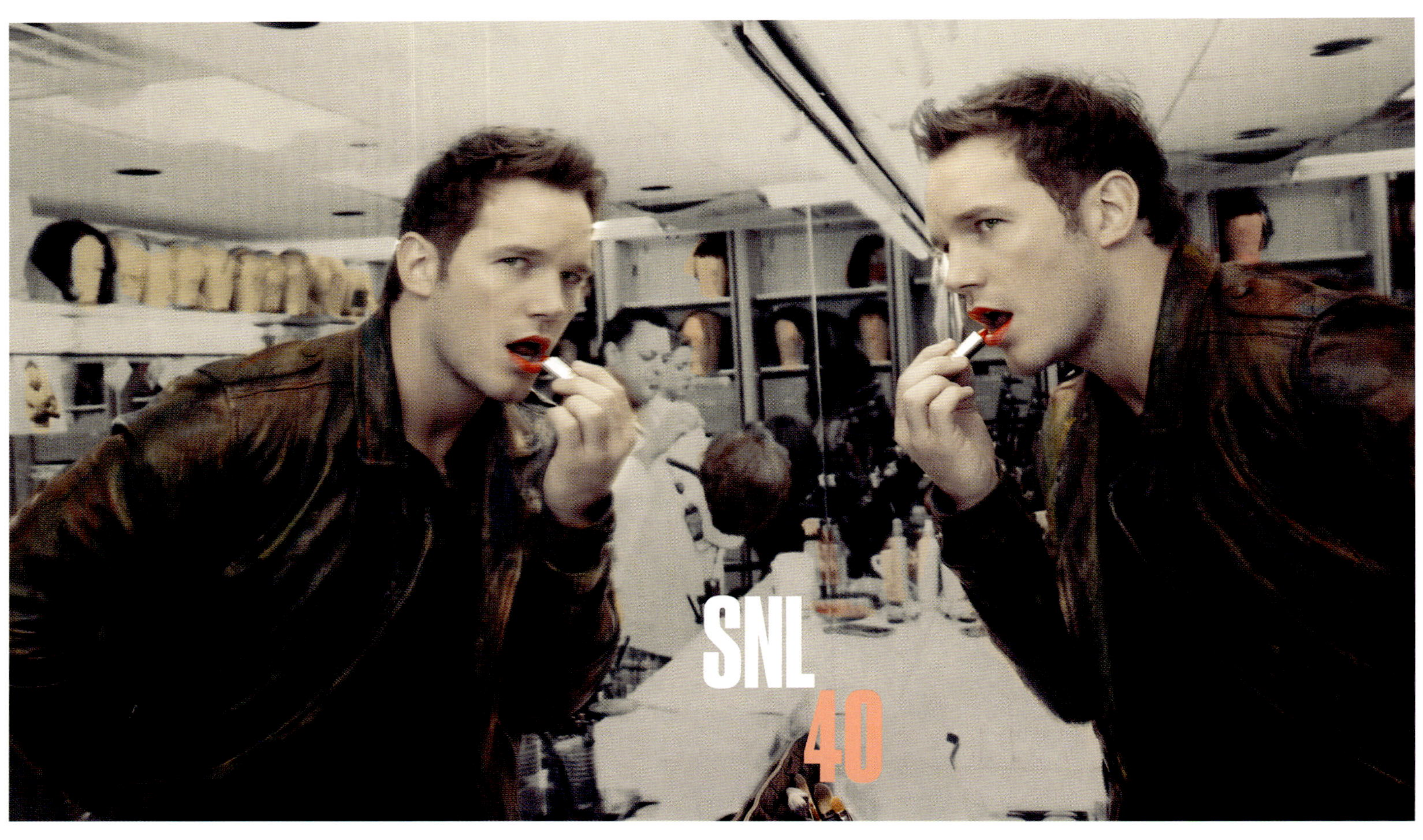
SNL
40

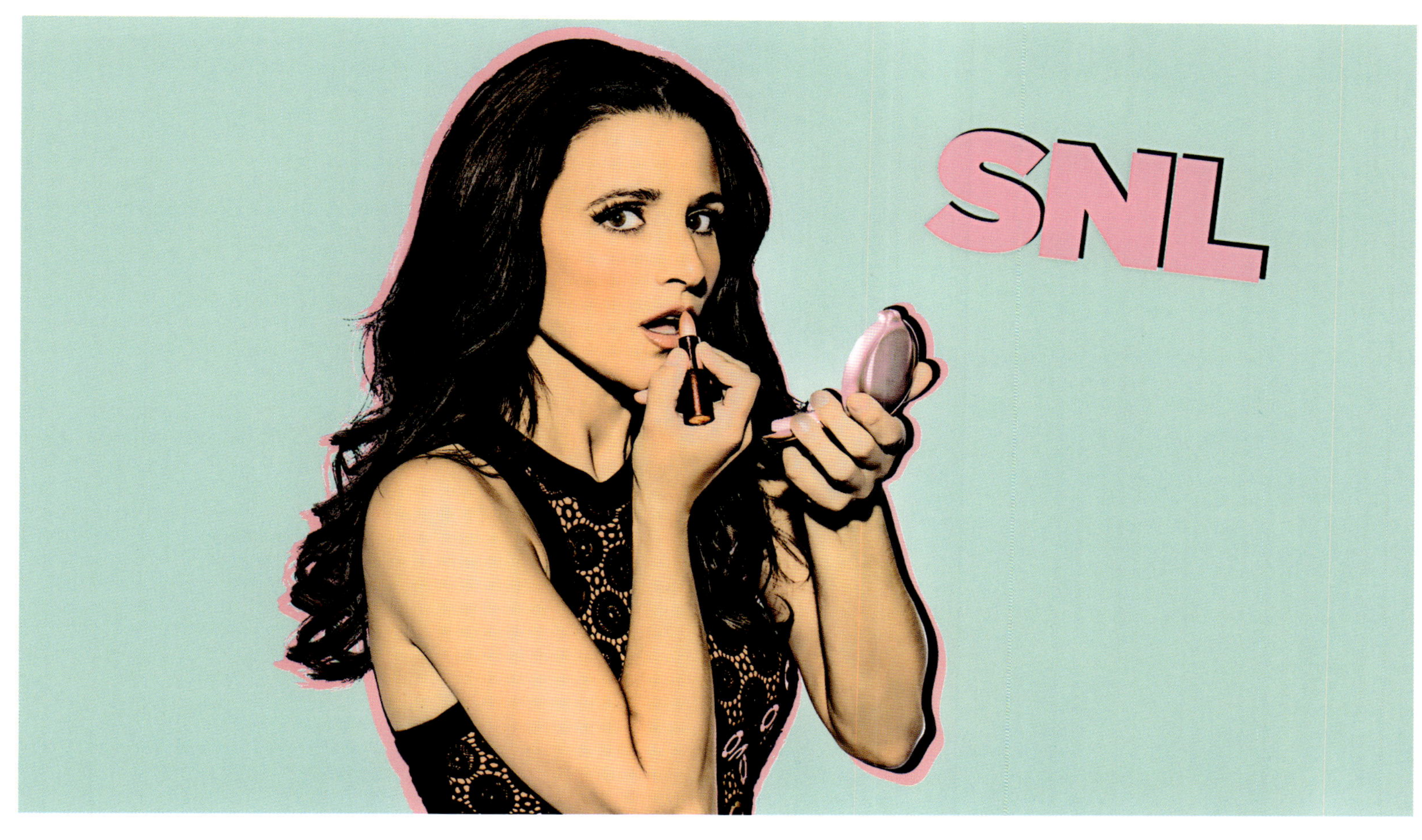
SNL

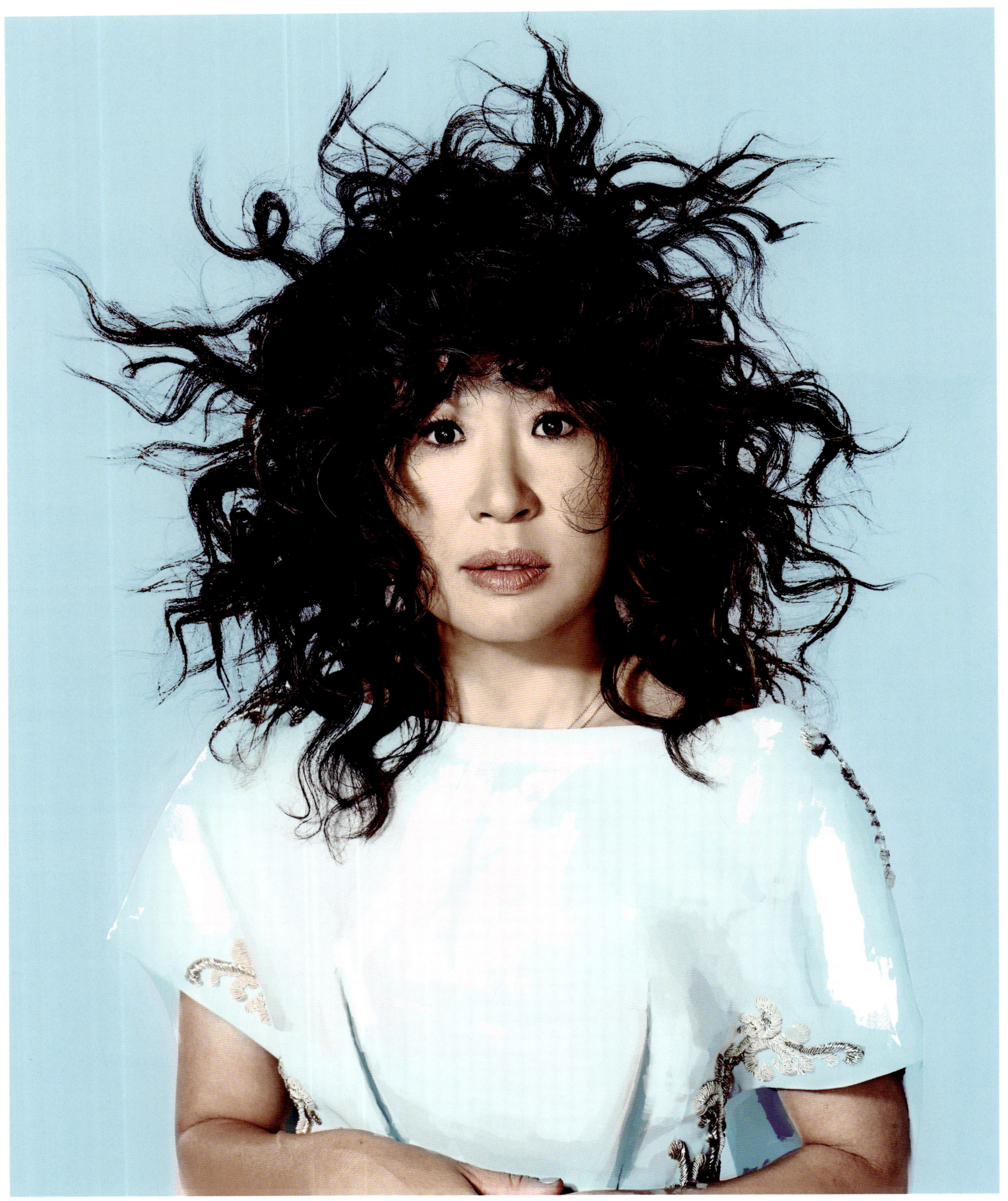

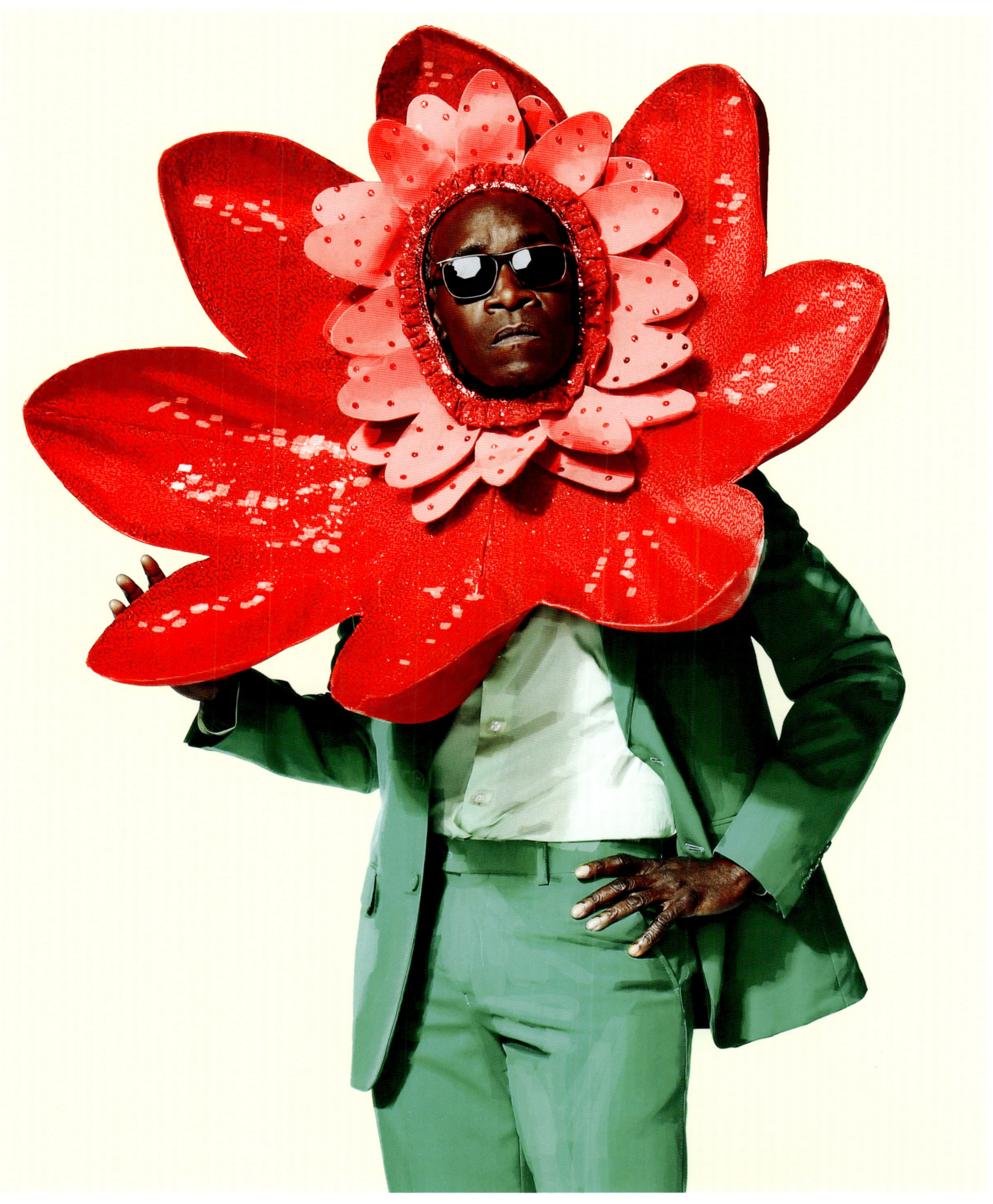

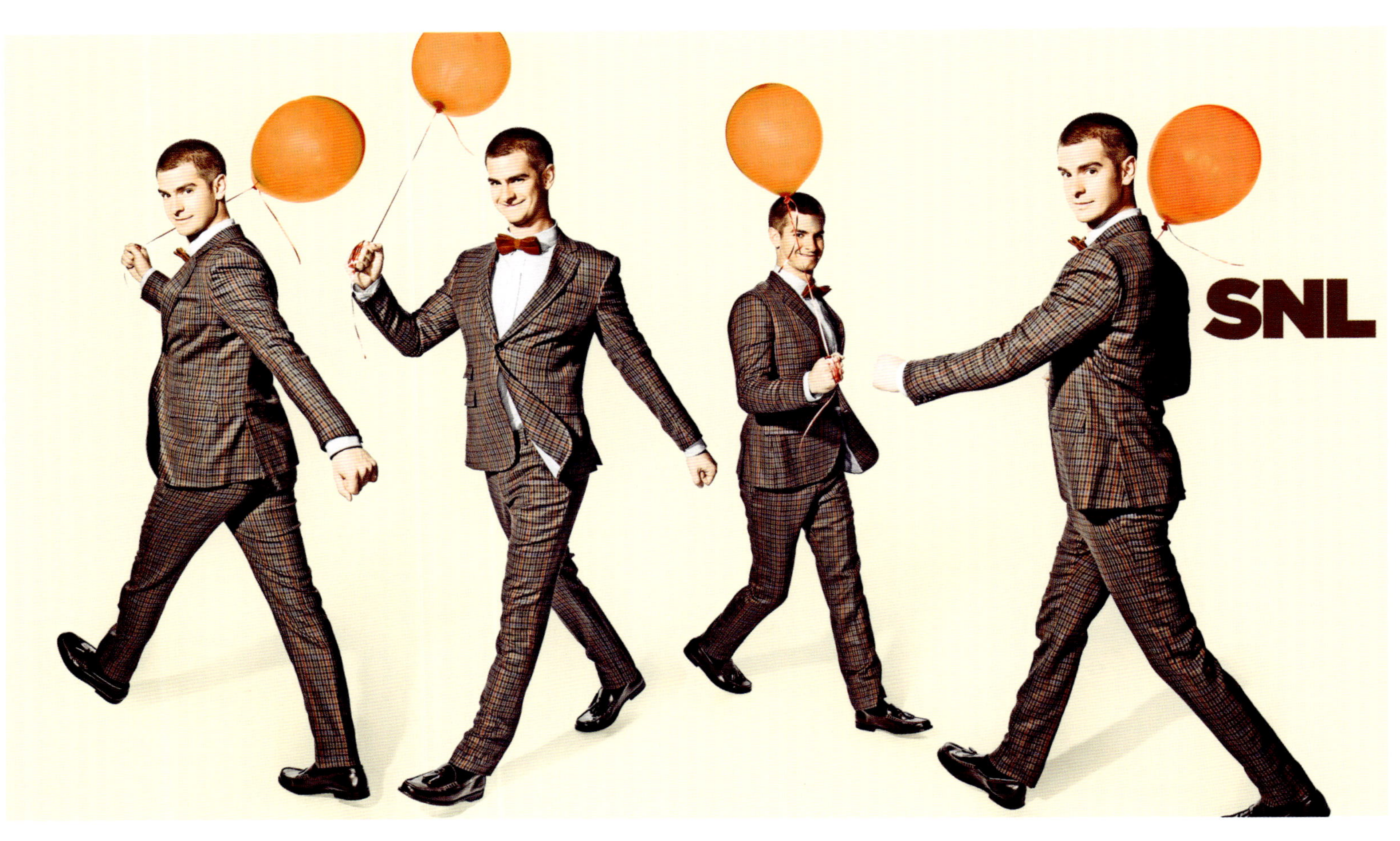
SNL

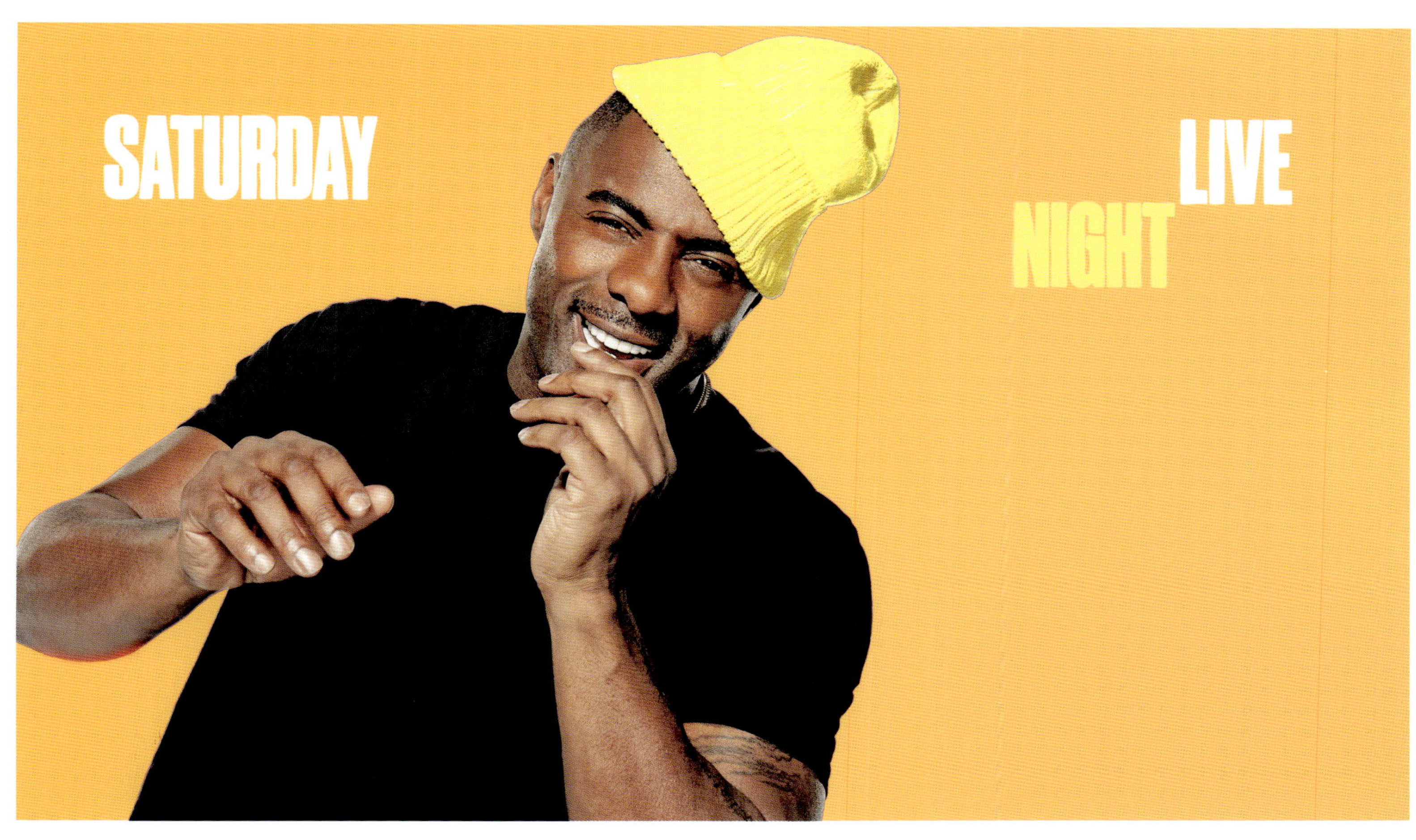
SATURDAY
LIVE
NIGHT

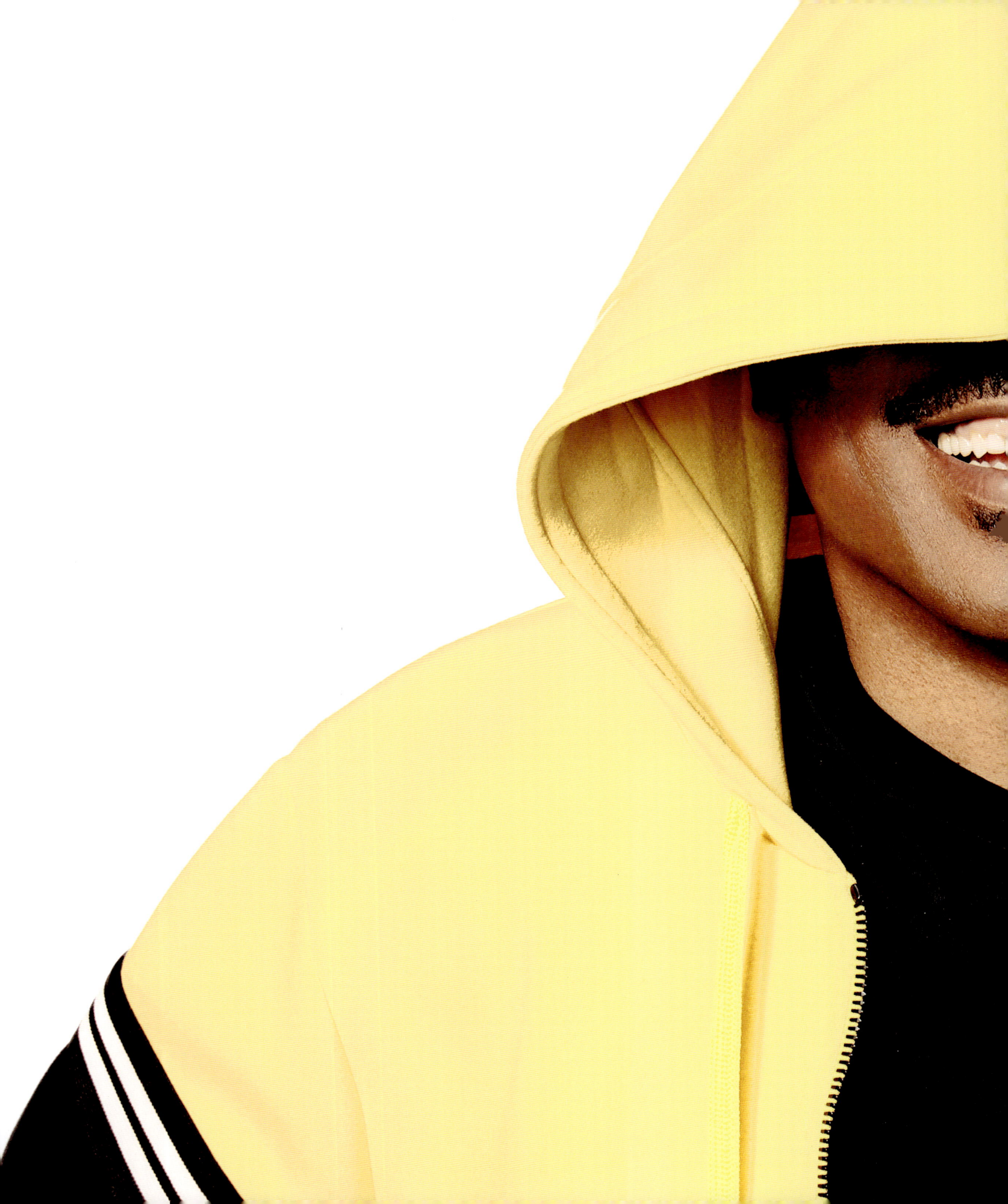

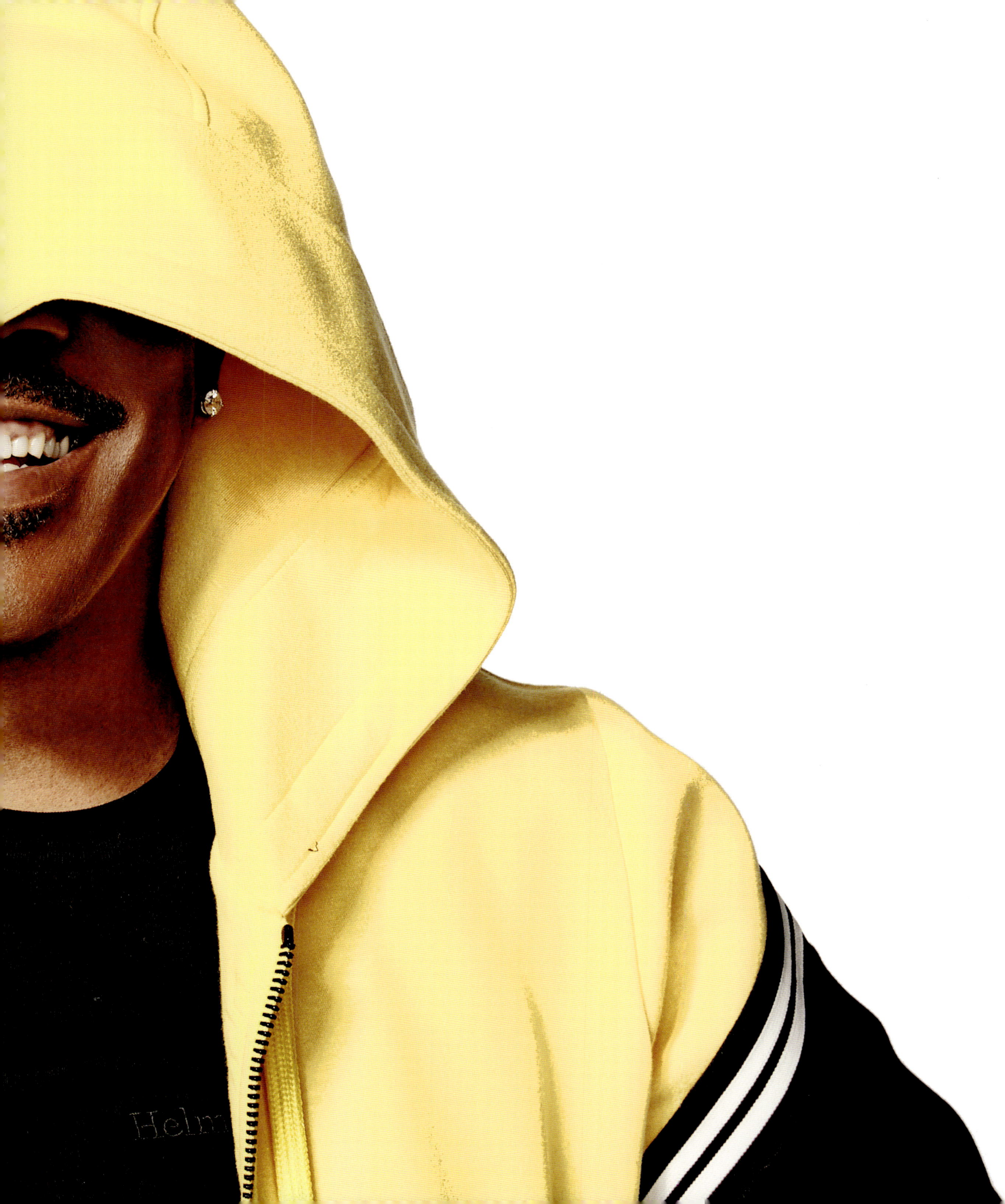
Helm

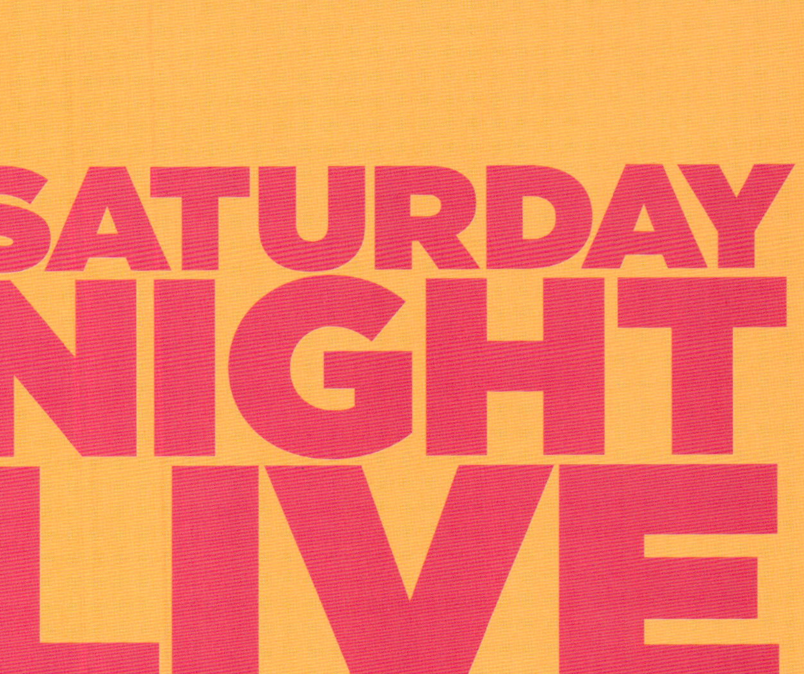
SATURDAY
NIGHT
LIVE

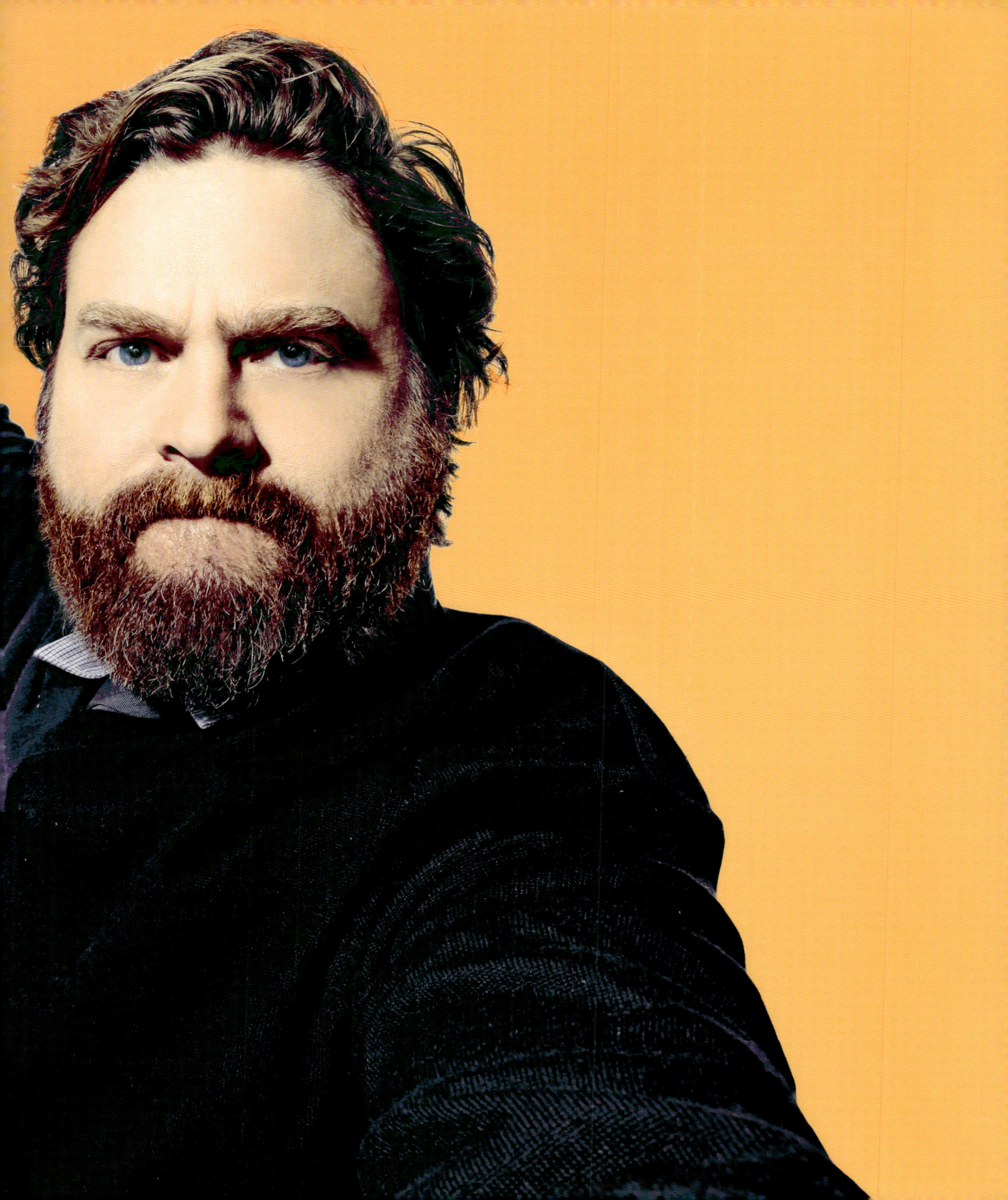

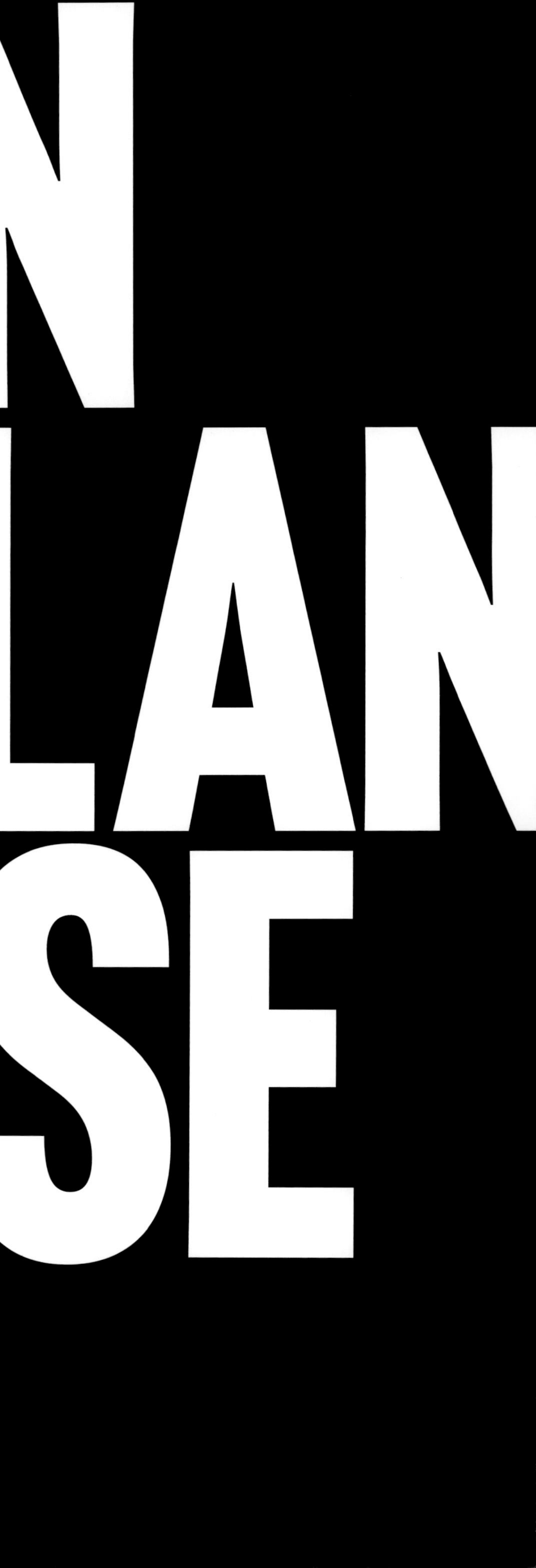

EY:

STUDY

Comedian, actor, producer, and writer John Mulaney has hosted SNL five times since the end of his tenure as a writer for the show in 2013. Over these five shows, he and Matthews have staged many brilliant and sometimes elaborate bumpers drawing on a wide variety of references. Their collaboration has been so extensive that it merited its own chapter within this book. Mulaney is not only game to try things, but often comes up with ideas of his own for the shoots. "It's my favorite part of the week, hands down," he says. "Oh my god, I love it. For the show, you're trying on these iconic looks and tropes and styles, but it's for a sketch, and it's ephemeral and it's moving fast. And it's live TV. Whereas [shooting bumpers] is like, 'Oh, I want to do Lou Reed *Transformer*' and Mary Ellen nails it perfectly."

Most shoots take place Thursday afternoon in a very crowded Studio 8H, where the entire live show takes place. Tensions run high in the run up to the live show, but Matthews makes a point to insist on creating a fun atmosphere during her shoots. For her, the job has always been about creating joy. "How fun it is and how much fun she's having is just infectious—at a place where people aren't always having fun, a place where people aren't always that upbeat about the creative side of things. She gives off that she just loves what she's doing. Certain days people love what they're doing, but they just don't exude it. And you know, she's doing it in the middle of midtown traffic."

With all of the activity going on, Studio 8H may not sound like an ideal setting for photoshoots—surprisingly little about how SNL is done would seem "ideal" from the outside—yet it just works. "This stage is so busy, the studio floor is so busy, as she's trying to get these flats up and have all of the carpenters and painters hold the work that they're doing just so we can hear what she's saying. The band's doing soundcheck for their techs and running their songs . . . Thursday afternoon is so crowded—you have to shoot promos, too. As crazy as things are done [at SNL], It really is best there [in the studio]. You go "this is insane, and it's the best option."

In the following pages, Mulaney shares his recollections of working with Matthews.

“That’s what *Saturday Night Live* feels like, like you’re at 20,000 feet in a paper airplane.”

THIS SPREAD
So beautiful. I love the scarf. I love my excitement. And how clean that paper airplane is. Love it.

NEXT SPREAD
This one was great. The original [Chuck Close painting of Philip Glass] is so iconic to me. But when we got into it, it was like, you know, there’s almost nothing going on. But it was like, “Oh, the shirt’s very simple. The expression is what it is.” I mean, it just sort of has stood the test of time as an image. My ears also stick out more than Philip Glass’s. And I love how the hair is shaped around my ears. It’s a little monkey-like in a way that I enjoy.

FOLLOWING SPREAD
This one was a lot of fun, because this is a bit of a nod to this annual event: at *Saturday Night Live* where we all have to go to the Museum of Natural History benefit, because Lorne Michaels is on the board of it. And I remember being at one of these, and they have all these auction items. And one is twenty-five front row seats near the museum for the Macy’s Thanksgiving Day Parade, then one of them is tickets to *Saturday Night Live*, which are very hard to get. One year they auctioned off that you could have your name on the plaque of a black Kodiak bear diorama. And I was like, “No one’s gonna bid on this.” Compared to a sleepover for your kids and all their friends under the squid in the whale at the museum . . . As soon as they announced it, it was like, bam, bam, bam, fifty-thousand, sixty-thousand, seventy-thousand, a hundred, two hundred, two-fifty, bam, bam, bam, bam, half a million bucks. And I said, “What the hell’s going on?” And Steve Higgins said, “All they want is immortality. And this is a plaque.” I always thought of that auction with this one.

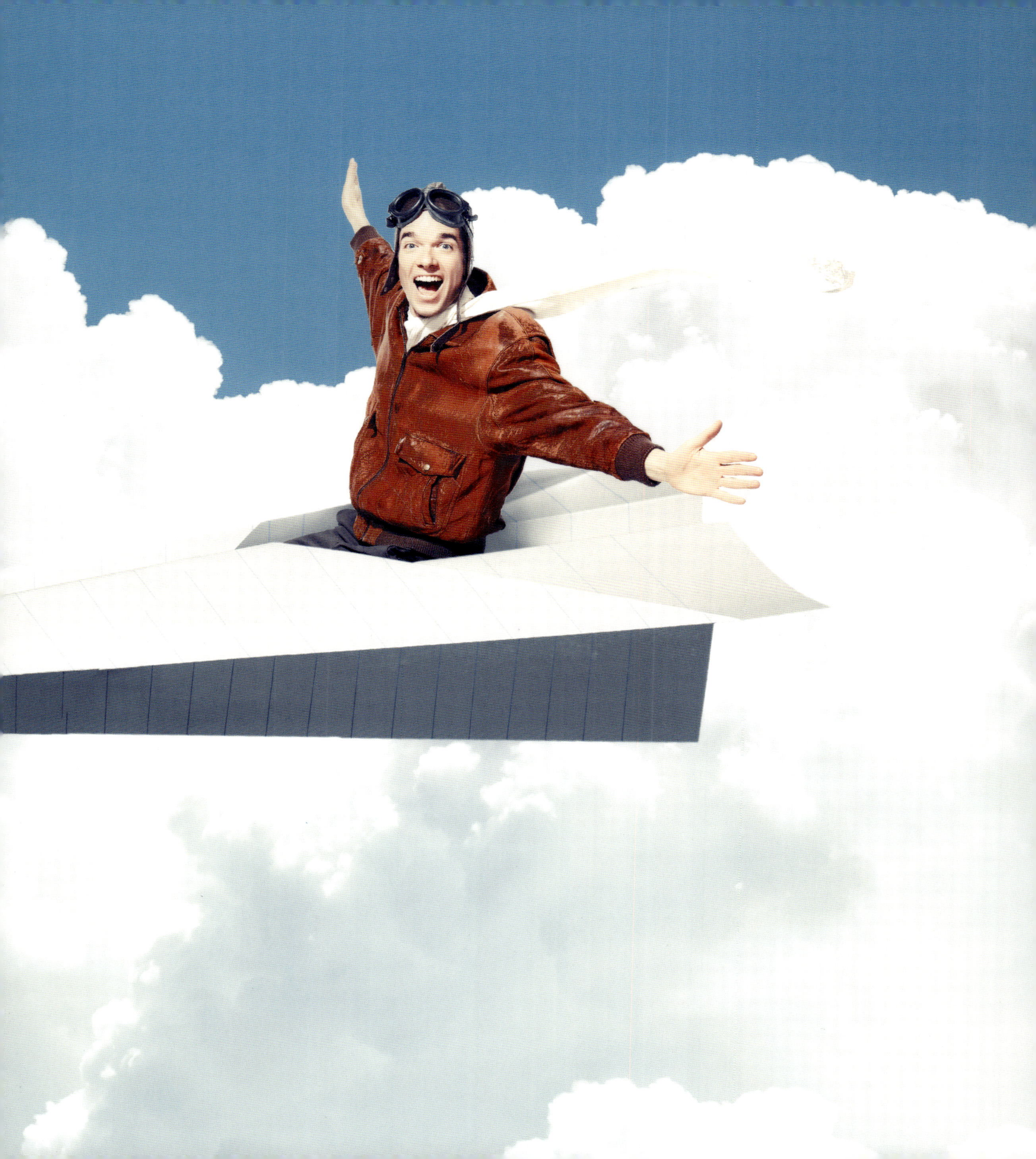

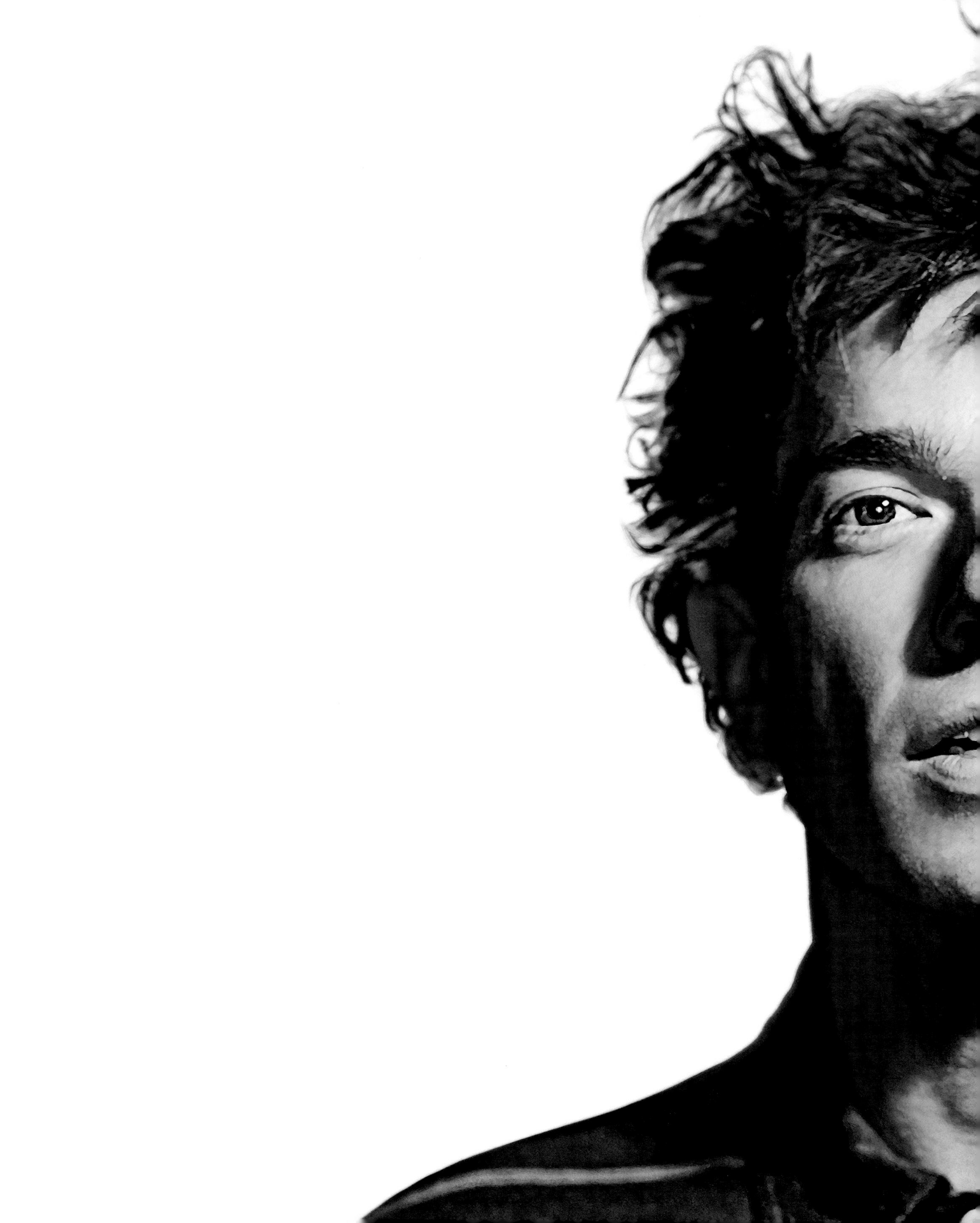

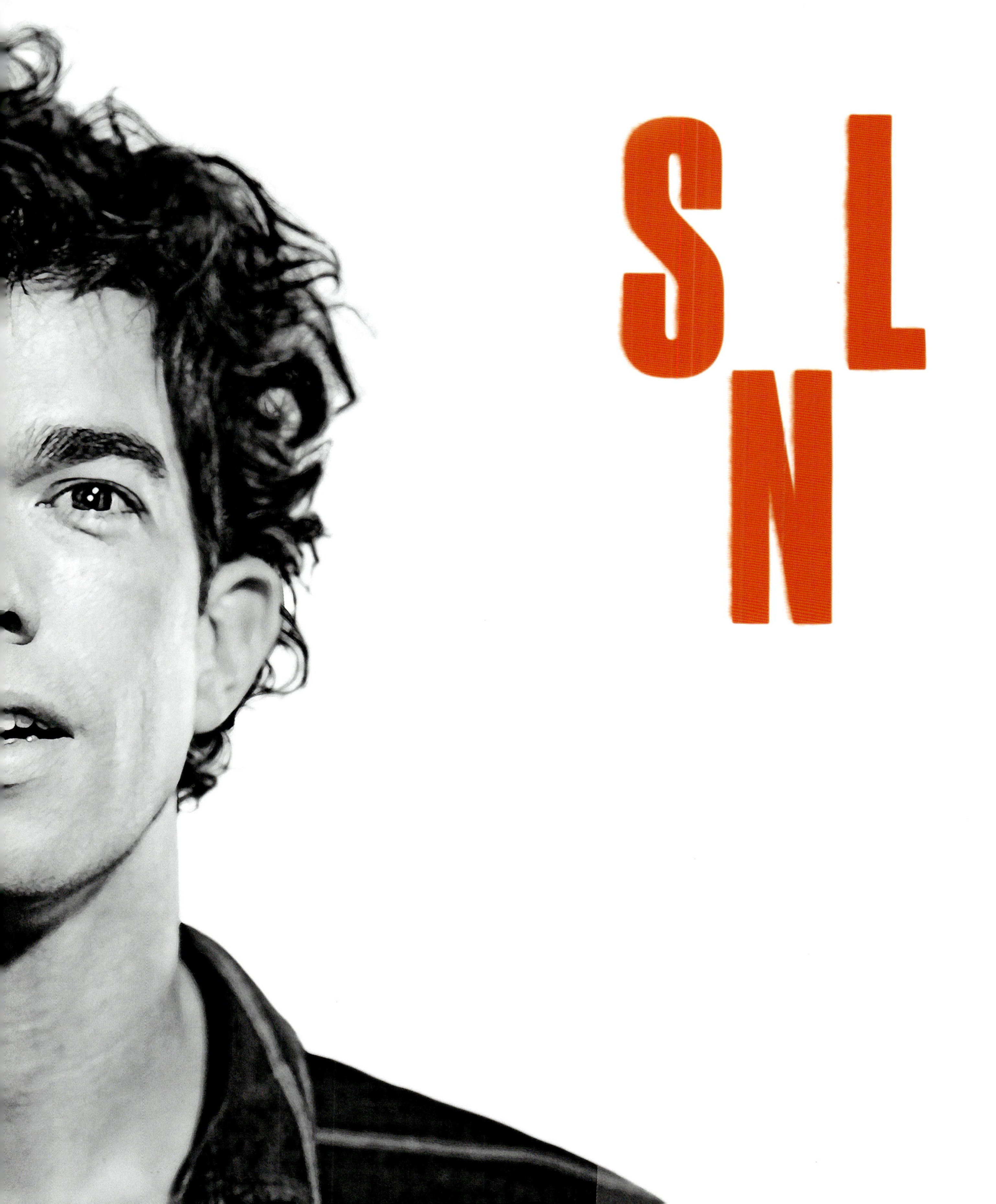
SNL

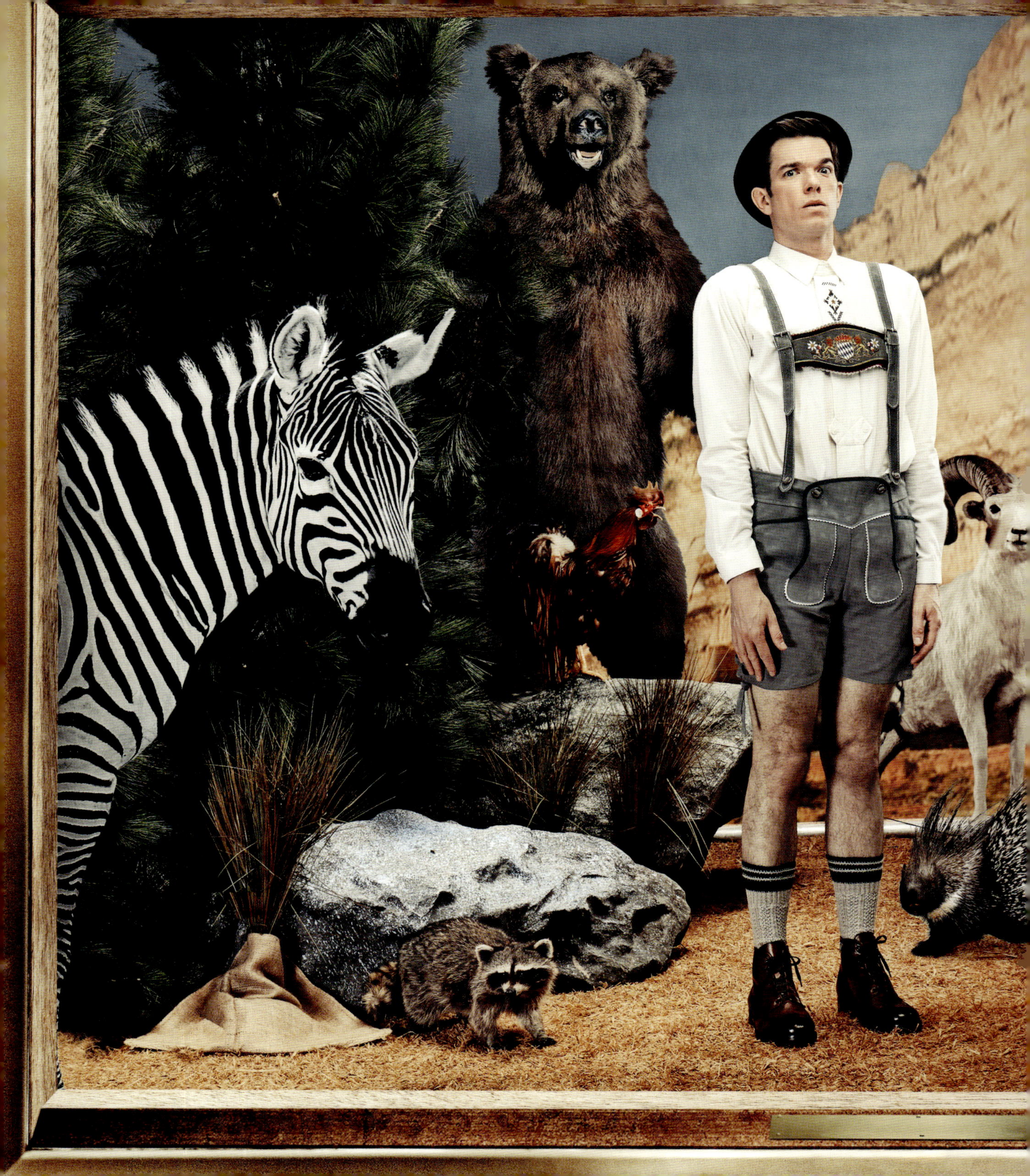

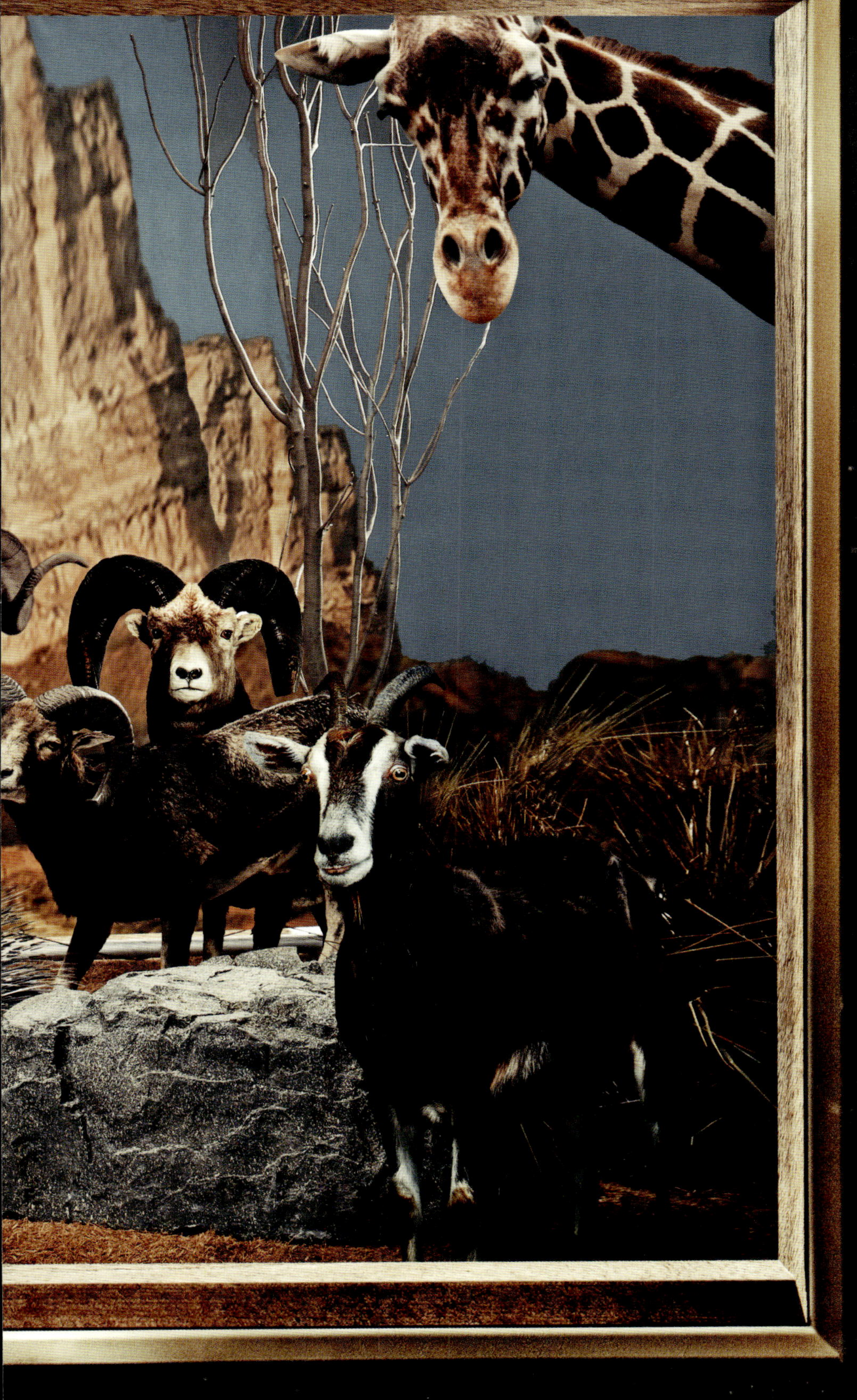

S L
N

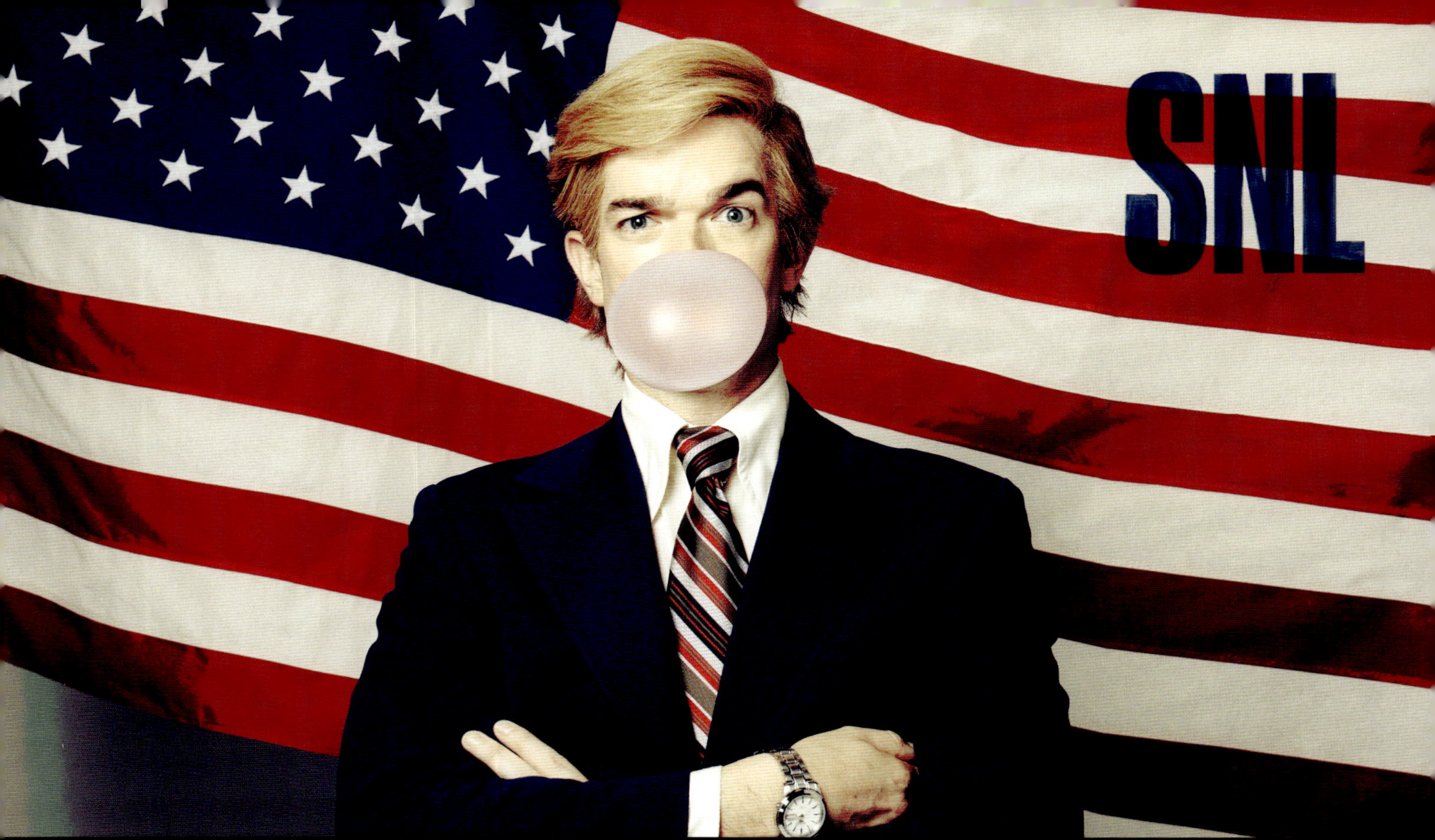

SNL

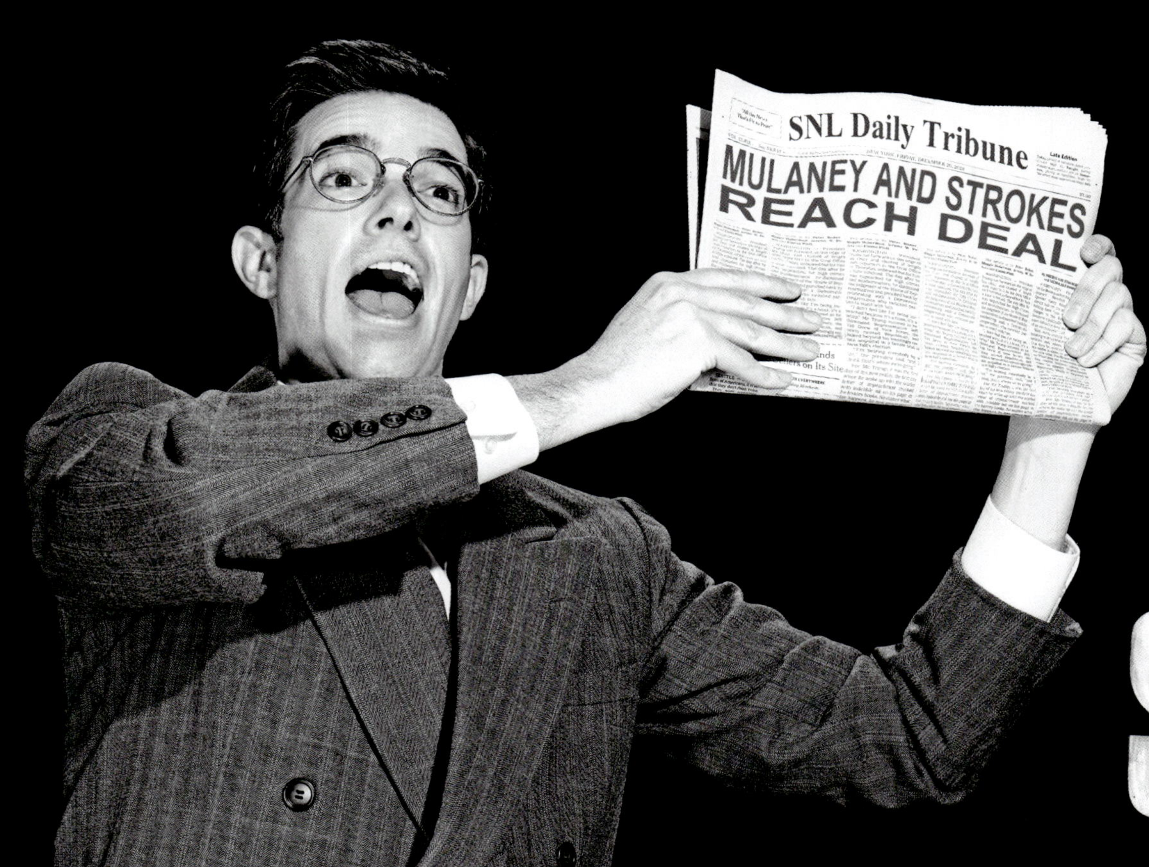

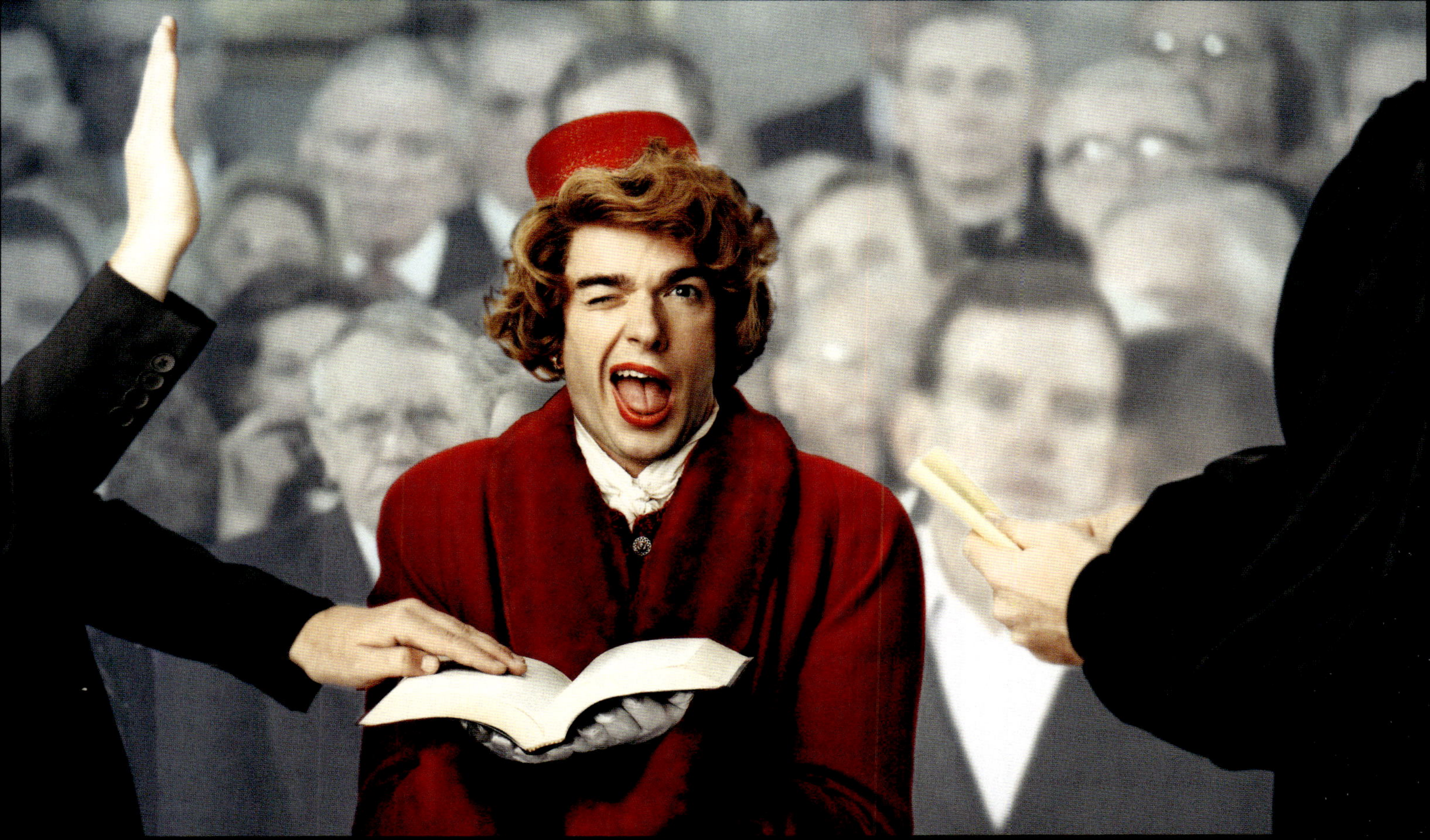

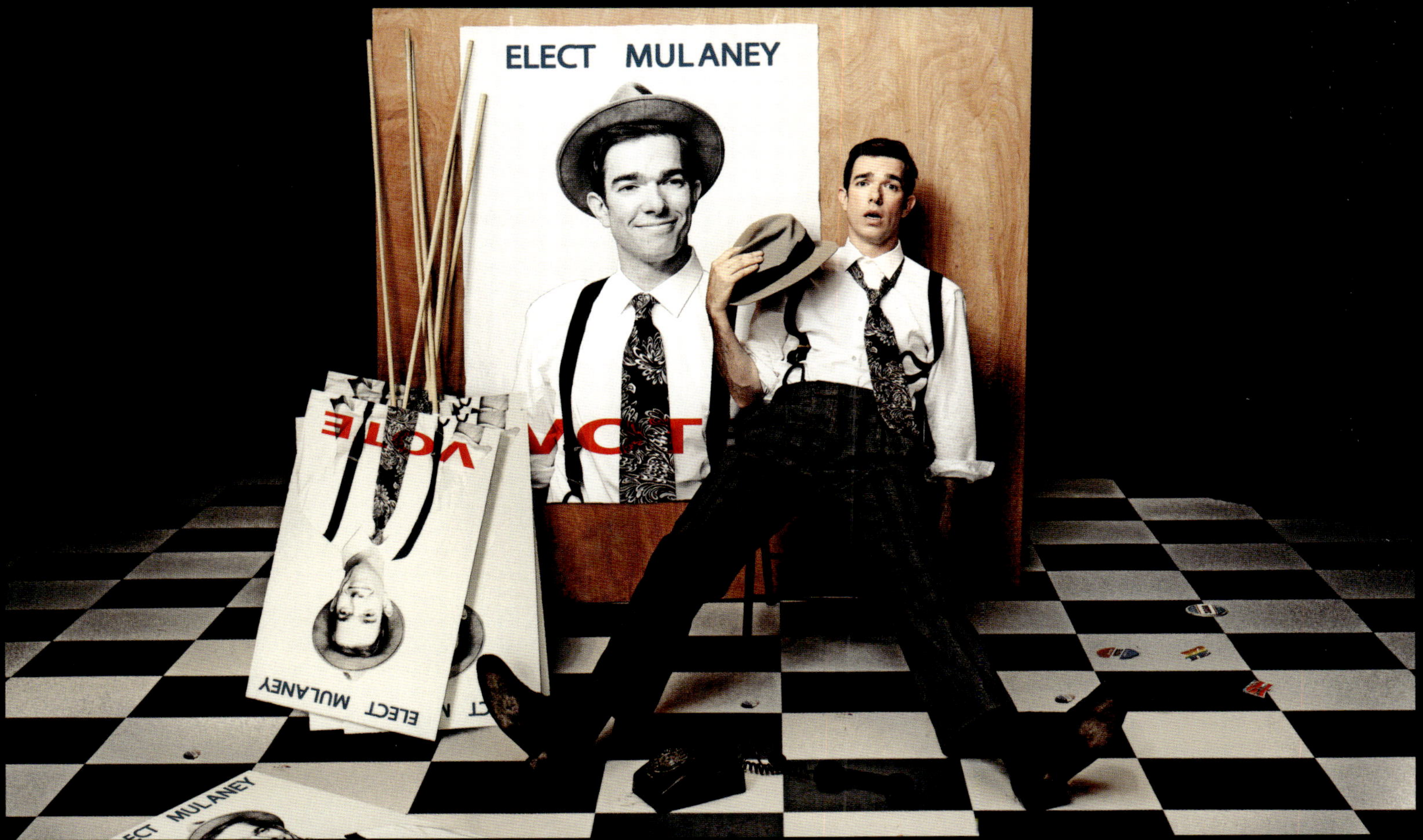

ELECT MULANEY

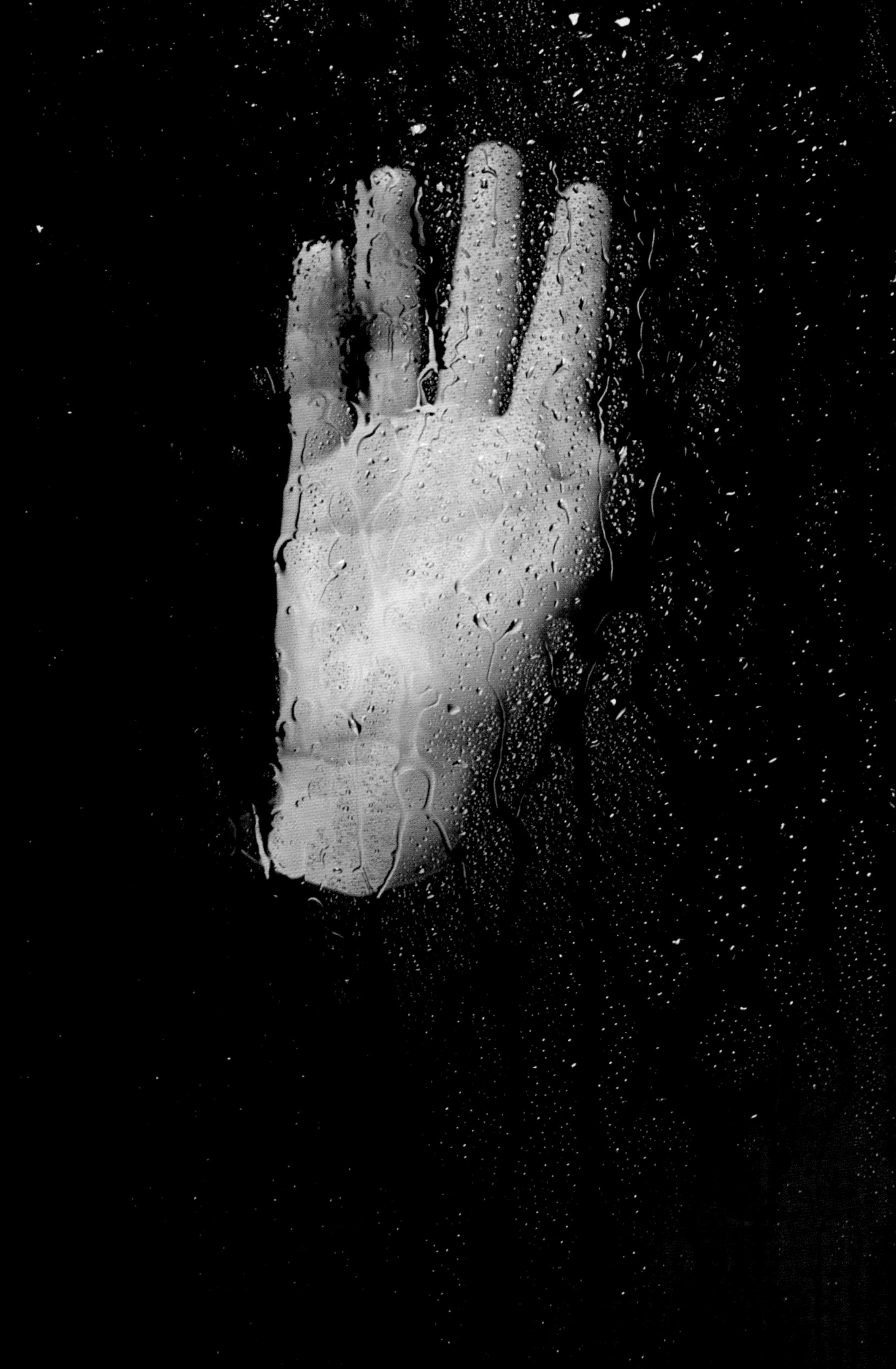

PREVIOUS SPREAD
TOP LEFT This was *The Candidate*, Robert Redford. It was the Halloween show 2020, so it was a COVID show. Whenever we do these, we really do it practically. That's not meant to sound ike I'm some Olympian, but I would alway think, "It's way harder to recreate this than I thought." definitely had some trouble blowing the bubble. had a lot of gum in my mouth to achieve that.

TOP RIGHT Nancy Reagan was a lot of fun. I had to do several things that day in and out of that wig, but in that makeup and with the wig cap on. And had to make several decisions and go into several different meetings, because we were interrupted. just remember being in a lot of things in a wig cap with that makeup and feeling like, "This actually looks pretty cool."

BOTTOM LEFT That's obviously "Dewey Defeats Truman" and it's really a great, simple photo when you do it. The placement of it's really good. Yeah, imple. But really, glasses are really nice.

BOTTOM RIGHT This was another one of the October 2020 ones, the last show before the election. That hat, by the way, was [late music supervisor] Hal Willner's hat. That was really special. I mean, the whole photo is fantastic. love the upside down posters. I love that even in good times his smile isn't that sincere, a bit of a half-assed smile.

THIS SPREAD
s it a car window? Is it a window window? There's something about the blue tie with the rain over hat black shirt and black background. I think about the tie a lot. I've actually worn versions of this outfit a lot since we took this. Now, whenever 'm unsure what to wear, I wear a black shirt with a blue tie and a blue suit. I am struck now by the drops of rain with the tie. So I think Mary Ellen and Tom [Broeker, costume designer] must have worked closely on that.

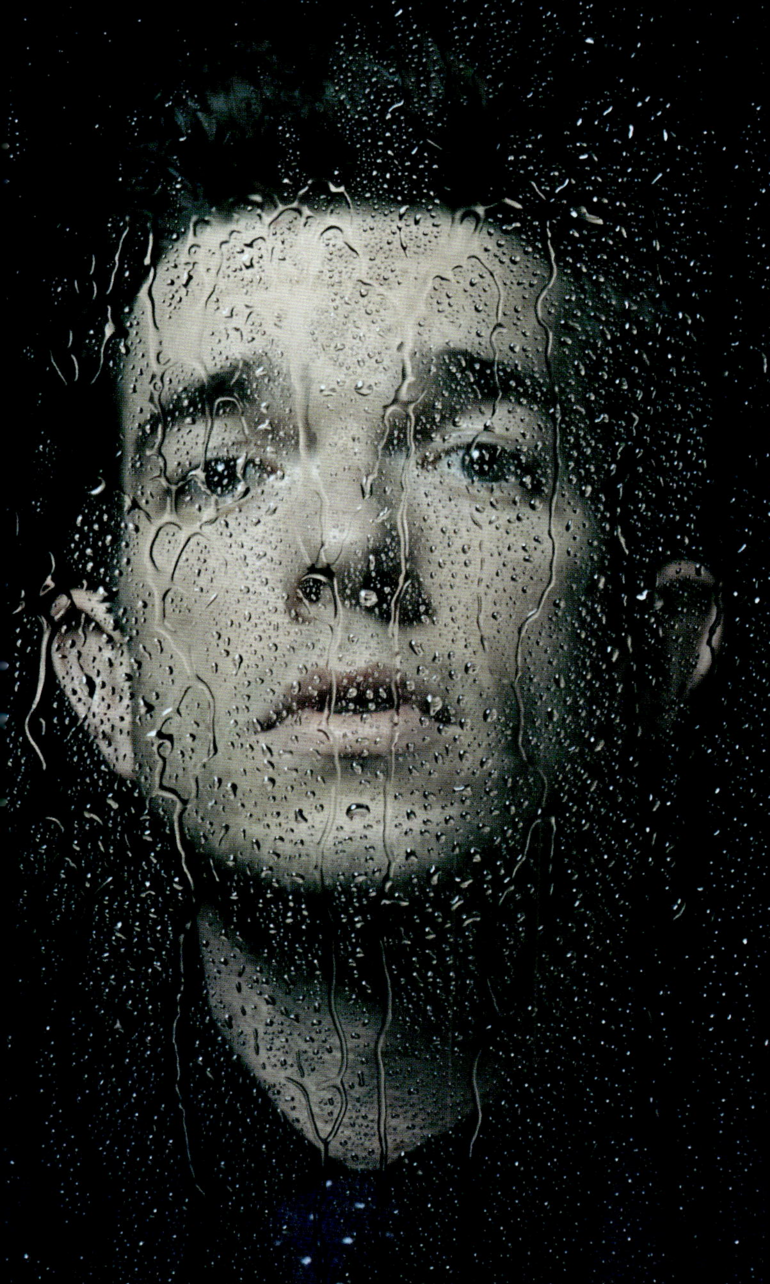

SNL

THIS SPREAD
This is a very fitted suit. And the jump in those shoes on a concrete floor. While it doesn't look that big of a thing, at that point in time, I had a tear in my hip. I'd been working so much, and then doing the show, I was often in terrible physical condition.

NEXT SPREAD
TOP LEFT The eyeshadow does [the heavy lifting], the jacket does too. The guitar is really high. There's so much going on. I loved doing this one. I think I pitched [the *Transformer* record cover] because Lou Reed is like my absolute favorite thing ever. I like everything about him.

BOTTOM LEFT This was so fun. That whole episode. It was February 29, leap year, and David Byrne was the musical guest. It was like pure fantasy camp that he was doing the music. I don't even think I appreciated music when I first saw *Stop Making Sense*. I saw it as a very young kid. I loved the staging of it. I love this fascinating guy. Even before he puts on the big suit, he looked like a vampire to me. It was really intriguing. So any way to do the big suit was super fun. I had a slight hesitation, though. I thought, "Man, if I bump into David on the studio floor, I'll be a little embarrassed because I don't know how much he wants to always reference that kind of work." But I thought, I'm not asking him to do it. I'm taking the photo. It's a fun nod and he ended up walking out onto set and we did a little moving image vignette of him teaching me some of the *Stop Making Sense* dance moves. So cool. It's really special to me. So this photo I just love so much. And I love that song, "This Must Be the Place," when he's dancing. Yeah, that whole sequence is so cool. The suit is spot on. It's a really nice fabric. I always thought about the fabric in *Stop Making Sense* because it moved really, really well. I wondered if it was the same as Steve Martin's suits, which I wrote down somewhere what they were made of—he says in his book. I have suits where I go, "That's what I'll wear tonight because I have a big stage and I really have to move."

RIGHT There's this version of me without the [Patti Smith] wig on that should be my funeral pic. I actually got one framed. I remember Mary Ellen being like, "She's standing straighter than you can imagine. So if you're standing normally, you're basically hunched over." I remember her giving me this cue to stretch my neck out. And I think that kind of added to the facial expression. Just ramrod straight. She said, "Imagine you have a string on the top of your head that's pulling you upward." I remember what she said, and I always use this for my own posture.

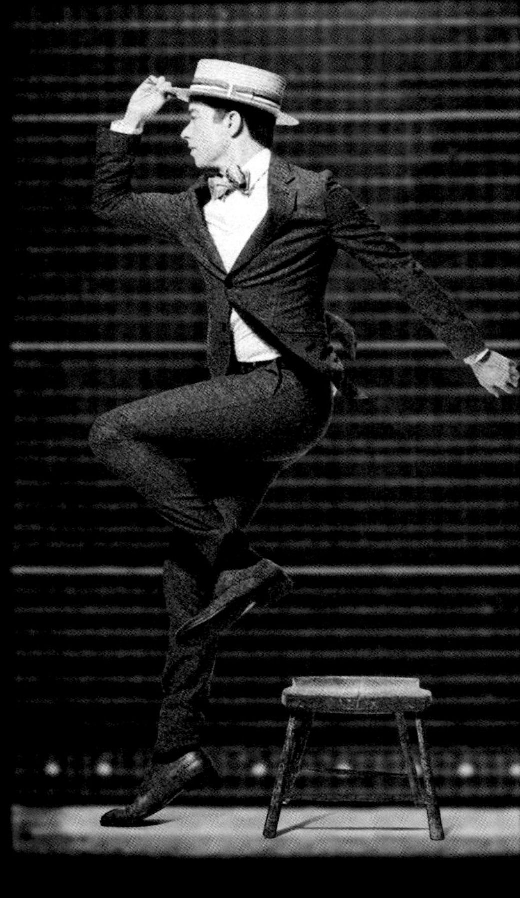
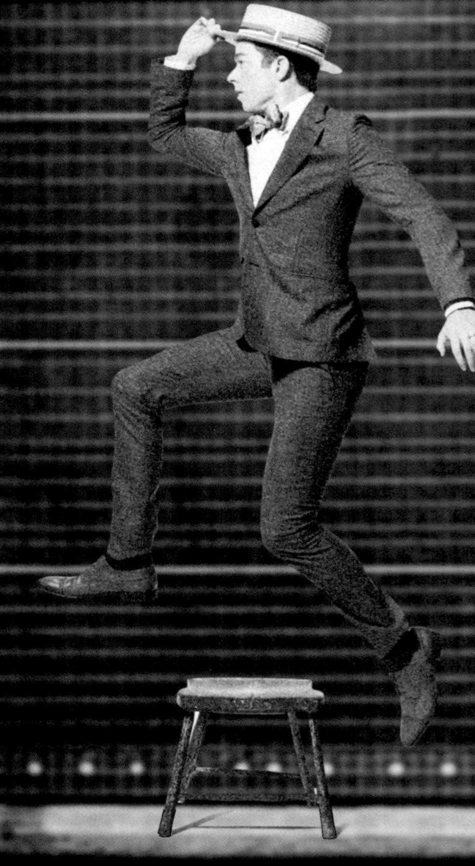
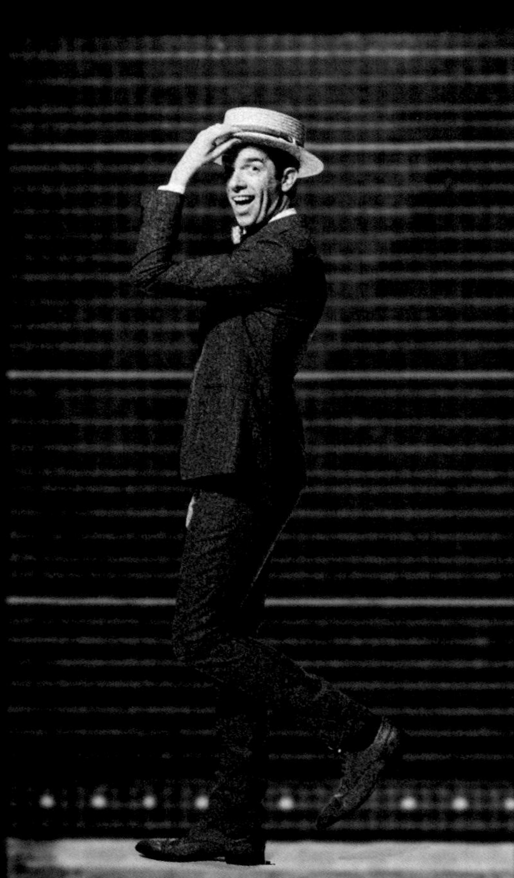
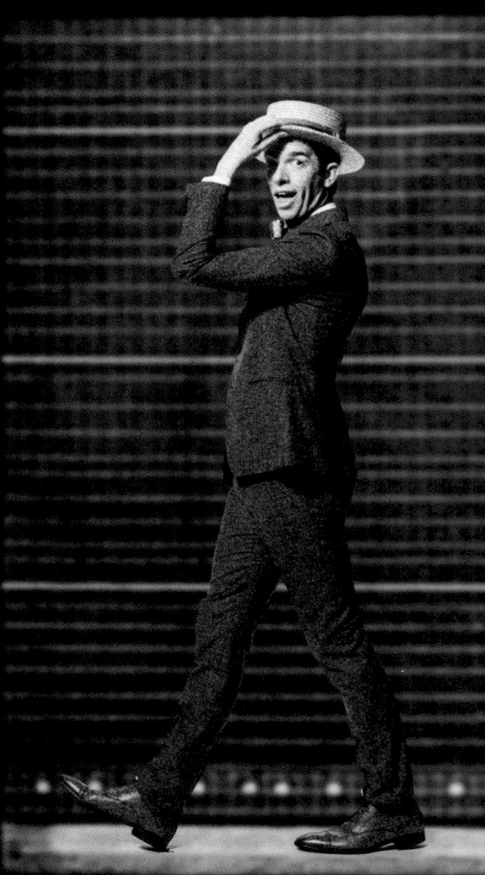

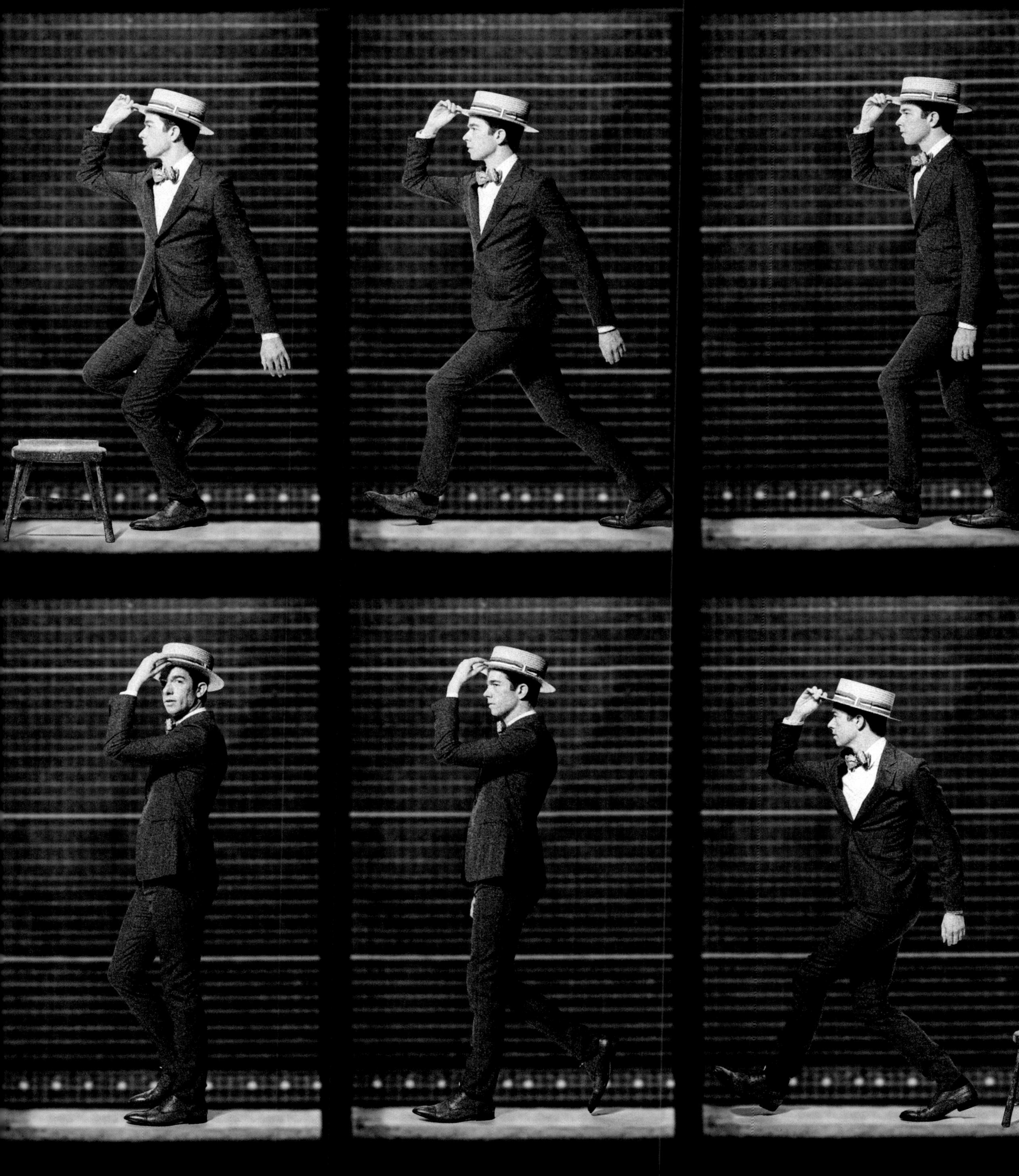

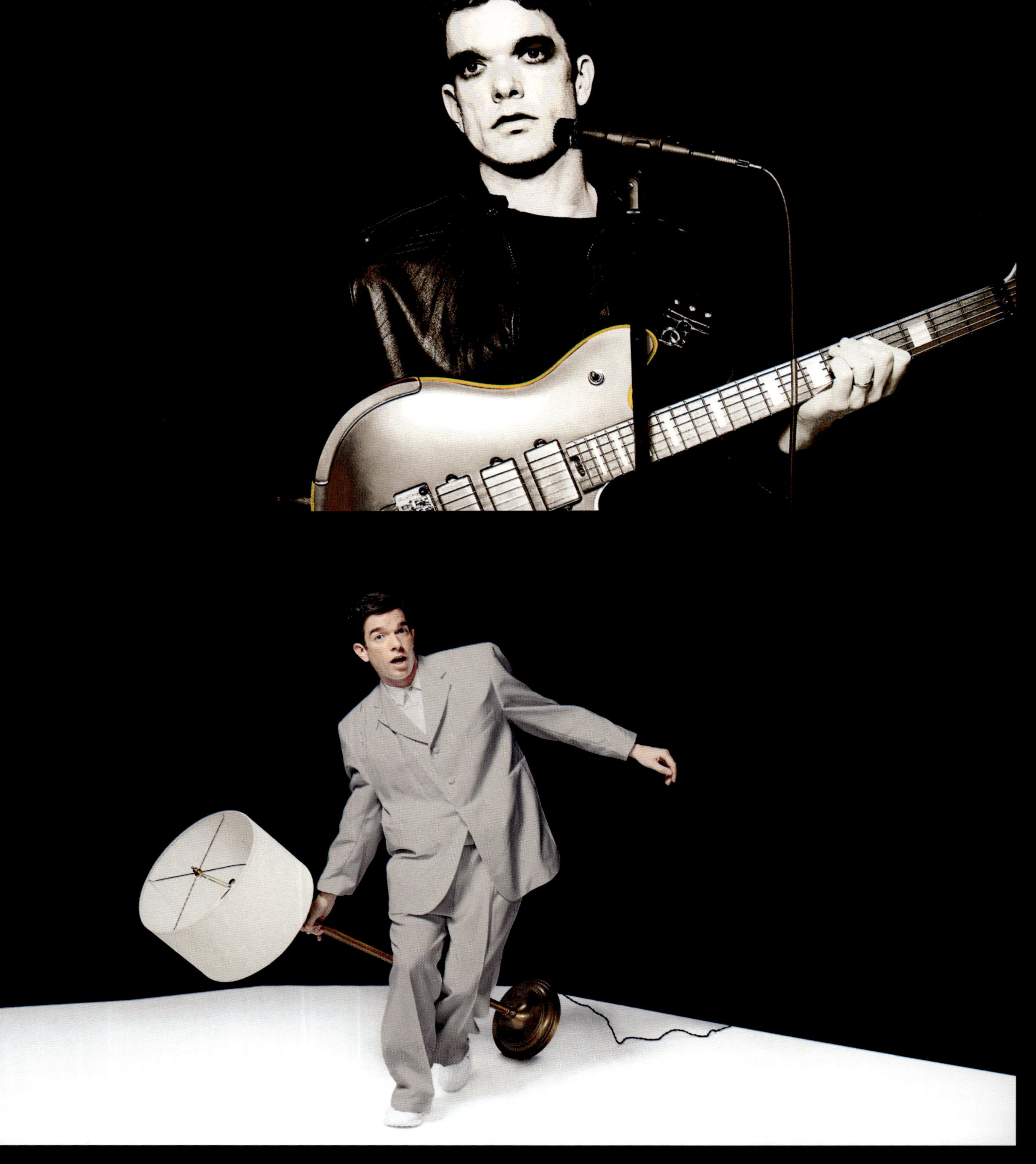

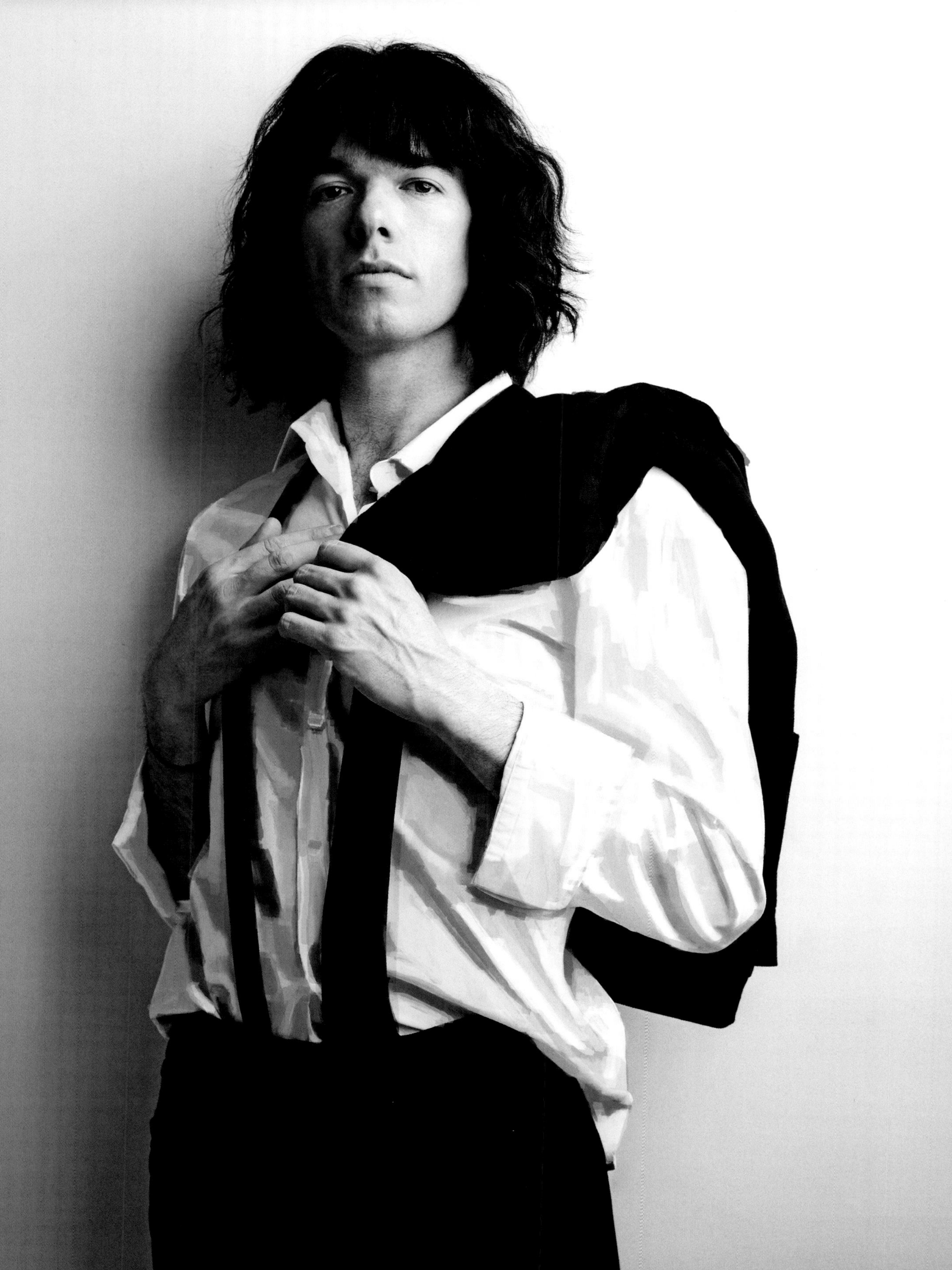

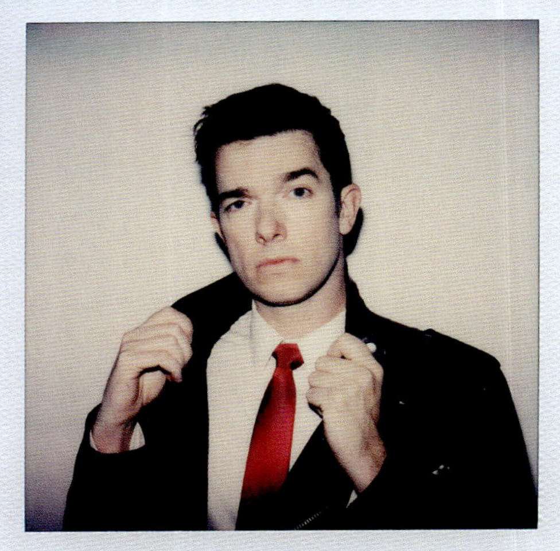
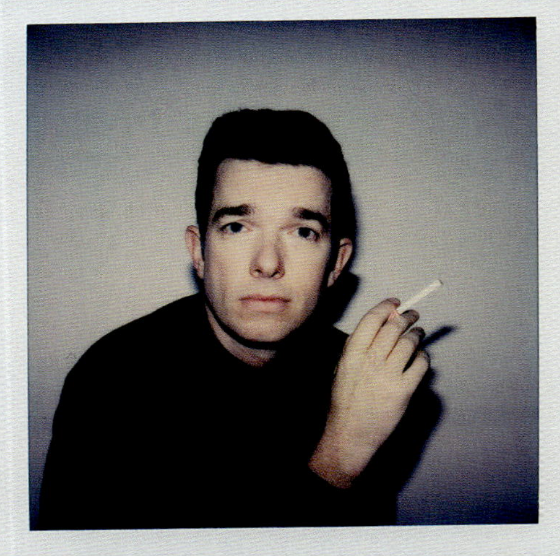
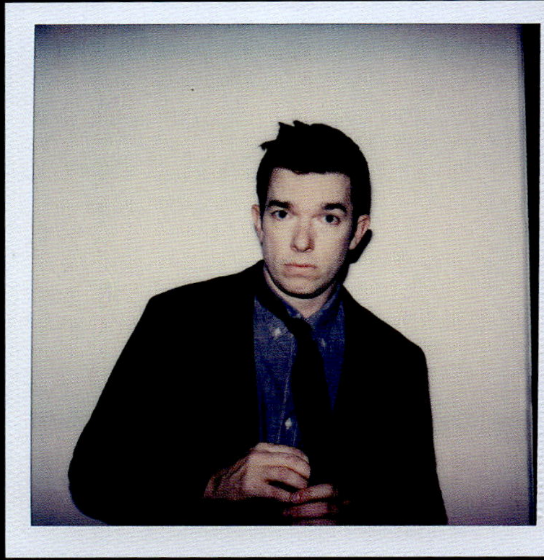
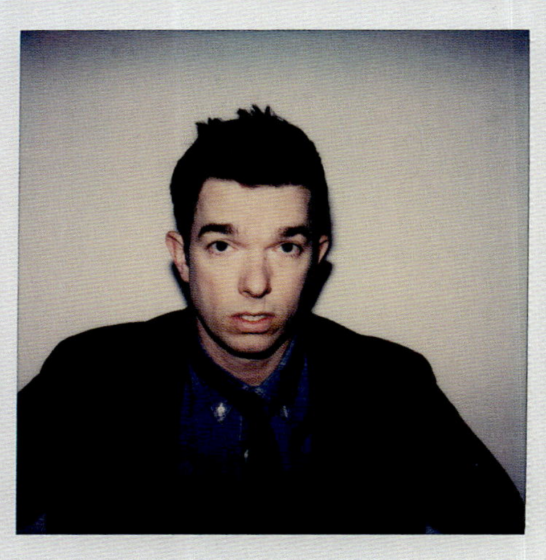
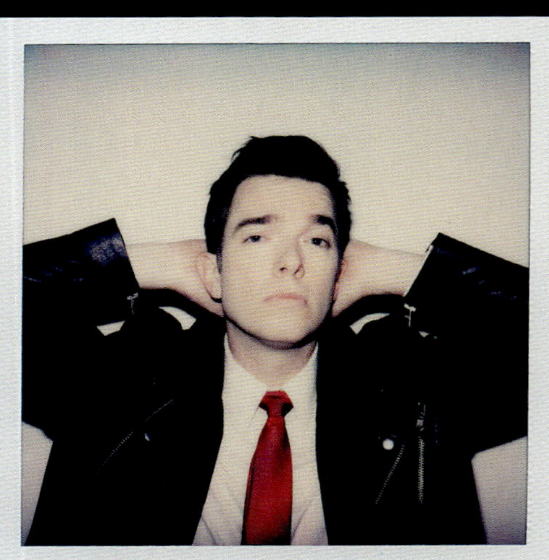
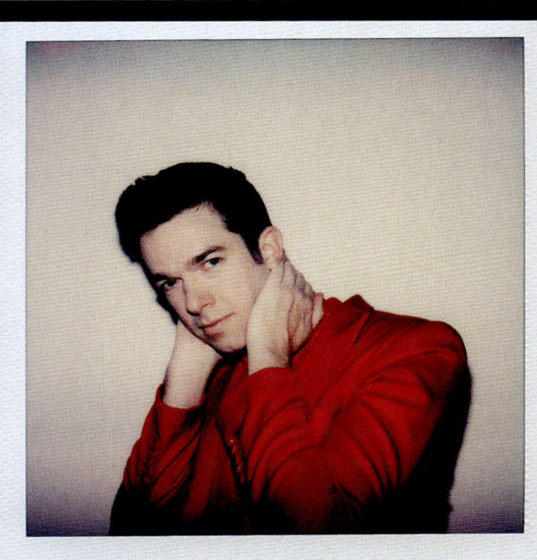
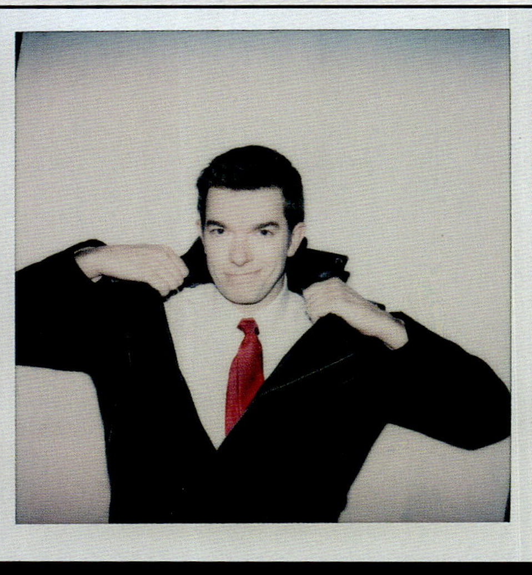
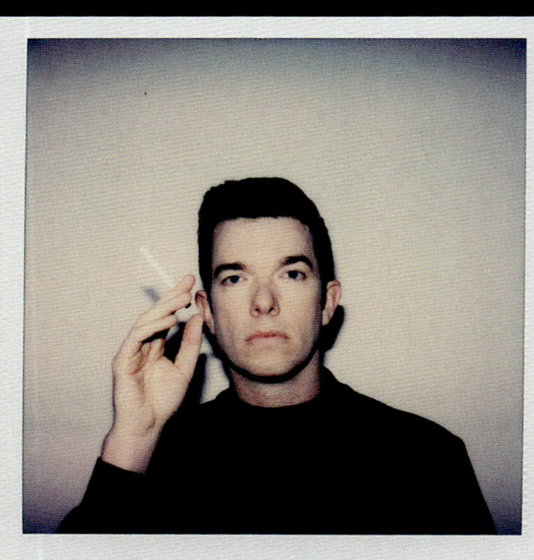
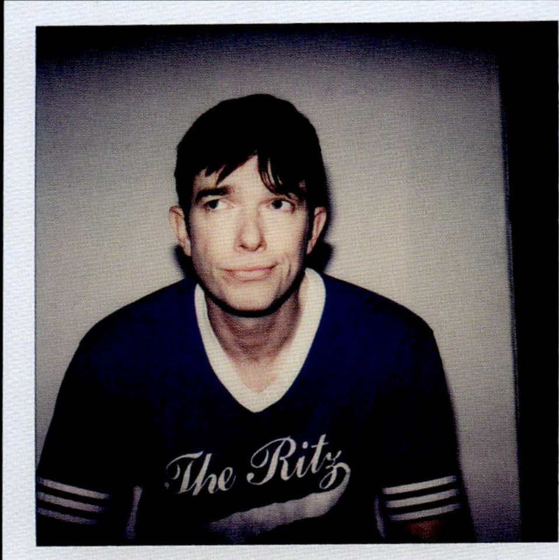

THIS SPREAD

ABOVE This is the only Warhol-y thing we've ever done. This was the late-in-the-show shot. I believe the guy with the cigarette is based on Halston. I believe Andy himself was in these photos wearing the red tie and white shirt and jacket.

OPPOSITE This ended up being the one they framed on the wall for that time hosting. A really cool, straightforward shot. You always kind of need some that are recognizable. Good haircut that day! And a fun Magritte-like move of the legs. I like that it's a busier, heavy shoe. The balance of it is so great. I think about this photo a lot. Every time I cross my legs I think about this series. I can never get over what a simple idea it is, but how compelling it is.

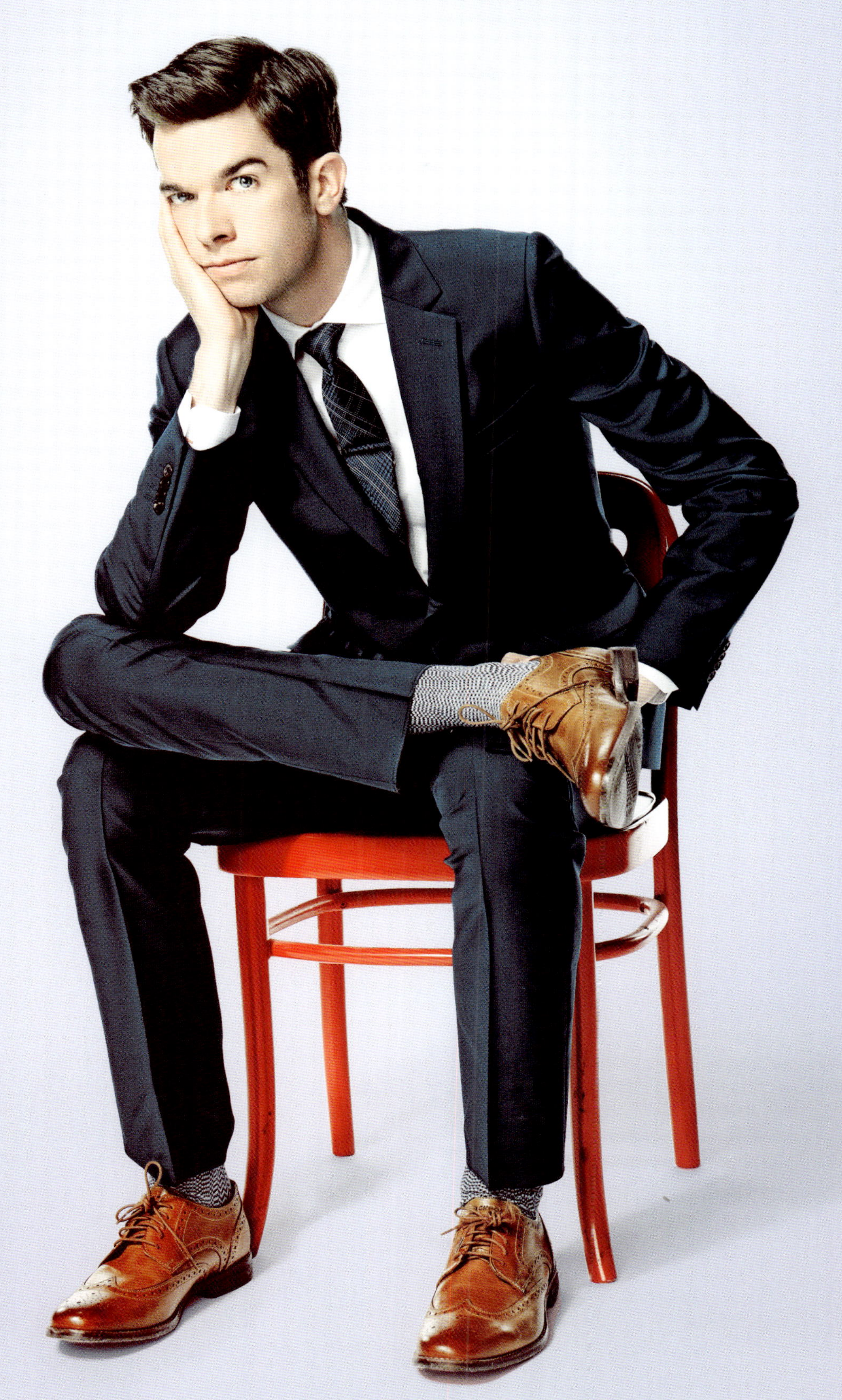

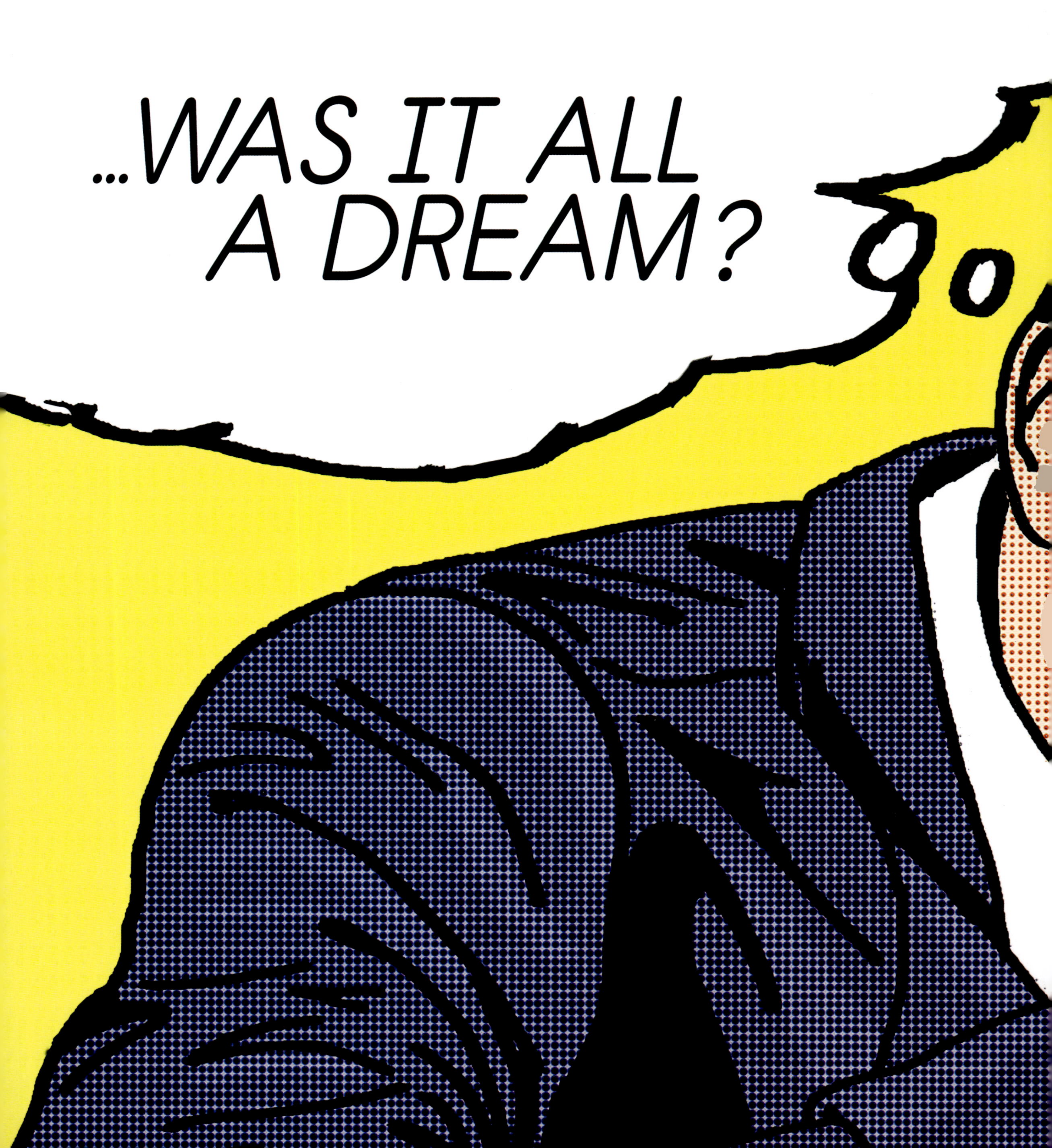
...WAS IT ALL
A DREAM?

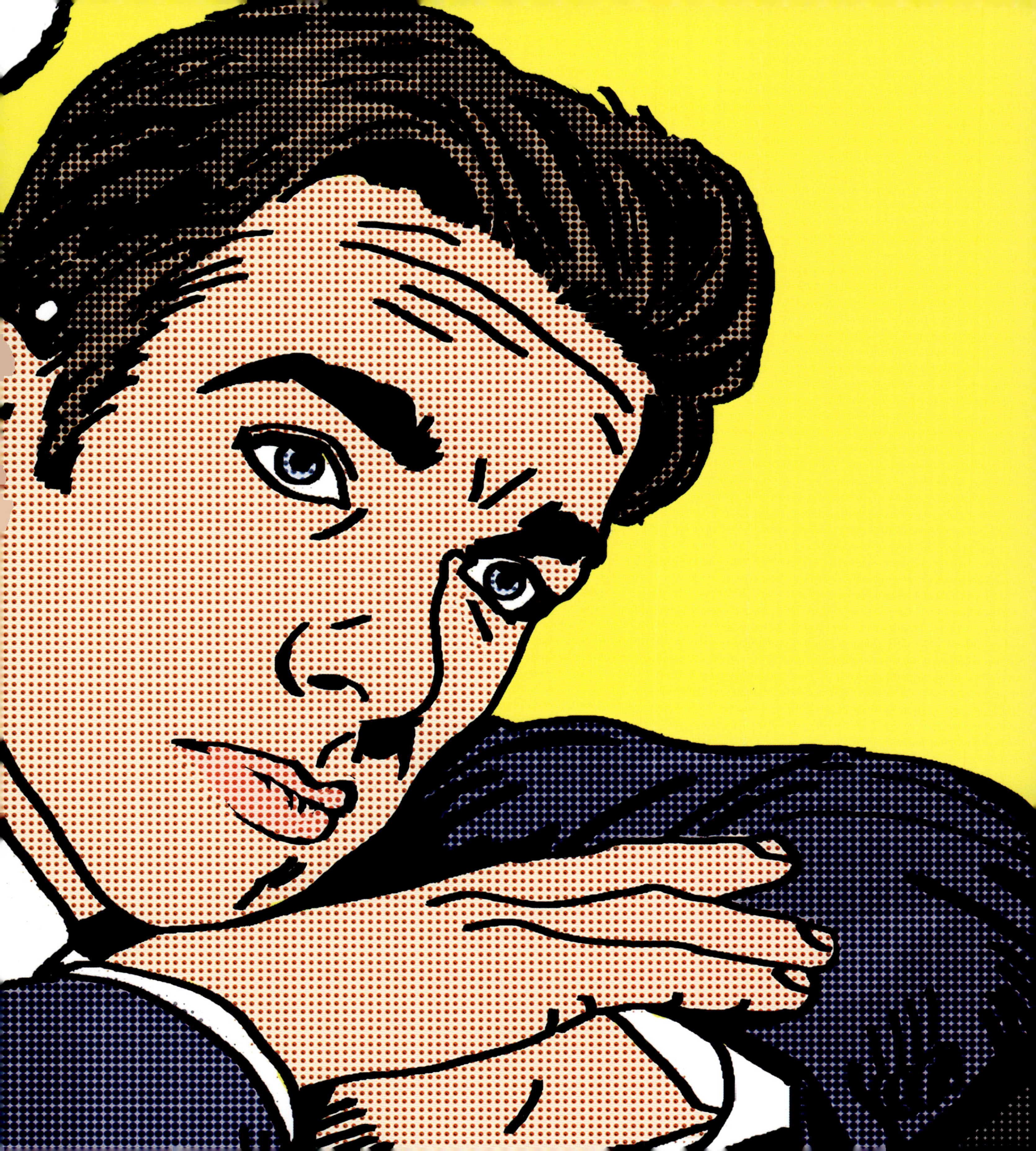

BEHIND

THE SCENES

An exclusive peek at Mary Ellen Matthews's creative process and an homage to the teamwork that helps make the shoots come together. See what it's like to be on set, whether in Studio 8H or on location in New York City.

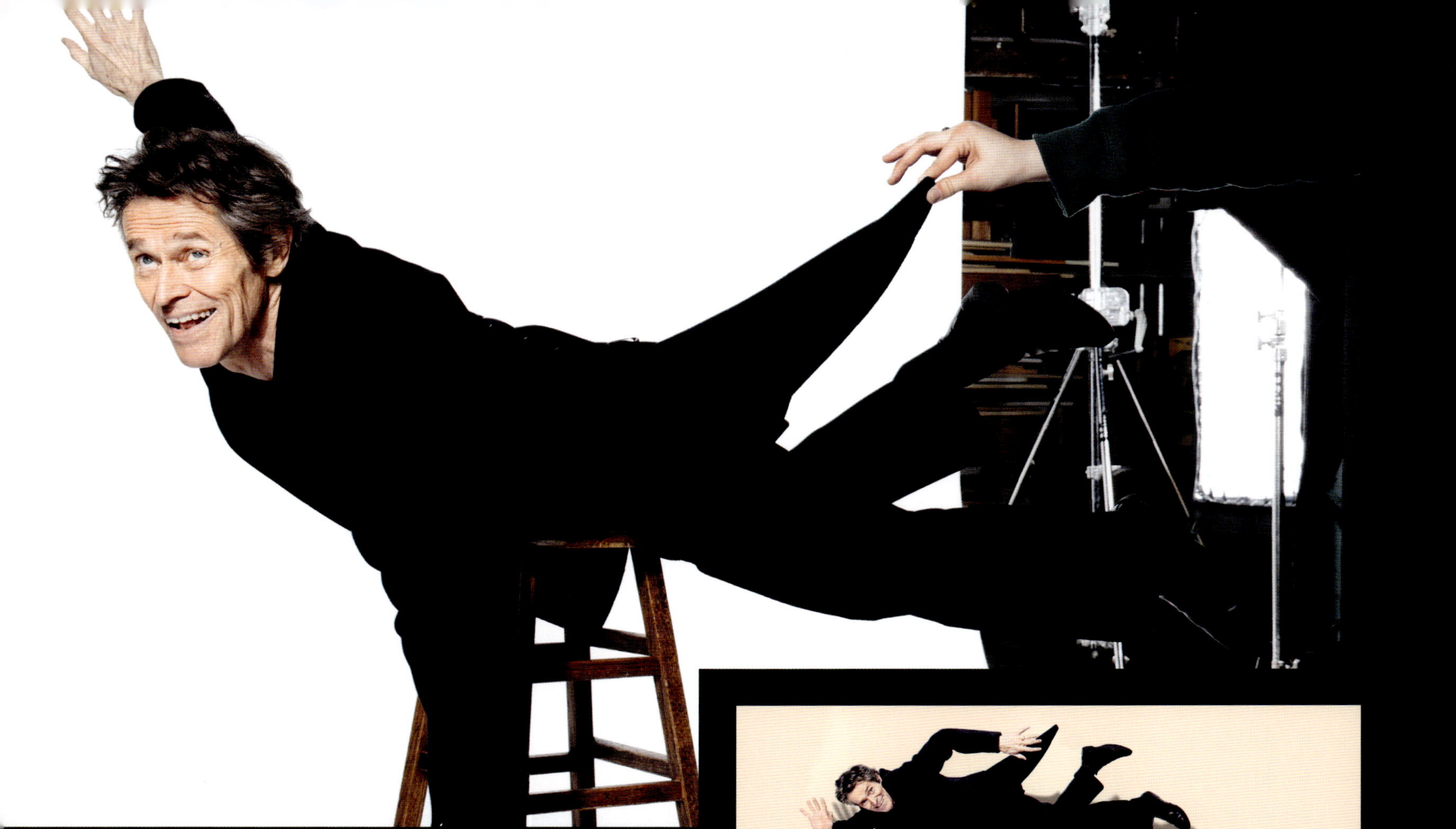

Willem Dafoe →

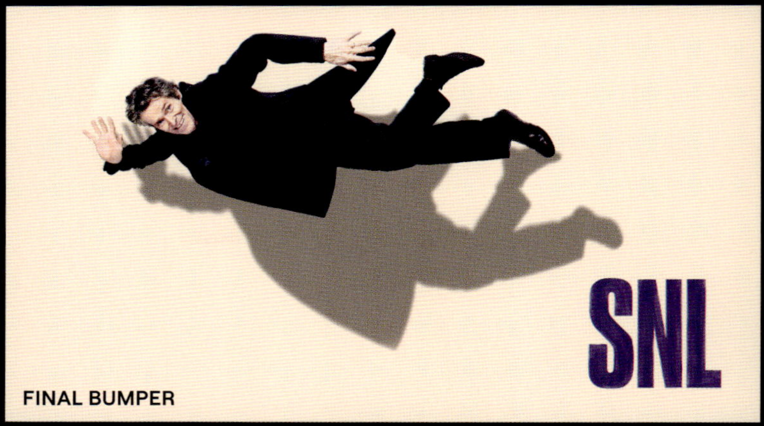

SNL

FINAL BUMPER

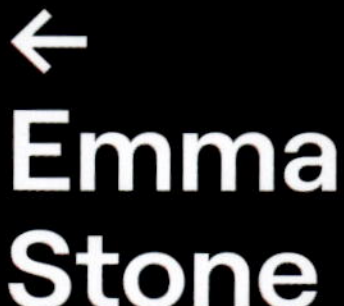

← Emma Stone

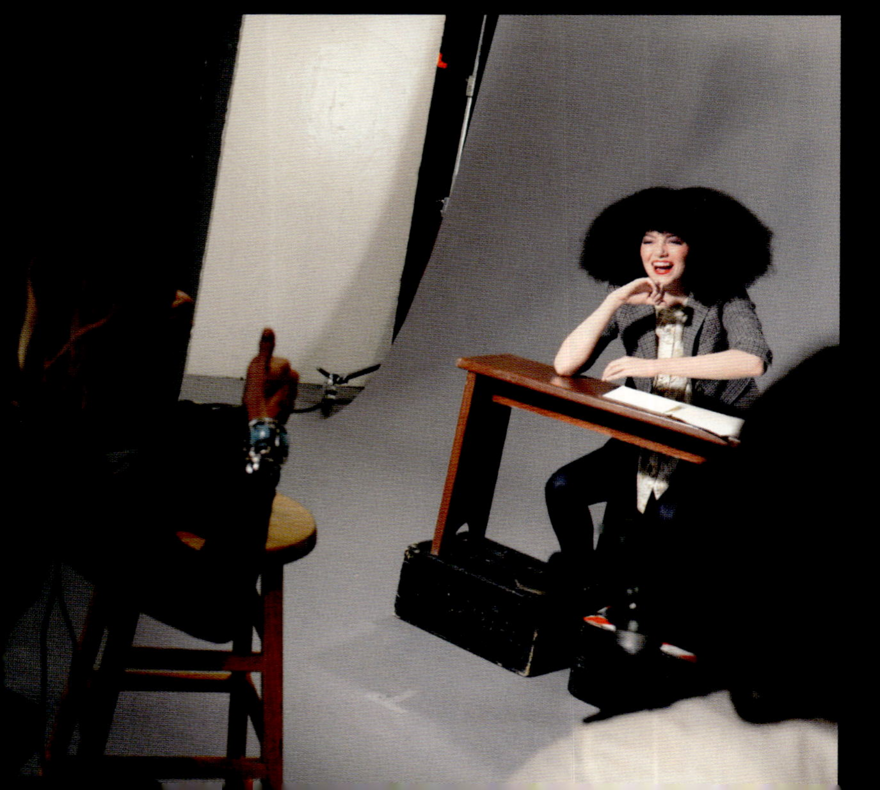

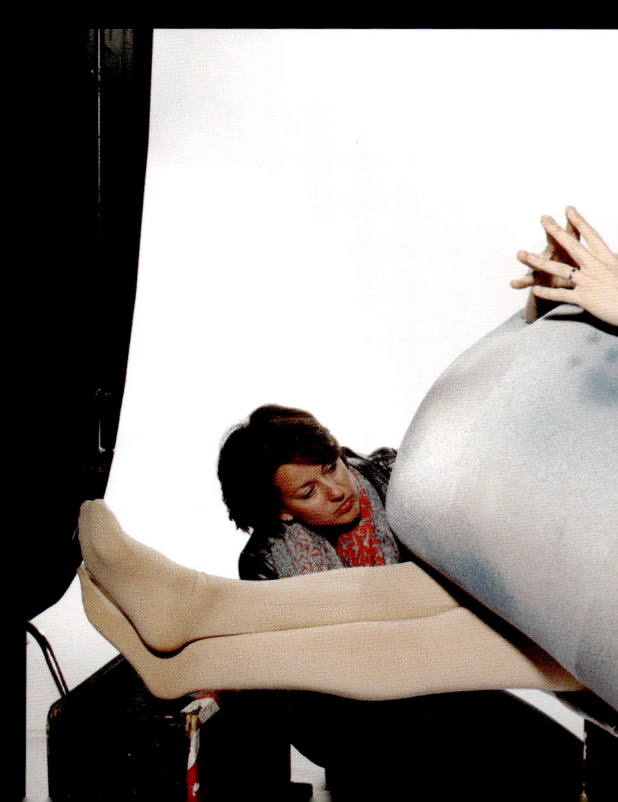

“ANYBODY WHO WAS NEAR THIS SHOOT WAS IN STITCHES LAUGHING.”

↓ Tina Fey and Amy Poehler

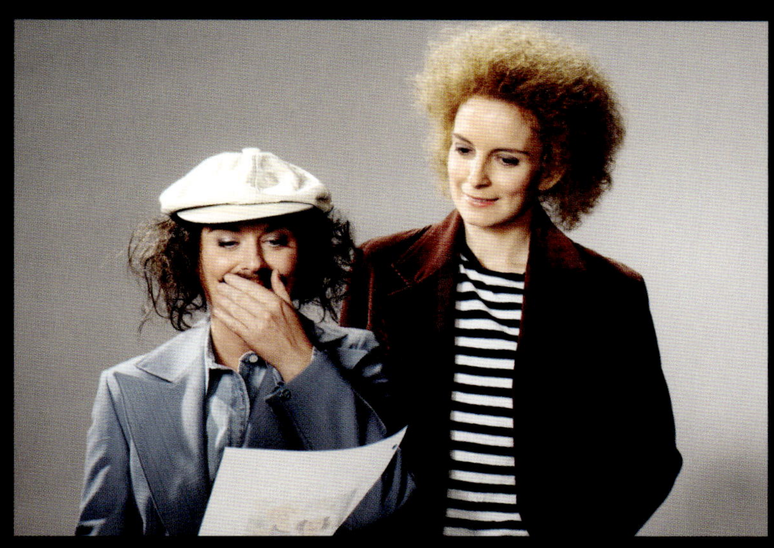

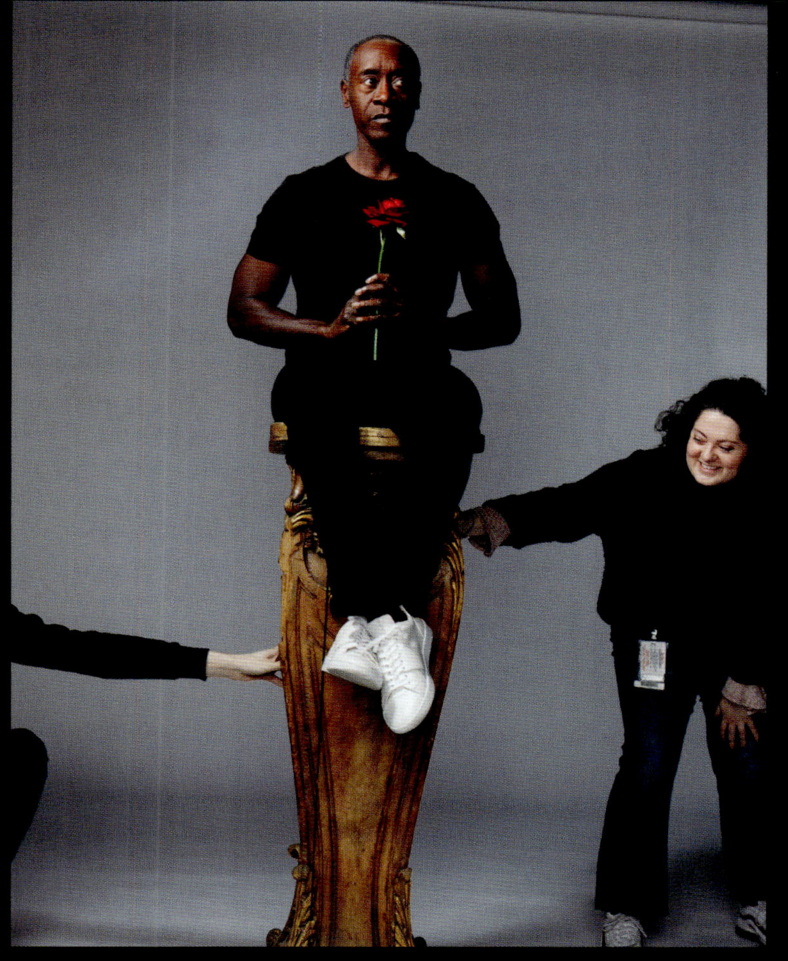

↑ Don Cheadle

↓ Andy Samberg

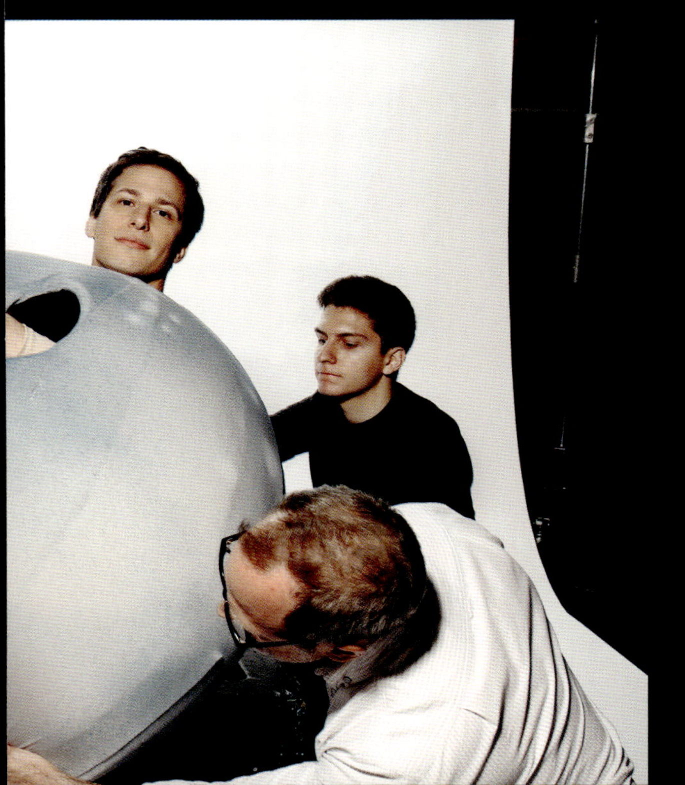

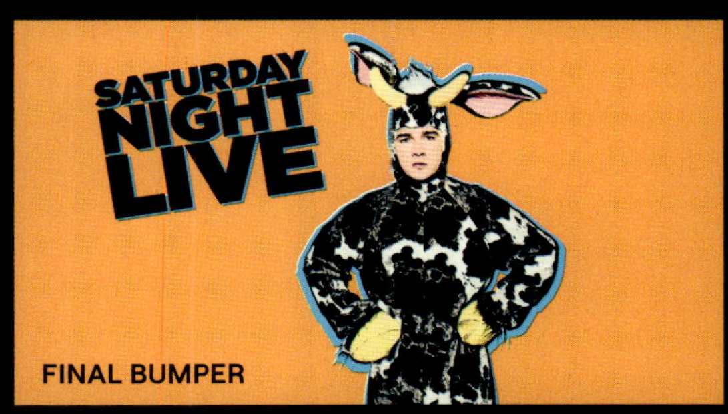

Shia LaBeouf →

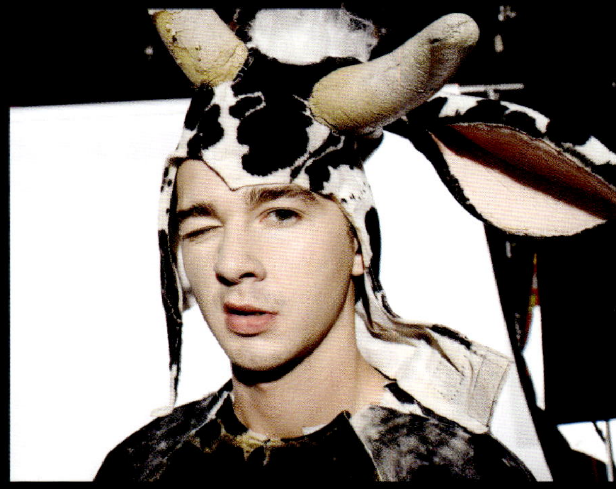

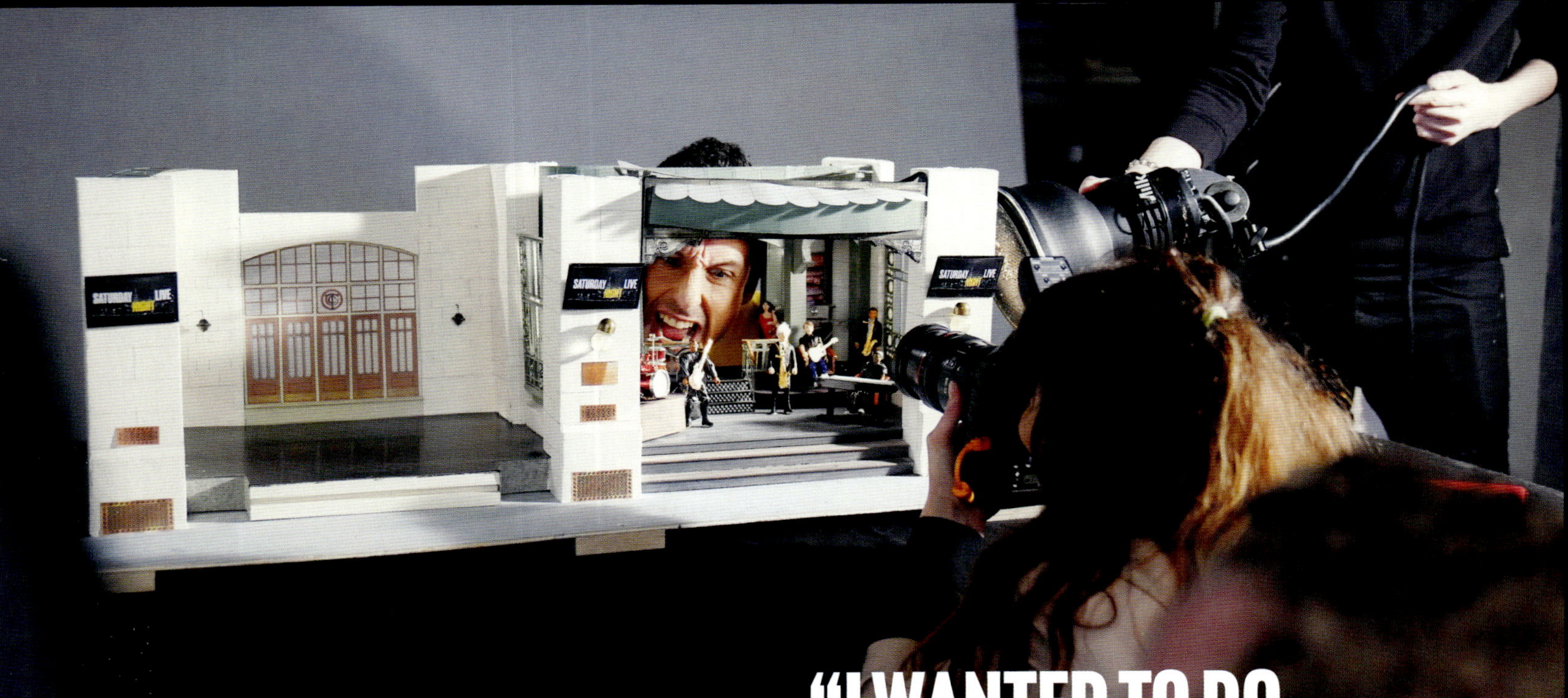

↑
Adam
Sandler

"I WANTED TO DO SOMETHING SPECIAL FOR ADAM, WHICH I ESPECIALLY LIKE TO DO WITH CAST WHEN THEY COME BACK."

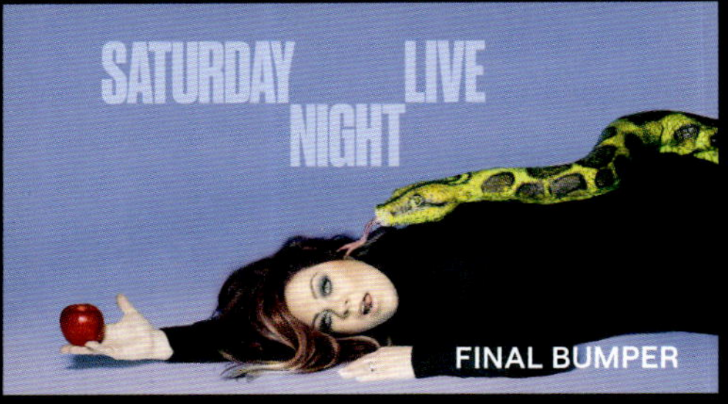

FINAL BUMPER

↑
Melissa
McCarthy

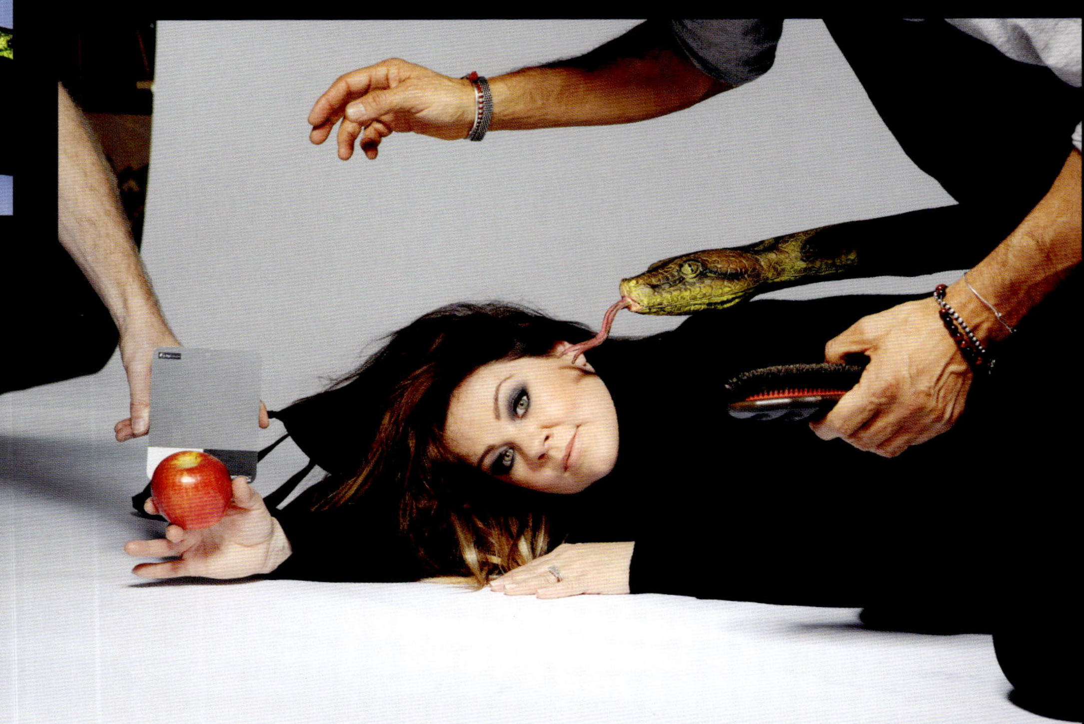

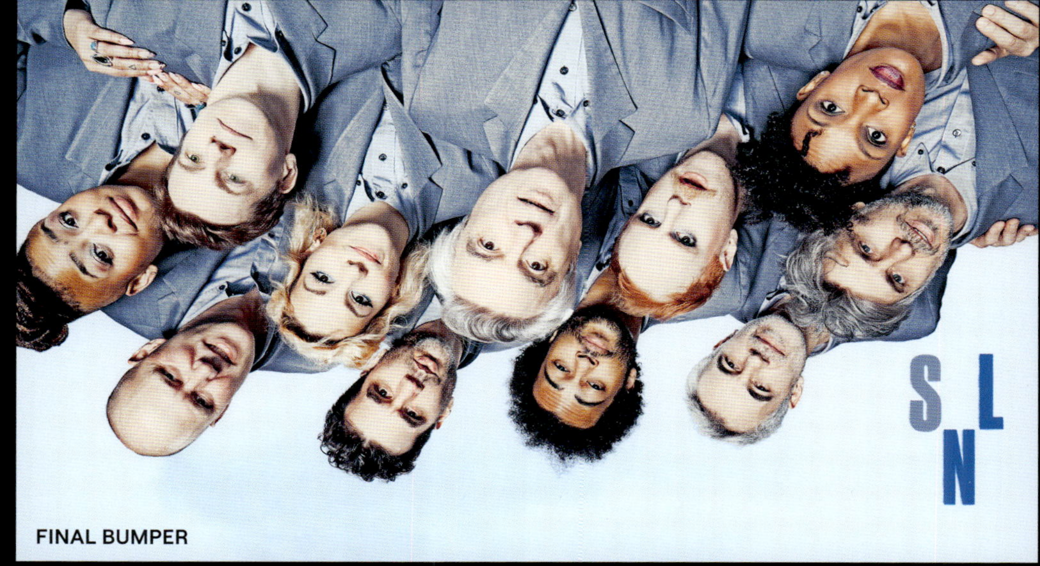

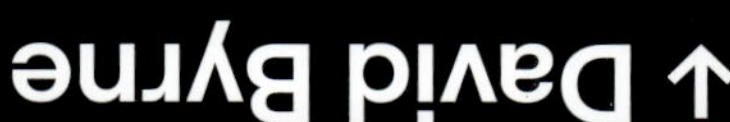

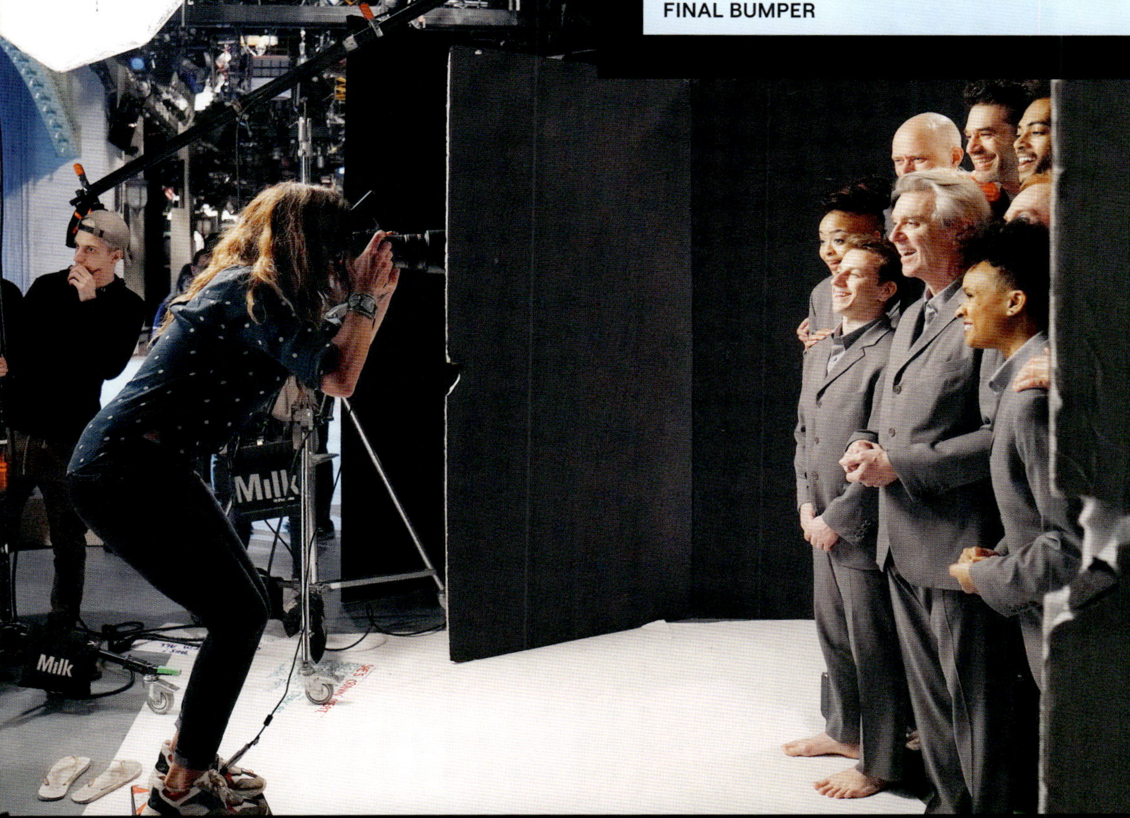

Justin Timberlake
↓

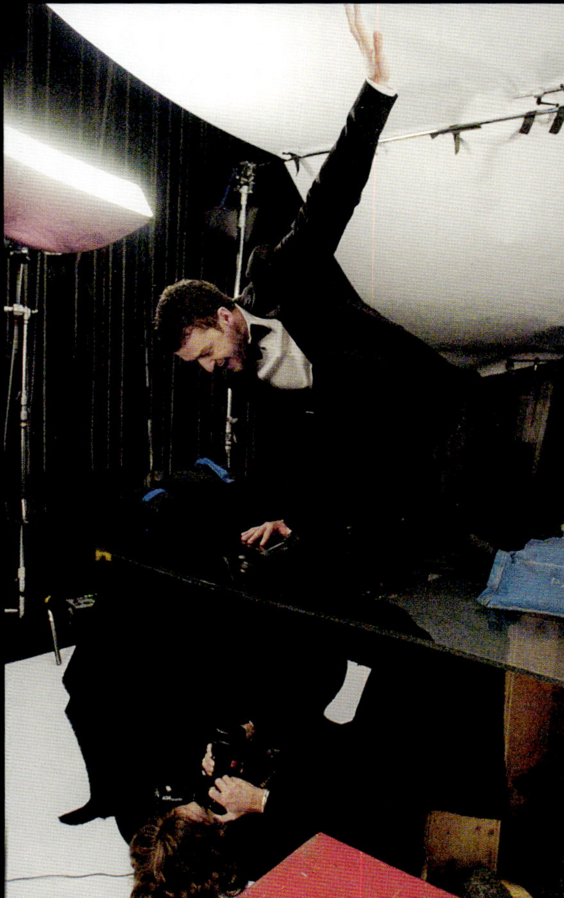

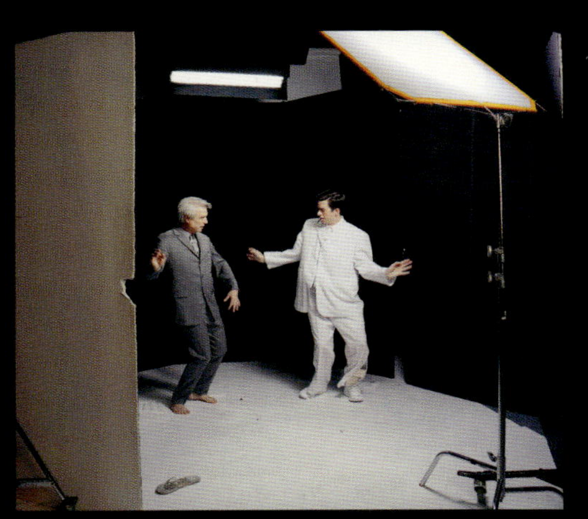

←
David Byrne & John Mulaney

"WE DID THIS OUTSIDE ON THE NBC MARQUEE AND I DIDN'T GET THE CORRECT PERMISSION SO WAS IN A BIT OF TROUBLE FOR THAT. OOPS."

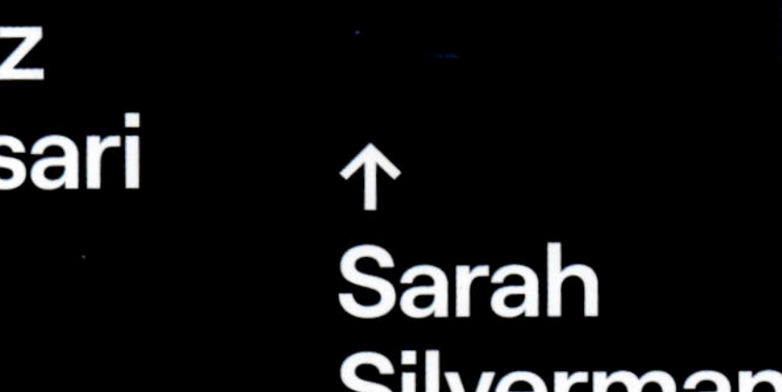

↑ Sarah Silverman

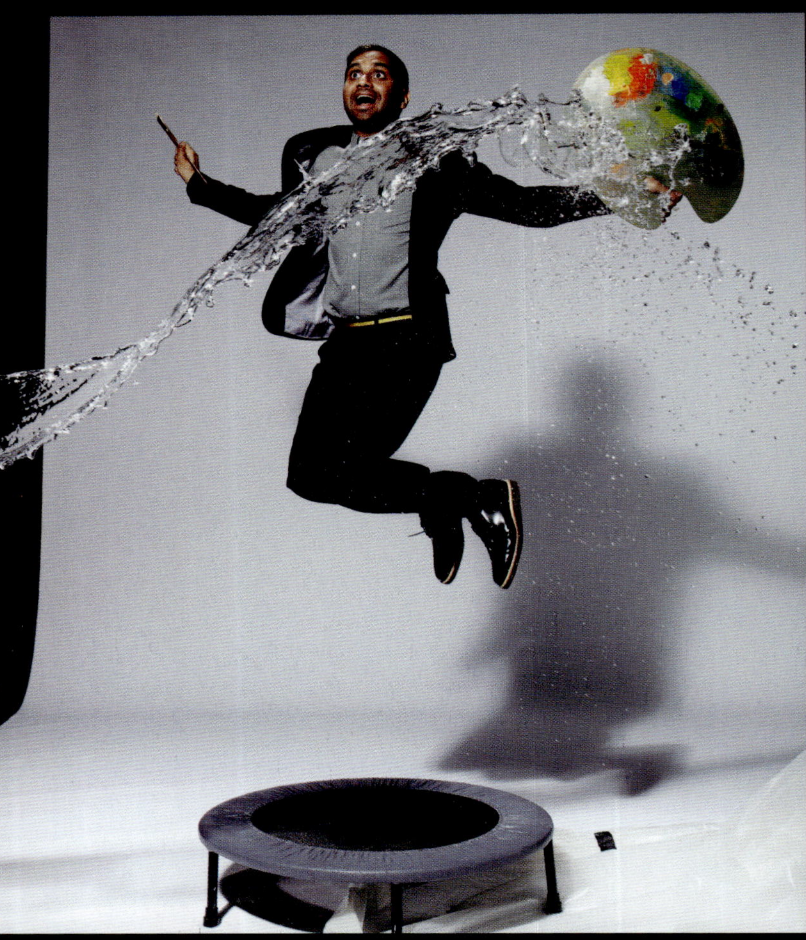

← Aziz Ansari

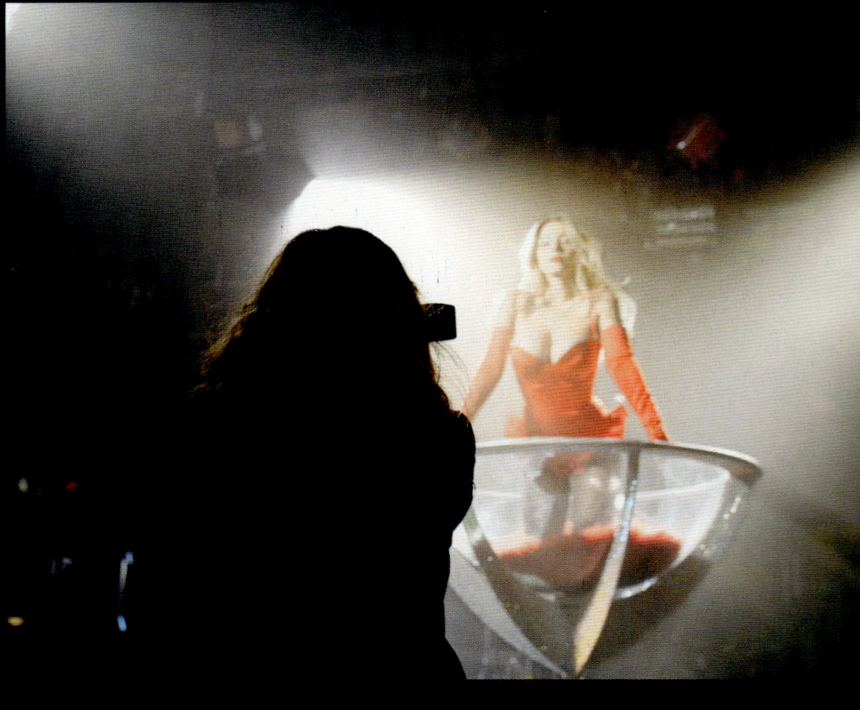

↑ Sydney Sweeney

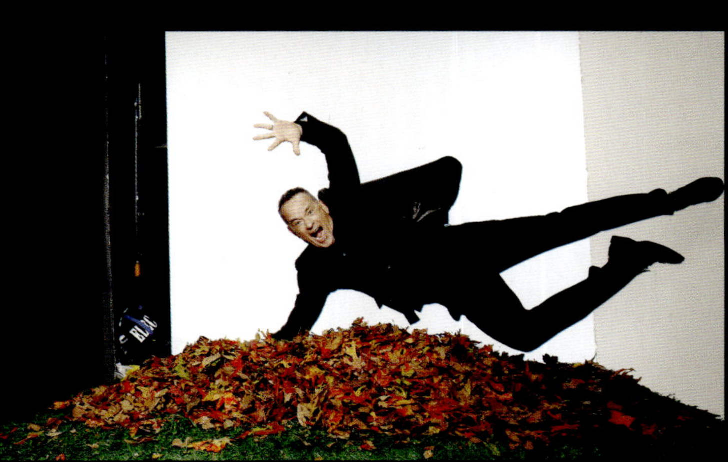

← Tom Hanks

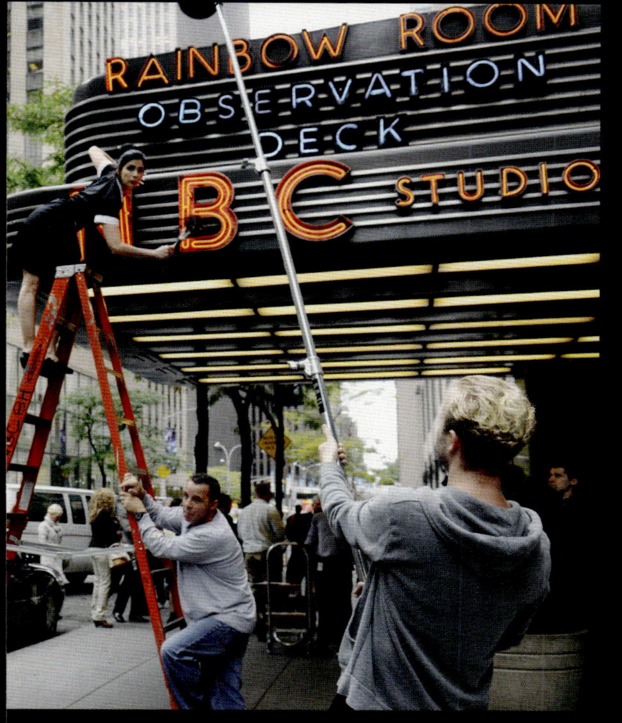

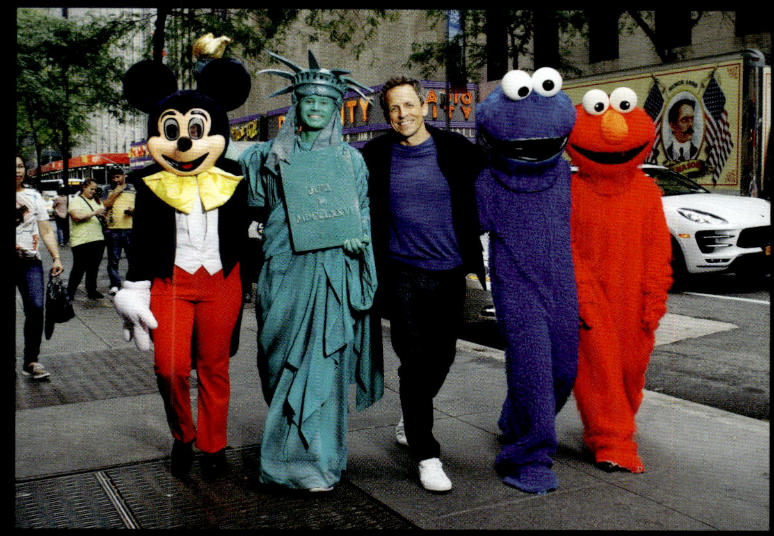

↑ Seth Meyers

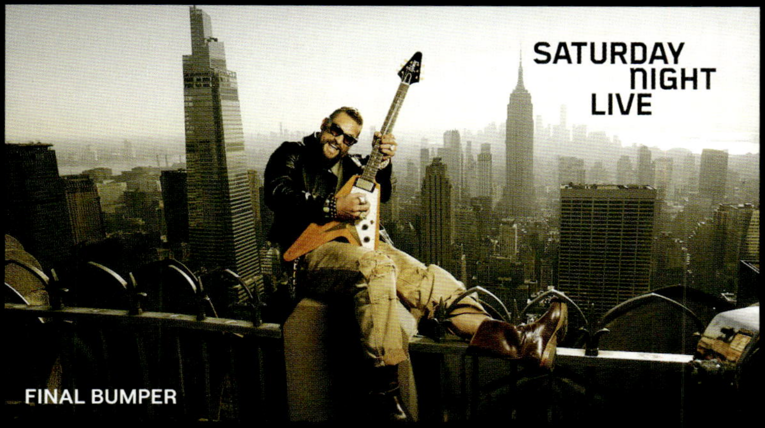

SATURDAY
NIGHT
LIVE

FINAL BUMPER

Jason
Momoa
↓

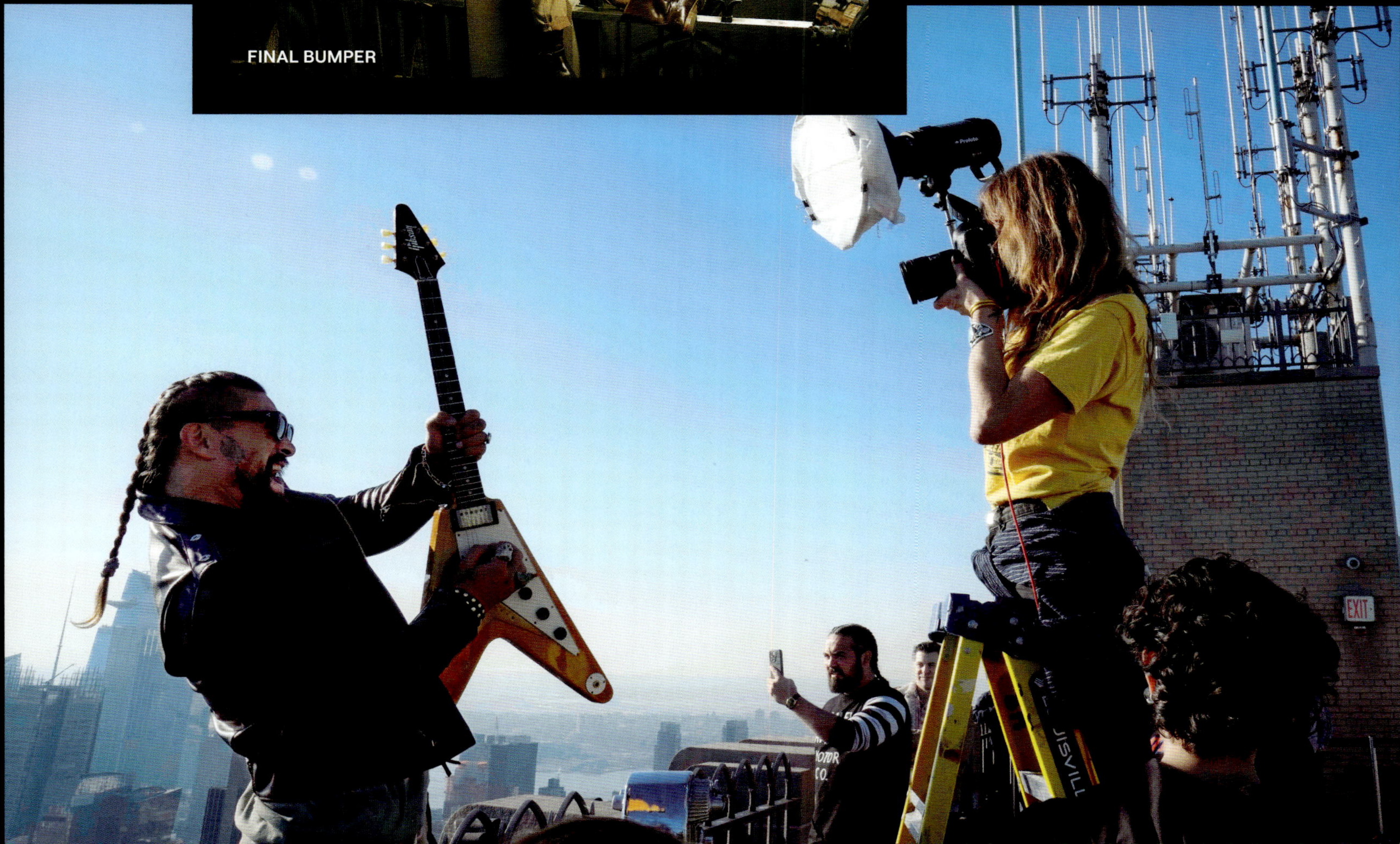

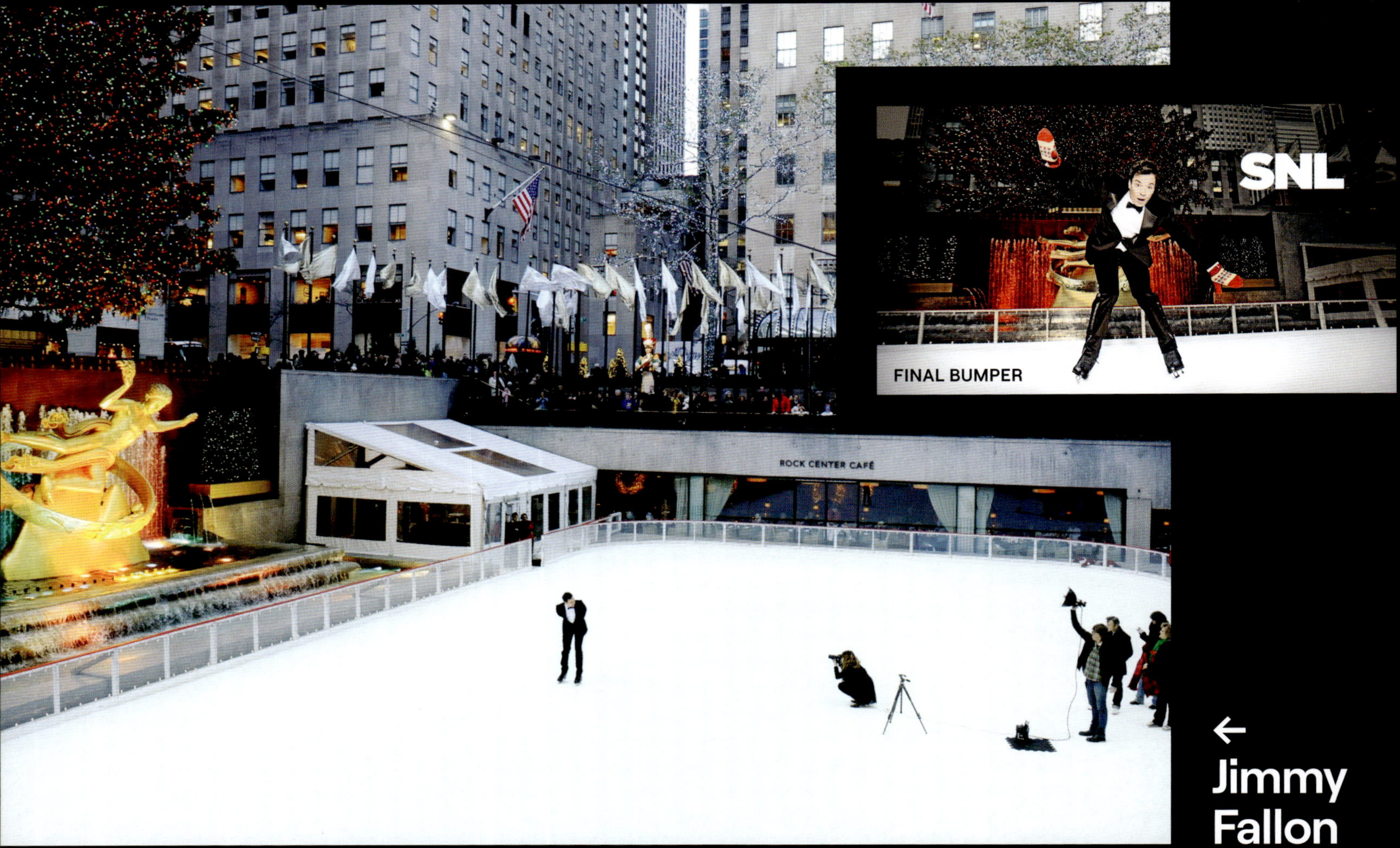

FINAL BUMPER

← Jimmy Fallon

↓ Jim Carrey

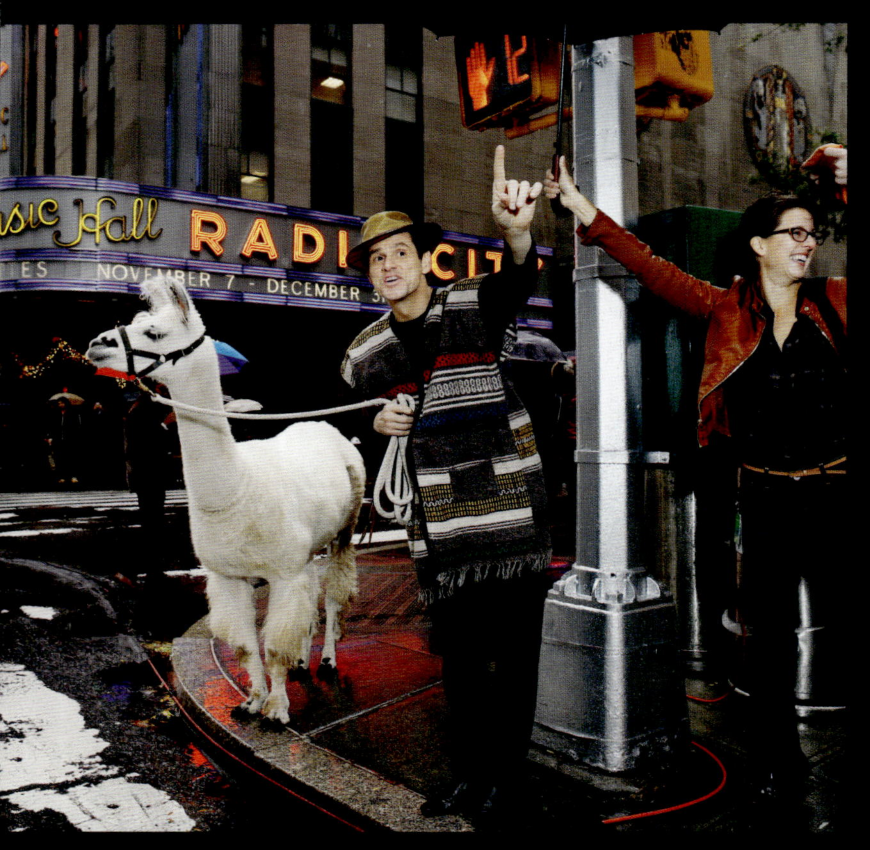

↓ Aubrey Plaza

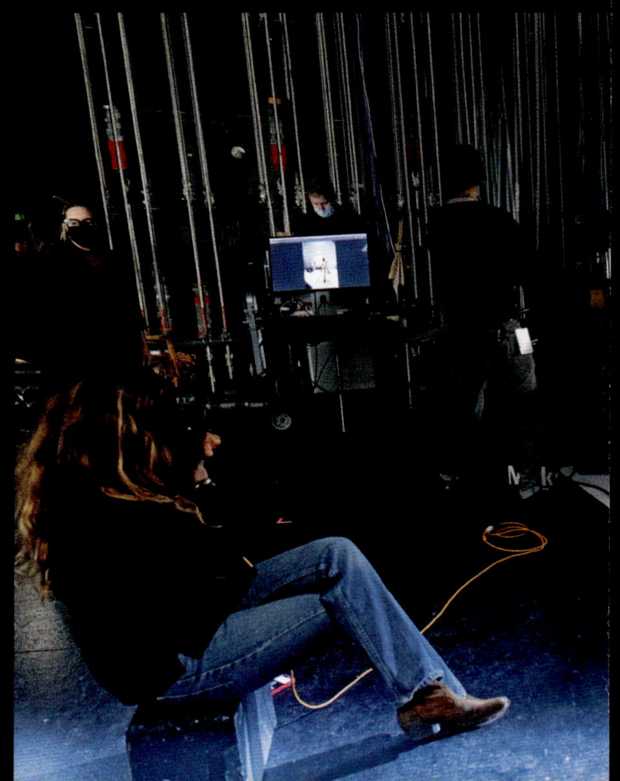

“MY TEAM LIT THIS SO WELL IT LOOKS LIKE IT WAS SHOT IN A STUDIO AND COMPED TOGETHER.”

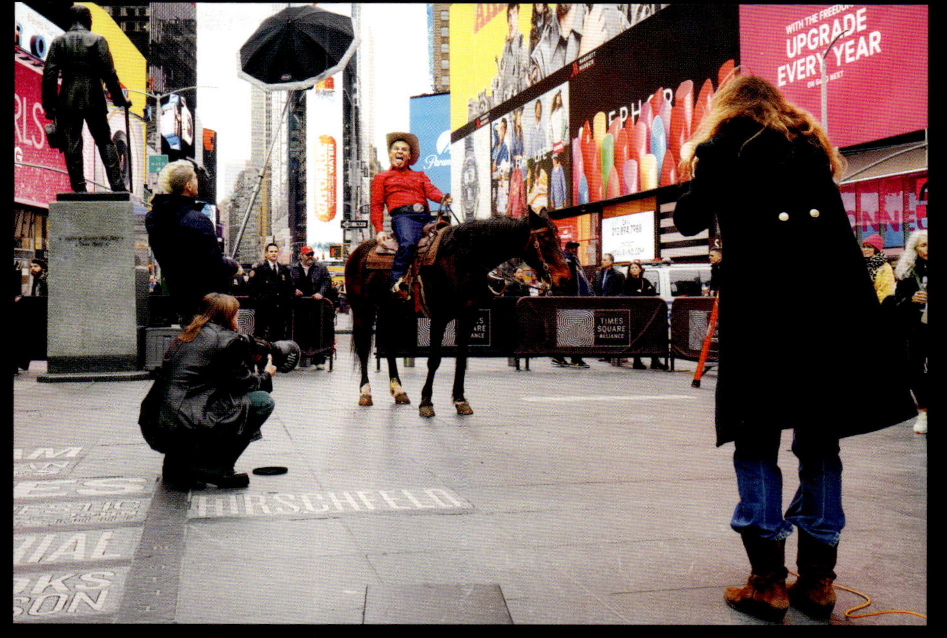

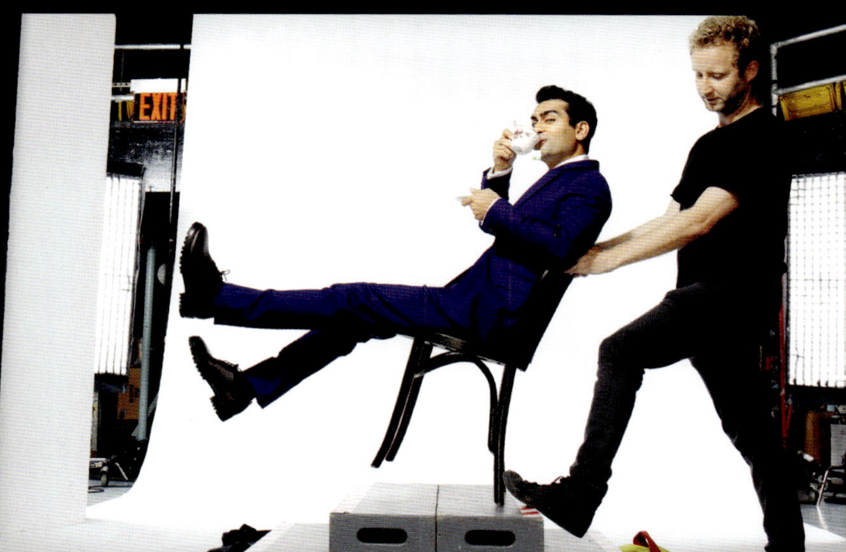

← Kumail Nanjiani

↑ Josh Brolin

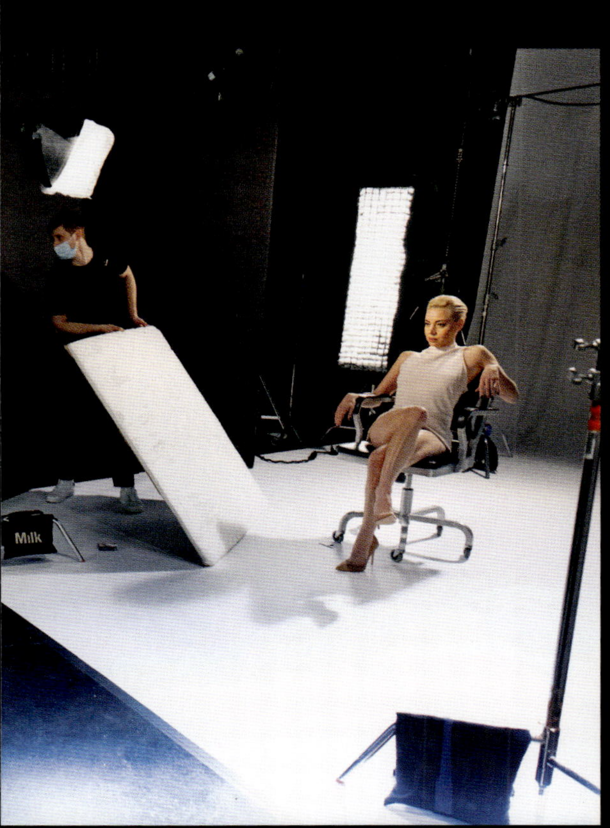

SNL

FINAL BUMPER

↑ Sabrina Carpenter

PHOTO INDEX

COVER ANDY SAMBERG

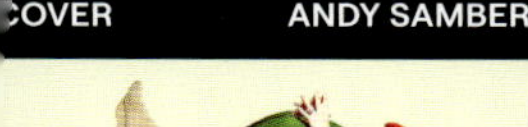

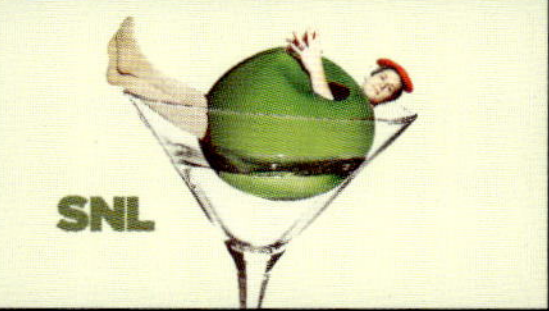

S39 | 05/17/14

I love martinis, and I always thought it would be funny to have somebody as the olive. When I saw Andy Samberg was booked to host, it made perfect sense to me to ask him to be said olive. Tom Broeker had the round costume, although it wasn't green. As the genius he is, he added the red pimiento beret. We estimated the size of the olive and the angle of his legs in the glass and we propped his legs up on a couple of apple boxes and hoped for the best. Such a simple idea given to the right person who can deliver the right expression, and his casual hands on the olive's belly just make magic.

2 SCARLETT JOHANSSON

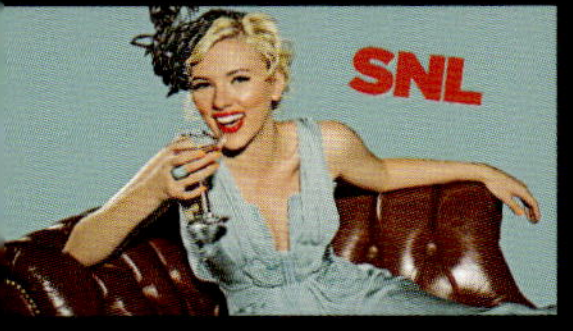

S32 | 04/21/07

Comment from Scarlett Johansson: *"Mary Ellen loves a prop. Somehow she always manages to pull out the most fun and perfect prop to make a whole scene out of nothing, [like] a martini glass and a fun, silly hat. It's what I love most about working with her. Her playfulness is infectious."*

6 WILL FERRELL

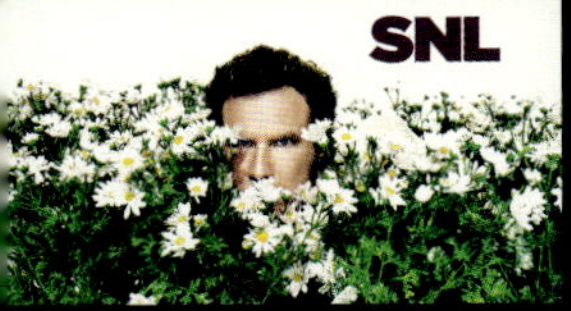

S34 | 05/16/09

18 EMMA STONE

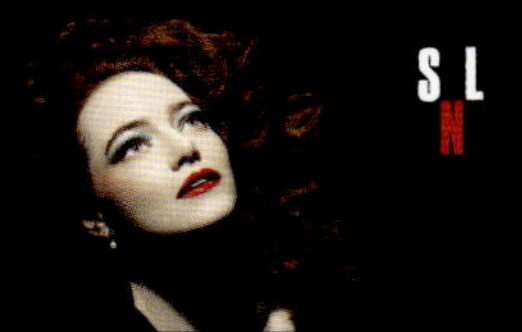

S44 | 04/13/19

I wanted to do something super glamorous, almost old Hollywood, a tribute to George Hurrell. I just adore his lighting style. And to Emma: I'm sorry you had to look into that light.

20 DANIEL CRAIG

S45 | 03/07/20

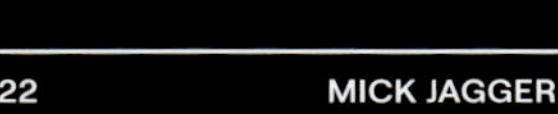

22 MICK JAGGER

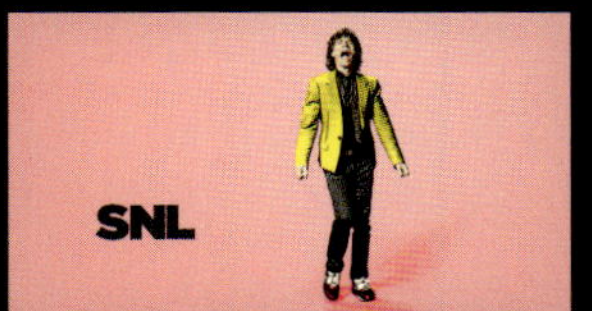

S37 | 05/19/12

One of the most intimidating shoots of my life, he's my absolute hero and such a sweetheart!

24 LARRY DAVID

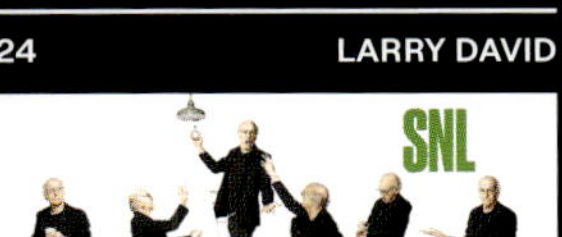

S41 | 02/06/16

26 ISSA RAE

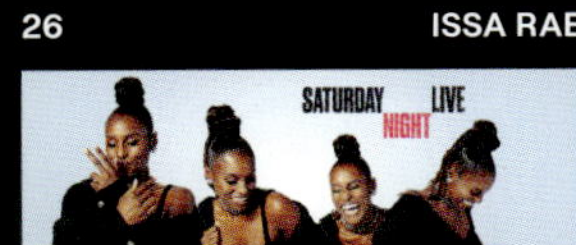

S46 | 10/17/20

27 KENDRICK LAMAR

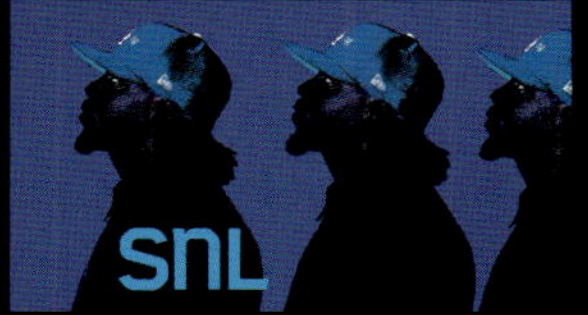

S48 | 10/01/22

28 MACHINE GUN KELLY

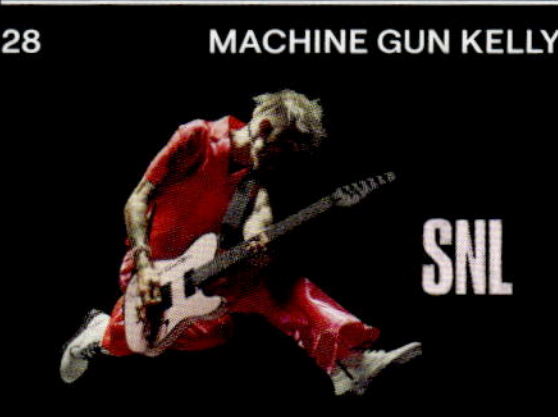

S46 | 01/30/21

29 DAN LEVY

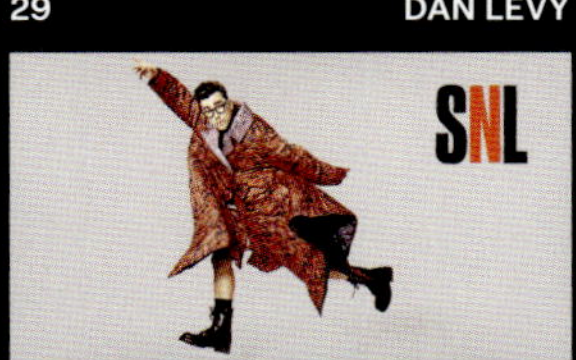

S46 | 02/06/21

30 ANDERSON .PAAK

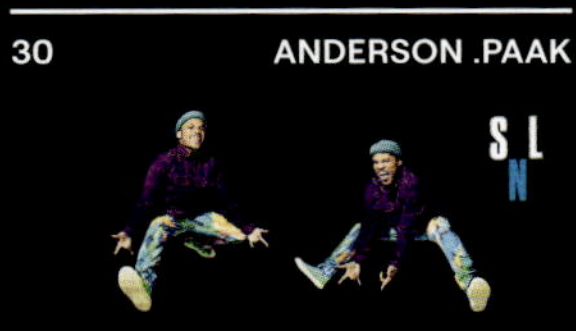

S44 | 12/01/18

32 JUSTIN BIEBER

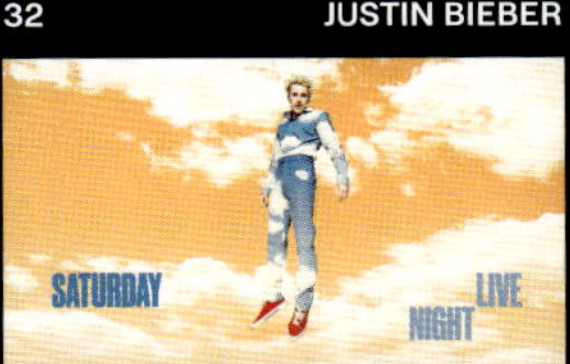

S45 | 02/08/20

I love the way it feels like he's falling out of the sky.

33 BENEDICT CUMBERBATCH

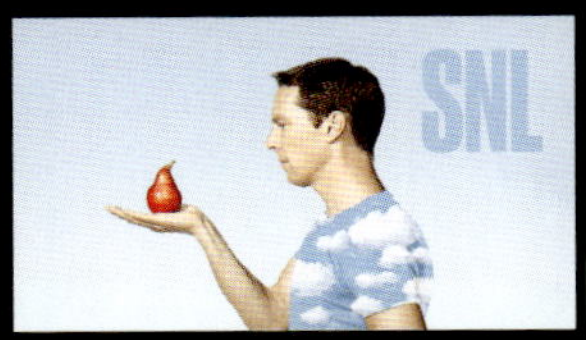

S42 | 11/5/16

We happened to have a pear on set and I think I said, "Consider the pear." The clouds got added in postproduction to give it a Magritte feel.

34 AYO EDEBIRI

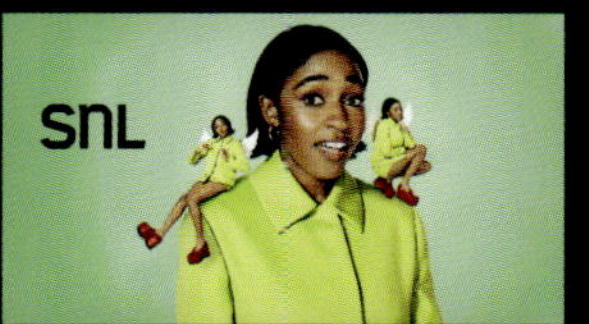

S49 | 02/03/24

This was Ayo's idea. She wanted to do angel and devil, but I had done that with Ryan Gosling, so we did two angels, because she's an angel. Of course a last-minute dash to costumes to get the wings!

35 JASON MOMOA

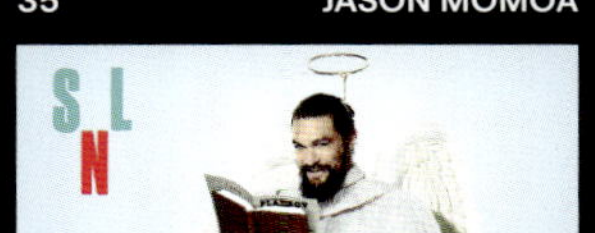

S44 | 12/8/18

36 DREW BARRYMORE

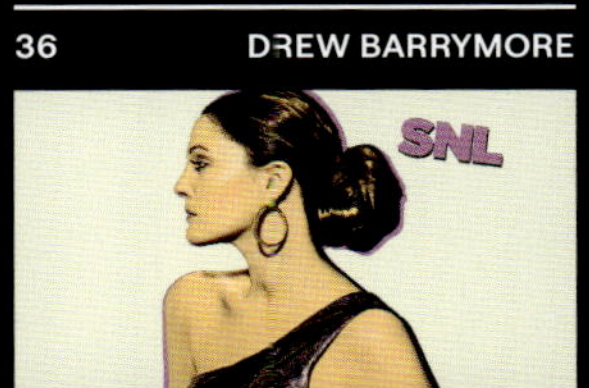

S32 | 02/03/07

38 ALEC BALDWIN

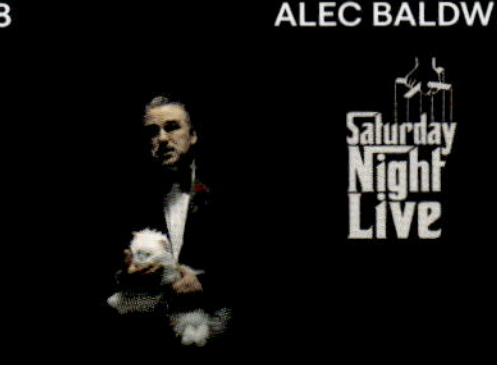

S34 | 02/14/09

This was Alec's idea to do *The Godfather*, and I suggested the stuffed cat instead of a real one, which puts it in the world of SNL. I don't like to make these recreations too close to the original, to me it's got to have something that's off or not quite right.

Comment from Alec Baldwin: *"Usually, we would shoot two types of looks. One was a more natural portrait. Then we'd do something silly like this. I always loved when Mary Ellen would attempt this kind of thing. I love this picture."*

40 JIM CARREY

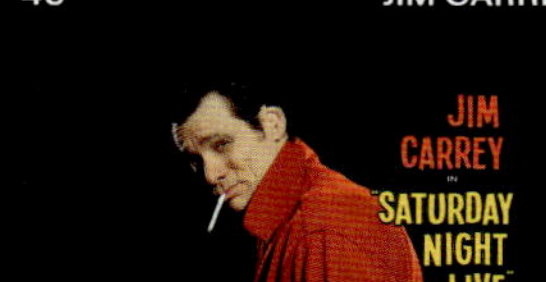

S36 | 01/08/11

I can't remember which of us had the idea for him to be James Dean. Tara Donnelly in the graphics department made the text look like the *Rebel Without a Cause* poster and it came out great.

42 JONAH HILL

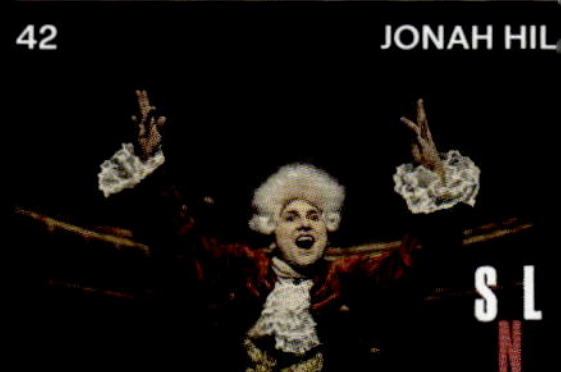

S44 | 11/04/18

We were talking about movies and Jonah said that *Amadeus* was one of his favorites. So I spoke to the costume and wig departments and thankfully was able to make it work. I used a shot of Studio 8H's balcony seating for the background, but made it look like a centuries-old theater in Photoshop.

43 LADY GAGA

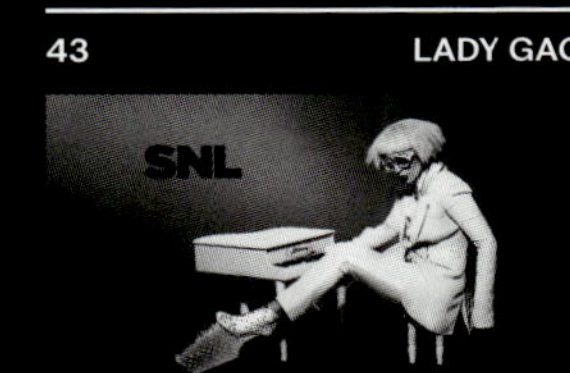

S39 | 11/16/13

44 JIMMY FALLON

S37 | 12/17/11

Both Jimmy and I are huge music fans, so we decided to do a Bowie tribute. This is actually a still from an animation where he opens his eyes.

46 **LCD SOUNDSYSTEM**

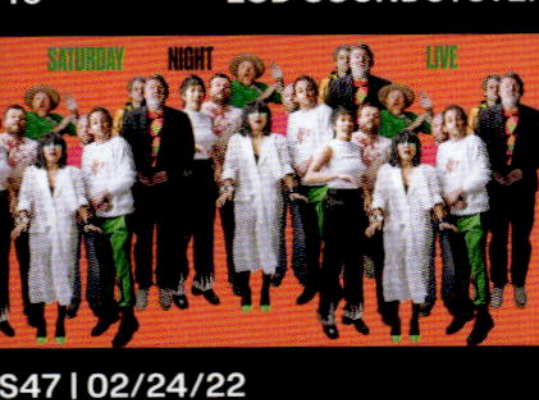

S47 | 02/24/22

48 **FRANK OCEAN**

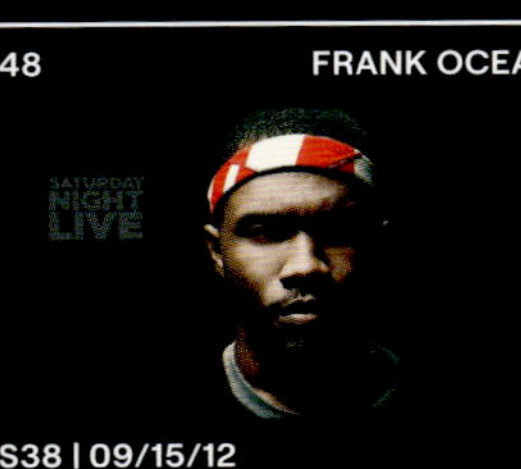

S38 | 09/15/12

50 **LARRY DAVID**

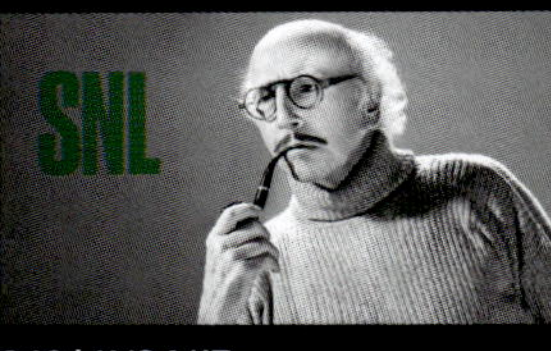

S43 | 11/04/17

I wish we came up with a name for this fellow. I think LD uses this photo as his current headshot.

52 **TINA FEY & AMY POEHLER**

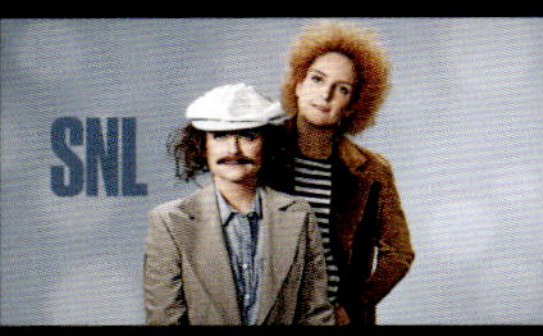

S41 | 12/19/15

This is a direct reference to the Simon & Garfunkel image, and anybody who was near this shoot was in stitches laughing. Every time Amy and Tina caught a glimpse of themselves they would just break. I don't know how they managed to keep a straight face for the photo.

53 **TOM HANKS**

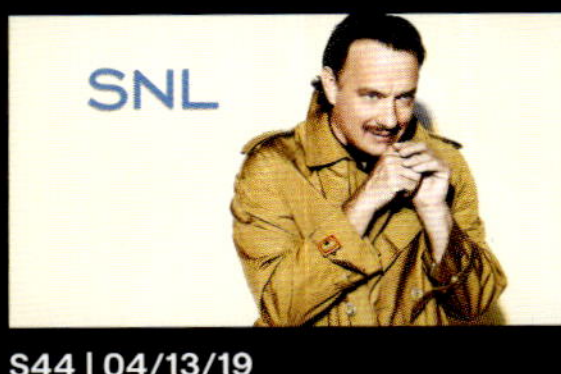

S44 | 04/13/19

Comment from Tom: *"Those photos taken by Mary Ellen capture the very specific moment in time—the week of doing SNL. There is the specific facial hair, the look of each played-up photo, with the sessions coming right smack in the midst of getting the show up. I look at the photos and am transported to the world and energy of doing that LIVE Show, then and there."*

54 **EMMA STONE**

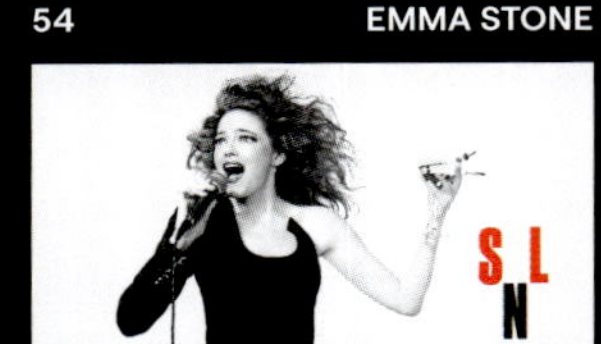

S44 | 04/13/19

55 **WILL FORTE**

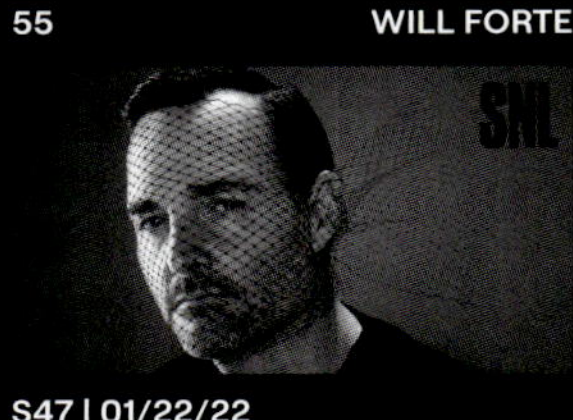

S47 | 01/22/22

56 **DWAYNE JOHNSON**

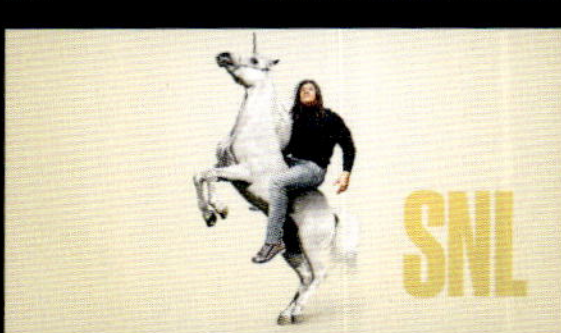

S42 | 05/20/17

Dwayne was actually dressed in this outfit for another bumper we did, where he reenacts an old photo of him wearing a fanny pack that had become a meme. Then I thought about him in the same outfit but wearing a wig and riding a stallion with the horse's mane flowing. So I asked Jodi [Mancuso, hair designer] if she had a long black wig lying around and luckily she did. I had him sit on a stool and gave him directions for how to pose, then used a stock photo of a horse, and at the last minute I added the unicorn horn.

57 **FRED ARMISEN**

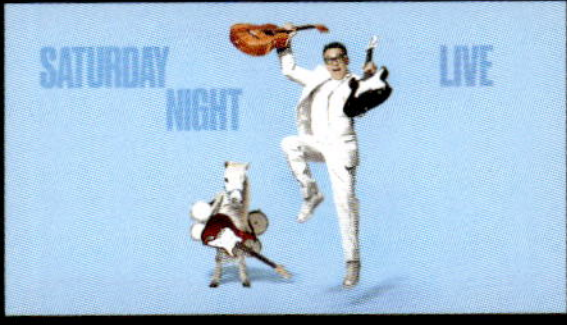

S41 | 05/21/16

This is a spoof of the cover of the Rolling Stones album *Get Yer Ya-Ya's Out!* Having the little pony in the studio was a big hit.

58 **TINA FEY**

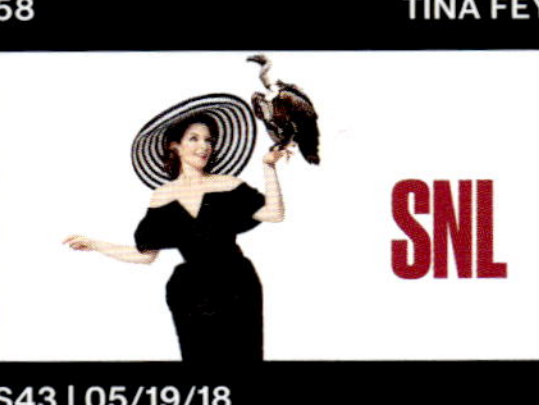

S43 | 05/19/18

The inspiration was: a very pulled-together gal from a vintage high fashion magazine holding a little canary, but have it be a huge vulture instead.

59 **AMY SCHUMER**

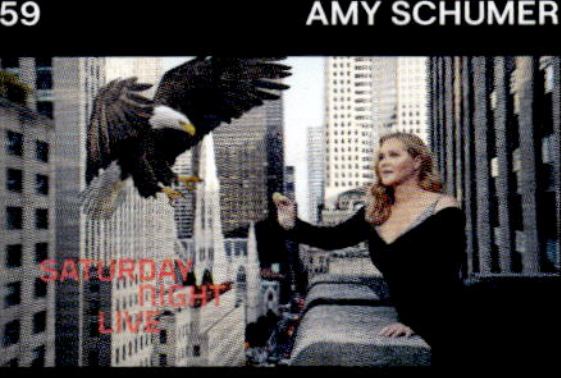

S48 | 11/05/22

I was going after a Marilyn Monroe type shot, similar to the one I had done with the mop for SNL at Home. We brought some bread to attract pigeons but it didn't really work. And then I thought it would be so much funnier if there was a big ridiculous bird than the reality of a pigeon. And the stock photo eagle fit the bill.

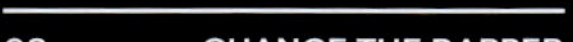

60 **CHANCE THE RAPPER**

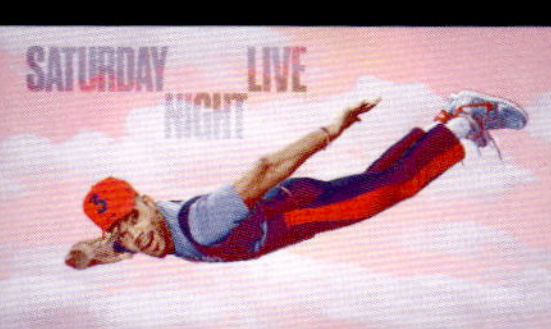

S43 | 11/18/17

62 **DANIEL RADCLIFFE**

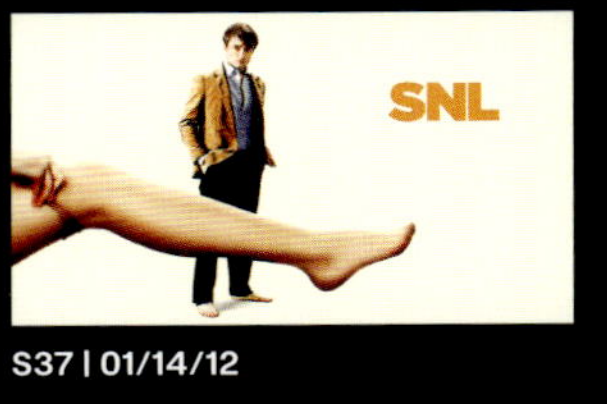

S37 | 01/14/12

We actually had an NBC page volunteer her leg for this takeoff of the *Graduate* poster.

64 **AUBREY PLAZA**

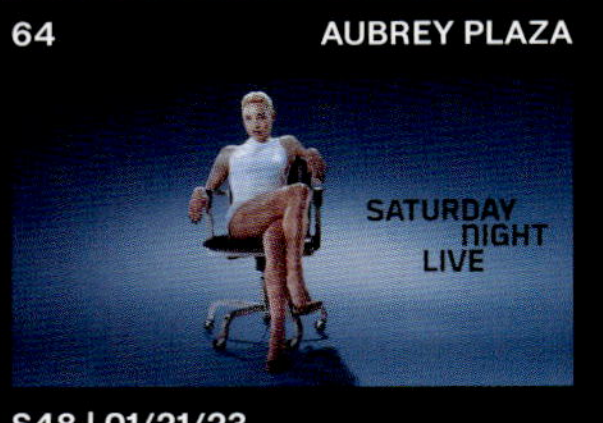

S48 | 01/21/23

I was in a cab on the way to the shoot and had this last-minute thought to have Aubrey to give us a *Basic Instinct* moment by portraying Sharon Stone in that iconic scene. She loved the idea and said, "Do you know who's here today?" And it turned out that Sharon Stone was actually in the studio, rehearsing with Sam Smith, which was an unbelievable coincidence. And thankfully, we had a similar chair lying around to pull off the image so quickly. We referenced the original scene and my lighting crew, Alex and Will, got it perfect.

66 **PETE DAVIDSON**

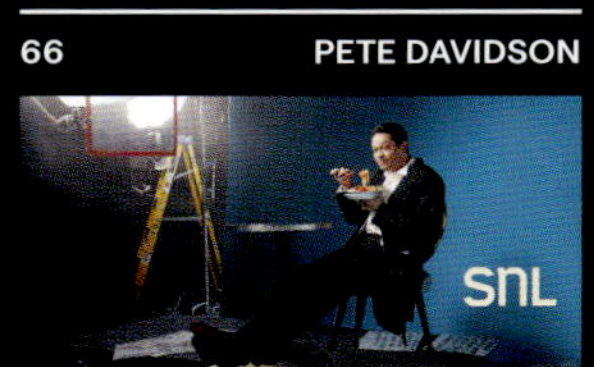

S49 | 10/14/23

68 **KATE MCKINNON**

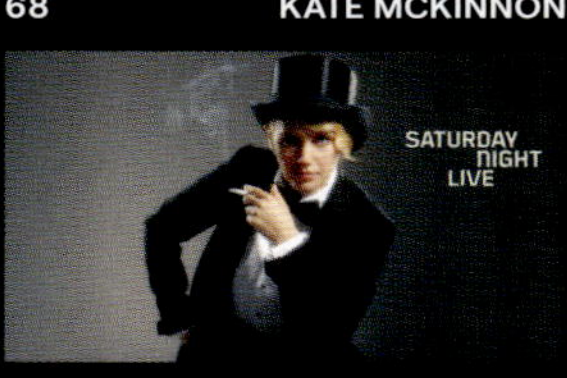

S49 | 12/19/23

Kate McKinnon as Marlene Dietrich.

70 **DAVE CHAPPELLE**

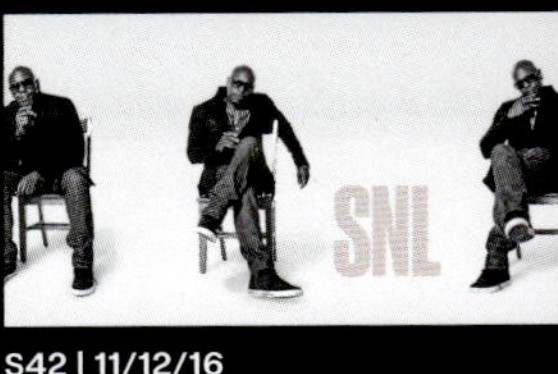

S42 | 11/12/16

Dave is the only person who's allowed to smoke real cigarettes in the studio.

72 **JACK WHITE**

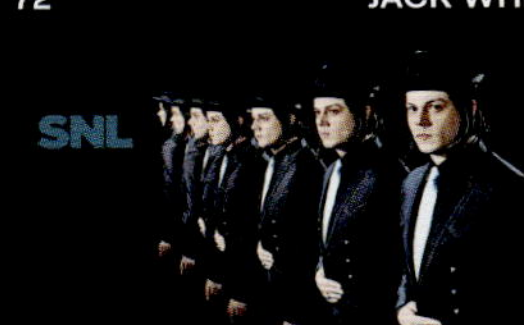

S42 | 03/03/12

This one the first times I started doing bursts. The camera takes many frames per second so they can be used as a little animation. Instead of using them as a moving image, I thought it was interesting to see them all spread out as a still.

73 **STEVE LACY**

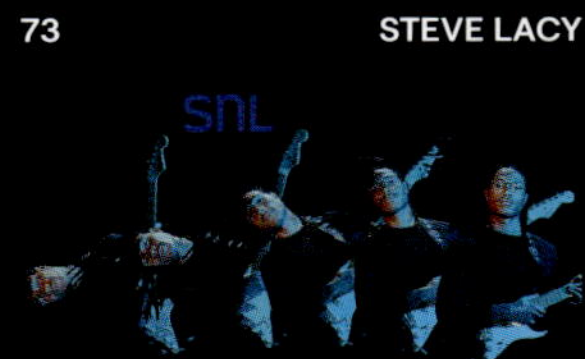

S48 | 11/05/22

Another example of a burst used as a still.

74 **SETH MEYERS**

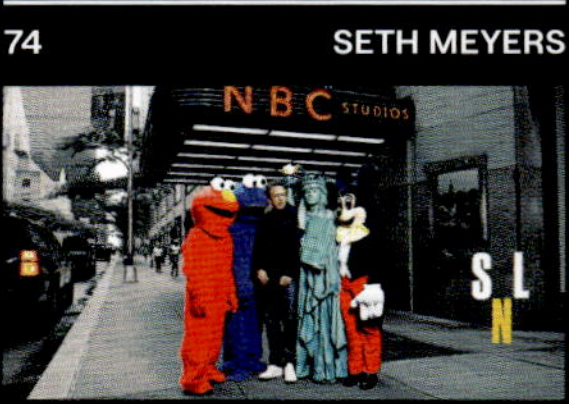

S44 | 10/13/18

Some of these were hired straight from Times Square and some were interns wearing costumes but I can't remember who was who.

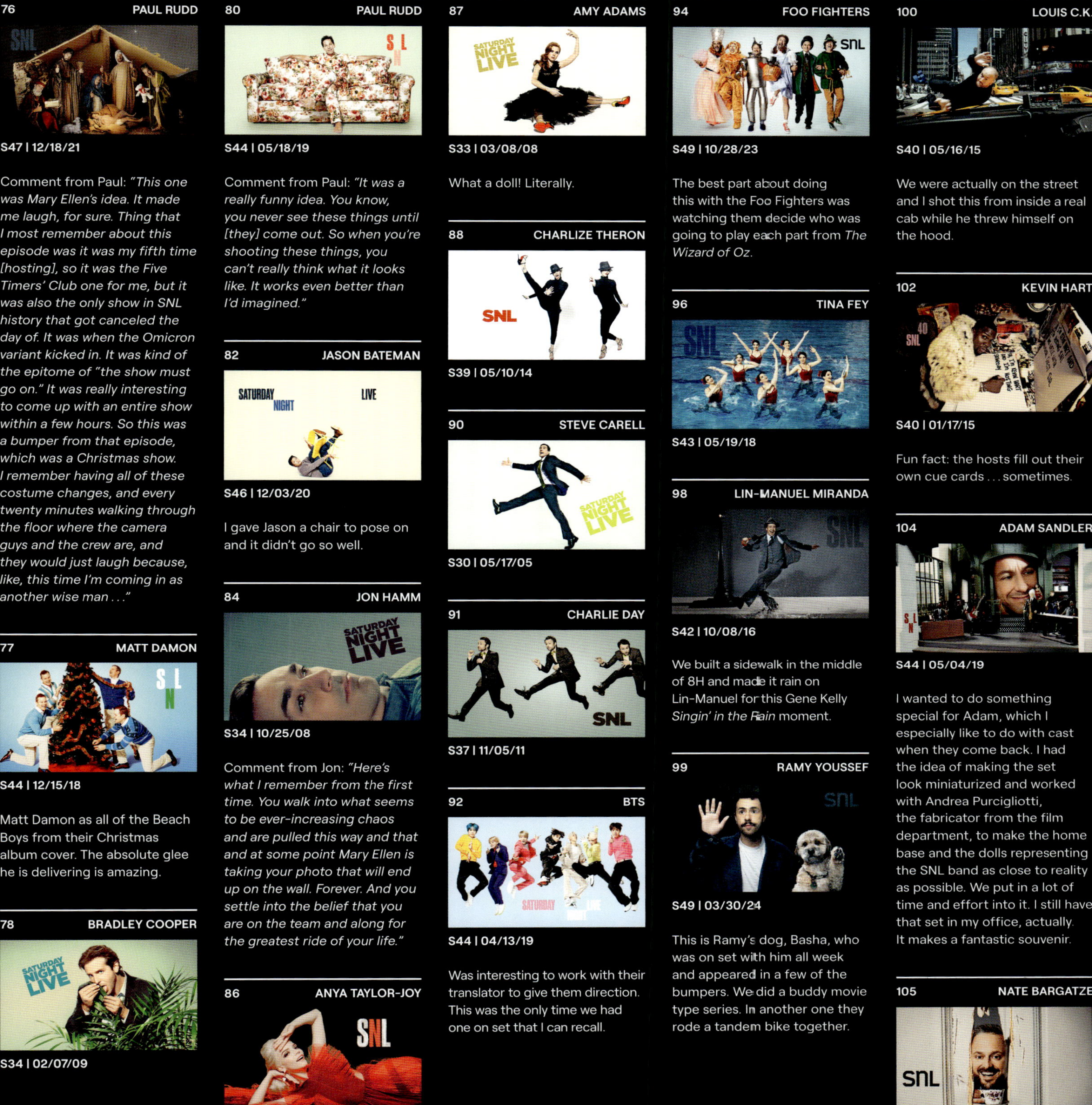

76 **PAUL RUDD**

S47 | 12/18/21

Comment from Paul: *"This one was Mary Ellen's idea. It made me laugh, for sure. Thing that I most remember about this episode was it was my fifth time [hosting], so it was the Five Timers' Club one for me, but it was also the only show in SNL history that got canceled the day of. It was when the Omicron variant kicked in. It was kind of the epitome of "the show must go on." It was really interesting to come up with an entire show within a few hours. So this was a bumper from that episode, which was a Christmas show. I remember having all of these costume changes, and every twenty minutes walking through the floor where the camera guys and the crew are, and they would just laugh because, like, this time I'm coming in as another wise man . . ."*

77 **MATT DAMON**

S44 | 12/15/18

Matt Damon as all of the Beach Boys from their Christmas album cover. The absolute glee he is delivering is amazing.

78 **BRADLEY COOPER**

S34 | 02/07/09

80 **PAUL RUDD**

S44 | 05/18/19

Comment from Paul: *"It was a really funny idea. You know, you never see these things until [they] come out. So when you're shooting these things, you can't really think what it looks like. It works even better than I'd imagined."*

82 **JASON BATEMAN**

S46 | 12/03/20

I gave Jason a chair to pose on and it didn't go so well.

84 **JON HAMM**

S34 | 10/25/08

Comment from Jon: *"Here's what I remember from the first time. You walk into what seems to be ever-increasing chaos and are pulled this way and that and at some point Mary Ellen is taking your photo that will end up on the wall. Forever. And you settle into the belief that you are on the team and along for the greatest ride of your life."*

86 **ANYA TAYLOR-JOY**

87 **AMY ADAMS**

S33 | 03/08/08

What a doll! Literally.

88 **CHARLIZE THERON**

S39 | 05/10/14

90 **STEVE CARELL**

S30 | 05/17/05

91 **CHARLIE DAY**

S37 | 11/05/11

92 **BTS**

S44 | 04/13/19

Was interesting to work with their translator to give them direction. This was the only time we had one on set that I can recall.

94 **FOO FIGHTERS**

S49 | 10/28/23

The best part about doing this with the Foo Fighters was watching them decide who was going to play each part from *The Wizard of Oz*.

96 **TINA FEY**

S43 | 05/19/18

98 **LIN-MANUEL MIRANDA**

S42 | 10/08/16

We built a sidewalk in the middle of 8H and made it rain on Lin-Manuel for this Gene Kelly *Singin' in the Rain* moment.

99 **RAMY YOUSSEF**

S49 | 03/30/24

This is Ramy's dog, Basha, who was on set with him all week and appeared in a few of the bumpers. We did a buddy movie type series. In another one they rode a tandem bike together.

100 **LOUIS C.K.**

S40 | 05/16/15

We were actually on the street and I shot this from inside a real cab while he threw himself on the hood.

102 **KEVIN HART**

S40 | 01/17/15

Fun fact: the hosts fill out their own cue cards . . . sometimes.

104 **ADAM SANDLER**

S44 | 05/04/19

I wanted to do something special for Adam, which I especially like to do with cast when they come back. I had the idea of making the set look miniaturized and worked with Andrea Purcigliotti, the fabricator from the film department, to make the home base and the dolls representing the SNL band as close to reality as possible. We put in a lot of time and effort into it. I still have that set in my office, actually. It makes a fantastic souvenir.

105 **NATE BARGATZE**

06 MAYA RUDOLPH

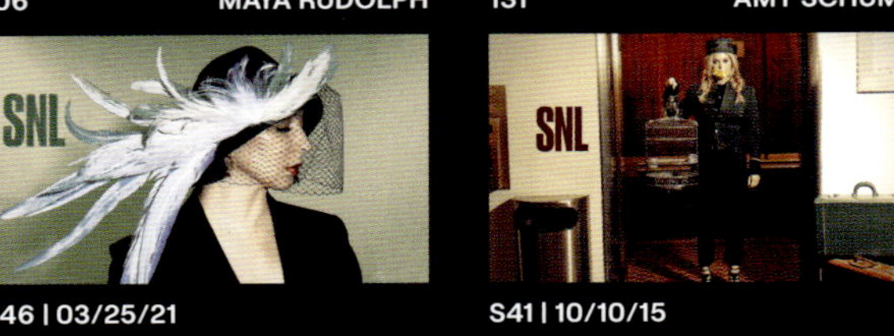

46 | 03/25/21

love to include quiet moments or bumpers. Gives a bit of a breath during the show.

07 EMMA STONE

37 | 11/12/11

Emma is a huge Gilda Radner fan and wanted to do this tribute. Major props to the hair, makeup, and wardrobe team here.

28 SARAH SILVERMAN

40 | 10/04/14

We did this outside on the NBC marquee and I didn't get the correct permission so was in a bit of trouble for that. Oops. Apologies all around but it was worth it!

30 JONAH HILL

41 | 03/05/16

This is a classic type of thing where I take a famous reference and insert it into our SNL world. There is a certain amount of enthusiasm to using Studio 8H for these kinds of shoots. In this case, luckily, it was a Tuesday instead of the usual Thursday, otherwise the studio would have been full of activity.

131 AMY SCHUMER

S41 | 10/10/15

This was an animation where she spits out fake yellow bird feathers. It's always fun to use the areas around the studio.

132 BILLIE EILISH

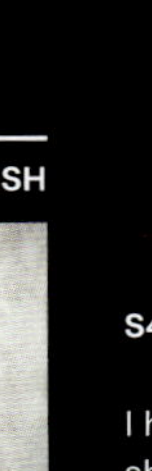

S49 | 12/19/23

We actually started out doing a snow angel but it turned into more of a snow pile over her. Love her sparkly eyes!

133 BAD BUNNY

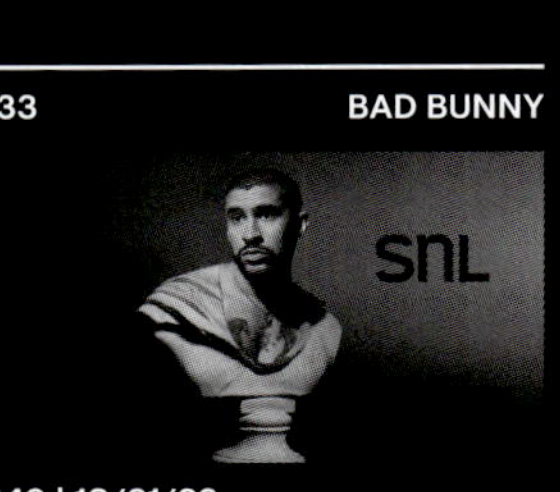

S49 | 10/21/23

134 STEVE CARELL

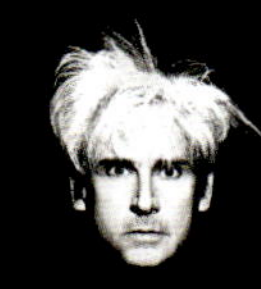

S44 | 11/17/18

136 LARRY DAVID

S43 | 11/04/17

Larry David seems like a work of art to me, so I thought, "Let's lean into that and play around with different artistic styles." I experimented in Photoshop and it became apparent that the Cubist style was right for Larry. It came together with my incredible retoucher, Ted Blumenschein

137 STEVE BUSCEMI

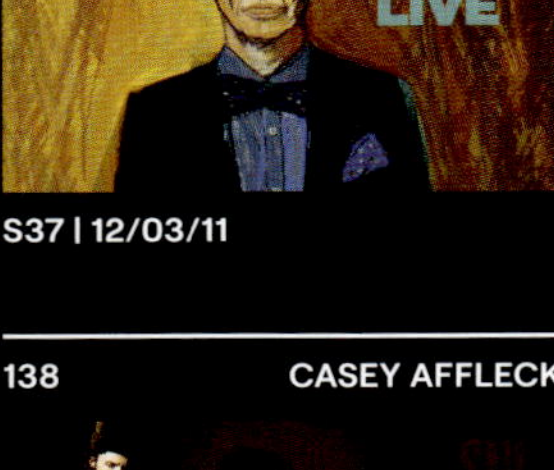

S37 | 12/03/11

138 CASEY AFFLECK

S42 | 12/17/16

I had just seen the Caravaggio show at the Met and came up with the idea of having Casey play each part in one of his paintings, but of course adding a bit of modern humor with the telephone.

140 AZIZ ANSARI

S42 | 01/21/17

Yet another example of how fun it is to take famous artworks and bring them into the world of SNL, add the comedy, add the ridiculousness, in this case the stuffed cats and the cue cards. We threw the water and he jumped at the same time, but because we threw it in front of him, he didn't even get wet. We didn't have to do this more than a couple of times. I'm quite practiced at timing for things like this, luckily, because if we got the studio really wet it would have been a pain in the ass for the crew to have to clean it up.

141 TIMOTHÉE CHALAMET

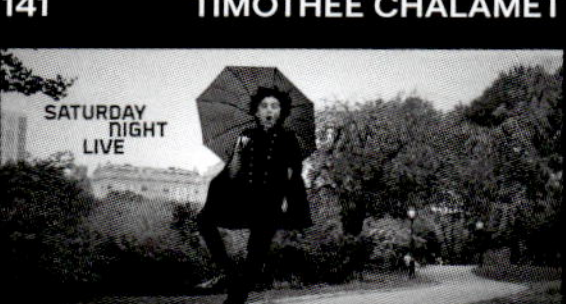

S49 | 11/12/23

Such a fun day in Central Park. We ran around trying to dodge paparazzi and people with their camera phones. He was so much fun and I love this adorable jump.

142 JOSH BROLIN

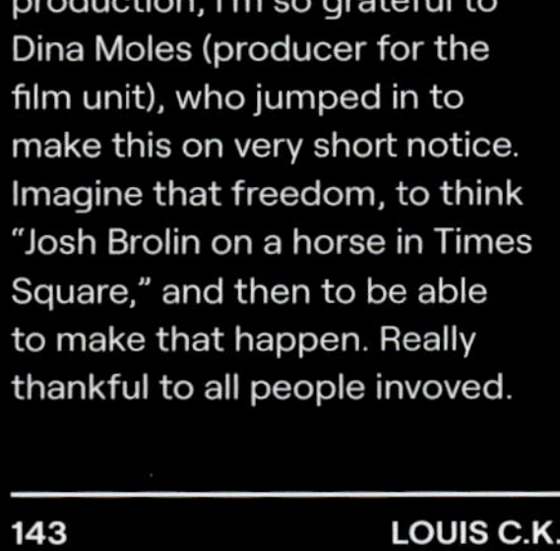

S49 | 03/09/24

Well, first of all, this is not Photoshop. This is an actual horse and the actual Josh Brolin. My team lit it so well it looks like it was shot in a studio and comped together. We had to work really fast, I think we did the whole thing in about fifteen minutes. We had security in place and we worked with the mayor's office to lock down the area so we could get the shot. For a shoot with this level of production, I'm so grateful to Dina Moles (producer for the film unit), who jumped in to make this on very short notice. Imagine that freedom, to think "Josh Brolin on a horse in Times Square," and then to be able to make that happen. Really thankful to all people invoved.

143 LOUIS C.K.

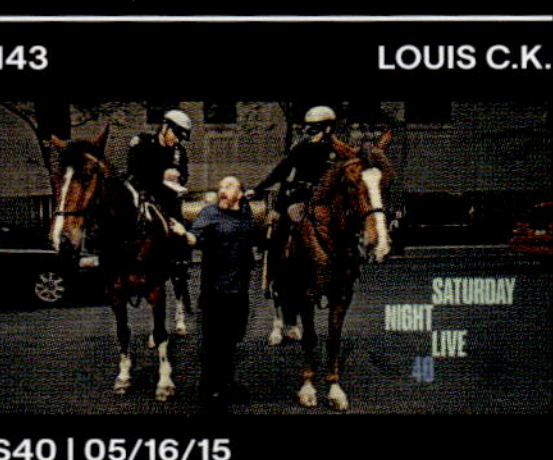

S40 | 05/16/15

I'm a big horse person, so I try to include them whenever I can. Someone arranged for mounted police officers to come by so we could grab a shot with Louis.

144 JAKE GYLLENHAAL

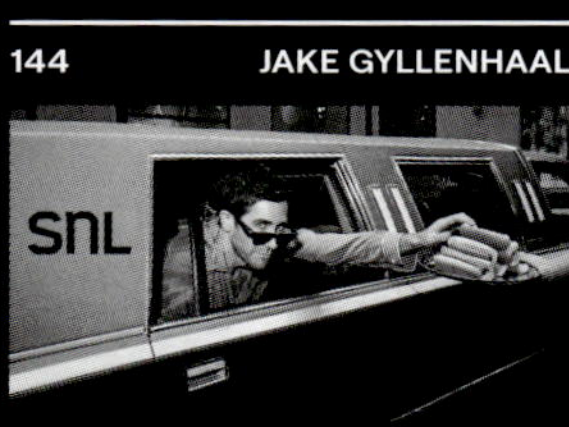

S49 | 05/18/24

We had started out for Jake's shoot on location at the Oyster Bar at Grand Central Terminal and then in this old-school limousine, the concept being "'70s movie star style." And hot dogs are emblematic of NYC, so it seemed funny that he would be served a hot dog from a silver tray.

145 JACOB ELORD

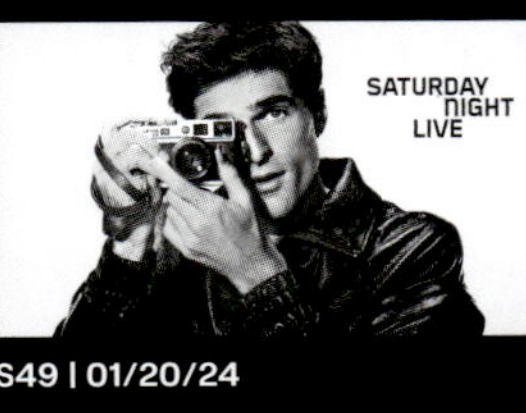

S49 | 01/20/24

That is Jacob's own Leica. He was shooting a lot during the week. I had camera envy.

146 ARCADE FIR

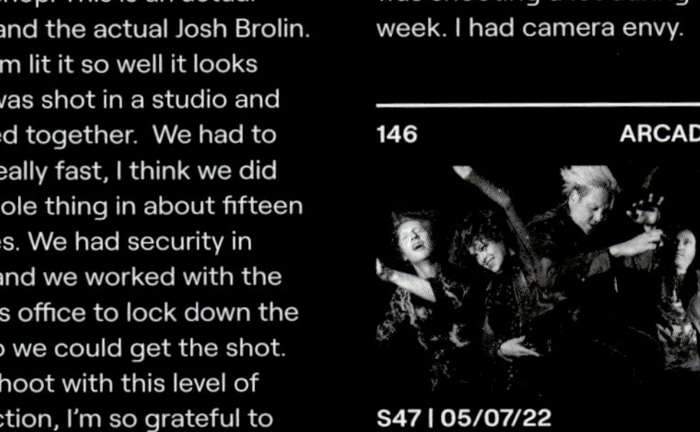

S47 | 05/07/22

I shot each of them separately because I wanted a big energy across the screen. I explained the idea and they were all on board, so they gave me these big jumps with different positions. It was a lot of effort for them, but I comped it together quickly on set to show them and they were digging it. It conveys all of them as this big whirly bird of rock 'n' roll energy

147 U2

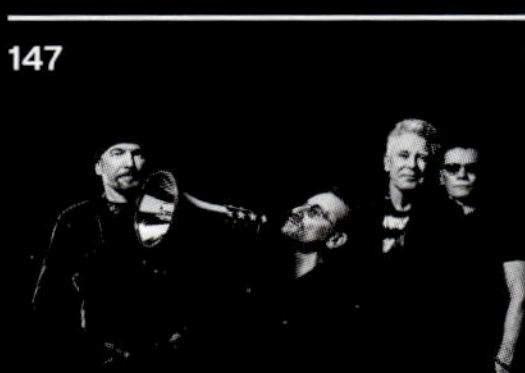

S43 | 12/02/17

Getting to work with U2 is always such a thrill. I love the black-and-white graphic quality of this.

148 RIHANNA

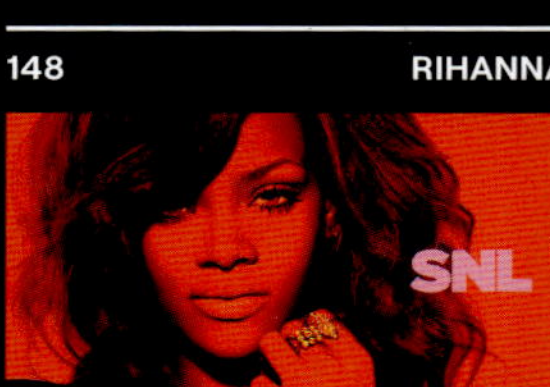

S36 | 10/30/10

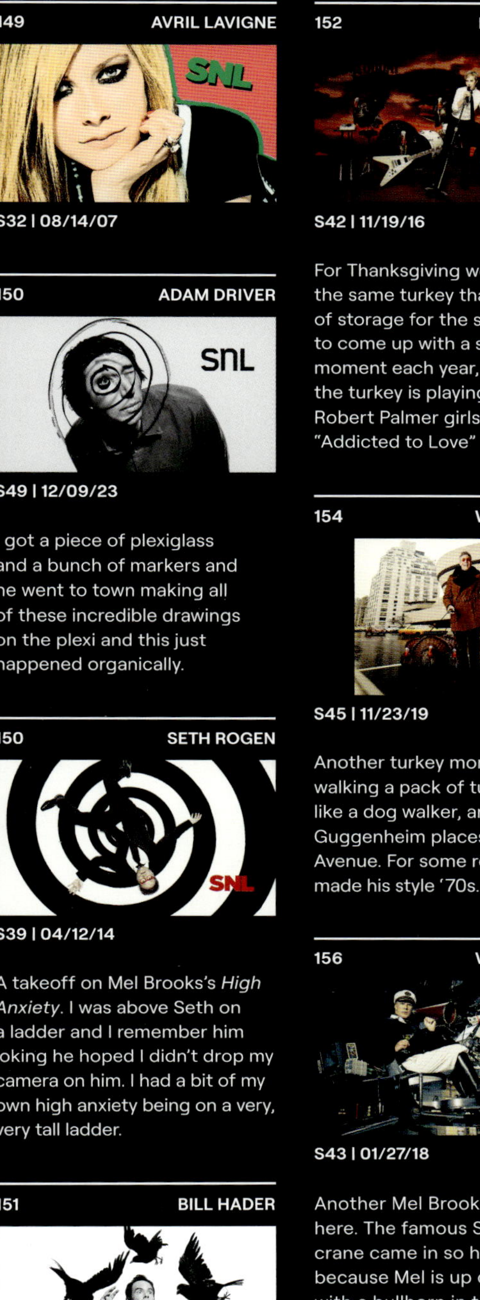

149 **AVRIL LAVIGNE**

S32 | 08/14/07

150 **ADAM DRIVER**

S49 | 12/09/23

I got a piece of plexiglass and a bunch of markers and he went to town making all of these incredible drawings on the plexi and this just happened organically.

150 **SETH ROGEN**

S39 | 04/12/14

A takeoff on Mel Brooks's *High Anxiety*. I was above Seth on a ladder and I remember him joking he hoped I didn't drop my camera on him. I had a bit of my own high anxiety being on a very, very tall ladder.

151 **BILL HADER**

S43 | 03/17/18

This is a spoof of *The Birds*. It was an animation and we had the crows bouncing around on a fishing line and it looked absolutely ridiculous. Bill was hilariously overreacting in terror to them.

152 **KRISTEN WIIG**

S42 | 11/19/16

For Thanksgiving we always use the same turkey that we get out of storage for the show. I try to come up with a silly turkey moment each year, and here the turkey is playing all of the Robert Palmer girls from the "Addicted to Love" video.

154 **WILL FERRELL**

S45 | 11/23/19

Another turkey moment: Will walking a pack of turkeys like a dog walker, and the Guggenheim places him on 5th Avenue. For some reason we made his style '70s. No idea why.

156 **WILL FERRELL**

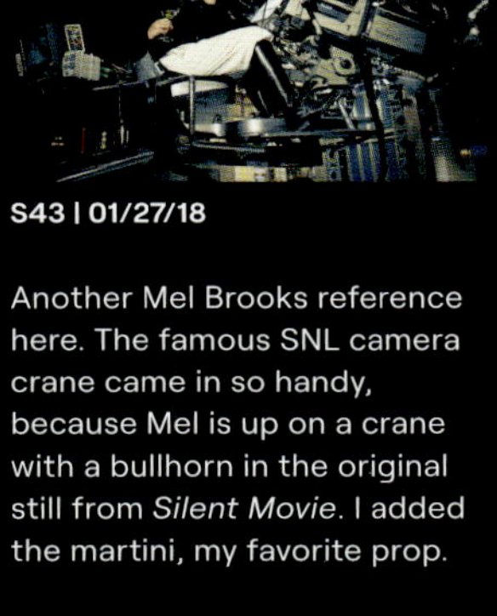

S43 | 01/27/18

Another Mel Brooks reference here. The famous SNL camera crane came in so handy, because Mel is up on a crane with a bullhorn in the original still from *Silent Movie*. I added the martini, my favorite prop.

156 **WILL FERRELL**

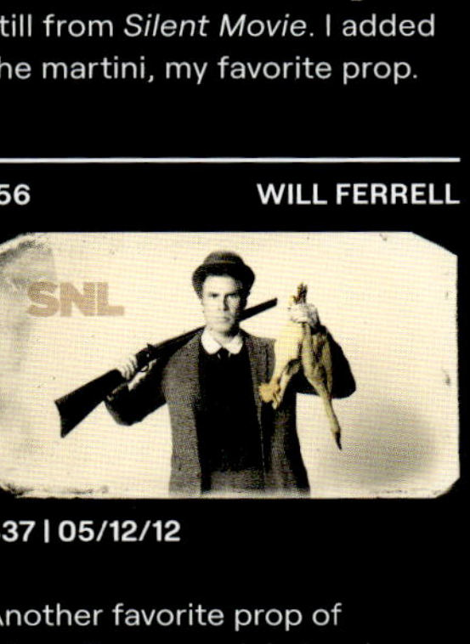

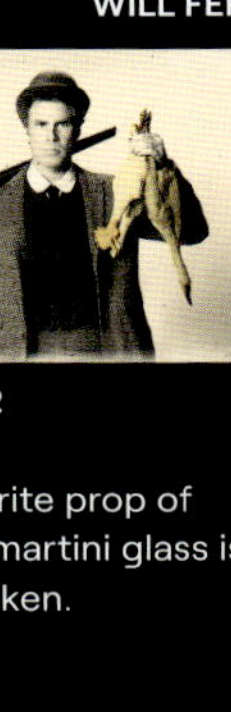

S37 | 05/12/12

Another favorite prop of mine after a martini glass is a rubber chicken.

157 **WILL FERRELL**

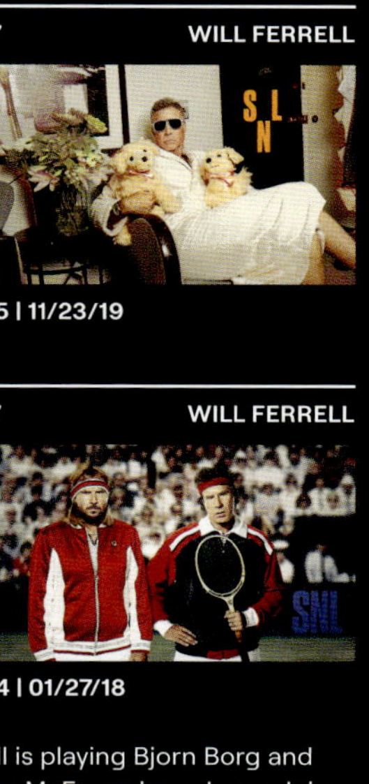

S45 | 11/23/19

157 **WILL FERRELL**

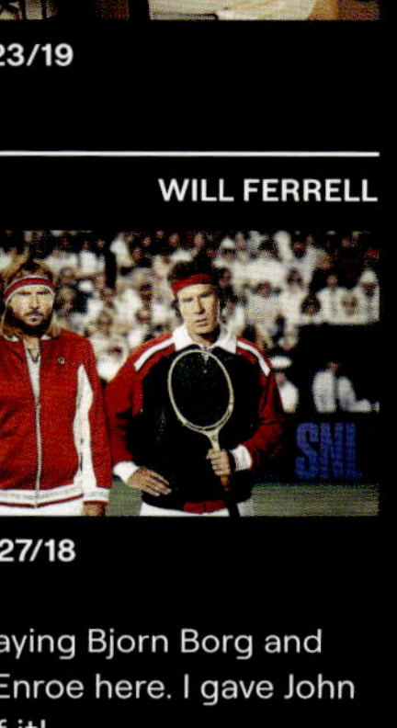

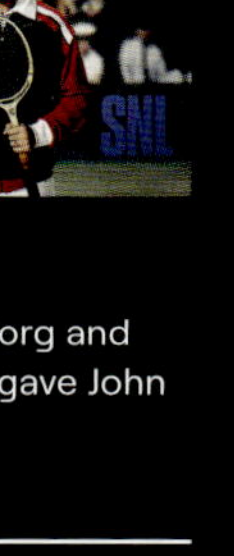

S44 | 01/27/18

Will is playing Bjorn Borg and John McEnroe here. I gave John a print of it!

158 **MELISSA MCCARTHY**

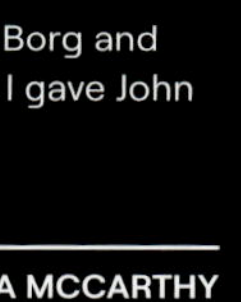

S42 | 05/13/17

Melissa was the perfect comedy genius to make an SNL version of the famous Diane Arbus photo.

160 **POST MALONE**

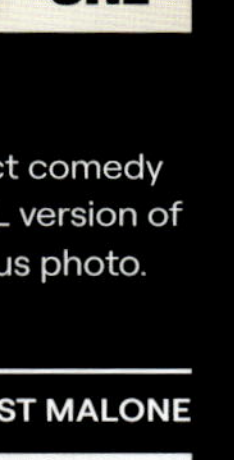

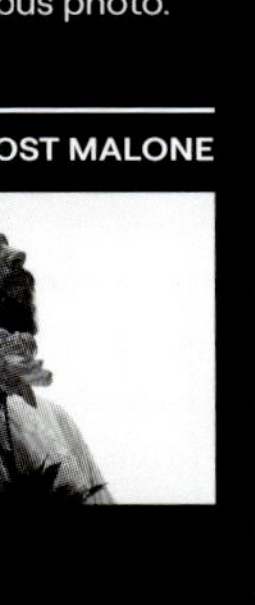

S47 | 05/14/22

I love his rhinestone earring. I love that he says "ma'am."

161 **EMMA THOMPSON**

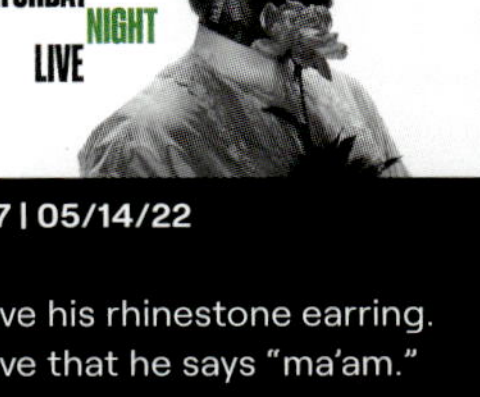

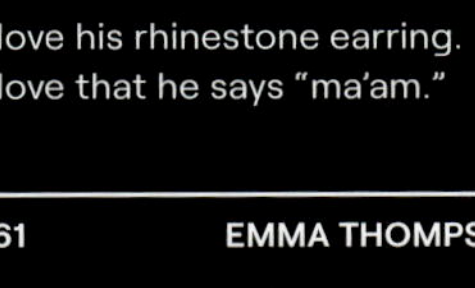

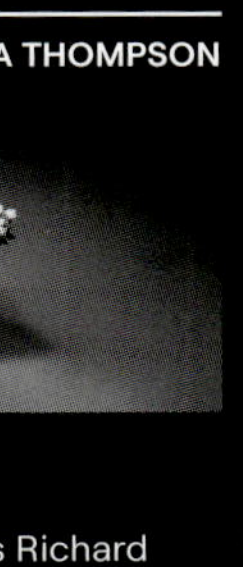

S44 | 05/11/19

One of my heroes is Richard Avedon. I had the idea to recreate his portrait of Judy Garland and it was an amazing opportunity to be able to do it with Emma.

162 **BLAKE SHELTON**

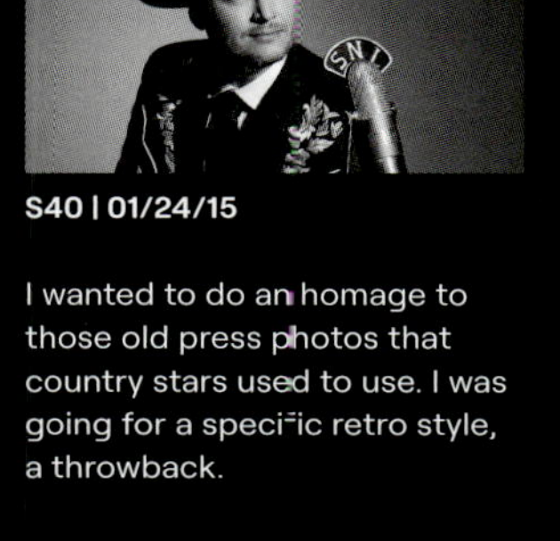

S40 | 01/24/15

I wanted to do an homage to those old press photos that country stars used to use. I was going for a specific retro style, a throwback.

163 **A TRIBE CALLED QUEST**

S42 | 11/12/16

164 **JACOB ELORDI**

S49 | 01/20/24

165 **JOSH HUTCHERSON**

S39 | 11/23/13

This was actually a tiny chair that I used, although the idea was for him to be on a giant chair.

166 **BILL BURR**

S46 | 10/10/20

I wanted to see Bill in a painterly way, as a work of art. There was no direct reference, but I had the frame and somehow we ended up here with the fly swatter.

168 **TRAVIS KELCE**

S48 | 03/05/23

For this one I was thinking about how Jimi Hendrix lit his guitar on fire, and what if Travis lit his stogie off of his flaming football. Very badass.

170 **HALSEY**

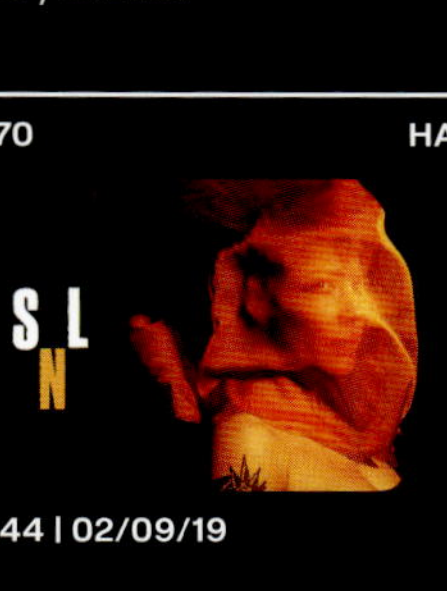

S44 | 02/09/19

172 **DONALD GLOVER**

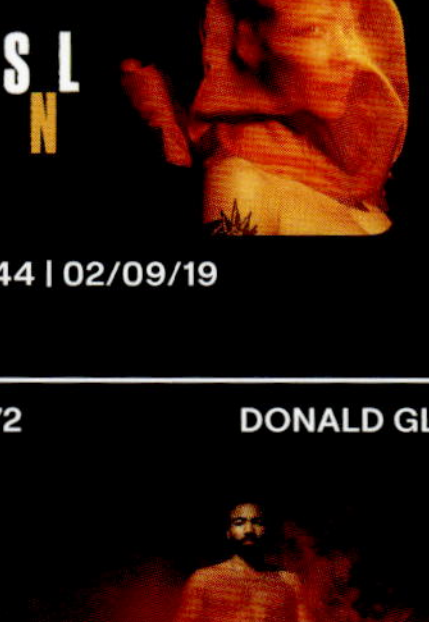

S43 | 05/05/18

179 **KIM KARDASHIAN**

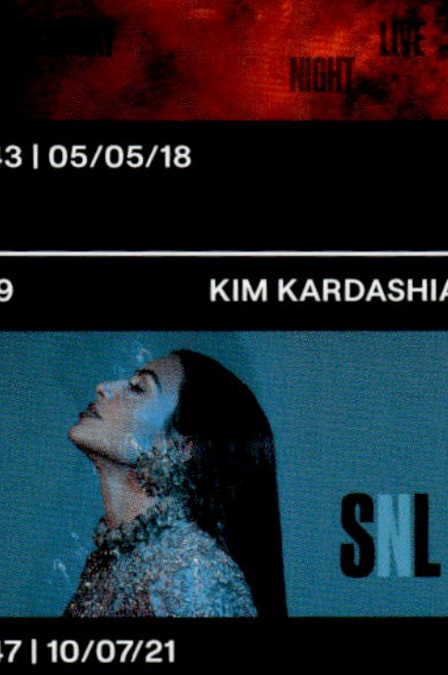

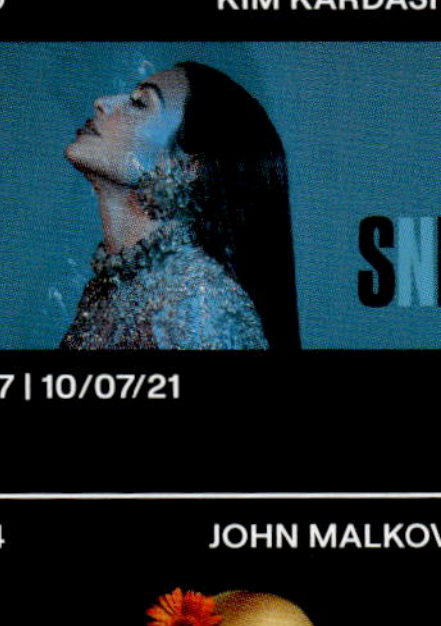

S47 | 10/07/21

174 **JOHN MALKOVICH**

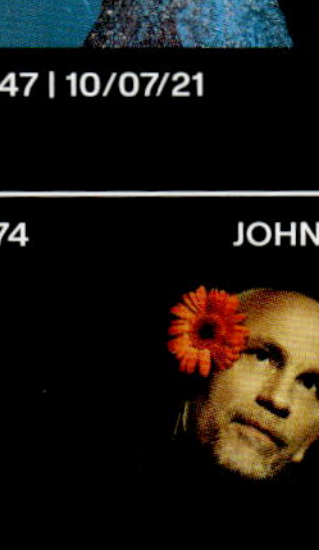

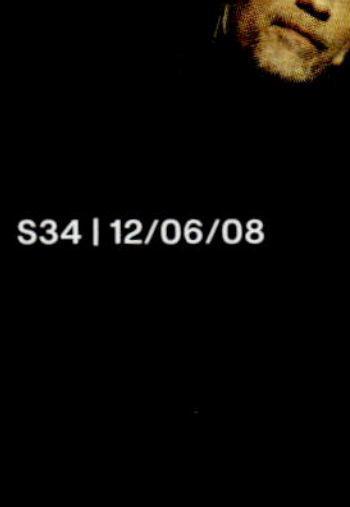

S34 | 12/06/08

75 **BAD BUNNY**

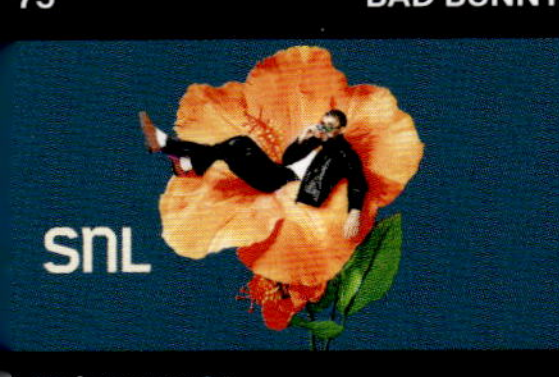

S49 | 10/21/23

Flor de Maga is the national flower of Puerto Rico, so I requested one specifically for Bad Bunny.

76 **KIERAN CULKIN**

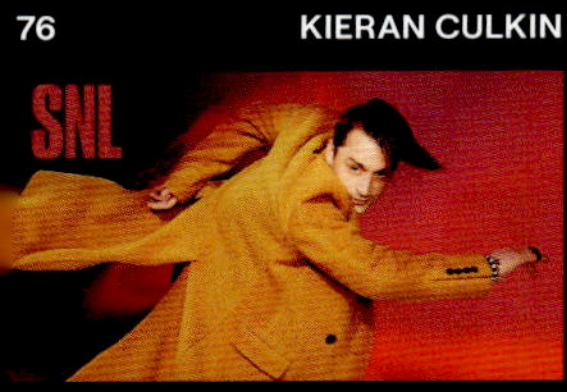

S47 | 11/06/21

I love the movement here. We were using color gels and a slow shutter speed during this season.

78 **TAYLOR SWIFT**

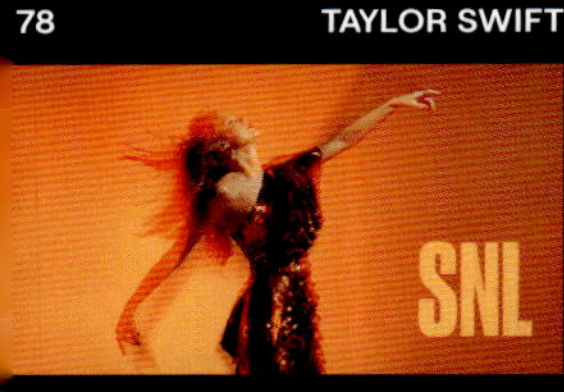

S47 | 11/11/21

80 **JACK HARLOW**

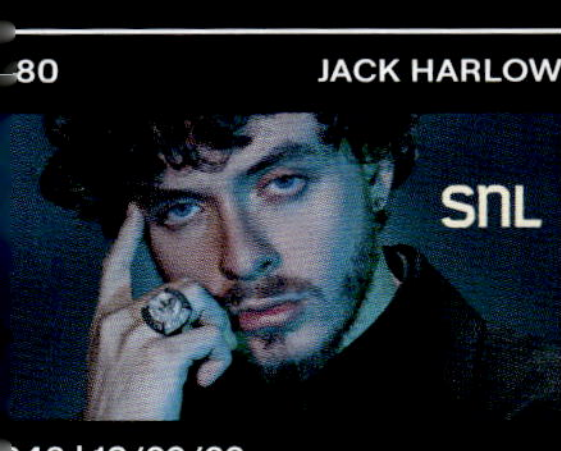

S48 | 10/29/22

Jack was so much fun. We sang a Gerry Rafferty song together during the shoot. We both knew all the words. *Right Down the Line*, I think it was.

81 **JENNIFER LOPEZ**

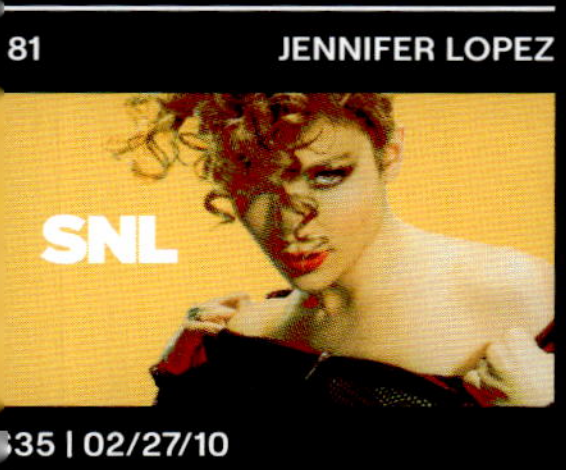

S35 | 02/27/10

182 **KRISTEN STEWART**

S45 | 11/02/19

We played around with paints and paint brushes as props. She painted on the seamless paper and then we had the idea to put paint on her face and create something super artistic.

184 **TIMOTHÉE CHALAMET**

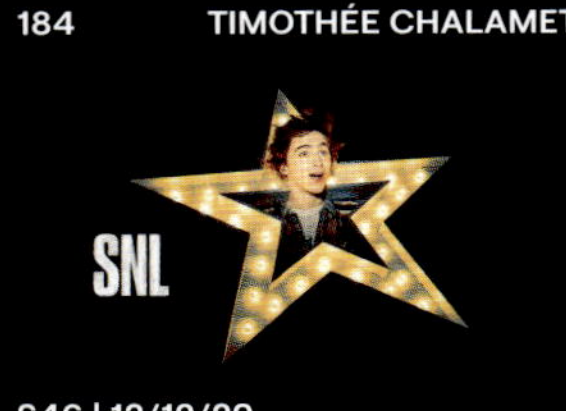

S46 | 12/12/20

185 **SYDNEY SWEENEY**

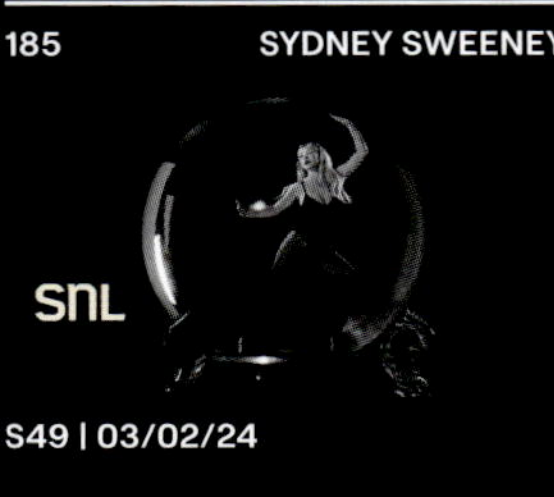

S49 | 03/02/24

186 **JACK WHITE**

S48 | 02/25/23

This was done entirely in camera. We swung a flashlight around his head while keeping the shutter open and balancing the light. He had to stay verrrry still.

188 **JANELLE MONÁE**

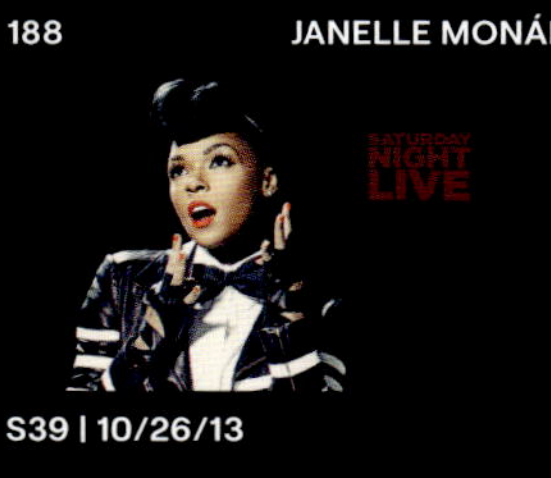

S39 | 10/26/13

189 **JANET JACKSON**

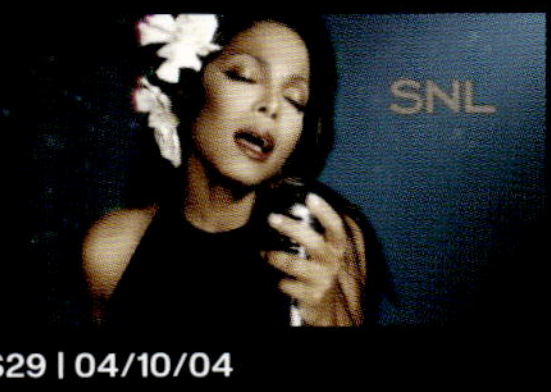

S29 | 04/10/04

Had the idea to have Janet play Billie Holiday. It's quite a thing to watch someone transform in front of your eyes.

190 **MILEY CYRUS**

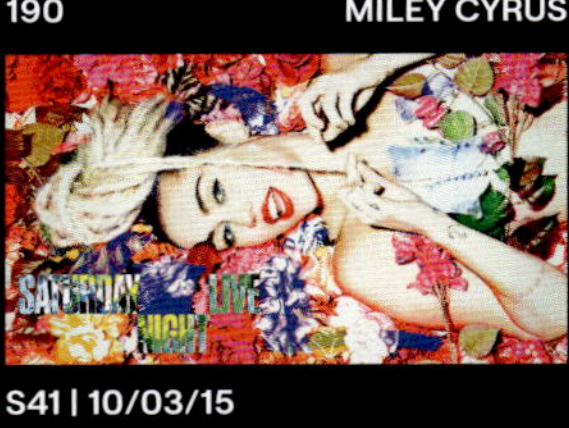

S41 | 10/03/15

192 **YOUNG THUG**

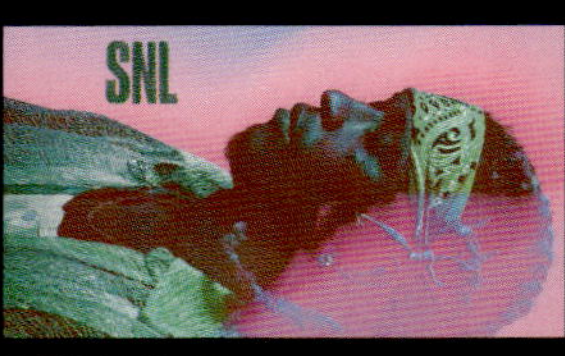

S47 | 10/16/21

194 **KRISTEN STEWART**

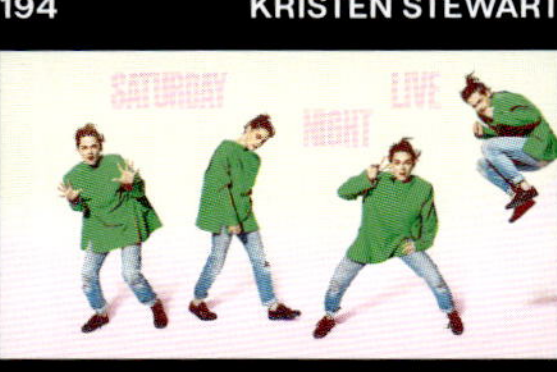

S42 | 02/04/17

196 **LIL WAYNE**

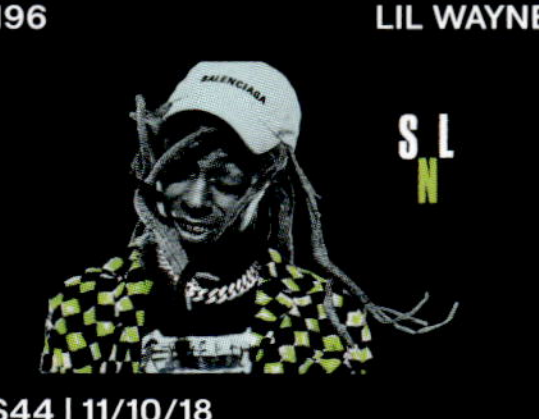

S44 | 11/10/18

198 **PAUL RUDD**

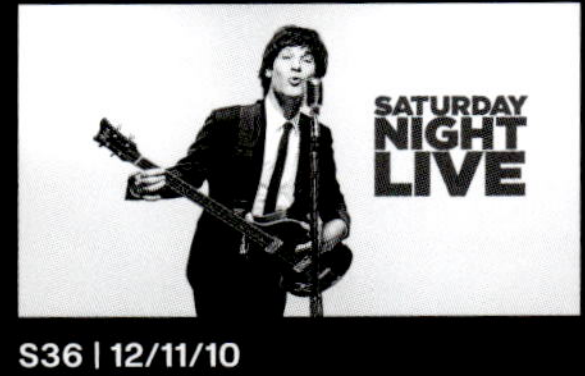

S36 | 12/11/10

Comment from Paul: *"This was a really cool, fun picture to take because McCartney was the musical guest. The band usually [does their] soundcheck while you're getting your pictures taken for these bumpers. I'd never met Paul McCartney, but I mean, the Beatles are the greatest band of all time and I couldn't believe I was actually doing the show with Paul McCartney. So Mary Ellen and I were taking pictures and I'm thinking the entire time that Paul McCartney is going to come in with the band in five minutes. I know the schedule. And sure enough, he did. And Mary Ellen, who understandably is working on a tight schedule, looks to me and I look at her and she said, "We're gonna go with Paul McCartney here. We're not going to take these right now." I said, "Yeah, let's do that." And so we went down and watched him rehearsing with his band. He was just figuring out what songs he was going to sing, and they wheeled down on the main floor a grand piano. And as soon as he got done playing his songs, he came down and sat at the piano and I was standing over his left shoulder about ten feet back and looking at him going, "Oh my god, it's Paul McCartney." And then he just started playing "The Long and Winding Road." I couldn't believe where I was standing. And Mary Ellen and I were looking at each other like, this is incredible. And he finished the song and there's probably about twenty people in the room, the camera guys that were kind of setting up, you know, figuring out the shots, and we all applauded. And then he went right into "Lady Madonna." I remember Lorne coming in, and Lorne seldom even comes in when the band is doing this. And [Paul] wound up giving us a mini Beatles concert. He probably played about seven or eight songs and that was all during our photo shoot. So then I went back and got dressed up as him and did this."*

199 **PAUL MCCARTNEY**

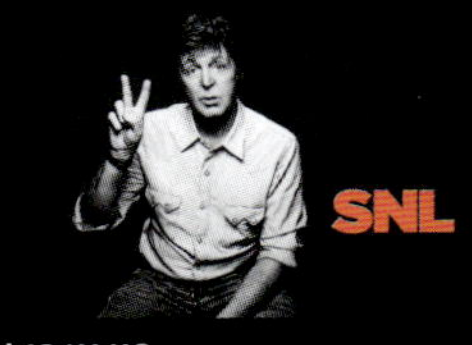

S36 | 12/11/10

200 **CHRIS ROCK**

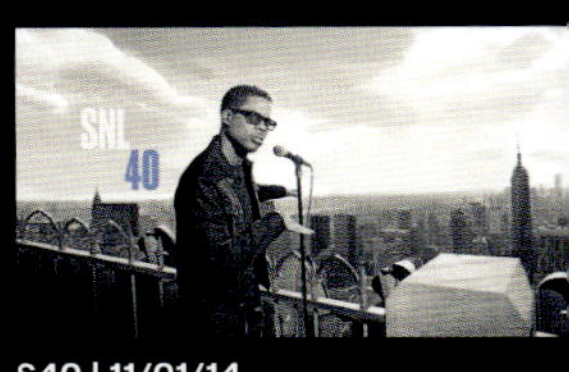

S40 | 11/01/14

Chris Rock at the Top of the Rock. We've done a few people up there but he was the first. He looks like he's just about to do a set for the city of New York.

202 **MEGAN THEE STALLION**

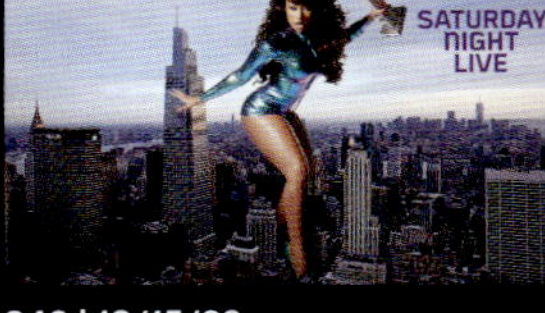

S48 | 10/15/22

Megan takes New York, literally. A takeoff on *Attack of the 50-Foot Woman.*

204 **ZOË KRAVITZ**

S47 | 03/10/22

205 **RYAN GOSLING**

S41 | 12/05/15

We had two people standing behind Ryan holding the props. I believe it was Will Heath and Tom Broeker. Like for Zoe, we did this all in camera.

206 **DWAYNE JOHNSON**

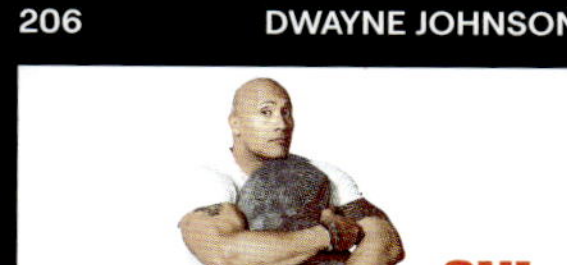

S42 | 05/20/17

Rock . . .

207 **DANA CARVEY**

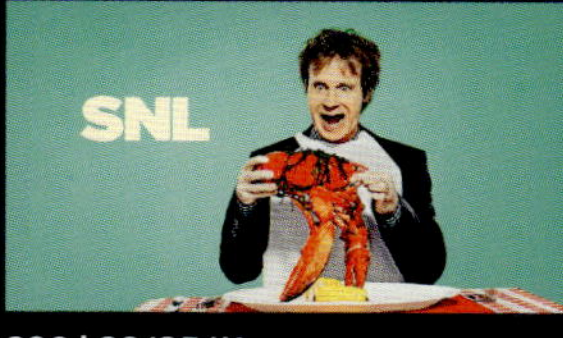

S36 | 02/05/11

. . . Lobster

208 **PEDRO PASCAL**

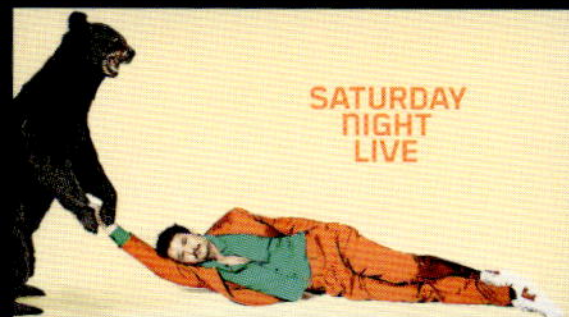

S48 | 02/04/23

209 **EDDIE MURPHY**

S45 | 12/21/19

210 **CHARLES BARKLEY**

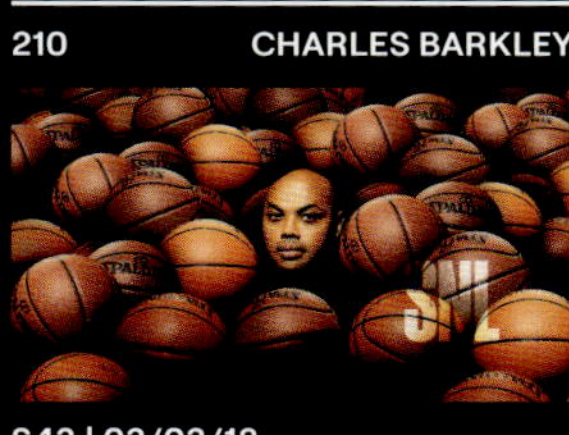

S43 | 03/03/18

211 **ELI MANNING**

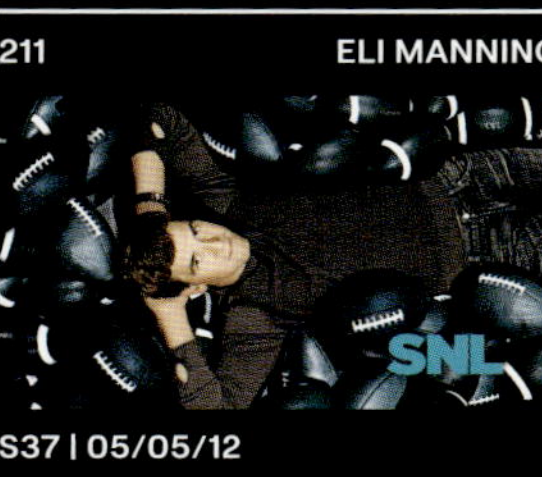

S37 | 05/05/12

212 **PAUL RUDD & ONE DIRECTION**

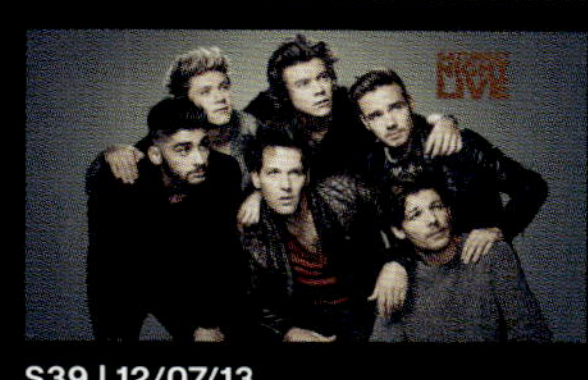

S39 | 12/07/13

Comment from Paul: *"I said [that] I'd like to take a picture with One Direction and just pretend that I'm in the band. I've had crazy, great musical guests, every time that I hosted. This was the third time I hosted and they were the band. And I knew they were massive. It was at a time when people were sleeping out on the streets because they just wanted to see One Direction. They were really sweet. They were great guys, and completely game. I worked the hardest on my hair, and I remember acting like it's a real boy band photo when, you know, clearly they never really considered themselves that and they really weren't. They were funny dudes, and really sweet."*

214 **MARGOT ROBBIE**

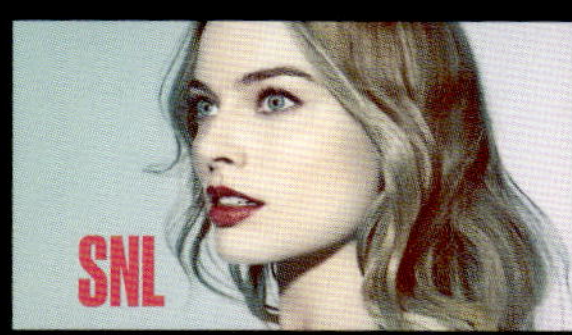

S42 | 10/01/16

216 **AUSTIN BUTLER**

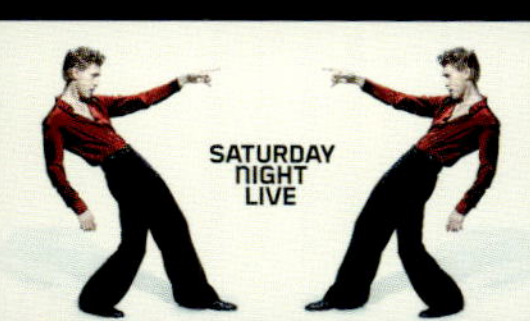

S48 | 12/15/22

So handsome and boy can he move. I love putting two images together that create cool shapes and have the person interacting with themself.

218 **MARTIN SHORT & STEVE MARTIN**

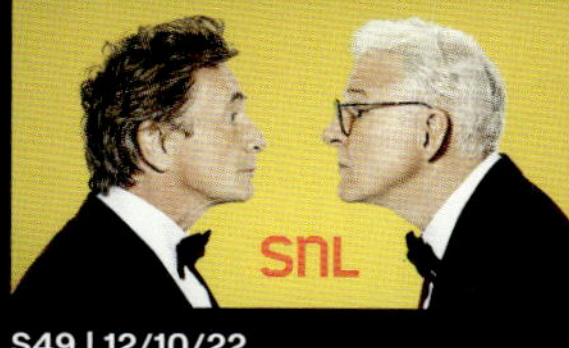

S49 | 12/10/22

From a design perspective, having them look at each other with tuxes on I thought would be an impactful image, and I knew that once they got in that position, they would nail the facial expressions.

220 **CHRIS PRATT**

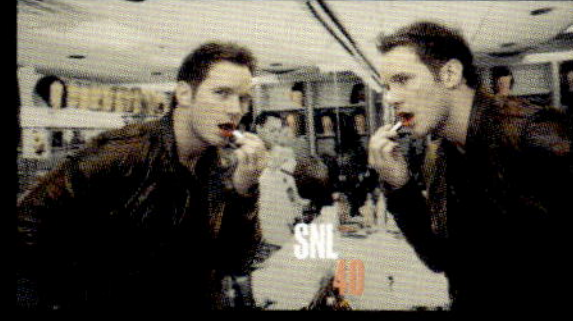

S40 | 09/27/14

This is kind of a throwback image, taken in the hair and makeup room. During the 40th season I was inspired by Edie Baskin's hand tinted technique from the early days of the show.

221 **JULIA LOUIS-DREYFUS**

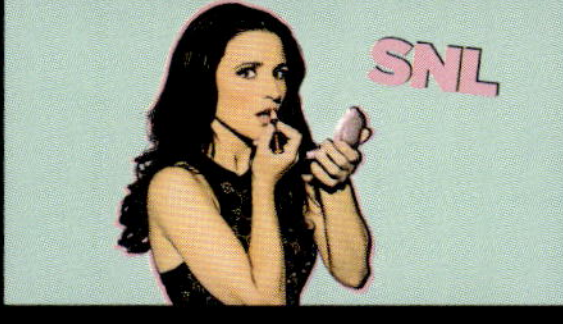

S32 | 03/17/07

I really love this treatment I was doing for season 32 almost as much as I love JLD.

222 **SANDRA OH**

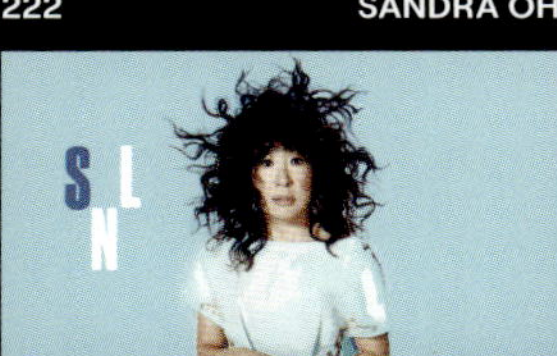

S44 | 03/30/19

I asked Sandra to mess her hair up, and she and her glam team really ran with that idea.

223 **DON CHEADLE**

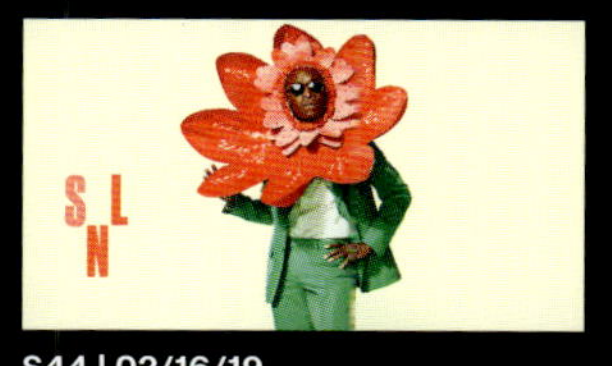

S44 | 02/16/19

I actually made a sketch of Don as a flower and I thought this would make such a sweet photo, and then he made it cooler than I could have imagined by adding the sunglasses and that swagger.

224 **ANDREW GARFIELD**

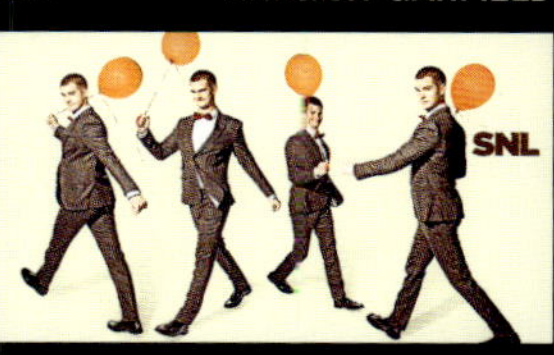

S39 | 05/03/14

Sometimes I don't know what the image will ultimately be until I can play around and see how things work together. I like that he is heading in different directions here.

225 **IDRIS ELBA**

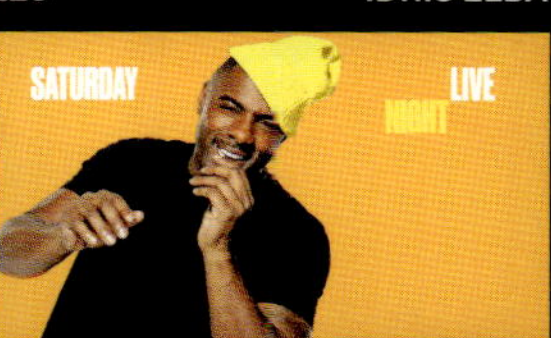

S44 | 03/09/19

I wish I could remember what we were laughing about here!

226 **EDDIE MURPHY**

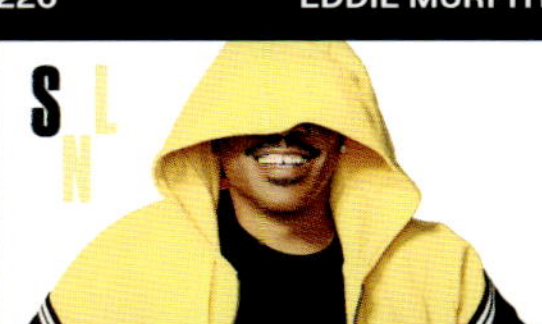

S45 | 12/21/19

The most recognizable smile.

228 **ZACH GALIFIANAKIS**

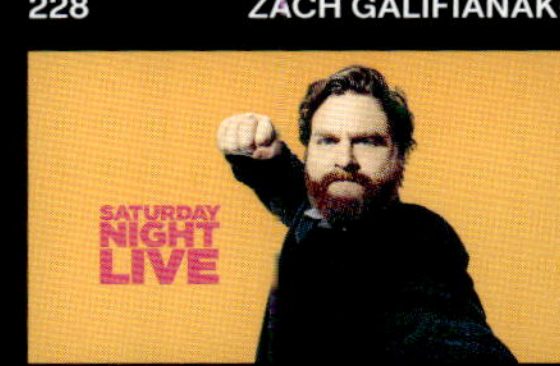

268 **BETTY WHITE**

S35 | 05/08/10

I feel so lucky that I got to work with Betty White. She was so gracious and really handled that boombox!

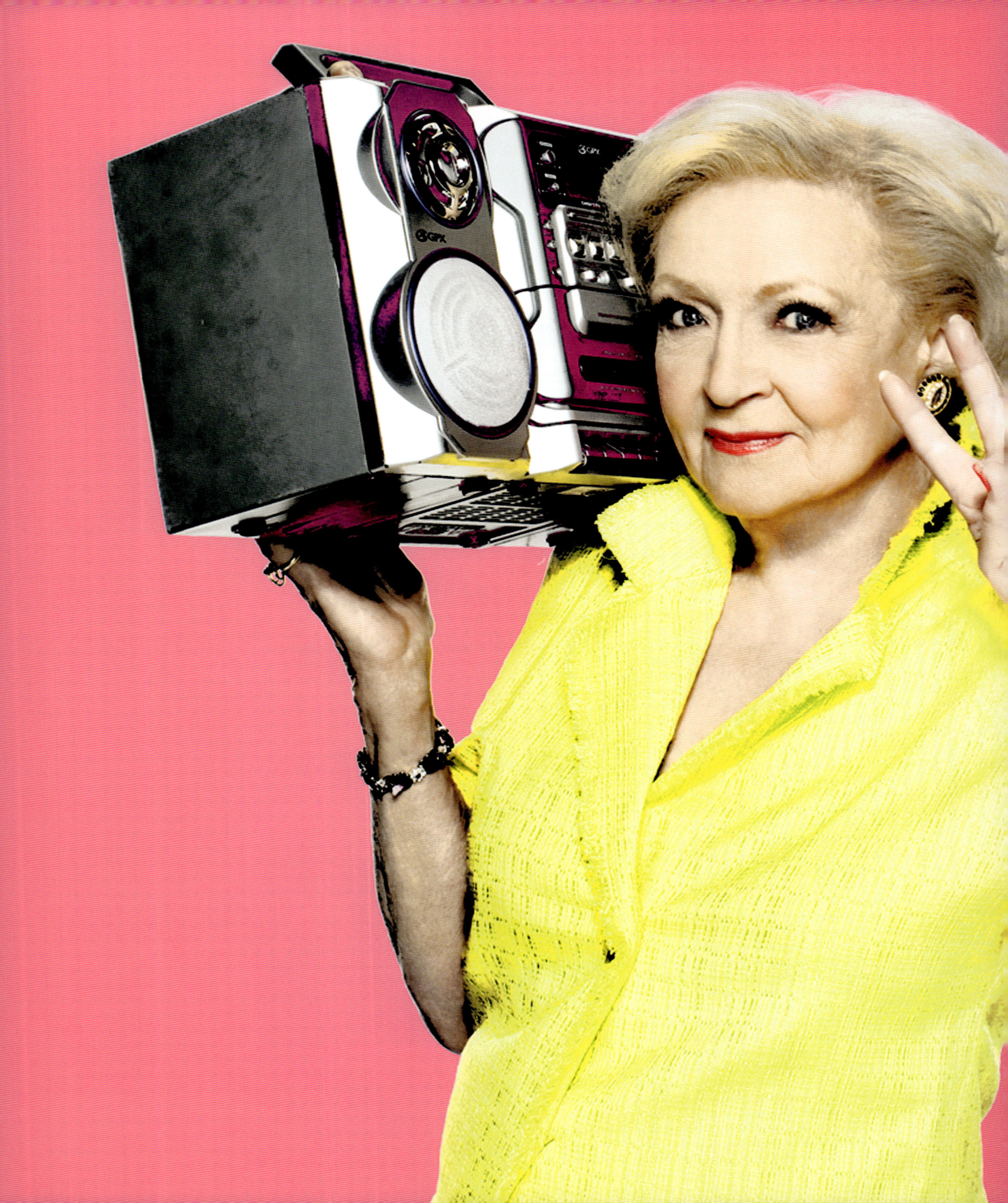
GPX
GPX

SNL 35

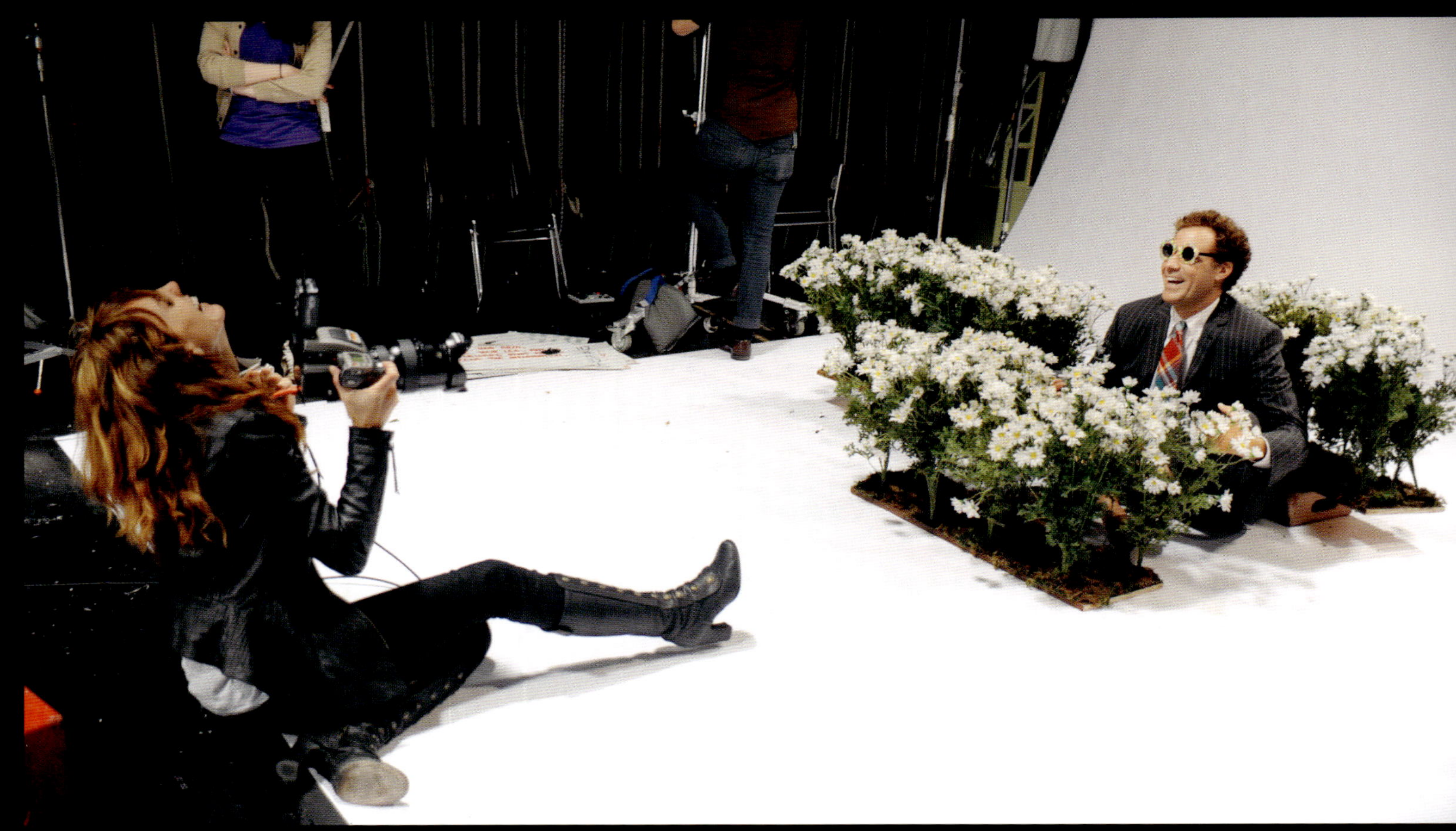

Matthews and Will Ferrell shooting
the daisies bumper (2009).

ACKNOWLEDGMENTS

To Edie Baskin and Lorne Michaels: thank you for changing my life. Thank you for letting me create week after week. Thank you for the inspiration and thank you for the opportunity to belong to the SNL family.

To Alison Castle: thank you for your keen eye, your fluid words, and your astute understanding of what is cool and important. Could not have done it without you.

To Emily Oberman: Thank you for being the most dope and brilliant person in the room who always knows exactly which decision is the right one. You are always so giving of your time and talent. I am lucky to call you my dear friend. This book 100% could never have happened without you. Thank you for taking this project on and endless gratitude to your team: Laura Berglund, Elizabeth McMann, Chad McCabe, Mira Khandpur, and Samantha Infante.

To my crew over the years, Will Heath, Rosalind O'Connor, Alex Schaefer, Will Crakes, Bella Baskin, Dana Edelson, Norman Ng, and the infinite number of interns and photo PAs: thank you for always letting me switch back to the fresnel and for your patience and enthusiasm.

A huge thank-you to the SNL hair, makeup, and costume departments. Tom Broecker, you are such a genius and such a well of support and knowledge. You quite simply make it all come together. Thank you, Jeri Grieco, Jodi Mancuso, Louie Zakarian, and your teams, for always coming through when all these ideas come out of nowhere at you and always at the last minute.

To all talent department members and producers from 2000 to 2024 who helped me wrangle, persuade, manage expectatioins, and generally get 'er done: thank you, x

Thank you, Dina Moles and your team, for always making it happen out in the wild.

To the studio crew in 8H, thank you for all your willingness to jump in and help with electricity, lighting, stage management, and special effects, and for everyone's incredible support over the years.

To the props department, Larry and Steve Demmler, Eamon Cunningham, and Margaret Viani: you all are awesome.

Thank you to all of the outside glam artists, stylists, makeup artists, hair stylists, manicurists, and all their support people: I am grateful for your artistry.

Thank you, Ted Blumenschein, for your artistry and endless creativity. We've been working together for twenty-four years! Thank you for being available at all hours and for your commitment to always seeing the over three thousand images through, none of which would have made it to air without your efforts.

Thank you, Bryan Tallevi, Katie Hockmeyer, Megan Startz, Shayne Mifsud, Geoff Katz, and Marc Jacoby, for taking care of all the business.

To Rosalind O'Connor: thank you for handling everything beautifully.

To Shawn Patrick Anderson: You are a cold stone genius, and I thank you for all of those nutty ideas and all things prop-tastic. Thanks also to your entire team at Acme.

Thank you to Launa Eddy for your insane talent working on the tiny cities for SNL at Home.

A very special thanks and love to Marci Klein, Keith Raywood, Bob Golden, and Copious Management.

And of course, thank you, Michael Sand and Deb Wood and the team at Abrams, for publishing my first book.

Last but not least: Thank you to all of the hosts and musical guests who were so generous with your time and talent. This book is for you!

Pentagram Design Team:

Emily Oberman
Laura Berglund
Elizabeth McMann
Mira Khandpur
Chad McCabe
Samantha Infante

Abrams Team:

Editor: Michael Sand
Design Manager: Deb Wood
Managing Editor: Nate Lee
Production Manager: Denise LaCongo

Library of Congress Control Number: 2024943699

ISBN: 978-1-4197-8253-4
eISBN: 979-8-88707-664-5

Published in 2025 by Abrams, an imprint of ABRAMS.

Printed and bound in China
10 9 8 7 6 5 4 3 2

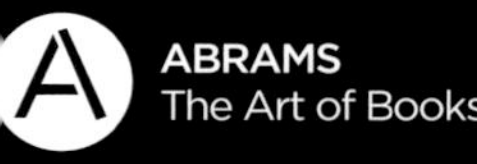

195 Broadway
New York, NY 10007
abramsbooks.com

ABRAMS is represented in the UK and Europe by Abrams & Chronicle Books, 1 West Smithfield, London EC1A 9JU and Média Participations, 57 rue Gaston Tessier, 75166 Paris, France. abramsandchronicle.co.uk and media-participations.com
info@abramsandchronicle.co.uk

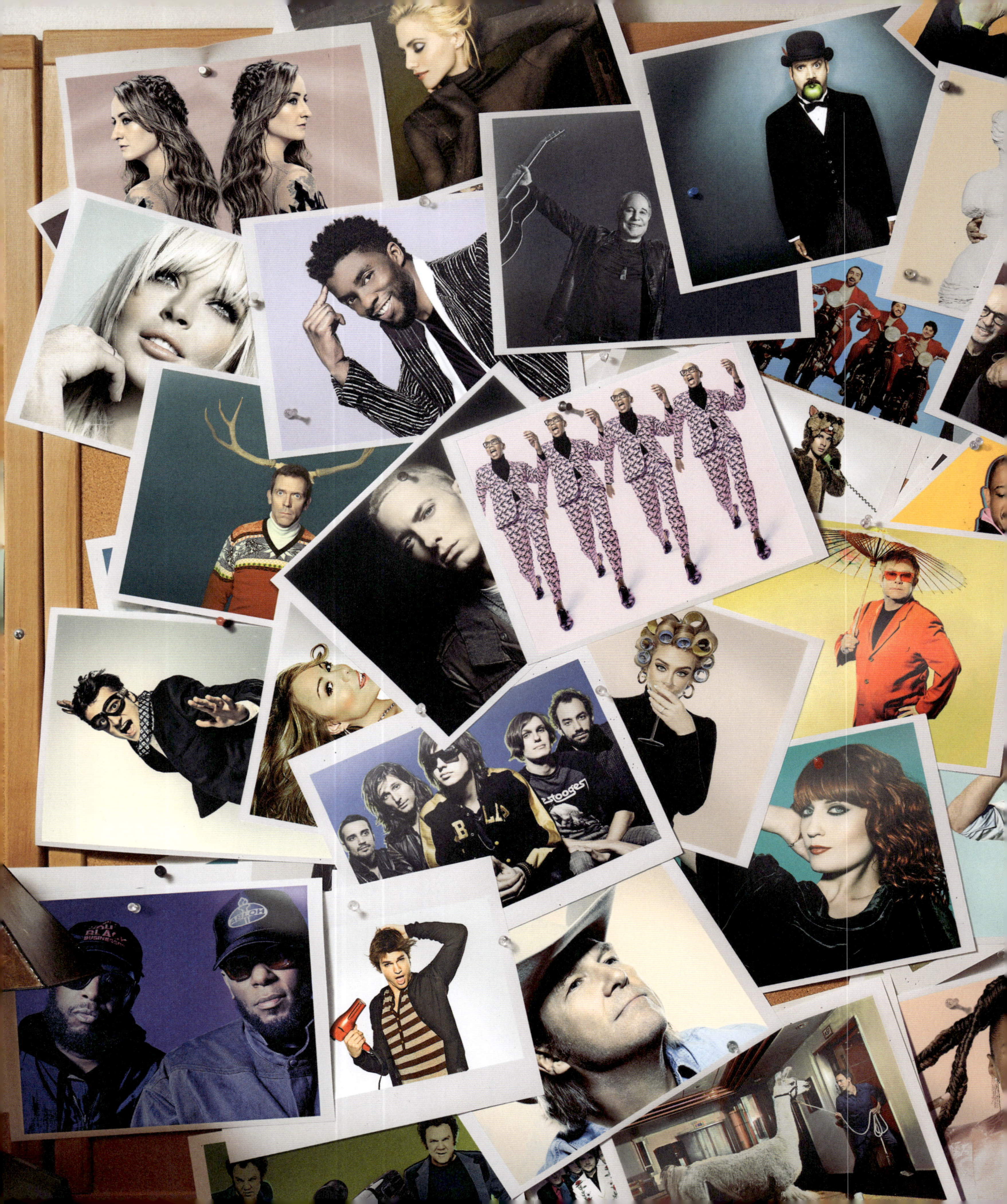
Stooges